Nuclear Weapons, Nuclear States, and Terrorism

Fourth Edition

Nuclear Weapons, Nuclear States, and Terrorism

Fourth Edition

Peter R. Beckman

Paul W. Crumlish

Michael N. Dobkowski

Steven P. Lee

Hobart and William Smith Colleges

2007
SLOAN PUBLISHING
Cornwall-on-Hudson, NY 12520

Library of Congress Control Number: 2006927114

Beckman, Peter R. et al.
  Nuclear Weapons, Nuclear States, and Terrorism, 4th Edition / Peter R. Beckman, Paul W. Crumlish,
    Michael N. Dobkowski, and Steven P. Lee
    p.   cm.
  Includes bibliographic references and index.
  ISBN 1-59738-006-7

Cover designer: Amy Rosen
Cover art: Drawing by Susumu Horikoshi, a survivor of Hiroshima, who observed the
mushroom cloud from a mountain village twenty miles north of Hiroshima. Courtesy
of the Hiroshima Peace Memorial Museum.

To our children and all children

© 2007
Sloan Publishing, LLC
220 Maple Road
Cornwall-on-Hudson, NY 12520

Previous editions published by Prentice Hall, a division of Pearson Education, under the title
The Nuclear Predicament.

Printed in Canada
10 9 8 7 6 5 4 3 2 1

ISBN 1-59738-006-7

Table of Contents

Part III: The Second Nuclear Age (1991–)

Preface

The Changing Nature of the
Nuclear Predicament

Fifty years ago, in the heat of the Cold War, many of the earth's inhabitants justifiably feared that they might die in a sudden, catastrophic nuclear war. When the Cold War sputtered to a peaceful end in the early 1990s, they celebrated their escape from a terrifying moment in human history and looked forward to a peaceful millennium. Nuclear weapons continued to exist, but the lesson of the first nuclear age seemed to be that humans had the capacity to tame the terror inherent in those weapons.

September 11th and the rise of a terrorist movement with a global reach rekindled fears that nuclear weapons would remain a prominent factor in the human future. In the second presidential debate of 2004, when the moderator, Jim Lehrer, asked the two candidates, "If you are elected president, what will you take to that office thinking is the most serious threat to the national security of the United States?" John Kerry responded by saying, "Nuclear proliferation. Nuclear proliferation." Given his opportunity to respond, President Bush initially began to defend his administration's initiatives in the face of Kerry's criticism, but quickly swung back to Lehrer's question: "Well, first of all, I agree with my opponent that the biggest threat facing this country is weapons of mass destruction in the hands of terrorist networks." Lehrer appeared surprised that there was general agreement on the nature of the threat and asked the two candidates to confirm that "the single most serious threat you believe, both of you believe, is nuclear proliferation." The president interjected, "In the hands of a terrorist enemy" and Kerry said, "Weapons of mass destruction, nuclear proliferation."

We concur. Beyond all the other ills that currently plague human kind, there still looms the specter of nuclear weapons. During the Cold War, we, George W. Bush, John F. Kerry, and the authors of this text, along with billions of other humans, lived with the reality that the United States and the Soviet Union had the capacity to destroy human civilization and that those two states had fashioned policies that could bring about that destruction. Today, in the world most of the readers of this text have grown up in, what we call the Second Nuclear Age, such an outcome is unlikely. Neither Russia nor the United States is poised to wage war against the other, and the other nuclear weapons-possessing states have too few weapons to endanger the planet. But we live in an uncertain era. The key question for us is: Will the peoples of the world be able to control the temptation to use nuclear weapons? Or are we merely marking time until a nuclear device explodes somewhere, and that explosion so emboldens others to consider nuclear weapons as just another munition, appropriate for advancing or defending the political interests of a state or group, that we plunge into a new, violent, more dangerous era, a Third Nuclear Age?

Some of the individuals who will help answer that question are now reading these words. You, however, like the generations immediately before you, confront a predicament concerning nuclear weapons. A predicament is a dangerous situation from which there seems to be no escape. Every proposed solution seems to either make the danger worse or puts at risk other things that we value highly. During the Cold War, the principal predicament was this: In order to prevent nuclear war, nuclear-armed states believed that they had to threaten to wage nuclear war, yet nuclear war threatened to destroy everything that those states valued. But if they did not make the option of waging war very real, they believed that other states might deprive them of the very things they cherished, particularly their independence and their way of life. To put that predicament in colloquial terms, during the Cold War, it seemed appropriate to say of nuclear weapons, we can't live with them and we can't live without them.

The end of the Cold War reduced the urgency of that fundamental predicament, but it remains, lingering in the shadows. For instance, one option, getting rid of nuclear weapons, seems dangerous because disarmed nations would be at the mercy of any nation that cheated on its disarmament commitments. But the other option, keeping the weapons, is also fraught with danger because there is the risk that, through proliferation, the weapons will fall into the hands of irresponsible leaders or terrorists who would use them. The end of the Cold War also brought new versions of the predicament, none of which carries the society-destroying potential of the original, but each of which threatens to degrade the human condition for millions. Three stand out: (1) Can any threat deter terrorists from using a nuclear device, and even if it could, might not the onerous nature of such a threat drive thousands more individuals to become terrorists? (2) Can nuclear weapons states, particularly the United States, avoid the pressure to develop a greater variety of small-scale nuclear weapons, and perhaps use them, weapons that in certain circumstances might seem to be the answer to the challenges it faces? (3) How can the United States prevent states hostile to it from acquiring nuclear weapons when American pressure may be the very thing that convinces such states that they need nuclear weapons to deter the United States from attacking them?

When we wrote the first edition of this book, we were not certain that anyone would be able to read these words 20 years later. You now know, as we did not then, that nations would be able to devise a workable response to the predicament during the first nuclear age. One of the concerns of this text is to explore how earlier generations found a response to the predicament, and to suggest that it was done with no small measure of luck and that it was an imperfect solution. Nonetheless, our surviving the first nuclear age should hearten all of us. A meaningful response to today's predicament may be possible. We took to heart then, as we do now, Albert Einstein's warning that "the unleashed power of the atom has changed everything save our modes of thinking, and thus we drift toward unparalleled catastrophe." This book thus represents our effort to help all of us challenge our modes of thinking, to

Albert Einstein at Princeton, September 1943. *National Archives*

better understand what has happened and what is happening, and to explore alternatives for the future.

So deep and tangled has the nuclear predicament been that even now it is difficult to discern the lessons of history, particularly about the Cold War. We do with modest confidence suggest that these are four basic lessons learned during the first nuclear age, lessons learned not only by scholars but by presidents, prime ministers, and concerned citizens as well:

- The real secret of nuclear weapons is that they can be made. Getting rid of nuclear weapons can never blot out that critical knowledge; they cannot be "disinvented." We will always live in a nuclear age.

- Nuclear weapons, even in relatively small numbers, can produce catastrophic damage against which there is no adequate defense.

- A full-blown nuclear war must never be fought. Because no one knows when the use of a few nuclear weapons would escalate to a large-scale use, it is wiser to err on the side of caution and not use nuclear weapons at all.

- It is important to keep alive the nuclear taboo, a general belief that nuclear weapons are fraught with awesomely horrific and morally unacceptable consequences, and it is important to prevent nuclear proliferation, the spread of nuclear weapons to states not possessing them.

This is hard-won and imperfect knowledge. Not everyone will agree that the lessons are correct, and not everyone will be aware of the lessons; some will deny that they are applicable to the second nuclear age. Moreover, such lessons do not always provide us much guidance about many difficult, day-to-day policy decisions. When Bush and Kerry debated in 2004, for instance, they both placed nuclear weapons at the top of their concerns for the security of the United States. But even then both disagreed on what the United States should do in response. Kerry argued that we need to pay far more attention to the vast but poorly secured Russian nuclear arsenal, while the president wanted to emphasize a continued offensive against terrorists. Each would have criticisms of the other's approach. In the best of all possible worlds, we might do both, of course, but money, time, and attention are scarce commodities for all governments, and leaders usually need to emphasize one policy approach rather than another.

It is in those choices, as well as in the broad kinds of conclusions that we draw about the nuclear age we live in, that we will shape our nuclear future. Our worst fear is that we might stumble into a Third Nuclear Age, one in which the use of nuclear weapons is relatively frequent and the lives of millions are sacrificed or stunted. We have organized this text to help you make informed choices about the nuclear predicament that confronts you and the planet's other inhabitants. In the first part, "Then and Now," we examine three basic topics. Chapter 1 discusses what it is like to be the victim of a nuclear attack and, at the extreme, what fate the earth as a whole might experience from a nuclear war. Chapter 2 recounts how humans were able to unleash the power of the atom and how they came to do so; it also identifies the states that have chosen to become nuclear weapons states. Chapter 3 assesses how humans have made the decision to use nuclear weapons, and not to use them. It explores several hypothetical pathways that rational humans might follow to unleash nuclear war. These chapters balance the historical experience with our present-day concerns, from Hiroshima in 1945 to al Qaeda's current efforts to acquire a nuclear device.

Part Two of the text, comprising Chapters 4 and 5, addresses the first nuclear age, that period from 1945 to roughly 1990, when states acquired nuclear weapons and increasingly sophisticated methods of delivering them against targets. During that time, leaders fashioned plans to wage nuclear war, sought to exploit the nuclear weapons in their arsenals in order to provide more clout to their foreign policies, and then, as it became apparent that a nuclear war would be deadly, cautiously fashioned an understanding of how nuclear-armed states had to behave in order to avoid the catastrophe. The first nuclear age coincides with the Cold War between the United States and Soviet Union. We try to gauge the role of nuclear weapons in bringing about and ending that Cold War.

Part Three then turns to our contemporary condition, the second nuclear age. Chapter 6 explores how the older nuclear weapons states have responded to the new age. What role can nuclear weapons play in their military strategies when their former foe is no longer a threat while the new threats from terrorists and rogue states seem far less amenable to traditional responses? Chapter 7 examines how concerns about nuclear weapons shape the foreign policies of various states, particularly those of the United States. That state chose to wage war in 2003 to keep nuclear weapons out of Saddam Hussein's hands, and has alternated between threat and reward in an attempt to end the nuclear aspirations of Iran and North Korea. Chapter 8 examines the crucial question of whether more states will attempt to become nuclear powers and why, whether they are likely to succeed, and whether we can devise responses that will lessen the likelihood that proliferation will take place. Chapter 9 turns to the other pressing question of the second nuclear age: Will terrorists be able to acquire nuclear devices and, if so, can they be deterred from using them?

Part Four changes our perspective from the challenges we confront in the second nuclear age to our cultural and moral capability to respond. Do we have the ability, as Einstein called for, to refashion our modes of thinking so that we can begin to shape our nuclear future anew? Chapter 10 describes the way American culture has responded to nuclear weapons and the threat they pose. It suggests that our way of thinking about the nuclear world, or of avoiding that thinking, might be at the heart of the problem. Chapter 11 discusses nuclear weapons from a moral point of view and asks if there are fundamental moral guidelines we should use when making our nuclear policy choices.

Part Five presents and critiques three basic nuclear policy responses that the United States in particular might adopt in the second nuclear age. Chapter 12 argues for essentially the Bush administration approach of continuing pressure and threats (and sometimes force) directed against hostile states with nuclear ambitions and directing warfare against terrorist groups that have attacked the United States. Chapter 13 harkens back to the experience of the first nuclear age to argue for negotiated constraints on nuclear weapons and negotiated understandings of how all states will behave internationally (and possibly domestically). Chapter 14 proposes the abandonment of nuclear weapons as the best policy. Although they cannot be disinvented, they can be removed from the world's arsenals and the capacity to rebuild them can be blunted, reducing greatly the risk of their use and freeing nations to get on with solving more basic problems confronting them.

The Epilogue reflects our judgments about how the world might respond to the coming of the Third Nuclear Age, should this occur. Our policies should be designed to avoid such an event, but if it were to occur, and no policy can guarantee that it will not, what would the response to it be like? Would the response make our situation better or worse?

It is our contention, and our motivation behind the writing of this book, that as Americans we have a special responsibility to think carefully about the nuclear future because, while the United States alone cannot dictate that future, it has a powerful voice in shaping that future. You must, of course, reach your own judgments on these matters. There is not and probably can never be a clear answer to the nuclear predicament that will achieve universal assent. We believe, however, that better answers come from individuals with a sense of history, who take the time to examine the implications of their policy preferences, and heeding Einstein's injunction, look for new modes of thinking. When Condoleezza Rice made the argument for war against Iraq, one of the key elements in her thinking centered on Iraq's nuclear weapons program. In arguing for the war, she said, "We don't want the smoking gun to be a mushroom cloud." In fact, there was at the time no Iraq nuclear weapons program, and there was no direct evidence that it existed, so we might well fault the administration for weak thinking. But for all of us, as we edge further into the second nuclear age, her caution, generalized beyond the context in which she expressed it, still holds: we do not want a mushroom cloud to be the sign of our failure to think carefully and choose wisely about the nuclear predicament.

ACKNOWLEDGEMENTS

This book is a collaborative effort of four individuals who approach the nuclear predicament from different perspectives. Our discussions and debates for more than two decades have been nourished by Hobart and William Smith Colleges' emphasis on interdisciplinary study. We are grateful for Larry Campbell's permission to use the materials on the physics of nuclear weapons that appeared in the first three editions and his guidance on updating that chapter. We want to thank John Farrance, who provided much valuable assistance in the final preparation of the manuscript. We also want to recognize Harmon Dunathan's encouragement at the beginning of this project and Rene

Schoen-Rene's aid in drafting the first edition. Louise Bond continued to provide her patient support for a four-author effort that must have seemed perpetual. We also want to thank Bill Webber of Sloan Publishing for his energetic interest in bringing out a new edition of the book. We benefited from reviewers whose comments helped shaped this edition, Patrick J. Haney, Miami University; Robert L. Pfaltzgraff, Jr.,The Fletcher School, Tufts University; and Dan Reiter, Emory University. We also thank reviewers of previous editions, among whom are: Larry Elowitz, Georgia College; Donald S. Will, Chapman College; Mark Reader, Arizona State University; George Hunsinger, Bangor Theological; and John F. Stack Jr., Florida International University. We must, of course, lay claim to the errors that remain.

1

Hiroshima and 9/11
The Nuclear Predicament

Before dawn on August 6, 1945, the B–29 bomber *Enola Gay*, piloted by Colonel Paul Tibbets, took off from Tinian in the Mariana Islands in the Central Pacific and headed for southern Japan. On board was a single atomic bomb nicknamed Little Boy. At 8:16 A.M., the bomb, armed during the flight, was released over Hiroshima. It exploded 43 seconds later 1,900 feet above the city, as it had been set to do, to increase the area of destruction. "I had a definite job to do," Colonel Tibbets later remarked. "I did it. I had orders to carry out…. When I passed through the town wiped out by the atomic bomb, my only reaction was: good job well done! That is, I had done my job thoroughly."[1] On target, on time—the mission was technically a perfect success.

By present standards the bomb, with an explosive yield of 12,500 tons of TNT, was a small one, equivalent to a battlefield weapon in today's nuclear arsenals. Yet it was powerful enough to transform a city of some 340,000 people into a plain of devastation in a matter of seconds. The first nuclear age had dawned for all the earth's inhabitants.

Although the residents of Hiroshima had expected American conventional bombing because an air base and military factories were located in the area and they had not yet been extensively bombed, the surprise and shock were absolute. The citizens of this densely populated urban sprawl on wide river plains had prepared shelters and cleared fire lanes in anticipation of an American air raid. But they were unprepared for what was to occur. About 7 A.M. on August 6, Japanese radar detected a group of approaching planes (the lead weather reconnaissance plane and the *Enola Gay* accompanied by two observation planes), and officials sounded an air raid alert for the area. But only the single weather plane circled at high altitude over the city. Most people believed the all-clear signal issued at 7:31, when the weather plane left the area, and emerged from shelters to set about their daily tasks. The authorities and general population assumed that the three planes that appeared shortly before 8:15 were on a routine reconnaissance mission and hardly anyone went to the shelters. Instead, fathers set off to work, children to school, and soldiers to their appointed jobs.

Their world suddenly disintegrated. A blinding flash of white light, like an exploding sun, was instantly followed by a searing heat and tremendous blast. A huge fireball of several million degrees centigrade vaporized people and poured radiation in all directions. Debris and smoke sucked up by the ascending fire ball spread a dark pall over the city and fell for hours in a radioactive "black rain." Fires erupted everywhere and, fanned by the swirling winds set up by the explosion, burned for six hours and consumed 3.8 square miles of homes and offices. In a few seconds, 13 square miles of city had been flattened or set aflame. Of 76,000 buildings in Hiroshima, 70,000 had been damaged or destroyed, 48,000 totally. Up to 130,000 people had been killed or mortally injured by wounds and radiation burns. Among the casualties were tens of thousands of children. Most of the survivors who emerged from the holocaust believed that they had survived a direct hit. As one survivor recalled:

> Then it happened. It came very suddenly…. It felt something like an electric short—a bluish sparkling light…. There was a noise, and I felt great heat—even inside the house. When I came to, I was underneath the destroyed home…. I thought the bomb had fallen directly upon me.[2]

But, of course, he was wrong.

Gradually, the extent of the devastation came into focus. As a survivor noted: "Hiroshima was no longer a city, but a burnt-over prairie. To the east and to the west everything was flattened. The distant mountains seemed nearer than I would ever remember…. How small Hiroshima was with its houses gone."[3] Another said: "I climbed Hijiyama Hill and looked down. I saw that Hiroshima had disappeared…. I was shocked by the sight….What I felt then and still feel now I just can't explain with words."[4] The survivors encountered massive suffering and horror wherever they looked. "I and mother crawled out from under the house. There we found a world such as I had never seen before, a world I'd never even heard of before…," a world that another survivor called "an uncanny world of the dead."[5]

On August 8, the Soviet Union declared war on Japan, and one day later the United States dropped another atomic bomb, this one of plutonium, nicknamed Fat Man on Nagasaki, killing or injuring 100,000 people. Japan surrendered five days later. World War II was over at last, after nearly six years of total war and 40 million deaths. (See Figure 1–1.)

The survivors of Hiroshima and Nagasaki are the only people in the world who have endured the wartime use of atomic weapons. Damage done to them and to their cities has been exhaustively studied by scholars and governments. The number of deaths that occurred, both immediately and over a period of some months, will probably never be fully known, but is variously estimated from 180,000 to 300,000 or more. In addition to those killed immediately, tens of thousands of people began (within hours and days after the explosions) to manifest the ill effects of toxic radiation—vomiting, diarrhea, bloody stools, fever, inflammation, ulcerations, bleeding from body cavities, loss of hair, low white blood cell counts—and many died. In subsequent years, increased incidences of leukemia, other types of cancer, and birth defects were noticed and documented among the *hibakusha*, or "explosion-affected persons." Additional debilitations have been either demonstrated or suspected to have been caused by exposure to the radiation, including various blood diseases, endocrine and skin disorders, damage to the central nervous system, premature aging, and general weakness. The hibakusha are still, psychologically, a group set apart. From this information on the results of two small bombs, we can extrapolate and even predict the effects of a nuclear war today, when the power of nuclear arsenals is measured in units of millions of tons of TNT. As Robert Jay Lifton has argued, Hiroshima is our text.[6] It is the template of the first nuclear age, a period that witnessed nu-

Figure 1–1   *Left*: "Little Boy," a gun-assembly type atomic bomb using U-235, was dropped on Hiroshima on August 6, 1945. It had never been tested. *Right*: "Fat Man," an implosion- type bomb using Pu-239, was dropped on Nagasaki on August 9, 1945. Its prototype had been tested at Trinity. *Department of Energy/Office of History & Heritage Resources.*

clear-infused competition between the two super powers, the United States and the Soviet Union, Cold War tensions, nuclear brinkmanship and the policy of Mutual Assured Destruction or MAD, the threat to destroy the world in order to keep the peace. Although the world today is very different, with a diminished threat of global nuclear conflict since the dismantling of the Soviet Union, it is not without risk and volatility. What are some of the potential new "Hiroshimas" we face?

THE SHADOW OF NUCLEAR TERRORISM

On this warm September day, a brilliant blue filled the sky above New York City. The offices of lower Manhattan teemed with their usual quota of workers; school children were settling into their class-room routines, and across the rest of the nation, families were waking, getting ready for the day, watching the morning television programs. The initial reports were that an airplane had crashed into one of the Twin Towers, leaving a lengthening trail of smoke from the impact site. An accident, surely, but unsettling none the less. And then, the dramatic moment when a fireball erupted in the sec-ond tower, coupled with reports of hijacked aircraft and an explosion at the Pentagon. Much of Amer-ica sat transfixed, watching in real time the unfolding attack on the United States.

The television images of September 11, 2001 are indelibly stamped on our minds, when in a sec-tion at the tip of lower Manhattan, now called Ground Zero, recalling the point of detonation of nu-clear explosions, day was suddenly transformed into night. Aaron Brown of CNN, watching the collapse of the first tower, called the great rush of smoke and ash "a mushroom cloud"—nuclear allu-sions seemed appropriate for this tragedy. We saw people running in panic, their faces masks of fear. Chasing them—gaining on them was a black cloud of dust and debris, all that was left of the once proud Twin Towers of the World Trade Center. We have images of desperate office workers falling to their deaths, trying to escape a more horrible death by fire or from buildings imploding and shattering thousands of human beings into particles of rubble and dust. We read countless stories of who the innocent victims were before that fateful moment—workers from more than 86 countries doing their jobs in the World Trade Center towers; hundreds of firemen, police, and other emergency workers rushing in and being trapped by their last gesture of mercy; civilians and military personnel serving their country at the Pentagon; four plane loads of business people and retirees, children, parents, and grandparents, flying across the country. It was as bad as we remember it; as bad a day as Americans have experienced in their history. Contemporary Americans did not have living memories of what it means to flee a city enveloped by flames and debris. Now we do.

We do not yet have a name for the era ushered in by September 11. Scholars in the future may call it the Age of Terrorism, or the Age of Weapons of Mass Destruction or the Age of Anxiety. Whatever we call it, 9/11 has forced a reconsideration not only of who we are as a nation, but the very nature of American security. It gave pause to the belief that Americans are safe behind secure borders. September 11 left nearly five times as many Americans dead as all terrorist incidents of the previous three decades combined. The carnage was 30 times greater than what an American terrorist, Timothy McVeigh, had inflicted on Oklahoma City in 1995 and about double that of those whom the Japanese killed at Pearl Harbor in 1941. There were earlier precedents, but this attack on American soil seemed new and transforming.

And the threat is not going away. The world is much smaller and much less secure, and political movements hostile to the United States have not abandoned their goal of harming the United States or its allies. On July 7, 2005, Islamic extremists detonated bombs on three subway trains and a double-decker bus in London, leaving over 50 dead and 700 injured. Inevitably, we must confront the possibility and the fear that terrorists will attempt to use a nuclear device against the United States.

The Second Nuclear Age began at the same time that a new and more deadly form of terrorism emerged as well. September 11 was, in retrospect, a step in this resurgence and evolution. On the morning of February 26, 1993, international terrorists attacked the 110-story World Trade Center with a truck bomb in the Center's underground parking facility, killing six and injuring over a thousand. Had that explosion succeeded in undermining the structural foundation of that building as intended, thousands of people might have died, as they did eight years later. In April 1995, McVeigh used a truck bomb against Oklahoma City's Alfred P. Murrah Federal Office Building, killing 168 men, women, and children, making it, at that point, the worst domestic terrorist attack in American history. For weeks the press projected images of the scoured-out office building, of bleeding babies and shocked survivors and relatives, their faces drained of hope and color. The same news photograph of a firefighter carrying the limp body of a dead child from the collapsed day-care center on the building's first floor appeared on the covers of *Time* and *Newsweek*. These images are reminiscent of some of the early photographs of Hiroshima and its survivors, days after the August 1945 attack.

Overseas, on August 7, 1998, two powerful truck bombs exploded within minutes of each other, targeting the American embassies in Nairobi, Kenya, and Dar es Salaam, Tanzania, killing 257 innocents and wounding more than 5,000 (mostly citizens of those countries). Americans were targets of similar attacks in June 1996, when a fuel truck packed with thousands of pounds of explosives detonated at the King Abdul Aziz Air Base near Dhahran, Saudi Arabia, killing 19 Americans and injuring hundreds. And in October 2000, terrorists detonated an explosive-laden rubber boat against the hull of the *USS Cole*, in Aden, Yemen, killing 17 and wounding 39.

Since September 11th, there have been hundreds of terrorist attacks against American forces, officials, and civilians in Iraq as well as terrorism against Iraqis, Afghans, and others. Many of these attacks have been linked to al Qaeda, the organization established by a Saudi rebel, Osama bin Laden, who oversaw the September attack on the World Trade Center. For instance, on March 11, 2004, a Moroccan Islamist terrorist cell linked to al Qaeda, set off ten bombs on commuter trains in Madrid, Spain, killing 191 people, and in October 2002, members of Jemaah Islamiyah, a terrorist group allied with al Qaeda, set off powerful explosions that killed more than 200 people in Bali, Indonesia. The same group bombed the J. W. Marriott Hotel in Jakarta in August, 2003, leaving twelve people dead. On May 12, 2003, there were bomb attacks at three western housing complexes in Riyadh, Saudi Arabia which killed 35 people.For Osama bin Laden, the thousands of his followers, and millions of those who sympathize with his extreme Islamist ideology, America is the hated enemy. In their view, there is no distinction between Americans in uniform or people going about their daily tasks. There are no innocent civilians. It is a duty for every Moslem to kill Americans wherever they can be found, according to this view. Those who died on September 11 were infidels, the enemy who deserved to perish. Some observers have concluded that these militants loath Americans for who they are and what they represent, making peace or even reconciliation very difficult. Thus al Qaeda and its supporters pose a real threat, even if they represent a distinct minority of the Moslem world.

In such a world view, terrorism becomes the weapon of choice for al Qaeda. Terrorism is the deliberate killing of innocent people for political purpose. Many see it as a crime against humanity because it negates the very value and sacredness of human life itself. Few if any moral standards have deeper roots than the prohibition against taking innocent life. Whatever differences may exist in culture, religion, class, race, or any of the other categories by which human beings seek to establish their identities, this rule transcends them. Terrorism pays no heed to this principle and subjects its victims or potential victims to paralyzing fear. A terrorist, simply, is one who sows terror. As the political theorist Michael Walzer maintains, terrorism's "purpose is to destroy the morale of a nation or a class, to undercut its solidarity; its method is the random murder of innocent people. Randomness is the crucial feature of terrorist activity. Death must come by chance."[7]

What the attack against the World Trade Center, the Pentagon, and earlier the Federal Building in Oklahoma City demonstrated to Americans is that terrorism can now strike anywhere in America, from the icons of military and financial power to a quiet southwestern city far removed from national or international politics. The shock, the fear, the anxiety produced by these deadly incidents only begin to suggest what the impact of the explosion of a nuclear device in the United States or the detonation of a conventional explosive contaminated with radioactive material (a "dirty bomb") would have on the fabric of American society.

Do terrorists seek this "ultimate" weapon? Al Qaeda has claimed to have access to dirty bombs—conventional explosives combined with radioactive materials—and one of its operatives was arrested in Vancouver attempting to smuggle dirty bomb-making material into the United States, making the second scenario entirely plausible, as we discuss later in the chapter. *The 9/11 Commission Report* noted that al Qaeda tried to acquire or make nuclear weapons for at least ten years. Many experts believe that al Qaeda has mounted a determined effort to purchase or steal either nuclear material or possibly even a small (10-kiloton) weapon from Russian sources. It has negotiated for the purchase of uranium, its operatives have traveled repeatedly to Central Asia to buy weapons-grade materials, and there has been significant al Qaeda chatter about an "American Hiroshima." In the public portion of his February 2004 worldwide threat assessment to Congress, George Tenet, then Director of the CIA, warned that al Qaeda, "continues to pursue its strategic goal of obtaining a nuclear capability." Tenet added that more than two dozen other terrorist groups are pursuing nuclear and other weapons of mass destruction. *The 9/11 Commission Report* concluded that "a trained nuclear engineer with an amount of highly enriched uranium or plutonium about the size of a grapefruit or an orange, together with commercially available material, could fashion a nuclear device that would fit in a van like the one… parked in the garage of the World Trade Center in 1993. Such a bomb would level Manhattan."[8] The possibility of an American Hiroshima has taken on a new aspect and urgency. Many experts believe that nuclear terrorism has a better-than-even chance of occurring in the next ten years. The Aspen Strategy Group, a bi-partisan policy think tank, concluded in the summer of 2004 that the danger of nuclear terrorism is real and that the American government has not done nearly enough to reduce it. Harvard University scholar, Graham Allison, agrees. In his 2004 book, *Nuclear Terrorism* he argues that " …a nuclear terrorist attack on America is more likely than not in the decade ahead. With a ten-kiloton nuclear weapon stolen from the former Soviet arsenal and delivered to an American city in a cargo container, al Qaeda can make 9/11 a footnote."[9]

During the Cold War, many Americans feared dying in a Soviet nuclear strike. We lived with that fear (a topic we explore fully in Chapter 10), sometimes choosing to ignore it, sometimes choosing to believe that our threatened retaliatory destruction of the Soviet Union would keep the unthinkable from happening. Now, in the still-pulsing reverberations of 9/11, the continuing war in Iraq, and the terrorists' seeming disregard of commonly accepted moral standards coupled with their repeatedly demonstrated willingness to die to inflict suffering on others, the fear has been renewed and heightened. As the journalist Bill Keller wrote in May, 2002: "All September 11 did was turn a theoretical possibility into a felt danger. All it did was supply a credible cast of characters who hate us so much they would thrill to the prospect of actually doing it—and, most important in rethinking the probabilities, would be happy to die in the effort. All it did was give our nightmare legs."[10]

In the scramble to make America secure after 9/11, Americans discovered that as a country, it was quite vulnerable, that the world in which they lived harbored real danger. Terrorists might acquire a nuclear weapon or bomb-making material, perhaps by theft from Russian stockpiles, or perhaps bought on the black market in Pakistan, or purchased from some other state desperate for cash, such as North Korea. It might be brought into the United States undetected in the hold of a container ship to New York harbor or some other port. Or extremists might attack a facility in the United States where highly radioactive waste was stored, detonating the waste with high explosives, sending radioactive materials into the atmosphere. In a world where many are willing not only to kill but die along with their victims for a cause; in a world where 9/11 demonstrated how vulnerable the U.S. economy and social fabric is to attack, it now seems prudent if horrifying to expect that terrorists or even states that are unwilling to comply with international norms (called "rogue states") would attempt or threaten to use nuclear weapons or other weapons of mass destruction against the United States. The American public supported the Bush administration's war against Saddam Hussein and Iraq in the spring of 2003 largely because of a feared connection between weapons of mass destruction, Saddam Hussein, and terrorists. The panicky aftermath is still with us.

NUCLEAR PROLIFERATION

Americans have to contend with more than the threat of nuclear terrorism. Nuclear proliferation—the acquisition of nuclear weapons by states that did not previously have them—has created a new set of anxieties. In 1998, India's newly elected Hindu nationalist government detonated five nuclear test blasts. Two weeks later, Pakistan followed suit. These two South Asia nations had been in a tense military standoff over the disputed province of Kashmir. An escalation of that conflict now clearly threatened to produce a nuclear exchange and the growing religious fundamentalism in both states threatened to fan animosities to higher levels.

The open proliferation by Pakistan and India was complemented in the Second Nuclear Age by a creeping proliferation by other states, particularly North Korea and Iran (countries the United States has labeled rogue states). The governments of these states had covertly re-energized their programs to produce nuclear weapons. In 2002, the North Korean government shook the world by admitting it was pursuing a nuclear weapons program despite its 1994 pledge to halt the program. At the time we write this, North Korea claimed to have a half-dozen nuclear warheads. A next step would be to engineer the warheads to fit North Korea's missiles—missiles that are growing in both sophistication and reach, and which have been sold to other countries. As we shall see, the United States has been engaged in an effort to bring about the end to North Korea's nuclear program, but with little success.

American concerns about proliferation are also directed toward Iran. Iran's missile program—drawing on North Korean expertise and materiel—has produced a missile, the Shahab-3, capable of reaching some 900 miles, bringing Israel and the American forces operating in Iraq and Afghanistan under its threat. The ongoing nuclear program in Iran—ostensibly to produce electrical power but capable of being diverted to weapons production—may be able to produce a nuclear weapon in three to five years. The Bush administration has declared that Iran's possession of nuclear weapons would be unacceptable. While denying that it intends to produce nuclear weapons, the Iranian government has repeatedly asserted that, as a sovereign state, it has all the rights that other sovereign states have and would exercise those rights.

The United States and its citizens seem to be on a collision course with North Korea and Iran regarding nuclear weapons. Nuclear proliferation thus creates a set of difficult challenges for the United States. But the issue is far broader than just American sensitivities and concerns. Consider the following scenario: The mullahs (the Islamic religious leaders) who control Iran conclude that their goals of the expansion of militant Islam and keeping the West at bay would be greatly enhanced if the Islamic Republic of Iran succeeded in obtaining nuclear weapons. Moreover, it has not been lost on the Islamic Republic that the differences between American approaches to Saddam Hussein's Iraq (the United States attacked), and Kim Jong Il's North Korea (the United States sought to negotiate) stemmed from the American belief that Kim may have had nuclear weapons in hand while Saddam had only a program to produce them. Having nuclear weapons thus provides security obtainable in no other way. The hard-core mullahs' abiding hatred of the United States and its threatening liberal culture would be freer to express itself.

How might Iran exploit its nuclear strength? The scenario suggests that Iran might threaten the West or any of its neighbors outright, just as American leaders suspected Saddam Hussein would do once his weapons of mass destruction had been produced. Let's rewrite history for a moment. Imagine a *nuclear-armed* Saddam Hussein seizing Kuwait in the summer of 1990 (as he did), and then telling the West as well as the alarmed Arab states to accept the change in the status quo or face nuclear retaliation. Or imagine Hussein with more expansive goals than just Kuwait—say, in seizing northern Saudi Arabia (which the first Bush administration feared the non-nuclear Iraq would do in 1990). Or imagine Saddam now moving to crush Israel, a long-trumpeted Iraqi goal (recall that he did use Scud missiles to attack Israel in 1991).

We can imagine American fears and threats and mobilization to try to restore the status quo in Kuwait (which it did in 1990). Armed with nuclear weapons, Saddam refuses to withdraw from Kuwait (as he refused in 1990). Perhaps he threatens to strike neighboring capitals like Riyadh or cities like

Tel Aviv or to destroy oil-loading facilities in the Persian Gulf if the United States contested the oc-cupation of Kuwait. Israel, concerned that it would be the next victim of Iraqi aggression and worried that the United States would not stand firm against Iraq, attacks Iraqi military facilities and all suspected nuclear weapons sites, perhaps using some of its nuclear weapons. Or perhaps the United States acts first—both to destroy Iraqi power and prevent Israel from acting in a way that would raise tensions dramatically throughout the region.

Our look at Iraq assumed, contrary to reality, that Iraq in 1990 had nuclear weapons. That was not true in 1990 (nor in 2003 either). But now consider Iran, clearly committed to creating a capacity to produce nuclear weapons if it chose to do so in the future. Now feeling more secure, the Iranian clerics might seek to recover some of the power and dynamism of Iran's earlier years. They might court a confrontation to do so—just as the radical clerics under the Ayatollah Khomeini did in 1979 when Iranian students seized the American embassy. But there are other options open to nuclear-armed Iran.

Iran's leaders may decide instead that a direct confrontation with the United States or Israel would provoke horrible retaliation against Iran and therefore avoid clearly provocative acts. But they might consider resorting to indirect intimidation, manipulating the possibility of a nuclear attack by using any number of Islamist terrorist groups such as Hezbollah and Islamic Jihad, with which it has influence. Such groups nullify in large measure the need to have air power or missiles as delivery systems. They will be the delivery system. In the worst of such scenarios, the consequences may not be a fertilizer bomb but a nuclear device in front of a building in a yet-to-be-targeted American or Israeli city.

To the degree that you believe Iranian leaders might be so tempted, proliferation gives "our nightmare legs." These scenarios may be unlikely, surely, but they are not impossible. As we will see, nations historically have threatened to use nuclear weapons—and they have contemplated the use of nuclear weapons to advance their goals and interests.

There are, of course, other reasons to be concerned. If nuclear proliferation continues, there are some potential nuclear states that may not be politically strong and stable enough to ensure control of the weapons and control of the decision to use them. If neighboring, hostile, perhaps politically unstable states such as India and Pakistan have them, the temptation to strike against traditional rivals may be too hard to resist. When the weak fear the strong, the weaker party often does what it can to maintain its security. Pakistan has fought three wars with its larger and more powerful neighbor, India. If it feels threatened, it might be tempted in the future to act preemptively. Many fear that states that are radical at home, say North Korea, will recklessly use their nuclear weapons in pursuit of revolutionary ends abroad. In some of the new nuclear states, civil control of the military may be weak. Nuclear weapons may fall into the hands of military officers more inclined to use them.

So we now face a wider range of contingencies. There is the possibility that nuclear weapons will proliferate to "rogue" states and terrorists. There remains the risk of accidental or unauthorized use by nuclear states. This threat increases if more states or groups have access to the weapons. Finally, there is the possibility of deliberate use of nuclear weapons by existing states and threshold states; Israel could believe itself sufficiently threatened to resort to a nuclear strike; Russia could feel itself threatened by neighboring states or China; an India-Pakistan war could erupt; North Korea could feel itself threatened by a South Korea emboldened by the nuclear umbrella provided by the United States. And the United States, ironically, may feel itself "liberated" to use nuclear weapons after 9/11, particularly if it perceives an imminent threat from terrorists. Many Americans responded initially to the September 11 attacks with a desire for revenge, retribution, and deterrence. We know that political and military leaders are working hard to think through the implications of these new threats, but only the most sanguine observer can assume that they will get it right on every occasion. But what would "getting it wrong" mean?

BREAKING THE NUCLEAR TABOO

We can only speculate on what impact the exploding of a nuclear terrorist device would have. Three things seem clear, however. First, it would break *the nuclear taboo*, the universal, deeply ingrained sense that has developed since 1945 that nuclear weapons are not to be used. Once the taboo is broken, it might make it easier for others to use nuclear weapons. Second, the sheer scope of the ensuing tragic loss of life, the random arbitrariness of the deaths of those unlucky enough to be the victims, the surprise and shock of the event, and the economic and social disruption would probably undermine confidence in the government. Pervasive fear and anxiety would become the order of the day. The targeted city would eventually be rebuilt, like Hiroshima and Nagasaki, but there would be deep psychological, emotional, and political scars left over that would take much longer to repair. Third, there would be calls for revenge, bloody revenge against the perpetrators or presumed perpetrators and any others who were deemed hostile by the attacked nation. The Bush administration's assertion after 9/11 that Saddam Hussein was in league with the terrorists and would himself attack the United States at some point resonated with many Americans who sought to punish Saddam by killing him or at least driving him from power. How much more revenge-minded might a populace become after nuclear terrorism?

A nation attacked by nuclear weapons will surely seek some form of retaliation if it has the means at hand. Some Americans called for "nuking" Afghanistan after 9/11 and any other regime that "supported" Osama bin Laden. President Bush himself suggested that retribution and punishment are necessary. "Whether we bring our enemies to justice or bring justice to our enemies, justice will be done." The phrase is ambiguous enough to suggest that "justice" might even require the use of nuclear weapons if the situation warrants it. There has been more nuclear "talk" coming out of Washington in recent years suggesting a change of orientation towards the use of these weapons. Some analysts fear that being the only hegemonic superpower in the world may actually increase the likelihood that the United States would consider using nuclear weapons, perhaps even before its opponents do so. The nuclear taboo is under great strain.

THE EFFECTS OF NUCLEAR WEAPONS

To understand why the nuclear taboo emerged after the American use of nuclear weapons against Hiroshima and Nagasaki in 1945, we need to examine the effects of nuclear weapons. Suppose that instead of the truck filled with hundreds of pounds of fertilizer and fuel oil used in Oklahoma City or the aircraft filled with thousands of gallons of jet fuel that crashed into the Twin Towers and the Pentagon, terrorists had acquired 100 pounds of highly enriched uranium, smaller than a soccer ball. Now sitting amidst furniture packed into a rental truck parked on a city street, it could produce a blast equivalent to 10,000 to 15,000 tons of TNT, about the size of the Hiroshima bomb. Under normal conditions, this would devastate a three-to-four-square-mile urban area. Much of Oklahoma City, for instance, would have disappeared, leaving hundreds of thousands dead or seriously injured. In a denser urban environment, such as lower Manhattan, the tip of Manhattan, including all of Wall Street reaching up to Grammercy Park, would have been destroyed, with over a million casualties. Moreover, within days after the blast, people far from the scene of devastation reaching portions of New Jersey, upstate New York, and Connecticut would become ill, some dying, some becoming incapacitated, others passing serious genetic mutations on to their off-spring.[11]

How is it that this explosive technology damages human life and society in ways not imagined before World War II? What is it that has made nuclear weapons so feared—feared in the profound sense that in them we see the possible death of civilization as we know it? Our only experience with the use of nuclear weapons in war was the attacks on Hiroshima and Nagasaki, two unprepared urban targets. Japan's surrender allowed the U.S. government to make an intensive investigation of the impact on those cities, but the United States decided that it needed to be "on the ground" in order to observe the effects of nuclear explosions. In 1953 and 1955 it conducted extensive tests against a variety of objects: houses and buildings, vehicles, electrical and communications transmission systems, and animals. From the theoretical understanding of the bomb, its use against Japan, and this postwar curiosity came the most concrete knowledge we have about nuclear weapons as weapons of mass destruction.

Assume that a nuclear device is used in an urban area where you are living. As that weapon detonates, there would be a brilliant flash of light as the release of nuclear energy occurred. Temperatures on the order of tens of millions of degrees would heat the air around the blast to create a glowing fireball that would expand and rise into the sky, creating the familiar mushroom-shaped cloud.

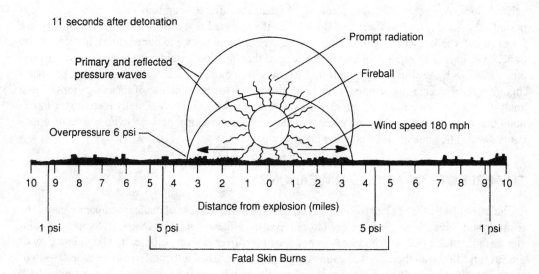

Figure 1–2   This figure shows a one megaton explosion eleven seconds after detonation.
Adapted from K. Lewis, "The Prompt and Delayed Effects of Nuclear War," *Scientific American, 241* (July 1979): 36.

The energy released by the weapons would take three forms. At the instant of detonation, 5 percent of the energy would be invisible radiation (in the form of neutrons and gamma rays), which would travel out for a relatively short distance from the point of blast.[12] This is called prompt radiation. The visible light would be thermal (or heat) radiation, accounting for 35 percent of the bomb's energy. Another 50 percent of the weapon's energy would be converted into a shock wave of air created by the superheated air in the vicinity of the detonation. (A detonation close to the ground would also create a shock wave of lesser strength transmitted through the ground.) And finally, 10 percent of the energy would be in the form of very small radioactive particles created by the blast. If the blast occurred close enough to the ground surface, small pieces of earth would be sucked up by the fireball as it rose; the radioactive particles would fuse to those pieces of dust and debris. Carried aloft in the fireball and then pushed away from the blast site by prevailing winds, these radioactive particles would eventually fall out of the atmosphere. The result—radioactive fallout.

The effects of a single nuclear blast do not end with atomic and thermal radiation and blast (shock) effects. Unlike conventional weapons, a nuclear device multiplies its destructiveness. The initial shock wave from an airburst, for instance, can "echo" off the ground and combine with the shock wave as it travels outward to produce a more powerful wall of pressure that smashes what it encounters. Moreover, behind the shock waves are intense winds that exert a dynamic, relatively long-lasting pressure on structures that can topple them just as a hurricane does. The air will fill with flying debris.

Thermal radiation will be intense enough to start fires, but the main source of fires after a nuclear attack in an urban area is more likely to be from ruptured natural gas lines in buildings. The fires are likely to spread, creating a blazing inferno as they move outward as conflagrations. Or, if the heat from the fires in a particular area is strong enough, oxygen will rush in from surrounding areas and create a firestorm that consumes everything in the area.

Another effect, which seems minor compared to the physical damage of a nuclear blast, is EMP, or electromagnetic pulse. As a nuclear weapon detonates, it creates an intense, brief surge of electrical energy. Such energy is likely to disrupt or destroy communications systems driven by micro-chips and devices with unshielded electronic components.

Imagine being at ground zero, the point directly underneath an exploding nuclear device. Thermal and atomic radiation and the shock wave radiate outward in all directions from this point. As they move outward, they diminish in strength or destructiveness. Therefore, we can image a series of concentric circles of destructiveness ranging from ground zero out for some distance. Figure 1-2 illustrates the effects of a one megaton warhead (a very large nuclear device, one found historically in the arsenals of the superpowers).

One rough index of destructiveness is the pounds per square inch index (known as *psi*). At the earth's surface, the atmosphere normally puts approximately 15 pounds of pressure on each square inch of surface. The shock wave of a nuclear blast creates its own pressure, called "overpressure." One conventional reference point is 5 psi of overpressure. Within a circle with this much overpressure, it is expected that 50 percent of the individuals will die and that "lightly constructed commercial buildings and typical residences are destroyed; heavier construction is severely damaged."[13] It is not the blast (or overpressure) itself that accounts for all the destruction of human lives or property, although that will contribute. Rather, the 5 psi ring indicates where falling buildings, fires, wind-driven debris, and other effects will cause such devastation to those people and things unfortunate enough to be within that circle. Further out from ground zero, the casualties from the blast itself will decrease.

Other casualties will come from radiation. Those close to ground zero, if they survive the effects of blast and thermal radiation, will immediately receive lethal doses of nuclear radiation. The range of nuclear radiation, however, is limited; the range of thermal radiation is greater but still limited. For instance, a one-megaton explosion can produce third-degree burns up to five miles; death is likely if such burns cover more than a quarter of the body's surface. These, then, are the "prompt" effects of a nuclear blast.

To this point, we have looked at the impact of a single nuclear weapon on an urban area. The range of nuclear explosiveness is quite varied, from several kilotons to many megatons. Tactical nuclear weapons like the W33 artillery shell can deliver from 1 to 12 kilotons against a target; the Lance short-range missile could deliver 1 to 100 kilotons. The example in the preceding paragraphs spoke of a one megaton weapon, a weapon far larger than the Hiroshima or Nagasaki weapons and one beyond the hopes of any terrorist organization. But the ability to destroy the heart of a city—like Hiroshima and Nagasaki were destroyed—lies within the capacity of any group or state possessing nuclear weapons. Cities, of course, need not be the only target. The more rural the target, the less the comparative damage; such a target might be a military unit or a key transit point. The debris and conflagration would be minimized, but all the other effects would occur. As the explosion is likely to be an airburst (to maximize the area covered by the blast effects), the amount of fallout would be decreased, due to less debris in the mushroom cloud.[14]

Finally, as military establishments considered how they might protect their assets—particularly weapons, communication facilities, and key personnel—they began to dig deeper into the earth, putting tons of reinforced concrete between these valued assets and a nuclear device at or near ground level. The technologies of nuclear attack have responded. For instance, the United States has begun development of a nuclear warhead that would penetrate some distance below the surface of the earth, through concrete, before detonating. If such a warhead can be delivered accurately (and with the Global Positioning System developed by the United States, it can), the nuclear device can be relatively small and, because the explosion would occur far underground, the blast, radiation, and fallout effects would be largely, but not completely, contained.

The effects of nuclear weapons on human bodies and on humans' handiwork from bridges to buildings represent the physical damage created by such weapons. There is also the *psychological damage*. Survivors will forever carry the memory of terror. Individuals far from the site will draw on what they are told and what they see in the media to form images of the event. The only experience humans have had with a nuclear attack came at the end of a long and bloody war; the Japanese in both cities expected to be attacked and in a devastating way as other large portions of other cities had been burned to the ground by American bombing attacks.

It is likely that the next nuclear explosion will come as a surprise to its victims and other members of a society, for the most likely scenario for such an explosion will be the opening hours of a war or in the single heartbeat of a terrorist attack. Historically, wars began with a powerful attack against an opponent's military capabilities (as at Pearl Harbor). Now wars between nuclear-armed nations are likely to begin with nuclear attacks against urban areas as they are also the site of military facilities, centers of economic production, and the political heart of a society. Terrorists, with access to far fewer nuclear weapons, will be unwilling to waste a nuclear device; the maximum impact will be achieved by attacking a heavily populated target.

The victims of the attack—both those who survive the detonation and those fellow citizens who are horror-struck on learning that it has occurred—will ask, why us? What did we do to deserve this?

Burying the dead would also create major logistical and psychological nightmares. The overall psychological impact could be so significant that a victimized nation or region might not have the will or the capability to pull itself back to some level of normality for many years. And as indicated earlier, it would be difficult to contain these social, political, and psychological effects to the nations involved.

If the nuclear attacks are very limited and only on one or two cities, eventually there would be recovery. The Japanese reconstructed Hiroshima and Nagasaki relatively quickly and they are now normal, functioning cities. The issue of global impact and ultimate recovery arises if there are additional weapons used and of significantly larger power. For example, the recovery of the Japanese cities was largely dependent on outside assistance. Comparable Indian or Pakistani cities, such as Madras, Pondicherry, or Karachi, could expect outside assistance, if it were available. If the detonations, however, were more numerous, widespread, and potent, then sufficient sources of outside help would be more difficult to enlist. That certainly is the case if we were to contemplate the prospects of a more global conflagration.

Throughout the Cold War (roughly 1945–1990), there was a real prospect of such a global nuclear war. Even today, nuclear powers possess over twenty thousand nuclear weapons. If even a small portion of these weapons, most of which are far more powerful than the weapons which destroyed Hiroshima and devastated Nagasaki, were actually used in nuclear war, the ensuing holocaust would dwarf the worst human tragedies in history.[19] A World Health Organization study estimated that a nuclear war fought with about one-half of the present arsenals would cause one billion immediate deaths and seriously injure an equal number, most of whom would eventually die due to the effects of radiation exposure, lack of food and uncontaminated water, shortages of medicine and medical care, and the general collapse of the social, economic, and political infrastructures of society.[20]

Government officials in the United States and the Soviet Union gave thought to what nuclear war might look like—and what could be done to survive it. The prospects were sobering, as multiple explosions created major systemic effects.[21] One class of systemic effects concerns radioactive fallout. It is perhaps the effect that we know most about because extensive above-ground nuclear tests by both superpowers produced measurable fallout patterns. Multiple detonations with a significant proportion of ground bursts would likely produce extensive fallout over populated areas and farming areas. As the radioactive fission fragments decay (that is, as they emit particles to move toward stable, nonradioactive isotopes), they release doses of radiation that may be lethal for unsheltered people and animals. Even in shelters, unless the shelter is well shielded and closed off from air-transported radioactive dust, radiation will be a problem. In areas far removed from the blast sites and not in the central plume of fallout it might be safe to emerge in the open after two to three weeks. The amount of radioactivity would still greatly exceed what we now consider to be safe, but would not produce short-term deaths. In the direct plume areas, depending on the distance from ground zero, two to ten years would be required for the radiation to return to levels considered safe.

Fallout itself can produce death or sickness that so weakens the body that it falls prey to other diseases. In the long run, those individuals who survive radiation deaths will most likely suffer greatly increased cancer rates and pass on genetic defects to their offspring. Such effects, of course, are not confined to humans. Indeed, as most animals, domestic or wild, will not be sheltered, we can expect extensive deaths of livestock and game, depriving humans of food, power, and transportation. The killing off of birds may prove quite serious, as birds are natural controls for insect populations. Ironically, insects are the most immune to radiological effects. They would become a serious threat to food crops.

likely, the message day after day would be one that brings no hope. While radiation levels would, within several weeks, fall below lethal levels in many areas, deaths would continue to mount from those with radiation sickness and other illnesses that attack bodies weakened by radiation damage, foul water, hunger, and cold. The medical profession and its support facilities—hospitals, drug manufacturing, and distributing operations—would be greatly reduced in number by a major attack. Food, or its absence, would be another continuing reminder that the future is precarious. Even if food were available for a while in some areas, disruption of transportation systems will keep it out of the mouths of many.

A major nuclear war would severely test political leaders and governments, as well as the society's economic system. Modern economies are generally resilient, finding ways to cope with shocks, creating new solutions to problems as they emerge. But the strength of such economies also points to a key problem: the interdependence of a large number of individuals on each other for their continued economic well-being. A catastrophic disturbance in one area of the economy is likely to ripple through the entire economy. More traditional economies are not as interdependent; significant disruption in one area does not necessarily imperil the rest. Yet traditional economies often operate close to the boundary between economic sufficiency and extreme scarcity. Widespread nuclear attacks would likely plunge entire societies into monumental privation.

At some point a nuclear attack would likely move the economy past the point where it could regenerate itself. Even with government efforts, it could not produce enough to sustain the survivors at a subsistence level. Every day would be a losing struggle to keep warm, dry, and fed enough to prevent death through starvation and disease. An interest in the future would be an early victim. Similarly, at some point a nuclear attack would push the political system beyond recovery, even if the nation is said to be the "victor" in the nuclear exchange. If the political structure survived relatively intact, it would still be overwhelmed with immense problems. The political process would be expected to put together the shattered economy. If this were not challenge enough, the traditional governmental functions themselves would be under challenge. Who would have the right to issue orders? Who would be willing to obey? Public order would be precarious. Parts of the nation would be awash with refugees from devastated areas, who would fall upon areas ill prepared to receive them, and animosities would escalate as shortages increased and demands grew that resources held by undamaged areas and individuals ought to be redistributed.

These bleak images haunted the imaginations of many during the Cold War. They had a basis in fact: the United States and the Soviet Union planned to stage massive attacks against the other if it came to war. Had such an exchange come to pass, there would be no future. As former Soviet leader Nikita Khrushchev once remarked, the living would envy the dead.

THE SECOND NUCLEAR AGE

We are clearly living in a different nuclear world, a second nuclear age, where the threat of such doomsday scenarios has significantly declined. With the fall of the Berlin Wall in 1989 and the disintegration of the former Soviet Union in the early 1990s, the chances of unlimited thermonuclear exchanges between major nuclear powers have diminished to the point that remarkably few even worry about them anymore. The conventional wisdom suggests that the world is a much safer place now that communism has expired and, with it, the expansionist Soviet adversary that served as the fixed point for the American foreign policy compass for four decades of Cold War. The threat of nuclear war is over or greatly diminished, people say.

We believe that conclusion to be a bit premature, even a case of wishful thinking. A certain form of the nuclear threat, namely, a global nuclear conflagration initiated by the superpowers, may have been lessened by recent events, but not the threat itself in other guises. It can be a fundamental and analytically mischievous error to confuse the end of the Cold War with tranquility or predictability. Peace is quite compatible with trouble, conflict, racism, inequality, injustice, xenophobia, and genocide—and therefore with chaos, uncertainty, and unpredictability. We have seen extraordinary changes in the former Soviet Union, Eastern Europe, South Africa, and the Middle East. What is equally extraordinary is that no one foresaw these changes. The leaders and the experts were caught unaware. History has an abiding capacity to undermine our certitudes. No one predicted September 11. The most obvious conclusion to emerge from these events is that the geopolitical and military power of the United States is no longer sufficient to ensure its security. We live in aftermath, an aftermath that has adopted the concept of "homeland security" as synonymous with national security and the irony is we feel less secure than ever. We should approach predicting the future, therefore, with some caution and humility.

As a result of the dramatic political transformations of the 1990s, and the 9/11 attacks, has the likelihood that a nuclear weapon will explode somewhere in the world decreased? Probably not. Even as the probability of large-scale nuclear war between the United States and Russia has decreased dramatically, the probability that a nuclear weapon will detonate in Russia, or Asia, or the Middle East, or even the United States, may have increased. But because this new threat comes in a form so different from prior experience, and because the instruments and policies needed to address it are so unlike the familiar Cold War approaches, Americans have had difficulty awakening to the new reality. The Aspen Strategy Group concluded in 2004 that the danger of nuclear terrorism is much greater than the public believes.[27] What was striking about September 11 was not only the lethal success of the operation, but the combination of will, planning and execution with a religiously motivated martyrdom. We confront, therefore, individuals and organizations who not only have the desire and skill to inflict great harm, but are not impeded by the normal constraints of their own mortality. The common assumption held before that fateful black Tuesday that terrorists would not resort to weapons of mass destruction because they would lose their own lives in the process and unleash the full power of the United States in response is no longer comforting.

The winding down of the superpower nuclear arms race may, ironically, produce two distinct types of threat in the twenty-first century: the more traditional problems of proliferation and of how to prevent former Soviet warheads and missiles from falling into the "wrong" hands; and the newer, perhaps more daunting task of dealing with large quantities of loosely controlled fissile material from which nuclear weapons can be made, material that is a profound security and ecological hazard and that terrorists covet. The collapse of Soviet power and the failure of totalitarian institutions certainly open up long-term possibilities of democratic transformation. But in the short term, the prospects may be for continued political upheavals, dislocation, and economic distress, an environment that may allow some of this material to be purchased by those interested in a quick nuclear "fix." The periodic economic and political crises Russia has faced since 1991 are an indication of how unstable the situation can become. The news is not entirely grim. But as long as Russia continues to be buffeted by turbulence, corruption and economic instability, the threat of nuclear leakage will persist.

This situation is complicated by the possibility of future breakdowns in Arab-Israeli relations; the growth of Moslem extremism and the use of terror; ethnic conflict in the Balkans and Africa; a volatile and aggressive regime in North Korea; the emergence of regional nuclear powers like India and Pakistan; technological advances in the Chinese nuclear arsenal; and the proliferation of sophisticated and deadly weaponry, including chemical, biological, and nuclear weaponry, around the globe and the desire to use them by extremist groups if they can.

The United States has obviously emerged as the only superpower after the Cold War. However, there are a number of countries—Japan, Taiwan, South Korea, Argentina, and Brazil, to name a few—that are now capable of equipping themselves with nuclear armaments and of constructing or purchasing sophisticated long-range missiles. When we add the so-called "rogue" nations like Iran, Syria, Sudan, and North Korea, for instance, that have either actively pursued nuclear capability, or provided havens for terrorists, we have a growing list of nations that could pose a real threat to the security of their neighbors, not to mention the interests of the major powers. Furthermore, it may be premature to envision a new era of permanent cooperation and peace between the United States and Russia. The political, ethnic and economic volatility of that region is still troubling. It remains to be seen if Russia's challenge to the West is truly over, or for that matter the challenges raised by Communism or some other brand of authoritarianism. German reunification is a fact and it is unlikely that Russia will regain its influence over Poland, Hungary, or the Czech Republic. The situation in the Balkans, however, is less stable or predictable. It is possible that at some time in the future the struggle between different national or ethnic groups might lead to regional conflict. It is possible that such a struggle might encourage the Russians or the Germans to extend their influence in the Balkans. Turmoil in Albania and in Serbia's Kosovo province in late 1998, remains a potential concern, as are the irredentist populations in some of the former Soviet republics.

THE NUCLEAR PREDICAMENT

The predicament we face in the second nuclear age, simply put, is that even with the relaxation of tensions between the superpowers, the United States, Russia, Great Britain, France, and China still possess nuclear weapons of awesome destructive capability. Furthermore, India, Pakistan, Israel and a growing list of countries including Iran and North Korea possess or may soon possess weapons, that if ever used, could precipitate a regional nuclear exchange that could destroy millions of lives.

There is also the specter of nuclear terrorism—particularly worrisome given the events of September 11 and the continuing threats posed by al Qaeda and its Islamist agenda. It is unclear, as well, whether the revolutions of the late 1980s in Eastern Europe and the Balkans will be stabilizing in the long term given the emergence of long-suppressed nationalisms and ethnic rivalries. So, although humans created this awesome technology of death, they have not yet been able to devise a method of insuring that it will never be used again in an attempt to achieve military or political objectives, deliberately or accidentally. Simply put, the predicament is that nuclear weapons exist, but we have not found unambiguous and universally accepted ways of controlling them and most proposed solutions have embedded within them potential or actual risks and problems. Whether means will be found to force nation-states armed with weapons of mass destruction to change before they destroy themselves remains to be seen. That nuclear powers have not engaged each other in war since 1945 is some consolation, but it is no guarantee that accident or miscalculation could not at anytime draw

Figure 1–3   Hiroshima in October 1945. *National Archives.*

them into a conflagration. The decision to use the atomic bomb against the Japanese (discussed in Chapter 3) reveals many of the features of the nuclear age in which we live, and begins to form the questions we need to ask for today and tomorrow. We are in the nuclear predicament largely because our modes of thought and our nuclear weapons policies are based on pre-Hiroshima categories of reflection. Because of Hiroshima, we must recognize the truth in Albert Einstein's insight that although reality has been transformed, our ways of thinking about reality have been relatively unaffected. "The unleashed power of the atom has changed everything save our modes of thinking, and we thus drift toward unparalleled catastrophe."[28] By relying on assumptions, values, methods, objectives, and policies rooted in the prenuclear age and solidified in the first nuclear age, we run the risk of missing or misconstruing the singular nature of the nuclear threat in the second nuclear age. Unless we overcome the conceptual and psychological problems of comprehension and action, we may not be in a position to fashion an appropriate and imaginative nuclear weapons policy consistent with the uniqueness of the nuclear predicament.

SUMMARY

On the morning of August 6, 1945, a single atomic bomb destroyed Hiroshima. On August 9, a second bomb destroyed Nagasaki. Humans, no matter where they lived, had been hurled into the first nuclear age. The mushroom-shaped cloud became the signature of the times, casting its shadow on the future, not only for the victims of those two attacks, but for all of the earth's inhabitants. It quickly became apparent that nuclear weapons could destroy much of what humans had painfully amassed as societies and cultures—and possibly lead to the extinction of the species. This chapter has reviewed what has happened and what might happen again if and when nuclear weapons are used. You know, as earlier generations did not, that the direst of outcomes would not occur, that the nuclear-infused Cold War would melt and douse the fire that the United States and the Soviet Union threatened to unleash on each other. But you also know, as they did not, that global terrorism is possible and that in the not-to-distant future, it may be nuclear-armed.

In the second nuclear age we confront new challenges, challenges that seem as perplexing as those of the first nuclear age. Those challenges, however, like the responses that humans crafted to meet them, are rooted in the first nuclear age. That is where our analysis must begin, with a description of how nuclear weapons are made, who has the capacity to make them, and who at the present time has them. We then return, in Chapter 3, to the fundamental question of why leaders might choose to use nuclear weapons, which brings us back to Hiroshima and Nagasaki and the agonizing birth of a new world.

ENDNOTES

[1]Quoted in Fernand Gignon, *The Bomb* (New York: Pyramid Books, 1958), p. 13.

[2]Quoted in Robert Jay Lifton, *Death in Life: Survivors of Hiroshima* (New York: Random House, 1967), p. 21.

[3]Michihiko Hachiya, *Hiroshima Diary* (Chapel Hill: The University of North Carolina Press, 1955). p. 8

[4]Lifton, *Death in Life*, p. 23.

[5]Quoted in Richard Rhodes, *The Making of the Atomic Bomb* (New York: Simon and Schuster, 1986), pp. 723-24.

[6]See Robert Jay Lifton and Greg Mitchell, *Hiroshima in America: Fifty Years of Denial* (New York: G.P. Putnam's Sons, 1995)

[7]Michael Walzer, *Just and Unjust Wars*, (New York: Basic Books, 1977), p. 197.

[8]*The 9/11 Commision Report* (New York: W.W. Norton & Co., 2004), p. 380.

[9] Graham Allison, *Nuclear Terrorism* (New York: Henry Holt and Co., 2004), p. 203

[10]Bill Keller, "Nuclear Nightmares," *New York Times Magazine*, May 26, 2002. See also Nicholas D. Kristof, "An American Hiroshima," *The New York Times*, August 12, 2004, p. A19, "The Nuclear Shadow," *The New York Times*, August 14, 2004, p. A20.

[11]Jessica Stern, *The Ultimate Terrorists* (Cambridge: Harvard University Press, 1999), p. 2.

[12]These are approximations for an airburst of a fission device. Samuel Glasstone and Philip Dolan, ed. *The Effects of Nuclear Weapons*, 3rd ed., (Washington, D.C.: U.S. Government Printing Office, 1977), pp. 7–8. The single most important source of effects.

[13]Office of Technology Assessment, United States Congress, *The Effects of Nuclear War* (Washington, D.C.: U.S. Government Printing Office, 1979) pp. 18–19.

[14]Ibid., pp. 64–75.

[15]See Grigori Medvedev, *The Truth About Chernobyl* (New York: Basic Books, 1991).

[16]Mary Makarushka, "Journey to Chernobyl," *On Wisconsin*, Vol. 106, No.1 (Spring, 2005), p. 27.

[17]World Health Organization report; www.who.int/mediacentre/news/releases/2005/pr35/index

[18]International Atomic Energy Agency, International Conference: One Decade After Chernobyl," April, 1996, www.iaea.org/worldatom/programmes/safety/Chernobyl/conclus. 17

[19]*SIPRI Yearbook 2004, World Armaments and Disarmament* (New York: Oxford University Press, 2004), p. 629.

[20] International Committee on Experts on Medical Sciences and Public Health. *Effects of Nuclear War on Health and Health Services* (Geneva: World Health Organization, 1984), p. 5. See also Eric Markusen, "Genocide and Total War," in Isidor Wallimann and Michael Dobkowski eds., *Genocide and the Modern Age* (Westport, Conn: Greenwood Press, 1987), p. 99.

[21]R.P. Turco et. al., "Nuclear Winter: Global Consequences of Multiple Nuclear Explosions," *Science*, vol. 222 (December 23, 1983), pp. 1283–1291. See also Stephen H. Schneider, "Climate Modeling," *Scientific American* (May 1987), pp. 72–80, and Markusen, "Genocide and Total War," p. 99.

[22]Paul Ehrich, Carl Sagan, Donald Kennedy, and Walter Orr Roberts, *The Cold and the Dark* (New York: W.W. Norton, 1984); Paul Ehrich e. al., "Long-Term Biological Consequences of Nuclear War," *Science*, vol. 222 (December 23, 1983), pp. 1293–1300.

[23]Stephen Schneider, "Climate Modeling," *Scientific American 256* (May 1987), p. 80.

[24]Ehrlich, *Cold and Dark*, pp. 50–51.

[25]John Hersey, *Hiroshima* (New York: Bantam Books, 1946, 1973), p. 55.

[26]Office of Technology Assessment, Effects, p. 87.

[27]Graham Allison, *Nuclear Terrorism* (New York: Times Books, 2004), pp. 1–15.

[28]Otto Nathan and Heinz Norden, eds., *Einstein on Peace* (New York: Schocken, 1986), p. 376.

2

Building the Bomb

The "Gadget" (Figure 2-1) stood fully assembled atop a 100-foot steel tower in a remote section of the Alamogordo Air Base in New Mexico[1]. It was roughly spherical in shape with a diameter of about six feet, with electrical cables draped crazily over its surface. Inside the metal casing, 2.5 tons of high explosives surrounded a 13.5 pound plutonium core, no larger than a grapefruit. The final assembly had taken place under unusual and ominous weather conditions, amid heavy rains, thunder, and lightning. Code-named *Trinity*, this was to be the first full-scale test of the Manhattan Project's highly secret atomic bomb research.

On July 16, 1945, at 5:30 a.m., electrical signals ignited the explosives, which sent a powerful shockwave into the plutonium core, compressing it into a supercritical mass. In less than a millionth of a second the resulting chain reaction in the plutonium was over, the temperature of the core had

Figure 2–1   The "Gadget" in place at the top of the tower at the Trinity test site. Los Alamos National Laboratory

Source: Photo at http://www.lanl.gov/history/atomicbomb/images/GadgetS.GIF

risen to about 100 million degrees, and its pressure had risen to about 100 million atmospheres. Shining many times brighter than the noonday sun, the glowing core of hot plasma became a rapidly expanding fireball (Figure 2-2), vaporizing everything in its path, and lighting up the clouds and nearby mountain ranges with an eerie brilliance. Pound for pound, the nuclear explosive yielded more than a million times as much energy as the chemical explosives in conventional bombs. Trinity was a complete success, exceeding the expectations of most of its builders. The assembled scientists who were, or were to become, the luminaries of American physics were jubilant. The gray skies, however, bore silent testimony to a future more ominous than anyone there could have foreseen.

The bomb represented the confluence of three forces: 50 years of scientific research to understand the physics of the atom, the political lobbying of individuals who wanted to arouse the United States to the danger of science in the service of Nazi Germany, and the ability of the U.S. government to organize the massive engineering effort needed to build a deliverable nuclear explosive. Critical nuclear experiments on the heavy metal uranium—the beginning point for all nuclear weapons—had been done in a Berlin laboratory since 1934. Scientists there and elsewhere had discovered that when uranium was bombarded with neutrons, different elements had appeared in the sample that had not been there before bombardment. In late 1938, two German scientists, Otto Hahn and Fritz Strassmann, were finally able to identify two lighter elements in such a sample. Hahn communicated the results to a former colleague, Lise Meitner, in Sweden, a refugee from Nazi anti-Semitism. She and her nephew, the physicist Otto Frisch, quickly hypothesized that the large mass uranium atoms had split or "fissioned" (Frisch's term) into those two smaller mass elements. Their published conclusions and personal communications among the network of scientists, particularly those who had led left fascist Europe and emigrated to the United States, spurred further scientific investigation.

Figure 2–2   Trinity test site .016 seconds after the "Gadget" was fired. Los Alamos National Laboratory.
Source: Photo at http://www.lanl.gov/history/atomicbomb/trinity_gallery/images/TR18_2.jpg

Physicists realized that fissioning or "splitting" of uranium atoms released extraordinary amounts of energy per atom, so that if the fissioning could be made self-sustaining, unprecedented amounts of energy might be quickly released, and that in turn suggested a military application for this new phenomenon. Several refugee scientists urged Albert Einstein, their most famous colleague in exile in the United States, to write President Franklin Roosevelt. Although Einstein was a consistent advocate of pacifism and world government, as a German emigré his fear that Hitler might obtain the atomic bomb was so great that he agreed to do so, alerting the President to the military potential of nuclear fission and urging him to provide government support for further research. Roosevelt's support helped bring the "Committee on Uranium" into existence along with a modest allotment of funds ($6,000) in November, 1939, two months after Nazi Germany invaded Poland. When France and Britain had come to Poland's defense in early September, Europe entered its second World War.

Initial government interest in the fissioning process in the United States—and in Germany and the Soviet Union—was cautious.[2] The political and military leaders of the time did not know that it would be possible to create nuclear weapons. Indeed, the very idea that one could achieve a self-sustaining fission process and then build that into a deliverable weapon of war was but an untested hypothesis. As these nations were at war—or in the case of the United States, laboring to rearm—other claimants for government revenues could make a much more convincing case that the then-existing technologies, be they in warships or tanks or aircraft, would provide the war-winning weapon, if only enough funds, resources, and personnel were devoted to these enterprises. As it would happen, the right combination of individuals, resources, and organization in the United States (with significant help from Great Britain[3]) first revealed the secrets of the enormous destructive force that we saw in Chapter One.

In this chapter, we briefly explore how the bomb works, not only in terms of the physics of nuclear weapons, but also in terms of the technologies that are necessary for a state or a group to build nuclear weapons. As you come to understand the problems faced by the nuclear physicists and engineers, their ingenious solutions, and the extraordinary physical conditions created by nuclear explosions, you will be able to appreciate the fascination that this subject holds for them, a fascination that undoubtedly played some role in the development of nuclear weapons. Nuclear weapons are a consequence of a widespread human endeavor to know and control the physical world. They are an artifact of the human experience.[4] Moreover, to understand how nuclear weapons came to be built is to appreciate the role that governments and the publics they represent play in the process. Nuclear weapons are the result of political decisions made by humans. Finally, to understand nuclear weapons is to demystify them. To see them as any other human artifact gives us the power to see that control of nuclear weapons is possible.[5]

THE DISCOVERY OF A NEW WORLD

The science that would produce nuclear weapons was a young science, coming of age at the dawn of the twentieth century when scientists in Europe made crucial discoveries.[6] Henri Becquerel found that the heavy metal uranium gave off strange rays that would darken photographic plates. Subsequent experiments on other naturally occurring radioactive elements by Marie and Pierre Currie and Ernest Rutherford, among others, revealed that three physically distinct types of rays were being given off. Because the properties and nature of these emissions were poorly understood, they were simply designated by the first three letters of the Greek alphabet: *alpha*, *beta*, and *gamma rays*. (This is the *natural radioactivity* of uranium.) How, they asked themselves, could an element, presumably the smallest, indivisible and permanent manifestation of matter, produce such effects? Rutherford concluded that upon emitting its radiation, a radioactive element such as uranium transformed itself into a different chemical element. That transformation was possible only if a uranium *atom* itself was composed of several parts that could undergo change. The challenge was to identify the parts, how they were arranged, and what held them together.

By the early 1930s, physicists had developed what came to be called the planetary model of the atom's parts. (See Figure 2-3.) In the atom's center is the *nucleus*, composed of small, heavy, positively charged particles called *protons* and other small, heavy particles with no electric charge called *neutrons*. Collectively, the protons and neutrons are called the *nucleons* of an atom. 99.95 percent of an atom's mass or weight is due to its nucleons. Surrounding the positively charged nucleus are light, negatively charged *electrons* orbiting at relatively large distances from the nucleus, just as the Earth and the other planets orbit the sun. If an oxygen atom, for instance, were enlarged until the nucleus was the size of a baseball, the atomic electrons could be found as far as almost a mile away. Electrostatic attraction (now called the Coulomb force) between the positively charged protons and negatively charged electrons keeps the electrons in orbit. While this model of the atom has been superceded by a more sophisticated one,[7] it provided physicists of the time with a fruitful insight into the world of the atom.

The chemical properties of each element such as hydrogen, oxygen, and uranium are unique and are determined by the number of electrons surrounding the nucleus, which must in turn equal the number of protons in the nucleus. However, the number of neutrons can vary somewhat. Indeed, an element such as uranium may exist in more than one form, differing only in the number of neutrons in

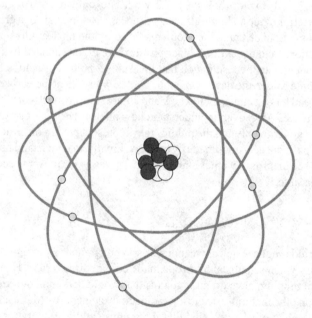

Figure 2–3   Bohr's planetary model of the atom. Nitrogen is illustrated here.

the nucleus. Such different forms of a particular element are known as the *isotopes* of that element. Different isotopes of an element are chemically almost identical, despite the slight differences in weight—the difference in weight of the isotope depending upon the different number of neutrons in the nucleus.

Any particular isotope is completely specified by giving its element name and its atomic mass number, as in uranium-235. All uranium atoms have 92 protons, which means that an atom of the isotope uranium-235 consists of a nucleus of 92 protons and 143 neutrons ($235 - 92 = 143$), surrounded by 92 electrons. By the same token, uranium-238 consists of a nucleus of 92 protons and 146 neutrons, surrounded by 92 electrons. These seemingly trivial differences would make all the difference in the world when it came to making nuclear weapons.

This model of the atom, as insightful as it was, seemed to be built upon a critical contradiction: All the positively charged protons crammed into the nucleus should repel each other because of the electrostatic repulsion of the Coulomb force. This force increases rapidly as the distance between like-charged particles decreases, so that the protons clustered in the nucleus must repel each other very powerfully. The model of the atom now had to include a much stronger attractive force (not surprisingly called *the strong nuclear force*) capable of resisting the Coulomb repulsion and holding the protons in the nucleus. This force between the nucleons would be very strong when they were together, but rapidly drop to zero if they moved even a small distance apart. Each proton finds itself attracted by only three or four protons in its immediate neighborhood, but is repelled by all the other protons in the nucleus (as the Coulomb force of repulsion acts over very large distances).

The *neutrons* in the nucleus help to hold the protons together as well, because they contribute to the strong nuclear force between adjacent protons and neutrons, but as they have no electrical charge, they do not contribute to the repulsive Coulomb force. Thus, having more neutrons than protons in the nucleus can—up to a point—help keep the nucleus stable because they help overcome the ever-present Coulomb force. If, however, one were able to destabilize the nucleus—to weaken the hold of the strong nuclear force—the protons would fly apart with great velocities and the repulsion energy would be released. How might this be accomplished?

For large nuclei such as uranium, the strong nuclear force barely keeps the protons together. Suppose we sent a neutron toward a U-235 nucleus. Neutrons are critical for nuclear weapons as they have no electrical charge; thus the protons in the uranium nucleus do not repel neutrons as they approach the nucleus. If a neutron enters a U-235 nucleus and disturbs the nucleons in such a way that the strong nuclear force is briefly diminished, the repulsive Coulomb force will begin to drive the protons apart, further weakening the strong nuclear force and accelerating the protons even more. The nucleus of the heavy uranium atom then splits apart (or fissions), creating two lighter elements and a few left-over neutrons that move apart at great velocities, carrying away great amounts of energy. If the strong nuclear force in other uranium atoms can be disrupted at the same time, in a very brief moment we have the makings of a very powerful explosive device.

The schematic diagram of Figure 2-4 illustrates what happens in the process of *neutron-induced fission*. A relatively unenergetic neutron collides with a U-235 nucleus and is absorbed, temporarily forming the isotope U-236. However, the energy and disruption which it brings with it is too great for this precariously unstable nucleus, which spontaneously breaks into two main pieces and a few free neutrons.

What are the important features of this fissioning process? First, the smaller nuclei and neutrons that emerge from the reaction come off with great velocities and energies. It is this energy that is utilized in a nuclear explosion—and in nuclear power plants designed to generate electricity. Second,

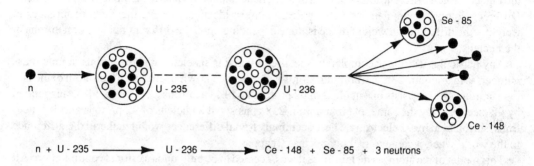

n + U - 235 ——————→ U - 236 ——————→ Ce - 148 + Se - 85 + 3 neutrons

Figure 2–4   Unstable U-236 breaks up into Se-85 and Ce-148. This is only one of many possible sets of fission fragments.

the neutrons that emerge from the fissioning may collide with other heavy nuclei, causing them to fission, thus leading to the possibility of a self-sustaining *chain reaction* and the release of great amounts of energy. Nuclear weapons (and power plants) must be able to create and control this chain reaction. Third, when heavy nuclei fission, they break into two different nuclei, but not always the same two. In fact, more than 300 different isotopes of 36 light elements have been found in the products of nuclear fission. These fission products are themselves unstable, and undergo further transformations, creating the *radioactivity* that is a central aspect of nuclear weapons.

RADIOACTIVITY

Isotopes of unstable elements spontaneously reach stability by emitting energetic particles and electromagnetic radiation. This is the radiation that early physicists observed when uranium was placed near photographic plates. An *alpha ray* (now called an alpha particle) is frequently emitted by very heavy nuclei which are unstable by virtue of their large size. The alpha particle turned out to be a small nucleus consisting of two protons and two neutrons bound tightly together. This emission transmutes the original element into another. For example,

U-238 ——→ Th-234 + alpha particle

In this way, the uranium nucleus quickly loses two destabilizing protons and four units of mass, becoming the element thorium in the process. Subsequent emissions may occur until the atom reaches stability.

Beta rays turned out to be electrons with either a negative or positive electric charge (the *positron*). Protons can turn into neutrons and neutrons into protons, in the process creating positrons and electrons, respectively, which are then ejected from the nucleus. The transmutation moves the new element closer to stability. Finally, a radioactive element may emit a *gamma ray*, very energetic photons of "light," a light with frequencies well beyond the visible and ultraviolet regions of the electromagnetic spectrum. Nuclei emit gamma rays, thereby reducing their energy without changing their proton and neutron composition.

These natural transformations continue to occur in all unstable or radioactive elements. Each radioactive element has a characteristic property called its *half-life*. A half-life is the time needed for half of the unstable atoms in a sample to transform themselves into stable atoms. For example, one of the isotopes of tin, Sn-121, has a half-life of 27 hours while one isotope of silver, Ag–97, has a half-life of 23 seconds. Uranium-238, on the other hand, has a half-life of 4.5 billion years. This naturally occurring half-life decay has implications for nuclear weapons as well. Tritium, an isotope of hydrogen (H–3), found in many modern nuclear warheads, has to be replenished periodically for in roughly 12 years, half of it will have become Helium-3.

When uranium fissions in a nuclear weapon or a power reactor, the fission fragments (two lighter elements) are radioactive isotopes, which will give off alpha, beta, and gamma rays. In a nuclear explosion, these fission fragments will be blown into the environment, fused to dust and debris and carried into the atmosphere by the fireball and updraft from the heat of the explosion, falling back to earth many miles from the point of detonation. These unstable elements will move toward stability by continuing to shower the contaminated area for years with radioactivity, damaging the living cells in humans, animals, and plants that they strike.

ENGINEERING THE BOMB

Although Hahn and Strassmann's discovery of nuclear fission in 1938 immediately suggested to physicists the possibility of an energy-releasing fission chain reaction, there was no clear answer to *how* this might be done. As it turned out, practical chain reactions could be achieved, but only with great difficulty. The effort and expense needed were so great that in the 1940s, only a major national power could marshal the needed scientific, technical, and economic resources. In recognition of the large industrial effort called for, in August 1942, the American Army Corps of Engineers established a unit called the Manhattan District to oversee all work on the bomb.[8] General Leslie Groves was placed in command of what would come to be a far-flung enterprise, with research and test facilities constructed at Los Alamos, production facilities in Hanford, Washington and Oak Ridge, Tennessee, and continuing nuclear research at the University of Chicago, the University of California, Princeton University, and Columbia University, to name a few.

There were four basic challenges that the Manhattan Project (or any effort to acquire nuclear weapons) had to solve: (1) It had to collect sufficient *fissile material*—material capable of being fissioned. (2) That material and the way it was put together had to release enough neutrons to sustain the process of fissioning and thus produce a *chain reaction*. (3) Once the chain reaction started, the fissile material had to *stay intact* long enough to complete the reaction rather than being blown apart and ending the explosion in a "fizzle." (4) *The device had to be small and rugged enough to be deliverable to the target*.

Let us first consider *the problem of a sustained chain reaction*. As we have already seen, nuclear fission itself releases neutrons. Those neutrons may collide with other unstable nuclei and cause them to fission, producing yet more itinerant neutrons. If one fissioning atom can, by releasing a neutron, cause another fission, which releases another neutron, and the process continues, we say that the fissile material has reached a *critical mass*. That would be enough to sustain the heat-generating activities of a nuclear reactor, but it does not produce an explosion. We need to accelerate the fissioning process by having more than one neutron being released in each fission. For the two most commonly used fissionable isotopes in nuclear weapons, uranium-235 and pluto-nium-239, the average number of new neutrons per fission is about 2.5 and 3 respectively, and so this requirement is satisfied.

Simply freeing more neutrons is not enough, however, for each itinerant neutron can do something other than strike the nucleus of the fissile material:

1. It may leave the fissionable material entirely before causing another fission.

2. The very act of beginning the chain reaction may blow the fissile material apart. Many neutrons no longer encounter another nucleus to fission.

3. The neutron may be absorbed by a nonfissioning nucleus before causing another fission. For example, there may be impurity atoms in the material whose nuclei absorb neutrons without fissioning.

How do bomb makers cope with these three problems? Consider the impurity problem. Uranium itself is at the heart of this problem. Uranium-235 has a high probability of capturing a neutron and fissioning, but uranium-238 can capture a neutron without fissioning at all. Because naturally occurring uranium is 99.3 percent uranium-238 and only 0.7 percent uranium-235, a significant number of neutrons would be lost to the U-238 in a sample of natural uranium, and sustaining a chain reaction would be rendered more difficult. For this reason, natural uranium is usually processed to remove some of the U-238 to produce reactor-grade uranium for electrical power generation or to remove most of the U-238 for weapons-grade or Highly Enriched Uranium (HEU). Weapons-grade uranium is typically enriched to 95 percent U-235 whereas uranium enriched to 4 percent U-235 is adequate for most power reactors. Beyond the presence of U-238, great care is taken to eliminate other neutron-absorbing impurities from power plant fuel rods and nuclear weapon cores.

There are four techniques to deal with the problem of neutrons' leaving the sample of fissile material: (a) Make the sample of fissionable material larger. This provides the neutron with more chances of meeting a fissionable nucleus before it arrives at the boundary of the sample. (b) Surround the sample with a neutron reflector, like beryllium, so that neutrons are reflected back in as they try to escape. (c) Choose a shape for the sample that minimizes the surface area through which neutrons may escape. A sphere, for instance, has the minimum surface area for a given volume. (d) Increase the density of the sample by judicious choice of its chemical form or by compressing it. If the atoms are packed closer together, there is a greater chance that a neutron will run into a fissionable nucleus before escaping entirely.

As for the problem of the *premature blowing apart of the fissile material*, we need to look more closely at the nature of the problem to understand the technical solutions to overcome it.[9] Consider the speed of a nuclear chain reaction. A fission-produced neutron in highly enriched fissionable material takes only about .01 microseconds (.01 millionths of a second) to be captured by a fissionable nucleus and to produce another fission. Let us suppose that on the average two neutrons from each fission survive to produce additional neutron-induced fissions.

A single trigger neutron, after .01 microseconds, will have caused one fission, released 180 MeV (180 million electron volts) of energy, and sent two neutrons flying through the material to fission more nuclei. After an additional .01 microsecond, two more nuclei will have fissioned, producing 360 MeV of prompt energy and four more neutrons. Each .01 microsecond results in a new generation of fissions and neutrons, and the number of fissions grows rapidly. This is analogous to the population explosion that occurs when a birth rate is significantly greater than the death rate, though on a much shorter time scale. Within the first .5 microseconds, there will be a significant release of energy—enough to scatter the fissile material far and wide (and do great damage to the immediate vicinity) but without producing an explosion equivalent to, say, 20,000 tons of TNT (20 Kt) that can destroy the heart of city. That power will be released in roughly the next .2 microseconds, but only if the fissile material remains intact long enough.

The trick to making a fission explosion is to take a mass of fissionable material that is not critical, suddenly turn it into a critical mass and keep it critical long enough for the reaction to produce the desired energy. The simplest way to do this is to take two sub-critical masses, each of which is too small to be critical, and rapidly bring them together to form a critical mass. The earliest American design accomplished this by the so-called *gun assembly technique*, in which a precisely shaped piece of uranium-235 is shot down a gun barrel into a larger piece of uranium-235 at the other end. The larger piece contains a hole to receive the smaller slug. The speed of the driven slug must be sufficiently high to continue its progress into the other mass long enough after the reaction has begun to produce the desired energy yield. The weapons designers were so confident of this design that it was not tested before its use on the city of Hiroshima, where it produced a 12.5 Kt explosion.

The weapons tested at Trinity and dropped on Nagasaki employed a different design and produced explosions of about 22 Kt. In this design, a critical mass is achieved by taking a sphere of Plutonium-239 that is not critical, surrounding it with specially shaped conventional high explosives, and detonating all of the explosives simultaneously. This produces a powerful shock wave that drives inward and compresses the fissionable material until it has reached a density sufficient to make it critical, giving the name *implosion device* to this type of weapon. Figure 2-5 illustrates this and also introduces a few additional features. Most of the fission weapons in the current arsenals of the major powers are of this type. (Uranium-235 can be used in place of PU-239).

The detonators are placed at strategic positions around the shell of explosives and must be triggered simultaneously so that the implosion will be symmetrical and compress the core uniformly from all sides. Otherwise, the core may be blasted into a nonspherical, noncritical shape. The layer of uranium-238, which is very dense and heavy, is given a high inward velocity and acts as a driver. It is the inertia of this high-speed heavy metal that helps to keep the compression of the core proceeding, even after the nuclear chain reaction has begun, and thus keeps the core at a supercritical density long enough for the requisite number of generations of neutrons to be born. The vacuum layer shown in the diagram allows the uranium to achieve full velocity before hitting the core. The U-238 driver also acts as a neutron reflector and aids in making the compressed core supercritical.

The complete fission of 2.2 pounds of fissionable material would produce a 17.5 Kt explosion. Because fission explosions never succeed in fissioning all of their material, a typical 17.5 Kt bomb would require larger amounts of fissionable material, the exact amount depending on the efficiency of the bomb design.

The Manhattan Project scientists kept in mind that a nuclear device that could not be delivered to a target would not be an effective weapon of war. It had to fit into the bomb-bay of the largest American aircraft of the time, the B-29 (which by 1945 had demonstrated great effectiveness in penetrating Japanese air defenses). It had to remain sub-critical during transport to the forward operating base and on the flight, then become critical only at the moment it reached the target. And it had to work reliably. Both the gun assembly and implosion devices met these requirements.

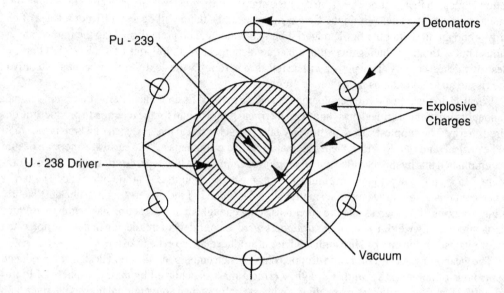

Figure 2–5   Schematic diagram of an implosion device.
Adapted from Howard Morland, *The Secret That Exploded* (New York: Random House, 1981)

ACQUIRING FISSILE MATERIALS

Access to uranium in sufficiently large quantities is the first step in making nuclear weapons. Uranium is a naturally occurring heavy metal whose concentrated deposits were initially thought to be relatively scarce; today we know they are relatively abundant and widespread globally. The metal when mined is intermixed with other elements that need to be separated from the uranium ore through a mechanical and chemical process that typically leaves a compound of uranium, uranium oxide, that goes by the name *yellowcake* from its yellow or orange tint.

Naturally occurring uranium, however, is not going to make a bomb as most of it is U-238 which does not easily fission. How can we separate the fissionable U-235 from the much more abundant U-238? U-235 is chemically almost identical to U-238, so there is no practical chemical method to effect this separation.

There are four *mechanical* methods to accomplish what is now called the *enrichment process*, where the proportion of U-235 is increased in the sample of the material. Each of them is technically difficult and time-consuming.

Gaseous diffusion utilizes the fact that when a gas of atoms is forced through a porous medium with very small pores, the lighter isotopes make their way through somewhat more easily, and so the gas emerging from the other side is slightly richer in the lighter isotopes. Because U-235 is fractionally only slightly lighter than U-238, the enrichment after a single pass through such a filter is very small. Therefore the gas must be passed repeatedly through a series of filters before a significant enrichment is achieved. The development of suitable filter materials was a technical problem of considerable difficulty, and a suitable gaseous form of uranium had to be found. Uranium hexafluoride, a very corrosive gas at elevated temperatures, was the only practical candidate.

The Manhattan Project built an enormous gaseous diffusion plant at Oak Ridge, Tennessee, consisting of cascades of diffusion units each feeding a subsequent one. Thousands of pumps were needed, specially designed to resist the highly corrosive effects of the uranium hexafluoride and possessing seals that were effective in keeping lubricants out of the gases and the gases from leaking out of the system. Thousands of kilowatts of electrical power were needed to run these pumps, and one of the largest steam power plants ever built was constructed at Oak Ridge to provide the necessary power. After the enriched gas leaves such a gaseous diffusion separator, it is chemically converted into uranium metal or an oxide of uranium suitable for use in a reactor or a weapon. This became the principal method for enrichment by the United States during the Cold War.

The *electromagnetic separation* method consists of producing a gas of uranium ions and accelerating them in a vacuum chamber into a large magnetic field. The trajectories of moving charged particles in a magnetic field are circles whose diameters depend on the mass of the particles. This means that U-235 and U-238 would follow different trajectories, and by placing a collector at the correct position in the magnetic field, U-235 ions could be collected ion by ion. Large-scale versions of such separators, known as calutrons, were built at Oak Ridge and provided U-235 for the first uranium bomb.

The *centrifuge* method also takes advantage of the differing weights of the atoms of U-235 and U-238. Uranium hexafluoride gas is introduced into a long vacuum tube inside of which a rotor spins at extremely high speed. With its three more neutrons, the slightly heavier U-238 is pushed away from the rotor, increasing by a small amount the proportion of U-235 toward the center of the tube. The gas in the center of the tube is moved to another vacuum tube and the process is repeated over and over through a cascade of tubes until the amount of U-235 reaches the percentage desired. The Manhattan Project gave up on this approach but over the last several decades it has become a favored route for the creation of HEU.

Laser separation methods are the newest candidate for enriching uranium.[10] A finely tuned laser, for instance, can ionize one isotope of uranium which can then be withdrawn as a gas from the sample. While these technologies are available, they have yet to demonstrate a capacity to produce enriched uranium more cheaply than the older methods. A state interested in acquiring nuclear weapons, however, may be willing to pay the cost of laser separation. Iran, for instance, has contracted to purchase an AVLIS (atomic vapor laser isotope separator) from Russia, a sale that the United States has pressured the Russian government to reverse.

Each of these methods uses unusual and highly specialized equipment (such as ultra-high speed centrifuges) in large numbers, often located in large buildings, and requires large amounts of electrical energy. Tracking the flow of these materials into nations and observing the construction of facilities by satellite or aircraft reconnaissance can provide some degree of warning that a state is engaged in a uranium enrichment program which is the precursor to the development of nuclear weapons. Of course, during World War II, the United States was able to produce its own enrichment machinery, and the intelligence systems of the Axis were unable to observe construction of large-scale facilities like Oak Ridge. Soviet intelligence organizations, aided by the fact that the United States was an ally of the Soviet Union, did keep watch on American efforts during the war. Today, U.S. satellites and communications monitoring systems watch the globe for tell-tale uranium enrichment activities.

PLUTONIUM

Soon after the discovery of the fissioning of U-235 in 1938, there was speculation about other isotopes that might be fissionable. In particular, it was predicted on theoretical grounds that a hitherto undetected element with a fissionable isotope could be produced from U-238. This new element, *plutonium*, can be produced in the reaction shown below. A nucleus of U-238 absorbs a neutron and becomes U-239. The U-239 is unstable but does not fission; rather, it decays to neptunium-239, which in turn decays to plutonium-239, emitting an electron and a neutrino (a subatomic particle with rather unusual properties) in the process.

$$N + U\text{-}238 \longrightarrow Y\text{-}239 \rightarrow Np\text{-}239 + e^- + neutrino$$
$$\downarrow$$
$$Pu\text{-}239 + e^- + neutrino$$

Pu-239 itself is unstable, decaying to U-235 by expelling alpha particles. It has a half-life of 24,000 years. This accounts for the fact that no Pu-239 is found occurring naturally on the earth. Any Pu-239 with which the solar system may have been endowed at its inception has long since vanished. This means that every single atom of plutonium used in the production of nuclear explosives has to be produced artificially. Once created, however, it becomes a candidate for nuclear weapons as it is fissionable.

What is needed for the production of Pu-239? Only a copious supply of neutrons and U-238. U-238 is quite plentiful, of course, which leaves only the problem of producing neutrons in large quantities. That can be done, as we have seen, by fissioning U-235, this time in nuclear reactors where the speed of the fissioning is carefully controlled by using control rods to absorb some of the neutrons, thus preventing an explosion. The Manhattan Project constructed a large Pu-239 producing facility at Hanford, Washington. Reactor production of Pu-239 and its subsequent chemical separation from the other elements in which it was embedded proved successful, providing the fissile material for the Trinity and Nagasaki weapons.

After the war, weapons-grade plutonium would be made in nuclear reactors specifically designed for this purpose. But there is an alternative route. Nuclear power reactors that supply electrical energy use uranium in which U-238 is the principal component. They thus produce plutonium as a by-product of their operation. For this reason, fears about nuclear proliferation center on the widespread availability of nuclear power reactors and the possibility of their being used to produce weapons-grade plutonium. We shall return to this problem shortly.

THE HYDROGEN OR FUSION BOMB

We conclude our technical consideration of nuclear explosives with an account of the hydrogen bomb. As we shall see in Chapter 4, after the successful development and testing of fission devices, a debate arose in governmental, scientific, and military circles as to whether or not the United States should proceed with the development of yet more powerful nuclear explosives based on the *fusion* of light nuclei. Edward Teller, one of the physicists active in the nuclear weapons project from the beginning, tirelessly promoted the project.

Just what is an H-bomb, and how does it differ from the fission bombs we have been considering? The H-bomb derives its energy from *fusing* small nuclei together to form larger nuclei rather than from splitting large nuclei to produce smaller ones. Consider two small nuclei, those of hydrogen, for example. Each consists of a single proton. Because the Coulomb repulsion of two protons is not very great compared to the strength of the strong nuclear force, why does the strong nuclear force not pull them together to form a single nucleus? It is because the nuclear force has a short range and is not felt until the protons come very close together. Under ordinary circumstances, the Coulomb repulsion will keep nuclei from approaching each other that closely. However, if we succeed in bringing two nuclei sufficiently close together, the nuclear force will completely overwhelm the Coulomb repulsion, and they will come crashing together, releasing energy in the process.

How can we bring light nuclei close enough to allow the strong nuclear force to take over? Our sun and the other stars accomplish this feat in their interiors, supplying the energy that keeps them radiating. We can duplicate this by *heating light nuclei* to a temperature high enough to form a gas of particles with thermal velocities great enough to produce close encounters of protons in spite of the Coulomb repulsion. It is for this reason that fusion weapons are also called *thermonuclear* weapons.

The temperatures needed are in the tens of millions of degrees, temperatures found ordinarily only in the interior of stars—and since 1945 in the initial fireball of a fission bomb explosion. The trick then is to detonate a fission device in the vicinity of some light nuclei, heat them to a very high temperature and then allow the resulting fusion reaction to proceed. It was not easy to devise a way to heat the fusion material hot enough before the force of the explosion blew it away. The U.S. solution to this problem was devised by Teller and other scientists. It was one of those very "sweet" (meaning beautifully ingenious) technical ideas that so exhilarates scientists and engineers.

The technical details of nuclear weapons designs are highly classified secrets. However, there is much information in the public domain, which, when considered in the light of known principles of physics, can give rise to educated guesses that are probably not too far from the truth.[11] The H-bomb description that follows, including the diagram in Figure 2–6, is based largely on these sources, particularly Howard Morland's work.

Stage 1 of the device (the upper stage) consists of an ordinary fission bomb of the sort we have already considered. It provides the high temperatures needed to initiate fusion in the second stage. Stage 2 consists of a heavy U-238 tamper shell, which encloses the fusion material. A rod of fission material (U-235 in Figure 2–6) is imbedded at the center of the fusion fuel, and the space between the tamper shell and the outer casing is filled with a polystyrene-type foam. A heavy shield between stages 1 and 2 helps to protect stage 2 against the direct blast for a brief instant. X-rays from the stage 1 blast, traveling at the speed of light, are reflected from the casing walls onto the polystyrene-type foam which absorbs them to become a hot plasma, imploding on the stage 2 fusion material, simultaneously heating and compressing it.

The heavy U-238 tamper provides the inertia that keeps the implosion moving inward and the reaction contained long enough for it to proceed to completion. The fusion material, which consists of lithium deuteride (LiD), is an interesting feature of the device, and worthy of some explanation.

The most easily attained fusion reaction uses two isotopes of hydrogen: deuterium (D), which is hydrogen–2, and tritium (T), which is hydrogen–3. They can fuse via the following reaction:

$$D + T \rightarrow He\text{–}4 + N + 17.6 \text{ MeV}$$

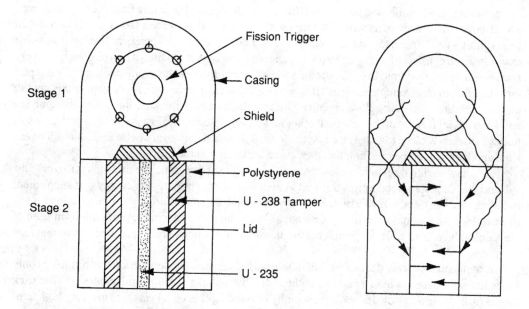

Figure 2–6   Schematic diagram of a possible configuration of a fusion (thermonuclear) bomb.
Adapted from Howard Morland, *The Secret that Exploded* (New York: Random House, 1981)

Unfortunately, both deuterium and tritium are gases at ordinary temperatures and pressures. Gases have very low densities and so require large volumes if an appreciable mass is to be achieved. One way to achieve a large mass with a small volume for the hydrogen isotopes is to liquify them by cooling them to temperatures near absolute zero. The first successful U.S. fusion device utilized liquid hydrogen isotopes, weighed 62 tons and included cryogenic equipment to keep the deuterium and tritium liquified. Obviously such a device is not suitable as a deliverable weapon. The Russians and the Americans, apparently independently, arrived at the same solution to this problem.

The solution consists of using another element for the fusion fuel which is stable and solid at ordinary temperatures and which is converted into tritium when it is bombarded with neutrons. The light element Lithium-6 (Li-6) is such an isotope, undergoing the following reaction upon neutron bombardment.

Li–6 + N → Li–7 → H–3 (tritium) + He–4

Where do the neutrons come from? This is where the rod of fissionable material buried within the fusion material comes into play. It is compressed to supercriticality and begins to fission, in the process providing neutrons to begin transforming lithium to tritium. As the fusion reaction progresses (D + T → He–4 + N) the neutrons which it produces continue the process of converting lithium-6 into tritium.

But where does the deuterium (H-2) come from? Lithium hydride (LiH) is a solid compound of lithium and hydrogen. If this compound is made from the Li-6 isotope of lithium and the H-2 (deuterium) isotope of hydrogen, one has LiD which incorporates the necessary fusion fuel isotopes in close proximity and in convenient physical form.

There is yet a third stage to many thermonuclear devices. U-238 incorporated into the bomb can be made to fission by the high energy neutrons which are produced by the D + T fusion reaction. Thus the U-238 tamper will fission, and if the casing of the device is also made of U-238, it too will fission. In this way the energy of the fusion neutrons can be turned into blast energy and the yield of the weapon increased. Thus a typical thermonuclear explosion is a fission-fusion-fission device, in which about half of the energy comes from fusion and the other half comes from fission.

Fusion can also be used in other ways. To make a "clean" bomb—one that does not create high levels of long-lasting radioactivity, one makes the stage 1 fission trigger as small as possible and removes any uranium from stage 2. In this way, the fission fragment production is reduced to a minimum, but the flood of neutrons that shower the blast region will kill or incapacitate individuals in the vicinity by damaging their central nervous systems. This type of weapon has been popularly called the neutron bomb.

Fusion is also used to "boost" fission bombs. If some gaseous deuterium and tritium are introduced under pressure into a small volume in the center of an ordinary implosion-type fission device, the heat from the fission reaction will cause them to fuse, emitting high-energy neutrons. These neutrons in turn produce additional fissions in the fissionable material. Additionally, because of the high energy of these neutrons, the fissions they produce give off more than the usual number of free neutrons which enhances or "boosts" the subsequent chain reaction. The energy coming directly from the fusion process itself does not make a significant contribution to the boosted weapon's output. The fusion reaction simply makes the fission reaction more efficient, so that a greater fraction of the fissionable material actually undergoes fission before the reaction ends.

The yield of a fusion-boosted weapon is adjustable by varying the amount of tritium and deuterium in the core. This can be done in the field and makes possible the dial-a-yield weapons which are widely deployed today. (This is the tritium that needs periodic replacement as it has a half-life of 12.3 years.)

As the technology to produce thermonuclear weapons demands a greater effort by a society, states with fission bombs do not automatically move on to develop fusion devices. At the present time, only the original big five of the nuclear club (the United States, Soviet Union/Russia, Great Britain, France, and China) have demonstrated a thermonuclear capability. The essential secret of these weapons, however, is known to everyone: they can be produced if the state is willing to commit its resources to do so.

BECOMING A NUCLEAR POWER

The Manhattan Project marshaled the science and technology to solve the principal problems of procuring fissionable material and then assembling it into an explosive device. The choice of the Los Alamos site for a bomb design laboratory in November 1942 provided a focus for the project. J. Robert Oppenheimer, the director of the laboratory, arrived at the site in March 1943 and was soon followed by a stream of scientists, technicians, and support personnel. To Los Alamos came the U-235 and Pu-239 being produced at Oak Ridge, Tennessee, and Hanford, Washington, at first in a trickle, and later in increasing amounts. To Los Alamos came the results of measurements at Chicago and elsewhere of neutron absorption probabilities, critical masses, neutron reflectors, and a host of other matters. And from Los Alamos came the "Gadget" (Figure 1–1), "Little Boy," and "Fat Man" (Figure 1–2) which demonstrated so dramatically the feasibility of a self-sustaining nuclear fission reaction of enormous power.

The detonation of the "atomic bomb" over Hiroshima marked the beginning of the nuclear age for everyone, for the basic secret was out: A nuclear bomb could be built. The United States had produced a nuclear weapon from scratch in three and a half years. Is the ability to do so—and perhaps as quickly as that—within the reach of any nation or group, relying on its own efforts? The U.S. government was interested in that question. In May 1964, one of its labs selected several young physicists who had no background in nuclear weapons and no access to the secrets of the weapon. In seven months of research and testing (the "testing" consisted of answers provided by weapons experts to the research tests proposed by the participants), the physicists discovered and passed over the gun-type as too easy to build and went for the more interesting implosion device—not knowing that both avenues had been adopted by the Manhattan Project and that implosion remained the preferred approach. In 18 months, they had a rough design for a plutonium bomb; in 27 months, blueprints. The weapons experts concluded that their design would work.[12] Given the materials, well-trained physicists anywhere can design nuclear weapons in short order.

The bottleneck remains the acquisition of fissile materials. To enrich U-235 or create Pu-239 demands engineering and production capabilities and technologies of a relatively high order (or the wherewithal to purchase them, often clandestinely, as there are usually prohibitions or restrictions on the sale of materiel that has the potential to create nuclear weapons). Such requirements have been met by ten states who have gone on to produce nuclear weapons, but many other states are candidates for nuclear status. It is the case that most industrialized states can, given the time and money, solve the engineering and production problems, and relatively wealthy but less industrialized states (such as China, India, and Pakistan) can as well.

The processes of *proliferation*—the expansion of the number of nuclear weapons states—is a key part of the nuclear predicament and a central feature of the first nuclear age. Proliferation remains a central if not *the* critical issue of the second nuclear age. In Chapter 8 we will discuss the reasons why states might choose—or not choose—to proliferate. Here we are concerned with the *pathways to proliferation*. What approaches are open to the political and military leaders?

1. *A crash program to match a rival's capabilities*: A state can mimic the Manhattan Project by concentrating its efforts to build a nuclear weapon in a short period of time. The Soviet approach is the only other example we have of such a pathway. (The U.S. had no *nuclear* rival when it undertook their project.) While Joseph Stalin had ordered a small pilot project begun in 1942, it took Hiroshima to push him to action. "A single demand of you, comrades," he said to the officials involved in the Soviet effort. "Provide us with atomic weapons in the shortest possible time. You know that Hiroshima has shaken the whole world. The balance has been destroyed. Provide the bomb—it will remove a great danger for us."[13] Soviet scientists told Stalin in August 1945 that it would take five years to produce the bomb. It took four. The successful Soviet test of a fission device came in August 1949.

2. *Longer-term programs to create nuclear weapons*. This pathway involves an early, conscious choice to go nuclear, but the program is not driven by a sense of impending destruction at the hands of an opponent. Britain's development of the bomb in 1952 and China's in 1964 are the two programs that best fit this category. Pakistan's approach appears to fit here as well, as does the South African effort (although among all the nuclear powers, it alone subsequently decided to scrap all of its weapons). Iraq, until its defeat in 1991, had embarked on a similar pathway. As

we shall see in Chapter 7, the case of the Democratic People's Republic of Korea ("North Korea") is ambiguous, possibly reflecting this or the following pathway.

3. *Longer-term programs that make a nuclear option possible*. This pathway gives the state the option to go nuclear at some point without actually committing the political leadership to develop the weapon at the start of the project. Avner Cohen suggests that the French and Israeli governments took this approach to nuclear weapons. David Ben Gurion, the first Israeli prime minister, took the position of minister of defense as well so that he could secretly launch a program that could produce a nuclear weapon, and only later revealed his plans to selected political and military leaders. Cohen notes that "apparently Ben Gurion himself was not clear in his own mind those days how far Israel should go with its nuclear pursuits." Similarly, he notes that "under the [French] Fourth Republic, important nuclear activities were made piecemeal by sympathetic politicians and administrators acting on their own, while the official government could maintain, and rightly so, that no final political decision on nuclear weapons had been made."[14]

Both, however, did ultimately choose to develop such weapons, the French publicly and the Israel government secretly. Israel became a nuclear state during the period 1968–1971. It has never tested a device, and has publicly said that it would not be the first to introduce nuclear weapons in the region. There is every reason to believe, however, that Israel has at least 50–100 warheads, possibly 200, in its arsenal. Refusing to acknowledge being a nuclear power even though most informed observers and governments are convinced that the state is a nuclear power has been called *opaque proliferation*.

India's approach to nuclear weapons is similar. In 1974, it tested a nuclear device that demonstrated its capability, but the government declared itself interested in nuclear devices for peaceful purposes only (such as the excavation of large areas as conventional blasting does). It did not build a nuclear weapons force and refrained from any further tests until the 1990s. The Indian government was, however, "a screwdriver away" from having nuclear weapons after 1974 (although it would still take some time to develop the wherewithal and military organization to deliver such quickly constructed weapons to their targets). Iran seems to be following this pathway at the present.

4. *Acquiring nuclear weapons from others*. States have sought to acquire nuclear weapons from their possessors. China, for instance, sought to become a nuclear weapons state through its alliance with the Soviet Union. The Soviets refused to give or sell nuclear weapons to the Chinese but for several years the USSR did help Chinese scientists with indigenous development. President Nasser of Egypt, fearing that the Israelis would develop nuclear weapons, apparently asked the Soviet government to sell atomic bombs to Egypt. The Soviets refused, but may have offered to protect Egypt with their nuclear weapons. (Such an approach is called *extending the nuclear umbrella*.) There were reports during the 1970s that Libya sought (unsuccessfully) to purchase nuclear weapons. In the early 2000s, many expressed the fear that North Korea's Kim Jong Il would sell nuclear weapons to whomever had the cash.

While the direct delivery of nuclear weapons has not yet occurred, there has been a recurrent pattern of the transfer of nuclear plans and technologies between states. In some cases, it came with the cooperation of an existing nuclear weapons state, as the Soviet Union initially aided Chinese efforts, and China and North Korea probably aided Pakistan in the development of its weapons by sharing technical expertise and materials. Pakistan provided similar help to North Korea in return for the North's missiles. Currently there are fears that North Korea remains amenable to such transfers. Some observers have expressed concerns that if Islamic militants come to power in Pakistan, they might be willing to transfer nuclear technologies if not the weapon to other Islamic states.

These government-to-government exchanges are but one avenue to proliferation, however. When Libya ended its nuclear program in 2004 and submitted to inspections, the world learned that Libya was able to order centrifuges for U-235 enrichment through commercial suppliers who attempt (often successfully) to avoid the controls placed on such sales. Indeed, Libya seemed at the time to be on the verge of acquiring a turn-key plant to enrich uranium. The history of the nuclear age, however, suggests that technology transfer also happens not only on the black market but in the open market as well, where states have acquired nuclear weapons technologies or so-called "dual use" items that can be used for non-nuclear purposes as well as to build a nuclear weapons program.. And the most open transfer of technologies and expertise came with the sale or gift of nuclear-power plants and research reactors by their developers. Granted, these latter transfers do not provide the weapon or its technologies, but they move the recipients closer to acquiring the weapon.

NUCLEAR POWERS AND NUCLEAR ASPIRANTS

How many states have attempted to go nuclear? How many have seen their programs through to fruition? Table 2-1 summarizes nuclear weapons histories of various states. By spring 2006, nine states had entered the nuclear club: the United States, the Soviet Union, Britain, France, China, Israel, India, South Africa, and Pakistan.[16] (Soon after acquisition, the South African government destroyed its small nuclear arsenal.) In 1991, the nuclear club momentarily expanded as the Soviet Union collapsed and three newly independent republics (Belarus, Ukraine, and Kazakhstan) inherited parts of the Soviet nuclear arsenal along with the new Russian state. By the fall of 1996, however, all the warheads were back in Russia and none of the three governments actually had control over the warheads, as they remained under a military organization controlled by the Russian government. North Korea has declared that it is a nuclear weapons state, making it the tenth nation to have acquired the bomb—if in fact it has actually produced the weapons.

Table 2–1 shows that a large number of states began nuclear weapons programs or followed the "option" pathway but then decided against constructing nuclear weapons. Many of those states such as Germany and Japan are leading industrial and technological powers. Given access to fissile materials (in many cases readily available, as we shall see, from nuclear power plants within those states), those states could proliferate very quickly if the political leadership decided to do so. And as the cases of Iraq, North Korea, and Iran demonstrate, *any* state with sufficient funds, an indigenous scientific establishment, access to fissile materials, and the political will, can undertake a nuclear weapons program with a strong probability of producing a nuclear device. With all these factors in place, a state starting essentially from scratch might count on a working fission device after 4–5 years of a crash program, and 7–15 years in a normal (but still costly) program.

A state could accelerate the process by using espionage (as the Soviets did in their penetration of the Manhattan Project during and immediately after the war) or through theft (as the Israelis did in acquisition of some fissile materials) or by purchasing dual-use equipment on the open market (as Iraq did) to reduce the time to reach nuclear status. Or states might acquire materials covertly from existing nuclear states—for instance, through the semi-official Pakistani network run by A. Q. Khan, the developer of Pakistani nuclear weapons. Covert programs (like Libya's and Iraq's) that must rely on such networking and shadowy suppliers are likely to take on the characteristics of Libya's program: "ambitious, [but also] disorganized, incomplete, and likely years away from producing actual nuclear warheads."[17]

TABLE 2–1   STATES WITH NUCLEAR WEAPONS PROGRAMS

THE NUCLEAR CLUB

United States	Tested in 1945 (program begun in early 1940s)
Soviet Union/Russia	Tested in 1949 (program begun in early 1940s)
United Kingdom	Tested in 1952 (program begun in early 1940s)
France	Tested in 1960 (program begun in late 1940s)
China	Tested in 1964 (program begun in mid–1950s)
India	Tested in 1974, 1998 (program begun in mid–1960s)
Pakistan	Tested in 1998 (program begun in early 1970s)

SELF-PROCLAIMED PROLIFERATORS

North Korea — Program possibly begun in 1970s; no test; CIA estimated 1–2 weapons in mid–1990s; self-proclaimed possessor in 2003

OPAQUE PROLIFERATORS

Israel — Nuclear capable, 1967–1971; no test; remains nuclear-armed
South Africa — Nuclear capable, 1979–1981; no test; de-nuclearized in 1991

TEMPORARY PROLIFERATORS BY INHERITANCE

Belarus, Ukraine, and Kazakhstan — 1991 breakup of the USSR left former Soviet nuclear weapons within territory; all returned to Russia by mid-1990s

NUCLEAR ASPIRANTS

Historical (No current nuclear weapons programs; No weapons produced)

Germany	Canada	Libya
Japan	Argentina	Syria
Sweden	Egypt	South Korea
Switzerland	Iraq	Taiwan

Current (on-going program rumored; no weapons known)

Iran

Brazil

Acquisition of nuclear weapons by a terrorist group would be far more difficult but not impossible, a topic we take up in Chapter 9. Such a group could not make its own weapons unless it had the physical facilities to do so, and those would have to be under relatively long-term protection of a host government to have the time to follow a production pathway. Most potential host governments would probably be extremely reluctant to permit such an operation because of the high probability of attack by other states. Purchase or theft are more likely pathways for terrorist groups, but still quite difficult at the present time given the safeguards that nuclear weapons states have created around their existing weapons. In the second nuclear age, however, Russia became a cause for concern as Chechen terrorists fighting the Russian government have demonstrated an ability to bribe Russian officials to overlook the shipment of conventional weapons or to disregard security regulations which allowed suicide bombers on planes. While Russian nuclear weapons are controlled by an elite force, there have been reports that in the breakup of the Soviet Union, a number of small tactical nuclear devices could not be accounted for.

As for a nuclear weapons state or a governmental organization within such a state giving a nuclear device to a terrorist group to promote its policy goals, we believe such risks are low. The donor state is likely to be identified if the weapon were detonated and it would face severe—probably nuclear—retaliation. Moreover, the nuclear device might end up in the hands of a group hostile to the donor nation itself (for terrorists pursue their own agenda), which might produce a very frightful outcome for the donor. Therefore, at this moment, the more immediate threats are the theft of a nuclear weapon (perhaps with the connivance of low-level officials) and the use of radioactive materials to create a radiological device or "dirty bomb" (discussed below). Terrorist organizations currently seem to be most likely to obtain such devices through theft or bribery.

Why states or terrorist organizations seek a nuclear weapons capability is a crucial question that we explore in depth in Chapter 9. The history of the first nuclear age demonstrates that some states have felt *compelled* to acquire them and the advances in physics and engineering made such weapons conceivable and feasible. We expect such compulsion will continue for some governments and leaders far into the future. Ironically, the growing demand for energy means that globally, more governments will have an interest in nuclear matters, for it is likely that the controlled fission of the atom will become a principal source of electrical energy. Nuclear power plants, however, provide fissile materials for nuclear weapons and an ever-growing source for a particular type of radiological bomb. We now turn to that part of the story.

THE ROLE OF NUCLEAR POWER GENERATION IN PROLIFERATION

Without enriched uranium-235 or plutonium-239 there is no bomb. But both of these are natural parts of the nuclear power industry. In recent years, concerns about global warming from fossil fuels, the desire for independence from foreign oil imports, and the largely unmet need of less-developed countries for energy have renewed general interest in nuclear power. Europe and Japan have committed themselves to nuclear-produced electricity to a much greater extent than the United States has, but even in the latter, as current nuclear power plants reach obsolescence and the demand for energy continues to mount, there is a renewed interest in the construction of new nuclear reactors. Such a trend is not likely to be reversed in the near future.[18] Even if it turns out that the nuclear power industry does not return to a high-growth state for one reason or another, the currently existing reactors (about 430 worldwide) and the steady diffusion of technical expertise will continue to afford opportunities for proliferation.

Most civilian nuclear reactors are fueled with a mixture of U-235 and U-238, contained in long thin rods that are inserted into the reactor core in an array which leaves space for water to circulate between them. The U-235 slowly fissions, heating the water to produce steam, which then directly drives a turbine to generate electricity (a boiling water reactor), or the steam is piped to a heat exchanger where a separate supply of water is boiled to drive the turbine (a pressurized water reactor). Unlike a nuclear explosive, the uranium in a power reactor need not be highly enriched in U-235. In fact, natural uranium, containing only 0.7 percent U-235, will do if the water circulating in the reactor core is replaced with *heavy water*. Heavy water is D_2O where the usual hydrogen atom has been replaced by the heavy hydrogen isotope deuterium whose nucleus contains a proton and a neutron. Lacking the neutron, ordinary water (called light water) has too great a probability of absorbing the neutrons needed to fission the U-235 unless more highly enriched U-235 is used.

Canadian nuclear reactors are generally heavy water reactors, employing natural, unenriched uranium as their fuel. Canada has exported this technology to other countries, enabling them to build and operate nuclear reactors without having to engage in the difficult uranium isotope separation process, although in this case they must obtain a significant quantity of heavy water in addition to the natural uranium. Heavy water does occur naturally, but the quantities needed generally mean that it must be imported, thus often making a state dependent upon foreign sources of supply for both the uranium and deuterium-rich water.

If, on the other hand, one uses ordinary water, then the fuel rods must contain uranium enriched to 3–4 percent in U-235. States with such light-water reactors therefore must be able to enrich uranium or to purchase enriched uranium from supplier nations who generally exercise tight supervision over its use. For energy deficient states, the building of uranium enrichment facilities is justifiable in terms of meeting legitimate energy needs—and it is the right of any sovereign state to do so. This has been Iran's basic claim in its confrontation with the United States regarding the former's attempt to create a nuclear power-generating capability.

The ability to separate the isotopes of uranium for enrichment purposes is the first step towards nuclear power independence—and towards a nuclear weapons capability. Enrichment to weapons grade (approximately 90 percent U-235) takes greater effort but is prefigured in the initial mastery of the enrichment process. Nuclear weapons, however, can be built with far less U-235, but they will be bulkier—and therefore more difficult to deliver to the target—and less efficient.

One other route to nuclear weapons or the expertise to develop them has come from *research reactors* which typically operate at 80–90 percent enrichment. Many of these reactors have come from the major nuclear powers, but donor states usually exercise tight control over the HEU fuel rods and the overall amount of HEU is quite small. Currently, however, there are about 275 active research reactors in nearly 70 countries.[19]

The second connection between nuclear power reactors and nuclear weapons is the Pu-239 which nuclear reactors create. Because the fuel rods contain an abundance of U-238, a significant amount of U-238 is converted into Pu-239 by the neutrons produced in the fissioning of the U-235. The Pu-239 can be chemically separated from spent fuel rods, but the extreme radioactivity of the rods makes such reprocessing a dangerous and technically sophisticated operation. Furthermore, commercial power reactors are designed to be refueled infrequently, with the rods left in the reactor for about a year. This results in the buildup of Pu-240, another isotope produced when U-238 is bombarded with neutrons. The presence of Pu-240 mixed in with the Pu-239 (and these isotopes cannot be chemically separated) renders the product ill-suited for nuclear weapons use. It is for this reason that nuclear weapons states obtain their plutonium from reactors which are specially designed to produce plutonium and not power.

This is not to say that a plutonium device with a surfeit of Pu-240 cannot produce a bomb of sorts, if one were willing to settle for a bomb of very low yield (say, from under 1 to perhaps 3 kt).[20] In fact, in 1962 the United States successfully tested a nuclear device made with reactor-grade plutonium. Weapons-grade plutonium, however, is typically 6 percent Pu-240 and 93.5 percent Pu-239, while reactor grade plutonium is typically 23 percent Pu-240. The Pu-240 fissions too quickly, blowing the material apart prematurely, thus producing a nuclear fizzle; heat, blast, and prompt radiation would reach about a third of a mile from the point of detonation. The critical limitation, however, on building a weapon of reactor grade plutonium is the high radiation from Pu-240; it is intense enough to severely injure anyone working with the bomb. Of course, if technicians who assembled the bomb and those who were to deliver it accepted their deaths as a part of the mission, reactor-grade plutonium might be fashioned into a crude nuclear weapon.

The reprocessing of fuel rods to extract the Pu-239 is a relatively well-known technology because it was initially feared that the world's supply of uranium would run out. Thus, the major nuclear powers invested in programs to reprocess plutonium to be used in power reactors in place of uranium. Indeed, a properly designed reactor can produce more new nuclear fuel than it consumes—such reactors are known as breeder reactors. Even though the world's supply of uranium is nowhere near exhaustion, plutonium reprocessing continues (in part because it liberates the reprocessor from having to depend on imports of uranium).

The nuclear weapons states (and those that have sought nuclear weapons) have pursued both the uranium isotope separation strategies and the reprocessing of plutonium as the route to nuclear weapons. Plutonium reprocessing seems to have been the Israeli choice. In South Asia, "India's route... would be based on plutonium derived from its natural uranium fueled, heavy water cooled and moderated reactors, and separated in its established reprocessing facilities."[21] North Korea has pursued both uranium enrichment and plutonium separation to develop a nuclear capability.

RADIOLOGICAL WEAPONS

We have seen how radioactive materials constitute severe health risks to individuals exposed to the alpha, beta, and gamma rays they emit as they decay toward greater stability. Fissioning U-235 produces a vast array of such radioactive isotopes. Among these are cesium-137, cobalt-60, and iridium-192 (which today have uses in medicine and industry). In the early days of the Manhattan Project, when no one knew if *deliverable* nuclear weapon could be made, the U.S. Army considered combining such radiological materials and high explosives in a bomb. The blast would scatter the radioactive material, making the contaminated area uninhabitable.[22] While the Americans lost interest in the approach as they were able to build nuclear weapons, Iraq's inability to build a nuclear weapon led that nation to build and test "a dirty bomb in the 1980s before abandoning the program on the grounds that it was ineffective against military targets, according to U.N. weapons inspectors."[23]

The idea of a radiological or "dirty" bomb has re-emerged in the second nuclear era, as terrorist groups such as al Qaeda have shown an interest in such a device[24]—indeed, going so far as to give an

American, Jose Padilla, the mission in 2002 of staging a dirty bomb attack against an American city. (Padilla was apprehended before he could begin the assignment.) On the other hand, Chechen rebels fighting for independence from Russia did leave a radiological device in a Moscow park. Russian authorities rendered it harmless after the Chechens revealed its location, but the point was made. Dirty bombs were potential parts of a terrorist arsenal.

Terrorists seeking nuclear materials through purchase or theft are more likely to acquire the materials for radiological bombs than fissile materials for a nuclear weapon, as the former are in widespread use around the world. For instance, in the United States, there are an estimated two million licensed locations using radioactive materials.[25] The former Soviet Union, however, is the treasure trove for such materials, often weakly protected. In the first nuclear age, Soviet scientists explored a wide variety of applications of nuclear physics. "The Soviets are known to have produced tens of thousands of radioactive devices for uses ranging from medical diagnostics to military communications, and many were simply abandoned after the Soviet breakup in 1991. Some regions are so littered with such devices that published tourist guides caution travelers to watch out for them."[26] Agricultural experiments, for instance, used cesium-137, a highly radioactive isotope, to determine the effects of radiation on plants and seeds. The cesium was available at many sites, not all of which could be identified and secured. Calculations suggest that roughly 2 ounces of cesium-137 (with a half-life of 30 years) could, if dispersed by a conventional explosive, make the area ten miles from the detonation point radioactive enough to cause people to abandon the area for years unless there was a very expensive clean up.

Trafficking in radioactive isotopes has become a significant part of the criminal smuggling in the new republics in the Caucuses, with much of the activity centered in Georgia. For instance, in May 2003 police discovered a cab about to unload lead-lined boxes containing strontium and cesium at the railroad station in Tbilisi, the capital, for transhipment to unknown individuals.[27] (Georgia also has been the site of smuggling of kilogram quantities of uranium as well). As Georgia was in political turmoil and wracked by violent independence movements, such smuggling may have served as a means of raising money by selling such materials to other terrorists or as a way of raising the stakes in the confrontation with the Georgian government. The American government became so concerned that a radiological device may have already made its way into the hands of al Qaeda that in December 2003 it sent technicians to four (perhaps more) large American cities with equipment hidden in briefcases and golf bags to detect radiation from a radiological device.[28] None were found, but the growing consensus has been that such an attack may be increasingly likely in the near future.

Terrorists or states seeking to inflict radiological damage on their enemies need not, however, transport a dirty bomb to their target. Bennett Ramberg's book title captured an important truth: *Nuclear Power Plants as Weapons for the Enemy.*[29] Any nation that has a nuclear reactor has a radiological bomb in place. There are 65 sites in the United States with a total of 103 nuclear reactors. Around the world there are 438 commercial units. In the reactor core are the fissile materials and the radioactive byproducts of the fission process. As a rule, the core is shielded behind heavy concrete walls that are designed to withstand some forms of attack, but apparently most were not designed to withstand the impact of a large jet liner fully loaded with jet fuel.

Even more worrisome are the spent fuel rod storage areas located at the reactor sites in the United States. The fuel rods, depleted of their uranium, but now containing highly radioactive plutonium and fission fragment isotopes, are kept in cooling pools of water. The loss of water—say, from an attack on the storage pool—could lead to an uncontrollable fire that would dump cesium–137 and other radioactive particles into the air. One estimate is that if a fire broke out at a Connecticut storage site, 29,000 square miles (including New York City and Long Island) might become uninhabitable.[30]

There are 40,000 tons of spent fuel in storage facilities in the United States. 11,000 tons will be added in the next several years. The U.S. Department of Energy planned to begin moving spent fuel rods to a massive underground storage facility at Yucca Mountain, Nevada. Political opposition to opening this site, however, will delay their transfer and the 2010 target date for opening the facility is likely to be missed. Moreover, there are 33,000 tons of spent fuel rods that Brazil, the Czech Republic, India, Japan, Mexico, Slovenia, South Korea, Switzerland, Taiwan, and member states of the European Union had originally obtained for their reactors from the United States and that the U.S. had pledged to take back. Political opposition in the United States may make that impossible now. Even if the United States were willing to do so, it will take time before those rods are removed from their individual storage sites. Russia has proposed to build a massive spent-fuel rod storage site and store the rods for a price. In the meantime, Russia's nuclear waste is stored (often haphazardly) at nuclear power stations; in the vicinity of the cities set up as centers of nuclear research, fissile material production, and weapons making; and at military bases.

It might be modestly comforting to report that only in the former Soviet Union is there a danger of theft or removal of fissile or radiological material from nuclear sites. The danger is real there, but it is not absent in the United States. The Nuclear Regulatory Commission (NRC) has the responsibility to oversee the security at nuclear power plants in the United States. The NRC sets security guidelines and mandates periodic tests in what are called force-on-force exercises to see if a simulated terrorist group could reach the vital components of the reactor where it might be able to damage the controls or operating mechanisms sufficiently to produce a meltdown of the core or other events that would release radioactivity into the environment. In the recent past, the "terrorists" have reached those components in 50 percent of the tests, even when the security guards knew that a test was to be conducted at the site.[31]

In similar force-on-force tests conducted at sites under the Department of Energy's control where fissile materials are stored, the failure rate has been roughly the same. The details can be disheartening:

> [In a 1998 test] Navy SEALs successfully entered the site through a perimeter fence, gained entrance to a nearby building, 'stole' a significant quantity of plutonium, exited the building, and escaped through the fence, all without being caught. After this embarrassment, Rocky Flats management stipulated that in future tests the SEALs could not leave by the same way they came in. Instead, they were required to take the plutonium, climb a guard tower, and rope the material over the fence.[32]

The guards successfully defended the site in the re-test.

Given the heightened worldwide concern over terrorism, we might expect that security at sensitive sites such as power reactors or fuel rod storage ponds would be enhanced, so that the chances of diversion of or attacks on radiological or fissile material is likely to diminish. Such security, however, is costly and seeks to prevent relatively unlikely events. When economic conditions deteriorate and budgets become strained, societies are less likely to pay the extra cost until after the unlikely has happened.

CONCLUSION

Given the laws of physics, it may have been inevitable that humans would discover nuclear weapons. Their creation reflected the innate human curiosity about the natural world, coupled with increasingly powerful ways to understand that world. How and when they would emerge was far less predictable, but in retrospect it seems natural that the great war that engulfed the world in 1939 would spur the harnessing of this new nuclear science to war-waging. Equally important, many of the world's inhabitants perceived the war as a struggle between good and evil, a struggle in which the very survival of nations, peoples, and life-sustaining beliefs was in peril. Finding the war-winning weapon was imperative.

That nuclear weapons would emerge first in the United States was something of a surprise. Europe had been the heart of the golden age of physics, when humans began to make remarkable progress in understanding the basic building blocks of matter—what they consisted of and the forces that held them together. But Europe was also the heart of the rising threat of totalitarian fascism. Ironically, it was this shadow that drove the center of nuclear science to the more tranquil shores of the United States, where European physicists, American industrial might and engineering ingenuity, and the looming war converged to produce the awesome weapons of destruction.

The closing days of World War II ushered in the first nuclear age. Its arrival closed one chapter of this remarkable scientific and technological story. A new story then unfolded. Like the other fruits of science, nuclear fission was available to all, for this kind of human knowledge flows across frontiers without a passport. Scientists and engineers in other nations sought to duplicate the feats of the Manhattan Project, and U.S. scientists turned their attention to warhead efficiencies, missile delivery systems, and harnessing nuclear fusion.

The arrival of the first nuclear age is not, however, just a story of the creation of nuclear weapons. It is also a story of how humans came to use that weapon. In Chapter 3, we explore how the Truman administration decided to use nuclear weapons against Japan and how future leaders might choose to use the nuclear weapons at their command.

ENDNOTES

[1]For extensive accounts of the Trinity Test and the scientific and technological developments which led to it, see the following: Henry DeWolf Smyth, *Atomic Energy for Military Purposes: The Official Report on the Development of the Atomic Bomb under the Auspices of the U.S. Government, 1940-1945* (Princeton, NJ: Princeton University Press, 1945) and Richard Rhodes, *The Making of the Atomic Bomb* (New York: Simon & Schuster, 1986). For the early and later periods, see Gerard DeGroot, *The Bomb: A Life* (Cambridge, MA: Harvard University Press, 2005), and Charles Loeber, *Building the Bomb: A History of the Nuclear Weapons Complex* (Washington, DC: U.S. Government Printing Office, 2002).

[2]For the German experience with nuclear weapons see Thomas Powers, *Heisenberg's War: The Secret History of the German Bomb*, (New York: Knopf, 1993); Mark Waller, *German National Socialism and the Quest for Nuclear Power*, 1939-1949 (Cambridge, UK: Cambridge University Press, 1989); and Paul Lawrence Rose, *Heisenberg and the Nazi Atomic Bomb Project, 1939-1945*, 2nd ed. (Berkeley, CA: University of California Press, 2001).

[3]British contributions are detailed in Ferenc Morton Szasz, *British Scientists and the Manhattan Project: The Los Alamos Years*, (New York: Palgrave Macmillan, 1992).

[4]It is the case that nuclear physics emerged when it did out of a Western cultural tradition that chooses to see the world in a particular fashion, but it strikes us as implausible that other cultural traditions would not have come to the same understanding and same weapons, though perhaps at some other time. It may be, however, that how nuclear weapons became part of the political and cultural history of the times does reflect their birth within a Western culture.

[5]Howard Morland captured this nicely in the subtitle of his article, "The H-Bomb Secret: To know how is to ask why." *The Progressive* (November 1979), p. 245.

[6]See Diana Preston, *Before the Fallout: From Marie Curie to Hiroshima* (New York: Walker, 2005), for a history of the physics and people involved. Earlier studies include J. G. Feinberg, *The Story of Atomic Theory and Atomic Energy* (New York: Dover, 1960); Emilio Segre, *From X-rays to Quarks: Modern Physicists and Their Discoveries* (New York: W. H. Freeman, 1980). For personal accounts, see Laura Fermi, *Atoms in the Family* (Chicago: University of Chicago, 1954) and Eve Curie, *Madame Curie* (New York: Garden City Publishing Co., 1943).

[7]The development of quantum mechanics by Werner Heisenberg and Erwin Schrodinger replaced Bohr's "planetary" orbits of the electron with something called quantum states. The quantum state describes the probability of finding the electrons at different locations about the nucleus. There are a great many different quantum states available to electrons. For an in-depth presentation see Kenneth Krane, *Introductory Nuclear Physics* (New York: Wiley, 1987).

[8]For general accounts of the Manhattan Project, see Smyth, *Atomic Energy for Military Purposes*; Vincent C. Jones, *Manhattan: The Army and the Atomic Bomb* (Washington, D.C.: U.S. Army Center of Military History, 1985); and David Hawkins, Edith Trulow, and Ralph Carlisle Smith, *Project Y: The Los Alamos Story, Vol. II of A Series in the History of Modern Physics 1800-1950* (Los Angeles: Tomash Publishers, 1983). For the individuals, see Gregg Herken, *Brotherhood of the Bomb: The Tangled Lives and Loyalties of Robert Oppenheimer, Ernest Lawrence, and Edward Teller* (New York: Henry Holt, 2002); Kai Bird, *American Prometheus: The Triumph and Tragedy of J. Robert Oppenheimer* (New York: Knopf, 2005); Jennet Conant, *109 East Palace: Robert Oppenheimer and the Secret City of Los Alamos* (New York: Simon & Shuster, 2005); and Robert S. Norris, *Racing for the Bomb: General Leslie R. Groves, the Manhattan Project's Indispensable Man* (South Royalton, VT: Steerforth Press, 2002).

[9]For more extended treatments of the physics of nuclear weapons, the following books will be helpful: Samuel Glasstone and Philip J. Dolan, *The Effects of Nuclear Weapons* (Washington, DC: Department of Defense and Energy Research and Development Administration, 1977); Smyth, *Atomic Energy for Military Purposes*; Thomas B. Cochran, William M. Arkin, and Milton M. Hoenig, *Nuclear Weapons Databook Vol. I: U.S. Nuclear Forces and Capabilities* (Cambridge, MA: Ballinger, 1984); Kosta Tsipis, *Arsenal: Understanding Weapons in the Nuclear Age* (New York: Simon & Schuster, 1985); MIT Faculty, *The Nuclear Almanac: Confronting the Atom in War and Peace* (Reading, MA: Addison-Wesley, 1984), pp. 195–204, 447–494.

[10]For a fascinating though technical report by Iranian physicists, see P. Parvin et al., "Molecular Laser Isotope Separation Versus Atomic Vapor Laser Isotope Separation," *Progress in Nuclear Energy*, Vol. 44 (No. 4, 2004), pp. 331–345.

[11]Howard Morland, a former Air Force pilot who had taken some engineering courses while in college, engaged in this kind of sleuthing and published his conclusions in the November 1979 issue of *The Progressive*. The government sought unsuccessfully to obtain a court injunction to restrain its publication but did succeed in delaying publication for half a year. Morland has written an interesting book chronicling his pursuit of the secret and his efforts to see it published. Howard Morland, *The Secret That Exploded* (New York: Random House, 1981). This was followed by a book entitled *Born Secret: The H-Bomb, the Progressive Case and National Security*. See also A. DeVolpi, G. E. Marsh, T. A. Postol, and G. S. Stanford, *Born Secret: The H-Bomb, the Progressive Case, and National Security* (New York: Pergamon, 1981).

[12]Dan Stober, "No Experience Necessary," *Bulletin of the Atomic Scientists*, Vol 59 (2, March/April 2003), pp. 57–63.

[13]Quoted by David Holloway, *The Soviet Union and the Arms Race* (New Haven, CT: Yale University Press, 1983), p. 20. In 1979 or 1980, a close advisor to the Ayatollah Khomeini reportedly used very similar language in speaking with an Iranian official in charge of the Shah's nuclear program: "It is your duty to build the atomic bomb for the Islamic Republican Party... . Our civilization is in danger and we have to have it." Quoted in Leonard Spector and Jacqueline R. Smith, *Nuclear Ambitions: The Spread of Nuclear Weapons 1989-1990* (Boulder, CO: Westview, 1990), p. 208.

[14]Avner Cohen, "Israel's Nuclear Opacity: A Political Genealogy," in Steven L. Spiegel, Jennifer D. Kibbe, and Elizabeth G. Matthews (eds.), *The Dynamics of Middle East Nuclear Proliferation*, (Lewiston, NY: Edwin Mellen, 2001), p. 191. For an extensive analysis of the Israeli program, see Avner Cohen, *Israel and the Bomb* (New York, NY: Columbia University Press, 1998).

[15]Janice Gross Stein, "Proliferation, Non-Proliferation, and Anti-Proliferation: Egypt and Israel in the Middle East," in Spiegel et al. (eds.), *Dynamics*, p. 44, footnote.

[16]For a current accounting, see Joseph Cirincione, Jon B. Wolfsthal, and Miriam Rajkumar, *Deadly Arsenals: Nuclear, Biological, and Chemical Threats*, 2nd ed. (Washington, DC: Carnegie Endowment for International Peace, 2005).

[17]*Washington Post National Weekly Edition*, March 8-14, 2004), p. 16.

[18]For a recent discussion, see James A. Lake, Ralph G. Bennett, and John F. Kotek, "Next-Generation Nuclear Power," *Scientific American*, Vol. 286 (January 2002), pp. 72–81.

[19]See Alexander Glaser and Frank N. von Hippel, "Thwarting Nuclear Terrorism," *Scientific American* (February, 2006), pp. 56–63.

[20]The following is adapted from Milton Heonig, "Terrorists Going Nuclear," in Yonah Alexander and Milton Hoenig (eds.), *Superterrorism: Biological, Chemical, and Nuclear* (Ardsley, NY: Transnational Publishers, 2001), pp. 32-36, especially footnote 5, and Dan Stober, "No Experience Necessary," *Bulletin of the Atomic Scientists*, Vol 59 (2, March/April 2003), pp. 62–63.

[21]P. R. Chari, *Indo-Pak Nuclear Standoff: The Role of the United States* (New Delhi, Manohar, 1995), p. 38.

[22]The Army also was developing the ability to use chemical warfare against the Japanese in a land invasion of Japan.

[23]Joby Warrick, "Tracking a Dirty Bomb," *Washington Post National Weekly Edition*, (December 8–14, 2003), p. 6.

[24]See Michael A. Levi and Henry C. Kelly, "Weapons of Mass Disruption," *Scientific American*, (November 2002), pp. 76–81.

[25]Charles D. Ferguson and William Potter, The Four Faces of Nuclear Terrorism, (New York: Routledge, 2005); research cited in Charles Hanley, "Study: Dirty Bombs Highly Likely for U.S." Durham, NC *Herald-Sun*, June 19, 2004, p. A2.

[26]Joby Warrick, "The Hunt for a Deadly Legacy," *Washington Post National Weekly Edition*, November 18-24, 2002, p. 16.

[27]Warrick, "Tracking," pp. 6–7.

[28]John Heilprin, "Experts Walk Streets to Detect Dirty Bomb," Durham NC *Herald-Sun*, January 8, 2004, p. A2.

[29]Bennett Ramberg, *Nuclear Power Plants as Weapons for the Enemy: An Unrecognized Military Peril* (Berkeley, CA: University of California Press, 1984).

[30]Robert Alvarez, "What about the Spent Fuel?" *Bulletin of the Atomic Scientists*, (January/February, 2002), pp. 45-47. See also Elizabeth Kolbert, "Indian Point Blank," *The New Yorker* (March 3, 2003), pp. 36–41 and Shankar Vedantam, "A Radioactive Secret," *Washington Post National Weekly Edition*, April 4–10, 2005, p. 29.

[31]Daniel Hirsch, "The NRC: What, Me Worry?" *Bulletin of the Atomic Scientists*, Vol. 58 (January/February, 2002), pp. 39–44. See also Mark Hertsgaard, "Nuclear Insecurity," *Vanity Fair*, (November 2003), pp. 175–184.

[32]Danielle Brian, Lynn Eisenman, and Peter D. H. Stockton, "The Weapons Complex: Who's Minding the Store," *Bulletin of the Atomic Scientists*, (January/February, 2002), p. 51.

3

The Decision to Use Nuclear Weapons

Secretary of War Henry Stimson returned to Washington, D.C. on April 12, 1945 after inspecting a top-secret nuclear facility in rural Tennessee. Stunned to learn that President Franklin Roosevelt had just died, Stimson went to the White House where Harry Truman waited to be sworn in as president. Once that had been done, Truman spoke briefly to Stimson and the other hastily assembled cabinet members, telling them that he would continue Roosevelt's policies and would look to them for advice, but that "all final policy decisions would be mine."[1]

Truman recalled that the cabinet members then

> rose and silently made their way from the room—except for Secretary Stimson. He asked to speak to me about a most urgent matter. Stimson told me that he wanted me to know about an immense project that was under way—a project looking to the development of a new explosive of almost unbelievable destructive power. That was all he felt free to say at the time, and his statement left me puzzled. It was the first bit of information that had come to me about the atomic bomb, but he gave me no details.[2]

Stimson was a very knowledgeable cabinet officer, responsible for the Manhattan Project, then rushing toward the test and production of the atomic bomb. On April 25, he and General Leslie Groves, who directly oversaw the project, met with Truman. In a way, it was an anticlimactic meeting. Others had spoken to Truman about the bomb and its potential. For instance, the day after Stimson had first broached the subject, Truman had spoken with James Byrnes (whom Truman planned to appoint as Secretary of State). Byrnes had told him "that the weapon might be so powerful as to be potentially capable of wiping out entire cities and killing people on an unprecedented scale. And he added that in his belief the bomb might well put us in a position to dictate our own terms at the end of the war."[3]

Secretary Stimson now confirmed the bomb's extraordinary power and indicated that "in all probability" it would be available within four months. In a short period of time, Harry Truman would be the first leader faced with making a decision about using a nuclear weapon. We know that he chose to do so. How and why did he come to that decision? How and why might *other* leaders decide that they, too, must use nuclear weapons?

MAKING CHOICES

In war—as in politics—things happen because individuals make choices. Sometimes, of course, individuals believe that they have no choice; they are simply implementing decisions made by others. The personnel in command of nuclear-tipped missiles, for instance, may believe that if they receive authenticated orders to launch their missiles, they have no choice but to comply. But they, in fact, do have a choice not to comply, although they may not be aware that a choice exists. Similarly, leaders of nations may believe that they have no choice. Roosevelt and his advisors felt that once the Japanese attacked Pearl Harbor on December 7, 1941, they had no choice but to wage war against Japan. There were, however, other choices open to them, such as attempting to negotiate with Japan or simply retiring to the West coast and building a "Fortress America."[4]

Similarly, the use of nuclear weapons will always constitute a choice for leaders to make. The key question is, Will they recognize that they indeed have a choice? That is, will they recognize that they do have a range of options open to them and give serious consideration to options other than the use of nuclear weapons? To say that choice always exists does not mean that all options would be equally attractive. On the contrary, leaders often face pressures that narrow the range of choice to what seems politically viable and strategically sound. However, even though they may see themselves as constrained by circumstance to make a particular choice, they may still recognize that a choice exists. Indeed, they might even wish to make a choice different from the one they feel compelled to make. Did Truman see that he had a choice, or were nuclear weapons so compelling that he saw no other options?

Some choices, of course, seem so fraught with risk that they encourage a careful examination of the options. Given our contemporary understanding of nuclear weapons, we might imagine that their possible use would create a great deal of debate among the decision makers. Debate tells us that people perceive a range of choices (though they in the end may feel constrained to use the weapon). Was there a debate among Truman's advisors? Did the new President closely question his advisors so that he might become aware of different opinions about what should be done? Did he encourage a discussion that would clarify the strengths and weaknesses of the nuclear option? We might imagine that a newly installed leader might be just the person to ask such question and probe.

To answer these questions we will use a general model to understand decision making regarding the use of nuclear weapons:

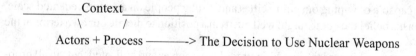

Our model says that we must ask (1) who are the decision-makers and advisors (the actors) and (2) how did they interact with each other to produce that choice (the process)? In addition, we need to ask, (3) what are the conditions surrounding the decision-makers (the context)? One of the critical features of the context in 1945 was the difficult position Harry Truman was in. Vice-president for only three months and essentially a stranger to Roosevelt, Truman knew about Roosevelt's foreign and military policy only by reading the newspapers. His sudden accession to the presidency meant that he had a lot to learn—and quickly—as Stimson's mysterious comments after the swearing-in suggested.

Moreover, leadership is more than just holding title to an office; it is the ability to command respect and loyalty from one's subordinates. Truman's statement at the swearing-in about "making all the final policy decisions" was both an attempt to ensure that the room full of Roosevelt appointees understood that he was President in more than just name, and to assure them that he would, in fact, make decisions—that he would be a leader.

In such a context, a new leader in the short run is likely to adopt the perspectives and preferences of his or her predecessor and of the predecessor's advisors. If the people around Truman believed that the bomb was a legitimate and very effective means of waging war, we would expect Truman to be quite disposed to adopt this view because this was the received wisdom of his advisors. If there were no debate among them, a new, untried, and ill-informed leader might be quite reluctant to raise questions that would spark such a debate and thus create dissension among the advisors, or to create a suspicion in their minds about the new leader's soundness on the issue or about her or his capacity to lead. Finally, even if the new leader might have some personal reservations about using the bomb, he or she might feel pressured to use the bomb for these reasons as well.

Truman's insistence that "all final policy decisions would be mine" should not be taken to mean that the relationship between leaders and advisors is one where advisors offer dispassionate advice and the leader weighs the evidence like a judge to select the best option. Rather, it is usually better to see advisors as *advocates* of particular options.[5] If the actors are the heads of bureaucracies, their advocacy often reflects the interests of the bureaucracy they lead. We would expect Secretary of War Stimson, for instance, to reflect the interests of the U.S. Army and Army Air Force, as he was their civilian boss, but not the interests of the Navy or the State Department.

A key bureaucratic interest is to insure that the organization continues to receive adequate funding and be given important missions to accomplish. The atomic bomb was the Army's project, and the Army saw a role for the bomb in the coming invasion of Japan, so it would be a proponent for its use. Within the Army, moreover, was an organization fervently interested in using the bomb: the Manhattan Project. Congress had allocated two billion dollars—an enormous sum at the time—to a project that was so secret that very few members of the Congress knew what the money was for. Many of the Project's military men and civilian scientists wanted to demonstrate their contribution to the war effort—one made far from the battle front—in a compelling way. As well, they wanted to see their labors through to a conclusion. For many Manhattan Project members, only by using a bomb against a real target—most importantly a city—could they demonstrate and measure the power of their creation. Stimson would represent this interest in the councils of government.

Advisors usually reflect more than just institutional interests, however. They often advocate their personal policy preferences. Stimson, for instance, wanted to convince Truman that the critical issue was not whether to use the bomb (he was convinced it should be) but how to establish some international control over nuclear weapons once the war was over. Moreover, many advisors have personal political or career ambitions. They want to be associated with a winning policy, or to avoid being tied to a failing policy. Stimson, a man with extensive government experience and political clout of his own, was probably beyond political ambition; that fact may have given him greater influence with Truman as he did not constitute a rival to the untried president.

As a consequence of their institutional connections and personal perspectives, advisors often engage in a *political process*, attempting to influence each other and the leader to adopt their preferred policies. In such an environment, the leader often finds that he or she too must engage in the same political process—of attempting to influence others to agree with what the leader wants done, because the selection of any option may be disliked by some advisors and bureaucracies who can cause trouble for the leader or stymie the implementation of the policy.

This political process often produces a *compromise* decision, a combining of the elements of several options. Such a compromise accommodates the interests of a number of powerful or persuasive actors. The leader's preferences are usually central in that compromise, but he or she often makes policy concessions to the interests of others.

Making compromises within a political process is often the hallmark of democratic political systems. In such an open political system, where there is often a dispersion of power among various individuals and groups, advisors will compete intensely and the leader often must engage in politicking to set the agenda, create the options, or get her or his perspectives and preferences accepted by others. In open systems, therefore, leaders help shape national policy. Rarely do they dictate it. What about authoritarian regimes? Can we expect politicking and compromise as well there? We can. Even the relatively closed political system of an imperial Japan that attacked the United States in 1941 had a degree of openness. There were powerful factions in the Japanese political and military elite whose consent was usually necessary to reach decisions. The Emperor had enormous prestige, but the norms of the political system severely constrained him from openly advocating the policies he preferred. Similarly, other closed political systems, such as the Soviet Union, particularly after Stalin's death in 1953, are open enough to have politicking within the elite. The same seems to hold true within terrorist organizations. Within al Qaeda, for instance, some of the senior leaders openly argued against Osama bin Laden's planned attack on Washington and New York, insisting that consolidation of Taliban control over Afghanistan had to be accomplished first.[6]

TRUMAN'S DECISION TO DROP THE BOMB

Beyond Truman's newness to the presidency in an open political system, how might the context have further set the conditions for the decision that he would reach? A crucial part of the context was the status of the war.[7] By the spring of 1945, the United States had been at war against Japan for three and one-half years. Japan's ally, Nazi Germany, was collapsing and would surrender unconditionally to the United States, Britain, and the Soviet Union on May 7. American forces had gradually carried the Pacific war closer to Japan. By April 1945, when they invaded the island of Okinawa, 300 miles off Japan, they essentially commanded the seas around the Japanese home islands. In March 1945, the new bomber commander in the Pacific, Curtis LeMay, had ordered his B-29s to stage low-level fire-bomb attacks against Japanese cities, causing extensive death and destruction. There were, however, large Japanese armies in the home islands and in China and Manchuria. In every engagement with the Japanese army, American forces suffered heavy casualties as most Japanese chose to die rather than surrender.

Surrounding this context of immediate events was the larger context of how Americans thought about war. While we examine this point in more detail in Chapter 4, we need to note here that the

United States sought a decisive victory. Franklin Roosevelt had pledged in January 1943 to force Germany and Japan to surrender unconditionally—to submit to any and every Allied demand. Behind this goal of complete victory over Japan were elements of racism,[8] a desire for revenge for being humiliated at Pearl Harbor, and an American conviction that unless an enemy were thoroughly defeated and reorganized according to the winner's dictates, the enemy would rise again to threaten the survival of the United States (as had Germany after World War I).

The American public had accepted unconditional surrender as the paramount war goal, but such a goal can exact an enormous price. The next step in the military plans called for a series of invasions of the Japanese home islands in the late fall of 1945 to compel Japan's unconditional surrender, invasions that would likely have huge casualty tolls. While Roosevelt's advisors had grimly accepted the idea of invasion as necessary, by the time of Truman's accession differences of opinion had begun to appear among the military leadership.[9] The Navy, now effectively blockading Japan and beginning to stage carrier air raids against the home islands, had concluded the blockade would force Japan's surrender at some point, and at low cost in American lives. The Army Air Force leadership, determined to become a separate entity from the Army and to have a large peace-time force of bombers and fighters, was counting on massive conventional bombing as the way to end the war and secure the Air Force's future. Thus, in their eyes, an invasion would be unnecessary. As the atomic bomb did not fit into the plans of the Navy and Air Force, its leaders were less interested in its use, less likely to see it as a war-winning weapon, and, for a few, a weapon shrouded in moral issues, particularly concerning the extensive civilian casualties that would likely come with its use.

On the other hand, the Army, given its method of fighting wars, pressed its view that only "boots on the ground" end wars, especially if one sought unconditional surrender. For the Army, the key question was, How do we minimize American casualties in the coming invasion? The atomic bomb seemed to be part of the answer. Army planners counted on up to nine atomic bombings to "soften up" Japanese defenses prior to the invasion.

The final part of the context that would shape the decision was the Soviet Union. Roosevelt had gained Stalin's promise to enter the war against Japan soon after Germany surrendered. At the time, American military planners felt it essential to keep Japan from redeploying its armies from Manchuria and China to aid in the defense of the home islands. By the late spring of 1945, American officials were of different minds about the need for Soviet intervention. Some still felt that the Japanese armies on the continent had to be pinned down, but did not want the Soviets to advance too far into the region. The Soviets had disregarded American wishes for the reconstitution of the states of Eastern Europe, installing communist-dominated governments rather than allowing for democratic elections. These officials worried that the Soviet invasion would bring similar attempts in Asia. Some feared that the Soviets would insist on participating in the occupation of Japan, making decision-making more contentious (as it was becoming in occupied Germany). And there were some who eyed Soviet military strength, remembered the past hostility shown to the capitalist West, and began to see the Soviet Union as the next major threat to the United States. But in general, no one wanted to disrupt the wartime alliance with the Soviet Union because all the plans for a post-war world—symbolized by the United Nations, whose Charter was being negotiated in San Francisco—rested on the premise of a working relationship between the United States and the Soviet Union.

Considered as a whole, the context surrounding Truman and his advisors favored the use of nuclear weapons. Indeed, *any perfected weapon* (nuclear or otherwise) that a military service found a role for in the on-going war would likely be used *unless* (1) influential actors found a compelling reason not to use it (because it seemed contrary to their interests or their conception of the national interest) and (2) those actors had access to the key decision-makers and were willing to pay the political costs for making their opposition known. While the leadership of the Navy and Army Air Force did not see the necessity for the bomb, they had little reason to oppose its use—or to disrupt the comity of the military services by opposing the Army's project and plans. General George Marshall, the Army Chief of Staff, was not convinced that the bomb would end the war, but it was an important part of the overall invasion plans. Secretary of War Stimson hoped that its use would make the invasion unnecessary.

Within the State Department, the acting Secretary of State, Joseph Grew, had come to the conclusion that an invasion might not be necessary if the Japanese were told that if they did surrender unconditionally, they could keep the Emperor as the symbolic head of the Japanese nation. Stimson and Truman were interested, for it might make an invasion with its prospect of appalling casualties unnecessary. But others within the State Department and the military were opposed and Truman recognized the political danger if he seemed to back away from unconditional surrender, especially in this regard. Many Americans and their elected officials saw the Emperor as the incarnation of the evil.

Thus by the early summer of 1945, the critical question was not whether to use the bomb, but how to get Japan's unconditional surrender. The bomb was part of the picture, of course, but not part of the debate within the administration. The debate had gravitated toward whether to modify the unconditional surrender terms, and if a modification were to take place, what should the Japanese be told and when. The actors were divided and willing to contest that matter. The Army's interest in using the bomb moved ahead.

If there are to be challenges to the momentum pushing actors toward the bomb's use, those challenges might come during the process of resolving important *implementation questions* such as "What would be the target of the bomb?" and "How long would an atomic campaign go on against Japan?" Wars (and peacetime politics) always involve a number of such implementation choices. The process of making choices on those matters provides additional opportunities to raise questions and provoke debate and thus reveal a broader range of choice to the leaders.

The bomb's targets had been identified by Air Force planners: the major Japanese cities that had yet to be extensively attacked by conventional bombing raids and that had some military significance. But they were to be cities, and hence civilian casualties would be great. Target identification had occasioned the one instance when top civilian leaders interfered in these implementing decisions. Stimson insisted over strong opposition from the American military that Kyoto, a religious site as well as the old capital, be removed from the list. Truman backed him up, noting that "even if the Japs are savages, ruthless, merciless and fanatic, we as the leader of the world for the common welfare cannot drop this terrible bomb on the old capital or the new [Tokyo]."[10] But the debate about specific targets had not been enough to raise the basic question of whether the bomb should be used or not. In seeing America's opponents as "savages, ruthless, merciless, and fanatic," Truman was less inclined to think about them either as humans (Should one use such a "terrible weapon" against fellow humans?) or as people who might respond rationally to their worsening military situation by suing for peace without the use of the bomb.

While the top American leadership seemed to have moved easily toward a decision to drop the bomb, at the middle levels of the government there were occasions when divergent views came to the table. For instance, in late May 1945 an advisory committee that Stimson had created explored the possibility of forewarning the Japanese and then dropping the bomb on an uninhabited island. The committee concluded that the approach had too many drawbacks, including the limited number of weapons that the United States would have and the Manhattan District's desire to observe the actual effects of the weapon. It endorsed the use of the bomb as soon as possible, without warning, against a real target. A similar discussion a month later among a panel of scientists drew the same conclusion.

Ideas can reach top leaders without passing through the filtering process of committees and bureaucracies, however, and Truman did learn of the "demonstration option." But he displayed little interest in it except to endorse the emerging compromise among his advisors in late June that Japan should be *warned* of "utter devastation of the Japanese homeland" if it did not surrender unconditionally and accept the military occupation of Japan, a warning issued on July 26, 1945, as a part of the Potsdam Declaration. As to the question of the future of the Emperor, the Declaration's compromise language now stated that the occupation would end once the Allies had completed the demilitarization of Japan, punished the war criminals, and "there has been established in accordance with the freely expressed will of the Japanese people a peacefully inclined and responsible government." In the Japanese government, a minority leaned toward surrender as long as the Emperor's position was safeguarded. The military, in particular, insisted on fighting on, to create enough American casualties to force better terms than unconditional surrender. The Japanese rejected the Potsdam terms.

While the debate within the administration regarding the language of the Potsdam Declaration entered its final stage, Truman learned of the successful test of the technologically complex implosion device at Alamogordo, New Mexico, and that it had released significantly more energy than had been predicted. Military planners told him that a second plutonium bomb and a second type of bomb (the untested gun-type uranium bomb) would be ready for use in early August and a third by late August. The Army Air Force had conducted practice runs over the selected target cities. The question now before Truman was not whether to use the weapon but how quickly. Speed seemed of the essence. Secretary of State Byrnes wanted the bomb as a follow-up to the Potsdam Declaration—to show that the Allies meant what they said. General Groves, anxious to use the bomb before Japan surrendered, sent Truman a glowing report of the Trinity test to encourage quick use. The leadership worried about Soviet entry into the war, now just days away. Stimson endorsed the bomb's use. The Navy and Air Force leadership, however much they might have seen it as unnecessary, apparently chose not to make it an issue.

The president essentially agreed to allow Groves and the Air Force officials in the theater to pick the time and place for the attack following general guidelines that he endorsed: "The 509th Composite Group, 20th Air Force, will deliver its first special bomb as soon as weather will permit visual bombing after about 3 August 1945 on one of the targets: Hiroshima, Kokura, Niigata, and Nagasaki. … Additional bombs will be delivered on the above targets as soon as made ready by the project staff."[11] Actual target selection was left up to the Air Force—and in fact to the aircrews themselves: Kokura was spared on August 9 because it was obscured by smoke. The B-29 pilot elected to try the second target on his list, Nagasaki, even though his plane was running low on fuel and clouds covered that site, forcing him to use radar to bomb the target—something that Groves wanted to prevent. Radar bombing was relatively inaccurate, thus spoiling the Project's ability to judge the damage the plutonium bomb could do to a city.[12]

After the Hiroshima attack, the administration awaited any word from Japan. As the Japanese made no move to capitulate, the execute order remained in force, and the second bomb struck Nagasaki. After the second bomb, the Japanese emperor personally intervened in the tense debate within the Japanese government and compelled it to accept the surrender terms.

Thus the first two uses of nuclear weapons did not, at the top levels, occasion much of the process that we often associate with critical decisions. The top leadership did not struggle with the basic question, "Should we use the bomb or not?" They did not examine the costs and benefits of those two options. This is not to say that Truman or his advisors such as Stimson treated the matter lightly. All the top leadership were concerned with the costs of the impending invasion of Japan. Any weapon that offered to reduce that cost dramatically would, without much thinking, recommend itself. The leadership of the Navy and the Army Air Force did have their own proposed solutions to how to force the unconditional surrender of Japan and questioned the necessity of using the bomb, but their solutions would not be quick nor could they guarantee success on the terms the U.S. government had stipulated.

Truman had sided with Stimson and Army Chief of Staff Marshall on the issue: The United States had to move forward with the invasion as it held the most promise to produce a quick, unconditional surrender. The other services were mollified because they were permitted to continue with their preferred options. The Navy sank every Japanese ship it could find and LeMay continued the systematic destruction of Japan's major cities by fire-bombing. At the least, the bomb would be the opening shot in the upcoming invasion of the Japanese home islands. If the United States got lucky, Japan might offer unconditional surrender before the first American waded ashore under fire.

THE DEBATE ABOUT THE USE OF THE BOMB

After the war a debate arose about the use of the bomb on Japan and continues to this day.[13] It centers around three intertwined questions: (1) Was dropping the bomb necessary? (2) What were the real reasons for doing so? (3) Did Truman and his advisors violate important moral or ethical principles in deciding to use the bomb? We need to look at this debate, not only to understand the nuclear past, but also because this debate, to one degree or another, established *a context for future decisions* about the use of nuclear weapons in the Cold War and beyond. Decision makers who contemplate using nuclear weapons are likely to find that these questions become prominent in their decisions, as will the competing answers.

Critics of the decision to use the bomb against Japan answer the three questions in these ways:

1. The use of the bomb was not necessary because Japan was on the verge of surrender. Cut off from its sources of raw materials, particularly oil, and with its cities being burned out by American bombers, it was only a matter of time before the Japanese war machine ground to a halt, forcing capitulation. The Japanese had sought Soviet diplomatic help in securing peace terms with the Americans and were stunned when the Soviets declared war on Japan on August 8. This set of circumstances, the critics argue, would have produced a quick decision for surrender. The use of the bomb was a rushed decision. Truman could have waited to see if Japan would recognize its helpless condition. The bomb may have been unnecessary; the loss of life was therefore unacceptable.

    The critics also point out that the administration's refusal to accept explicitly the continuation of Emperor made it impossible for the peace faction within the Japanese leadership to meet the American terms. The tragedy is that the American government did, in fact, permit the emperor to remain once Japan surrendered. Moreover, Truman gave the Japanese elites very little time to probe the ambiguous language of the Potsdam Declaration, having given the Air Force the order to commence bombing a week after its issuance.

Other critics modify this argument by saying that perhaps the bomb was necessary, but the demonstration option was the correct choice. Japanese national pride, which allowed the war to continue in spite of an unrelenting string of losses, would have been overcome by the demonstration of a powerful weapon that the Japanese did not have. Realism would have overcome national pride—even a prideful nation can legitimately give in to such unanswerable power.

2. While the Truman administration did want to end the war quickly, some critics allege that the real motivation was to force the Japanese to surrender before the Soviet Union became actively involved in the war and therefore able to make demands for full participation in settling Japan's future. Even more importantly, use of the weapon was meant to cow the Soviet Union into accepting the American definition of a desirable post-war order. Japan was forced to pay the terrible price for the beginning of the Cold War.

3. Finally, some critics condemn the Truman administration's lack of moral vision. For the first time weapons were used that were inherently indiscriminate in their terror and destructiveness. Even accepting the premise that dropping the atomic bomb on Hiroshima and Nagasaki saved tens of thousands of American lives and countless Japanese lives by obviating the need for an invasion, the invasion would at least have been a legitimate form of warfare. Dropping the bomb, on the other hand, without fully understanding all the possible scientific, medical, ecological, and political consequences, was to break with accepted practice and unleash the destructive genie.

Moreover, the critics charge, Truman and his advisors lost sight of what this war was all about. The war was a struggle between the Hitlerites on the one hand, who claimed that only the brutal survived and therefore anything a state did to ensure its survival was legitimate, and the democrats on the other hand who argued that democracy and humane values could not survive in the world of the brutal. Decent human beings, therefore, had to ask if the means one chose—even in the cause of defending democratic moral values—were so repugnant as to make one indistinguishable from a Hitler. To condemn children to die—and massive bombings of cities by conventional or nuclear weapons ensured that thousands would die—was to allow the Hitlerites to win the war. It was Hitler's terror which had triumphed, not the democrats' vision, which said that moral people simply could *not* do all that was possible to do in war.

The members of the Truman administration rejected these allegations, claiming that the critics were factually wrong, or were working from hindsight, or laboring under a misunderstanding of how leaders actually make decisions. The administration and scholars supporting its decision assert that the better answers are these:

1. In July and August, 1945, most American policy makers believed that the Japanese were not about to surrender on terms acceptable to the United States. Though clearly losing the war, the Japanese continued to fight on. The symbol of their resoluteness was the *kamikaze*, the Japanese aviator who willingly piloted his explosive-laden plane into an American ship. Their appearance in large numbers in defense of the Japanese island of Okinawa, along with a stubborn and effective ground resistance that produced 75,000 U.S. casualties, seemed to indicate that the Japanese were developing a potent form of resistance. It seemed clear that it would take a devas-

tating blow to compel Japan's surrender. No one could predict in advance how the Japanese would react to a Soviet declaration of war. No one could predict in advance whether the Japanese would quickly surrender once a land invasion began. Thinking it prudent to assume the worst case, the administration saw the bomb as the reasonable alternative to a prolonged, bloody invasion. From all the information that the administration had at the time, say its defenders—and the administration's code breakers were reading Japanese diplomatic messages—the Japanese were saying to themselves that there would not be an unconditional surrender. Not only was the Emperor's position to be safeguarded, but there was to be no occupation of the home islands.

2. There were no other primary motives that led to the bomb's use. The administration, the defenders acknowledge, was wrestling with a variety of issues as the war came to its climax. One of those problems was how to deal with what Washington perceived to be Russian demands and obstructionism. The bomb might have useful consequences for dealing with the Russians, but that never was a prominent feature of the top leadership's thinking. Their focus then, as it had been for more than three years, was the defeat of Japan.

   There *was*, of course, a more basic political motive. If the administration had not used the bomb, large numbers of Americans, after surveying the casualty lists created by the invasion of Japan, might have turned on the administration, condemning it for withholding the one weapon that might have minimized the loss of U.S. life. But acting politically is the price, so to speak, of governing a democracy: Political leaders must give weight to what the public wants (or to their best estimates of those wants).

3. War always threatens the ethical standards of a society, the defenders of the administration would argue. The key question is, in the face of *competing* moral standards, which standard outweighs the others? The Truman administration viewed the bomb as another weapon, horrible like other weapons, but used for clearly moral purposes: to end a brutal Japanese imperialism and to bring the suffering of war to an end as quickly as possible. Civilians would die in large numbers—and no one denied that fact, even though one might try to soften its reality by thinking of the Japanese cities as military targets. But that was the price one had to pay to wage war successfully in the middle of the twentieth century, argued some defenders. In the end, without success in this war, the world would have been left with a monstrous tyranny in Europe and Asia dedicated to the extirpation of the very values the critics sought to protect. What moral condemnation would then fall on the administration? These moral dilemmas continue unresolved to this day, as we shall see in Chapter 11.

This post-war debate about the appropriateness of the use of the bomb cannot be definitively resolved. We cannot replay history to see what might have happened if the bomb were not dropped. Nor can we watch over the shoulders of decision-makers as they thought their way through all the issues surrounding nuclear weapons. We might fault them for not asking the questions that would have led to a full-scale review of the alternatives or to a more careful examination of what would cause the Japanese to surrender. But we can also recognize that *our criticism comes from having lived in the nuclear world*, an experience denied Truman and his advisors. And we can recognize that unlike the abundance of time we have to formulate our criticisms, they were continuously engaged in waging a world war, and everyone wanted the killing over with as quickly as possible.

THE IMPLICATIONS OF HIROSHIMA AND NAGASAKI

After Hiroshima and Nagasaki, after the early months and years of living in the first nuclear age, a new context emerged. Knowledge of the bombs' effects and the controversy surrounding their use influenced the leaders of all nuclear-armed states. Using the bomb became stigmatized as an unacceptable act, creating the nuclear taboo.[14] Leaders contemplating a decision to use nuclear weapons would first have to overcome their own moral scruples or those of powerful people around them. There would likely be a debate among the decision-makers about the wisdom of any use of nuclear weapons. Leaders would have to be convinced that the use of such weapons would in fact achieve vital goals and be convinced that incurring the opprobrium of the international community and possibly of their own societies was politically bearable. President Dwight Eisenhower's comment when a member of his staff presented a report recommending use of nuclear weapons in Vietnam to support the French effort to remain in control reflects the restraint that the past imposes on leaders: "You boys must be crazy. We can't use those awful things against Asians for the second time in less than ten years. My God!"[15]

The citizenry of nuclear-armed states may also have serious reservations about using nuclear weapons. For instance, on the fiftieth anniversary of dropping the bomb, 43 percent of American respondents told pollsters that if the decision had been theirs to make, they would have ordered the bombs dropped on Japan, but 50 percent said they would have tried some other way.[16] Leaders contemplating the use of nuclear weapons would have to consider (and debate) what a divided public might mean for the use of nuclear weapons and how the public might be brought to accept the use of such weapons.

There was, of course, another feature of the first nuclear age that would encourage intense debate among the leadership of a nation: the possibility of devastating nuclear retaliation by the victim or by its nuclear-armed ally. In the Truman administration's case, there was no concern about Japanese retaliation. In a world of several nuclear states, the leadership would have to consider whether the use of nuclear weapons would recklessly and irresponsibly risk the nation's existence.

Off-setting this constraint in the first nuclear age was the impression that nuclear weapons were a powerful means to gain one's policy objectives. Recall that the supporters of Truman's decision saw the destruction of two Japanese cities as the factor that compelled Japan to surrender on terms the Americans found acceptable. Today, Osama bin Laden apparently has used this conclusion to spur al Qaeda's efforts to secure a nuclear device, arguing that its use would drive the Americans from the Islamic world.[17] Is this impression accurate? There are two key questions here: (1) Did nuclear weapons in fact compel Japan's surrender? (2) How did they do so?

It is *not* clear that the bombs *must* have compelled the Japanese leadership to accept the inevitable. The Japanese government in the summer of 1945 was deeply divided between those who wanted to fight until the U.S. offered far better terms and those who wanted to end the war as quickly as possible. The stalemate between these factions perpetuated the status quo—the continuation of the war. Only after two bombs had dropped did the Emperor feel that he must take the highly unusual step of intervening directly into the governmental debate, now confident that the die-hards in the military would not challenge his request to accept the American terms. But there were still important Japanese military leaders who wanted to continue to resist *in spite of* the bombs. (And, as it happened, a small group of renegade military officers did attempt a coup against the Emperor to prevent the surrender; it failed.)

The bombs did change the political dynamics within the Japanese elite. In the future, the use of nuclear weapons may change the influence and initiative of those in the enemy government, but there is no guarantee that the internal balance of power will change, or that those willing to concede or surrender will gain the upper hand. Indeed, if history had been slightly different—if there were a more timid Emperor who could not find the political will to intervene, or if the process of decision-making within the Japanese government had been more prolonged—we might have drawn quite different lessons about what the bomb can do. Indeed, it is possible that the Japanese die-hards might have recovered their power if days slipped by without a further attack and then the subsequent attacks were few and far between.

It is also possible that in the only case we have of nuclear use, *the bombs themselves were not enough*. They may have been a *culmination* to a series of losses that the United States had inflicted on Japan since the carrier battle at Midway in June 1942. If atomic bombing made the difference, it was only because all the other defeats had come before. Alternatively, we might see the bombs as part of a combination of defeats *occurring at roughly the same time*: the loss of Okinawa, the devastating air raids, the Soviet entry, and the bombs. Without the force of all those roughly simultaneous blows, the two bombs might not have had the kind of impact they appear to have had on the Japanese leadership. (After all, LeMay's fire raids were causing even more casualties and devastation in some Japanese cities than the two atomic bombs caused.)

Thus, the ability of nuclear weapons to compel a government to surrender may be more problematic than this one historical example might suggest. Having said that, we suspect that the current image of Hiroshima and Nagasaki that rests in the minds of today's leaders and citizens (including yourself) is that nuclear weapons were the *war-winning weapon* (even when used in small numbers). To believe that nuclear weapons could quickly resolve important but seemingly intractable political issues would encourage leaders to consider nuclear weapons as an option in spite of their moral stigma and to lessen the intensity of debate within governments. Moreover, it has become fashionable to lump nuclear weapons with chemical and biological weapons as "weapons of mass destruction." This tames nuclear weapons and makes them appear less threatening, for chemical and biological weapons can be defended against (the chemical suits issued to American troops invading Iraq in 2003 are emblematic), making them seem like other weapons of war. And as America's potential adversaries are likely to have very small stocks of nuclear weapons, these weapons lose their image as the potential destroyers of nations. Today, the context may be less likely to spur debate within the U.S. government than it would have during the first nuclear age.

NEAR USES OF NUCLEAR WEAPONS

Since 1945, no leader of any nuclear-armed state has decided to use nuclear weapons. Was one use enough? Was the nuclear option never seriously considered by policy-makers after that? Or did it remain an option, only to fall to the wayside after careful deliberation and debate, even in the face of an impending political or military loss? And if there were occasions when leaders contemplated the use of nuclear weapons, can we find some pattern that would better help us understand when and why leaders move toward explicit decisions about using the bomb? We have examined the historical record for some answers.

Our focus is on *near-use decisions*—those occasions when the top leadership of a nation *actively considered using nuclear weapons*. We examined the historical record to detect such cases, concentrating on periods of war or intense crisis in which one of the states involved was nuclear armed, and on periods when a state stood on the brink of becoming a nuclear power, an event of some concern to the other members of the nuclear club. We were able to identify 25 occasions when considerations of nuclear use *would be most likely* to occur. Table 3–1 reports the results. We found, in 10 cases, some evidence that the nation's leadership actively considered the use of nuclear weapons.[18]

The table suggests that near-use decisions are relatively rare. One might have imagined that nuclear weapons are so central that in time of war or crisis they would *automatically* become an option to be considered. That is possible, of course, but we found little evidence for such an assertion. Sometimes policy makers agreed only to consider the use option at some later time, as the Eisenhower administration did in October 1953: "In the event of hostilities, the United States will consider nuclear weapons to be available for use as other munitions."[19] Such an orientation may create a context which might encourage a decision to use nuclear weapons but is not itself a near-use decision.

Similarly, the military of a nuclear state always plan for the use of nuclear weapons. We discuss such plans in the next chapter; here we need only note that while military establishments may make the nuclear option *available* to the top leadership, unless the top leadership actively considers using the capability provided by the military, we do not have a near-use decision. Making nuclear weapons a prominent part of a military plan does, however, increase the likelihood of active consideration.

In addition to the near-use decisions presented in Table 3-1, you might ask about two other circumstances that would seem to be clearly near-use decisions but do not appear in the table. The first occurs when leader *threaten to use* nuclear weapons to secure policy goals—a relatively frequent behavior by the United States and Soviet Union during the 1950s and early 1960s. For instance, in 1953, the United States warned the People's Republic of China that it would use atomic weapons against Chinese forces if the Chinese did not agree to armistice terms to end the Korean War. In these cases, however, the leadership considered the option of *making the threat*, not the option of using such weapons. Indeed, in cases of nuclear threat-making, the top leadership usually did *not* want to have to use the weapons. We do not include such cases of threat-making except where the top leadership actively discussed the use of nuclear weapons.

Second, there are the cases where the leadership felt that it had to present *an image* of having considered nuclear use for public relations purposes. The classic case of this came in November 1950, when Chinese intervention in the Korean War threatened to bring defeat to U.S. and South Korean forces. A reporter asked President Truman at a news conference if the atom bomb was under consideration as a means to deal with the worsening military situation.

Truman: That includes every weapon that we have.

Reporter: Mr. President, you said "every weapon we have." Does that mean that there is active consideration of the use of the atomic bomb?

Truman: There has always been active consideration of its use. I don't want to see it used. It is a terrible weapon, and it should not be used on innocent men, women, and children who have nothing whatever to do with this military aggression. That happens when it is used.[20]

There is no evidence that the bomb was, in fact, under active consideration by Truman or his top advisors, but Truman may have felt that, politically, he could not say otherwise. After all, American lives were on the line. McGeorge Bundy suggests that Truman's concluding statements showed his

TABLE 3–1   POTENTIAL NEAR-USE DECISIONS

Category	Event	Nuclear Actors	Evidence from the Historical Record
Wars in Which Nuclear Actors Were Direct Participants	Korean War (1950–1953)	United States	**Case 1:** Eisenhower administration considers nuclear weapons in conduct of war and to force an end to the stalemate.[1]
	Suez War (1956)	Great Britain	Nuclear weapons were not considered as an option.
	Algerian War (1960–1962)	France	No evidence of consideration of nuclear weapons.
	Vietnam War (1963–1973)	United States	Johnson and Nixon administrations did not consider nuclear weapons use at the highest level.
	Egypt-Israeli War (1970)	Israel	No evidence of consideration of nuclear weapons.
	Yom Kippur/Ramadan War (1973)	Israel	**Case 2:** Probably consideration after Israeli counterattack initially failed.[2]
	Sino-Vietnamese War (1979)	China	No evidence of consideration of nuclear weapons.
	Afghan War (1979–1989)	USSR	No evidence of consideration of nuclear weapons.
	Falkland/Malvinas War (1981)	Great Britain	No evidence of consideration of nuclear weapons.
	Gulf War (1990–1991)	United States, Great Britain, France	No evidence of consideration of nuclear weapons.
	Afghan War (2001)	United States	No evidence of consideration of nuclear weapons
	Iraq War (2003–)	United States, Great Britain	No evidence of consideration of nuclear weapons.
Crises Directly Involving Nuclear-Armed States	Berlin Blockade (1948–1949)	United States	No evidence of consideration of nuclear weapons.
	Indochina War (1946–1954)	United States	**Case 3:** Eisenhower administration considered using nuclear weapons to prevent French defeat by Vietminh (April/May 1954).[3] **Case 4:** Eisenhower administration considered using nuclear weapons if Chinese intervene in Indochina war.[4]

Event	Countries	Case Description
Quemoy Crisis (1954–1955)	United States	**Case 5:** Eisenhower administration considered likelihood of using nuclear weapons if Chinese attack two islands off China's coast.[5]
Quemoy Crisis (1958)	United States	**Case 6:** Eisenhower administration again considered nuclear weapons to defend the off-shore islands.
Berlin Crisis (1961)	United States, USSR	**Case 7:** Kennedy administration reviews plans for nuclear use.[6]
Laos Civil War (1959–1962)	United States	No evidence of consideration of nuclear weapons.
Cuban Missile Crisis (1962)	United States, USSR	**Case 8:** Kennedy administration pledges to respond with nuclear weapons against USSR if any Cuban-based missile is launched.
Vietnam (1961–1965)	United States	No evidence of consideration of nuclear weapons.
Arab–Israeli War (1973)	United States, USSR	No evidence of consideration of nuclear weapons.
India–Pakistan Crisis (1990)	India, Pakistan	No evidence of consideration of nuclear weapons.
India–Pakistan Crisis (1999)	India, Pakistan	No evidence of consideration of nuclear weapons.
India–Pakistan Crisis (2001–2002)	India, Pakistan	Possible alert for nuclear forces; no evidence that top leadership actively considered using nuclear weapons.
Chinese Nuclear Program (1955–1970)	United States, USSR	**Case 9:** Kennedy administration considers a nuclear attack on Chinese facilities and asks for Soviet views (May 1963).[7] **Case 10:** Johnson administration considers a nuclear attack on Chinese facilities (September 1964).[8] **Case 11:** Brezhnev Politburo considers a nuclear attack on Chinese facilities (spring/summer 1969).[10]
Pre-emptive Strike against Nuclear Facilities by Current Nuclear State[9]		
Indian Nuclear Program (1960s–1979)	China	No evidence of consideration of nuclear weapons.
Iraqi Nuclear Program (1970s–2003)	Israel	No evidence that Israeli government considered nuclear weapons; did use conventional bombs in 1981.

		Nuclear weapons not considered.
Pakistani Nuclear Program (1970s–2003)	United States, India	No evidence that India considered nuclear weapons in considering an attack on Pakistani nuclear facilities.
North Korean Nuclear Program (1980s–)	United States	No evidence of consideration of nuclear weapons.
Iranian Nuclear Program (1980s–)	United States, Israel	No evidence to date of consideration of the use of nuclear weapons.

[1] See evidence cited in this chapter.

[2] See Seymour Hersh, *The Sampson Option* (New York: Random House, 1991) and Yair Evron, *Israel's Nuclear Dilemma*, (Ithaca, NY: Cornell University Press, 1994), p. 72.

[3] See McGeorge Bundy, *Danger and Survival* (New York: Random House, 1988), pp. 260—270.

[4] Stephen E. Ambrose, *Eisenhower, Vol. 2: The President* (New York: Simon & Schuster, 1984), pp. 205–206.

[5] Bundy, *Danger and Survival*, p. 274.

[6] See evidence cited in this chapter.

[7] See Gordon H. Chang, *Friends and Enemies* (Stanford, CA: Stanford University Press, 1990), pp. 243–245.

[8] Chang, *Friends and Enemies*, p. 250.

[9] Dates are the time period when the participants had nuclear weapons. In cases of pre-emptive strikes, dates are from nuclear program inception to approximately five years after test or termination of program.

[10] Arkady Shevechenko, *Breaking with Moscow* (NY: Knopf, 1985), p. 166; Henry Kissinger, *White House Years* (Boston, MA: Little, Brown, 1979), p. 183.

unwillingness to think of such weapons as meaningful options.[21] Perhaps the destruction of Hiroshima and Nagasaki made Truman the *least* likely leader to entertain that option again.

PATTERNS OF USE AND NEAR-USE OF NUCLEAR WEAPONS IN THE FIRST NUCLEAR AGE

An examination of the historical record from 1945 until 2005 in Table 3-1 suggests these hypotheses about the use or near-use of nuclear weapons.

1. While nuclear weapons may have been ever-present in the minds of policy makers, they rarely became an option that received serious consideration by top policy makers and, in all but one case, the policy-makers rejected the use of nuclear weapons.

2. The U.S. decision in 1945 suggests that nuclear weapons are most likely to be used when a state is engaged in a protracted major war that begins with conventional weapons, proves to be costly, and spurs one or both combatants to seek a rapid and victorious end to the war—and particularly likely if the weapon becomes available during that war. In the post-Hiroshima period, only the 1980–1988 Iran-Iraq war meets the criterion of length and cost—and both sides had nuclear weapons programs. Neither side, however, achieved a nuclear weapons capability before a truce ended the fighting.

3. "Young" nuclear powers—that is, states in the first 15–20 years of their lives as nuclear weapons states—seem most prone to near-use decisions. Historically, a young nuclear power caught up *in a stalemated war* has considered using nuclear weapons against a non-nuclear foe, even if the foe had a nuclear patron. For instance, in 1953 President Eisenhower himself suggested "the use of tactical atomic weapons on [Chinese forces in] the Kaesong [Korea] area, which provided a good target for this type of weapon"[22] and asked his advisors if enemy airfields in North Korea "might not prove a target which would test the effectiveness of an atomic bomb. At any rate, said the President, he had reached the point of being convinced that we have got to consider the atomic bomb as simply another weapon in our arsenal."[23] This was in spite of both China and North Korea's being in an alliance with the nuclear-capable Soviet Union.

4. A young nuclear power will consider the nuclear option in times of a crisis with a *non-nuclear* power. (Cases 3–6 during the Eisenhower administration.)

5. The leadership of an "older" nuclear power, on the other hand, has rarely considered using nuclear weapons. Even under the relatively dire circumstance of a stalemated war, the nuclear-use option has remained off the table. We can find no evidence that the top leadership of the United States considered using nuclear weapons against North Vietnam[24] or that the Soviet leadership considered using nuclear weapons against Afghan insurgents.[25]

6. Historically, nuclear powers young and old did not consider nuclear use against other nuclear weapons states in times of crisis. The Berlin and Cuban crises are models of caution in this regard although both states were still relatively young. (We examine these seminal events in Chapter 5.)

7. Nuclear powers, even older nuclear weapons states, will consider nuclear weapons as an option to keep another state from going nuclear or to destroy a small nuclear arsenal. In 1963 and 1964,

the U.S. government considered attacking Chinese nuclear facilities to prevent China from acquiring nuclear weapons[26]; the Soviet government in 1969 debated a proposal to attack the fledgling Chinese arsenal.[27] While such attacks might spark a wider conflagration, policy-makers apparently saw the nuclear option as constrained to a particular time and place—a limited use of nuclear weapons.

In the first nuclear age, then, there were occasions when governments made decisions about the use of nuclear weapons. In all but one case, active consideration did not lead to use. In the next several chapters, we will explore some of the reasons why the top leadership of nuclear-armed societies has been unwilling to use the power at its disposal. But it is clear that nuclear use *has been actively contemplated*. Given the right kind of situation (wartime, crisis, or unsettling nuclear proliferation), top policy-makers have seen the merits of nuclear use, especially in the "youth" of a nuclear weapons state.

COLD WAR VISIONS OF NUCLEAR USE

Ironically, the two major nuclear powers of the first nuclear age *assumed* that their opponent was *continuously entertaining the nuclear option*, waiting for the propitious moment to launch its attack or, in a spasm of fear, rushing to destroy the other before a rain of nuclear-tipped missiles reached its cities. In the hot-house atmosphere of the Cold War, U.S. and Soviet leaders and academics imagined how the opponent might make the decision to attack—or how they might be forced to initiate nuclear war against their wishes. These Cold War scenarios are useful for two reasons. First, they remind us how rational leaders and planners saw the world, and they provide us with how today's and tomorrow's leaders might come to a decision to use nuclear weapons.

Scenario I: Nuclear Escalation to Achieve Goals.   This scenario argued that decision makers might, at some point, use nuclear weapons to achieve goals that were being thwarted by the opponent. The several cases of near-use in the Eisenhower administration are the closest historical counterparts to this scenario, contemplating as they did nuclear escalation against a non-nuclear power (China or the Vietnamese insurgents) to achieve a goal such as ending the Korean war or preventing the fall of territory to the Communists. In Europe, the United States and several of its NATO allies *planned to use nuclear weapons first* if Soviet-led Warsaw Pact forces invaded Western Europe; NATO judged it likely that the Pact's armored forces would quickly over-run NATO units unless tactical nuclear weapons were used.

This escalation from conventional to nuclear weapons on the battlefield raises the issue of *thresholds* on the *escalation ladder*.[28] (See Figure 3-1.) In a crisis or war, there will be pressure on leaders to escalate the severity, the location, or the nature of the conflict to achieve their goals. At some point, escalation would involve behavior quite different in character from previous actions, thus crossing a threshold (or a firebreak). The idea of a threshold implies that leaders will be forced to think long and hard before making such a move because they recognize and fear that a different kind of conflict lies across the threshold, a conflict in which the risks might be much greater and the likelihood of success more in doubt.

Scholars and decision makers have suggested that there is a significant threshold between the use of conventional weapons and nuclear weapons *on the battlefield*. Leaders might be reluctant to cross

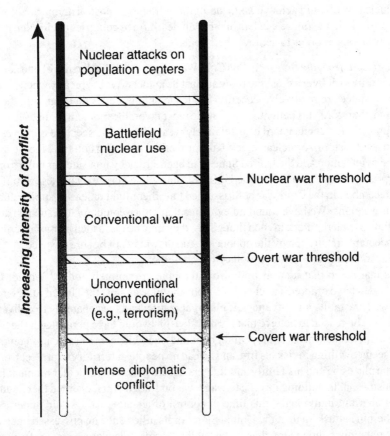

Figure 3–1   Escalation Ladder

that threshold if they had reason to believe that (1) their nation would not benefit from the increased destruction (as the enemy might retaliate with its nuclear weapons), or (2) once the battlefield threshold had been crossed, there would be a great temptation to cross the next threshold—to use nuclear weapons against *the homeland* of the other state, particularly its cities.

Crossing the threshold between conventional and nuclear war thus seemed to offer a possibility of securing one's goals in war, but with the very great risk that the cost of doing so would be catastrophic. On the other hand, to the degree that leaders felt that there was a *strong* threshold between battlefield and homeland use, they might be tempted to use nuclear weapons *on the battlefield*. They might, of course, seriously misjudge the strength (or weakness) of a particular threshold and face catastrophe for that misjudgment, but their decision to use nuclear weapons would be based on the assessment that the opponent would not retaliate for fear of further escalation.

One thing should be apparent from our discussion: Rational leaders in the pursuit of seemingly rational goals (such as the defense of West Germany) were expected to contemplate the use of nuclear weapons. Put another way, using nuclear weapons—even against an opponent with the capability to retaliate—was not judged to be a sign of madness, even when it came to be recognized that a full-scale nuclear war could achieve *no* meaningful political purpose. Therefore, we should not be terribly surprised if, in the future, leaders of other nuclear-armed countries decide that they, too, must use nuclear weapons in order to achieve their goals.

Scenario II: Bolt from the Blue.   In this Cold War scenario, the leadership of one nuclear state decides that it is time to deliver a crushing blow against its nuclear rival, typically when the relations between the two states are relatively peaceful. The leadership believes that war with the opponent is inevitable and, therefore, it is better to attack at the most favorable moment for oneself—presumably when the opponent lowers its guard or is relatively weak. This is the scenario of *preventive nuclear war*. It begins with a surprise nuclear attack—the proverbial lightning bolt from the clear blue sky.

Both the Soviet Union and the United States had been struck by non-nuclear bolts from the blue in 1941: a surprise German invasion of the USSR in June and a surprise Japanese air attack on Pearl Harbor in December. In the Cold War both assumed the other might unleash a similar attack, but now with nuclear weapons. We have found no evidence that either contemplated such an attack. If they had—or if future leaders entertain such thoughts—they may be dissuaded by moral scruples and by a fear of unacceptable retaliation by the opponent. And they may not be sure of success. After all, Germany and Japan paid dearly for their bolts-from-the-blue.

But does that mean that nuclear bolts-from-the-blue are unlikely today? Would, for instance, Osama bin Laden have ordered a nuclear bolt-from-the-blue against the United States in 2001 rather than a far less devastating aircraft attack if his organization had the capability to deliver such an attack? There may be reason to believe that his moral vision would have permitted it (he had called for an attack on Americans wherever they might be found), and his fears of retaliation might have been modest (he seemed willing to risk his life, and he had no people or territory to protect from retaliation other than the places he and his family and fighters occupied at any particular moment in time). The Bush administration, in building its case to wage war on Iraq in 2003, claimed that Saddam Hussein was another aberrant individual—this time in control of a state—who would undertake a nuclear bolt-from-the-blue attack against the United States or its allies once he possessed nuclear weapons. We should remember, however, that states with "normal" leaders have in fact considered a bolt-from-the-blue nuclear attack against another state: Both the United States and the Soviet Union considered a surprise nuclear attack on Chinese facilities to destroy China's budding nuclear arsenal.

Scenario III: Fear-Induced Preemption.   Fear-induced preemption may occur in any number of ways, but its central feature is the worsening of a crisis to the point that one side *fears* that it is about to be struck with nuclear weapons and *decides therefore to strike first*. In striking first with nuclear weapons, one hopes to blunt the power of the expected attack, perhaps even defeat the enemy in one decisive blow. Historically, there have been no near-use decisions that have the earmarks of preemption. Looking retrospectively at the Soviet-U.S. relationship, however, there were any number of conflicts that might have led to preemption. Consider the Cuban missile crisis of 1962. Suppose that the United States had invaded Cuba (as it planned to do if the Soviets had not withdrawn the missiles). Unknown to the United States, Soviet commanders in Cuba had battlefield nuclear weapons. Suppose that the Soviet government had authorized its commanders to use them against an invasion force, but now, with the American forces coming ashore, the Soviet leadership sees a deadly peril: Kennedy had threatened that any Soviet missile launched from Cuba would bring a full retaliatory response against the USSR. Fearing that the U.S. would do so once their forces in Cuba had been hit with nuclear weapons, Moscow orders its nuclear forces to begin a massive attack on the United States.

What characterizes fear-induced preemption scenarios is the assumption that, as the likelihood of war increases, the fear of being the victim of the first nuclear blow increases. The remedy is to strike first. Such a decision can be justified in a number of ways:

- The nation that strikes first at the military assets of the opponent may lessen the damage the opponent can deliver through retaliation.

- A quick strike might so disrupt the opponent's government and military command system that enemy retaliation would be insignificant.

- The enemy government would be so anxious to save what was left that it would not launch a retaliatory strike.

- If one does not strike first, one's own weapons are likely to be destroyed by the opponent's attack, thus leaving one at the mercy of the opponent.

- And, given the emotional perspective of the leadership (the enemy has, after all, seemingly ordered the destruction of much of one's society), it is easy to see the enemy as so monstrous as to deserve such punishment.

Thus fear leads to a decision to act, and that action is buttressed by what sounds to fearful men and women like compellingly rational arguments for action. Fear, of course, is internal. It may rest directly on what others *are* doing—or on what one *believes* others are doing. The rush to war because of fear is nothing new—it seems to have been a critical ingredient in the beginning of World War I. If the leadership of a nation believes that nuclear war is to come, a first strike is a reasonable option under the circumstances. Even a leadership loath for war may decide on war.

Scenario IV: Inadvertent Nuclear War. The last Cold War scenario that we will consider is one in which war is thrust upon the leadership of a nation by mistake. Some mistakes are the results of an *unintended error*. Suppose that the monitoring service of a nation interprets radar signals incorrectly and reports that an attack is coming. During the Cuban missile crisis, "U.S. radar operators mistakenly warned that a missile had been launched from Cuba and was about to hit Tampa. Only after the expected detonation failed to occur was it discovered that an operator had inserted a training tape into the system."[29] Similarly, what might be *innocuous behavior* at one time might be perceived by others as anything but at another time. During the Cuban missile crisis, the U.S. Air Force "deployed nuclear warheads in nine of ten test silos at Vandenberg Air Force Base and then launched the tenth missile in a previously scheduled test, oblivious to the possibility that the Soviets might have been aware of the warhead deployments and could have confused the test for a nuclear attack."[30]

If leaders launch their weapons *in response to such false information or innocuous behavior*, we have an accidental or inadvertent nuclear war. The nation which so launches its weapons is actually acting as the fear-induced preemption scenario stipulates; the nation on the receiving end would see this as a bolt-from-the-blue. The key aspect of this scenario is that decision makers *erroneously* assume that nuclear war has *already begun* and they are only acting in response to the decision of the other, whereas in reality, their own actions initiate nuclear war.

Historically, the superpowers experienced these kinds of accidents, but built-in safeguards and a measure of luck have prevented accidental war. Even the demise of the Cold War did not end the risk. In 1995, a meteorological rocket launched by Norway was misread by Russian monitoring systems. According to press reports, for the first time the top Russian leadership was warned that it was about to be struck by a nuclear warhead.[31] Fortunately, the leadership discovered the truth, but the press reports indicated that President Yeltsin felt that he had very few minutes in which to make a decision—even when the terrors of the Cold War had presumably dissipated.

An inadvertent war may also begin with the *unauthorized* use of nuclear weapons by subordinates. A common scenario depicts subordinates' attempting to force the national leadership into a full-scale war. In Stanley Kubrik's classic film, *Dr. Strangelove*, renegade Air Force General Jack D. Ripper ordered his bomber wing to attack the Soviet Union. He calculated that the American government would order a follow-on attack in order to blunt Soviet retaliation and thereby defeat the growing Communist threat. Unbeknownst to General Ripper, the Soviets had just completed installation of a "Doomsday bomb"—a super-weapon that would automatically detonate if any nuclear attack took place on the Soviet Union. Here was a scenario for inadvertent war and the inadvertent destruction of the planet. It's a must-see. We discuss it further in Chapter 10.

Are such forms of inadvertent nuclear war likely? Although there is always the possibility that erroneous information might bring on nuclear war, the experience of more than 50 years suggests that decision makers are reluctant to react to warnings that an attack is about to happen until further checks are made on the reliability of the information. This may be especially true if the information has an element of strangeness to it—such as the launch of a single missile. Indeed, it is likely that decision makers may be prepared to suffer a single such attack as a mistake and negotiate the next stage of the ensuing crisis rather than respond in kind.

Moreover, in well-maintained monitoring systems, the chance of erroneous reporting is likely to be low. As such systems degrade (for instance, as personnel go unpaid, morale drops, and training decreases, as Russia experienced in the second nuclear age), the leadership may see the system as unreliable and therefore put less credibility in its reporting (which reduces the likelihood of erroneous messages having an impact). *In a crisis*, however, a leadership faced with an erratically operating monitoring system may be more likely to treat seriously any warning such a system produces.

As to "rogue" elements in a nation's military establishment using nuclear weapons to force the hand of the leadership, well-ordered military establishments that are responsive to civilian oversight are not likely to go astray in such ways. Indeed, states have maintained the tightest security and controls over their nuclear forces, a topic we take up in Chapter 4. A disintegrating military organization may have less ability to control its subordinates, however. They may decide that they will re-write the nation's foreign policy using the weapons at their disposal, or sell them to others who are willing to use them. Unfortunately, even in well-ordered military systems there does seem to be the possibility that military personnel will seek to circumvent controls on their capabilities in the belief that they are acting responsibly: During the Cuban missile crisis, American "officers at Malmstrom Air Force Base jerry-rigged the launch system to give themselves the ability to launch their Minuteman missiles without higher authorization."[32]

NUCLEAR DECISIONS IN THE SECOND NUCLEAR AGE

The Cold War came to an abrupt and unexpected end between 1989 and 1991. The Cold War scenarios no longer seemed plausible for the five major nuclear powers; the probability of nuclear use by one against the other dropped quite close to zero. The world had entered the second nuclear age. New questions soon emerged, however, about how and why states might make a decision to use nuclear weapons. The dramatic emergence of India and Pakistan as full-fledged nuclear weapons states in May 1998 meant that two states with a long history of bitter conflict between them (including three wars) would now have to contemplate the nuclear dimension as a part of their decision making. North Korea and Iran appeared determined to challenge the American assertion that they would not be permitted to have nuclear weapons. The American government attacked Iraq to destroy its nuclear capabilities. Al Qaeda sought to acquire a nuclear device and threatened to create an American Hiroshima. While we examine the dynamics of these conflicts in later chapters, here we are interested in the potential scenarios for nuclear use that might emerge in these circumstances.

It seems to us that the four classic Cold War/first nuclear age scenarios we just discussed are as robust as ever in the second nuclear age, although the nations involved might be different. Table 3-2 provides some updated—albeit hypothetical—scenarios. Are there, however, *new patterns* of decision making that might emerge in this second nuclear age? This speculative exercise is important because we need to imagine to be able to head off the nightmare scenarios. That was one of the utilities in the Cold War thinking about the classic scenarios. While they may have been developed as projections of what a malevolent enemy might do (such as stage a bolt from the blue), they also became cautionary tales about what *we* had to do *to avoid a nuclear catastrophe*, a point we examine in Chapter 4.

You may have noticed in Table 3–2 that the actors have changed in a significant ways in the old scenarios. First, there may be *an asymmetry in the power* of the states in conflict, such as a very powerful United States and a much weaker state such as North Korea in Scenario III. The former can threaten the devastation of the opponent's entire country, while the weaker can only threaten local devastation. Does such a nuclear asymmetry make the leadership of one state more fearful than the other? Does this mean that North Korean leaders will be more likely to avoid a confrontation, or, conversely, that they will be more reckless in confronting the United States precisely to demonstrate that they are not afraid of American threats? That recklessness may drive one of the participants into a decision to preempt because it fears that the last actions of the opponent are the tipoff that it intends to attack.

A second difference from the classic scenarios is that when the nuclear states in conflict are themselves not great powers, their nuclear decisions may be designed to affect the great powers as well as the opponent. In Scenario I, we might imagine that the Pakistanis use nuclear weapons not only in escalation to keep from losing the ground war, but also to compel the great powers (particularly in this case, the United States and China) to intervene in some fashion against the Indians before the situation on the subcontinent spins totally out of control. Thus, we might suggest a new scenario for the second nuclear age:

Scenario V: Forcing the Great Power's Hand.   A state's leaders may decide to use nuclear weapons (perhaps only one) to force the great powers, particularly the United States, to become involved in resolving the crisis on terms better than the state could bring about on its own. Of course, the state might miscalculate. Its opponent, if nuclear armed, might retaliate, thus making the situation far worse. Or the great powers may intervene against the state using the nuclear weapon, precisely because it broke the nuclear taboo. But those are risks the leadership first using the weapon might consider but discount, believing that doing nothing would produce a worse outcome, while using a nuclear weapon would galvanize others into action to stop the conflict.

TABLE 3–2   CLASSIC COLD WAR SCENARIOS OF NUCLEAR USE
APPLIED TO THE SECOND NUCLEAR AGE

Scenario I: Nuclear Escalation Achieve Goals	Chronic tension between India and Pakistan produces a conventional shooting war along the border of the two nations. An Indian offensive overwhelms Pakistani forces in the south, threatening Karachi. Pakistan uses several nuclear weapons to blunt the offensive and force the Indians to withdraw.
Scenario II: Bolt from the Blue	Iran watches with concern as a new Iraqi government comes to power, one dominated by Shi'ia who appeal to Iraqi nationalism rather than relying, as the past Shi'ia led-cabinet has, on their sectarian ties with Shi'ia Iran. There has been growing agitation among Arabic-speaking Iranians in the provinces along the Iraqi borders "to join with their Iraqi brothers." American support has continued to build the power of the Iraqi army. And Teheran is awash with the allegation that the United States plans to make Iraq the staging area for an impending attack on Iran (although none is planned). The Iranian government decides that time is not on its side and orders an attack with its small nuclear arsenal against military targets in Iraq.
Scenario III: Fear-Induced Preemption	A nuclear North Korea enters a profound internal crisis. Factions within the North Korean military establishment now appear to be free of political control; those officers in command of nuclear weapons units call for an all-out offensive to reunite the two Koreas. The American government, fearing that nuclear strikes are about to occur against American forces in the South, orders nuclear preemption, judging conventional weapons incapable of ensuring the destruction of the North Korean arsenal.
Scenario IV: Inadvertent Nuclear War	The new president of Taiwan announces that Taiwan will seek international recognition as an independent state. The Chinese begin a new round of test-firings of missiles into the waters around Taiwan and begin amassing an invasion fleet. The United States steps up its naval patrols in the straits. At this point, a malfunction in the Chinese radar system erroneously reports multiple launches of cruise missiles headed for the fleet assembly area. The Chinese order a limited nuclear strike against the American fleet.

In addition to the reworking of the classic scenarios, the second nuclear age appears to hold new pathways to nuclear use in the scenarios described below.

Scenario VI: The demonstration use.   As you will recall, in 1945 the American government considered detonating the bomb against a relatively uninhabited area in Japan to show American power and thus persuade Japan to accept American demands. We imagine that more leaders of nuclear states will be tempted to demonstrate to an opponent their power and resolve through a similar use of a nuclear device, a device perhaps directed against a relatively uninhabited area within an opponent's territory, or at sea but within sight of the opponent's major port. Such a nuclear use forces the targeted state to fear that if it does not comply, the next step will be an attack against a far more valuable target, but at the same time the destruction is relatively minor—perhaps just a toe over the threshold. (It may also force other states to intervene diplomatically, in which case Scenario V is at work.)

Scenario VII: Reprisal.   Inflicting injury in retaliation for an action by another nation has long been a practice in world politics. Such punishment is not war-waging (that is, designed to affect the outcome of a particular conflict), nor necessarily to force the violator back into compliance (though no one would object if that occurred). Rather, the use is purely punishment—to exact some cost for a transgression of the rules. To this point in history, nuclear weapons have remained outside the range of acceptable means of reprisal, but we suspect that this may be changing. In the Gulf crisis of 1990–1991, for instance, President G. H. W. Bush threatened to retaliate with nuclear weapons if the Iraqis used chemical or biological weapons against coalition forces—weapons generally judged unacceptable.[33]

Scenario VIII: Internal politics.   Governments have, from time to time, employed their military's weapons in political crises *within* their states, ranging from conventional high explosives to more exotic weapons, such as Saddam Hussein's use of chemical weapons against dissident Kurds within Iraq. In the future, governments may see their nuclear arsenals as "another weapon of *internal* war" to destroy or subdue internal opponents. Alternatively, the internal use of nuclear weapons may come as part of a military establishment's coup d'etat, or as part of the jockeying for power among a highly factionalized military, or as a part of the struggle by nuclear-armed warlords to dominate regions of a fracturing state.

Scenario IX: Terrorism and Counter-Terrorism.   Chapter 1 made the case that we are living in an age of terrorism, and that terrorists are likely to consider nuclear weapons as a means to promote their political goals. In Chapter 9 we explore when and why terrorists might decide to use nuclear (or radiological) weapons. We note here the salient features of many terrorist groups that have nuclear implications. First, terrorism attempts to find a force-multiplier to compensate for its relative weakness vis a vis the society and government that it is attacking. Nuclear weapons hold the promise of being force-multipliers par excellence, far more than the high-explosive vest worn by a suicide bomber. Second, the weakness of terrorists makes the creation of fear a desirable tactic—and perhaps the only one available to them—for only fear seems to have the power to dissolve the social patterns that give strength to the governments they oppose. Nuclear-weapons are fear-creating.

Third, like any other political movement, terrorists must be able to recruit individuals. Recruitment depends upon the attractiveness of the political message and the aura the terrorist movement can create about its capability to inflict great damage and its willingness to do so. Detonating a nuclear weapon may be the strongest recruiting message possible, for in addition to the demonstration of power and will, the movement may well enshroud itself in the mantle of inevitable victory.

Added to these incentives for terrorists to use nuclear weapons are the presumably diminished constraints operating on terrorists. Most governmental leaders would fear retaliation if they used nuclear weapons, a retaliation directed at them personally or against the society that they control and have responsibility for and from which, in one way or another, they derive their power. Such constraints may be attenuated for terrorists, especially those who are themselves willing to be martyrs to their cause. The fear of dying may have no hold on them, and in serving an idea rather than serving living humans, they may more easily accept the death of "their people" from retaliation as the unfortunate price that good people must pay to protect and advance the idea. Finally, terrorists may be quite willing to re-interpret the common moral injunction against killing innocent people by claiming that many of the so-called innocents are as evil as those opponents who openly wear the uniform of the enemy, for those "innocents" sustain the enemy's soldiers. Moreover, the very culture that the "innocents" carry and propagate may be the evil that the terrorist seeks to eradicate.

These assessments should not be read as asserting that terrorists would thoughtlessly use nuclear weapons if they acquired them. We expect that the model that we presented at the start of this chapter will still hold. Within al Qaeda, we imagine the top leadership wrestling with critical questions such as these: If we successfully detonate a nuclear device in the harbor of New York City, will the United States mobilize itself to wage a total war of extermination against us? Will such a mobilization cripple the movement, or will the very act of sending more American forces into the Islamic world give us more adherents to send against the Americans? Will the United States retaliate against things we hold dear, such as the religious shrines in Mecca and Medina, for instance, or will they fear an uncontrollable backlash throughout the Islamic world for such sacrilege? Will *our* use of nuclear weapons so disturb Muslims that they will fall away from our cause, drying up our funding and sanctuaries? Different individuals within al Qaeda, reflecting different organizational interests and personal perspectives, are like to provoke a debate about the decision to use a nuclear device. A use decision is not inevitable.[34]

Just as terrorism adds a new scenario to the possible use of nuclear terrorism, so too might counter-terrorism. It may be that as terrorists find more horrific ways to attack societies and thereby seem to put themselves far beyond the norms of civilized nations, there may be a temptation to use nuclear weapons against terrorist formations, particularly leadership cells. As we write this, al Qaeda's leadership appears to be hiding in the very rugged mountainous terrain along the Afghan-Pakistan border, sparsely populated and difficult for either nation's government to control. If the leadership were located with some precision, but in an area too remote for quick ground attack or too rugged for effective conventional bombing, would the option of a nuclear attack suggest itself to the U.S. leadership? It is useful to recall that the Bush administration began the second war against Saddam Hussein in 2003 with a bombing strike against a building complex that intelligence indicated was Saddam's location that evening. The temptation to use actionable intelligence was overwhelming, for if this conventional decapitation strike worked, the policy-makers felt that it might shorten the war.

DECISIONS REGARDING "DIRTY BOMBS"

Terrorists and governments with nuclear ambitions could assemble radiological devices as an interim step towards a full-fledged nuclear capability. The decision to stage a radiological attack might be "easier" in the sense that proponents could argue that it does not squarely fall under the nuclear taboo and that while the havoc caused by such a device might not be as great as the explosion of a nuclear device, there would still likely be some deaths from radiation and the contaminated area would serve as a long-lasting and powerful reminder of the terrorists' capabilities and commitment. Nonetheless, the reaction of the target and the target's allies is likely to be intense. Indeed, the use of a radiological device, though it would still be many orders of magnitude less lethal than a nuclear weapon, might be taken by the targets of the attack as an indication that the terrorists intended to cross the nuclear threshold, driving the target state to redouble its efforts against the terrorists. On the other hand, a terrorist group might judge such a device as a less costly way of forcing the target to comply with some of its demands.

CONCLUSION: MAKING A NUCLEAR DECISION AND THE ODDS OF ITS BEING MADE

Our decision-making model argued that the context, the actors, and process of making decisions are the critical factors that lead to a decision to use or not use a nuclear weapon. Generally, we expect that a decision to use nuclear weapons, whether it be by a constituted government, a terrorist organization, or a rebellious military command, will occur when

- the context is one in which the social unit sees itself in intense conflict and there is general agreement that extremely important matters are at stake.

- influential actors conclude that the use of the bomb will produce a desired result effectively and with less cost than other means, that the long-term consequences are manageable, and that, overall, the world will not be a much more dangerous place for them than it is now.

- key actors conclude that the use of the bomb promotes particular interests, be they national (or group) interests, bureaucratic or organizational interests, or personal interests.

- key actors can live with the moral consequences by seeing a higher moral value being served than those values that will be adversely affected by the use of the bomb.

- key actors are able to persuade significant other actors who claim to have a voice in making the decision to adopt or accede to their views, usually with some compromise constituting the final decision.

The emphasis in our discussion has been to identify how and why the next nuclear weapon will be used against a target—an event we have not seen for more than 60 years. This emphasis is grounded in our belief that the next use will be critical for the future of the world. Given one set of circumstances, the next use may completely shatter the nuclear taboo and lead others to give the nuclear option far more prominence in their decision making. The scenarios that we have sketched above may then *all* quickly come to pass. On the other hand, any nuclear use may intensify concern about the threat nuclear weapons pose, enough so that citizens and leaders work to manage if not resolve the dilemmas of living in a nuclear world.

We conclude this chapter with our best estimate of the likelihood of a nuclear use in the next 25 years. Recall that the presence of nuclear weapons in the arsenals of any state gives decision-makers *the option* to use such weapons. In the next 25 years, there are likely to be as many nuclear-capable states as there are now, if not more. Use, therefore, remains possible. Also recall that the historical record reveals that young nuclear nations are more likely to *consider* using such weapons. As states join the nuclear club, they will need to pass through a period of maturation in which there will be the temptation.

Recall also that states have historically conjured up images of opponents' using nuclear weapons against them. In the Cold War, the scenarios that leaders and scholars devised to understand the predicament provided the intellectual and emotional justifications for why a nation —itself loathe to consider using nuclear weapons—might have to do so, even to the point of actually striking first. We've suggested that new nuclear weapons states are likely to see their opponent(s) in similar terms, thus giving new life to the old scenarios. In addition, changed circumstances have raised the possibility of new scenarios coming into play, thereby increasing the pathways by which the next nuclear use might come about.

In looking at the history of the first nuclear age, we are struck by the conclusion that basically rational leaders might decide to use nuclear weapons. This is not to deny the importance of irrationality. We might imagine, for instance, that in a circumstance such as panic, even rational leaders might respond instinctually rather than thoughtfully. Instinct or emotion, however, need *not* produce a decision to use nuclear weapons. A decision *not* to use them may be made on an emotional, non-rational basis. Indeed, as McGeorge Bundy argues, the *fear* of nuclear weapons may be what keeps leaders away from the decision to use them.[35] But rational calculations may impel them to do so in spite of their fears. We expect, therefore, that *future* use decisions will be made by men and women who think and behave in essentially rational ways.

No matter the pathway that leads to use, we estimate that the probability of the use of nuclear weapons in the next 25 years is relatively high, on the order of .2 to .3.[36] That is, there is a 20–30 percent chance that in the next 25 years you will witness the use of a nuclear device, not necessarily against your society, but some place in the world.[37] In comparison, the likelihood of Earth's being struck by an asteroid or comet large enough to have a major regional or global impact is roughly one out of a thousand (.001) in the next 75 years,[38] of a top major league baseball player hitting safely is approximately .329 (or roughly three out of ten times),[39] and of a 30-year-old American citizen reaching 85 years of age is better than .6 (or better than six out of ten chances).[40] In other words, we are speaking of a relatively strong possibility of such an event. A batter doesn't get a hit every time up of course, and we may well pass the next 25 years without a nuclear use. But the risk is great that we won't be that lucky.

The hostile use of nuclear weapons, after more than 60 years of abstinence, will push us into a *third nuclear era*, one where it may take dramatic if not heroic efforts to re-stabilize international political life. Failure to do that may bring more uses, and the calamities that we pointed out in Chapter 1 may come to pass, not just for the immediate victims of the detonation of a nuclear weapon, but for many of us in a more uncertain, more perilous world.

Our pessimism underscores one of the paradoxes of the nuclear age in which we live. We have weapons at our disposal that seem to pose the greatest threat imaginable to the things we value. Historically, a state has sought more powerful weapons to provide greater security to its homeland, its population, and its treasured cultural values—a people's way of life. How have states attempted to make nuclear weapons serve that role of providing security—both to keep the peace and, if necessary, to win the war—yet knowing that in doing either, they have risked total destruction? We now turn to that part of the predicament.

ENDNOTES

[1]Harry Truman, *Memoirs, Vol. 1: Year of Decisions*, (Garden City, NY: Doubleday, 1955), p. 10.

[2]Truman, *Memoirs, Vol. 1*, p. 10.

[3]Truman, *Memoirs, Vol. 1*, p. 87.

[4]Geoffrey Blainey, *The Causes of War* (New York: Free Press, 1973) ably argues for the existence of choice. Congresswoman Jeanette Rankin of Colorado was the only vote in the Congress against the declaration of war against Japan, but she, along with 49 other members of the House members, had also voted against American entry into World War I. She and they had recognized a choice. See Hannah Josephson, *Jeannette Rankin: First Lady in Congress* (Indianapolis, IN: Bobbs-Merrill, 1974).

[5]For a fuller exposition of this way of thinking about policy-making, see Graham Allison and Philip Zelikow, *Essence of Decision: Explaining the Cuban Missile Crisis*, 2nd ed. (New York, NY: Longman, 1999), Chapters 3 and 5.

[6]*The 9/11 Commission Report, Authorized Edition* (New York, NY: W. W. Norton, 2004), pp. 250–252.

[7]For histories and analysis of the end of the Pacific War, see Herbert Feis, *The Atomic Bomb and the End of World War II* (Princeton, NJ: Princeton University Press, 1966), Gregg Herken, *The Winning Weapon* (New York: Knopf, 1980), Leon Sigal, *Fighting to a Finish: The Politics of War Termination in the United States and Japan, 1945* (Ithaca, NY: Cornell University Press, 1988), Samuel Walker, "The Decision to Use the Bomb: A Historiographical Update," *Diplomatic History*, Vol. 14 (Winter, 1990), pp. 97–114; John Ray Skates, *The Invasion of Japan* (Columbia, SC: University of South Carolina Press, 1994); Richard B. Frank, *Downfall: The End of the Imperial Japanese Empire* (New York: Random House, 1999); and Tsuyoshi Hasegawa, *Racing the Enemy: Stalin, Truman, and the Surrender of Japan* (Cambridge, MA: Belknap Press, 2005).

[8]John W. Dower, *War Without Mercy: Race and Power in the Pacific War* (New York: Pantheon Press, 1986).

[9]This discussion draws on Sigal, *Fighting to a Finish*; see also Richard B. Frank, "Why Truman Dropped the Bomb," *The Weekly Standard* Vol. 10 (August 8, 2005).

[10]Diary entry, Harry Truman, *Off the Record*, ed. by Robert H. Ferrell (New York: Harper and Row, 1980), pp. 55-56, quoted by McGeorge Bundy, *Danger and Survival* (New York: Random House, 1988), p. 79.

[11]Quoted by Sigal, *Fighting to a Finish*, p. 213.

[12]Frank Chinnock, *Nagasaki: The Forgotten Bomb* (New York: New American Library/World Publishing, 1969), pp. 65-69; Sigal, *Fighting to a Finish*, p. 216–218.

[13]For the debate, see among others Gar Alperovitz, *Atomic Diplomacy* (New York: Simon & Schuster, 1965); McGeorge Bundy, *Danger and Survival*, G. Alperovitz, *The Decision to Use the Atomic Bomb and the Architecture of an American Myth* (New York: Knopf, 1995); Barton Bernstein, "The Atomic Bombings Reconsidered," *Foreign Affairs*, Vol. 74 (January/February 1995), pp. 135–152; Frank, "Why Truman Dropped the Bomb"; and the other entries in Note 7.

[14]See Peter Gizewski, "From Winning Weapon to Destroyer of the World: The Nuclear Taboo in International Politics," *International Journal*, Vol. 51 (Summer 1996), pp. 397–419; T. V. Paul, "Nuclear Taboo and War: Initiation and Regional Conflicts," *Journal of Conflict Resolution*, Vol. 39 (December 1995), pp. 696–717.

[15]Meeting of May 1, 1954 with Robert Cutler; quoted by Stephen E. Ambrose, *Eisenhower, Vol. 2, The President*, (New York: Simon and Schuster, 1984), p. 184.

[16]"If the decision about dropping the bomb had been yours to make, would you have ordered the bombs to be dropped, or would you have tried some other way to force the Japanese to surrender?" *The Gallup Poll Monthly*, No. 359 (August 1995), p. 3.

[17]Steve Coll, "Jihadis' Nuclear Ambitions," *Washington Post National Week Edition* (February 14–20, 2005), pp. 22-23.

[18]What constitutes a "case" does determine what our count of such near-use decisions will be. Generally, we say a separate case occurs when three conditions are met: there is some separation in terms of time between deliberations about the use of nuclear weapons, the goal sought (or problem being responded to) is different, and the participants have a sense that a decision has been reached (rather than a decision postponed). For this reason, we treat the series of discussions about nuclear use in Korea in 1953 as one case, but the two decisions in the spring 1954 regarding French IndoChina as two cases.

[19]NSC 162/2, October 23, 1953; quoted by Bundy, *Danger*, p. 246.

[20]Truman news conference of November 20, 1950; *Public Papers of the Presidents: Harry S. Truman, 1950* (Washington, DC: Government Printing Office, 1965), p. 727.

[21]Bundy, *Danger*, pp. 231–232.

[22]Summary of February 11, 1953 NSC meeting; *Foreign Relations of the United States 1952-1954*, Vol. 15 (Korea), Part 1 (Washington, DC: Government Printing Office, 1984), pp. 770.

[23]Summary of NSC meeting of May 6, 1953; *FRUS*, Vol. 15, Part 1, p. 977. Eisenhower's military commanders generally opposed the use of nuclear weapons; an armistice agreement soon ended the war.

[24]James G. Blight notes that "in a recent interview Nixon told Roger Rosenblatt that he gave the use of nuclear weapons serious consideration on four occasions: (1) during the Vietnam War, (2) during the 1973 Middle East War, (3) during the 1969 Soviet-Chinese border dispute, and (4) during the India-Pakistan War

of 1971. See Rosenblatt, *Witness: The World Since Hiroshima* (Boston: Little, Brown, 1985), pp. 78–79. …In subsequent interviews, however, Henry Kissinger gently suggested that when a president (in this case his former boss) says he 'considered' going to nuclear war, one must take it with a grain of salt." James G. Blight, *The Shattered Crystal Ball: Fear and Learning in the Cuban Missile Crisis* (Savage, MD: Rowman & Littlefield, 1990), pp. 107–108; footnote 41, p. 187. As far as we can tell, these four instances did not go beyond Nixon's mental processes, and thus do not qualify as a near-use decision.

[25]These two cases are also ones in which the opponent of the nuclear state had its own nuclear backers—China and the Soviet Union in the case of Vietnam; the United States in the case of the Afghan resistance. It may simply be that as a nuclear state grows older, its opponents find working relationships with other nuclear weapons states, thereby inducing caution in the aging nuclear state.

[26]See Gordon H. Chang, *Friends and Enemies: The United States, China, and the Soviet Union, 1948-1972* (Stanford, CA: Stanford University Press, 1990), p. 243–250.

[27]Reported in Soviet defector Arkady N. Shevchenko's account, *Breaking With Moscow* (New York: Knopf, 1985), p. 166; Henry Kissinger, *White House Years* (Boston: Little, Brown, 1979), p. 183.

[28]For a discussion of thresholds and escalation, see Herman Kahn, *On Thermonuclear War* (Princeton: Princeton University Press, 1961).

[29]Steve Fetter and Kevin T. Hagerty, "Nuclear Deterrence in the 1990 Indo-Pakistani Crisis," *International Security* Vol. 21 (Summer 1996), p. 178.

[30]Fetter and Hagerty, "Nuclear Deterrence," p. 178.

[31]Bruce Nelan, "Nuclear Disarray," *Time*, May 19, 1997, p. 46.

[32]Fetter and Hagerty, "Nuclear Deterrence," p. 178.

[33]Chemical and biological weapons have been judged unacceptable by many societies, and their use proscribed by more than 130 nations who signed the conventions of 1972 and 1993 outlawing them.

[34]We recognize that al Qaeda has become more like a franchise operation, where local leadership may have far more control over resources and decisions than Osama bin Laden and the al Qaeda elite do, although the latter are likely continue to provide general direction, funding, and encouragement.

[35]McGeorge Bundy, *Danger and Survival*.

[36]We define nuclear use as the intentional detonation of a nuclear weapon to affect an opponent's calculations or behavior. Nuclear tests can, of course, be intended to produce similar effects (Pakistan's 1998 tests were a clear warning to India) but what we mean by nuclear use is a detonation that is clearly outside a test site.

[37]For another attempt to estimate the probabilities of nuclear use, see Ike Jeanes, www.nukefix.org.

[38]NASA Ames Space Science Division, "Asteroid and Comet Impact Hazard," *Executive Summary, 1995*; www.impact.arc.nasa.gov/report/neoreport.

[39]Average of the American League batting champion, 1980–1993; *The World Almanac 1995* (Mahwah, NJ: World Almanac, 1994), p. 944.

[40]Interpolated from "How Long Will I Live?", *The Participant*, November 1997, pp. 12–13.

4

Planning to Wage Nuclear War
Deterrence in the First Nuclear Era

On the morning of August 7, 1945, Bernard Brodie, who at age 35 had a reputation as one of the nation's foremost writers on naval strategy, stopped in a drugstore to buy *The New York Times*. After reading just two paragraphs in the *Times* story on the bombing of Hiroshima, he turned to his wife and said, "everything that I have written is now obsolete."[1]

Brodie saw that the atomic bomb had changed forever the nature of war. He observed that "everything about the atomic bomb is overshadowed by the twin facts that it exists and its destructive power is fantastically great."[2] Since it exists, it cannot be "dis-invented." Even if every scientist and engineer who knew how to build a bomb were put to death, everyone knows the basic fact of the bomb—that it works. Thus it can be reinvented given time and resources. Brodie looked ahead to the day when all the world's major powers would be armed with atomic weapons.

Furthermore, because the bomb is so very, very powerful, any defense against the bomb would have to be perfect to be useful. During World War II, for instance, British defenses were able to stop, at best, 96 percent of the German V-1 guided missiles launched against England. These missiles, armed with a modest warhead of conventional explosives, were never more than a nuisance with little effect on the Allied war effort. However, if even 4 percent of a flight of nuclear weapons reached their targets, the resulting losses would be unacceptable. Brodie felt, therefore, that no defense was possible against an atomic attack.

In a paper published in 1945, Brodie set out his remarkably farsighted predictions about how life would differ in a nuclear age. He observed that in the future a nation

must remain constantly prepared for war; there would be neither the time nor the surviving industrial machinery to mobilize once the atomic bombs start exploding. This constant readiness may encourage aggression, exacerbate world tension, or possibly even spark in some minds the luring temptation of a "preventive war"—that is, to strike first to destroy an adversary before it can grow powerful enough to be a threat. Then again the calamity that would certainly ensue if the other side struck back with its own atomic bombs would be so grimly devastating, its very anticipation might deter a potential aggressor from attacking in the first place.[3]

Jacob Viner told the conference at which Brodie presented his paper that "the atomic bomb makes surprise an unimportant element of warfare." As he later pointed out, it will make no difference "whether it was Country A which had its city destroyed at 9:00 a.m. and Country B which had its city destroyed at 12:00 a.m. or the other way around...Retaliation in equal terms is unavoidable and in this sense the atomic bomb is a war deterrent, a peace making force."[4]

Brodie and Viner had glimpsed the new truths of the nuclear age—nothing could be gained by a nuclear war. Yet in spite of this momentous change in the nature of war, the United States and Soviet Union along with several other states prepared to wage nuclear war and made threats to do so in order to advance their national interests. Moreover, both nations would build more powerful and more numerous nuclear weapons, targeted in large measure on the civilian populations of its adversaries. The United States, like other nations of the otherwise civilized world, had come to regard the civilian population of its adversaries as legitimate targets. How did this come about? Einstein's assertion that everything had changed except our ways of thinking seemed most true when it came to critically important individuals—the political and military leaders of the nations of the world.

In this chapter we examine the development of nuclear weapons in the arsenals of the United States and Soviet Union and their efforts to find strategies for the use of these weapons. They, like all nations that create nuclear arsenals, had to confront four fundamental questions:

1. Does the state need nuclear weapons in peacetime?

2. If it does, how many and of what kinds?

3. What plans should be made for the use of nuclear weapons in the event of war?

4. How can nuclear weapons be used to promote the national interest?

There have not yet been, nor are there likely to be, final answers to these questions. Each generation of leaders and each nation with the capability to build nuclear weapons has had to find the answers appropriate for its time and place. In the United States, the search for these answers has gone forward both in the context of its military traditions and in the light of the experience of fighting two world wars, as well as in its perception of the nature of the world. The answers the United States and others fashioned for these questions gave shape to the first nuclear age, not only in terms of the vocabulary and images we use today, but more profoundly in terms of the issues and problems that we still must cope with. Understanding how and why they reached the answers they did also alerts us to critical processes by which nations and leaders reach such fundamental decisions and to the promises and pitfalls of their efforts. We begin with the historical legacy bequeathed to U.S. and Soviet leaders.

THE LEGACY OF TWO WORLD WARS

Ironically, to think about war during the twentieth century meant using the theory and concepts of a nineteenth century German military officer, Carl von Clausewitz, who fought against Napolean and spent the rest of his short life developing a theory about war. For Clausewitz, the purpose of war was "to compel our opponent to do our will." But that act of force does not exist in isolation. It was meant to serve the political interests of the nation. Indeed, for Causewitz "war is a continuation of political activity by other means."

"If you are to force the enemy, by making war on him, to do your bidding," Clausewitz argued, "you must either make him literally defenseless or put him in a position that makes this danger probable. It follows, then, that to overcome the enemy, or disarm him must always be the aim of warfare."[5] He identified three objectives when seeking to disarm an adversary: the enemy's armed forces, the enemy's country, and the enemy's will. If the aim of the war was the complete overthrow of the enemy,

> the fighting forces must be destroyed: that is, they must be put in such a condition that they can no longer carry on the fight. The country must be occupied; otherwise the enemy could raise fresh military forces. Yet both these things may be done and the war cannot be considered to have ended so long as the enemy's will has not been broken.[6]

The notion that the will of the enemy is decisive, and therefore a justifiable and, in some cases, necessary target for attack became a basic assumption about warfare in the Twentieth Century.

The irony of the twentieth century was that while war became more absolute—employing all the resources of industrial states—it became far more difficult to compel an opponent to do one's will. World War I (1914–1918) revealed that irony, but at a staggering price. France and Germany each lost 1.5 million men; the British Empire nearly a million; Russia lost more than all the rest combined. The battle lines in France and Belgium never fluctuated more than a few miles in the generals' quest for a decisive battle that would produce a victory, with the same terrain changing hands again and again, in spite of the loss of some 4 million lives.

Figure 4–1 Canadian forces leaving their trench, World War I. *U.S. Department of Defense*

Two revolutions—the democratic revolution, ushered in with the French Revolution, and the Industrial Revolution—had transformed the face of war. The democratic revolution unleashed the forces of nationalism, making wars not simply the business of kings, but the concern of every citizen. "National wars are fought by the people as a whole, and no longer by professional armies; the stakes are no longer dynastic interests or the fate of a province, but the future of the collective society or its ideals."[7] The patriotism of ordinary citizens increased exponentially the will of a society to resist and provided a large pool of individuals willing to die in that resistance. States refined techniques to use these manpower resources with increasing effectiveness, creating large standing armies and quickly mobilizable reserves. Thus, over 6 million troops were hurled into battle within two weeks of the beginning of World War I.[8] Even today, many states maintain large military establishments. Nationalism continues to make it possible to sustain large numbers of men (and, increasingly, women) in the world's armies.[9]

The Industrial Revolution had profound ramifications, leading to what Walter Millis called the industrialization of war.[10] Mechanized agriculture released large numbers of men from the production of food to industrial production—and provided the manpower for mass armies. It made communications more rapid and more reliable, making effective command of large armies and fleets possible. It provided ever more deadly weapons. But the most radical change brought by the Industrial Revolution was the transportation revolution of the mid-nineteenth century, in particular the railroad. During the U.S. Civil War, the Union commander, General Grant, proved it possible to maintain indefinitely an army in constant contact with the enemy, even while being defeated on the battlefield with heavy losses. If served by either railroad or steam-powered water transport, an army could be fed, re-supplied, and, most importantly, reinforced with newly raised troops as long as there were resources and a political will to continue. As Theodore Ropp said, "it was the railway, in short, which made mass armies practical."[11]

The effect of these revolutions was to strengthen the position of the entrenched defender to the point, that, by 1914, an attack had little prospect for success against a prepared and supplied defender unless the attacker had an overwhelming superiority in numbers; even then, the attacker would pay a high price in casualties. Thus, war had become a matter not of brilliant generalship, but of *attrition*. The first nation to exhaust its manpower resources, or lose the will to continue the struggle, became the loser. As a nation could make claims on the entire manpower resources of its population, it was necessary to destroy a substantial portion of the available manpower resources before a nation would consider surrender.

World War I challenged the idea that war could serve the nation's interests. What society would be willing to pay these enormous costs again? As the British poet Robert Graves (who served in the trenches as an infantry officer) suggested, because of the suffering and eventual disillusionment, after World War I "you just couldn't get men to do that again." Both political and military leaders feared that, after World War I, their people no longer had the will to sustain a prolonged war. As a result, the world's military establishments spent the ensuing years searching for alternatives to the stalemate of trench warfare, and their solutions ranged from the smallest scale to the grandest, from the tactical to the strategic.[12]

One alternative to avoid the prolonged attrition of trench warfare would be to strike directly at a nation's ability to sustain an army in the field. This grew in part from observations that Germany had surrendered in World War I with its armies in the field still undefeated, because it could no longer sustain these armies and the government and public lost the will to continue the struggle. The advocates of this approach looked to the bombing airplane as the weapon to wage such a war, going over the heads of the adversary's army. This strategic air power would strike at an adversary's ability to sustain its armies in the field, and by striking directly at the enemy's population, destroy the adversary's most vulnerable target—the will to persist. Civilian suffering might be a cause of defeat—not just a consequence.

The proponents of strategic air bombardment believed that there could be no effective defense against such an offensive. "I think it is well for the man in the street to realize," said British cabinet minister Stanley Baldwin in 1932, "that there is no power on earth that can keep him from being bombed. Whatever people may tell him, the bomber will always get through."[13]

But the experience of World War II showed that strategic air bombardment had limitations. The strategic bombing campaigns did impair the efficiency of the enemy's economy, forcing the dispersal of industries, and producing raw material shortages and transportation bottlenecks. Continued bombing did require the nations under attack to divert considerable resources to defending themselves against air attack. By 1944 some 2 million German soldiers and civilians were employed in antiaircraft defense and some 30 percent of guns manufactured in 1944 were for antiaircraft use.[14] But a well-organized and resolute defender could mount a very effective defense against a strategic air offensive, as the air battles over Britain in 1940 and the three-year bombing campaign against Germany demonstrated.[15] Although the Allied air forces attacked "panacea target" after "panacea target" (first ball-bearing plants, then petroleum production facilities, and then railroad rolling stock and bridges), the decisive point whose destruction would bring the enemy to its knees eluded the leaders of the air forces, just as it had the leaders of the ground armies in World War I.

Strategic bombing was no more effective in destroying the will of the German people to resist the Allied forces. The morale of civilian populations under continued air bombardment proved remarkably resilient. After the initial panic, bombing apparently stiffened the civilian will to resist and aided government efforts to mobilize civilians. Thus the attempt to force the surrender of an enemy by inflicting pain on its population may have had the opposite effect of strengthening an enemy's willingness to persist. Even though the United States and Britain dropped some two million tons of bombs on Europe, "those who expected bombing to win the war on its own were frustrated by events."[16] The strategic bomber in World War II proved itself not to be "an instrument of a decisive early blow, but as another weapon of attrition."[17]

When World War II ended, the images of war and what it took to achieve victory were clearer than they were in 1918. The stalemate in the trenches could be avoided; men were still willing to die in the millions for their nations. But the price would continue to be enormous: There were at least 30 million killed in the Allied nations waging war against Germany and Japan, fairly evenly divided between military and civilian deaths.[18] Moreover, the new technologies meant that vast areas, including cities, would come under devastating attack. The material and cultural losses from World War II were unprecedented. (See Figure 4-2) So the old question remained. How could one hope to achieve victory in war at a reasonable cost?

With the atomic bomb, proponents of strategic air bombardment felt they finally had the absolute weapon. Clausewitz had spoken of *absolute* war as an ideal or abstraction which could not be obtained in practice because of the frictions of war: imperfect intelligence, imperfect control of troops, and chance. The atomic bomb appeared to be an instrument that could finally make absolute war achievable. The conventional bombs dropped on Britain, Germany, and Japan, although causing immense damage, were dropped over several years and at widely scattered targets. The damage sus-

Figure 4–2   Germany, 1945: The destruction shown here is typical of that suffered by cities across Europe during World War II.

tained could be repaired, factories and railroads restored to use, and resources from undamaged parts of a country used to aid the worst hit areas. However, an extensive atomic attack would inflict damage simultaneously across the country, making recovery impossible, as we pointed out in Chapter 1. The atomic bomb would therefore shatter both the enemy's ability to wage war and its will to do so. To the proponents of strategic air bombardment, this was at last the war-winning weapon.

EXPLAINING DECISIONS REGARDING NUCLEAR WEAPONS AND STRATEGY

In Chapter 3, we suggested that *the context* in which the United States found itself in 1945 helped explain why the United States used nuclear weapons. The post-war environment created a new context that would help drive new decisions regarding strategy and weapons choices. World War II had ended the dominance of Great Britain, France, Germany, and Japan as the traditional great powers and had elevated the United States and the Soviet Union as the key actors in world politics. While we will discuss the Soviet-American relationship in Chapter 5, it is important to note that within three years of the defeat of Germany, the U.S. and Soviet governments had each come to see the other as a dire threat to its national interests and, increasingly, to see the other as preparing to wage war. Each seemed to the other to be expansionist in nature. The Soviets had overrun Eastern Europe as consequence of their war against Hitler and imposed communist regimes in their wake, creating a bloc of satellite states responsive to Soviet direction. Their strong influence over local communist parties who mounted both peaceful and violent challenges to governments friendly to the United States suggested that Soviet interests were global. Soviet challenges to American policy toward occupied Germany, even to the point of courting war with the United States by blockading Western access to Berlin, reinforced American fears. From the Soviet perspective, the United States had used World War II to become *the* global state, erecting a military presence around the Soviet Union, stretching from occupied Germany in the west to occupied Japan in the east, with rapidly evolving political and military interests in Greece, Turkey, Iran, and China. The United States had engineered the formation of the North Atlantic Treaty Organization (NATO) as a military alliance directed at the Soviet Union. The Soviets feared that America's sole possession of the atomic bomb would embolden it and make it more aggressive.

These perceptions—and the behaviors that flowed from them—created what has come to be called the Cold War, lasting roughly until 1990. With hindsight we know that no hot war would occur between the two states, but tensions and competing interests between the two were strong enough to make war seem likely. That meant that their political and military leaderships would have to develop strategies to wage such a war and to prepare weapons to do so successfully. Nuclear weapons would be a part of that strategy, for they seemed to solve the problem of achieving victory at an acceptable cost, but now the nation had to decide on how many were required, how would they be delivered, and what strategy could be devised for their use that would advance the political interests of the nation.

In examining the history of the nuclear choices the United States and other powers have made, we find that there are four types of explanation that help us understand the particular choices made. Our presentation to this point has emphasized a particular type of context explanation: Policy-makers often respond to *the lessons of the past*, in this case, to avoid the costs of attrition warfare. This is not to say that everyone sees the past with the same eyes or comes up with the same solutions, for they do not. After World War I, for instance, German military planners emphasized blitzkrieg tactics of fast-moving columns of tanks while French planners emphasized sophisticated defensive fortifications. These were two different responses to the same problem—avoiding the grinding attrition of modern warfare. Nuclear weapons seemed in 1945 to be the answer for American military planners.

A second type of explanation looks for an *action-reaction sequence*. It argues that states act principally in response to the behavior of other, salient states. We saw this in Chapter 2, as Stalin ordered a crash nuclear weapons program as a reaction to the dropping of the American bombs on Japan. Such action-reaction processes can continue across time, producing relatively stable patterns of behavior. The nuclear arms race is an oft-cited example. As one state builds more nuclear weapons, the other side is driven to at least match if not exceed the efforts of the first, which in turn provokes a response by the first state. Such races can branch out from a competition of numbers to a competition of technologies (as moving from bombers as the delivery system to missiles).

A third type of explanation examines *bureaucratic interests*. What states do regarding nuclear weapons and strategy, this explanation argues, is principally the result of bureaucracies pursuing their particular interests. We saw in the last two chapters how committed the Manhattan Project both was in creating nuclear weapons, and in seeing those weapons used against Japanese cities. This explanation generally expects bureaucracies to have an interest in perpetuating their existence by acquiring resources and being assigned important missions. And, they will seek to acquire more missions and resources if doing so does not challenge the vested interests within a bureaucracy. Thus, to understand decisions regarding nuclear weapons, we would look for pressures emanating from bureaucracies.

Lastly, a focus on *leadership* itself, as we offered in Chapter 3, provides an explanation for decisions regarding nuclear weapons and strategies. This explanation points to individual leaders and their perceptions, goals, and persuasiveness within the political system. Recall that in our analysis of the American decision to drop the bomb on Japan, it mattered greatly that Harry Truman was new to the presidency and determined to show his cabinet—all appointees of Franklin Roosevelt—that he was the president in more than just name. Individual leaders respond to inner drives and to their environment—their immediate colleagues and subordinates, other powerful actors in their political system, and the public at large. With these four explanatory approaches in mind, we now turn to the key decisions regarding nuclear weapons and doctrine that emerged in the Cold War.

AMERICAN WEAPONS AND STRATEGY AT THE START OF THE COLD WAR

In March 1947, President Truman acknowledged the existence of a cold war and pledged U.S. assistance in containing the reach of the Soviet Union. The United States would provide weapons, advisors, and economic aid to friendly governments trying to cope with Communist insurgencies (as in Greece) or external pressures (as in Turkey, where the Soviets were pressing the Turks to return former Russian territory to the Soviet Union). Several weeks later, Truman assembled the commissioners of the Atomic Energy Commission, the newly created agency responsible for the production of the atomic bomb, to hear an assessment of the state of the nation's atomic arsenal. Not only was the president dismayed at how few bombs had been produced, but he heard the chairman of the commission report: "None of these bombs is assembled. The highly technical operation of assembly hitherto has been effected by civilian teams no longer organized as such. Training of military personnel to effect assembly is not complete." As reported by a commissioner who was present, the president blanched; he realized his atomic arsenal was empty—the United States had no deliverable atomic bombs.[19]

In a little more than a year and a half, American nuclear capabilities had atrophied—as had much of its military establishment. Without a nuclear opponent, the United States assumed that if war broke out, the U.S. government could re-mobilize its resources, assemble its bombs, deploy them and the bombers close to the Soviet Union, and begin the strategy that it had inherited from World War II—a continuous attack against Soviet cities, this time with nuclear rather than conventional explosives. Whatever gains a Soviet ground offensive was able to reap would be soon overturned by the destruction of the Soviet Union. And as the Soviets could make the same calculation, war seemed unlikely.

In the spring of 1948, following a Communist coup in Czechoslovakia and during a time of increasing concern over Soviet pressure against U.S., British, and French control of a divided Berlin, the military commanders of the U.S. armed forces, the Joint Chiefs of Staff,[20] reached the conclusion that the Soviet Union would risk war with the Western nations to advance its interests. As one participant noted,

> Neither we nor the prostrate nations of Western Europe could match Russia's land army, man for man, or tank for tank, on D-Day without total peacetime mobilization which was practically out of the question. Given the military spending limits, we were forced to rely principally on our atomic monopoly.[21]

Nuclear weapons were more palatable politically than a very expensive, large standing army equipped with conventional weapons that would require substantial dislocation in the lives of the youth of America. This emerging American commitment to nuclear weapons was, in part, a way to "wage war on the cheap." As Walter Lippman pointed out at the time, atomic weapons appeared

> the perfect fulfillment of all wishful thinking on military matters: here is war that requires no national effort, no draft, no training, no discipline, but only money and engineering know-how of which we have plenty. Here is the panacea which enables us to be the greatest military power on earth without investing time, energy, sweat, blood and tears, and—as compared with the cost of a great Army, Navy and Air Force—not even much money.[22]

The reliance on nuclear weapons as the foundation of U.S. military security rested on nuclear plenty. In April and May 1948, the United States conducted tests of improved weapons designs that made more efficient use of fissile material; the success of these tests meant that more bombs could be produced than the Joint Chiefs had called for.[23] Now the nation could have as many nuclear weapons as it wished.

Thus by the end of 1948 two of the four questions that confronted the U.S. government had been answered. The United States had decided it was necessary, in view of the growing tension with the Soviet Union and in light of the apparent U.S. inferiority to the Soviet Union in conventional arms, to maintain stocks of atomic bombs in peacetime, and to stockpile as many bombs as it was possible to produce. What it also needed to answer was the question of how they might be used. A strategy, to be effective, must identify targets to be attacked, determine how these targets are to be attacked, and decide to what end those targets are being attacked. The first strategy adopted by the United States was to destroy the capability of the Soviet Union to wage war against the United States, and the responsibility for its execution in event of war was assigned to the Air Force Strategic Air Command. Based on World War II experience, primary emphasis in a series of war plans drafted from 1947 to 1949 was to identify urban-industrial centers for attack. The targets whose destruction was thought to most disrupt the Soviet Union's war-making capability were the liquid fuel, electric power, and atomic energy industries—all located in Soviet cities.

Still unresolved was the debate over the basic aim of strategic nuclear bombing: Was it to destroy the enemy's *ability* to wage war or its *will* to wage war? In May 1949 a committee from all three services reviewed the ability of existing nuclear weapons to "bring about capitulation, destroy the roots of communism or critically weaken the power of the Soviet leadership to dominate the people."[24] It concluded that bomb did have the capability to inflict "serious damage to vital elements of the Soviet war-making capabilities," but rather than undermining the will of the Russian people, however, the committee suggested the bomb might have the opposite effect: "For the majority of Soviet people, atomic bombing would validate Soviet propaganda against foreign powers, stimulate resentment against the United States, unify these people and increase their will to fight"[25]—just as Allied bombing had led German and Japanese citizens to rally to their leaders.

In addition to a nuclear attack on the Soviet Union, the Strategic Air Command (SAC) was assigned a second mission as the American commitment to aid its allies in Western Europe grew with the signing of the North Atlantic Treaty in 1949. That mission was to retard Soviet advances in Western Europe in the event of a Soviet invasion. The North Atlantic Treaty was the first formal commitment by the United States to defend Western Europe and the treaty implied that American troops would be sent back to Europe (four divisions were, in fact, committed there by 1951). However, in 1949, "the nuclear stockpile was still too small and the weapons too large and unwieldy to be used against true tactical targets such as troops and transportation bottlenecks."[26] Thus, to defend Western Europe, nuclear weapons would have to be used against the Soviet Union.

Strategic thinking took a new turn in the fall of 1949. On September 23, 1949, the White House announced that it had confirmed evidence that the Soviet Union had tested its first atomic weapon. American aircraft, flying between Alaska and Japan to sample the atmosphere downwind from the most likely Soviet test sites, had detected increased levels of radiation during September 1949. The conclusion was inescapable—the Soviet Union had a working nuclear device.[27] No one had doubted that the Soviets would obtain nuclear weapons. The surprise was in the timing. But American military planners were not greatly dismayed; they had expected Soviet proliferation at some point, and it was obvious that some years would pass before the Soviet Union would have a sufficient stockpile of deliverable nuclear weapons and the means to deliver those weapons against the United States.

PREPARING FOR NUCLEAR WAR

The Soviet test foreshadowed the world of the first nuclear age: two hostile states each with the power to annihilate the other (and their neighbors). American and Soviet leaders now faced parallel problems: What would the opponent do with its nuclear weapons? Would they consider war? What strategy and what nuclear weapons would be necessary to wage a war successfully, a war thrust on it by the nuclear armed opponent? Much of what we know about how the United States wrestled with these questions comes from documents prepared for or by the National Security Council.[28] These documents, milestones in policy formation, provide a window into the thoughts and values of the times. One of the first of these policy documents to consider the circumstances under which nuclear weapons might be used was *U.S. Policy on Atomic Warfare* (NSC-30). (Previous plans had been contingency plans drawn up by military staffs.) Approved in September 1948 by President Truman, NSC-30 recognized that the military "must be ready to utilize promptly and effectively all appropriate means available, including atomic weapons."

NSC-30 also stipulated that the decision to employ atomic weapons in the event of war rested with "the Chief Executive when he considers such a decision to be required."[29] This established the principle of presidential control of nuclear weapons. Moreover, the custody of the nuclear warheads themselves initially rested with a civilian agency, the Atomic Energy Commission, rather than with the military services, creating a bureaucratic safeguard against unauthorized use. NSC-30 is still in force today, but as we shall see, the exact manner in which presidential control is exercised has changed over time. Beginning in 1951, custody of the weapons was gradually transferred to the services, until, in 1967, all nuclear weapons had been delivered to the military.[30] Nonetheless, nuclear states recognized early on that control over nuclear weapons—in terms of both command authority and custody—were key issues. Stalin's approach was similar: he would make any decision regarding use, and the NKVD—Stalin's internal security forces— would be the custodians of the warheads, not the Soviet military.

With evidence of the Soviet test, President Truman in January 1950 directed the Secretaries of State and Defense "to undertake a reexamination of our objectives in peace and war and the effect of these objectives on our strategic plans, in the light of the probable fission bomb capability and possible thermonuclear bomb capability of the Soviet Union."[31] The resulting document, titled "U.S. Objectives and Programs for National Security (NSC-68)," was submitted to the National Security Council in April 1950. One of the document's chief architects, Secretary of State Dean Acheson, frankly admitted in his memoirs that the "purpose of NSC-68 was to so bludgeon the mass mind of top government that not only could the president make a decision, but that decision could be carried out,"[32] thus recognizing that senior officials can do much to delay and obstruct the implementation of presidential directives with which they do not agree.

Though it is difficult to know how much influence such a policy statement actually has, NSC-68 certainly expressed the temper of the times and its rhetoric reflected the basic assumptions that fueled the Cold War for years to come. It portrayed the Soviet leadership as "inescapably militant...because it possesses, or is possessed by a world wide revolutionary movement, because it is the inheritor of Russian imperialism and because it is a totalitarian dictatorship" which "requires a dynamic extension of authority and the ultimate elimination of any effective opposition." The United States, as "the principal center of power in the non-Soviet world," is "the principal enemy whose integrity and vitality must be subverted or destroyed... if the Kremlin is to achieve its fundamental design." Thus the world is divided by "the underlying conflict" between the "free world" of the West and the "slave society" behind the Iron Curtain.[33]

NSC-68 foretold that when "the Kremlin calculated that it has sufficient atomic capability to make a surprise attack on the U.S., nullifying our atomic superiority and creating a military situation decisively in its favor, the Kremlin might be tempted to strike swiftly and with stealth." NSC-68 predicted that the year of maximum danger of such a bolt-from-the-blue would be 1954, when the Soviet Union was expected to have amassed 200 atomic bombs and "an atomic bomber capability... in excess of that needed to deliver the available bombs," thus giving the Soviet Union the capacity to seriously damage "the vital centers of the U.S. by surprise attack." Given the assumption that the Soviets possessed an overwhelming superiority in conventional military forces, NSC-68 rejected a policy of no-first-use of nuclear weapons: "in our present situation of relative unpreparedness in conventional weapons, such a declaration would be interpreted by the USSR as an admission of great weakness and by our allies as a clear indication that we intended to abandon them."[34] The United States would have to go nuclear in the early stages of a conventional Soviet assault.

It is important to note some of the important aspects of nuclear thinking in NSC-68. American planners assumed that its nuclear opponent would be constantly calculating its nuclear strength and assessing the possibility of a successful surprise attack. They expected that an opponent committed to "subverting or destroying" the United States would naturally wage nuclear war. They assumed that just 200 nuclear weapons—a small number—would constitute the peril point. (As a point of comparison, by 1960 the U.S. arsenal alone would reach over 12,000 nuclear weapons and the U.S. nuclear stockpile peaked in 1966 at an estimated 32,200 nuclear bombs and warheads.[35]) They calculated that such a Soviet arsenal (and its necessary delivery systems) would be available in five years, a relatively short time. Doing nothing would be the route to disaster.

There is no evidence that the Soviet leadership did in fact make such calculations about the payoffs from a bolt from the blue. The U.S. government did not succumb to nuclear paranoia (although there were middle level officials who did propose waging a preventive war). It is not known if in fact there is some magic threshold number (like 200 nuclear devices) that would move a nuclear state to the point of deciding whether to begin a nuclear war. Though that did not happen in the Soviet-American relationship, there is no reason to assume that that might not happen in another. And others may well adopt the American decision regarding first use; Pakistan, for instance, may have concluded that it too faces in India an opponent with superior conventional capabilities, and therefore it must employ a strategic doctrine that emphasizes first use.

NSC-68's prescriptions to protect American security not unsurprisingly called for increased military spending, improved air and civil defense, and an increase in the U.S. atomic capability. Expan-

Figure 4–3   U.S. cannon firing a 15 kiloton nuclear projectile. U.S. Department of Energy

sion is always expensive, and that provoked an intense debate in Washington, a debate that was ended in June 1950 by the invasion of South Korea by communist North Korea. Coming as it did less than a year after the triumph of the Communist Chinese in completing their conquest of mainland China, the North's invasion seemed to Washington a clear sign that the Soviet Union was willing to use force to extend the area under its domination. The Truman administration chose to use U.S. forces under the aegis of the United Nations to repel the invasion, and to begin a serious expansion of U.S. nuclear capabilities.

By 1953, because of the high priority given to developing a strategic nuclear weapons delivery capability, the American Strategic Air Command (SAC), under General Curtis LeMay, had become a formidable force, matched by the growing sophistication and power of nuclear weapons. The 10,000 pound implosion-type Mark III atomic bomb had been replaced by atomic bombs weighing under 3,000 pounds, yet 25 times more powerful. Soon to be available was a 1,000 pound bomb, easily carried by most Air Force fighter-bombers and Navy attack planes and usable as a warhead on short-range guided missiles, in shells for long-range artillery (as shown in Figure 4-3) and as atomic demolition mines.[36] The U.S. stockpile of nuclear weapons has been estimated as 1,000 weapons by the summer of 1953,[37] virtually doubling again by 1955.[38]

THE "SUPER"

The detonation of the first Soviet nuclear device also drove another nuclear decision. Less than two months after evidence of the Soviet explosion reached the United States, the General Advisory Committee (GAC) of the Atomic Energy Commission reviewed a proposal to create a "Super bomb," a bomb based on nuclear fusion.[39] The committee recommended strongly against diverting effort from the fission bomb program toward development of a fusion bomb, and it made strategic and moral arguments for not proceeding with the development of the "Super." It pointed out that there would be no limit to the explosive power of a fusion bomb, producing a weapon having the explosive force of hundreds of existing fission bombs. In the Committee's view, the Super would be a weapon only of genocide. "It is not a weapon which can be used exclusively for the destruction of material installations of military or semi-military purpose. Its use, therefore, carries much further than the atomic bomb itself the policy of exterminating civilian populations."[40] The GAC instead recommended developing small atomic bombs for tactical or battlefield use against strictly military targets. The chairman of GAC, Robert Oppenheimer, continued to press for increased production of tactical nuclear weapons, in hope "battle could be brought back to the battlefield."[41]

The Joint Chiefs of Staff, in their response to the report of the General Advisory Committee, argued "that there is a possibility that such a weapon might be a decisive factor if properly used and [we] prefer that such a possibility be at the will and control of the United States rather than of an enemy." The Joint Chiefs warned "that the United States would be in an intolerable position if a possible enemy possessed the bomb and the U.S. did not." In response to the argument of the GAC that the Super was intrinsically immoral, the Joint Chiefs of Staff said that "in war it is folly to argue whether one weapon is more immoral than another. For, in the larger sense, it is war in itself which is immoral, and the stigma of such immorality must rest upon the nation which initiates hostilities."[42]

Truman sided with the Joint Chiefs. On January 31, 1950, he authorized the development of the hydrogen, or thermonuclear, bomb as well as an increase in the production of fission weapons, including tactical battlefield weapons. Thus when presented with divided counsel, the president chose both courses of action. As a result, the U.S. strategic retaliatory force is now armed with fusion weapons, and the United States eventually deployed over five thousand tactical nuclear weapons in Europe during the Cold War.

It is important to realize that seldom in the real world are important policy decisions made in a vacuum by disinterested officials objectively weighing the pros and cons of a policy. It is also essential to be aware of the temper of the times—the context in which this decision was made. This was a time of rising anti-Soviet hysteria, fueled by what some saw as the Truman administration's perfidious abandonment of China to the Communists, and the Soviet Union's successful test of an atomic bomb, using secrets pilfered from the Manhattan Project. In these times, some regarded any dissent as treason. For Lewis Strauss, AEC Commissioner who had voted for moving ahead on the Super, "opposition to the Super was less a case of mistaken judgment than a crime."[43] Subsequently, after a four-year campaign, Strauss drove Oppenheimer out of the atomic program.[44]

Nor were the scientists who urged the construction of the Super free of self-interest: a second laboratory—the Livermore Lab—was created in 1952, dedicated to building the H-bomb, dissipating resources to the detriment of the atomic program.[45] The stakes were considerable for the scientists involved: Ernest Lawrence, pioneer of the cyclotron, bought a new Cadillac each year with the cyclotron slush fund.[46] A high-profile project such as the Super brought scientists not only an escape from the routine of teaching and a chance at exciting research, but other perks as well: expense accounts, travel, and—most seductive—access to leaders in government and business. It was disgust with scientists' incessant lobbying that led President Eisenhower to warn in his farewell address as president in 1960 that "we must also be alert to the… danger that public policy should itself become captive of a scientific-technological elite."[47]

The step from fission to fusion bombs was at least as significant as the earlier step from the largest conventional bombs to fission bombs. The bomb dropped on Hiroshima had a force of 12.5 kilotons or 12,500 tons of TNT and was more than one thousand times as powerful as the largest "blockbuster" bomb used in World War II. There would be fusion bombs in the U.S. inventory of almost ten megatons, or almost one thousand times as powerful as the Hiroshima bomb. To illustrate the difference between a fission and a fusion bomb: "A fission bomb of 15 Kilotons dropped on the Statue of Liberty in New York harbor would do little more than break windowpanes at the distance of Time Square (some seven miles away). A ten megaton hydrogen bomb dropped at the same place would utterly devastate all of Manhattan [shown in Figure 4-4] and indeed the entire New York City and harbor area."[48]

The Super came at the point when the U.S. monopoly on fission weapons had been broken. Now the United States had a new lead and, as its production of nuclear weapons increased, the United States was entering *an era of nuclear plenty*—it had the ability to wage total war, to destroy not only the enemy's capability and will to fight a war, but the enemy itself.

Figure 4–4   New York City as a target. A 10-megaton thermonuclear weapon would completely devastate the area shown.
Copyright © Corbis

A DOCTRINE FOR WAGING NUCLEAR WAR

As more weapons became available, military leaders (and eventually, civilian leaders as well) re-evaluated how these weapons would be used in time of war. Everyone expected nuclear war to be relatively short. There is not time in the midst of a crisis to begin selecting targets and matching them to weapons, so for the United States, the drafting of detailed plans for the use of nuclear weapons in the event of war had begun as early as 1947. By the 1950s such planning had become a full-time occupation for large staffs of officers in the Air Force, the Navy, and the Army. Planning is a labor-intensive and time-consuming process, requiring identification of potential targets, determination of the exact location of the target, assignment of the appropriate weapon to the target (size of weapon, altitude of detonation, and so forth), determination of the method of delivery of the weapon (strategic bomber, carrier aircraft, missile, and so forth), mapping the exact route and timing for each bomber sortie to minimize the effectiveness of Soviet air defenses,[49] and finally the writing and distributing detailed orders to each ship, aircraft, and missile launch control center.

Such detailed plans as well as the general strategic guidance provided by documents like NCS-68 provide the options available to the U.S. government if war should come. By their very nature they are secret. At the same time, American officials have judged it useful for the sake of discouraging a potential adversary from attacking the United States to present particular visions of how the United States might wage war. These public statements have been called *declared national policy*. During the first nuclear age, for instance, the U.S. government explicitly rejected *preventive war*, which is a war begun with an unprovoked attack on a potential enemy for fear that the enemy might someday have sufficient power to threaten U.S. security. NSC-68 characterized preventive war as morally repugnant and contrary to the American tradition of not acting as an aggressor. There is no evidence that the top leaders of the United States ever seriously considered a preventive war against the Soviet Union, even when the United States had overwhelming nuclear superiority, as it did from the late 1940s through the 1950s.

But preventive war must be distinguished from *preemptive war*. While a preventive war is waged against a state that poses no imminent threat (though it may pose a threat in the future), a preemptive war is waged by a state that is *under threat of imminent attack*. The United States was not adverse to preemptive nuclear war against the Soviet Union. In 1961, Daniel Ellsberg was studying the Single Integrated Operational Plan (SIOP), the secret document that would direct the nation's nuclear forces in the event of war, as part of the review of national defense by the incoming Kennedy administration. At first he was baffled by the apparent illogic of the plan, but he came to the realization that it was based on the assumption that the United States would be the nation to strike *first* in a nuclear war, when there was positive evidence an attack was about to be mounted against the United States or possibly even its closest allies.[50] This strategy of preemption was recognized in NSC-68: "The military advantage of landing the first blow ... required the U.S. to be on the alert in order to strike with our full weight as soon as we are attacked, and, if possible, before the Soviet blow is actually delivered."[51] Using "our full weight" meant an all-out attack on the Soviet Union. A preemption doctrine obviously made *war-planning before the war* a crucial activity.

But to publicly declare that one followed a preemption strategy had its own risks. Declared policy is intended in part to send signals to potential adversaries, warning them that certain actions could bring a nuclear response from the United States. One can imagine that to declare publicly a policy of preemption would make the United States seem excessively bellicose and might actually increase the risk of a surprise attack against the United States. On the other hand, starting with NSC-68 in 1950, the United States has consistently refused to declare that it would not be the first to use nuclear weapons in a conflict. Preemption, after all, depends upon first use. This ambiguity was intended to warn the Soviet Union and its Warsaw Pact allies that if they invaded Western Europe, they would risk a nuclear counterattack by the United States, even if they did not use nuclear weapons themselves.

We emphasized in Chapter 3 that if that moment came, the leadership of a nation might decide *not* to follow through on its plans and the threats it had issued. Who would make the decision to refrain from implementing a nuclear strategy—or to order the preemptive strike? Normally, we think of the American president as the individual who would, as he or she is the constitutionally designated commander-in-chief. However, who exactly would have a finger on the metaphorical "button" has been a contentious issue. The military services and their leaders have some freedom of action. Consider this episode: In 1957, Robert Sprague, a representative of President Eisenhower, observed a practice alert of the entire Strategic Air Command (SAC) bomber force. In six hours, not a single bomber had been able to take off. Sprague pointed out to SAC commander Curtis LeMay that in a real attack, the planes would have been destroyed by the Soviets before they could take off. LeMay responded that "the United States had airplanes flying secret missions over the Soviet territory 24 hours a day picking up all sorts of intelligence information, mostly communication intelligence and Soviet military radio transmissions." LeMay went on to say, "If I see that the Russians are amassing their planes for an attack, I am going to knock the shit out of them before they take off the ground."[52]

LeMay's response was in line with the undeclared national policy of preemption. What shocked Sprague was that LeMay would *himself* order an attack on Soviet air bases. Sprague pointed out that this was not national policy. NSC-30 declared that the decision as to the employment of atomic weapons in the event of war was reserved to the president. Furthermore, NSC-30 did not say that electronic surveillance evidence in itself would automatically trigger a preemptive attack. LeMay replied that he did not care; "It is my policy—that is what I am going to do."[53]

LeMay's assertion raises the problem of exactly how much control a president can exercise over the military establishment, both in peacetime and in a crisis. It also points out a dilemma that has concerned leaders of all the nuclear states since the dawn of the atomic era—the problem of the *command and control* of nuclear weapons. Command and control are often lumped together with the problem of maintaining reliable communications and obtaining timely intelligence during a crisis or war, labeled the "Command, Control, Communications and Intelligence" problem, abbreviated C^3I. Although control of a nation's armed forces has always concerned national leaders, until the advent of nuclear weapons there was a limit to the irreversible harm a military commander acting without authority could do. Armies could always be recalled, invaded territory evacuated, apologies made, and reparations paid. Because nuclear weapons are so very destructive, however, the commander of even a small unit—a missile squadron, for instance—has the power to do irreparable damage and even precipitate a full-scale nuclear war.

Thus, by the end of the 1950s, the American government had over 12,000 bombs, a doctrine for war-waging which called for the obliteration of the Soviet Union in a massive, pre-emptive attack, and a president nominally in command of the nuclear establishment, but with enough service autonomy to suggest that in fact there were several fingers near the nuclear button. The United States Air Force and its commanders (particularly of SAC) would have a strong institutional interest in having the maximum flexibility to safeguard the nation. The size and complexity of the strategic nuclear establishment meant that actual control over the execution of strategy would remain untested, but fraught with unsettling possibilities.

This unannounced doctrine of massive preemption had many sources. The lesson of World War II seemed to be that strategic bombardment was the route to victory, with nuclear weapons being the winning weapon. After Pearl Harbor, the nation would never again allow itself to be the victim of the first blow. A long-standing American strategic tradition that set the annihilation of the enemy as the only legitimate war aim played its part as well. The doctrine also carried a moral assumption that aggressors should be punished for striking the United States.

During this period, the Soviet Union had come to the same strategic conclusion as the United States, that pre-emption (which necessarily meant first use) was the central doctrine for nuclear war. We suspect that this is likely to be the approach of many "young" nuclear powers. The underlying assumption is that nuclear wars can be waged, and waged successfully, as long as one is able to detect and successfully preempt the attack being readied by the opponent.

THE STRATEGIC ASYMMETRY OF THE 1950s

While American and Soviet strategies were symmetrical in that they relied on preemption, there was a fundamental difference. Unlike the Soviet Union, the United States had, by the late 1950s, largely "solved" the problem of how to deliver a preemptive attack against its opponent's homeland. U.S. technological developments had enhanced the effectiveness and reduced the vulnerability of the U.S. bomber force. By 1959, all of the older bombers had been replaced with the B–52 (Figure 4–5), which required very little warm-up before takeoff, thus reducing the risk of a surprise attack eliminating the American bomber force. With a combat radius of over 3,000 miles, the B–52 made possible the basing of the U.S. retaliatory bomber force in the United States with airborne refueling where needed to permit the bombers to reach targets deep in the Soviet Union. One-third of the bomber force was maintained on ground alert in the United States and would take off at the first sign of a Soviet strike. They would then proceed along emergency war plan routes toward their targets, but their missions would be aborted at pre-specified points unless they received a "go code" to continue.[54] In addition there were continual improvements in the U.S. strategic intelligence-gathering capability including overflights of the Soviet Union by U2 aircraft from 1956 through 1960 and finally the success of the Discoverer and Samos reconnaissance satellites in 1961.[55]

The Soviet Union, on the other hand, lacked a bomber force capable of reaching the United States in any strength, and had no allies close enough to the United States for forward-basing of its shorter-range strike aircraft. In reality, then, its preemptive actions would be taken in Europe, against American forces stationed there and against America's allies. It did, however, have a public program to build a strategic bomber fleet. The 1950s, in fact, were characterized by increasing American concern that the Soviet Union was acquiring the capability to destroy a large enough portion of the U.S. retaliatory capacity in a single bomber strike that it could initiate a nuclear war with relative impunity. This concern was based in part on a 1955 Soviet ruse when the Red Air Force flew a portion of the long-range bombers in its inventory over Moscow several times. Using the inflated report of Soviet bomber production, United States Air Force Intelligence predicted that the Soviet Union would have 600 to 800 long-range bombers by 1960, a sufficient number to destroy all of the U.S. strategic bomber force on the ground.[56] (The Soviets, in fact, produced only a small bomber force; they would come to rely on missiles as their primary delivery system.)

In sum, then, in the 1950s there was a decided *strategic asymmetry*: the United States had a growing stockpile of fusion bombs and a growing bomber force that could deliver the weapons against the

Figure 4–5   B–52 Strategic bomber refueling in flight. *U.S. Air Force*

Soviet Union. The Soviets had a growing fusion stockpile as well; in November 1955 the Soviets tested their first true Super of 1.6 megatons.[57] From that point on, the megatonnage of Soviet tests steadily increased to nearly 50 megatons before atmospheric testing ended. But they lacked the ability to deliver these warheads against the United States: The U.S. strategic nuclear monopoly still existed in practice.

The strategic asymmetry of the 1950s also had an impact on the foreign policies of the two nations. In Chapter 5, we focus on how nuclear-armed states dealt with each other during the Cold War. Here we note that at the height of the golden age of the American monopoly in the mid-1950s, the *declared* nuclear policy of the United States was to respond to traditional forms of military aggression with a threat of "massive retaliation." As defined by Eisenhower's Secretary of State, John Foster Dulles, massive retaliation meant a capability to "retaliate, instantly, by means and at places of our own choosing."[58] Dulles was quick to suggest that he did not mean that every aggression anywhere would be met with nuclear weapons, or that we would necessarily attack the Soviet Union in response to its Chinese ally's invasion of Taiwan, but rather that the United States reserved the option of responding to actions it declared unacceptable with nuclear weapons. The administration hoped that the threat would suffice to deter such actions. This declared policy was partially in response to the frustrations of fighting a limited war in Korea where Chinese manpower prevented the United States from reuniting Korea under a non-communist government after the United States had repelled an attempt to seize the state by the communist North Korean regime. It also reflected the administration's conclusion that the Chinese finally accepted an armistice to end the fighting in Korea only after the incoming Eisenhower administration threatened to use nuclear weapons if they did not do so.

Massive retaliation lasted only several years as a declared policy. It seemed both too bellicose and not particularly credible as a threat. The Soviets, on the "short end" of nuclear asymmetry, countered in the mid-1950s with a declared policy of "peaceful coexistence." States with radically different so-cial systems could keep the peace even though they might be intensely competitive in non-violent ways. While nuclear weapons might be necessary to ensure the peace, nuclear war was too destruc-tive to contemplate. Thus nuclear weapons had no legitimate role in day-to-day politics. There was, of course, a great propaganda advantage to such a position (the Soviet Union seemed to be the cham-pion of peace), and the Soviet leadership within several years chose to "rattle its rockets" in its own threat-making, but "peaceful coexistence" did suggest a framework that might move nuclear strategy away from preemption.

The doctrine of massive retaliation as held out by Dulles was, in some ways, simply a public state-ment of the implications of Eisenhower's military policy called the "New Look."[59] The new formula-tion assumed that "the basic Soviet objectives continue to be consolidation and expansion of their own sphere of power and the eventual domination of the noncommunist world," but contrary to NSC-68, it did not expect that the Soviet leadership would deliberately embark on a general war: "The uncertain prospects for Soviet victory in a general war, the change in leadership [Stalin had just died], satellite unrest and the United States' capability to retaliate massively makes such a course im-probable." Given that breathing room, Eisenhower felt that the United States had to slow the pace of the American military build-up—particularly in conventional arms—as he feared "seriously weak-ening the United States economy or undermining our fundamental values and institutions."[60] Loath to become involved in another Korea and cutting back on conventional forces, nuclear threat-making seemed a necessity.

COMING TO UNDERSTAND THE REALITY OF THE NUCLEAR AGE

By the end of the 1950s, the Eisenhower administration decided to consolidate the various plans de-vised by the military services into a Single Integrated Operation Plan (SIOP) for the coordinated waging of nuclear war. The Strategic Air Command acted as the agent of the Joint Chiefs of Staff in preparing and updating the plan each year. The first SIOP, SIOP-62, approved in December 1960, re-flected SAC's perspective. SIOP-62 envisioned that when the president ordered the use of the na-tion's strategic nuclear force, the United States would launch the entire nuclear alert force at one time, a massive "Sunday punch" aimed at destroying the communist world's ability and will to wage war. There were no options open to the president for striking selected targets nor of withholding at-tacks on Soviet allies, such as the People's Republic of China, that might not have joined in the Soviet action that provoked the U.S. strike. In practice, SIOP-62 would likely be preemptive—a first strike—aimed at the opponent's military and civilians. Faced with the certainty of such an over-whelming attack, it seemed reasonable to expect that the Soviet Union would be deterred from ag-gression.

The first SIOP was a curious document. While it reflected both growing American power and a growing American interest in rationalizing the planned use of nuclear weapons, it was oblivious to the rapidly approaching end of the American strategic monopoly as the Soviet Union continued to develop its nuclear weapons and delivery systems. Indeed, decisions made in the 1950s by both nu-clear powers produced a new reality that dramatically changed military planning and the nature of the nuclear world. We will examine four critical areas: command and control, the credibility of one's retaliatory forces, the development of the intercontinental ballistic missiles, and the development of a "triad" of delivery systems.

Command and Control. Codifying the preparations for nuclear war into the American SIOP made clearer a dilemma that has concerned leaders of all the nuclear states since the dawn of the atomic era—the problem of the *command and control* of nuclear weapons. When the Sunday punch was *the* nuclear option, the president had an incentive to make sure that he and he alone could order such action. As it became clear that the president might need *a range of options*, control became a critical issue. The U.S. government has not relied solely on the expectation that subordinate officers would be unfailingly responsive to the chain of command. Most U.S. nuclear weapons were eventually equipped with Permissive Action Links (PALs)—devices that require the use of a unique code to arm or to launch the weapons. Military personnel in possession of the weapons would be sent the code only when ordered to use the weapons. Entering an incorrect code into the PAL would disable the weapon permanently.

During the Cold War, the famous locked briefcase, nicknamed the "football," always accompanied the president—an omnipresent symbol of how close the world was then to Armageddon. This briefcase contained the *SIOP Decision Handbook*, which, along with the special codes identifying the president to the nuclear commanders who would actually disseminate the *Emergency Action Messages* ordering a nuclear strike, would enable the president to launch a nuclear strike. These authentication codes are still provided only to the president and his designated alternates or successors (known collectively as the National Command Authority) and to certain specified senior military commanders.[61]

On the other hand, there are risks in concentrating control of nuclear weapons in too few hands, lest an enemy be tempted to seek to eliminate the top command in a single strike (called *decapitation*) and thereby immobilize the nation's nuclear forces. Which senior commanders have the codes authorizing the launch of U.S. missiles has not been made public. Although the number is not large, it includes the SAC Airborne Command Post code-named "Looking Glass." For almost 30 years, from February 1961 to July 1990, one of a fleet of nine planes was always in the air with a battle staff aboard with the means to prepare and disseminate an Emergency Action Message, the coded orders to execute the nuclear war plan, and with the required authentication codes.[62] Therefore, even if the president were eliminated, a retaliatory strike could still be ordered by the surviving successor to the president or even by the commander of the Strategic Air Command.

By the end of the Cold War, a sizeable and expensive infrastructure had grown up to ensure, in the jargon of the nuclear age, "continuity of government." For example, by 1980, "there were reportedly more than seventy-five sites around" the United States, "all manned twenty-four hours a day"[63] where American leaders could find safety and still direct a war after the United States was attacked. In addition, during the Cold War years, captains of missile-carrying submarines (with the cooperation of their crews) had the capability to launch their missiles without presidential codes, if all communication with their fleet commander were lost. Thus, any potential attacker would know that even if it eliminated the president, his successors, and the entire command structure of the military forces, it could still receive a retaliatory strike from the missiles on submarines.[64] During this period, the Soviet Union recognized the same problems and also took elaborate steps to insure proper command and control.

Maintaining the Ability to Retaliate. While a concern about command and control emerged with the first nuclear weapons, concern about America's retaliatory capability awaited the moment when U.S. strategists began to worry about Soviet progress in developing an intercontinental strike capability. When American strategists in the 1950s finally began to plan for the day when the Soviet Union would have the weapons and delivery systems to stage a massive attack on the United States, they assumed that the Soviets would first attack American nuclear weapons and their delivery systems, destroying enough of them so that the United States could not retaliate. The Soviets would then be able to conduct, or threaten, a nuclear campaign against the United States (presumably its cities) and so compel it to surrender. The key was the devastating first strike that would disarm the United States. The appropriate response seemed to be to find ways to preserve the nuclear capabilities of the United States *even if* the Soviet Union struck first, and *so preserve the ability to retaliate.*

In the decade of 1950s, retaliation rested on the bomber fleet, and the question was how to ensure its survival. Fears of the Russian threat to U.S. retaliatory forces took a new and more disturbing direction in October 1957, when the Soviet Union launched the first artificial earth satellite, *Sputnik*, with a second following a month later. It was clear that a nation that had rockets powerful enough to put a satellite into orbit around the earth could use these same rockets to deliver nuclear weapons directly to the United States with no warning and no possibility of interception. Thus the Soviet Union had found a way to create nuclear symmetry with the United States. Nuclear-tipped missiles would make the United States defenseless and vulnerable.

The U.S. intelligence community pondered how soon the Soviets would have an operational missile force. They made the same sort of inflated prediction about Soviet strategic missile production that they had about Soviet bomber production. Air Force Intelligence predicted that the Soviet Union could build and deploy 500 intercontinental ballistic missiles (ICBMs) by 1961.[65] What were the implications for the American retaliatory capability lodged in its bomber fleet? Most SAC bombers were located on only 44 bases, and two to six Soviet ICBMs would be needed, it was estimated, to destroy an air base.[66] It was therefore assumed by the most pessimistic analysts (which of course included those in both Air Force and SAC Intelligence) that the Soviet Union could, and possibly would, launch a disarming first strike against the United States when it had some 250 operational missiles, thus completely destroying the U.S. strategic retaliatory capacity. The United States would then have no choice but to capitulate or be faced with the destruction of its cities by the remaining Soviet ICBMs and bombers.

This continual tendency to overstate Soviet capabilities was in some ways a legacy of Pearl Harbor and the adoption of "worst-case analysis" as a planning tool by the U.S. military after World War II. A legitimate methodology if responsibly used, worst-case analysis sought to establish as a baseline for planning what would be the most damaging course of action that an enemy could take. Thus, in the 1950s the U.S. intelligence community sought to determine how many aircraft, missiles, or nuclear weapons the Soviet Union could build if they devoted the maximum possible resources and if their programs were perfectly successful. This worst case could then serve as an upper limit on U.S. measures to counter the enemy threat. Concentrating on the worst case, however, obscures the question of how likely the worst case is to occur. Organizations with vested interests to promote usually do better when the worst case is accepted as the basis for a decision. A commission examining American bomber vulnerability responded by urging the building of a large offensive missile force, protected from attack by dispersal and hardened shelters.[67] The Air Force's mission would expand dramatically, as missiles now seemed to be the answer for both sides to the central question: how could one protect one's ability to retaliate?

Intercontinental Ballistic Missiles. The guided missile revolutionized nuclear weaponry. Modern military rocketry had emerged in Germany during World War II with the V-2, essentially a rocket-powered artillery shell which expended all of its energy in the initial part of its flight, reaching a great height above the earth and then falling to its target in a ballistic trajectory (a trajectory whose path is determined by the missile's initial velocity and the force of gravity). Attaining speeds as high as 15,000 miles per hour as it approached its target, the ballistic missile was at last a delivery system "that would always get through," as Stanley Baldwin had foretold 20 years earlier.

Given the scarcity of atomic weapons and their great cost in the 1940's, the judgment of Vandevar Bush that "one does not trust them to a highly complex, possibly erratic carrier of inherently low precision" was probably justified and therefore the early postwar decision to subordinate missiles to manned aircraft, most importantly jets, was probably appropriate at the time.[68] However, as defensive measures such as radar-controlled surface-to-air antiaircraft missiles were improving in effectiveness, the ability of a manned conventional subsonic bomber to reach a defended target was becoming increasingly doubtful. The ballistic missile was virtually invulnerable to enemy countermeasures and continuing technological innovation suggested that with time it would become a very accurate weapon.

The irony was that the Air Force, which had a monopoly over the strategic bombardment mission in the United States, showed great reluctance to develop the strategic missile. The Air Force was committed to manned aircraft, particularly manned bombers, and refused to change.[69] Because of this resistance, research on long-distance ballistic missiles was canceled in 1947 and was not to be revived until 1951, and then only at a minimal level.[70] "Before 1954, the Air Staff was interested in long-range strategic missiles only when they perceived a threat from an enemy or from a sister service. And of the two, threats from the Army or Navy seemed to motivate the Air Staff more."[71] The Air Force position did carry some weight as thermonuclear weapons—ideal for the planned massive preemptive attack—were heavier than fission weapons and could only be carried by large manned bombers, of which the Air Force alone was permitted to have.

However, increasingly lighter and more powerful thermonuclear weapons proved successful in tests in 1954. These and other advances in weapons technology as well as increasing intelligence evidence of Soviet missile development made it impossible for the Air Staff to resist civilian pressure both to establish an organization outside normal Air Force channels to develop an operational ballistic missile and to give this program a high enough priority to permit it to go ahead, in some cases at the cost of existing programs. By 1958 this effort produced an American Intercontinental Ballistic Missile (ICBM) capable of reaching the Soviet Union from bases in the United States, adding a missile component to the Strategic Air Command. But the bomber remained in the inventory as well.[72]

At the same time, in an attempt to gain a role in strategic weapons delivery, the Navy and the Army had joined together on the development of a liquid-fueled intermediate-range ballistic missile (1,500 mile range) for use on land or on board surface ships or submarines. The Navy realized that only submarines could approach close enough to the Soviet Union to launch their shorter-range missiles at strategic targets deep within the Soviet Union and quickly saw the unsuitability of liquid-fueled missiles on submarines. Therefore, in December 1956 the Navy severed its connection with the Army liquid-fuel project and began work on the solid-fueled Polaris, designed to be launched from submerged submarines.

Given the impetus of Sputnik, the Navy had no difficulty getting adequate funding to press development of these capabilities. As this development was not in competition with existing Navy weapon systems, there was little resistance within the Navy to the Polaris. This is in contrast with the Air Force, where missiles threatened to make obsolete the hard-won skills, training, and experience of an entire officer corps of pilots, navigators, and bombardiers. Quite the contrary, the submarine-launched ballistic missile greatly enhanced the value of the Navy's other principal technological innovation of the post-World War II period—the nuclear-powered submarine. The nuclear-powered submarine could stay submerged at sea, practically limited only by the crew's psychological endurance. The solid-fueled Polaris missiles could be fired while the submarine remained submerged, aimed by an inertial navigation system that keeps very accurate track of the submarine's position. (See Figure 4-6.)

The Triad. By March 1958, both President Eisenhower and Congress had accepted ballistic missiles as the answer to the vulnerability of U.S. retaliatory forces, in spite of opposition from the Air Force.[73] The issue became not whether, but how soon and how many, missiles would be built and deployed. The 1960 presidential campaign rang with Democratic party assertions that there was a "missile gap" that favored the Soviet Union.[74] The Eisenhower administration countered that there was no missile gap, but chose not to provide evidence to support its accurate claim as that would reveal American intelligence capabilities to the Soviets. The incoming Kennedy administration soon learned the truth. By September, 1961, according to CIA estimates, the Soviet Union had only 10 to 25 ICBMs deployed.[75] At that time, including intermediate range missiles in Europe and Turkey, the U.S. had some 223 missiles capable of reaching Soviet territory.[76] By the time of the Cuban Missile Crisis in October 1962, the Soviet Union had at most about 30 ICBMs, while the United States had about 200 ICBMs, including 20 solid-fueled Minutemen, deployed.[77] These counts were somewhat misleading, as reliability for these early missiles was woeful. For instance, only 4 to 20 percent of the U.S. first-generation ICBMs were likely to reach their targets, or to detonate if they did.[78]

Figure 4-6   SLBM missile tubes on an American Trident submarine, the USS Ohio.
U.S. Department of Defense.

Nonetheless, missiles were now a permanent part of America's strategic arsenal. They, along with the manned bomber fleet, constituted "the Triad," so named because American strategic capability rested on three legs: land-based ICBMs buried in underground concrete silos to provide protection against attack, submarine launched ballistic missiles (SLBMs), and manned bombers. It fell to the Kennedy administration to decide on the number of delivery systems each leg of the triad would have. The Soviets adopted a similar mix, although their bomber force was a smaller proportion. Table 4–1 reports numbers for both states at their height.

The creation of the American Triad reflected the interplay of an organization loath to give up its traditional mission (the Air Force's fixation on the manned bomber) and of inter-service rivalry (the Navy's attempt to find a strategic mission). Nonetheless, the virtues of having three different delivery systems of very different characteristics came to be recognized. The Triad made the simultaneous destruction of all the U.S. retaliatory capability in a disarming first strike virtually impossible, and protected the country against any single technological breakthrough that would render the entire U.S. retaliatory force vulnerable.

In addition, each component of the Triad had particular advantages, useful in certain situations. Land-based ICBMs were for decades the most accurate and the most quickly useable should the president require the option of a nuclear strike against a specific target. However, land-based ICBMs, in spite of increased "hardening" or reinforcing of the silos to withstand attack (Figure 4-7), would be increasingly vulnerable to a disarming first strike as missile accuracy improved. The submarine-launched ballistic missiles were an extremely invulnerable retaliatory force, as the possibility of an enemy simultaneously destroying all the continually moving, constantly submerged, missile-carrying submarines at sea was very remote. At the height of the Cold War, about 20 U.S. subs were at sea at any one time, and perhaps 10 Soviet subs. The submarines, however, were much more expensive to maintain, and submarine missiles were inherently less accurate than land-based missiles, and carried smaller warheads. In addition, communications with submarines are slower and less reliable than with land-based missile batteries.

TABLE 4–1   DEPLOYED STRATEGIC WARHEADS: 1987

Russian:	
Intercontinental Ballistic Missiles:	6,612
Submarine-launched Ballistic Missiles:	2,804
Manned Bombers:	855
Total:	10,271
United States:	
Intercontinental Ballistic Missiles:	2,458
Submarine-launched Ballistic Missiles:	5,760
Manned Bombers:	2,353
Total:	10,571

Source: U.S. Arms Control and Disarmament Agency. START I aggregate numbers of strategic offensive arms as compiled from individual data submission of parties.

Figure 4–7   An MX ICBM emerges from its protected silo in a test firing. *U.S. Air Force*

Both long-range land-based bombers and, for the United States, short-range carrier-based naval aircraft could be assigned new targets in flight or even choose their own targets, or they could be ordered to return to base without dropping their bombs. Once launched, ICBMs or SLBMs cannot be recalled or destroyed[79] or re-routed in flight. Bombers could be kept on airborne alert during a crisis, a very invulnerable position for a brief time. On the other hand, manned bombers were becoming increasingly vulnerable to air defenses, to the point that their ability to penetrate the defended Soviet air space was becoming very doubtful.

This mix, offering flexibility and survivability, has become the standard—at least for relatively wealthy states. Less wealthy states have tended initially to rely on aircraft delivery (as most states have an air force), later adding land-based missiles, and, in the case of France and Britain, ultimately moving their strategic strike forces to submarine-carried missiles.

THE ARMS RACE

The expansion of the American and Soviet nuclear establishments fits a well-known historical phenomenon of an *arms race*, the relatively continuous growth in the quantity and quality of armaments. Some of the expansion is driven by the action-reaction dynamic of two states in a competitive relationship: what one has, the other must have. But to have quantitatively more or qualitatively better weapons appears to add a margin of safety for the possessor, encouraging the upward spiral. Some of it is driven by the internal pressures that emerge with organizations or in the competition between organizations (as in the Navy's search for a strategic mission). Some of it emerges in the interplay of domestic politics (as when there are allegations of a bomber gap or a missile gap). Whatever the driving forces, once nuclear weapons appeared and demonstrated their power, there would be intense pressure on governments to acquire these new weapons. As Table 2-1 suggested, many states initially responded with programs to build those weapons.

Arms races—especially involving nuclear weapons—are at the heart of what has been called the *security dilemma*: The very attempt to enhance one's security by acquiring more or better weapons threatens the security of another state, who in turn responds with similar actions, once again imperiling the security of one's own state. And the costs of arms-racing can be staggering. The United States spent, according to the most authoritative estimate,[80] about $ 5.5 trillion (in constant 1996 dollars) building and maintaining nuclear weapons and nuclear weapons-related programs from 1940 to 1996. This was about 29 percent of all military spending by the U.S. during this period—which included World War II, the Korean War and the Vietnam War—and about 11 percent of all government spending. (By comparison, the U.S. national debt was $ 8.3 trillion at the beginning of 2006.[81]) Unfortunately, it is not possible to obtain—even now—hard data about Soviet expenditures for nuclear weapons, except the very rough estimate that "one may nevertheless infer from the scale of the effort that costs were quite high, perhaps even roughly comparable to those in the United States."[82] This leaves open one of the most intriguing questions of the entire Cold War: could the United States afford this $ 5.5 trillion, and the Soviet Union not? Did, in fact, the Cold War end the way it did simply because the United States had the deeper pockets and could sustain the arms race longer than the Soviet Union?

States have searched for alternatives other than an arms race to meet their security needs. Going to war has been one "solution"—destroying the opponent's capability rather than trying to match it. Forming alliances with other states has been another. Yet another has been in reaching mutual agreements to limit weapons through arms control negotiations. (We examine these approaches in Chapter 5). Whatever avenue they take, however, states have looked first and foremost to their security interests. The problem in the nuclear age is that the power of nuclear weapons challenged the basic notion of security. How could a state secure itself if nuclear weapons would, if used, obliterate society?

NUCLEAR DETERRENCE

It is well to keep in mind that, despite the accelerating arms race and each side's perception of the other as a mortal enemy, neither the United States nor the Soviet Union sought nuclear war. Their wish to preserve the peace, however, *had to reckon with the fear that the other was in fact willing to contemplate nuclear war.* Thus each prepared to wage nuclear war if it were forced on them by the other. At the same time, each sought to persuade the other that there would be no benefit from starting a nuclear war. That is, each sought to *deter* the other from using its nuclear arsenal. A condition of *nuclear deterrence* occurs when a state contemplating nuclear aggression determines that, even if it struck its opponent first, it would still suffer retaliation so devastating that there would be no possible gain to be had from initiating nuclear war.

Thus, for deterrence to work, the *ability* to retaliate must be apparent to one's opponent, and this requires a capacity of a nation's retaliatory forces to survive a first strike. The key question was how *vulnerable* was one's existing retaliatory force. Those U.S. planners who could envision the Soviet Union's initiating a general nuclear war as a calculated act argued that deterrence was *delicate*—that the American retaliatory capability was always, in Soviet eyes, questionable. In this light, effective deterrence depended on the continued increase of the U.S. nuclear striking force and continued efforts to protect the U.S. retaliatory capacity.[83]

The other point of view was that no nation would ever deliberately initiate a general nuclear war, even if the ability to retaliate were uncertain, as there was no possible end whose attainment would be worth *even the risk of a nation-destroying retaliatory strike*. This position held that deterrence was rugged and that only by miscalculation or in desperation could a general nuclear exchange ever occur. In this view, strenuous efforts to increase both force levels and invulnerability were wasted effort—or worse. Such efforts could be read by the opponent as an attempt to achieve a *first-strike capability*, that is, the capability to destroy in a first strike a rival's ability to retaliate, which could precipitate a preventative or preemptive war.

We expect that this debate over whether nuclear deterrence is delicate or rugged will recur in the future. Deterrence rests on the *perception* of whether the other side has both the physical capability and the will to retaliate. Perceptions are, by their nature, subjective, so there can be no objective verification that deterrence is working. For example, if the opponent is acting in a restrained fashion, is this because deterrence is rugged, or because the opponent has no aggressive intentions? If the opponent is acting aggressively, is deterrence delicate, or is the opponent simply probing to determine what it can get away with, all the while having a deep respect for deterrence?

The debate is also fueled by differing interpretations of *the role of uncertainty and risk* in nuclear strategy. For instance, those who held that deterrence is rugged contended that unless the Soviet Union could be positive that its first strike could destroy every retaliatory weapon, it would not dare launch an attack. Because the bomb is so very powerful, if even a few weapons were fired in retaliation, they would do incalculable damage to Soviet society. All that is necessary to maintain deterrence was to create doubt in minds of the Soviet leaders that they could stage a surprise attack and emerge unscathed. That doubt could be achieved with a modest nuclear arsenal. Meanwhile, the United States could seek to reduce tensions with the Soviet Union and reach agreement on areas of mutual interest.

Those who held that deterrence is delicate contended that the Soviet Union was controlled by leaders whose values differed so profoundly from the leaders of the United States that the Soviet leaders would have to be absolutely convinced that they had no prospect of success for deterrence to succeed. There were many in the United States who insisted Soviet leaders were godless men who put no value on human life. On the other side, there were many in the Soviet Union who contended that the United States was unalterably committed to the destruction of the Soviet Union as a threat to capitalism. That meant an energetic build-up of nuclear weapons systems, and a continued demonstration of resoluteness to challenge the other. Tension was inevitable.

MAD: THE MCNAMARA REVOLUTION

When the newly elected John Kennedy received his briefings on SIOP-62, he was startled to learn that the president's options for waging nuclear war were essentially one: to deliver a massive Sunday Punch against the Communist world. He was aghast at the only two choices he had: do nothing or commit mass murder, including the murder of citizens of innocent Soviet allies who had chosen to stay out of the conflict. And, as the Soviets developed their own nuclear forces, America's policy of a massive attack meant its own suicide if it were to launch that attack on the Soviet Union. Kennedy insisted on having more options.

His Secretary of Defense, Robert McNamara, led the administration in rethinking nuclear doctrine, pulling together the evolving ideas about deterrence and its degree of ruggedness, and created a vocabulary and a set of assertions about nuclear weapons that defined discussion, policy, and negotiations regarding nuclear arms. While it is not clear if the second nuclear era will produce its own vo-cabulary and assertions or continue to adopt the McNamara definitions, any change will likely use these ideas as points for departure.

The discussion of strategic doctrine focused on certain key aspects of nuclear weapons, as de-scribed in the following sections:

1. *Weapons could be classified as either first- or second-strike weapons.* First-strike weapons are weapons that are not likely to survive an enemy attack. Their only use is in a preventive or pre-emptive war. Deterrence, however, is best assured by a large number of second-strike weap-ons—weapons likely to survive an attack and deliver a retaliatory response. A weapon's status could change with time and advances in technology. Missiles buried in silos initially were sec-ond-strike weapons. However, as missile accuracy improved, and satellite reconnaissance pin-pointed the location of all Soviet and U.S. silo-based ICBMs, such weapons were unlikely to survive a nuclear attack; they became first-strike weapons. On the other hand, ballistic missile submarines, cruising silently deep beneath the surface of the ocean, were and still are very diffi-cult to destroy, and therefore are second-strike weapons.

2. *Nuclear weapons can be classified as counterforce or countervalue weapons. Counterforce weapons*, those best suited for the destruction of an enemy's military forces, are typically very accurate, because military targets, particularly an enemy's strategic nuclear striking forces and their command and control facilities, are likely to be small in size and well protected, buried in the earth or protected by concrete structures. Only a warhead detonated very close to such a tar-get is likely to damage it significantly. In addition, a weapon intended to destroy counterforce targets must have a relatively brief flight time, leaving the opponent with insufficient time to launch its missiles or fly off its bombers. *Countervalue weapons*, on the other hand, are those best suited for use against what an enemy values—a euphemism for an enemy's people, eco-nomic base, and all the networks that make a society. In this century, those values are predomi-nantly found in urban areas, so countervalue weapons are essentially weapons targeted against cities. Such weapons can be relatively inaccurate and their flight time is irrelevant. Cities do not move, and it makes little difference whether a multimegaton weapon with a destructive radius of 20 miles lands in the exact center of a city.

3. *Counterforce weapons are likely to be first-strike weapons; countervalue weapons would most likely be second-strike weapons.* Counterforce weapons thus strain deterrence, making it more delicate; countervalue weapons make deterrence more rugged.

These refinements in thinking about nuclear weapons allowed McNamara to tackle the question of a reasonable nuclear strategy. Initially he rejected SIOP-62 with its single option and in its place offered a strategy called *Flexible Response*, providing a range of nuclear options in response to prov-ocation or aggression. Flexible response was an explicit *counterforce* strategy, predicated on "city avoidance." It sought a means of limiting damage to the United States.[84] The principal objective in the event of war would be "the destruction of the enemy's military forces, not of his civilian population." Striking only at the opponent's military forces and minimizing civilian casualties, all the while maintaining a reserve sufficient to destroy the opponent's cities, would give the opponent "the strongest possible incentive to refrain from striking our own cities."[85] Thus an opponent's population would be maintained as hostage to discourage it from attacking the U.S. population, while at the same time demonstrating U.S. ability to destroy the opponent's cities if it wished. War would become a demonstration of the capacity to hurt. War would be terminated by bargaining, with the United States having the upper hand—the opponent's nuclear weapons destroyed, its cities vulnerable to incineration.

Although the policy of flexible response or city avoidance was attractive to McNamara for a brief period of time, its problems quickly became apparent. It required a considerable counterforce capability. A large arsenal of highly accurate nuclear weapons would make an opponent extremely nervous, for if they were used in a first strike, they might be able to destroy the opponent's nuclear weapons, leaving it defenseless and open to nuclear blackmail. The opponent might then be driven to preemption if it perceived any sign that a first strike from the other side was in the offing. Deterrence would become delicate indeed.

Moreover, McNamara's analysts calculated that even a limited nuclear war, one in which each side deliberately refrained from striking the other's cities, would still entail loss of life on an unprecedented scale (from fallout on cities downwind from military targets and from near misses), thereby making the effect practically indistinguishable from an unlimited nuclear exchange. In addition, as the Soviet Union increased the survivability of its retaliatory forces by protecting its ICBMs in concrete underground silos and by dispersing its missiles in submarines at sea, McNamara realized that counterforce strategy would do little to protect the United States against intolerable damage from a retaliatory Soviet second strike.

Thus McNamara arrived at what would become *the* strategy of the first nuclear era: *assured destruction*. In his words, the basic objective of U.S. strategic military forces had become "to deter a deliberate nuclear attack upon the United States or its allies by maintaining at all times a clear and unmistakable ability to inflict an unacceptable degree of damage upon any aggressor, or combination of aggressors—even after absorbing a surprise first strike."[86] McNamara felt that assured destruction would be reached when surviving American forces could "destroy 20% to 33% of the Soviet population and 50% to 75% of the industrial capacity."[87] This policy called for second-strike, countervalue weapons.

A doctrine of assured destruction, if adopted by both sides of a nuclear relationship, could produce a condition of *Mutual Assured Destruction* (MAD). If each side adopted the strategic view that the only nuclear capability that mattered was the ability to assure the destruction of the other in a retaliatory second strike, the symmetry of military doctrines would achieve a stable, non-threatening balance. *The only use then that nuclear weapons would have would be to deter an attack*. MAD thus made the point that *the only reason for the existence of nuclear weapons was that they were not to be used*.

The policy of MAD fit well with the triad of land-based ballistic missiles, submarine-launched ballistic missiles, and manned bombers, and met the political interests of the military services. The policy also provided a guideline for how many weapons were needed, in the face of the services routinely arguing for more. McNamara was able to craft a compromise of 1,000 land-based solid-fueled Minuteman, the 54 liquid-fueled Titan ICBMs previously deployed, 41 missile submarines, each carrying 16 missiles, and about 600 B-52s.[88] As you might suspect, these numbers were in part a political decision negotiated between rival services and with an eye to an American public that had perceived the previous administration's program, about half as ambitious, as inadequate. But they were also based on serious and systematic strategic thought. McNamara's staff had concluded that anything "beyond the level of around 400 1-megaton-equivalent delivered warheads would not significantly change the amount of damage inflicted." Doubling the number of delivered 1-megaton-equivalents would increase the destruction of Soviet industry by only 1 percent.[89]

SECOND THOUGHTS: CHALLENGES TO MAD

MAD, like its very acronym, always had an air of unreality to it, although it in general has remained the de facto nuclear policy of the United States. It was vulnerable to challenge. For MAD to work, the opponent needed to accept its requirements, particularly its argument that nuclear weapons exist only to be left unused. For some time, Soviet military doctrine seemed to be more oriented toward waging nuclear war in the belief (or hope) that the Soviet Union would *prevail* if war were thrust on the USSR. Soviet doctrine emphasized preemption, itself fraught with the dangers discussed in the last chapter regarding the misreading of an opponent's actions. Some Americans feared that Communist party leaders would accept large losses of their citizens' lives to advance their political agenda; those leaders would thus not be deterred by threats of U.S. retaliation against Soviet cities.

Moreover, MAD removed the possibility that nuclear weapons might be used to advance American political interests in the foreign policy realm as they had under Eisenhower and Dulles. Some U.S. officials wanted to deter the Soviet Union from provocative acts by making Soviet leaders uncertain whether the United States would respond to a provocation with a limited use of nuclear weapons. Some wanted to maintain a flexible response capability to better deal with contingencies such "as accidental acts, the escalation of conventional conflicts, a challenge to a nuclear test of wills by ill-informed or cornered and desperate leaders involving the nuclear equivalent of shots across the bow." In particular, as more states acquired nuclear weapons, particularly those labeled as "rogue nations," some leaders felt nuclear weapons might be necessary to shape outcomes acceptable to the United States.

And then there were America's allies who looked to the American nuclear arsenal for their protection. From the start of the nuclear age, the United States brought Western Europe and Japan under its *nuclear umbrella*, threatening to treat a Soviet attack on those allies as an attack on the United States itself, which would trigger American nuclear retaliation against the Soviet Union. This *extended deterrence* has always been vexed by a question of credibility. Was the United States prepared to lose New York to defend Paris? The French government assumed that no rational leader would do so, and opted for their own nuclear force—targeted on Soviet cities (and anyone else, it declared, who attacked France). The stationing of American forces in Europe under the aegis of the North Atlantic Treaty Organization (NATO) was designed to serve as a trip-wire, a way of having the United States committed to the defense of Europe in case of a Soviet invasion—and thus give credibility to the threat to use nuclear weapons.[90] Providing nuclear weapons to U.S. forces stationed in Europe made the point even clearer. But to rely on MAD and its argument that nuclear weapons are not to be used appeared to call into question American threats to go nuclear in case of a Soviet invasion.

Finally, there were always groups within the American government—more or less influential depending upon the party and man in control of the White House—who argued that flexible response was the only policy that made sense—that the United States had to adopt a war-waging doctrine for nuclear weapons. They argued that deterrence against attacks on the homeland would still hold (because of the threat of massive mutual devastation) even when tactical nuclear weapons were used on the battlefield (which in any case would most likely be Central European real estate).[91] They felt reasonably confident that the threshold on the escalation ladder would hold, because no rational leader would want to engage in mutual city-killing.

The shift away from MAD had begun under the Nixon administration and reached its apogee in the first years of the Reagan administration.[92] In 1981 President Reagan signed National Security Decision Directive 13 which set the goal of *prevailing in a protracted nuclear war of up to 180 days*. This assumed that the Soviet Union would be deterred from war only if they feared that any war with the United States would be lost, no matter at what level the Soviet chose to wage it. In the succeeding eight years, the SIOP went through six revisions, each giving a greater emphasis to threatening the destruction of Soviet political and military command and control systems. President Reagan described these changes in this way: "Our targeting policy... places at risk those political entities the Soviet leadership values most: the mechanisms for ensuring survival of the Communist Party and its leadership cadres, and for retention of the Party's control over the Soviet and Soviet Bloc peoples."[93] These values—rather than a concern for the lives of Soviet citizenry—were, in that administration's view, what deter a Soviet attack against American cities, while American plans to defeat the Soviet Union on any battlefield of its choosing would deter a Soviet attack anywhere.

This war-waging orientation claimed that assured destruction alone was inadequate. It might deter an all-out attack, but it was insufficient to deter less extensive nuclear use; indeed, it might encourage such use. But there was strong criticism of the war-waging doctrine: First, it is likely that every nuclear explosion would constitute a powerful blow for escalation across the threshold to total war. Second, if a nation's leaders believed nuclear war could be controlled, those leaders would be more likely to use nuclear weapons. Third, a war-fighting doctrine has to emphasize counterforce weapons, which would raise fears on the part of the opponent of a first strike or of attempted coercion based on the first-strike capability. Fourth, there would be a tendency to forget that the primary objective of nuclear strategy was to avoid wars, not to fight them.

As we shall see in Chapter 5, by the end of the Reagan administration, the president had come to a new understanding of the Soviet Union, which while it did not dramatically change American plans to deter and wage nuclear war, it did reduce the likelihood of such a war. That was but a prelude to the end of the first nuclear era, when, in the space of months, the Soviet Union dissolved, and with it, the threat of major power nuclear war dissipated.

TECHNOLOGY'S IMPACT ON DOCTRINE

As we have seen, the changing technology of nuclear weapons and their delivery systems has played a key role in changing doctrine—and politics and organizational interests. For instance, in the early years of the Kennedy administration, nuclear weapons could only be aimed effectively against cities rather than military (counterforce) targets. Deterrence based on assured destruction reflected the technological capability of the time. But very quickly, technological advances made precise counterforce strikes technically possible. The increasing *accuracy* of missiles made more precise attacks possible (going from an average miss distance of more than half a mile to now less than 500 feet).[94] *Intelligence collection capabilities*, particularly by satellites, meant that every land-based missile silo could be located with precision, and thus effectively targeted—as could all major military, scientific, and manufacturing, and transportation facilities. Intelligence had far greater difficulty in locating mobile missile launchers, however, as satellites themselves—and their communications—are vulnerable to attack.

The most important of the technological developments was the multiple independently targetable reentry vehicle system (MIRV). In the early 1960s, each ballistic missile carried only one warhead in one reentry vehicle (the container that protects and carries the warhead from launch to target). Later in the 1960s, as both the United States and the Soviet Union began work on various antiballistic missile defenses (ABM), missile designers looked at ways to counter these defenses. Their solution was to increase the number of warheads on each missile (Figures 4-8 and 4-9)—now possible because the increased accuracy of missiles reduced the destructive power of the warhead needed to destroy a target. At the same time, continued advances in warhead design made warheads smaller and lighter. For example, the Titan carried a warhead with a yield of 9 megatons (and weighing over 8,000 pounds), while the Minuteman III missile carries warheads with yields between 300 and 475 kilotons, weighing less than 800 pounds each.[95] (But keep in mind that these 800-pound warheads are still over 30 times more powerful than the bomb dropped on Hiroshima.) More warheads would overwhelm the defense systems by the weight of numbers. Moreover, each warhead could be aimed at a separate target. Any defense system would have to attack each warhead separately. Even after both the United States and the Soviet Union discontinued work on ABM defenses, the deployment of MIRV went ahead, with deployment of U.S. MIRVed missiles beginning in 1970. The United States eventually deployed 550 three-warhead Minuteman III missiles (out of 1,000 Minuteman). The submarine-launched Poseidon (successor to the Polaris missile) carried ten or more warheads, while the currently deployed Trident submarine missile deploys 5 warheads.[96]

MIRV thus provided missiles with the counterforce capability they previously lacked, just at the time that doctrine was moving away from an emphasis on counterforce weapons.[97] Counterforce planners assumed that at least two warheads would be required to guarantee destruction of an enemy ICBM in its silo, given the uncertainty of each warhead striking its target. Given rough parity in the number of missiles deployed by each superpower, as long as each missile had only one warhead, the side that initiated a counterforce attack would use up all of its missiles before the other side's force of ICBMs was destroyed. However, with multiple warheads, one missile could destroy more than one enemy missile, raising again the specter of a disarming first strike, at least as far as fixed-based

Figure 4–8   Three MIRV warheads. *U.S. Department of Defense.*

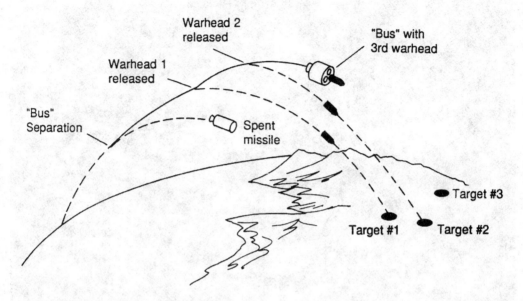

Figure 4–9   MIRV flight patterns

ICBMs were concerned. MIRV thus created a problem for ICBMs in fixed silos and led to a proliferation of proposals for mobile ground-launched ICBMs. None of these schemes—ICBMs on moving railroad cars, on trucks, in cargo aircraft parked on the ends of runways—were ever deployed by the United States. Given the triad, and SLBM systems in particular, the possibility of a disarming first strike remained negligible.

The possibility of maintaining a "secure strategic reserve" was considerably improved by the other major technological innovation of the 1970s—the cruise missile, a jet-powered, pilotless aircraft capable of carrying nuclear weapons. Advances in computer technology enabled the cruise missles to match the radar profile of the terrain it flew over with radar images stored in its memory, allowing it to make course corrections in flight and achieve great accuracy.[98] Small in size (roughly 20 feet long), relatively cheap, and easily carried to within 1500 miles of the target by aircraft, surface ships, and submarines, cruise missiles in large numbers could overwhelm any defense system. (See figures 4-10 and 4-11)

DEFENSE AGAINST MISSILES

In contrast to these successful technologies, success eluded the other technological effort in the nuclear realm—the attempt to create defenses against missile warheads. In a speech broadcast on March 23, 1983, President Reagan surprised most of the country and some of his own advisors with these closing words:

Let me share with you a vision of the future which offers hope. It is that we embark on a program to counter the awesome Soviet missile threat with measures that are defensive...What if free people

Figure 4–10 Air-launched cruise missile emerges from a B-52.   Copyright © *Corbis*

Figure 4–11   A sea-launched cruise missle begins its flight after launch from a submarine.
U.S. Department of Defense.

could live secure in the knowledge that their security did not rest upon the threat of instant U.S. retaliation to deter a Soviet attack, that we could intercept and destroy strategic ballistic missiles before they reach our own soil or that of our allies...I call upon the scientific community in our country, those who gave us nuclear weapons, to turn their great talents now to the cause of mankind and world peace, to give us the means of rendering these nuclear weapons impotent and obsolete.[99]

Although officially called the Strategic Defense Initiative (SDI), the press quickly dubbed the President's plan "Star Wars" after the 1977 George Lucas science fiction movie, because it depended on the development of advanced technology such as satellite battle stations using particle beams and lasers to fight a defensive war in space.

Secretary McNamara's analysts had estimated that 200 Soviet warheads detonating in the United States would kill 50 million Americans. Given that there were some 10,000 ballistic warheads in the Soviet strategic arsenal in the 1980s, a defense would have to destroy at least 98 percent of the warheads in a Soviet all-out strike to limit damage significantly in the United States. There are formidable obstacles to an effective ballistic missile defense: the short time during which the missiles are vulnerable to attack, the long distances across which the attacks must be made, the ruggedness of the warheads, and the thousands of warheads and decoys an attacker could send against the United States. To have any prospect of success, the defense system would have to be layered, with different defensive methods to attack the missiles and incoming warheads at different stages of their flight. A large, complex, and robust battle management system would be required to take on the task of coordinating and controlling the entire defense system. It would consist of sensing satellites, ground and satellite communication links, and computers, whose task it would be to track and identify targets, decide on optimum ways of meeting the attack, distinguish real warheads from decoys, assign defensive weapons to particular targets, detect hits and misses, and reassign targets that had been missed.

The critics of SDI challenged the feasibility of such a system on a number of grounds. First, some of the necessary technologies, such as particle beam weapons and directed energy weapons powered by nuclear explosives, did not exist and might not ever work. Second, the system could not be tested under realistic conditions (a large-scale surprise attack) and would have to work perfectly the first time it was needed. Third, countermeasures to missile defenses are readily available, less technically demanding and much less expensive than the missile defenses themselves. For example, lasers, the most promising weapon for attacks during the initial stage of missile flight, can easily be countered by giving the missile a reflective coating or causing the launch vehicle to rotate as it ascends so the laser could not remain focused on one spot.[100] Finally, missile defenses rely on satellites, communications, and multiple computers linked together, which are all quite vulnerable to attack.

Critics also warned that SDI might make a nuclear attack *more likely*. Though it could not be effective against a large scale first strike, it might be able to contend with a severely degraded retaliatory second strike. Thus, if the United States chose to initiate a counterforce strike against the Soviet Union, a "ragged response" by surviving Soviet missiles would do little damage. There might be occasions when the United States would be tempted to launch such a first strike, believing it could deal with the consequences. Far more threatening was the fear the Soviet Union might suspect that deterrence had weakened greatly for them, thus increasing the pressures on the Soviet leadership to strike first. Even beginning deployment of such a system, critics warned, might lead the Soviets to conclude that they had no alterative but to launch a preemptive strike before the U.S. missile defenses were operational. Thus, SDI, instead of making life in the United States more secure, might precipitate the very attack it is meant to defend against.[101]

By 1987, even the scientists working on SDI had come to admit that the dream of a perfect shield against missiles was unobtainable. They realized that the exotic technologies needed were going to require decades to develop and might prove never to be practicable. But, as we shall see in Chapter 6, the dream of missile defenses remains alive in the second nuclear era.

SUMMARY

The debate over doctrine has been a function of the great power of the weapons, the rapid pace of technological change, and the growing belief that nuclear war is to be avoided but with great uncertainty about how to make deterrence work. Changes in doctrine reflected the attempt to devise ideas that could make sense out of the unfathomable, ideas that could provide some coherence to military policy. At the same time politics and organizational interests played crucial roles. As a candidate John Kennedy recognized the power of the perceived "missile gap" after Sputnik as an issue to use against the Republicans, and candidate Ronald Reagan used claims of a similar nuclear gap against the Carter administration. The military services as a rule wanted more weapons; McNamara's formulation of assured destruction was in part an attempt to head off an Air Force request for thousands of missiles. And, as we have just seen, technology played a role as well.

As the Cold War intensified and a war economy became a permanent feature in both countries, the defense establishments came to represent a major portion of government expenditures, and defense industries a significant segment of the total economy. For example, by 1985, U.S. expenditures for defense constituted 28 percent of its national budget and 7 percent of its Gross National Product.[102] In the U.S., a sizeable portion of the economy became dependent on government defense contracts. This economy created special interests, both within and outside the military service, that had, and continue to have, a major stake in the continued development and procurement of more weapons. President Eisenhower in his farewell address in January 1961 warned the nation:

> against the acquisition of unwarranted influence...by the military-industrial complex. The potential for the disastrous rise of misplaced power exists and will persist. ... The conjunction of an immense military establishment and a large arms industry is new in the American experience. The total influence—economic, political and even spiritual—is felt in every city, every statehouse, every office of the federal government.[103]

In his memoirs, Eisenhower also warned against parochial political interests: "Each community in which a manufacturing plant or a military installation is located profits from the money spent and the jobs created in the area. This fact constantly presses on the community's political representatives—congressmen, senators, and others—to maintain the facility at maximum strength."[104]

The irony of the creation of a permanent war economy in the United States is that the continued buildup of U.S. military strength also created an arms industry with considerable economic, and therefore political, power, able to exert considerable influence on decisions to acquire new weapons. Each purchase of new weapons by the U.S. government provides the arms industry with even more resources to influence future decisions to purchase more weapons. We see these forces continuing to work in the United States today as the aerospace industry continues its very effective lobbying campaign for missile defense funding, even though all previous missile defense programs have yielded nothing but expensive failures.[105] In Chapter 6, we will look at criticisms of the George W. Bush administration's proposals to make sizeable investments in very high-tech military hardware of no use in the current war on terror.

At the start of this chapter, we asserted that nuclear weapons states must fashion answers to four key questions. The historical record indicates that the United States and the Soviet Union both reached similar answers. During the first nuclear era, they both decided that they needed nuclear weapons in peacetime—to wait until war broke out might be a deadly mistake. They needed a large number (ultimately in the thousands) and a variety of such weapons (principally carried by aircraft, missiles stationed in below-ground silos or on mobile launchers, and aboard submarines).

As to plans for using the weapons, there were a variety of answers, but they all revolved around a core argument, one that Bernard Brodie had sensed at the start of the nuclear age:

> Thus far the chief purpose of our military establishment has been to win wars. From now on its chief purpose must be to avert them. It can have almost no other useful purpose.[106]

But just how nuclear weapons could avert wars was open to debate. There was a general consensus that the opponent had to be deterred from using its nuclear weapons, but the crucial, vexing question was how deterrence was to be accomplished.

Some claimed that only by having the ability to fight across the full spectrum of nuclear war, ranging from a limited nuclear war up through a major nuclear exchange, could a nation demonstrate to an opponent that at any level the opponent chose to wage war, it would face military defeat. Predicting defeat no matter the level of violence it employed, the opponent would be deterred from launching any aggression. Such a *flexible response* or *prevailing* or *war-fighting strategy* requires a massive strategic arsenal (and a very robust conventional force), containing a large number of quite potent counterforce weapons, as well as a very survivable strategic reserve, committed to the defense of the nation and its allies. Others argued that the only use for nuclear weapons in war was as instruments of retaliation, *to assure the destruction of an attacker.* The principal requirement for the nuclear forces is that a sufficient number be able to survive any attack an enemy might consider making. Strategies for fighting war with them were not necessary. The key becomes possessing a secure retaliatory capability and manifesting the will to deliver such retaliation. That retaliation was to be directed principally at whatever was judged most valuable by the would-be attacker's leadership, be it the mass of people who constituted the nation or the leadership itself. It may be that these two strategic approaches, assured destruction and war-fighting, are the twin poles between which every nuclear nation's doctrine will oscillate, as new nuclear powers retrace the same route that the United States and the Soviet Union traversed in the Cold War. Or it could be that France and China, with their much smaller nuclear arsenals and their implicit assured-destruction approach, represent a pattern to which future nuclear nations may adhere.

At the end of the first nuclear era, the world knew that it had escaped nuclear catastrophe. *How* it had been able to do so, however, remains a matter of controversy. Was it because deterrence works?

We have no empirical evidence that any nuclear power, from the beginning of the nuclear era through the dissolution of the Soviet Union, seriously contemplated using nuclear weapons against another nuclear state and then stayed its hand for fear of the second-strike retaliation it would receive or that it judged it could not prevail in the military conflict at any level that it chose to use. If there was never a test of deterrence, we cannot conclude that it works.

Second, if there never has been a test, we have no way of knowing whether one of the two poles of deterrence strategies is a better strategy—better in terms of promoting deterrence. If both might work equally well, then we might adopt the one that is the least costly and the least provocative, which would lead us to McNamara's ultimate choice, assured destruction. But absent a test of deterrence—and surely we would all hope to avoid such a test—we are left with having to make uncertain choices.

The fourth question with which we began the chapter asked: How can nuclear weapons be used to promote the national interest? Nuclear powers struggled to find an answer for their defense strategies. But nuclear weapons were present during times of general peace as well. Was there a way to build them into a state's foreign policies that would advance the nation's interests? We now turn to that part of the experience of the first nuclear era.

ENDNOTES

[1]Fred Kaplan, *The Wizards of Armageddon* (New York: Simon & Schuster, 1983), pp. 9, 10.

[2]Quoted in Lawrence Freedman, *The Evolution of Nuclear Strategy*, 2d ed. (New York: St. Martin's Press, 1989), p. 427.

[3]Quoted in Kaplan, *Wizards of Armageddon*, p. 26.

[4]Quoted in Kaplan, *Wizards of Armageddon*, p. 27.

[5]Carl von Clausewitz, *On War*, ed. and trans. By Michael Howard and Peter Paret (Princeton, NJ: Princeton University Press, 1976) Bk. I, chap. 1, p. 77.

[6]Clausewitz, *On War*, p.90.

[7]Raymond Aron, *Century of Total War* (Garden City, NY: Doubleday and Company, 1954), p.19.

[8]A. J. P. Taylor, *First World War, an Illustrated History* (New York: Putnam, 1963), p. 22.

[9]Nationalism has also proved to be a devisive force as well; in multi-ethnic nations such as Yugoslavia, societies have fragmented into warring factions, each creating its own military force by drawing on the patriotism of its ethnic group.

[10]Walter Millis, *Arms and Men; A Study in American Military History* (New York: Capricorn, 1987, c1956) .

[11]Ropp, *War in the Modern World*, (New York: Collier, 1962), p. l61.

[12]A pair of terms that is used in a very general sense in everyday conversation, but in a military context have very specific meanings: strategy and tactic. Traditionally "tactics" has been used to describe the handling of troops in contact with the enemy and "strategy" to mean the handling of troops not in contact with the enemy. More recently, strategy has been defined as "the art of distributing and applying military means to fulfill ends of policy." Basil H. Liddell Hart, *Strategy: the Indirect Approach*. (London: Faber & Faber, 1968), p. 334.

[13]Quoted in Freedman, *The Evolution of Nuclear Strategy*, p. 5.

[14]R.J. Overy, *The Air War, 1939-1945* (New York: Stein and Day, 1980), p. 122.

[15]In fact, the peak month for tank production by Germany was October 1944 and for aircraft production was November 1944, in spite of a protracted and intensive bombardment by Allied air forces.

[16]Overy, *The Air War*, pp. 119–20.

[17]Freedman, *The Evolution of Nuclear Strategy*, p. 12.

[18]*The New Encyclopedia Britannica* (Chicago: 1998) v. 29, p.1023.

[19]Richard Pfau, *No sacrifice Too Great; the Life of Lewis L. Strauss* (Charlottesville, VA: University Press of Virginia, 1984), pp. 94–95.

[20]The Joint Chiefs of Staff (JCS) is an organization within the Department of Defense under the supervision and control of the secretary of defense. The JCS are the primary military advisors to the president, the

National Security Council, and the secretary of defense and consist of the Chairman of the Joint Chiefs, the chief of staff of the Army, the chief of Naval Operations, and the chief of staff of the Air Force and on occasion the commandant of the Marine Corps. In addition, within the Department of Defense are the three military departments, the Department of the Army, the Navy (including the Marine Corps), and the Air Force, each of which has its own civilian secretary. B. Thomas Trout and James E. Harf, eds., *National Security Affairs. Theoretical Perspectives and Contemporary Issues* (New Brunswick, N.J.: Transaction Books, 1982), pp. 169–170.

[21]Omar N. Bradley and Clay Blair, *A General's Life; an Autobiography by General of the Army, Omar N. Bradley* (New York: Simon & Schuster, 1983.), p. 490.

[22]Quoted in Freedman, *The Evolution of Nuclear Strategy*, p. 48.

[23]Operation Sandstone; see Herbert F. York, *The Advisors: Oppenhiemer, Teller and the Superbomb* (San Francisco: Freeman, 1976), p. 20.

[24]David Alan Rosenberg, "Origins of Overkill: Nuclear Weapons and American Strategy, 1945 to 1960", *International Security 7*, no. 4 (Spring 1983), p. 16.

[25]Quoted in Freedman, *The Evolution of Nuclear Strategy*, p. 55.

[26]Rosenberg, "Origins of Overkill", p. 16.

[27]Lester Machta, "Finding the site of the first Soviet nuclear test in 1919". *Bulletin of the American Meteorological Society.* Vol. 73, No. 11, November 1992. pp. 1797–1806.

[28]Established by the National Security Act of 1947, the National Security Council (NSC) is the formal advisory body to the president on major national security issues. By law, the chairman of the NSC is the president and stated members include the vice-president and the secretaries of state and defense. In addition, there are a number of designated advisors to the NSC, including the director of Central Intelligence, the chairman of the Joint Chiefs of Staff, and the assistant to the president for National Security Affairs. Other members of the executive branch are invited to attend NSC meetings at the pleasure of the president. The staff of the NSC has varied in size and independence from time to time. Trout and Harf, *National Security Affairs*, p. 162.

[29]U.S.Department of State. *Foreign Relations of the United States: 1948, vol. 1, Part 2* (Washington, D.C.: U.S.Government Printing Office, 1976), pp. 624–628.

[30]Norris, Robert S. and William M. Arkin. "Nuclear Notebook: U.S. weapons secrets revealed" *Bulletin of the Atomic Scientists*, March 1993 p. 48.

[31]U.S.Department of State. *Foreign Relations of the United States: 1990,* vol. 1, (Washington, D.C.: U.S.Government Printing Office, 1976), p. 236.

[32]Dean Acheson, *Present at the Creation* (New York: W.W.Norton,1969), p. 371.

[33]U.S.Department of State. *Foreign Relations of the United States: 1950, vol. 1*, pp. 234–292.

[34]U.S.Department of State. *Foreign Relations of the United States: 1950, vol. 1*, pp. 234–292

[35]Norris "Nuclear Notebook: U.S. weapons secrets revealed"., Robert S.Norris, Steven M. Kosiak and Stephen I. Schwartz, "Deploying the bomb". in Stephen I.Schwartz, ed. *Atomic Audit; the costs and consequences of U.S. nuclear weapons since 1940*. Washington, D.C., Brookings Institution, D.C., 1998. p. 189, pp. 203–204.

[36]Rosenberg, "Origins of Overkill", p. 30.

[37]Rosenberg, "Origins of Overkill", p. 30.

[38]Gregg Herken, *Counsels of War* (New York: Knopf, 1985) p. 83.

[39]Pfau, *No Sacrifice Too Great*, p. 114. Work on the theory of a fusion device had begun before the explosion of the first fission device at Los Alamos, but had not been given a very high priority and had not produced a workable device.

[40]Quoted in Freedman, *The Evolution of Nuclear Strategy*, p. 66.

[41]Freedman, *The Evolution of Nuclear Strategy*, p. 68.

[42]U.S. Dept. of State, *Foreign Relations of the U.S. 1950, vol. 1*, pp. 506–511.

[43]Gregg Herken, *Brotherhood of the bomb: The tangled lives and loyalties of Robert Oppenheimer, Ernest Lawrence, and Edward Teller.* (New York: Henry Holt and Company, 2002), p. 213.

[44]Herken, op. cit. p 252.

[45]Herken, op. cit. p. 300. As late as two years later, following several embarrassing weapon test failures, the head of the GAC was still wondering if Livermore would ever "be an important lab."

[46]Herken, op. cit, p. 183.

[47]*U.S.President Public papers of the presidents of the United States: Dwight D. Eisenhower, 1960-61* p. 422

[48]Richard Smoke. *National Security in the Nuclear Dilemma: Introduction to the American Experience* (New York: Random House, 1984), pp. 58–59.

[49]In the 1950s and 1960s a considerable portion of the U.S. nuclear arsenal was committed to the destruction of Soviet air defenses to clear a path for aircraft on their way to attack strategic targets deep in Russia.

[50]Herken, *Counsels of War*, p. 144.

[51]U.S. Department of State, *Foreign Relations of the U.S.: 1950*, vol. 1, pp. 281–283.

[52]Kaplan, *Wizards of Armageddon*, p. 139.

[53]Kaplan, *Wizards of Armageddon*, p. 134.

[54]Rosenberg, "The Origins of Overkill," p. 49.

[55]Walter A. McDougall, *The Heavens and the Earth A Political History of the Space Age* (New York: Basic Books, 1985), p. 329; William E Burrows, Deep Black; Space Espionage and National Security (New York: Random House, 1986), pp. 110–111.

[56]Burrows, *Deep Black*, pp. 67–68.

[57]David Holloway, *Soviet Union and the Arms Race* (New Haven: CT: Yale University Fress, 1983), pp. 23–24.

[58]Freedman, *The Evolution of Nuclear Strategy*, p. 86.

[59]New Look:The "New Look" was set out in the National Security Council paper NSC-162/2 titled *The Basic National Security Policy*, and was approved in October 1953. U.S. Department of State, *Foreign Relations of the United States: 1952:1954* (Washington, D.C.: U.S. Government Printing Office, 1984), vol. 2, part 1.

[60]*Foreign Relations of the United States: 1952-1954*, pp. 578, 579–82.

[61]Schwartz, *Atomic audit, the costs and consequences of U.S. nuclear weapons since 1940*, p. 222.

[62]Eric Schmitt, "U.S. Curtails 24-Hour Duty of Its Flying Command Post," *New York Times* (July 28, 1990), p. 6.

[63]Schwartz, *Atomic audit*. p. 207.

[64]Daniel Ford, T*he Button; the Pentagons's Strategic Command and Control System* (New York: Simon & Schuster, 1985), p. 148; Ashton B. Carter, ed., *Managing Nuclear Operations* (Washington, D.C.: The Brookings Institution, 1987), p. 52.

[65]Kaplan, *Wizards of Armageddon* , pp. 161–162.

[66]Desmond Ball, *Politics and Force Levels: The Strategic Missile Program of the Kennedy Administration* (Berkeley: University of California Press, 1980), p. 9.

[67]*Gaither Commission repor*t; Kaplan, *Wizards of Armageddon*, p. 135.

[68]Beard, *Developing the ICBM*, (New York : Columbia University Press, 1976) p. 219.

[69]See Beard, *Developing the ICBM*, pp. 8, 167.

[70]Beard, *Developing the ICBM.*, p. 6.

[71]Beard, *Developing the ICBM*, pp. 11, 222.

[72]Beard, *Developing the ICBM*, p. 6. "The strategic bombardment function was still the most important in the Air Force. The chosen means to accomplish the mission remained the manned bomber fleet and would continue to do so with the future deployment of the B-52. Long range surface missiles were not im-

portant within the relevant furure of the Air Force. It was important, however, that other services not develop such weapons which could then compete with the Air Force responsibility and the chosen Air Force vehicle." Beard, *Developing the ICBM*, p. 105.

[73]Holloway, *Soviet Union ,and the Arms Race*, p. 43.

[74]Peter J. Roman, *Eisenhower and the Missile Gap*. (Ithaca, NY: Cornell University Press,1995.) p. 140–141.

[75]Sagan, "SIOP-63," p. 26.

[76]McDougall, *The Heavens and Earth*, p. 329.

[77]Ball, *Politics and Force Levels*, pp. 50,56.

[78]*Ball, Politics and Force Levels*, p. 52.

[79]A nation can, of course, deploy mechanisms aboard its missiles to give it the option of aborting the missile in flight or to prevent the warhead from exploding by send a radio signal, but have chosen not to for fear that the enemy might be able to send the abort signal.

[80]Schwartz, *Atomic audit; the costs and consequences of U.S. nuclear weapons since 1940*, p. 5.

[81]The debt to the penny http://www.publicdebt.treas.gov

[82]Schwartz, *Atomic audit*, p. 612.

[83]Albert Wohlstetter, "The Delicate Balance of Terror," *Foreign Affairs 37* (January 1959), pp. 211–234.

[84]"Damage limitation" as a concept had a more specific meaning: If the U.S. second-strike retaliatory force had counterforce weapons that were capable of destroying any of the enemy's weapons that were not used in his initial strike, the damage to the United States could be reduced in the event of a nuclear exchange. In the scenario McNamara envisioned, the Soviet Union might launch a limited nuclear attack on the United States, withholding some missiles for subsequent attacks if the United States did not accede to its demands. To limit damage to the United States in the Soviet follow-on attacks, McNamara would use counterforce weapons to destroy the remaining Soviet missiles.

[85]Robert S. McNamara, "Defense Arrangements of the North Atlantic Community", *Department of State Bulletin*, v. 47, no. 1202, July 9, 1962, pp. 67.

[86]Alain C. Enthoven and K. Wayne Smith, *How Much is Enough; Shaping the Defense Program, 1961-1969* (New York: Harper and Row, 1971), p. 174.

[87]Enthoven and Smith, *How Much is Enough*, p. 175.

[88]McDougall, *The Heavens and Earth*, p. 328.

[89]Enthoven and Smith, *How Much is Enough*, p. 207.

[90]Freedman, *Evolution of Nuclear Strategy*, p. 90.

[91]In the lexicon of nuclear strategy, "warfighting means the use of nuclear weapons for well-defined military purposes, as opposed to crude punishment with unbridled attacks on cities." Miguel Calder, *Nuclear Nightmare: An Introduction into Possible Wars* (Hammondsworth, England: Penguin Books, 1981), p. 18.

[92]In 1980, President Carter approved Presidential Directive 59, which set as the center of U.S. policy a countervailing strategy, defined as a strategy that denied an enemy the possibility of winning a nuclear war. Herken, *Counsels of War*, p. 301.

[93]Ronald Reagan, *National Security Strategy of the United States* (Washington, D.C., January 1988).

[94]Schwartz, *Atomic audit, the costs and consequences of U.S. nuclear weapons since 1940*, p. 149.

[95]Thomas B. Cochran, William M. Arkin and Milton M. Hoenig. *Nuclear Weapons Databook; vol. 1 U.S. Nuclear Forces and Capabilities*. (Cambridge, MA: Ballinger Publishing Co., 1984), pp. 55, 75, 122.

[96]Ted Greenwood, *Making the MIRV; A Study of Defense Decision Making* (Cambridge, Mass.: Ballinger, 1975), pp. 8–11.

[97]Kaplan, *Wizards of Armageddon*, p. 364.

[98]Richard K. Betts, ed., *Cruise Missiles: Technology, Strategy, Politics* (Washington, D.C.: The Brookings Institution, 1981), pp. 34–45.

[99]U.S.President, *Public papers of the presidents of the United States: Ronald Regan, 1983, Book I*, pp. 443–445

[100]Jeff Hecht, *Beam Weapons, the Next Arms Race.* (New York: Plenum Press, 1984) p. 177.

[101]President Reagan had proposed sharing SDI information with the Soviet Union to avoid this problem but never laid out a practical way in which this might be done.

[102]*Quadrennial Defense Review.* May 1997. *The Secretary's Message*, p. 1.

[103]*U.S. President, Public Papers of the Presidents of the United States: Dwight D. Eisenhower, 1960-61* (Washington, D.C.: U.S. Government Printing Office, 1961), p. 1038.

[104]Dwight D. Eisenhower, *Waging Peace, 1956-1961* (Garden City, N.Y.: Doubleday & Company, 1965), p. 615.

[105]The B–1 bomber presents a dramatic case of a weapon that was acquired in spite of determined opposition over a period of 30 years. It was opposed by four of the seven presidents, who considered that the day of the manned strategic bomber had passed, yet still more than $29 billion was spent to acquire this successor to the B–52. The economic and political rewards were enormous—during the seven years of the construction of 100 B–1 bombers an average of 40,000 workers in 48 states were employed by 5,200 companies in building the aircraft and its components. During the peak production year, 1986, 60,000 workers were employed, and the B-1 accounted for two-thirds of the income of the principal contractor, Rockwell International. Nick Kotz, *Wild Blue Yonder, Money, Politics and the B–1 Bomber* (New York: Pantheon Books, 1988), pp. 8, 222–223.

[106]Bernard Brodie, ed., *The Absolute Weapon: Atomic Power and World Order* (New York: Harcourt, Brace and Company, 1946), p. 76.

5

Nuclear Relations During the Cold War

It is 16 October 1962. President Kennedy has just learned that the Soviet Union is constructing nuclear missile sites in Cuba. His advisors are presenting their views on how the United States should respond. Robert Kennedy—the Attorney General and brother of the president—is speaking. Though we cannot give you the Boston accents, nor the styles of delivery, we can give you exactly what the people at the table said and how they said it, as their words were being secretly recorded. Reading the transcript aloud, taking the role of each person, is an education in how individuals actually responded to a nuclear crisis.[1]

Robert Kennedy: Mr. President, while we're considering this problem tonight, I think that we should also consider what, uh, Cuba's going to be a year from now, or two years from now. Assume that we go in and knock these sites out. Uh, I don't know what's gonna stop them from saying, 'We're gonna build the sites six months from now, bring 'em in… .'

Chairman of the Joint Chiefs Maxwell Taylor: Nothing permanent about it.

Robert Kennedy: Uh, … where are we six months from now? Or that we're in any better position, or aren't we in worse position if we go in and knock 'em out and say, uh, 'Don't do it.' Uh, I mean, obviously they're gonna *have* to do it then.

Secretary of Defense Robert McNamara: You have to put a blockade in following any limited action.

Robert Kennedy: Then we're gonna have to sink Russian ships. Then we're gonna have to sink Russian submarines. Now whether it wouldn't be, uh, the argument, if you're going to get into it at all, uh, whether we should just get into it and get it over with and say that, uh, take our losses, and if we're gonna … . If he wants to get into a war over *this*, uh … Hell, if it's war that's gonna come on this thing, or if he sticks those kinds of missiles in, it's after the warning, and he's gonna, and he's gonna get into a war for, six months from now or a year from now, so … .

McNamara: Mr. President, this is why I think tonight we ought to put on paper the alternative plans and the probable, possible consequences thereof in a way that State and Defense [Departments] could agree on, even if we, uh, disagree and put in both views. Because the consequences of these actions have *not* been thought through clearly. The one that the Attorney General just mentioned is illustrative of that.

President Kennedy: If the, uh, it doesn't increase very much their strategic strength, why is it, uh, … can any Russian expert tell us why they… . After all Khrushchev demonstrated a sense of caution [about] Berlin; he's been cautious, I mean, he hasn't been, uh ….

Unidentified speaker: Several possibilities, Mr. President. One of them is that he has given us word now that he's coming over in November to, to the U.N. If, he may be proceeding on the assumption, and this lack of a sense of *apparent* urgency would seem to support this, that this *isn't* going to be discovered at the moment and that, uh, when he comes over, this is something he can do, a ploy. That here is Cuba armed against the United States, or possibly use it to try to trade something in Berlin, saying he'll disarm Cuba if, uh, if we'll, uh, yield some of our interests in Berlin and some arrangement for it. I mean, that this is a, it's a trading ploy.

National Security Advisor McGeorge Bundy: I would think one thing that I would still cling to is that he's not likely to give Fidel Castro nuclear warheads. I don't believe that has happened or is likely to happen.

President Kennedy: Why does he put these in there though?

Why, indeed, would the Soviet Union put nuclear weapons in Cuba? Did it mean, as Robert Kennedy wondered, that the Soviets had decided on war with the United States? Or were they willing to risk war to get their way on contentious issues dividing the two states? Would the United States have to risk nuclear war to deal with the missiles? The Cuban missile crisis captures the central questions of this chapter: How did states attempt to make this new weapon a part of their international relations during the first nuclear age and what were the consequences?

We first concentrate on how states sought to exploit nuclear weapons to advance their national interests during what came to be called the Cold War. As policy makers quickly discovered, however, certain actions increased the likelihood of a nuclear war, thereby posing great peril to their societies. This recognition led policy-makers to devise nuclear "rules of the road" to lessen the risk of conflict and to establish controls on the weapons themselves in order to manage the threat they posed. We explore these developments as well.

THE NUCLEAR SHADOW

We might imagine that nuclear weapons would dramatically affect the thinking and behavior of the leaders of nuclear weapons states, and, as well, the thinking and behavior of the leaders of non-nuclear states having to deal with those nuclear-armed states. We call this effect *the nuclear shadow*—the changes that the very existence of nuclear weapons have wrought on relations between states. One indication of the shadow is the constant presence of a military officer near the president who carries a briefcase known as "the football," containing the coded messages authorizing a launch of U.S. nuclear weapons. The Russian president has a similar arrangement.[2] The football is a daily reminder of an inescapable shadow.

But did the shadow manifest itself in dramatically different behaviors by the leaders and the states they led during first nuclear age? The United States and the Soviet Union were able to keep a "long peace"[3] between themselves, and no great power waged war against another great power since 1945. Had nuclear weapons worked a fundamental revolution in world politics? There is no clear answer.[4]

There is, of course, the comforting *belief* that the long peace was a result of nuclear deterrence—of the fear that one would be destroyed or defeated if one used nuclear weapons. If that were the case, then nuclear weapons would have cast a dark, sharp shadow. But as we suggested in the last chapter, as neither Soviet nor American leadership actually contemplated waging war against the other, we cannot be sure that deterrence created the long peace. Thus, this aspect of the shadow also remains relatively unclear.

If we cannot say for sure that nuclear weapons kept the great powers from waging war against each other, perhaps we can suggest that the shadow's impact has been to make states more cautious in their foreign policies. Significant foreign policy blunders might lead to a nuclear confrontation and then to nuclear use. Therefore, it would seem reasonable to imagine that states became more risk-adverse in the nuclear world, making the world safer for all. Unfortunately, the evidence to support this claim is mixed.

In some cases, nuclear weapons did become a part of the considerations of decision makers, making them *less willing* to take actions if there was a risk of a nuclear war. In its Vietnam decision-making, for instance, the U.S. government took great pains to avoid any action that might suck China into the war, for the United States might then be forced to use nuclear weapons to counter Chinese manpower thrown into battle, or the Chinese might have used nuclear weapons, or the Soviets might become involved. "While no one can be certain," one American official reasoned, "the best judgment is that the Soviet Union could not sit by and let nuclear weapons be used against China."[5] At the same time, however, nuclear concerns did not prevent the United States from undertaking its massive military intervention in the Vietnam war.

Indeed, in some ways, the existence of nuclear weapons and nuclear deterrence made *intervention in Vietnam seem necessary*. American policy makers were convinced that deterrence rested on convincing the Soviets that the United States would respond to an attack on itself or its allies by striking the Soviet Union. Was such a threat credible? American leaders were concerned that if the United States did not keep its word in circumstances when it was costly to do so, then nuclear deterrence would be undermined. In facing the question in the summer of 1965 of whether to commit ground forces to the war in Vietnam, Lyndon Johnson saw this aspect of the shadow. He chose to escalate the war, a policy that he recognized was full of risk for the United States and himself politically. But, he said, "I was convinced that our retreat from this challenge would open the path to World War III."[6]

Moreover, the existence of nuclear weapons may have forced *non-nuclear or weaker* states to take *unexpectedly riskier actions* against a nuclear opponent. For instance, the People's Republic of China in the winter of 1950–1951 felt so threatened by U.S. military successes in the Korean War that it felt obliged to enter the war against the United States, even though the latter was nuclear-armed and the Chinese were not. Indeed, some states may feel that they *must* take risky actions when confronting a powerful nuclear-armed state in order to demonstrate that they will not be blackmailed by nuclear weapons. Nikita Khrushchev expressed the point this way: "…the fear of a nuclear war …can paralyze that country's defenses. And if a country's defenses are paralyzed, then war is really inevitable: the enemy is sure to sense your fright and try to take advantage of it. I always operated on the principle that I should be clearly against war but never frightened of it."[7]

The nuclear shadow has played on the surface of international relations in complex ways. If we step back to view the surface as a whole, do things become clearer? Was the Cold War itself a product of nuclear weapons. Did it remain cold precisely because of nuclear weapons?

COLD WARS AND NUCLEAR WEAPONS

The period of 1947 to 1991 marks an era in world history known as the Cold War, a period character-ized by the intense rivalry between the United States and the Soviet Union.[8] We think it useful to say that cold wars are a type of relationship that can exist between states, with the historic Cold War being just one prominent example.[9] In a cold war, the leadership of each state *believes* that the opponent has extremely hostile intentions against its own state and that the opponent contemplates waging war against it to accomplish those intentions, *but in reality* neither state's leadership desires war with the other. Thus, cold wars are "a mistake." They need not have happened, and might not have happened if the states in the relationship had a correct appreciation of the intentions of the other.[10]

In a cold war system, even though neither state intends war, there is a constant *threat of war*. The threat is partially created by the *perception* of the other state's hostile intentions: "They intend to attack us!" To keep war from happening, "we" make threats and brandish our weapons. And, as the other side only seems to understand the language of force, our foreign policy takes on strong mili-tary overtones. The other state, which finds itself in serious conflict with us, in turn sees our threats and our brandishing of weapons as ample proof of *our* hostile intentions, and it responds with threats of its own. Those reactive threats convince us that we were right in judging them willing to attack us.

In the historic Cold War, both sides came to see the other as having injurious intentions. George Kennan, an American diplomat in Moscow in 1946, presented an assessment that captured the Tru-man administration's thinking. The Soviet regime, he argued, had "learned to seek security only in patient but deadly struggle for total destruction of rival power, never in compacts and compromises with it."[11] Kennan's analysis became the intellectual underpinning of the U.S. response: the *contain-ment* of Soviet efforts to expand their control and influence so that, over time, internal contradictions within the Communist state would lead to a "mellowing" of Soviet goals and behavior, converting a revolutionary state into a traditional, status quo-oriented entity.

Soviet thinking ran in similar veins. Nikita Khrushchev, drawing on his ingrained Marxist per-spective, recalled that at the end of World War II, it was "difficult to judge what the intentions of the Allies were," but he surmised that "they wanted to take advantage of the results of the war and impose their will not only on their enemy, Germany, but on their ally, the USSR, as well."[12] Soviet policy be-came one of defensive probing for small advantages and insisting that Soviet interests be recognized, holding on for the time when the workers in the capitalist West would rise against the capitalist sys-tem and create socialist states—states that by definition would be friendly to the homeland of the pro-letariat, the Soviet Union.

In a cold war environment nuclear weapons make the opponent look more terrifying, for the oppo-nent possesses the capability to obliterate life. But they look terrifying precisely because of the as-sumption of very hostile intentions—they seem *willing* to obliterate life. In contrast, the United States and Britain possess nuclear weapons, but those weapons do not incite fear vis a vis the other. We suspect that readers today have very little fear of Russian or Chinese nuclear weapons.

While nuclear weapons do not make cold wars, they do inherently increase the risk of nuclear use, for they make war begun by the other seem quite likely. We saw in Chapter 4 how the emergence of Soviet and American military doctrine reflected the belief that the opponent stood ready to deliver a nuclear attack. Both sides prepared *preemptive* strategies that were based on the premise that if we suspected the other was *now* readying its attack, we would strike first.

No dire nuclear event occurred during the historic Cold War and the United States and the Soviet Union were able to keep the peace. Did nuclear weapons make war so perilous that, while they made the other appear more diabolical, they also kept the two from a hot war? Or do cold wars *by their nature* often remain cold, thus making the type of weapons the nations possess less important? We argue that cold wars can "dissolve" through the mutual recognition that the other state does not have the hostile intentions ascribed to it. Indeed, both parties in a cold war—neither of which plans to wage war on the other—may be very desirous to communicate that fact to the other. In the fall of 1948, for instance, as the Cold War was deepening, President Truman decided to take the highly unusual step of asking the Chief Justice of the Supreme Court, Fred Vinson, to talk to Stalin "man-to-man" (as Truman put it).

> I asked Vinson to point out to Stalin that the folly and tragedy of another war would amount to an act of national suicide and that no sane leader of any major power could ever again even contemplate war except in defense. Surely the next war—an atomic war—was as unthinkable as it was abhorrent.[13]

Truman diagnosed the problem as one of perceptions:

> The Russians simply did not understand—or *would* not—our peaceful intentions and our genuine desire to co-operate through the United Nations toward the establishment of a climate of peace; that we did not want to force and had no intention of forcing our way of life upon them or anyone else... .[14]

Similarly, immediately after Stalin's death in 1953, his successor as head of the Soviet Communist Party, Georgi Malenkov, sought to reassure the West of the Soviet Union's peaceful intentions. "At present," he declared, "there is no litigious or unsolved question which could not be settled by peaceful means on the basis of mutual agreement of the countries involved. This concerns our relations with all states, including the United States of America."[15]

These efforts to correct the perception of the other side are inherent in a cold-war situation, for each state knows that *it* does not plan to wage an aggressive war. If these efforts occur at the right time and in the right context, they may begin to undermine the belief that the other intends to attack. Further cooperative actions, now possible because of lessened fear, may reinforce and deepen this new perception to the point that both sides mutually recognize that the other does not intend to wage war, and thus help bring about an end to the cold war.

WAXING AND WANING OF COLD WARS

We would expect that across time there will be several points at which cold war states will edge toward a mutual recognition of pacific intentions, even though there may still be important conflicts between them. Indeed, in the late 1960s and early 1970s the United States and the Soviet Union did so, creating a period that came to be called *detente*, a term that captures the essence of a waning cold war as it means a relaxation of tensions. But then both states rediscovered reasons to be fearful of the intentions of the other, and the Cold War waxed again. We expect any cold war to show this fluctuation across time (indicated in Figure 5–1) as leaders come closer to the truth about their rival's intentions (a waning of the cold war), but then perceive that the other's willingness to wage war had not really abated (a waxing of the cold war, as occurred in the last years of the 1970s and early 1980s).

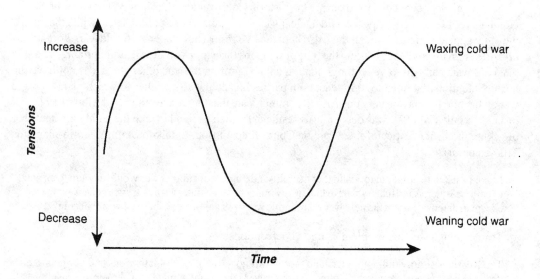

Figure 5–1 Waxing and waning of the Cold War

What causes a cold war to wax and wane? Cold wars wax for three central reasons. First, it is very difficult to sustain efforts to persuade the other side that one truly does not have deadly intentions. Consider what happened to Truman's and Malenkov's efforts. In Truman's case, he found that his Secretary of State strongly opposed the Vinson trip, and when the proposed trip leaked to the press, it was caught up in the whirlwind of a presidential election year, with Truman's Republican opponents accusing him of promoting a disastrous policy of appeasement. Vinson stayed home. Thus, *internal* disagreement and *domestic* politics can stifle cooperative gestures.

The Malenkov case reflects how difficult it is at times to change the ingrained mind-set of the other side. In the mid-1950s the Soviets made a number of cooperative gestures. The American Secretary of State, John Foster Dulles, believed as a matter of faith that the Soviets had very hostile intentions. When the Soviets made a concession, Dulles interpreted the action in one of two ways: (1) it was a trick to lull the United States into complacency while the Soviets prepared to attack, or (2) the Soviets made a concession because they were momentarily weak.[16] In neither case did the concession signal that the Soviets might *not* have hostile intentions.

And note this problem. If your opponent drew the conclusion that you made a concession because you *were* weak, your opponent *might act to exploit your presumed weakness*. You would then face a severe, *unnecessary*, and *self-created* challenge to your own survival. This is how Malenkov chose to interpret Dulles's responses to his offer to reach mutual agreement regarding their conflict. To Malenkov, the American leadership seemed

to regard the Soviet Union's efforts to safeguard peace among nations, its concern to lessen international tensions, as manifestations of weakness. It is precisely this preposterous assumption that explains the flagrantly unreasonable approach in certain U.S. circles to the settlement of international issues, and their policy of pressure and indiscriminate adventurism.[17]

In a cold war environment, leaders need to be very cautious about appearing weak, as that might trigger the very attack they fear.

The second reason a cold war can wax is that, even when the two states have taken some significant steps to communicate their true intentions to the other side, the normal processes of world politics intervene. Major powers, especially those with global interests or pretensions, will periodically find themselves in conflict over various issues because they see their interests in quite different lights. Consider the case of defeated Germany in 1945. The victorious allies—the Soviets, Americans, British, and French—agreed to divide the country into four occupation zones, with Berlin, wholly within the Soviet zone, divided into four sectors. The agreement gave the Western powers the right of transit across the Soviet zone to their sectors of Berlin. Disagreements soon arose between the wartime allies about the future of Germany. The Soviets wanted to keep Germany weak and under the thumb of the victors, as German military power had twice ravaged Russia in the preceding 30 years. The three western allies, on the other hand, wanted to revive Germany economically in order not to have to pay the bill to sustain Germany and to make Germans less susceptible to Communism. The three sidestepped Soviet objections by unifying their zones into one economic unit and moving toward a reconstituted German state. Stalin, to protect his interest in a weak Germany, would respond with a blockade of the isolated Western sectors of Berlin; the U.S., to promote its German policy and maintain its international standing, challenged the blockade. We look more closely at this crisis below: Our point here is that inevitable conflicts between great powers can reinforce the perception of the other as a state with very hostile intentions, thus deepening the Cold War.

The third reason that cold wars wax is that states explicitly try to integrate their weaponry into their foreign policies, whether those weapons be battleships, armored units, or nuclear weapons. They do so to remind opponents that diplomatic efforts may be followed by force, force of a most modern character. How would the possessors of nuclear weapons attempt to give their foreign policy more clout by making nuclear weapons—or the hint of nuclear weapons—a part of the diplomatic effort?

BRANDISHING NUCLEAR WEAPONS

In general, it has been the case that just having nuclear weapons has conferred a particular status on their possessor, a status that does not have to be openly articulated to work its influence. For example, when Stalin ordered the Greek communists and their Yugoslav supporters to end their insurgency in Greece in the late 1940s, he angrily told the Greeks, "What do you think, that Great Britain and the United States—the United States, the most powerful state in the world—will permit you to break their line of communication in the Mediterranean! Nonsense!"[18] The Truman administration had committed the United States to defeating the insurgency. Nuclear weapons were not a part of the commitment, but they were there in Stalin's eyes.

Prestige alone did not always carry the day, however. During the first 15 years or so of the first nuclear age, the nuclear states experimented with the explicit integration of nuclear threats into their foreign policy. This common pattern of threat-making we will call *the brandishing of nuclear weapons*. It featured displays of the weapons or the making of verbal statements that indicated that nuclear weapons might enter the picture if the state did not get its way on the issue at hand. The issue was not about the weapons themselves.

130   PART TWO The First Nuclear Age (1945–1991)

Brandishing nuclear weapons during the Cold War fell into four general patterns as described in the following sections:

1. *As a declaration of status.*   Repeated displays of nuclear hardware (or at least the delivery systems for nuclear weapons) such as the Soviets made during their annual May Day parade in Moscow were designed to reiterate the state's great power status. Nuclear testing can serve a similar purpose, especially when photos are released. Such displays constitute a demand to be treated as a major player in world politics and to have the nation's policy preferences accorded greater attention than might otherwise be the case.

2. *As an attempt to deter unwanted behavior by the opponent.*   Secretary of State Dulles' public warning in 1954 that the United States would consider "massive retaliation"—a vague term but taken by all to mean nuclear weapons—in case of further Vietnam-type insurgencies epitomized this form of brandishing. Coupling nuclear weapons to a foreign policy objective was meant to make clear that the leadership felt that the nation's vital interests were engaged and therefore the nation was resolute in its commitment to defend the status quo. Dulles's approach was called "nuclear brinksmanship": taking states to the brink of war by threatening to use nuclear weapons if the status quo were disturbed. While subsequent secretaries of state wanted to preserve the overall status quo (it was a part of American policy for much of the Cold War), none chose to wave nuclear weapons as a general warning as Dulles had.

Such brandishing to protect the status quo has occurred in specific circumstances as well. For instance, during the October (1973) War in the Middle East, the United States increased its nuclear alert status (something that the Soviets would immediately detect) to reinforce the American warning to the Soviet Union not to dispatch Soviet combat forces to the region. Indeed, displaying delivery systems of nuclear weapons such as the B-52 in non-routine ways was long a part of American foreign policy.

3. *In an attempt to compel a hostile state to do something it presumably would be unwilling to do.*   A notable example of this type of brandishing came in 1953 when the new Eisenhower administration quietly warned the Chinese that the United States would use nuclear weapons in the Korean War unless China and its North Korean ally agreed to accept the armistice terms the Americans were offering. Similarly, if Khrushchev had intended to reveal the presence of Soviet missiles in Cuba in 1962 and then demand that the West withdraw from its sectors in Berlin, he would be counting on the presence of the nuclear weapons to compel the West to rethink its posture in Berlin. (If the missiles were to be *offered in exchange* for Berlin, the display of nuclear weapons would be as a *bargaining chip*, which we discuss below.)

4. *To convey to opponents that one is personally tough-minded.*   For instance, the Kennedy administration decided in the summer of 1961 to deploy short-range nuclear missiles to Turkey in spite of advice not to, because this was a way of demonstrating toughness after the Vienna summit meeting; Kennedy feared that Khrushchev had concluded that he (Kennedy) was weak. Similarly, Khrushchev talked about using nuclear weapons against Western cities during the Berlin crisis of 1961, suggesting that he was tough enough to give the order. In July, for instance, he declared to the British ambassador that "six H-bombs would be enough to annihilate the British Isles and nine would take care of France."[19]

Historically, brandishing nuclear weapons to reinforce demands or signal resolution has been erratic in its effects. In some cases, brandishing seemed to have no effect. In Vietnam, for instance, in spite of Dulles's threat of massive retaliation, communist-led insurgency returned. In other cases, it was met with brandishing by the other side. When Khrushchev made his statement in 1961 to the British ambassador, the ambassador responded by rattling the British bombs: "You might destroy Britain, but we'll destroy your 20 major cities."[20] That would have put millions of Soviet citizens at risk. And in some cases, brandishing threatened to derail a far more important and desirable relationship. When the United States increased its nuclear alert status in October 1973 to reinforce its demand that Soviet forces not be sent to Egypt, the Soviet leadership was puzzled and angered by the American nuclear alert, for it seemed to fly in the face of American pledges to cooperate with the Soviet Union in resolving the conflict. The Soviet leadership chose to view this as a rash over-reaction on the part of President Nixon. Instead of countering with threats of their own, Leonid Brezhnev led the Soviet policy makers in the opposite direction: "What about not responding at all to the American nuclear alert?" he proposed. "Nixon is too nervous—let's cool him down."[21] Finally, the signal may provoke a very undesirable response: The Soviet Union deployment of missiles to Cuba was partially in response to the American deployment of missiles to Turkey.

Coupled with the erratic effect of brandishing nuclear weapons is the "cheapening" of the signal. If nuclear weapons are brandished repeatedly around issues that make it difficult to see *why* a nation's interests were so engaged as to warrant a nuclear threat, brandishing nuclear weapons loses its political punch. In 1956, for instance, the Soviets threatened to "rain rockets" on Britain and France to force them to end their attack on Egypt. Though it was clear that the Soviet Union very much wanted to bolster its developing relationship with Egypt, it seemed quite doubtful that it was really willing to risk Moscow and Leningrad to protect Cairo. Indeed, some commentators noted that the Soviet threat came only after the United States had declared its opposition to the Anglo-French military operation, thus condemning the operation to failure. Khrushchev's "rocket rattling" took on an aura of bluff and bluster, rather than commitment.

Brandishing nuclear weapons can also have undesirable effects on one's allies. In 1950, when President Truman incautiously told a news conference that "nuclear weapons were always under consideration" in the Korean conflict, an extremely worried Prime Minister Clement Atlee hurriedly flew to Washington to register Britain's concern. As it was, Truman was reacting defensively to a Korean situation turning sour—the Chinese had just intervened—and wanted to appear to the American public that he was considering all the options. He was not, in fact, considering nuclear weapons. That, however, was not known to the British, who feared that brandishing the weapons might bring the Soviets into the conflict, which then might escalate to Soviet attacks on Europe.

After the Khrushchev era (1954–1964), brandishing nuclear weapons became a more restrained practice, and has virtually disappeared among the major powers, but as we shall see in Chapter 7, it is alive and well between India and Pakistan and between the Democratic People's Republic of Korea (North Korea) and the United States. We expect the traditional nuclear states as well as the new ones that emerge to continue to explore its usefulness. Its most compelling drawback is that the signal may be disastrously misread by the other side—that it is *the preparation for a nuclear attack, which would give those states whose strategy emphasizes preemption the incentive to begin a nuclear war—the very last thing a signaler would want.*

NUCLEAR WEAPONS AS BARGAINING CHIPS

While nuclear weapons can be and have been used as threats, they have also become the medium by which states negotiate with each other to reach mutually satisfactory agreements. Sometimes the negotiations are with allies; nuclear weapons can be the means to cement a relationship or formal alliance. We saw in Chapter 4 how states have fashioned *extended deterrence*—a pledge to use nuclear weapons to defend an ally even at the risk of having one's cities destroyed by a nuclear opponent. In return for such a pledge, the ally is expected to coordinate its foreign policy with the protector and often forego the construction of its own nuclear arsenal.

Nuclear powers often have to go further, however, as the non-nuclear state may (rightly) question the willingness of its nuclear patron to risk its existence to defend the non-nuclear state. Nuclear powers have often had to provide access to nuclear weapons to ensure the loyalty of the non-nuclear state. That access is usually restricted, however. The U.S. government tried to reinforce the NATO alliance, for instance, by allowing its German ally to possess American nuclear weapons—weapons rendered inoperable by Permissive Action Links (PALs) until an American officer armed the weapon. Or that access might include providing the technology and materials to build nuclear weapons as the Soviet Union did for China. (States have resisted providing nuclear weapons to non-nuclear allies.) Provision of such nuclear aid usually comes with strings attached, so much so that the recipient often reacts negatively. Here is how the Chinese leader, Mao Tse-tung evaluated Soviet efforts, from its initial pledge of extended deterrence to direct aid for China's weapons program: "The Soviet Union is worried that we don't listen to them. They're afraid we might provoke the United States. But we're not afraid of getting into trouble with other countries. I will definitely develop the atom bomb. You can count on it. Nobody should try to restrict us."[22]

Nuclear weapons can also be bargaining chips in the diplomacy of hostile states. We saw at the beginning of this chapter how one American official suggested that the Soviets might be placing missiles in Cuba as a "trading ploy": the Soviets would remove the missiles in return for American concessions on the status of Berlin. In the second nuclear age, North Korea has made an art of offering to trade its budding nuclear capabilities for an end to U.S. efforts to keep the North isolated and under siege. The most prominent and sustained use of nuclear weapons as bargaining chips has come in the deliberations on arms control (which we discuss more extensively below). Not only are the weapons themselves at the heart of the negotiations, states have often deployed or threatened to deploy a particular weapons system in order to get the other side to make a concession to prevent the deployment.

In peacetime, nuclear weapons have been called upon to serve a number of purposes, and we can expect brandishing or bargaining with them to continue in the future. But we cannot overlook this basic point: The existence of nuclear weapons has not kept a state out of war with others or prevented a challenge to its interests. This holds true for the superpowers as well as others. Syria and Egypt decided to initiate war on Israel in October 1973 in spite of Israel's status as an opaque proliferator. They chose to run the risk of being struck with nuclear weapons, hoping perhaps that either Israel had no deliverable weapons, or would be constrained in using them, most likely by the United States. The Chinese chose to enter the Korean War in late 1950 in spite of the United States' clear nuclear weapons capability, its overall nuclear superiority over the Soviet Union, and its demonstrated willingness to use nuclear weapons against its enemies. For the Chinese, there seemed to be no other choice.

NUCLEAR CRISES

Brandishing nuclear weapons often seemed to exacerbate the Cold War, for it reinforced images of the opponent as having malevolent intentions. Using nuclear weapons to cement alliance relationships reinforced those images as well, as the alliance had the Soviet Union or the United States as its target. *Nuclear crises*, on the other hand, made the threat of nuclear war the central feature of the conflict between the United States and Soviet Union. These two types of threat-making lie along the continuum of threat, of course, as brandishing weapons may provoke a nuclear crisis. What separates them is that brandishing sees nuclear weapons as a means to a foreign policy end. In most cases, the state has no desire to use the weapons. *In a nuclear crisis, a state accepts that it may have to use its nuclear arsenal and the central issue is the survival of the state.*

During the late 1940s through the early 1960s, the United States and Soviet Union were on a nuclear collision course. President Kennedy estimated during the Cuban missile crisis that the likelihood of nuclear war was as high as fifty-fifty within ten years.[23] The existence of nuclear weapons probably performed one clear function: they made starkly vivid the kinds of costs that a state would pay if it engaged in war with its nuclear-armed rival. Nuclear weapons may have also forced decision makers to be more sensitive to the possibility that a crisis might escalate uncontrollably across the war threshold, and that once across, the outcome was likely to be disastrous for both sides. Thus it is likely that at some point in a waxing nuclear cold war there will be a crisis which, if passed without crossing the war threshold, will help both sides discover that they are in fact not mortal enemies. But—and it is a terrifying "but"—the de-escalation comes *after* the crisis, a crisis that, if Kennedy was right, could easily have gone in the other direction. We turn now to the two intertwined crises that decided the fate of the historic Cold War.

The near nuclear crisis over Berlin. The city of Berlin was a decades-long friction point between the United States and the Soviet Union.[24] Stalin imposed a blockade of the land and river routes from the western sectors of Germany to Berlin in June of 1948 to force an end to the Western powers' effort to restore the German state. Recall that the United States possessed a monopoly on nuclear weapons at the time. The Soviets, however, possessed an overwhelming conventional military advantage around Berlin.

Truman and his advisors concluded that nuclear weapons did not give them the ability to end the blockade.[25] If fighting did erupt—as it seemed it would if the American units tried to force their way to Berlin, the Soviets would seize all of Berlin and it would take a world war to restore the status quo. Berlin was not worth that cost, but because the Soviet Union and local communist parties seemed to be mounting a global challenge to the United States, and because 1948 was a presidential election year, the U.S. government felt that it had to respond in some way.

The key for the Truman administration—and this is true in any crisis—was to find a creative response of its own, one that would deal with the blockade on its own terms, yet not escalate the crisis across the war threshold (see Figure 5–2). That is, a state protects its interests and maintains some control over a crisis by discovering an option that lies *between* the opponent's action and the outbreak of violence. Truman decided to airlift supplies into Berlin, supplies that would sustain the allied garrisons and the citizens of the western sectors of Berlin as well. As long as the U.S. seemed willing to pay the costs of the airlift, Stalin now needed to find a creative option between the airlift and the outbreak of violence if he wished to push his point. It is here that nuclear weapons may have played a

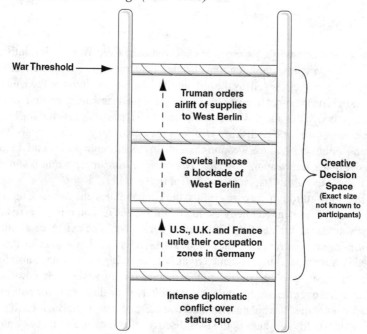

Figure 5–2 Escalation Dynamics. States attempt to ratchet up their challenge to an opponent without crossing the war threshold.

role, because to interfere with the airlift would have meant an attack on American military aircraft and personnel and thus seemingly cross the war threshold, to which the United States might respond with nuclear weapons against the Soviet Union. Seeing little "space" between the airlift and the opening of hostilities, Stalin ended the blockade in 1949.

The second Berlin crisis began in 1959 with Nikita Khrushchev's speech demanding that the United States, France, and Britain withdraw their troops from Berlin and terminate their occupation rights in the city. If the West failed to do so, the Soviets threatened to turn over control of the access routes to Berlin to the East German government. This, too, was unacceptable to the United States as it would force the United States to deal with the German Communist state which it had refused to recognize. Moreover, the East Germans, not party to any agreement about access to Berlin, could disrupt access as they saw fit. Washington expected them to do so in order to force recognition. It seemed that Khrushchev had found a creative option between the status quo that was unacceptable to the Soviets and crossing the war threshold.

The U.S. government rejected the Soviet demand, and while Khrushchev did not follow through on his initial six-month deadline, he kept alive Soviet demands and threats, trying to impress on the new U.S. President, John Kennedy, that the Soviet Union would not wait much longer, and issued nuclear threats (as we saw in his statement to the British ambassador). Kennedy reacted by mobilizing American forces and by asserting that the United States would not be driven from the city. Khrushchev reacted angrily, saying that Kennedy's statements were a preliminary declaration of war on the USSR, and he threatened to drop a 100-megaton bomb, the largest in anyone's inventory, on the United States and to destroy its European allies.

As it happened, a local event now came to drive events. As the crisis mounted, East Germans had flooded into the Western sectors of Berlin. In mid-August 1961, the East Germans began to seal off the Western sectors with a wall. The East Germans, however, did not deny Western military officials access to East Berlin nor did they interfere with access to West Berlin. U.S. tanks did face off against Soviet tanks at the Berlin checkpoints—the openings in the wall where controlled entry and exit took place. Washington grappled with the question of what would it do if the Soviets clamped a new blockade on the city.

In October 1961, the Kennedy administration finally reached agreement with itself on what it would do if a blockade occurred. Dubbed "Poodle Blanket," the U.S. prepared for four stages of escalation.[26]

> In case one response failed, we would go to the next and then the next, and so on. The first three phases involved pressures through diplomatic channels, economic embargoes, maritime harassment, and UN action, followed by or in combination with NATO mobilization and then conventional military measures, such as sending armed convoy probes down the Autobahn.... Phase four called for the escalating use of nuclear weapons.[27]

Phase four remained contentious and probably not developed. One of the plan's formulators, Paul Nitze, urged President Kennedy to consider by-passing tactical or demonstration uses of nuclear weapons in favor of a strategic strike on the Soviet Union if phase four were reached. If it were to be nuclear war, he argued, better for the United States to strike first. (Pentagon planners had estimated that a first strike on the USSR would limit U.S. casualties to 2–3 million, but as shorter-range Soviet missiles could not be immediately attacked, European casualties were likely to be in the "low tens of millions."[28]) Kennedy apparently remained non-committal—and probably quite worried.

As it happened, the Soviets chose not to escalate the issue and the crisis bumped along into 1962. The demands remained, exploratory talks could find no agreement, but the crisis did not worsen. Then came the Cuban missiles, which we discuss below. Some American policy makers saw the missiles as the next creative move by the Soviets to force the West out of Berlin: to trade Berlin for Cuba. But after Cuba, the Berlin crisis dissolved, enough so that by 1971, the United States had agreed to recognize East Germany and the status of West Berlin was accepted by all the parties.

The nuclear crisis over Cuba.   In the Berlin crises, nuclear weapons were in the background, a warning against crossing the threshold. In Cuba, they were at the heart of the crisis. In October 1962, an American spy plane detected the construction of Soviet missile sites in Cuba.[29] (See Figure 5–3.) Intelligence officers estimated that the Soviets would soon have 20–24 medium-range missiles carrying up to a 3-megaton warhead with a range of 1,200 miles ready to fire, and 4–12 intermediate-range missiles (5-megaton warheads) with a range 2,500 miles ready in two to four weeks.[30] The shorter range missiles could reach Washington, DC; the longer-range missiles, the United States east of the Rockies.

For Khrushchev and the Soviet leadership, the motivations for deployment were diverse. Some were concerned about restoring the strategic nuclear balance. In 1961, the Kennedy administration publicly announced that the balance was decidedly in the Americans' favor.[31] The trumpeting of American power seemed to foreshadow an attempt to exploit the imbalance, to blackmail the Soviet Union into acquiescing to American demands. Some Soviet leaders wanted to protect Cuba, now a Soviet ally. In 1961, Cuba had fended off a U.S.-sponsored attack by Cuban exiles at the Bay of Pigs.

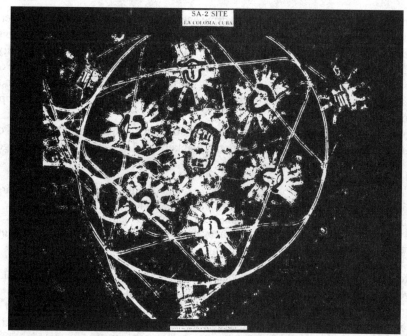

Figure 5–3 Cuban Missile Crisis.   Soviet surface-to-air missile site in Cuba. Photo-reconnais-
sance over Cuba in October 1962 discovered this characteristic pattern of SAM sites that the
Soviets built around their nuclear missile launching sites in the USSR, alerting American intelligence to the probable presence of similar nuclear missiles in Cuba.
United States Air Force

Now American forces seemed to be rehearsing invasion plans. Other officials worried about Soviet
prestige in the decolonizing Third World; it would collapse, they argued, if the Soviets failed to stand
up for Cuba. Moreover, the Chinese Communists, engaged in a bitter struggle with the Soviet Union
over the leadership of the world's communist parties, would excoriate any Soviet failure to protect
Cuba. And for some there was the festering Berlin problem.

Finally, there was intense desire—particularly felt by Khrushchev—to have the United States
treat the Soviet Union as an equal, as the superpower it aspired to be. The United States had deployed
its shorter range nuclear missiles in Italy and Turkey over the protests of the Soviet Union. Meeting
with Soviet Marshal Malinovsky in the Crimea in the spring of 1962,

> Malinovsky drew Khrushchev's attention to the installation of American missiles just over the hori-
> zon of the Black Sea in Turkey. He told Khrushchev that the American missiles in Turkey could strike
> the Soviet Union in ten minutes, whereas Soviet missiles needed twenty-five minutes to hit the
> United States. Khrushchev then mused on whether the Soviet Union shouldn't do the same thing in
> Cuba, just over the horizon from the United States. The Americans, after all, had not asked Soviet
> permission.[32]

The deployment of Soviet missiles to Cuba met the diverse interests of the Soviet elite. Soviet motives, understandable in themselves and on balance defensive in nature, were what we might expect

of a nuclear-armed state, particularly one at the short end of an asymmetrical relationship: trying to maintain a credible second-strike capability to ensure deterrence, to provide extended deterrence to an ally, and to engage tit-for-tat in missile deployment outside the home country. The motives, however, collided with American beliefs and politics.

The *covert* construction of the missile bases coincided with a major, *overt* Soviet conventional arms buildup in Cuba to show Soviet leadership of the socialist camp, to placate an anxious Fidel Castro, and to bolster deterrence against another U.S. attempt to remove Castro. These overt actions challenged the century-old American belief (symbolized by the Monroe Doctrine) that no hostile power should have any influence in the Caribbean—certainly not a Communist power. As the fall of 1962 was a congressional election year, President Kennedy found himself under intense pressure "to do something about Cuba." In particular, some Republicans alleged that there were nuclear weapons in Cuba. The President publicly and privately warned the Soviet Union that serious consequences would follow if the Soviet Union installed nuclear weapons in Cuba. Khrushchev, already having made the decision to deploy, repeatedly assured Kennedy that the Soviet Union would not deploy offensive arms in Cuba. Lacking a sensitivity to the beliefs and politics of the United States, actions reasonable from the Soviet perspective would create a fearsome crisis.

The Soviets compounded the crisis by apparently not considering what might go wrong in a complex operation to transport and erect missiles clandestinely in an area saturated by U.S. military assets. It is likely that the Soviet government assumed that the Unitd States would not learn of the missiles until the Soviet government revealed them, and the United States would then respond in ways that would promote Soviet goals (such as acquiescing in the existence of such missiles). Such fatuous assumptions are not unusual in the making of foreign policy.

The U.S. government did strive to avoid unthinking assumptions about likely Soviet responses during the crisis, but that care was off-set by a hasty rush to fashion a U.S. response. As we saw at the start of this chapter, Kennedy had asked for explanations of the Soviet behavior, but he allowed himself to be swept forward into a focus on the American response to what most of his advisors judged to be an extremely aggressive Soviet move. Thus the U.S. government deprived itself of the opportunity to consider other Soviet motivations (for example, that the Soviets were reacting defensively) or to think that this was a moment when it might be possible to work for some *mutually* acceptable understanding about security in a nuclear world. Robert McNamara, the Secretary of Defense, did broach the idea that the Soviet deployment did not change the basic facts about mutual assured destruction and that at some point, the Soviets would achieve a nuclear balance with the United States anyway, but no one wanted to work with the idea, for it suggested that the United States accept the deployment of missiles to Cuba. Moreover, the surreptitious mode of discovery (a U-2 overflight) and the estimate that the Soviets were just days from having operational sites created a sense of urgency to fashion a response, as did the congressional elections less than a month away.

The question then became a relatively narrow one: *How best to bring about the removal of the missiles?* A range of options suggested themselves: A diplomatic protest and demand for their removal, a blockade of Cuba, an air strike to destroy the missiles unilaterally, and an invasion of Cuba. On the first day of deliberations, the president and most of his advisors gravitated toward the air strike option. For Kennedy, the important question was how extensive the air strike should be (should it include, for instance, the Cuban Air Force and other military facilities?). His directive on that day was to prepare for an air strike:

I think we ought to, beginning right now, be preparing to. Because that's what we're going to do *anyway*. We're going to take out these missiles. The questions will be whether, what I would describe as number two, which would be a general air strike. That we're not ready to say, but we should be in preparation for it. The third is the general invasion. At least we're going to do number one. So it seems to me that we don't have to wait very long. We ought to be making *those* preparations.[33]

To the dismay of some of the individuals at the table, particularly the military, the president over the next several days changed his mind, partially at the urging of his brother Robert Kennedy and Secretary of Defense McNamara. They had accepted the idea that the missiles had to be removed, but they sought the creative response that would not cross the threshold into overt hostilities. The consensus reformed around a naval blockade of Soviet ships thought to be carrying additional missiles. The military were kept in line by the acknowledgment that they would be permitted to attack Cuba—most likely with more than just air strikes—if the blockade failed.

It is commonly thought that the blockade forced the Soviets to withdraw their missiles, thus ending the crisis. This is not the case. The blockade, in fact, failed. The Soviets sped up construction, rushing to bring the sites to an operational status. Khrushchev denounced the blockade as illegal and declared it unacceptable that the United States should tell Cuba and the USSR, two sovereign nations, what they could and could not do. The Soviets decided not to challenge the blockade, but for several tense days, there was the prospect of some kind of crisis at sea. An American warship attempting to board a Soviet freighter being escorted by a Soviet submarine might be the spark that pushed the two into direct hostilities.

As the crisis mounted, both sides worked behind the scenes to explore the terms for a diplomatic settlement. Such efforts ran into a serious roadblock. Kennedy was willing to pledge not to invade Cuba if the Soviets withdrew the missiles, but he balked at the Soviet demand that the U.S. withdraw its missiles from Italy and Turkey. Those missiles, Kennedy said, were tangential to the crisis, which in the U.S. view centered on unacceptable Soviet behavior in Cuba. The blockade, however, could not by itself force the withdrawal of the missiles and ending the blockade would not meet the Soviet demand for a parallel withdrawal of U.S. missiles from Turkey. A new impasse had developed.

The crisis ended because of two U.S. actions. First, the United States bluntly but privately warned the Soviets that unless there were a diplomatic settlement which secured the withdrawal of the missiles, the United States would invade Cuba within two days. Second, Kennedy agreed that while the United States could not formally agree to swap the missiles in Cuba for its missiles in Italy and Turkey, it would arrange for their withdrawal in the near future. This threat and concession brought Soviet agreement, thus ending the missile crisis.

Ironically, at the end of the crisis, the U.S. government stood poised to execute the air strike and invasion options that it had first considered, then set aside. There is every indication that Kennedy would have followed through with his threat. We can therefore say that the U.S. and USSR were two days away from some possible form of nuclear use. There was always the possibility that one of the Cold War scenarios we explored in Chapter 3 would have come to pass. Kennedy had declared that any missile launched from Cuba would bring a full retaliatory response from the United States on the Soviet Union. Who knows what the Soviet leadership might have ordered its personnel to do in Cuba—or what initiatives Soviet commanders in the field might have taken. Unbeknownst to the United States, the Soviets had also deployed tactical nuclear weapons to Cuba. While Moscow had refused to give its commanders the authority to use those weapons on their own volition during the crisis, who knows what might have happened if a U.S. invasion appeared in the offing. Imagine the shock to U.S. leaders on learning that American troops coming ashore in Cuba had been attacked with Hiroshima-sized atomic weapons, creating massive casualties. The odds of a nuclear Armageddon would have increased dramatically if there were no quickly negotiated compromise between the two nuclear powers, now engaged in combat with each other.

CRISIS LESSONS AND DETENTE

Foreign policy-makers and interested citizens are apt to draw lessons from the crises that they have passed through and, to the degree that those lessons are incorporated into the routines of governmental and military bureaucracies and are passed on the new members of society— particularly to the budding members of the political elite (you can look on this book and your reading of it as part of that process), those lessons will inform future decisions. The most powerful and long-lived crisis lesson of this century came from Adolf Hitler's challenge to the status quo in the 1930s. That lesson principally said that if one did not stop an evil leader's challenge to the status quo early enough, the world would be plunged into hell. It informed policy making during the Cold War and still shows up today, as in the George W. Bush administration's warnings about what would happen if evil leaders such as Saddam Hussein of Iraq were permitted to have weapons of mass destruction.

What lessons did the Berlin and Cuban nuclear crises teach the participants? A crucial lesson concerned the effectiveness of *nuclear compellence*: forcing a state to do something that it does not want to do under the threat of nuclear destruction. This is a form of blackmail diplomacy, itself a familiar pattern in world politics. Blackmail diplomacy was Hitler's method. He would insist, for instance, that Britain and France accept the termination of the Versailles treaty provisions limiting German armaments or, later, that they accept the loss of Czech territory to Germany, in order to avoid being thrown into another world war. The concessions Hitler demanded seemed far less costly than having to wage another world war. On the surface, then, adding nuclear weapons to the blackmail attempt would seem very attractive—here, surely, was a war to be avoided at all costs. We would expect that in the early years of nuclear relations, states will attempt to see if this is true.

Ironically, after the Berlin and Cuban crises, the answer in a nuclear age seemed to be the reverse. The power of nuclear weapons meant that while a leader might be willing to run the risk of a *conventional* war to achieve some relatively small concession (such as the annexation of part of Czechoslovakia or the end to Western control over Berlin), it seemed unlikely that a leader in a nuclear world would be willing to risk having his or her nation die as a result of an insistence on being granted that concession. That seemed to suggest *the nuclear defender of the status quo* had an advantage when it came to nuclear blackmail attempts. In addition, the defender of the status quo often has a greater capability to find the creative option lying between the action of the other state and the opening of hostilities.

But at the same time, it was clear that the United States *had* secured the withdrawal of the Soviet missiles by threatening to attack Soviet and Cuban forces in Cuba unless Moscow accepted Washingon's terms for resolving the crisis. The Soviets concluded that the United States was willing to do this because there was a *strong nuclear asymmetry* between the two states: The United States was the dominant nuclear power in 1962, at least if a nuclear war involved homeland attacks. Moreover, the Americans had been able to fend off the nuclear compellence effort to change the status of Berlin because of this asymmetry. "Never again," Soviet leaders declared, would they be forced to negotiate on such unequal terms; they redoubled their efforts to match the U.S. arsenal. The Cuban missile crisis thus accelerated the nuclear arms race.

The U.S. leadership, on the other hand, concluded that the U.S. nuclear *and conventional* strength mattered. The threat to invade Cuba was a real one because the United States had overwhelming conventional superiority in the region. The lesson was that a full-spectrum military establishment was essential, one that would be second to none.

There was another, more disturbing lesson that emerged out of the nuclear crises. In spite of strategic inferiority, the Soviet leadership, particularly Khrushchev, seemed to be willing to run extraordinarily high risks. Given how the crises played out, one might have concluded that it was all a bluff. Khrushchev appeared willing to march to the brink of war, but fully intended to back away if there seemed to be no give on the opponent's part. But would all leaders who created nuclear crises be bluffers? What if some leaders calculated the risks or costs of a nuclear exchange differently than the average person might? Might they not be more effective in a nuclear crisis? If, for instance, a leader were less than rational, he or she might be willing to accept what others might judge to be very high costs to accomplish one's goals. Richard Nixon toyed with the idea of presenting an image of being "a madman" in order to compel others to accept U.S. demands; madmen cannot be expected to make rational calculations of costs or risks. Similarly, if one appeared as reckless, willing to take big chances in the hope that one might win against the odds, one might be able to achieve nuclear compellence, forcing others to comply in order to lower the risk of disaster.

The fearsomeness of the Cuban crisis, however, led most political and bureaucratic leaders to conclude that a waxing Cold War was too great a threat. While the basic differences that separated the two states would not wash away, both had an incentive to make the world safer for themselves—to allow them to remain alive, to make deterrence work, and to promote their national interests. The crisis brought a recognition that the frightfulness of nuclear weapons was not enough to ensure a peaceful coexistence. Both had to take new steps to demonstrate one's peaceful intentions and a willingness to accept the existence of the other. Both now had a mutual interest in controlling nuclear weapons, both needed to avoid provocative actions with those weapons, and both needed to define the nuclear rules of the road that would allow them to promote their foreign policy interests without blundering close to the precipice as they had in the fall of 1962.

In the aftermath of the Cuban Missile Crisis, relations between the Soviet Union and the United States began to improve gradually, even though there were important issues dividing them, most notably the war in Vietnam. This relaxation in tensions or *detente* between the two nuclear powers would last for roughly 15 years, although by the middle of the 1970s tensions began to increase as each side accused the other of trying to take advantage of the other's restraint. In 1979, with the Soviet invasion of Afghanistan and Ronald Reagan's election to the presidency in 1980, detente chilled dramatically, so much so that in 1983 the Soviet leadership feared that the United States was on the verge of a nuclear attack. This waxing of the Cold War proved to be temporary, as Reagan and the new Soviet leader, Mikhail Gorbachev, in the middle of the 1980s began to modify their image of the opponent as intensely malevolent and hostile.

During the second half of the Cold War, both states did make progress in bringing their nuclear weapons under mutually agreeable restraints and in fashioning an understanding about how nuclear powers had to behave in order to avoid dangerous confrontations. As we shall see, both of these efforts had their genesis in the first part of the Cold War, but progress was slow as a waxing Cold War made both efforts seem foolish: a malevolent opponent would twist such efforts to suit its own purposes, perhaps even lulling its too trusting counterpart into complacency, and then into destruction by a bolt from the blue.

ARMS CONTROL IN THE FIRST NUCLEAR AGE

Arms control refers to agreements limiting the quantity or capability of weapons.[34] *Disarmament*, a form of arms control, envisions the abolition of the weapons (reducing the quantity to zero). While victors can impose a form of arms control on the vanquished (as Germany and Japan were denied the right to have a military establishment after World War II), most arms control rests on mutual agreement. That is, states must agree to be bound by a set of limitations. If a state refuses to sign such an agreement, it is not bound by the treaty's provisions. Moreover, the continued compliance with any agreement rests on the willingness of the signatories to adhere to the agreement (or on the power and willingness of some of the signatories to coerce that compliance from other signatories). Indeed, many agreements contain explicit escape clauses that legalize the renunciation of a treaty. For instance, the Nuclear Test Ban Treaty of 1963 stipulated that "each Party shall in exercising its national sovereignty have the right to withdraw from the Treaty if it decides that extraordinary events, related to the subject matter of this Treaty, have jeopardized the supreme interests of its country."[35]

The escape clause makes clear that arms control is expected to serve a nation's interests. Hence, a nation's definition of a desirable arms control agreement has usually been that which is most congenial to its position in the arms race. Typically, states have attempted to restrain the other side more than themselves. This parochial outlook on nuclear arms control has been driven by four forces: (1) Weapons makers and nuclear research laboratories have been very reluctant to have restraints put on their activities. Over time, they have developed close ties with influential members of the political elite who share their reluctance. (2) Conservative political leaders have usually been able to mobilize support for cautious approaches. The fear that others are untrustworthy and might put one's nation at risk by cheating or suddenly renouncing an agreement has created a constant pressure for insurance in the form of weapons or technologies that are not significantly constrained by an arms control agreement. (3) Arms control represents a diminution of state sovereignty. The state's ability to do what it wishes within its own borders, particularly for its own defense, is constrained. In periods of heightened nationalism, arms control can take on the appearance of an attempt by foreigners to interfere with that sovereignty. (4) Finally, the image of nuclear weapons as a war-winning weapon creates pressures to maintain them in the inventory "just in case."

Historically, nuclear arms control became a concern as the Manhattan Project entered its last stages. American leaders recognized that the American monopoly could not last indefinitely. It seemed better to seek some form of control when there was little risk to American security and when the American voice would dominate the negotiations. Interestingly, both the United States and the Soviet Union initially adopted the position that nuclear weapons should not be possessed by states at all. In June 1946, the American negotiator, Bernard Baruch, called for the destruction of nuclear weapons and the creation of an international agency to control all aspects of the peaceful development of nuclear energy from the mining of uranium to fissioning the atom.

Debate on the merits of the proposal was overshadowed by disagreement on how and when to abolish the existing U.S. weapons. Truman had told Baruch that "we should not under any circumstances throw away our gun until we are sure the rest of the world can't arm against us."[36] Until there was an effective international control agency, the United States would keep, build, and continue to test its weapons. The Soviet position reversed the sequence: The United States would destroy all of its nuclear weapons, then the nations would decide on a system of control. The Soviets, without nuclear weapons, wanted unilateral U.S. disarmament. Truman was not about to drop the gun.

The Baruch plan and the Soviet counterproposal came to naught. Neither side could find the formula to bridge the gap between the two positions. For a decade, the Soviet Union continued to demand complete and universal nuclear disarmament as the beginning point for negotiations, which ensured that the West would refuse (as it judged nuclear weapons critical in preventing a Soviet attack). Gradually, however, the Soviets began to explore with the West the possibility of reaching more limited arms control agreements. As it would happen, this step-by-step approach, coupled with the fashioning of "rules of the road" (discussed below), began to create what has come to be called *an international regime*—a common set of expectations, often reflected in treaties and agreements and in general patterns of behavior, that many states have about how states (including themselves) should behave.

In general, the emerging nuclear regime emphasized these expectations:

1. Nuclear weapons are undesirable and states should make an effort to at least control them if not to divest themselves of such weapons.

2. States should act to prevent the spread of nuclear weapons.

3. Nuclear-armed states should avoid making sudden challenges to the status quo.

4. Nuclear threats are unacceptable.

As the United States and the Soviet Union were the first and dominant nuclear powers during the first nuclear age, the arms control measures were often crafted by these two states, at times acting alone (for example, to limit the numbers of weapons each had in its arsenal), and at other times in concert with other states, both nuclear and non-nuclear (as in the Non-Proliferation Treaty). But in general, the negotiated aspect of nuclear relations depended upon the ability of the two superpowers to cooperate with each other. In turn, arms control agreements usually led to a period of more amicable relations between two, as general adherence to the agreements helped lessen the concern that the other had deadly intentions. At the same time, because every agreement was only a partial control on nuclear weapons and because negotiations had to finesse many technical details with ambiguous language, states would suspect that the behavior of others was, if not out-right cheating, then at least contrary to the spirit of the agreements. Arms control thus has encouraged a dialogue, contentious at times, that has helped clarify expectations. And it has provided a standard by which the international community could, to some degree, be mobilized against those states that chose to act outside of the expectations. But it has also led to mutual suspicions.

The broadest type of arms control consisted of *multilateral agreements* among a number of states. Two central treaties are the *Partial Test Ban Treaty* of 1963 and the *Non-Proliferation Treaty* of 1968. By 1963 atmospheric testing of nuclear devices had significantly increased the level of radioactive fallout around the world, making for a global political issue. The United States, the Soviet Union, and ultimately more than 120 other states signed the Partial Test-Ban Treaty which prohibited testing in the atmosphere, in outer space, and under water. The agreement did reduce atmospheric radioactivity in spite of the fact that some states such as China were not signatories and would test their weapons above ground. The treaty, however, allowed the arms race to go on underground.

The test ban was partial for two central reasons. First, no nuclear nation wanted to forgo all opportunities to test nuclear weapons. Progress toward lighter warheads was deemed important (and would be necessary if MIRVed systems were to be developed). Second, there were limitations on verification.[37] States are usually reluctant to agree to constraints on themselves unless they can be sure that others are, in fact, abiding by the same constraints—especially when it was feared that cheating regarding nuclear weapons might give the other side a critical advantage, thus tempting it to launch a devastating surprise attack. Both the United States and the Soviet Union could monitor atmospheric and underwater detonations because increased radiation would be detectable in the world's atmosphere. Underground testing, however, could not be detected reliably with the technology then available unless on-site inspections were permitted. The United States and the Soviet Union could not reach agreement on how that might be done. As verification capabilities increased (particularly through reconnaissance satellites), states felt more secure in establishing constraints on nuclear weapons, but the willingness to agree to a *comprehensive* test ban treaty proved elusive for decades. In Chapter 7 we examine its fate in the second nuclear age.

The Non-Proliferation Treaty (the NPT) emerged out of a recognition by the initial members of the nuclear club that their safety would be enhanced if there were no further additions to the club. They might, of course, unilaterally attempt to keep others from joining. As we saw in Chapter 3, the Americans and Soviets contemplated attacking the Chinese nuclear production facilities, and Israel did destroy Iraq's nuclear reactor in 1981. Less costly would be a negotiated agreement whereby the signatories would pledge not to acquire nuclear weapons, but non-nuclear states would demand compensation for giving up their sovereign right to have what others had. The NPT took this form: The non-nuclear signatories agreed not to receive nuclear weapons from others or manufacture nuclear weapons themselves, and accepted a form of monitoring by the International Atomic Energy Agency (IAEA) to prevent diversion of nuclear fuel from electrical energy generating nuclear plants to a nuclear weapons program. As compensation, they were to be given access to nuclear technology for peaceful purposes, principally energy production and basic research. Those with nuclear weapons agreed not to transfer such weapons to another state or to provide assistance in manufacturing such weapons. The states with nuclear weapons also agreed to negotiate in good faith to produce nuclear disarmament for themselves. Thus, the NPT pointed to a goal of a denuclearized world.

The NPT has proved to be the most widely accepted nuclear arms control agreement, ultimately getting more than 170 adherents. The initial holdouts were generally the states that had long been suspected of having a nuclear weapons program (as we saw in Chapter 3): Argentina, Brazil, Chile (a rival of Argentina and Brazil, but with no known program), Cuba, India, Israel, and Pakistan. Or they were states that had nuclear weapons and were involved in supplying the technology to produce such weapons to others (China, which became a signatory in 1992); or that made a practice of demonstrating independence from the two superpowers (France, also a 1992 signatory). Some states accepted the treaty, but with reservations. Germany, for instance, conditioned its adherence to non-proliferation upon NATO's ensuring its security.

Between NPT's entry into force in 1970 and a conference in 1995 to review the treaty and decide on making it permanent, there have been a number of disquieting events. First, the existing nuclear weapons states showed no interest in achieving nuclear disarmament. Second, proliferation by several signatories of the NPT seemed likely. Iraq, which had signed the treaty in 1969 and reached an agreement with the International Atomic Energy Agency to prevent diversion of nuclear fuels, had clearly gone ahead with a clandestine nuclear weapons program, only to be discovered and stopped in 1991. Iran, a 1970 signatory with similar IAEA safeguards, seemed to some to be pursuing a nuclear weapons program. And North Korea, a 1985 signatory with IAEA safeguards, ventured into the area of reprocessing plutonium, which would give it nuclear weapons capability, and publicly warned that it might be forced to develop such weapons. How those policies played out is covered in Chapter 7.

Many non-nuclear states wanted the NPT to include a declaration that the nuclear powers would not use nuclear weapons, particularly against them. The Soviet Union had unilaterally made a pledge that it would not be the first to use nuclear weapons—but it had a history of making nuclear threats against others. The United States and its NATO allies had rejected a "no first use" pledge. Their plans called for a first use of nuclear weapons to defend against a Soviet offensive into Europe. The United States had made nuclear threats against China. American opposition kept a no-first-use pledge out of the NPT.[38] But the political liabilities of such a posture were great enough to force the United States and Britain to provide NPT signatories with a "negative security assurance" that they would not use or threaten to use nuclear weapons against the non-nuclear states unless those states attacked the United States or Britain, their military forces, or their allies.

A narrower but still very important form of arms control has been *bilateral agreements*. While the principal participants have been the United States and the Soviet Union (and its successor, Russia), the early atomic age saw a promising step taken by Britain and the United States. In July 1943 President Roosevelt and Prime Minister Churchill agreed that the two states "will never use this agency [a nuclear weapon] against each other ...[and] we will not use it against third parties without each other's consent."[39] Four years later, the United States and Britain agreed to give up the veto power each had over the other's use of the weapon. In practice, each remained solicitous about the other's views regarding nuclear use, but neither was interested in constraining its ability to use nuclear weapons.

The United States and the Soviet Union, in spite of the Cold War, were able to take a series of steps to reach mutual controls on their nuclear weapons. The principal results have been SALT and START.[40] A Strategic Arms Limitation Treaty (SALT I) was first signed in 1972, with a follow-up (SALT II) in 1979. The United States judged that it had enough nuclear weapons to make deterrence work (hence building more made no sense economically, especially with the defense budget strained by the Vietnam war). By the early 1970s, the Soviet Union had successfully overcome the strategic inferiority that it had lived with since the start of the first nuclear age. Indeed, with the United States not building more missiles, the Soviet Union was forging ahead. SALT I capped the number of strategic missiles that both sides could have: 1710 ICBMs and SLBMs for the United States, 2358 for the Soviet Union. In a separate agreement, both sides agreed to limit the deployment of an anti-ballistic missile system to two sites (the ABM treaty).

Because such agreements have to be negotiated *within* the government as much as with the rival, they will have significant weaknesses as methods of control. In SALT I, for instance, President Nixon accepted fewer ICBMs and SLBMs than the Soviets would have as the price to get the Soviet Union to stop building. Such numerical inferiority would have been opposed by the American Air Force and Navy had it not been for the fact that SALT I purposefully left the number of nuclear *warheads* unconstrained. With multiple independent re-entry vehicle (MIRV) technology about to come on line, Nixon could argue that restrictions on the number of missile launchers did not really matter if more than one warhead could be put on each missile (and a good proportion of the missile force was in invulnerable submarines).

MIRV helped sell SALT I in the United States, but created a whole new problem for arms control. First, how destabilizing was a growing number of warheads? No one knew, but as we saw in Chapter 4, a plethora of accurate warheads created images of a first-strike capability (and possibly the temptation to launch such a strike). Second, how does one verify the number of warheads in a sealed nosecone of a missile? Verification was possible for SALT I because spy satellites watched the construction of missile bases in both countries and the construction of submarines capable of carrying SLBMs. Thus caps on the number of missiles could be effectively verified. What would it take to verify MIRVed systems?

SALT II increased the coverage of the treaty. Strategic bombers were now included, but the ceiling for all strategic delivery systems was increased to 2,400 for both sides (with a symbolic reduction to take place in three years to 2,250). A maximum of 1,320 systems could be MIRVed. Intelligence could determine which particular systems were *tested* in a MIRVed configuration and that became the "counting rule": if tested as a MIRVed system, all such deployments would be counted as MIRVed. Still missing, however, was a limit on the number of warheads that would be permitted in a MIRVed missile; the temptation would be to put more on each missile.

SALT II was concluded at the point when the Cold War began to wax again. President Carter did not dare submit it to the Senate for ratification, but both sides pledged to adhere to the agreement—a posture that both nations kept even during the Reagan reorientation of nuclear doctrine and foreign policy. Thus at the bilateral level as well, the nuclear regime which favored control over nuclear weapons continued. At the same time, creating arms control agreements had helped energize a growing network of individuals and organizations within various nations who would make arms control their life's work.

START (Strategic Arms Reduction Treaty), as the name implies, sought to reduce the number of strategic warheads, and to get rid of weapons systems that seemed dangerous because they had all the characteristics of first-strike weapons.[41] The Reagan administration, for instance, initially proposed that START set ceilings of a total of 850 ICBMs and SLBMs with no more than 5,000 warheads, of which only 2,500 could be on ICBMs. ICBM accuracy made them first-strike weapons. The Soviets had invested heavily in their ICBM force, which made it, in American eyes, dangerous. The Soviets rejected the American proposal as one-sided; with three-quarters of their warheads on ICBMs (6,000 in all), the Soviets would have to make radical changes in their force structure to meet the new ceilings, while the U.S. triad could much more easily accommodate the changes. Reagan's announcement of the effort to create a ballistic missile defense ("Star Wars") created even greater animosity. Not only would it challenge the ABM treaty, but American technology might be the first to produce such a system, making a U.S. first strike possible. An initial American surprise attack would destroy much of the Soviet ICBM force, allowing the Star Wars defense to defeat a ragged Soviet retaliatory strike. Then the Soviet Union would be forced to capitulate to avoid having its cities incinerated by the remaining American nuclear force.

By the end of the 1980s, however, both Reagan and Soviet leader Mikhail Gorbachev had come to accept the idea of a long-term goal of de-nuclearization, with a shorter-term goal of significant reductions in strategic delivery systems to 1,600 systems with 6,000 warheads. The American insistence on development of Star Wars led to an impasse with START, but in December 1987 both sides agreed to eliminate over three years all land-based missiles with ranges between 300 and 3,400 miles (the Intermediate-Range Nuclear Forces agreement). As we shall see in Chapter 7, the second nuclear age brought significant change to the bilateral approach to arms control.

In addition to multilateral or bilateral agreements, a state can pursue a variety of *unilateral tactics* to discourage proliferation or control the nuclear weapons of others by initiating actions in which its nuclear arsenal is not involved. In some cases, the action is *coercive*, as in the Israeli air attack against the Iraqi nuclear reactor in 1981. A far more common tactic is to threaten economic sanctions if a state undertakes a nuclear weapons program. American legislation for instance, mandates such sanctions, such as the cutting off foreign aid, but such sanctions have had a checkered history. In 1979 the Carter administration placed economic sanctions on Pakistan in the face of evidence that it was attempting to build a bomb. The Reagan administration reversed the decision when it needed Pakistan as the staging area for aid to the Afghan rebels fighting the Russians in Afghanistan. Both administrations chose to ignore clear evidence of the Pakistani program and extensive Chinese aid, and both certified, as American law required, that Pakistan was not building nuclear weapons.

Another form of unilateral action was the declaration of a moratorium on some nuclear activity, particularly nuclear testing, as long as other states exercised a similar restraint. Such moratoria were often declared *at the end* of an extensive set of nuclear tests and smacked of propaganda rather than an exercise in self-restraint or as an encouragement of reciprocal actions by the other side. More positively, states have terminated aspects of nuclear programs on their own. We saw in Chapter 4, for instance, that the United States unilaterally froze the number of missiles in its inventory when it reached a particular level. Moreover, the smaller nuclear powers (Britain, France, China, and Israel) have kept a relatively limited nuclear establishment without creating agreements with others to do so.

NUCLEAR RULES OF THE ROAD

Arms control begins with the fact that nuclear weapons exist, and asks, How can we manage these weapons? States have also tackled a broader question: How might we *reshape international politics to reduce the likelihood of nuclear use and, ultimately, reduce the attractiveness of nuclear weapons*? States have narrowly responded to this broader question by devising *nuclear rules of the road* that would reduce the likelihood of a confrontation between nuclear-armed states. They have also attempted a much more expansive answer: to devise *general rules of the road* to ensure the security of all states and to accommodate their national interests without warfare and massive military establishments.

As the most powerful state in the closing days of World War II, the United States attempted to create a set of general rules, rules that it felt were both appropriate and accepted by the other states in the coalition that was completing the destruction of German and Japanese military power. The American vision, enshrined in the United Nations Charter, set this basic rule: Aggression is forbidden. War could only be waged in self-defense. Members of the UN and non-members alike were to "refrain in their international relations from the threat or use of force against the territorial integrity or political independence of any state," and were, instead, to "settle their international disputes by peaceful means in such a manner that international peace and security, and justice, are not endangered."[42]

This basic rule challenged the traditional practices of world politics, as waging war was a right traditionally accorded to sovereign, independent states. It would be wrong to suggest that American power and persuasiveness were alone responsible for the fact that this rule won general acceptance in the international community. The carnage of two world wars, the threat of nuclear weapons, the organization of the world into two powerful blocs and a loose coalition of unaligned but weak states, and the fact of American power all worked together to create an environment that persuaded or coerced states to adjust their interests to fit the "no aggression" rule. When a state challenged the rule, as North Korea did in 1950 when it invaded South Korea and Iraq did in 1990, it found an international community generally united against it, and powerful states (led by the United States) willing to pay the price to enforce the rule.

The case of Iraq in 1990 is instructive.[43] From the perspective of the Iraqi leadership, the war against Kuwait was appropriate. Iraq had a long historic claim to Kuwait, which had detached itself from the Ottoman empire under the protection of the British navy at the end of the Eighteenth Century. In 1990, the Iraqi government faced an economic crisis that threatened to undermine the regime. It was attempting to rebuild a society devastated by eight years of debilitating war with Iran. The Kuwaitis had loaned Iraq the funds to wage war, but insisted on being repaid. Iraq wanted the loan forgiven, arguing that the war it fought alone against Iran also protected the Kuwaiti regime from the Islamic revolutionaries in Teheran. Additionally, Iraq depended upon oil sales to rebuild its society, but found that the Kuwaitis were flooding the oil markets in contravention of their agreed-upon oil quota, thus driving oil prices—and Iraqi revenues—downward. One need not enter the ambitions of Saddam Hussein into this mix to understand why the conquest of Kuwait might appeal to—and seem appropriate to—any Iraqi government. But such actions challenged the fundamental rule, and while there was no guarantee that the United Nations (or the United States) would come to the rescue, the probability was high that they would. If this rule held, non-nuclear states would presumably be less driven to acquire nuclear weapons and the chances of nuclear use would be near zero.

Historically, no major power challenged the no aggression rule, and it has passed into the second nuclear age as one of the basic rules of the road. (Chapter 7 assesses whether American actions against rogue states have begun to undermine the rule.) The basic rule of "no aggression" was insufficient, however, to address a fundamental crisis of the second half of the twentieth century—the struggles by peoples in the colonized world to liberate themselves from their European overlords. Some liberation efforts spiraled into war, with both insurgents and colonial overlords or their appointed successors seeking outside aid to defeat their opponents. Given Cold War perceptions, U.S. leaders began to see such decolonization conflicts as instances where the Soviet Union and the People's Republic of China used local proxies to wage indirect aggression to expand their "empires." To the United States and European powers, if Vietnamese communists, for instance, abetted by the Russians or Chinese, were able to seize the French colony of Indo-China, was this not the same as if Chinese forces crossed the border? The latter would be a naked act of aggression, and prohibited by the Charter. Even in more traditional violent political struggles against the government (as in the insurgency against the Greek government in the late 1940s), if communists were involved, the U.S. government saw the conflict as another attempt to evade the no aggression role, for it believed that communists coming to power would be subject to direction from Moscow. The two major post-1945 wars the United States fought (Korea and Vietnam) were predicated on the assumption that attempts by Korean and Vietnamese communists to re-unite their countries were acts of aggression forbidden by the UN Charter.

In the U.S. view, there needed to be a new rule that prohibited such "indirect aggression." The U.S. government fashioned one. One of its earliest expressions came to be called the Truman Doctrine. Truman declared to Congress:

One of the primary objectives of the foreign policy of the United States is the creation of conditions in which we and other nations will be able to work out a way of life free from coercion. ...I believe that it must be the policy of the United States to support free peoples who are resisting attempted subjugation by armed minorities or by outside pressure... . The world is not static, and the status quo is not sacred. But we cannot allow changes in the status quo in violation of the Charter of the United Nations by such methods as subversion, or by such subterfuges as political infiltration.[44]

A good part of the historical Cold War can be read as the attempt by the United States to impose this new rule on others. For the United States, internal change had to come essentially through peaceful means and reflect the will of the majority.[45] Others would find the rule unacceptable. As long as the Soviet Union or China was willing to render support to those who opposed the rule, the United States would find itself challenged by major opponents and always in risk of a collision with the nuclear superpower.

Moreover, as Soviet and Chinese power grew, weaker states that had cast off their British or French colonial overlords (often peacefully, it should be noted) came to see the USSR and China as needed counterweights to the United States or its French or British allies. Having such a counterweight also made it possible for weaker states to consider challenging the basic rule of no aggression embodied in the UN Charter. Egypt, for instance, found a Soviet connection useful to ward off British threats and to serve as a cover for threatening Israel. The United States, often linked to the local opponent (in this case, Israel), now found that a local conflict might drag the Soviet Union or China and the United States into the confrontation, creating the threat of a nuclear war at the superpower level. Hence there was a need for an additional set of rules to oversee this part of international relations as well, for a superpower collision arising from local rivalries seemed quite likely.

The near collision in Cuba along with the crises in Vietnam and the Middle East during the 1960s encouraged both the United States and Soviet Union (and in time the United States and People's Republic of China) to see if they could reach a mutually acceptable set of rules of the road for at least their bilateral relations. By 1972, the United States and Soviet Union had agreed on the "Basic Principles of Relations," signed by Richard Nixon and Leonid Brezhnev at the SALT summit in Moscow. The new rules adopted the Soviet formulation of "peaceful coexistence" that Malenkov and Khrushchev had promoted nearly 20 years earlier. Relations were to be based on "the principles of sovereignty, equality, non-interference in internal affairs, and mutual advantage." Furthermore, both sides pledged to "exercise restraint in their mutual relations, and will be prepared to negotiate and settle differences by peaceful means." They acknowledged "that efforts to obtain unilateral advantage at the expense of the other, directly or indirectly, are inconsistent with these objectives." They pledged to "avoid military confrontations" and "to do everything in their power so that conflicts or situations will not arise which would serve to increase international tension."[46]

Now it is the case that both sides soon thereafter concluded that the other was not adhering to this agreement, and as the Cold War waxed once again in the late 1970s, the agreement was set aside, *but it was not renounced*. Indeed, both sides accepted the rules but viewed the other as transgressing them while seeing its own actions as generally conforming to the rules. Most alleged violations occurred in the Third World. It was different in Europe, the place where a most deadly conflict might occur between the two heavily armed alliance systems. Both sides were able to begin and sustain a dialogue about security in Europe, including extensive talks to reduce their military forces in Europe and the to create "confidence-building measures" that would allay fears of a surprise attack. They agreed to create a Conference on Security and Cooperation in Europe which met periodically to reach agreements on the avoidance of provocative actions in that region (as well as to deal with such issues as human rights). At the Helsinki conference in 1975, for instance, NATO and the Soviet bloc states agreed to give 21-day voluntary advance notice of military maneuvers along frontiers if more than 25,000 troops were involved. This would prevent the other side from panicking when it suddenly observed large scale military movements. While the Reagan administration initially chose to see such agreements as foolish, believing that the Soviet Union could never be trusted to adhere to such rules, it did not deny that rules could be important for safeguarding the future.

OTHER MECHANISMS FOR CONTROLLING RELATIONS BETWEEN NUCLEAR-ARMED STATES

During the Cold War, other institutions and regimes emerged that, while not directly concerned with creating rules of the road for nuclear-armed states, did offer possibilities for reducing the likelihood of clashes between nuclear powers or between nuclear-armed and conventionally armed states. The United Nations, for instance, was a standing organization with worked-out mechanisms for dealing with the threat of war. The Charter gave the Security Council (composed of the five major nuclear weapons states as permanent members and other elected members—currently ten) the power to consider any threat to world peace and to authorize a response by the organization. The organization did have a modestly successful track record in dealing with the conventional forms of aggression that were outlawed by the Charter. It was occasionally able to intervene with modest success in internal conflicts that threatened to pull in outside powers. It was less willing or able to deal with what the United States claimed to be "unconventional" aggression (such as the communist insurgency in South Vietnam) but which many members of the United Nations saw as wars of liberation or unification.

Regional political organizations such as the Organization of African Unity or ASEAN (the Association of Southeast Asian Nations) also attempted to create mechanisms similar to those of the United Nations whereby nations in conflict can communicate and non-involved members of the organization can bring collective pressure to bear on the parties in conflict. Such organizations, again, had modest but important successes to point to. In addition, some regional military alliances created institutionalized forums for the coordination of security policies that served multiple purposes. NATO, for example, was designed to deter aggression by the Soviet Union, but also to control German power (a concern for the states that had been attacked by Germany in World War II) and to bind the United States tightly to Europe, to make its power committed to the defense and prosperity of Western Europe.[47] The existence of NATO helped maintain the no-aggression rule, but at a cost. The Soviet Union saw NATO as a means to wage aggressive war against it, or as a means to compel the Soviet Union and its allies to act in certain ways to avoid war.

Other formats have emerged over time to allow some form of consultation among political leaders. The wartime conferences between Roosevelt, Churchill, and Stalin became part of the process of post-war world politics. The tensions of the Cold War initially ended such conferences between the now rival nations, but the same tensions impelled the leadership to go to the "summit"—the first being held in Geneva, Switzerland in 1955. Summit conferences became a standard practice among the rivals since that time.[48] Even when rules were not on the agenda, summit meetings could help establish common perspectives and expectations, or failing that, to more clearly delineate the points at issue. Moreover, summits became a means of validating the status of the states. This function was quite important for the Soviet Union, for it meant that the United States in particular accepted the Soviet Union as a great power, and that implied that the latter's interests would be given due consideration.

To the degree that summits were places where confirmation of status and the validity of others' interests occurred, they could function as substitutes for explicit rule-making. To the degree that they raised unmet expectations, or they misled leaders about the interests and commitments of their opposites, summits posed some risk. The summit conference between Adolf Hitler and British Prime Minister Chamberlain in 1938 at Munich became synonymous with disastrous appeasement, and the Vienna summit between Kennedy and Khrushchev in 1961 led the former to think that he had not appeared tough enough, and the latter to assume that he could press harder. The Cuban missile crisis probably played itself out the way it did in part because of the "lessons" of the 1961 summit conference. Other summits, particularly during the Nixon administration, enhanced the effective management of nuclear weapons.

CONCLUSIONS

Our recent experience with arms control, the creation of rules of the road, and the shaping of international institutions such as the United Nations and practices such as summit conferences came about in a cold war environment. One might think that such an environment would be the worst circumstance in which to learn the basics of managing a nuclear world, for a cold war is based on the assumption that an opponent intends deadly harm—now with the most deadly of weapons. And yet the planet survived. Should we conclude that the nuclear predicament is less severe than we might have assumed, that humans and their governments do have the capacity to cope effectively with such weapons—with a few scares thrown in to remind us of the seriousness of our task? If so, the second nuclear age in which we now live should be a piece of cake.

We are not so sanguine. Perhaps our survival turned on the accident of who the two rivals were. The historic Cold War involved two states with no long history of bitter, conflictual relations (say, on the par of France and Germany). Indeed, both had just emerged from a very costly war in which they were allies. That past made it possible for the United States and the Soviet Union to discern, however dimly, that correct if not amicable relations were possible. Moreover, there was no event during the Cold War that made revenge the order of the day (as France's defeat in 1871 and Germany's in 1918 did). The Cuban missile crisis ended with a mutual compromise: no missiles in Cuba but a communist regime still in power. And both states had a political culture that was future-looking and predicted success for itself, as long as war could be avoided. Thus while there were pressures for a cold war to turn hot, there were historical features of *this* particular Cold War that encouraged its waning. Will the second nuclear age have similar saving graces?

The history we present here shows that the possession of nuclear weapons did not prevent nuclear rivals from taking provocative behavior toward each other; brandishing nuclear weapons became rather commonplace in the early years. Nor did the possession of nuclear weapons keep their possessors from waging debilitating conventional wars (the United States in Korea and Vietnam, the Soviet Union in Afghanistan). Indeed, in these instances, the possession of nuclear weapons failed to cow the "weaker" party into submission. On the other hand, having a nuclear arsenal probably encouraged a more ambitious Soviet foreign policy—or, at least, it encouraged the Soviets to think that the United States would accord them equal privileges as a world power. Some of the key conflicts in the Cold War were in good measure struggles to claim the rights of being a world power, the Cuban Missile Crisis being the most salient.

The possession of nuclear weapons in sufficient number did make one fact clear: *The possessor of deliverable nuclear weapons could not be forced to surrender like Japan at a cost its opponents would be willing to pay.* Thus, while nuclear weapons could not guarantee the achievement of foreign policy goals to change or protect the status quo, they could come close to ensuring the survival of their possessor—as long as nuclear weapons were not used. This is one profound aspect of the nuclear predicament: Nuclear weapons offered a kind of security undreamed of by the leaders of nations in earlier times, but only so long as nuclear weapons were not used. Security was simultaneously more available and more at risk.

In the long run, then, if nuclear weapons cannot be used in war and cannot with consistency produce foreign policy success, and if in the very attempt to make them part of foreign policy creates crises that imperil the society, and if nuclear weapons essentially make the rival unconquerable yet too dangerous to ignore, nuclear-armed states will be impelled to seek some form of understanding with the other—to manage the nuclear relationship with each other. And that in turn will necessitate negotiations. One logical place to negotiate is about the weapons themselves, thus making the weapons an almost inevitable avenue of contact and discussion. Another is to address the basic issue of how nuclear-armed states are to behave toward each other to minimize a potential conflict—which is a normal attribute of world politics—from escalating across the war threshold and, at the worst, across the nuclear threshold. Negotiations on these two matters helped impel the trajectory of the relations in a cold war first toward detente, and then toward the discovery that neither side wanted war, thus ending the reasons for a cold war.

In sum, over time in a nuclear relationship, there will be a constant pressure to move toward policies that accommodate the other side. Accommodation is likely because one cannot manage conflict successfully by insisting that one's own side always wins while the other side always loses. Bargaining with the other side to manage conflict means accepting, to one degree or another, *the other's definition of its security and its national interests.* The historic Cold War eroded rapidly during the last four years of the Reagan administration as both sides reached the point of accepting the idea that they needed to provide mutual security to each other.

But it was a very precarious security indeed, *one that demanded constant attention to the management of the relations between nuclear armed states.* Instead of allowing a state to isolate itself behind its wall of nuclear weapons, the possession of nuclear weapons forced nuclear rivals to be in perpetual contact with each other.

The early 1990s produced a revolution in world politics with the demise of the Soviet Union, which we turn to in the next two chapters. Its basic features are well known: the end of the Cold War and of the ever-present risk of nuclear war between the United States and Soviet Union. The Cold War had created a context for states to develop their military and foreign policy strategies. That context would now be absent. Would nuclear-armed states behave differently? If we conclude that, on balance, humans were adequate to the task in the first 40 years of a nuclear world, should we hope that they can do as well in the next 40?

ENDNOTES

[1]Transcript of White House meeting, October 16, 1962, 11:50 a.m.–12:57 p.m.. We have edited the transcript slightly, to remove interjections and the like that broke into conversations. The ellipses that appear are the original pauses of the speaker. Human speech is most definitely not like a movie script! The published version (which has edited the transcript even more) can be found in *The Kennedy Tapes: Inside the White House during the Cuban Missile Crisis*, eds. Ernest R. May and Philip D. Zelikow, (Cambridge: Belknap Press, 1997), pp. 99–100.

[2]Bruce W. Nelan, "Nuclear Disarray," *Time,* May 19, 1997, p. 46.

[3]John Lewis Gaddis, *The Long Peace* (New York: Oxford University Press, 1987); John Mueller, *Retreat from Doomsday: The Obsolescence of Major War* (New York: Basic Books, 1989).

[4]For several challenging hypotheses, see John Lewis Gaddis, *The United States and the End of the Cold War* (New York: Oxford University Press, 1992), pp. 106–118; and John Lewis Gaddis, *We Now Know: Rethinking Cold War History* (New York: Oxford University Press, 1997).

[5]Memo by George Ball, October 1965; quoted in Deborah Shapley, *Promise and Power: The Life and Times of Robert McNamara* (Boston: Little, Brown, 1993), p. 312.

[6]Lyndon Baines Johnson, *The Vantage Point* (New York: Holt, Rinehart, and Winston, 1971), pp. 147-48.

[7]Nikita Khrushchev, *Khrushchev Remembers*, translated and edited by Strobe Talbott (Boston: Little, Brown, 1970), p. 518.

[8]For recent studies of the Cold War, John Lewis Gaddis, *The Cold War: A New History* (New York: Penguin, 2005); Michael L. Dockrill, *The Cold War, 1945-1991* (New York: Palgrave Macmillan, 2006); David Miller, *The Cold War: A Military History* (London: John Murray, 1998); Ronald Powaski, *The Cold War* (New York: Oxford University Press, 1998); and Melvyn Leffler and David Painter (eds.), *Origins of the Cold War*, (New York: Routledge, 2005). A classic older study is Walter LeFeber, *America, Russia, and the Cold War, 1945-1992*, 7th ed. (New York: Mc-Graw-Hill, 1993).

[9]The Japanese-American relationship from 1931 to 1941 was another recent cold war, with this one ending in hot war as the Japanese decided that the American oil embargoes constituted a declaration of war, prompting them to open actual hostilities with a surprise attack on the American fleet at Pearl Harbor.

[10]This is not to say that with a correct appreciation there would be no conflicts between the two. States can be in conflict, and often are over many issues. The key question is whether each believes that other has truly injurious intentions and will wage war against it to secure those goals. Nor is this to deny that, from time to time, states will seek to destroy other states (Hitler's goal vis a vis the Soviet Union) or to shatter their power (Hitler's goal vis a vis France) by waging war. Nor, finally, is it to argue that goals are constant. At some point leaders may conclude that they now are ready to wage war to advance their goals. But a cold war is, first and foremost, a product of mistaken assumptions that another intends to wage war.

[11]Kennan telegram of February 22, 1946; *Foreign Relations of the United States 1946, Vol. VI* (Washington, DC: U.S. Government Printing Office, 1969), p. 699.

[12]Khrushchev, *Khrushchev Remembers*, pp. 223–224.

[13]Harry S. Truman, *Memoirs, Vol. 2, Years of Trial and Hope* (Garden City, NY: Doubleday, 1956), p. 215.

[14]Truman, *Memoirs, Vol. 2*, p. 214.

[15]Malenkov speech of March 15, 1953; *Documents on International Affairs 1953* (London: Oxford University Press, 1956), pp. 12–13.

[16]Ole Holsti, "Cognitive Dynamics and Images of the Enemy: Dulles and Russia," in D. Finlay, O. Holsti, and R. Fagen, *Enemies in Politics* (Chicago: Rand McNally, 1967), pp. 25–96.

[17]Malenkov speech of August 8, 1953; *Documents 1953*, p. 29.

[18]Meeting with East European leaders, February 1948, quoted by Milovan Djilas, *Conversations with Stalin* (New York: Harcourt, Brace and World, 1962), p. 182.

[19]Seminar transcript appearing in John P. S. Gearson, "British Policy and the Berlin Wall Crisis, 1958–61," *Contemporary Record* Vol. 6 (Summer 1992), p. 172.

[20]Gearson, "British Policy," p. 172.

[21]Victor L. Israelyan, *Inside the Kremlin during the Yom Kippur War* (University Park, PA: Pennsylvania State University Press, 1995), pp. 182–83. Ironically, Nixon did not order the alert; Henry Kissinger had while the President slept!

[22]Quoted in Li Zhisui, *The Private Life of Chairman Mao* (New York: Random House, 1994), pp. 206–207.

[23]Quoted by Arthur M. Schlesinger, Jr., *A Thousand Days* (Boston, MA: Houghton Mifflin, 1965), p. 802.

[24]For the first Berlin crisis, see Avi Shlaim, T*he United States and the Berlin Blockade, 1948-1949* (Berkeley, CA: University of California, 1983), Jean Smith, *The Defense of Berlin* (Baltimore, MD: Johns Hopkins, 1963) and Lucius Clay, *Decision in Germany* (Garden City, NY: Doubleday, 1950); for the second, see Vladislav Zubok and Constantine Pleshakov, *Inside the Kremlin's Cold War* (Cambridge, MA: Harvard, 1996) and Michael Beschloss, *The Crisis Years: Kennedy and Khrushchev* (New York: HarperCollins, 1991).

[25]Truman did approve the sending of a squadron of B-29s to Britain as an open reminder to the Soviets of the American nuclear monopoly and to make it clear that the United States would not be driven from Berlin. These B-29s, however, had not been configured to drop the bomb, nor were their crews trained to do so (although it is not clear whether Soviet intelligence was able to make this discrimination).

[26]See Fred Kaplan, "JFK's First-Strike Plan," *The Atlantic Monthly* (October 2001), pp. 81-86. It was during this crisis that Kennedy discovered the all-or-nothing nature of the existing SIOP and the military's orientation toward a first strike.

[27]Paul Nitze, *From Hiroshima to Glastnost: At the Center of Decision* (New York: Grove Weidenfeld, 1989), pp. 203–204.

[28]Gearson, "British Policy," p. 125.

[29]On the missile crisis, see, among others, Graham Allison and Philip Zelikow, *The Essence of Decision*, 2nd ed. (New York: Longman, 1999); James G. Blight and David Welch, *On the Brink: Americans and Soviets Reexamine the Cuban Missile Crisis*, 2nd ed. (New York: Noonday, 1990); Aleksandr Fursenko and Timothy Naftali, *"One Hell of a Gamble": Khrushchev, Castro, and Kennedy, 1958–1964* (New York: Norton, 1997); Roger Hilsman, *The Cuban Missile Crisis* (Westport, CT: Praeger, 1996); Mark J. White, *The Cuban Missile Crisis* (London: Macmillan, 1996).

[30]Top secret memorandum of 27 October, 1962 reported in Raymond Garthoff, *Reflections on the Cuban Missile Crisis*, Rev. ed. (Washington, DC: The Brookings Institution, 1989), pp. 202–203.

[31]At the time of the crisis, the US estimated that the Soviets had 60–75 ICBMs, no submarine launched missiles deployed along American shores, and 155 bombers capable of reaching the United States, but not deployed in significant numbers to do so. The US had 172 ICBMs, 112 SLBMs, and 1450 strategic bombers. In fact, the Soviets had only 25–45 ICBMs. In either case, the strategic balance was drastically in the Americans' favor. Garthoff, *Reflections*, pp. 206–208.

[32]Garhoff, *Reflections*, p. 12.

[33]Meeting of Tuesday, October 16, 11:50 am; *The Kennedy Tapes*, pp. 71-72.

[34]For general works and assessments see Bruce Russett and Fred Chernoff, *Arms Control and the Arms Race* (San Francisco: Freeman, 1985); Duncan Clarke, *Politics of Arms Control* (New York: Free Press, 1979); Bruce D. Berkowitz, *Calculated Risks: A Century of Arms Control, Why It Has Failed, and How It Can Be Made to Work* (New York: Simon & Schuster, 1987); and Patrick Glynn, *Closing Pandora's Box: Arms Races, Arms Control, and History of the Cold War* (New York: Basic Books, 1992). For treaty texts, see Jozef Goldblat, A*rms Control: The New Guide to Negotiations and Agreements* (Thousand Oaks, CA: SAGE, 2002) and Thomas Graham and Damien J. LaVera (eds.), *Cornerstones of Security: Arms Control Treaties in the Nuclear Era* (Seattle, WA: University of Washington Press, 2003).

[35]*United States Treaties and Other International Agreements*, Vol. 14 part 2, 1963 (Washington, D.C.: U. S. Government Printing Office, 1964), p. 1319.

[36]Harry Truman, *Memoirs Vol. 2*, p. 25.

[37]For verification, see John G. Tower, James Brown, and William K. Cheek (eds.), *Verification: The Key to Arms Control in the 1990s* (Washington, DC: Brassey's, 1992), Francesco Calogero, Marvin Goldberger, and Sergei P. Kapitza (eds.), *Verification: Monitoring Disarmament* (Boulder, CO: Westview, 1991); and Nancy W. Gallagher, *The Politics of Verification* (Baltimore, MD: Johns Hopkins University Press, 1999).

[38]Joseph Gallacher, "Article VII, The Treaty of Tlatelolco and Colonial Warfare in the 20th Century," *Arms Control*, Vol. 5 (No. 3, 1984), p. 75–76.

[39]Quebec Agreement, quoted in McGeorge Bundy, *Danger and Survival* (New York: Random House, 1988), p. 110.

[40]For SALT, see John Newhouse, *Cold Dawn: The Story of SALT* (Washington, DC: Pergamon-Brassey's, 1991), John Barton, *The Politics of Peace* (Stanford, CA: Stanford University Press, 1981), and Michael Krepon, *Strategic Stalemate* (New York: St. Martin's, 1984). For START, see Michael Mazaar, *START and the Future of Deterrence* (New York: St. Martin's, 1991), Kerry M. Kartchner, *Negotiating START* (New Brunswick, NJ: Transaction Books, 1992).

[41]One of the best sources for tracking arms control agreements and implementation are the yearbooks of the Stockholm International Peace Research Institute (SIPRI), *SIPRI Yearbook*, (Oxford, England: Oxford University Press). We have drawn on Shannon Kile and Eric Arnett, "Nuclear Arms Control," *SIPRI Yearbook 1996*, (Oxford, England: Oxford University Press, 1996), pp. 611–655.

[42]United Nations Charter, Chapter 1, Article 2, sections 4, 3. United Nations, *Yearbook of the United Nations 1995*, Vol. 49 (The Hague: Martinus Nijhoff, 1995), p. 1525.

[43]This assessment draws on Lawrence Freedman and Efraim Karsh, *The Gulf Conflict 1990-1991* (Princeton, NJ: Princeton University Press, 1993).

[44]Harry Truman, Special Message to the Congress on Greece and Turkey, March 12, 1947; *Public Papers of the Presidents: Harry Truman 1947* (Washington, D.C.: United States Government Printing Office, 1963), pp. 176–177.

[45]This is not to say that the United States accepted its own rule when it proved bothersome. In Cuba, for instance, Castro came to power in a popular revolution (ironically, supported by a number of American officials) and probably had the support of a majority of Cubans for years. Yet within two years of his accession to power, the United States was planning to wage a war of indirect aggression against his regime. Rule-makers often initially want to be able to drive anywhere they choose, while insisting that others keep to one side. In Chile, a Marxist, Salavador Allende, came to power in free elections; the Nixon administration could not accept the outcome and sought ways to topple him.

[46]Agreement of May 29, 1972; *Public Papers of the Presidents: Richard Nixon 1972*, p. 633.

[47]For NATO see Nicholas Henderson, *The Birth of NATO* (Boulder, CO: Westview, 1983); Lawrence S. Kaplan, *NATO and the United States*, updated ed. (New York: Twayne, 1994); Mark Smith, *NATO Enlargement during the Cold War* (New York: Palgrave, 2000); and Andrew M. Johnston, *Hegemony and Culture in the Origins of NATO Nuclear First Use* (New York: Palgrave Macmillan, 2005).

[48]For a review, see David H. Dunn (ed.) *Diplomacy at the Highest Level: The Evolution of International Summitry* (New York: St. Martin's, 1996).

6

Nuclear Strategy in an Age of Complexity

Imagine that you are the president of the United States. You have just called a meeting of your principal national security advisors to review options for dealing with Iran's apparent steps toward producing nuclear weapons. Moderated by the National Security Advisor, the meeting might go something like this:[1]

Director of Central Intelligence:
As we're all aware, for the past several months, Iran has refused to permit inspections by the International Atomic Energy Agency (IAEA) of some of its nuclear facilities. Iran has repeated its assertion that it is committed to the peaceful uses of nuclear energy, but that frequent IAEA inspections are just a cloak for CIA intelligence operations. If, as we suspect, Iran is enriching uranium to bomb grade levels in those facilities, it will in a relatively short period of time have enough to create one, possibly two nuclear weapons. They can easily put together a simple gun-type nuclear weapon—similar to the bomb we dropped on Hiroshima. That bomb didn't need testing because our people were certain it would work.[2] Therefore, we must assume that in two to three years, Iran could have a small yet sufficient number of nuclear weapons. Their dispersal would mean that we could not be sure any pre-emptive strike on our part would get them all. Even worse, we will have no way to know when Iran has produced its first nuclear weapons, or how many they have, let alone where they are stored. Time is not on our side.

Secretary of Defense:
An additional unknown is Iran's intentions towards Iraq. With a 1,000 mile common border with Iraq and considerable influence in Iraq's Shiite community, the largest in Iraq, Iran has the potential to make a hell of a lot of trouble for us in Iraq. Up till now, Iran has not given substantial aid or encouragement to a Shiite insurgency so the U.S. has had less resistance in Shiite-dominated regions. This could change if the U.S. were to move aggressively against Iran, forcing us to increase U.S. forces in Iraq.

Secretary of State:
A further complication is Israel, which has long said it could not tolerate a nuclear-armed hostile state within easy striking distance of Israel. Israel demonstrated in its raid on Iraq's nuclear reactor at Osirak in 1981[3] that it is willing to launch preemptive or even preventive strikes against perceived threats. Repeated statements by Iran's president challenging Israel's right to exist–remember, he quoted Ayatollah Komeini that Israel "must be wiped out off the map"[4]—has heightened Israel's fears.

National Security Advisor:
Wouldn't that be a plus for us? The Israelis do the dirty work; the Iranians direct their anger there rather than toward us and Iraq.

Secretary of State:
No, any action taken by Israel would have repercussions for us. Even if the U.S. had not approved the strike in advance, Arab states would assume that the strike had at least tacit U.S. support, given our long tradition of supporting the state of Israel. Besides, the raid would require overflight over other Middle East countries, including Iraq; permission would be difficult to obtain and violation of these countries' airspace by Israel would strain diplomatic relations with Israel's neighbors. We'd have to work like the devil to keep the Middle East stable, especially with Hamas controlling the Palestinian government.

You:
Well, could Israel take out those facilities militarily, or do we have to do it? General, what's CENTCOM's thinking?

Commander of Central Command:
As you know, CENTCOM is responsible for U.S. military forces and operations in the Middle East, so CENTCOM staff has given considerable study to Iran.

First, regarding Israel's potential for solving the U.S. dilemma, Central Command staff questions whether Israel in fact has the capability to launch a strike of this scale over this distance. Their earlier operations were much closer to Israel—the strike against the Osirak reactor in Iraq was less than half the distance, and the strike was against only one target, not nuclear facilities spread across a country four times as large as Iraq.

Now as to what we can do, Central Command staff has studied the following three alternatives for the use of U.S. military force. I direct your attention to the following PowerPoint slides.

OUR FIRST OPTION: A punitive strike against Iranian Republication Guards. This could be easily accomplished. The locations of Republican Guards units are readily determined and stealth aircraft, B-2 bombers based in the U.S. and cruise missiles would make the strikes, all in one night. These strikes would not, however, directly impact Iran's nuclear programs, but might force Iran to comply with our demands to avoid further loss.

OUR SECOND OPTION: A pre-emptive air strike against Iranian nuclear facilities. If 300 aim points were selected in Iran—that's roughly strikes against 125 nuclear facilities and the remainder would be strikes against command control and air defense sites—we'd need about five nights to complete the strikes, beginning with attacks on Iranian air defense capability. If we wait too long though, Central Command could not guarantee the destruction of every nuclear, bacteriological, or chemical weapon in Iran, and Iran would likely retaliate against our allies in the region with whatever weapons they have left.

OUR THIRD OPTION: Imposed regime change in Iran. Staff proposes a main-force assault across the border from Iraq, supported by a deception attack from the south, with airborne and special forces attacks from Afghanistan and cruise missile attacks from sea. As we did in Iraq, we would slice through the Iranian armed forces, capture the capital, Tehran, and topple the political and religious leadership. Air attacks would do most of the work against the nuclear facilities. Ground forces would do local reconnaissance of those facilities if necessary.

National Security Advisor:
What about stabilization operations after an invasion?

CENTCOM Commander:
We're not proposing that. Just in and out in 30 days. We destroy the nuclear facilities, smash up the bad guys, and let the Iranians sort things out.

If we're going to do Option Three, we need to begin the preparations now.

National Security Advisor:
So we just let Iran dissolve into chaos? That's not regime change, it's a recipe for anarchy—and that means we get a new breeding ground for terrorists.

Secretary of Defense:
Look, we've got hard choices to make. With current commitments in Iraq, we can't seriously hope to field a large force in Iran for any length of time, and our allies aren't going to put their forces in the line of fire either. But CENTCOM's plan gives the democratic forces in Iran a decent chance to come to power, and we make sure Iran has no nuclear program. We have to focus on that.

Secretary of State:
Won't Iran observe our buildup and know what's coming?

CENTCOM Commander:
No, Ma'am. We'll rotate troops into Iraq as we have been doing, but keep the troops in Iraq scheduled for redeployment stateside an additional 30 days. The rotation going in will need to be larger than usual, however.

National Security Advisor:
I don't see how we can keep this secret. We were able to do the Iraq buildup relatively publicly because everyone read this as a campaign to turn up the pressure on Iraq to permit the weapons inspectors to return. Now a buildup is going to set off alarm bells everywhere. Our allies will go ballistic, and Iran will mobilize support like Saddam never could. And there will be hell to pay if Iran starts playing the oil card and the Arabs call for a oil boycott against us.

Secretary of State:
The sad truth is that, at bottom, our allies and friends aren't likely to use force to deal with what everybody says will be a real danger for us all—Iran with the bomb. They're going to press the Iranians to live up to their pledges not to enrich uranium to bomb grade levels, but if anyone's going to do something, it's us or the Israelis.

Now, having heard all these arguments, what would you, as president of the United States do? You have heard the director of Central Intelligence say that he cannot promise you any firm intelligence if or when Iran actually begins producing nuclear weapons, or how many weapons, or where the weapons might be located. You have heard both the secretary of state and your military advisers tell you that you cannot rely on Israel to solve this dilemma for you. You have heard the military officer responsible for the forces that would actually be doing the fighting say that CENTCOM could bring the Iranian regime down in 30 days, but the United States lacks sufficient forces to ensure a stable government arises in its place. The general has given you three options to consider.

What do you chose to do? Is doing nothing a real option, or are there others that your advisors have not mentioned? Is force necessary at this moment? Do you, as president, have a responsibility to prepare for the worst case—that Iran will make as many nuclear weapons as quickly as it can, and it will use those as a cloak behind which to threaten vital American interests? And what if someone urges you to consider the use of nuclear weapons to ensure the destruction of the Iranian sites?

We have provided this scenario to suggest the complexity of the nuclear predicament in the second nuclear age and the awesome nature of the decisions the United States faces. During the Cold War, the United States also faced daunting challenges as well, for America's opponent had the capability to obliterate the United States. Today, the American president does not have to make decisions of that magnitude, but he or she has been and will continue to be confronted by states that pose some nuclear threat to the United States, or threaten to become nuclear weapons states. The use of force in such circumstances has become a live option, and in Iraq, it was the choice of the U.S. government. How did it come to this? What strategies are available to the U.S. government to deal with nuclear weapons and nuclear states in an age that seems to be remarkably distinct from its predecessor?

THE END OF THE FIRST NUCLEAR AGE

In Chapter 4, we examined how warfare in the twentieth century led the nations of the world to regard the civilian population of an enemy as legitimate a military target as the enemy's armed forces. We saw that nuclear weapons fit squarely within this tradition. Initial war-waging plans called for the obliteration of the enemy's society. Gradually, as the Soviet nuclear arsenal and delivery capability came to match that of the United States, both countries recognized that nuclear war meant nuclear disaster. Nuclear war could serve no meaningful purpose. Mutual assured destruction seemed to assure that both nations would survive. And then the unthinkable happened. The Soviet Union collapsed, pushing all the world's inhabitants into the second nuclear age. The old questions were back. How could the nuclear peace be maintained? Could nuclear weapons be used to advance the interests of a nation—or of a less-than-nation actor? Could states find their way anew, resolving the inevitable conflicts between them without encouraging the proliferation of nuclear weapons?

For all the promise that the second nuclear age began with, it quickly proved to be an age with its own complexities. In this chapter, we explore part of the American response, its military policy, and in the following chapter, its foreign policy response. The two salient events that define the current strategic environment are first, the sudden and unexpected collapse of the Soviet Union in 1991, which led to an accelerating reduction in the U.S. military establishment—a reduction in the size and nature of the U.S. strategic arsenal greater and more rapid than anyone could have realistically wished for during the height of the Cold War. The second was the attack on the World Trade Center in New York City on September 11, 2001, that profoundly changed the way the United States looked at the terrorist threat to the American homeland.

We provide more detail about the collapse of the Soviet Union in Chapter 7. The salient facts are these: The Soviet Communist party permitted reform movements to emerge in Eastern Europe in the late 1980s and encouraged an internal debate about how to transform a society suffering from economic and political stagnation. Political organizations challenged the party's monopoly on power, and the Soviet leadership accepted the idea that the party had to compete in elections for the right to rule—elections that they would lose. The spirit of freedom permitted long-suppressed local nationalism to manifest itself, so much so by 1991 that the Soviet Union broke up into 16 independent states. The new Russian state maintained control of the nuclear establishment, but as it had democratized and shed its command economy, Russia no longer appeared as a threat to the West. American nuclear strategy and a good part of its conventional war strategy now had no threatening opponent. The Cold War and its strategies and nightmare scenarios passed quietly into the history books.

The old Soviet military establishment, particularly its nuclear components, remained more or less cohesive and responsive to the top military command, dominated as it was by ethnic Russians and responsive to the new Russian state. This fact helped manage the transition to a new age. After protracted negotiations (aided by support from the United States), all Soviet nuclear weapons outside Russia were either returned to Russian territory or destroyed, a triumph for arms control virtually without precedent. Ukraine, Belarus, and Kazakhstan's willingness to divest themselves of nuclear weapons suggested that states might be willing to give up their nuclear weapons, in part because of rewards for doing so and in part because the costs of maintaining a nuclear arsenal can outweigh the benefits of having a nuclear arsenal.[5] It was a hopeful sign.

During the Cold War, some analysts had questioned the ability of the Soviet Union to sustain a military effort of the scale they had since World War II. The economic historian Paul Kennedy had asserted in 1987, for instance, that the Soviet Union simply lacked the resource base to maintain a global military presence.[6] The fundamental premise of the U.S. strategy of containment, beginning with the Truman Doctrine and NSC-68, was that all the non-communist world had to do was to contain the spread of communism, discourage Soviet adventurism, and avoid direct confrontation. Historical processes of moderation, along with the chronic demands on a nation's economy from an extensive military establishment, would eventually transform a revolutionary Soviet state into a far more traditional state. The strategy appeared to have worked. The U.S. Department of Defense noted with satisfaction:

> In the space of 25 months [November 1989 through December 1991], without a shot fired in anger, America's military security environment had been turned inside out. Gone was the 45 year threat of a massive Soviet/Warsaw Pact blitzkrieg across the divided Europe. Gone were the Soviet nuclear missiles stationed in Europe. Pledged to be gone were the nuclear arsenals inherited from the former Soviet Union by Ukraine, Belarus and Kazakhstan. In short, having been robbed of its only significant military competitor, at the end of 1991 the U.S. stood alone with the world's most powerful military force but without an adversary worthy of the name.[7]

The U.S. response to this revolutionary transformation of the Soviet bloc was interesting. In the decade before the collapse, Ronald Reagan had gone from the ideological Cold Warrior (pointing to an evil empire with which no one could or really should do business) to a president interested in reaching agreements with the Soviets. The first President Bush, also a long-time Cold Warrior, displayed caution in response to the collapse of Soviet/communist power, treating Russia with respect. President Clinton expended considerable effort to maintain the viability of Russia as a political and economic unit, including substantial American financial aid. In a sense, the United States passed a critical test of a nuclear relationship: *To help bring about political change equal to the consequence of war but without war and do so without a climactic nuclear confrontation.* Since then, the United

States has taken great pains to safeguard the existence of its long-time opponent—an opponent, one must note, that retained its nuclear weapons.

We saw in Chapter 5 how both states crafted arms control agreements that began to reduce their strategic arsenals, and that process has continued into the second nuclear age. We turn now to the composition of the U.S. nuclear arsenals. The old questions remained: How much is enough? Can we afford it?

THE CHANGING NUCLEAR ARSENALS

The collapse of the Soviet Union as an adversary accelerated a process of reducing the nuclear weapons in the arsenals of the United States and Russia that had begun under START and now continues under the Strategic Offensive Reductions Treaty (SORT). Russian progress in reducing strategic warheads since the dissolution of the Soviet Union has been substantial (see Table 6–1) although progress has been slower in the United States build down.

The negotiated reductions in warheads in the decade after the demise of the Soviet Union paralleled a reduction in U.S expenditures for defense.

> In 1985, America appropriated about $400 billion for the Department of Defense (in constant, fiscal year 1997 dollars), which constituted 28 percent of our national budget and 7 percent of our Gross National Product. We had more than 2.2 million men and women under arms, with about 500,000 overseas, 1.1 million in the Reserve forces, and 1.1 million civilians in the employment of the Department of Defense. Defense companies employed 3.7 million more and about $120 billion of our budget went to procurement contracts...

> Since 1985, America has responded to the vast global changes by reducing its defense budget by some 38 percent, its force structure by 33 percent, and its procurement programs by 63 percent. Today [1997], the budget of the Department of Defense is $250 billion, 15 percent of our national budget, and an estimated 3.2 percent of our Gross National Product.[8]

We might imagine that with a change in the world and the draw-down of U.S. forces, U.S. military strategies would adjust. Indeed, one might hope that strategic thinking would drive budget requests and allocations, creating a military establishment with the weapons and strategies (as well as the necessary training and support) that would meet the foreseeable threats to U.S. interests abroad. The U.S. government did try to create a mechanism for such a process by mandating the Quadrennial Defense Review (or QDR), a lengthy document produced every four years.[9] Each QDR report, 1997, 2001, and 2006, reveals the temper of its time, reflecting the national concerns at that moment in time and showing how the United States wishes to present itself to the world. At the same time, they are all intensely political documents, reflecting the particular administration's view of the domestic political environment and their view of the world, and behind both of these, the administration's ideology.

It is political in another sense as well. It is a document created in a competitive arena, where the military services and the secretary of defense and the secretary's office advance their particular perspectives on the world and the mix of strategy, forces, and hardware to best cope with the world seen in that light. As budgets are always limited (and during the first decade of the second nuclear age, decreasing), the perspectives reflect a mixture of service or organizational interests as well a more common understanding of what the military needs to prepare for. Given the vested interests within the

TABLE 6–1   WORLD'S CURRENT NUCLEAR ARSENALS

United States:	
Operational warheads:	
Strategic forces:	
Bombers:	1,050
ICBMs:	1,050
SLBMs:	2,106
Total strategic warheads:	4,116
Non-Strategic forces:	680
Total operational warheads:	4,796
Spare operational warheads:	315
Reserve warheads:	>5,100
Total warheads:	About 10,350
Russia:	
Strategic offensive forces:	
Bombers:	872
ICBMs:	2,436
SLBMs:	672
Total strategic offensive forces:	3,980
Strategic defensive forces:	1,100
Non-Strategic forces:	2,180
Total deployed warheads:	7,360
Reserve warheads or awaiting dismantling:	8,800
Total warheads:	About 16,000
China:	
Operational warheads:	
Strategic forces:	182
Non-strategic forces:	120
Total operational warheads:	More than 400
France: operational warheads:	348
Israel: warheads:	Up to about 200
United Kingdom: warheads:	About 185
Pakistan: warheads:	30–50
India: warheads:	30–40

Source: *SIPRI Yearbook 2005: Armaments, Disarmament and International Security*. (Stockholm International Peace Research Institute) Oxford: Oxford University Press, 2004 p. 636–637

services, the Congress, and the defense contractors that we discussed in Chapter 4, it should not come as a surprise that the budget allocations continued to give each service roughly one third, as it had for much of the Cold War period.

Chapter 4 also argued that such strategic formulations as the QDR are *instruments of declared national policy*, statements that are intended to give the world clear notice of what the United States will do in the event of attacks on the U.S. homeland, on U.S. forces abroad, on U.S. allies and friends, and on U.S. vital interests around the world. From the public portions of the QDR (most of which is classified), along with the public portions of the *Nuclear Posture Review*—a periodic public policy document setting out the country's policies for the U.S. nuclear arsenal—we gain a general view of the evolving American strategy in the second nuclear age.

In light of the reductions in its budget, the U.S. defense establishment reexamined the role of strategic nuclear weapons and the number and mix of weapons, their mode of deployment, and their command, control, and custody. On September 18, 1994, President Clinton approved *1993 The Nuclear Posture Review* which reaffirmed the U.S. commitment to the Triad and set the following as a goal for the nuclear arsenal:

> 14 Trident submarines, each missile armed with 24 D-5 missiles each with 5 warheads for a total of 1,680 SLBM warheads
>
> 450–500 Minuteman III ICBMs with single warheads
>
> 20 B–2 bombers with gravity bombs and 66 B–52 bombers carrying air-launched cruise missiles

The plan was to reduce U.S. strategic warheads by 59 percent and nonstrategic warheads by 90 percent. No nuclear weapons were to be in the custody of U.S. ground forces; nuclear warheads were no longer deployed on surface ships; and a number of development programs were terminated (for example the rail garrison scheme which would shuttle ICBMs around the countryside on rail lines).

The United States took further steps to reinforce Russian confidence in America's nuclear posture (and save money) by taking U.S. strategic bombers off day-to-day alert. The computer targeting systems for ICBMs and SLBMs would no longer be loaded with the coordinates of Russian sites (although given improvements in dynamic retargeting capability in recent years, this may have been more cosmetic than substantive). And the Navy worked to remove the ability of submarine commanders to launch SLBMs on their own volition by equipping the SLBMs with Permissive Action Links that disable a weapon permanently if use is attempted without the proper authorization code[10] and by equipping each submarine with special safes containing a vital launch key that cannot be opened unless and until a combination unlocking code is received from a higher authority.[11]

RETHINKING THE MISSION

At the same time, there was a hope that the Quadrennial Defense Review would occasion a comprehensive review of the doctrine and force structures of the armed services, building on various self-studies the military had made since the end of the Cold War. These self-studies did not recommend significant changes in the force structure of the services. Instead they produced "simply an agreement to all downsize in lock step, maintaining the basic division of the defense budget agreed to at the Key West conference in 1948."[12] Once again, as we noted in Chapter 4 where we examined the creation of the U.S. nuclear arsenal, the bureaucratic imperative—the need to protect individual service turf and service leaders' careers—took precedence over the nation's needs. As one commentator noted, "Since the end of the Cold War, there has been much activity on defense policy, but little change—other than reduction—in American military capabilities."[13]

For almost 50 years, the U.S. military had a single clear purpose: deter Soviet aggression. Each service, of course, defined the *national* priority in terms of its own specialty. The Air Force saw the nation's first priority as deterring the Soviet Union's use of nuclear weapons by maintaining a credible threat to destroy Soviet society in retaliation; this led the Air Force to develop its strategic nuclear forces, first exclusively bomber but later missile, at the expense of all other roles such as tactical ground support for the Army or long-range transport. The Navy saw a dual role for itself: It supported nuclear deterrence by maintaining a very secure retaliatory capacity while at the same time maintaining its traditional priority of command of the sea to ensure the ability to reinforce and supply U.S. forces and allies by sea and to project force around the periphery of the Soviet empire.

The Army's main priority was, in some ways, the simplest: to defend the Fulda Gap in Germany. This was the only practicable invasion route for the Soviet Army into western Europe. If the Army's power (along with NATO's contribution) were clear enough, the Soviet Union would be deterred from starting World War III. To meet this threat, the Army recreated the army of heavy armored and mechanized infantry divisions that had defeated the German Army in WWII, all well equipped with tanks and heavy artillery, with troops carried into battle in armored tracked carriers. To the old would be added the new: helicopter gun ships and tactical and theater nuclear weapons. But the armored vehicles, particularly the tank (such as the M-1 Abrams) and the self-propelled artillery (such as the 155-mm artillery firing 10 rounds per minute), defined the Army and its mission.

The end of the Soviet threat challenged the principal mission of each of the services, and all the planning, hardware, and doctrine that each had carefully crafted. But the post-Cold War provided new challenges that the nation's political leadership felt necessary to respond to, from attempting to restore order in civil war-torn countries ranging from Somalia in eastern Africa to Bosnia in southeastern Europe, to prevent genocide in Rwanda and Kosovo, to liberating Kuwait from Iraqi aggression.

Political leaders and the public were divided on the wisdom of military intervention during the 1990s, and that division played itself out in indecisiveness, in a slowness to respond (particularly in Rwanda and Bosnia), and in "mission creep"—the tendency for incremental decisions to expand the assignments given the military, thereby slowly pushing the United States into untenable positions, unless it chose a dramatic escalation. Somalia came to symbolize the problem. The result was often a poorly planned and poorly supported military mission that would take casualties for what seemed to be little purpose. The political leadership would quickly cut-and-run, leaving many to conclude that intervention was probably the worst course of action. To intervene and then leave precipitously would be the very thing most likely to encourage adventurism by the United States' adversaries.

The one bright spot in the first decade was the American-led military operation to drive Saddam Hussein's forces from Kuwait, which he had invaded in August of 1990. The attack, which included British, French, and Arab forces, proved to be overwhelming, quickly liberating Kuwait and putting Iraqi forces in peril of destruction. The first Bush administration decided against doing so, leaving the regime to survive another day. The war, however, seemed to validate the Army's ingrained belief that tanks and mechanized infantry in large numbers (600,000 were deployed) would carry the day, while the Navy and Air Force concluded that aerial bombardment and cruise missile strikes had secured these services' traditional missions far into the future. The end of the Cold War did not threaten the military's position—nor its way of doing things.

A NEW NUCLEAR DOCTRINE

After the first *Quadrennial Defense Review (QDR)* was presented to President Clinton in May, 1997, the president issued a Presidential Decision Directive in November, providing a new approach to American strategic policy, the first change in presidential guidance for nuclear weapons employment since 1981. In Secretary of Defense Cohen's words,

> Nuclear weapons play a smaller role in the U.S. security posture today than they have at any point during the second half of the 20th century, but … nuclear weapons are still needed as a hedge against an uncertain future, as a guarantee of U.S. security commitments to allies, and as a disincentive to those who would contemplate developing or otherwise acquiring their own nuclear weapons. Accordingly, the United States will maintain survivable strategic nuclear forces of sufficient size and diversity to deter any hostile foreign leadership with access to nuclear weapons.[14]

This "hedge against an uncertain future" contained some familiar elements. The United States would continue to rely on deterrence: the United States would have the capability to deny any attacker success as its society would be destroyed. The United States would maintain a wide range of retaliatory options to ensure that "the United States is not left with an all-or-nothing response." The United States would not maintain a hair-trigger retaliatory threat (one where the United States would launch its missiles the minute it received a warning that an enemy strike had been launched, as too many instances of erroneous warnings had occurred), but the United States reserved the right to launch its missiles before an adversary's nuclear weapons arrived. It remained to be seen if thinking about conventional weapons and military strategy would begin to change as well.

THE SHOCK OF 9/11

The attack on the World Trade Center's twin towers and the Pentagon on a bright September morning changed Americans' view of the world, as profoundly—and as unalterably—as had any event since the Japanese attack on Pearl Harbor 60 years earlier.

What died with those two events, in addition to the Americans killed, was America's innocence—the notion that the United States could wrap itself in its two oceans and ignore with impunity what was happening in the rest of the world. Pearl Harbor ended dramatically the American conceit that its oceans gave it immunity from the affairs of other nations and 9/11 ended the illusion that it was immune from other political currents surging in the world. Most Americans felt that both attacks were completely unprovoked and that both came with no warning. Most Americans believed that both attackers had acted entirely outside the rules that govern the conduct of civilized people in civilized states, even though both attackers later claimed that they had given the United States ample warning that if the nation persisted in its course of action, there would be consequences.

Against Japan, the United States waged a war of great violence, aimed at the subjugation of the Japanese people and the imposition of a political system the United States felt would keep the peace. Following the 9/11 attack, the United States invaded two independent nations, Afghanistan and Iraq, overthrowing their governments. The United States sought to create new governments that by their nature would be friendly to the United States and unlikely to seek nuclear weapons or harbor groups that did.

The 9/11 attacks molded a new American foreign policy and military policy. It forced consideration of a new dimension of world politics, one in which nuclear weapons played a significant role. The 9/11 attack was a calculated act of terrorism: "premeditated, politically motivated violence perpetrated against innocents" in the words of *The National Security Strategy of the United States of America*.[15] That violence came from unknown individuals (at least to the public at large), pursuing ends that seemed unknowable or at best irrational. (The attack on Pearl Harbor, on the other hand, was an act of war directed against the United States' armed forces, a legitimate target had the Japanese first declared war on the United States. The Japanese were very visibly engaged in a war of conquest in China, a familiar but regrettable aspect of world politics.) After 9/11, Americans were now forced to look on the world as a potentially hostile, mysterious place where no American was safe, regardless of where they were—in Kabul or New York City—and regardless of their personal role—as a member of the armed forces or a bond clerk at work at her desk in the World Trade Center.

For the past 50 years, the United States had relied on its nuclear weapons as its guarantee of safety, secure in the knowledge that any enemy who dared launch an attack of the U.S. homeland would meet with overwhelming retaliation that would destroy the attacker as a viable state. However, against an attacker with no homeland to put at risk, its nuclear weapons are of no use: A terrorist organization with no clearly traceable state sponsorship cannot be deterred by the threat of retaliation. In fact, stateless actors are entirely outside the usual international methods of control or constraint.

How would American military policy and American nuclear weapons fit into the new world? How might military force be used to safeguard American interests and help recreate a clear and comfortable view of the world?

THE MILITARY RESPONSE TO 9/11

We saw in Chapter 4 that the weapons and military forces that exist at any point in time constrain the choices available to any president contemplating the use of force, either as a part of a nation's foreign policy or in waging war. The 9/11 attacks amply illustrated that truism. The 9/11 attackers were quickly linked to al Qaeda, that had been waging a pinprick war against Saudi Arabia and increasingly against the United States. The American response had been to increase security measures, particularly at U.S. embassies and consulates, and to launch periodic cruise missile strikes at al Qaeda training camps in Afghanistan and against the al Qaeda leadership. Now the George W. Bush administration declared a War on Terror and sought to strike at the al Qaeda network in Afghanistan. The Administration demanded that the Taliban government of Afghanistan expel al Qaeda from the country. The Taliban leadership, itself dominant among the warring groups in Afghanistan still struggling to control that fractured state, had close ties with al Qaeda and shared its vision of the ideal Islamic state. It rejected American demands, which led to American operations in Afghanistan in support of the war lords still opposing the Taliban. The operations essentially consisted of CIA operatives, small detachments of Special Forces units, aerial attack, and sophisticated surveillance and reconnaissance, later supplemented by U.S. ground units. Ironically, Special Forces had its origins in the Cold War when its mission was to catalyze dissension among the Soviet Union's less-than-willing Warsaw Pact allies.

Backed by the United States, the warlords drove the Taliban from power in the cities and pushed its remnants, along with their al Qaeda supporters, into the more remote areas of the country, particularly in the east along the Pakistani border and in southern Afghanistan, where Taliban support was the strongest. But the truth was that the United States was only marginally prepared to wage a war on terror in this fashion, and without the aid of the anti-Taliban warlords, the contest would have been far more protracted. As it was, there were never enough U.S. forces in Afghanistan to ensure the destruction of the Taliban and al Qaeda, who regrouped and continue to hold out against Afghan government forces and the NATO forces who were subsequently deployed.

This willingness to intervene in Afghanistan was a part of a growing trend in military intervention by the United States. From 1945 through 1988—the 43 years of the Cold War—there were only six large-scale U.S. military actions abroad, one every seven years, while there were nine major U.S. military interventions in the 14 years from 1989 through 2003, one every year and a half.[16] This militarization of U.S. foreign policy had begun before 9/11, but it certainly has gained velocity since then and, most ominously, the imprecise way in which the administration of George W. Bush continues to talk about the current "Global War against Terror" suggests a war without end, a permanent condition with no fixed goal whose attainment would bring a return to peace and normalcy. Such a permanent state of war would institutionalize a war economy, a war society (think of the internal monitoring of cell phones, the color-coded threat alerts), and a war polity (where much of politics revolves around who can do the most for "national security")—just as did the Cold War for almost half a century.

The second major military response to 9/11, and one that became a far more salient feature in American life, was the invasion of Iraq in March, 2003. It, too, had part of its genesis in the war on terror, in that the Bush administration suspected and possibly believed that there was a connection between Saddam Hussein and al Qaeda, or that one would eventually be established, and that Iraq's reputed weapons of mass destruction would some day find their way into al Qaeda's or some other terrorists' hands. Whatever the truth behind the suspicions, American occupation of Iraq did provoke an insurrection by Iraqis that was joined by a growing al Qaeda network in Iraq. The war to avoid a terrorist threat now brought terrorist operations (as well as more conventional forms of guerrilla war) against U.S. and coalition forces, outsiders (such as aid workers and journalists), and the Iraqi people themselves.

The invasion of Iraq itself marked an important watershed for the U.S. military establishment. Since the end of the Cold War, and particularly with the arrival of Donald Rumsfeld as Secretary of Defense in early 2001, the military establishment sought technological "quick fixes" to make their performance on the battlefield more effective than ever before. This was touted by the arms industry and Pentagon bureaucrats as the "the revolution in military affairs" or "transformational warfare"—the continued search for ways to wage war with the minimum risk, the minimum forces and the minimum human resources in the field. Information collection systems would provide almost instantaneous presentations of the locations of friendly and enemy forces, enabling local commanders and military leaders far from the combat to understand what was happening at the moment and make changes in battle plans—when the systems worked. Precision-guided munitions became common during this war, giving the United States far more effective weapons, especially when tied into the information collection and command system. So confident were U.S. commanders in their new technologies and the training to make use of them (especially when confronting a demoralized Iraqi military apparatus that had been severely battered during the 1991 Gulf War and degraded by a decade-long arms embargo and continued air attack—Iraq was not even permitted to fly aircraft over two thirds of their country) that General Tommy Franks, CENTCOM commander in 2003, ordered a force roughly one-sixth the size of the force used against Iraq in 1991, to invade Iraq and converge on Baghdad.

The Pentagon has judged these technologies so successful that the latest QDR calls for further transformations in spite of the plentiful evidence to the contrary: Witness the bloody and unsuccessful assassination attempts against Iraqi leadership before the invasion of Iraq began. 50 air attacks targeted Iraqi leaders and not a single attack succeeded in killing its intended targets, in spite of dozens of civilian deaths.[17] For example, Rumsfeld proposes "moving 45% of U.S. air strike capability to unmanned aerial vehicles (UAVs)" and "doubling the number of unmanned aerial vehicles to increase persistent surveillance."[18] What is happening, of course, is that the American military is marrying new technologies to the old, Cold War divisions of heavy tanks and mechanized infantry. That partially transformed Army, had, with the Marines, found the winning weapon for the ground war in Iraq.

Neither the Army nor the Marine Corps was prepared for the military occupation of Iraq and the new requirement to stabilize the country long enough to create a democratic government and an Iraqi military and police force strong enough to replace the Americans. The military was not prepared for this constabulary role; the U.S. military did not have the arms, equipment, and the organization required. This level of warfare required lightly armed but very mobile forces with responsibility delegated to small unit commanders, not the tank and artillery-heavy divisions trained to fight set piece battles. It is not that no other army has confronted these same problems recently: both the British and Israeli army have developed both the tactics and the equipment to deal with insurgency, especially in an urban setting. These new requirements demanded a different doctrine, training, and view of the world—of policing rather than war waging. Accomplishing that mission has become the central challenge for the U.S. American military establishment. As we write this, the outcome is still in doubt.

The Bush administration, however, put a bold face on its experience in Iraq and with the war on terror. The 2006 Quadrennial Defense Review (QDR) trumpeted a new vision for the future. Its tone is relentlessly aggressive, with force to be employed quickly, without warning and without regard to the sovereignty of other nations, including "conducting wars in countries we are not a war with…"[19] and conducting "prolonged clandestine operations in denied areas, by proxy if necessary." The document argues that the United States will need to be able to maintain a "low-visibility presence in many areas of the world where U.S. forces do not traditionally operate."[20] Such low visibility operations would give greater prominence, the 2006 QDR said, to Special Operations Forces, which would be increased in size by 15 percent in personnel and one third in the number of battalions.[21]

Though the George W. Bush administration has increased the militarization of U.S. foreign policy and expanded the missions the military will be called on to perform, it is important to remember that pressures to do so have long played a role in American history. As Dennis Hart Mahan pointed out more than a century and a half ago, American citizens have had an aversion to maintaining a large standing army, especially one in which all Americans (or, historically, all male Americans) were expected to serve. Yet at the same time, Americans have been quick to insist that the United States use force to protect and advance its interests. We noted in Chapter 4 how quickly the United States embraced nuclear weapons for its war-waging; this was, in part, a way to "wage war on the cheap." We quoted Walter Lippman, who pointed out at the start of the first nuclear age that atomic weapons appeared "the perfect fulfillment of all wishful thinking on military matters: here is war that requires no national effort, no draft, no training, no discipline, but only money and engineering know-how of which we have plenty."[22] High-tech solutions—long-range strikes from the air or even from space and Special Forces sneaking around an enemy's back country, stirring up civil war, are simply the current manifestation of the search for war on the cheap.

THE NUCLEAR PART OF THE EQUATION AFTER 9/11

The terrorist attack on the United States and the U.S. response in Afghanistan and then in Iraq set the stage for the continuing evolution in U.S. strategy, particularly regarding nuclear weapons and nuclear threats. Indeed, the invasion of Iraq was intimately connected with nuclear weapons, as the Bush administration claimed that in spite of attempts to deny Saddam Hussein the capability to make nuclear weapons, Saddam had restarted the Iraqi nuclear program and at some point the Iraqi nuclear weapons might and probably would be used against a U.S. target or in some way fundamentally detrimental to American interests. And if there were no nuclear weapons in Iraq, then on the threat horizon were North Korea, which by the time of the invasion of Iraq had proclaimed itself to be a nuclear power, and Iran, which while asserting that its only interest in producing fissile materials was to generate electrical power, had already established itself as an untrustworthy state regarding its nuclear intention.

What role would nuclear weapons play in the evolving view of the world, now being shaped by the traumas of 9/11 and Iraq? Secretary of Defense Rumsfeld, on presenting the 2001 QDR, claimed that while most of the review had been completed before the 9/11 attack, "in important ways, these attacks confirm the strategic direction and planning principles that resulted from this review."[23] It emphasized the technological, high-technology reconnaissance and precision strike weapons taking the place of strategic bombers and intercontinental ballistic missiles. Just as strategic nuclear weapons carried by bombers and then by ballistic missiles in the first nuclear age relieved the nation of the burden of a large standing army, so presumably would global precision strike weapons on ballistic or cruise missiles, or on unmanned aerial vehicles loitering overhead, or even orbiting in space, along with spy satellites and robot aircraft tracking our enemies.

That is not to say that providing for the defense of the United States and its interests would turn out to be cheap in dollar terms. One critic charges that the United States spends more on its military than all the rest of the nations of the world together.[24] But even more conservative sources show that the U.S. spending is close to the total spending by all the rest of the world: for example the U.S. Congress authorized $466 billion in military expenditures for fiscal year 2004, while all the rest of the world spent about $500 billion on military expenditures. The growth of spending has been more dramatic; while military spending by the rest of the world remained relatively constant from 1998 through 2004, U.S. military spending increased by about two-thirds in the same period.[25] Making the latest technology the center of one's strategy, be it nuclear weapons in the 1950s or Predator drones in the 2000s, does have a cost, but it does not inconvenience many hundreds of thousands of American citizens who might otherwise be drafted to meet their nation's security needs.

It can be argued that these increases were forced on the United States by an ever-increasingly hostile world. President Bush has repeatedly had to ask for supplemental appropriations to cover the cost of the war in Afghanistan and Iraq, amounts that do not appear in the federal budget. For instance, the U.S. military budget received a $79 billion wartime supplement for fiscal year 2003 and a $87.5 billion wartime supplement for fiscal year 2004. $65 billion of the 2004 supplement was designated for military operations in Iraq and Afghanistan, with the remaining $22 billion designated for the support of the War on Terror.

However, if one looks closely at how money is being spent within the budget, it is clear that the United States is continuing to fund big-ticket weapons systems that have little to do with a war on terror or immediate threats to the United States. For example, the Special Operations Command, the center of the war on terror, received only $4.5 billion in the 2004 budget, while over $12 billion went to building new ships, including a new submarine while simultaneously converting two existing SLBM submarines to conventional guided missile carriers, and all this with no rival in sight that could be remotely capable of challenging U.S. dominance of the air and sea. Critics have noted that increasing the Army by 30,000 troops would cost between $4 billion and $5 billion a year, but rather than do that, the Pentagon is proposing to spend between $2 billion and $3 billion each on two destroyers employing stealth technologies that would make them nearly invisible to radar.[26] Stealth destroyers have no role to play in either a war on terror or in trying to stabilize Iraq. Increasing the size of the Army does. The real cost of this disconnect between meeting service interests and national commitments is in having a military establishment loaded with high-priced weapon systems for which there is no real need while not building an army adequately manned and appropriately trained and equipped for the missions it is being given. [27]

Those service interests would continue to provide the inertia and rationales for a continued flow of resources into the nuclear component of U.S. strategy. In his *Nuclear Posture Review* of December, 2001,[28] Secretary Rumsfeld announced that the new Bush administration would carry forward the Clinton administration policy of de-emphasizing the role of nuclear weapons in the nation's security. U.S. nuclear strategic forces in 2012 would look quite like that approved by President Clinton. There would then be an operationally deployed force of 1,700–2,200 warheads. "The planned force structure for 2012 comprises 14 Trident SSBNs (with two of the 14 in overhaul at any time) 500 Minuteman III ICBMs, 76 B-52H bombers, and 21 B-2 bombers."[29]

Rumsfeld proposed, however, to create a "New Triad." Rather than the Cold War Triad of long range bombers, intercontinental ballistic missiles and submarine-launched ballistic missiles, the New Triad places American security on three different conceptual legs:

- offensive strike systems, both nuclear and non-nuclear
- defenses, both active and passive
- a revitalized defense infrastructure

The secretary argued this triad would reduce U.S. dependence on nuclear weapons for deterrence, as non-nuclear attack systems, now with precision guidance and supported by greatly enhanced information collection systems, could be used in their place to destroy enemy weapons preemptively.

The second leg of the New Triad represented a significant movement toward the long-sought goal of President Reagan to elevate defense capabilities:

Missile defenses could defeat small-scale missile attacks intended to coerce the United States into abandoning an embattled ally or friend. Defenses that provided protection for strike capabilities of the New Triad and for other power projection forces would improve the ability of the United States and its allies and friends to counterattack an enemy. They may also provide the President with an option to manage a crisis involving one or more missile and WMD-armed opponents.[30]

The missile defense envisioned by the administration was ambitious in its scope: It would provide "defenses against attacks by small numbers of longer range missiles as well as defenses against attacks by larger numbers of short- and medium-range missiles." Ideally, this defense would be "able to intercept ballistic missiles of any range in all phases of their flight," from lift-off to re-entry. It would protect a wide variety of potential targets: "The President has stated that the mission for missile defense is to protect all 50 states, our deployed forces, and our friends and allies against ballistic missile attacks." The administration insisted that it need not be perfect. "Missile defense systems, like all military systems, can be less than 100-percent effective and still make a significant contribution to security by enhancing deterrence and saving lives if deterrence fails."[31]

Having a missile defense in fact rather than in hope would depend on meeting the enormous technological challenges. The United States currently has no such defense against most missiles; it has deployed an advanced Patriot anti-missile system, but its effectiveness has not been tested in combat and is only good for dealing with incoming warheads. (The original Patriot system was used in the 1990–1991 Gulf War and proved to be spectacularly unsuccessful.[32] The Iraqi missiles, however, were even worse in terms of accuracy.) The QDR claims that the prototype anti-missiles system may be available by 2010, further claiming that deployment of some interceptor missiles has already begun.[33]

A vital part of any missile defense system would be space-based assets to monitor missile launches and to track and attack the missiles in mid course. Moreover, with the growing dependence of American ground combat forces for real-time information and communication in order to maximize the power of smaller forces and unmanned reconnaissance and attack aircraft, space-based assets become even more critical. Thus the 2001 QDR suggests that "space control—the exploitation of space and the denial of the use of space to adversaries—will become a key objective in future military competition."[34] Indeed, we can well imagine that we are within a decade of increased emphasis on ensuring U.S. dominance in space, likely to be another costly proposition, spurring an arms race in space and ending a decades-long international consensus forbidding the militarization of space.

With the Bush administration still trying to bring about a successful outcome to its invasion of Iraq, the QDR for 2006 took up the thorny question of the spread of WMD. It set for the military establishment the objective of preventing "hostile states or non-state actors from acquiring WMD," including "active measure and the use of military force to deny access to materials, interdicted transfers and disrupt production programs."[35] The Review now argued that the United States needed the capacity to employ force against any state potentially hostile to the United States that acquires weapons of mass destruction. It envisioned a "deployable Joint Task Force" complete with assigned forces trained in the elimination of WMD.[36]

The QDR called for a Global Strike Capability, that is, the ability "to attack fixed, hard and deeply buried, mobile and re-located targets with improved accuracy anywhere in the world promptly."[37] These are planned to include SLBMs with conventional warheads.[38]

At the same time, the QDR indicated that nuclear weapons in the New Triad could play an offensive role denied nuclear weapons in the age of Mutual Assured Destruction: "Nuclear weapons could be employed against targets able to withstand non-nuclear attack, (for example, deep underground bunkers or bio-weapon facilities)."[39] Interestingly, while the 2001 QDR recognized the increased risk of clandestine introduction of nuclear weapons into the United States, neither it nor the *Nuclear Posture Review* contains specific measures to prevent smuggling nuclear weapons into the United States; instead, it defines the defense of the U.S. homeland in terms of ballistic missile defense.

The 2006 QDR now defined a more sweeping role for the U.S. military to deal with weapons of mass destruction: "To address such threats, the U.S. must be prepared to deter attacks; locate, tag & track WMD materials; act in cases where a state that possesses WMD loses control of its weapons, esp. nuclear devices; detect WMD across all domains; sustain operations even while under WMD attacks;...and eliminate WMD materials in peacetime, during combat, and after conflicts. National efforts to counter the threat posed by WMD must incorporate both preventive and responsive dimensions."[40]

THE NEW NUCLEAR ORDER

During the Cold War, nuclear planning for the United States had a central focus: deterring a Soviet nuclear strike and, if that failed (or appeared to be about to fail), waging nuclear war. Planners had to worry about how survivable their delivery systems were. Presidents had to worry about the flexibility in the plans to wage nuclear war. Today, those concerns are but memories. For the United States, nuclear relationships have been recast. There are no current major nuclear powers that the United States believes intend harm to the United States or to vital American interests such as access to oil. There are still disagreements with Russia, and China remains balanced between being a strategic partner and strategic competitor: China, notes the QDR, "has the greatest potential to compete militarily with the U.S. and field disruptive military technologies that over time could offset traditional U.S. military advantages."[41] The old friction between the United States and India has given way to a new relationship; the QDR now declares that "India is emerging as a great power and a key strategic partner."[42]

The nuclear threat to the United States has moved to a far more shadowy arena: weak states who may have a small nuclear arsenal or have aspirations to acquire one. But we need to recall that threat to the United States may be more the result of American perceptions than actuality (just as the belief that the Soviet Union would attack the United States was an American perception rather than a reality). We do not know if Saddam Hussein contemplated a nuclear strike on the United States or its allies, and we probably will not know if North Korean or Iranian leaders do now or might do so in the future. The threat from terrorists seems real in their intentionality, but still clouded in uncertainty about their capability.

We conclude this chapter with a sketch of the current nuclear states. We begin our presentation with those states who have clearly manifested a nuclear weapons capability, the declared nuclear weapons states.

Declared Nuclear Weapons States

It is useful to divide declared states into three subcategories: *first-tier* states that have sufficient nuclear weapons and a global delivery system that can cause massive, widespread damage if either chooses to wage nuclear war, *second-tier* states that can cause significant regional damage, and *newly arrived nuclear states* who have quite limited arsenals and problematic delivery capability.

First-tier States

Clearly occupied by the *United States* and *Russia*; these two states still possess arsenals large enough to destroy civilization on the planet and possibly destroy all life above the level of insects, notwithstanding the heartening progress in arms reduction and confidence building measures of recent years. (It has been estimated that even after all the START build-down goals have been reached, the Russian arsenal will contain about three times as much destructive capacity as all of the rest of the world's arsenal combined, the United States excluded.[43]) Therefore, as long as these arsenals exist, the fate of all humankind rests on the ability of the leadership of both countries to manage these arsenals.

Second-tier States

The United Kingdom (Great Britain), France and the Peoples Republic of China have all demonstrated, through repeated public testing and repeated public declarations, that all three have manufactured nuclear weapons and their delivery systems and that they intend to maintain their nuclear arsenals into the indefinite future. We will now look at these arsenals, their associated delivery systems and their possible uses:

United Kingdom. Britain currently produces its own warheads although it continues to rely on the United States for plutonium, uranium-235, and Tritium,[44] has performed all its nuclear testing since 1962 at the U.S. test site in Nevada,[45] and has purchased American missiles for its strategic submarines.[46] Its strategic nuclear retaliatory capacity is entirely submarine launched ballistic missiles on four submarines, each submarine carrying up to 48 warheads on 16 U.S. Trident missiles (which replaced earlier Polaris-missile carrying submarines).[47] Britain's stated policy is to maintain a total strategic retaliatory force of 160 operational warheads with at least one boat at sea at all times, two available for immediate sortie and one unavailable in overhaul.[48]

The critical question regarding Britain's nuclear forces is their relationship to both NATO and to the European Union. Britain has "subscribed" its principal nuclear forces to NATO "except where Her Majesty's Government may decide that supreme national interests are at stake," that is, when it would matter. It is difficult to think that use of strategic nuclear forces would even be considered in any case less than one involving "supreme national interests."

France. France has continued its independent nuclear posture that it adopted in the mid-1960s. It initially mimicked the American triad but today has retained 60 air-launched cruise missiles as a backup to its principal retaliatory force, four ballistic missile submarines. One of these four submarines will always be in refit, and one or two submarines will be on station at sea at all times, each submarine carrying 16 missiles with up to six warheads on each missile.[49]

France's stated targeting policy has been *tous azimut*—that is, targeting not one specific enemy, permitting political and operational flexibility. Its principal justification for its nuclear arsenal is to maintain military independence so it can independently deter invasions of France or threats to its vital national interests. To that end, the size of the arsenal, in French thinking, is independent of any military balance but is determined by "sufficiency," that is the "capacity to inflict unacceptable damage on any aggressor."[50]

China Since the mid-1960s, China's nuclear targets have increased as the range of its delivery systems increased, from U.S. bases in Japan to Soviet cities by the early 1970s, to intercontinental capability by the early 1980s (although it only deployed a handful of missiles). China apparently has not deployed multiple warhead missiles and its nuclear force remains rather modest: just 30 ICBMs, kept unfueled and without warheads—only 18 of which, all based in silos, are capable of striking targets throughout the entire United States, and another 50–100 medium range ballistic missiles, sitting unarmed in their garrisons with possibly another 150 tactical and theater nuclear weapons.[51] The number of Chinese strategic ballistic missiles deployed has actually declined, from 145 in 1984 to at most 80 today. Therefore, "a realistic estimate of China's nuclear arsenal... is 80–130 nuclear weapons."[52]

Second-tier states have in the past committed considerable resources to modernizing their arsenals, particularly their delivery systems, to make them more survivable, moving away from land-based ICBMs toward a submarine-based deterrent. China does have a number of modernization plans under way, but past plans have born remarkably little fruit, most notably their attempt to deploy nuclear-powered ballistic missile submarines. The first such submarine was launched in 1981 and is still not operational; a second submarine was either canceled or may have been lost in an accident. The only successful launches of submarine-based missiles were reportedly of test missiles, not operational missiles. China is also reported to have begun work on a new submarine but it is likely that deployment is "many years away" at best.[53] China is also committed to converting its land-based arsenal to mobile basing to enhance survivability, but its progress toward this end is uncertain.

Given the nature of the deployments by the second-tier states, we can reasonably infer that their core strategy is one of deterrence and the prevention of nuclear blackmail. China's existing arsenal, given China's industrial capacity to build a nuclear arsenal of almost any size, suggests that it has not adopted a nuclear-war fighting strategy nor intends to attempt to use nuclear coercion against either of the first tier states. That is not to say that nuclear intimidation (with its concomitant threat of use) is absent from Chinese strategy. Its arsenal is well suited to establish regional hegemony, that is, to dominate the western Pacific Rim and Indian subcontinent, including Japan (a vital American ally), and most critical to world peace, Taiwan and the waters surrounding that island. In a similar vein, the British government has stated its intention to deploy both strategic warheads of about 100 kilotons and smaller tactical warheads on their submarines, providing the government with the capability of using the small warheads both for the final warning, a "nuclear shot across the bow," and in regional conflicts such as the 1980 war with Argentina over the Falkland Islands if its opponent used tactical weapons against British forces. But in the main, these three older nuclear state have decided that deterrence is very robust, and that they can rely on a minimum deterrence with its limited economic costs and avoid the management and control problems that a large arsenal and hair-trigger delivery systems bring.

Newly Arrived Nuclear States

In 1998, *India* and *Pakistan*, by testing nuclear devices, demonstrated that they had a nuclear weapons capability and both asserted that nuclear weapons were part of their arsenal. India had tested a nuclear device in 1974 but had not publicly gone further in its weapons program. Pakistan probably had a nuclear capability in the 1990s—at least Indian strategists assumed that they did. Aircraft are the most likely delivery system, although both have deployed missile systems. There is some question whether either's devices are small and rugged enough to be mounted on those missiles. The aircraft ranges are sufficient to allow use on a battlefield or against the other's cities. Missile delivery systems would dramatically expand the range (particularly bringing much of China within range of Indian nuclear weapons). The size of the arsenals of the two states is open to conjecture, as neither has publicly stated either its current or projected number. It is likely that both have at least 50 available warheads, possibly 100, of Hiroshima size (roughly 15–20 kilotons).[54]

Given the relatively small size of the arsenals and relative youth of these states as declared nuclear weapons possessors, their strategies are likely to be similar in that each must plan to protect it nuclear arsenal against a disarming first strike by the other, and each must plan to wage a pre-emptive first strike of its own if it judges the other about to attack. Given that the two states share a common and disputed border and have engaged in three wars with each other in the last 50 years, and given that India has conventional military superiority, Pakistan is likely to make the use of nuclear weapons as part of its war-fighting strategy, at least as an option. When they will both come to the conclusion that the weapons exist solely for deterrence is open to question. Of all the nuclear relationships, this is the most unsettled; if nuclear use is to occur, this is one likely arena.

Pakistan/India and Israel are both instructive cases of the uses of nuclear weapons to insure national survival. It has been argued that Soviet Union/China/India/Pakistan are in effect a single system: a cascade of states that acquired nuclear weapons out of fear of another adversary state who they feared would use nuclear weapons to abridge their sovereignty. We have seen that Stalin had little interest in nuclear weapons until the United States had them and then ordered a crash program to acquire them, and there is evidence that fear of nuclear blackmail by the Soviet Union drove China's nuclear program. It can be argued that the exact choice of weapons and delivery system by China clearly indicates a felt need to deter the Soviet Union. So too, it has been argued that India's acquisition of nuclear weapons was in direct response to China's acquisition of nuclear weapons. India's program did not begin until after China's invasion of Tibet, the acquisition of a common border with China and the Indian Army's poor showing in the border clashes with the Chinese Army. It can be contended that the principal purpose of the Indian nuclear arsenal is to deter a Chinese invasion of India—a modest number of weapons with only limited-range delivery systems sufficient to impede an invasion but not enough weapons or long enough range to threaten China itself. Unfortunately, the same characteristics also describe an arsenal intended to threaten or even annihilate Pakistan—a smaller country much closer to India. This recognition has prompted Pakistan to develop its own capability but at quite some cost. As distances are short, sophisticated and long range delivery systems are not needed nor are large numbers of weapons to deter India from invading Pakistan or even from using nuclear weapons against Pakistan.

Opaque Nuclear Weapons States

These are states for which evidence exists that they have designed and built nuclear weapons but have not yet tested them (or if they have done so, the tests have escaped detection) and whose governments deny that they actually have weapons or declare, as the Israeli government does, that it would not be the first to introduce nuclear weapons into the region. Israel currently is the only state that fits under this designation. India and Pakistan left an opaque status with their open testing of military weapons in 1998. South Africa terminated its opaque status by 1991 after destroying the half-dozen or so weapons that it had built.[55] Opaque states generally are those who exist in condition of constant military tension and who have reasonable fears for their continued national existence (in Israel's case, its enemies reject the right of the state of Israel to exist). At the same time, their governments judge that it would be too provocative to reveal the existence of the arsenal, as revelation might force opponents to go nuclear in response and might force friends and allies to bring pressure to bear on the state to divest itself of nuclear weapons.

Israel. Israel is generally assumed to have a sizeable and sophisticated nuclear arsenal; estimates range up to 200 weapons,[56] although these weapons may in fact be stored not fully assembled, putting Israel a "turn of a screwdriver" away from an actual weapon. Given Israel's considerable scientific and technical infrastructure, the absence of testing is not evidence of an absence of weapons.

In fact, Israel's deliberately ambiguous statements about possible nuclear weapons and its handling of several security leaks in its nuclear program suggest that this ambiguity is part of a carefully studied policy to remind its enemies that it could have "a bomb in the basement." Israel has missiles capable of covering the entire Middle East and even possibly into Russia and has a sizeable and very effective Air Force that can also deliver weapons.

Israeli nuclear strategy is unknown. It may be that the Israeli arsenal is intended for battlefield use only. Given the paucity of information about the mix of weapons in their inventory, that question is unanswerable. It can also be argued that the Israeli weapons, by threatening the capital cities of its enemies, serve to deter a large scale invasion of Israel that might threaten its continued existence. It can also be argued that their arsenal is a "poison pill"—a warning that if the Israeli state is destroyed, no one will profit but that the entire Near East will be indefinitely uninhabitable.[57] Also, that the real target of Israeli deterrence could have been the Soviet Union—just as President Kennedy warned the Soviet Union during the Cuban missile crisis that the U.S. would hold the Soviet Union accountable for Castro's actions, Kennedy saying that he would regard any missile coming from Cuba as if it was coming from the Soviet Union. Similarly, the Israeli arsenal could have been intended to warn the Soviet Union that they must keep limits on their clients in the Mid-East.[58]

The existence of opaque nuclear weapons states reinforces Bernard Brodie's insight about the power of nuclear weapons: Any credible hint backed by the most circumstantial evidence such as an indigenous nuclear power industry, the acquisition of a nuclear reactor from abroad, any evidence of successful clandestine efforts to obtain nuclear material whether fissile or not, or the importation of technology that could be diverted to production of nuclear weapons may be sufficient to deter potential enemies. But at the same time–and this is at the heart of the nuclear predicament—the bomb's power is such that that any suspicion that an enemy has, or may obtain, nuclear weapons will be a powerful incentive for a rival to commit considerable resources—sometimes quite scarce—to efforts to build its own nuclear weapons, or at least make its enemies uncertain whether the state has nuclear weapons. India's reaction to China's acquisition of the bomb was to adopt the semi-opaque status of "we've tested a nuclear device but we are not building weapons," and Pakistan in turn became an opaque proliferator.[59]

States with Nuclear Aspirations

At one point in time, all current nuclear weapons states were nuclear aspirants. They made deliberate decisions to acquire a nuclear weapons capability and in so doing raised fears in portions of the international community. Over time, a norm began to emerge in the international community—reflected in the Non-Proliferation Treaty—that such nuclear aspirations were undesirable. The persistence by some states, particularly states that have for one reason or another challenged other key norms of international relations, to acquire nuclear weapons or their refusal to demonstrate unambiguously that they have no such aspiration, has created enormous tension in the second nuclear age. Iran and North Korea are the focus of the tension today. Iraq was until its defeat in 1991, and then again until 2003 when it was defeated again.

Indeed, Iraq became the warning sign. Iraq's defeat by the American-led coalition in 1991 exposed how much progress Iraq had made in its clandestine effort toward building nuclear weapons using a mix of imported and indigenous technology, and suggested how difficult it might be to identify and destroy nuclear facilities even when unlimited force was used. Although the allies had identified two Iraqi nuclear installations to attack during the intensive aerial campaign prior to the land invasion, UN inspectors after the war discovered over 20 undamaged Iraqi nuclear weapons facilities.[60] These discoveries upset the conventional wisdom of previous counter-proliferation efforts, forcing a recognition that states' clandestine efforts would not necessarily use the most efficient technologies for production of fissile materials, but rather those that are easiest to obtain and easiest to conceal.

North Korea. Although North Korea had a small Soviet-supplied research reactor since 1965, in 1985 U.S. reconnaissance satellites discovered the construction of a second, larger reactor well suited for the production of plutonium for weapons. Then, through the 1980s, U.S. intelligence discovered North Korea was building a plutonium reprocessing facility, conducting high explosive tests required to build implosion-style plutonium weapons, and erecting a third, giant reactor which could produce enough plutonium for several nuclear weapons every year. After an intense confrontation in 1994, North Korea and the United States reached an agreement that year (which we discuss in detail in Chapter 7), suspending North Korean activities but possibly leaving enough plutonium in their hands to construct several weapons. That agreement would fall apart with recriminations all around and the North would renew its efforts to acquire fissile materials, this time through uranium enrichment. In 2003 it withdrew from the Non-Proliferation Treaty and may have begun to reprocess the plutonium from reactor fuel rods. It is possible that the North has from a few to perhaps a dozen nuclear warheads, but North Korea's statements about its progress toward actually constructing nuclear weapons remain ambiguous.[61]

North Korea's strategic perspective remains unknown, but the American concern reminds us once again how potent nuclear weapons are, even when they may not exist. That a state like North Korea that cannot provide socks for its fighter pilots must still be feared as a potential nuclear power vividly summarizes the changes nuclear weapons have wrought.

Iran. Iran has harbored nuclear aspirations under two quite different regimes: that of the autocratic Shah and then under the rule of Islamic clerics. The fear is that in developing the capacity to reprocess the fuel rods used in nuclear power reactors to generate electrical power—a capacity that would include the enrichment of uranium and possibly the reprocessing of plutonium—Iran will then take the next step to build nuclear weapons.[62] The technology used to reprocess fuel rods and enrich uranium to serve as reactor fuel can also be used to enrich uranium to weapons grade uranium used to make nuclear weapons. As we shall see in Chapter 7, Iran has been involved in an extended conflict with the United States and key European states over this project. As we write this, Iran does not appear to have acquired fissile stocks to create a nuclear device, but the scale of their programs would allow the government, if it chose to do so, to construct perhaps 5–10 nuclear weapons a year. The Iranian government has repeatedly said that it has no intention of becoming a nuclear weapons state and that inspections by the International Atomic Energy Agency will verify continuing compliance with the Non-Proliferation Treaty, of which Iran is a signatory. And that treaty gives Iran the "unalienable right to research, produce, and use nuclear energy for peaceful purpose without discrimination."

Skeptics point out that Iran has ample oil supplies, which would provide cheaper electricity than a nuclear power plant could. They also point to what many take to be duplicitous behavior by the Iranians regarding its NPT obligations and the fact that it has attempted to hide its widespread nuclear facilities. (The existence of a uranium enrichment facility became known in 2002, for instance, only after an Iranian resistance movement provided the information.) In the words of Graham Allison, "Iran today is the leading example of country that is simultaneously exploiting the current nonproliferation regime and sneaking around it."[63]

DELIVERY SYSTEMS

For new states now acquiring, or seeking to acquire, nuclear weapons, the Triad simply is not obtainable. The seaborne leg of the Triad not only requires ready and secure access to the oceans but also demands a sophisticated naval establishment with long training in submarines. The Soviet Navy experienced considerable difficulty in maintaining its submarine fleet and the United Kingdom required substantial aid from the United States to develop its submarine-based nuclear retaliatory force.

Even maintaining an aircraft delivery system of sufficient robustness and reliability will challenge these aspiring states. The paradox of the modern age for the newly acquiring states is that building nuclear weapons puts less demand on their industrial and technical infrastructure than does maintaining a reliable and secure delivery system. Even China and India, the most sophisticated industrial states of the recent nuclear arrivals, have had little success with their attempts to create an indigenous aviation or submarine building industry.

For these reasons, land-based missiles, some easily acquired from abroad and not requiring a large industrial base to maintain, are likely to be the delivery system new nuclear states would prefer.[64] Though missiles might be the preferred delivery system, the warheads manufactured by recent nuclear arrivals are neither compact enough to fit into a missile warhead nor rugged enough to survive launching on a missile. Years of testing and engineering development were needed before warheads reached the ruggedness and miniaturization needed for missile warheads. Even after 15 years of nuclear weapons development, only a quarter of the American Polaris warheads were expected to detonate. Therefore, for the immediate future, recent nuclear states will most likely be forced to rely on aircraft for delivery with their attendant problems. Aircraft delivery requires large (and highly visible) airfields and an extensive infrastructure to support the operation, well-prepared and protected storage bunkers for the nuclear weapons, and sophisticated command and control mechanisms.

The newer nuclear weapons states are not likely to have the secure retaliatory capability that the triad provided. There is good reason to fear that in a crisis involving those states, the temptation to strike preemptively, rather than risk losing their entire arsenals, will be much greater than in U.S./Soviet crises of the past.[65]

If warheads can be made compact and rugged enough, there will be pressure in these states to go to missiles as the principal nuclear weapons delivery system as quickly as possible for cost-savings—the missiles themselves are easily obtainable from a host of willing arms suppliers and once in place, require substantially less upkeep than aircraft and, what may be even more important in third world economies, substantially less indigenous skilled manpower. But missiles in third world countries will bring with them the same problems encountered by the United States and Soviet Union.

If based on fixed sites, missiles will be vulnerable, even though more accurate than mobile missiles. It is unlikely that the newly arrived nuclear states will have the resources to go as far as the U.S. and Soviets in hardening their missile sites.

If mobile, then the missiles will be less vulnerable but less accurate—good for retaliation, less useful for a first strike. This is likely to make any nuclear exchange an exercise in the purposeful destruction of cities and therefore very costly in civilian lives.

TERRORISTS' NUCLEAR CAPABILITIES AND STRATEGIES

As we saw in Chapter 2, the basic concepts of nuclear weapons are well known. A very simple gun-type weapon, easy to plan, build, and detonate, requiring about 100 pounds of highly enriched uranium, need not weigh more than 600–700 pounds and exceed six feet in length. It could be delivered by an aircraft, a ship-carried cargo container, or a rented truck. The principal constraint on the spread of nuclear weapons up until now was the production of fissile material to fuel the nuclear device. Either enriching uranium to weapons grade, that is, sufficient to fuel a nuclear explosive, or creating plutonium are very demanding technologically and require a considerable industrial infrastructure, an infrastructure not easily hidden. A terrorist organization is never likely to have such a capability. There are, however, other routes to fissile material or nuclear weapons themselves, particularly theft or the transfer of such items with the connivance of officials having custody of them. Such acquisitions may be facilitated by a state that seeks to use the terrorist group to promote its own goals, but avoid a connection to the attack.

The collapse of the Soviet Union and the tight controls exercised by the Soviet state, coupled with the lack of funds to protect anything other than the nuclear weapons themselves, has made weapons-grade fissile material available within the former Soviet Union, not for overt sale, but available nonetheless.[67] A crude but effective nuclear weapon can be fashioned from roughly 25 to 60 pounds of fissile material, and it is estimated that there are some 1,200 metric tons of weapons-usable fissile material under the control of the Russian Ministry of Defense, the Minatom design and production agency, and the various users of weapons-grade fissile material in Russia such as naval reactors and research reactors. Those stocks are increased as more Russian warheads are dismantled (and partially decreased as U.S.-supported programs blend in unenriched uranium to render the uranium ineffective for weapons). This dismantling far exceeded secure storage available in Russia and stressed the Russian accounting system for keeping track of fissile material.[68] Fissile materials are also closer at hand, in research reactors supplied by the United States and the Soviet Union to other countries. Though the quantities are smaller than what might be obtained from Russian weapons, in these 60-some-research facilities there may be enough highly enriched uranium for over 1,000 nuclear weapons.[69]

As we write this, we have seen nothing to suggest that a terrorist group has obtained fissile material (or, less likely, a working nuclear device). Al Qaeda's leadership has publicly declared that it considered nuclear weapons acceptable in its effort to drive the United States and West from Muslim lands and it has made efforts to acquire fissile materials. It is probably just a matter of time before they, or the Chechen rebels fighting the Russian government, or someone else acquires sufficient materials to create a nuclear device. What happens next?

Here we must move into the realm of pure speculation but we can at least begin to suggest some of the decisions that terrorist leaders will need to make. It may be the case that they have franchised such an operation to a cell with orders to secure and use such a weapon, in which case the critical decision has been made. Otherwise, one of the early decisions the leadership must make is whether to hoard the weapon or the materials to make it until more are at hand, for one strategic consideration suggests that if one nuclear attack is convulsive, consider what several occurring in different locations or spaced out in terms of time might do to the enemy. Moreover, the first denotation is likely to tighten security sufficiently to degrade the chance of success for further attacks. On the other hand, given that terrorists are hunted by powerful forces, if they don't use it, they may lose it.

The use-or-hoard decision might depend as well on the strategy the terrorist leadership envisions for its nuclear devices. Does it envision that one or several nuclear detonations will force the United States (or some other target) to meet its demands, or does it read its opponent as likely to renew their counter-attack with greater vigor? If the latter, it may want to hoard in order to demonstrate that no matter how long the opponent tries to hold out, the terrorist will always be able to continue wrecking the opponent's society. Or does the terrorist group see its weapon as a device to extract concessions, concessions that build the terrorists' power and prestige? For instance, does it, perhaps after detonating one device, threaten to use others unless, say, all Muslims being held by American and Saudi authorities are released? On the other hand, we should not be surprised if terrorist leaders assume that their one or two nuclear weapons will be the "the war-winning weapon," especially if used when the United States remains mired in the chaos of Iraq and Israel confronts a Palestinian government led by the militant Hamas party.

Or the terrorists might adopt another compellence strategy: They might spread the word that there is a nuclear device already in place, to be detonated if the United States did not, say, accept the eastern border region of Afghanistan as Taliban/al Qaeda territory and refrain from attacking it. One might ask if the United States would be or should be willing to make such a trade? Is the threat, after all, credible? Given the bomb's power, what should one be willing to give up in order not to experience its effects? In other words, all the questions of the first nuclear age are with us, now in a new and frightening guise, and there are no easy answers. But in one way or another, terrorist leaders will have to make some critical judgments in their formulation of strategy.

Beyond strategic goals and options, terrorists would need to confront the issue of delivery systems. The 1993 truck bomb attack on the World Trade Center (which failed to do much damage) demonstrated that almost anything that moves could deliver explosives to a high-value target. An attack within the United States probably necessitates getting a nuclear device into the country. There is a delivery system ready. "The nuclear weapon that terrorists would use in the first attack on the United States is far more likely to arrive in a cargo container than on the tip of a missile." "Every day, 30,000 trucks, 6,500 rail cars and 140 ships deliver more than 50,000 cargo containers …from around the globe. Approximately 21,000 pounds of cocaine and marijuana are smuggled into the country each day."[70] Fifty pounds of highly enriched uranium no longer seems like an impossible delivery assignment.

CONCLUSION

We began this chapter asking you to imagine how you as president of the United States might deal with a state—a hostile state at that—on the verge of going nuclear. You were given a number of options, all involving the use of force against the would-be proliferator. Presumably your advisors believed that important issues were at stake, important enough to have the United States consider war-like actions. We ended this chapter with a brief consideration of the calculations terrorist leaders might make about using a crude but powerful nuclear advice to advance their political interests.

Clausewitz argued that "war is a continuation of political activity by other means." "When communities go to war," he said, "the occasion is always due to some political objective."

As we discovered in Chapter 4, the lesson that the United States and the Soviet Union learned was that while war was to serve a nation's political interests, nuclear war could serve no one's interest. At the same time, states had to threaten to wage nuclear war in order to prevent it. As we saw in Chapter 5, that could be a dicey business. But peace—at least nuclear peace—prevailed. Now, in the second nuclear age, we seem back where we started, asking the old questions. Can nuclear weapons, small or large, wielded by a superpower or by less-than-state actors or something in between, achieve some political objective after all? Do states need to prevent other states from going nuclear in order to keep the nuclear peace, or do those very attempts so challenge nations' security that nuclear weapons seem all the more necessary?

The nuclear predicament remains alive and well. The United States and the Russian Republic both have the ability, regardless of any damage that could be inflicted on their strategic nuclear forces by an attacker, to destroy that attacker's society. Mutual assured destruction therefore is a fact of life. For them. But probably not for Pakistan and India. It may never meaningfully exist for terrorist groups. It may never meaningfully exist for nuclear armed states such as North Korea, for while they can be obliterated, they cannot exact that kind of retaliation against the United States. At least not in the short run.

How concerned should the United States be about the nuclear arsenals and the nuclear ambitions of other states? Can it find a way to secure itself—to devise a strategy to secure itself—that avoids nuclear use?

There are the cynics who contend that current concerns over second-tier states' arsenals and the possible proliferation of nuclear weapons to other states are driven principally by bureaucratic imperatives: that organizations that have grown up to counter a specific threat, such as Soviet adventurism, must now search for another threat to protect the country from, lest we all recognize that these organizations no longer have a purpose and should be closed down, much as the March of Dimes had to discover children with birth defects to aid after the polio vaccine was invented. Some critics have asserted the Bush administration's concern over proliferation of nuclear weapons, especially in the absence of any hard evidence of proliferation, is the invention of the imagined threats that the administration can then protect the nation from.

However, any nuclear weapons in the hands of any other state does lessen the freedom of action the United States has in dealing with threats to U.S. interests and does heighten the risk of aggression in regional conflicts, possibly involving states the United States has pledged to protect. Consider, for a moment, another hypothetical case: Suppose Iraq had a small nuclear arsenal at the time it invaded Kuwait. Would the United States have been able to act as determinedly against Iraq? Would the U.S. have dared to concentrate troops on the ground and commit major warships as freely as it did? Would Iraq have been able to deter U.S. allies in the mid-East, such as Saudi Arabia, as well as Britain and France from supporting the invasion of Iraq? Would that not have destabilized the entire Mideast, a region recognized as vital to the U.S. interests? Would it not have caused U.S. allies there and in other regions to question their commitment to the United States as the U.S. showed its inability to stand behind its treaty obligations?

These are the unknowns of today and tomorrow. They are the threats and realities that the United States confronts in trying to navigate the nuclear future. In Chapter 7, we examine the political response of the United States in the second nuclear age and what choices it made to secure that future.

ENDNOTES

[1]This is loosely modeled on a simulation described in James Fallows, "Soldiers, Spies and Diplomats Conduct a Classic Pentagon War Game—With Sobering Results," *The Atlantic Monthly*, Vol. 294, Issue 5 (December 2004), pp. 99–110.

[2]Alexander Glaser and Frank N. Von Hippel, "Thwarting nuclear terrorism", *Scientific American,* Vol. 294, Number 2, February 2006, pp. 56–63.

[3]"Israeli and Iraqi statements on raid on nuclear plant", *New York Times*, June 9, 1981, p. A8.

[4]Nazila Fathi and Greg Myre, "Iran's new president says Israel must be wiped off the map", *New York Times*, Oct 27, 2005, p. A8.

[5]Other historical examples either involved development efforts that had not matured or one notable example, South Africa, where the nation was about to undergo a radical change of government and all parties recognized the wisdom of not burdening this transformation in government with the added responsibility of managing a nuclear arsenal.

[6]Paul M. Kennedy. *The rise and fall of great powers: Economic change and military conflict from 1500 to 2000*. (New York: Random House, 1987.)

[7]Center for Defense Information (1997 March) "The Quadrennial Defense Review: A Sense of Deja Vu." Retrieved May 31, 2006 from :// /dm/1997/issue2

[8]U.S. Department of Defense, *Quadrennial Defense Review 1997*. May 1997. The Secretary's Message, p. 1.

[9]Congress extended the deadline for the 2005 *Quadrennial Defense Review* report by a year in view of the ongoing conflicts in Afghanistan and Iraq. U.S. Department of Defense, *Quadrennial Defense Review* report 2006, p. A-3.

[10]U.S. Department of Defense, *Nuclear Posture Review,* March 1993.

[11]Stephen I. Schwartz, ed. *Atomic Audit; the costs and consequences of U.S. nuclear weapons since 1940*. (Washington, D.C.: Brookings Institution, D.C., 1998), p. 225.

[12]Richard A. Lacquement Jr., *Shaping American military capabilities after the Cold War* (New York: Praeger, 2003)

[13]Lacquement, *Shaping American military capabilities after the Cold War,* p. 177.

[14]U.S. Secretary of Defense. *Annual Report to the President and the Congress*, 1998. Chapter 5.

[15](September 2002) *The National Security Strategy of the United States of America*. Retrieved May 30, 2006 from http://www.state.gov/r/pa/ei/wh/15434.htm

[16]Andrew J. Bacevich, *The New American Militarism: How Americans are seduced by war*. (Oxford: Oxford University Press, 2005), p. 19.

[17]Douglas Jehl and Eric Schmitt, "Errors seen in early attacks on Iraqi Leaders," *New York Times*, June 13, 2004, p. 1.1. Dan Glaister, "High-profile air strikes 'killed only civilians,'" *The Guardian*, June 14, 2004.

[18]U.S. Department of Defense, *Quadrennial Defense Review Report 2006*, p. 6.

[19]*QDR report 2006,* p. vi.

[20]*QDR report 2006,* p. 22.

[21]*QDR report 2006*, p. 5

[22]Quoted in Lawrence Freedman, *The Evolution of Nuclear Strategy*, 2d ed. (New York: St. Martin's Press, 1989), p. 48.

[23]U.S. Department of Defense, *QDR report 2001*, p. v.

[24]Bacevich, *The new American militarism*, pp. 16–17, 229.

[25]GlobalSecurity.org, *World Wide Military Expenditures*, (last modified October 15, 2005), retrieved June 1, 2006 from http://www.globalsecurity.org/military/world/spending.htm.

[26]"Still shortchanging the troops," *New York Times*, February 10, 2006, p. A. 24.

[27]"Mr. Rumsfeld's flawed vision," *Washington Post.* February 23, 2006, p. A. 20

[28]U.S. Department of Defense, *Nuclear Posture Review* submitted to Congress on December 31, 2001.

[29]*Nuclear Posture Review 2001*, p. 19.

[30]*Nuclear Posture Review 2001*, p. 13.

[31]*Nuclear Posture Review 2001*, p. 25.

[32]Alexander Simon, *The Patriot Missile. Performance in the Gulf War reviewed.* (Center for Defense Information, July 15, 1998) http://www.cdi.org/issues/bmd/Patriot.html.

[33]*QDR 2006*, pp. 26, 49.

[34]*QDR 2006*, p. 16.

[35]*QDR 2006*, p. 33.

[36]*QDR 2006*, p. 6.

[37]*QDR 2006*, p. 49.

[38]*QDR 2006*, p. 6.

[39]*Nuclear Posture Review 2001*, pp. 12–13.

[40]*QDR 2006*, pp. 33–34.

[41]*QDR 2006*, p. 29.

[42]*QDR 2006*, p .28.

[43]Bruce D Larkin, *Nuclear Designs: Great Britain, France & China in the global governance of nuclear arms*, (New Brunswick, N.J., Transaction Publishers, 1996), p. 9.

[44]Larkin, *Nuclear Designs*, p. 165.

[45]Larkin, *Nuclear Designs*, p. 85.

[46]Larkin, *Nuclear Designs*, p. 32.

[47]"Status of the major nuclear-weapons states ballistic missile forces," *Arms Control Today*, June 2005, v. 35, issue 5, p. 11.

[48]*SIPRI Yearbook 2005: Armaments, Disarmament and International Security*, (Stockholm International Peace Research Institute) (Oxford: Oxford University Press, 2004), pp. 589–590.

[49]*SIPRI Yearbook 2005*, pp. 590–592.

[50]Larkin, *Nuclear Designs*, p. 38.

[51]Center for Defense Information, *Current World Nuclear Arsenals*. October 15, 1997. See also Jeffrey Lewis, "The ambiguous arsenal," *Bulletin of the atomic scientists*, v. 61, issue 3, May/June 2005, pp. 56–57 and David Shambaugh, *Modernizing China's military: Progress, problems, and prospects*, (Berkeley, California: University of California Press, 2002) p. 278.

[52]Lewis, "The ambiguous arsenal," pp. 56–57.

[53]Robert S. Norris and Hans M. Kristensen, "Chinese Nuclear Forces, 2003," *Bulletin of the atomic scientists*, v. 59, issue 6, November/December 2003, p. 78.

[55]Schwarz, *Atomic audit*, p. 615.

[56]*SIPRI Yearbook* 2004, pp. 645–646.

[57]During the Cold War, the real target of Israeli weapons may have been the Soviet Union. That is, the Israelis looked on the weapons as a way of compelling the Soviet Union to keep its Middle East client states from threatening the existence of Israel. See Seymour M. Hersh, *The Samson Option: Israel's Nuclear Arsenal and American Foreign Policy* (New York: Random House, 1991).

[58]Hersh, *The Samson option.*

[59]Michael J. Mazarr, *North Korea and the bomb: A case study in nonproliferation,* (New York: St. Martin's Press, 1995), p. 6.

[59]Michael J. Mazarr, *North Korea and the bomb: A case study in nonproliferation,* (New York: St. Martin's Press, 1995), p. 6.

[60]Devin T. Hagerty, "Nuclear Deterrence in South Asia," *International Security, v.* 20, no. 3, Winter 1995, p. 84.

[61]See Michael J. Mazarr, "Going Just a Little Nuclear: Nonproliferation Lessons from North Korea," *International Security*, Vol. 20 (Fall 1995), p. 94; Philip Shenon, "North Korean Nuclear Arms Pact Reported Near Breakdown," *New York Times*, December 6, 1998, p. 16; Graham Allison, *Nuclear Terrorism: The Ultimate Preventable Catastrophe* (New York: Henry Holt & Co, 2004), pp. 68, 80; and *SIPRI Yearbook 2004*, pp. 612–617.

[62]For a review of events, see *SIPRI Yearbook 2004*, pp. 605–609.

[63]Allison, *Nuclear Terrorism*, p. 161.

[64]Eric Arnett (ed.), *Military Capacity and the risk of war* (Oxford: Oxford University Press, 1987)

[65]Steve Fetter, "Ballistic Missiles and Weapons of Mass Destruction," *International Security*, v. 16, no. 1, Summer 1991, p. 19.

[66]*Avoiding nuclear anarchy; containing the threat of loose Russian nuclear weapons and fissile material*. Graham Allison et al. (CSIA Studies in International Security No. 12) (Cambridge, Mass.: MIT Press, 1996)., p. 57; Allison, *Nuclear terrorism; The ultimate preventable catastrophe*, p. 95.

[67]*Avoiding nuclear anarchy*. p. 2.

[68]See *Avoiding nuclear anarchy*. pp. 188 and 191 for examples.

[69]Allison, *Nuclear terrorism; The ultimate preventable catastrophe*, pp. 153–154.

[70]Allison, *Nuclear terrorism; The ultimate preventable catastrophe*, pp. 106–107.

7

Nuclear Relations During the Second Nuclear Age

The inspection team from the International Atomic Energy Agency gathered at its Baghdad hotel in the early morning light of September 24, 1991.[1] It would be another hot day, with the temperature expected to climb past 100 degrees. And it would be tense. The day before, David Kay from the Agency and Robert Gallucci from the U.S. State Department had led the inspectors to a nearby building pinpointed by Iraqi informants as part of Iraq's nuclear weapons program. Their search that day had turned up documents whose Arabic text most of the inspectors could not read but whose diagrams had the tell-tale configurations of nuclear weapons. Iraq had repeatedly and vociferously denied having a nuclear weapons program. The lie was now documented.

During that inspection the day before, the Iraqis who routinely accompanied the team had grown increasingly agitated as the team began to collect and inventory the documents. When Kay had ordered the documents to be loaded into the team's vehicles, the Iraqis seized the documents, saying that they would be returned in the morning. Kay and Gallucci protested. The United Nations had mandated that the inspectors be given full and free access to any materials that might be part of an Iraqi nuclear weapons program. In the end, however, Kay and Gallucci had given in. Some of the Iraqis were armed and the unarmed inspectors were in the heart of Iraqi-controlled Baghdad. But before the Iraqis had physically recovered all the documents, Kay had covertly given several to an IAEA inspector who had taken ill during the operation and had left Iraq that morning. Translated during the evening, the documents provided details of the Iraqi effort to create an implosion device—and indicated that another building nearby might be the headquarters of the entire Iraqi nuclear program.

Today's inspection was to enter that building, take possession of the documents held there, and to thwart any effort by the Iraqis to repossess them. The team climbed into their vehicles and roared off, closely tailed by their Iraqi minders, only to come to a sudden stop just down the street. They entered the targeted building without opposition and began collecting documents. Once again, when the team began to carry the documents to their vehicles in an adjacent parking lot, the Iraqis grew more agitated. Now an Iraqi official demanded that the documents be returned to the building. Someone on the IAEA team shouted that they should stuff the documents into their clothes. This would force the Iraqis to manhandle the inspectors physically to recover the documents. As many of the team members were much bulkier than their Iraqi minders, trying to enforce a strip search would be difficult. The Iraqi officials at the site mulled over the situation and then decreed that nobody could leave the parking lot unless the documents were turned over. Kay and Gallucci decided to wait the Iraqis out.

The team huddled under a tin roof covering part of the lot and in a bus that brought some of the team, rationing their bottled water and the American military's MRE food packets. A second and third day passed in the sweltering heat. The Iraqis organized several "popular" demonstrations against the inspectors, and the ring of Iraqi security personnel around the lot kept the threat of physical harm alive when the demonstrators marched off. Saddam Hussein's lieutenants counted on the threats, heat, and isolation to break the team's resistance.

The team, however, had satellite phones and remained in contact with the United Nations headquarters in New York. Headquarters in turn alerted journalists about the standoff in the parking lot, so whatever the Iraqis did would be covered live by broadcast news stations around the world. The United Nations formally warned the Iraqis that unless the inspectors were released with the documents and Iraq cooperated fully, there would be military retaliation. Saddam Hussein got the message. At sunrise on the fourth day, the Iraqis permitted the team to leave with the documents.

Those documents along with on-site inspections of known or suspected nuclear facilities allowed the IAEA to destroy the Iraqi nuclear weapons program. Inspectors located and removed fissile materials, oversaw the destruction of machinery for the production of fissile materials, consigned long-range missiles to the scrap heap, and rendered extensive building complexes inoperable. How was it that a budding nuclear power was disarmed by an international agency, an action mandated by the United Nations Security Council with the approval or acquiescence of the five major nuclear weapons states who sat as permanent members of that Council—states that ten years earlier found it difficult if not impossible to be of a single mind on many important security issues? How was it that in January 1992, the heads of many of the governments represented on the Security Council released a statement saying that "the proliferation of all weapons of mass destruction constitutes a threat to international peace and security" and, with India withholding its approval, they further asserted that there was a need to "prevent the proliferation in all its aspects of all weapons of mass destruction"?[2] How had this cooperation emerged? And why did it seemingly fall apart only a decade later when the question of the denuclearization of Iraq emerged once again in the United Nations?

The answers to these questions are bound up with the emergence of the second nuclear age. In the preceding chapter, we examined how military doctrine fitfully repositioned itself in response to end of the Cold War. This chapter examines how the states of the world began to re-examine and refashion their nuclear relations.

The emergence of a second nuclear age around 1990 did not mean, however, that the attitudes and practices of the first nuclear age were packed away in trunks for storage in the attic, to be looked at by latter generations with bemusement at their oddity. What it did mean is that the nuclear predicament had became more complex. There would still be the brandishing of nuclear weapons, but now it would often be the new nuclear states, with smaller arsenals, who would do so. Now relatively weak states would wave the threat of going nuclear to extract concessions from a superpower. And now terrorists would for the first time give credible evidence that they sought and would use nuclear weapons if they acquired them, vastly amplifying their threats.

How can we make sense of our current nuclear world? Where might we be headed? To answer these questions, we pick up the story of the end of the first nuclear age.

THE END OF THE FIRST NUCLEAR AGE

The first nuclear age began with a blinding flash of light in the New Mexico desert in 1945. In less than 50 years, the seemingly perpetual Cold War and the first nuclear age together passed into history, peacefully and unexpectedly. The great fear of nuclear incineration evaporated. Why had these changes occurred? What role did nuclear weapons play? We suggested in Chapter 5 that cold wars naturally wane in part because the leaders of nuclear armed states see the horrendous consequences of a cold war that spirals out of control. Was it this very fear of the consequences that made detente a permanent condition? No, something more fundamental took place. Mikhail Gorbachev, who became the Soviet leader in 1985, concluded that the Soviet economy was moribund.[3] In the decades since Stalin's death, the Communist Party had essentially reached a bargain with the Soviet people: If they would stay out of politics, leaving that arena to the party alone, the party would ensure that the economy provided an increasing standard of living for the people. Now the party was failing to deliver. Equally important, the faltering economy threatened the Soviet Union's status as a superpower, not only in terms of prestige, but also because the economy could not sustain a large, modern military and an active foreign policy. Gorbachev initiated a series of reforms that permitted a freer discussion of the society's ills and moved away from an economy controlled at the top. He hoped that the Communist Party could revitalize the economy and the party itself without jeopardizing its control. The hope proved illusory. The rage for reform began to challenge the Party's right to have a monopoly on power. The rage spread to Eastern Europe, either encouraged by the local Communist Party elites there or by popular movements seeking to negotiate with the entrenched Party elite.

Gorbachev refused to support repression in Eastern Europe or in the Soviet Union.[4] By the end of 1989, Communist parties no longer controlled most of the states of Eastern Europe, and the Soviet Union began to withdraw its military forces from those states—the very forces that protected the western approaches to the USSR from NATO. Gorbachev tolerated the emergence of political factions within the constituent republics of the Soviet Union, even when they began to announce a desire to leave the Union. By 1991, those factions had begun the breakup of the Soviet Union, with the Baltic republics of Latvia, Lithuania, and Estonia asserting that they were sovereign states, to be quickly followed by the independence of critical regions such as the Ukraine and Belarus. Gorbachev found himself the leader of the Soviet Union that no longer existed. Boris Yeltsin, the leader of the new Russian republic, soon became the voice of authority. Gorbachev's power base had evaporated, as had his personal prestige; many Russians blamed him for the collapse of the Soviet Union and the economic chaos that emerged as Russia attempted to turn itself into a market-based democracy. Yeltsin and democracy survived a coup attempt by disgruntled Party and military hardliners in 1991.

What role did nuclear weapons play in this transformation? Supporters of the Reagan administration argued that the president's accelerated military spending and modernization programs, including the Star Wars project discussed in Chapter 4, coupled with an aggressive challenge to Marxist governments around the world (most notably by aiding the Afghan resistance movement), pushed the archaic Russian economy into a futile and ultimately ruinous arms race. This was bankruptcy by design.[5] We suggest that nuclear weapons also had a more positive role. First, they gave the Soviet leadership and public a sense of security, allowing potentially risky experimentation because nuclear weapons would deter an American attack. Gorbachev could hold his party opposition at bay because he removed from their hands the most powerful rallying cry that Soviet leaders had ever developed: "If we weaken ourselves, the West will destroy us." Moreover, negotiations over nuclear weapons were a critical avenue by which both Reagan and Gorbachev came to see that images of a reckless, hostile opponent were misplaced.

Indeed, nuclear weapons had worked an unexpected magic on Ronald Reagan himself. When Reagan learned of a great Soviet fear in 1983 that the United States was about to stage a preemptive nuclear attack, he noted in his diary that he had learned "something surprising about the Russians." "Many people at the top of the Soviet hierarchy were genuinely afraid of America and Americans. Maybe this shouldn't have surprised me but it did." "I feel the Soviets are ... so paranoid about being attacked that without in any way being soft on them, we ought to tell them no one here has any intention of doing anything like that."[6] Furthermore, Reagan repeatedly disturbed his advisors by advocating the abolition of nuclear weapons and suggesting that he might not be willing to use them.[7] If anything, all the talk by members of his administration about nuclear war-fighting strategies made this president clearly alert to the perils of such a policy. Even if he were a pie-eyed optimist about being able to build a shield over the United States, he recognized that SDI was off in the future while the threat of nuclear weapons was now. Negotiations with the Soviets were, in the end, necessary.

Ironically, with the end of the Cold War, nuclear weapons became just another weapon in the inventory, not the glittering shield that stood between the nation and a threatening opponent. As we saw in Chapter 6, the military wrestled uncertainly with how nuclear weapons were to be a part of the nation's strategy. The international politics of the second nuclear age, however, would bring nuclear weapons to the forefront *as political issues*.

NUCLEAR RELATIONS IN A HEGEMONIC WORLD

While nuclear relations would take on a new complexion after 1990, the arrival of the second nuclear age did not wipe the slate clean. The patterns established during the first nuclear age would carry into the second. The international community continued to endorse the idea of nuclear non-proliferation. The United States and the new Russian state remained committed to reducing their nuclear inventories and living by the nuclear rules of the road they had crafted. The United States and Western Europe remained in their NATO alliance with its embedded nuclear weapons policy to defend Europe. Japan was still allergic to nuclear weapons, but maintained its strong conventional military forces and remained under the American nuclear umbrella. The United States and the People's Republic of China promoted the detente that had emerged between them and their growing economic relationship. The Chinese continued to field a nuclear arsenal with a minimal deterrent capability against the United States. The mutual hostility between Russia and China continued to diminish.

What did set the second nuclear age off from the first were two critical features. First, the new age was not the product of a world war with its devastation, its dramatic reworking of grievances, and its post-war attempts to fashion a new world out of the agony of the old. Second, there was only one superpower. By the mid-1990s, the United States stood alone, the most powerful state in the world, with five decades of experience in world politics. This is a *mature hegemony*, a world in which one state, considerably practiced in international politics, has preponderant influence. That influence plays itself out in the military realm as well as in the economic, the political, and the cultural realms.[8]

This is not to say that the other states accept the exercise of influence by the hegemon or that they necessarily do what the hegemon wishes. Indeed, there will always be a collection of states (and other groups, such as al Qaeda) that set themselves in opposition to what the hegemon wants or stands for. What hegemony does mean, however, is that:

1. the other states pay particular attention to the announced interests or policy positions of the hegemon,

2. it is far more difficult to achieve collective action if the hegemon is actively opposed,

3. the hegemon's leadership is often crucial for the creation of a collective effort, and

4. the hegemon from time to time will act in defiance of the wishes of other states.

Sergei Karaganov, a foreign policy advisor to Russian President Yeltsin, put it this way:

Look, many in the Russian leadership resent the United States, but they have decided that it is better to adapt to American power and do the best they can, because in the Middle East, Pakistan, and Iran—it can all go up in flames, in revolution and wars. So we have to have someone do the dirty job of keeping it all together. And that's the United States. And although you do stupid things, the United States is the only steamboat we can hitch ourselves to and go in the direction of modernity.[9]

Hegemons, however, are peculiar entities. The leaders and public of a hegemon often assume that they have the right and responsibility to lead by virtue of the state's power and by virtue of a national myth about being called to lead. The myth usually claims that the possession of great power is itself a consequence of possessing outstanding virtues (such as having the best economic system or political system, or as being blessed by a particular deity, or as being composed of a particularly favored group of human beings). In a more self-interested vein, a hegemon often recognizes that leadership is necessary in order to maintain its favored power position. Finally, the hegemon's great power relative to that of others often gives its leaders and public the impression that it can exercise leadership at modest cost.

One might expect that a hegemon would be constantly involved internationally, perhaps in a very forceful, often overbearing way. Even if it wished to act with a light hand, the power of the hegemon inevitably creates active opponents—states or groups that perceive the hegemon as the source of their difficulties or the obstacle to the achievement of their aspirations.[10] Those actors will work to undermine the hegemon's power, forcing the hegemon to pay attention to world politics and the protection of its power. In the long run, however, because a hegemon's resources are never infinite, its political elites and occasionally the public will worry about "imperial overstretch"[11]—the costs of leadership. Thus there will be a tension within a hegemon between those who focus on the bottom line (How much is this going to cost?) and those who focus on the international score (What will keep us on top?). We can expect some oscillation of power between these two camps, leading to lesser or greater international effort by the hegemon. Make the hegemon a democracy, where political parties criticize each other for neglecting the costs or the score, and the oscillation is reinforced. During the first ten years of the second nuclear age, American interests gravitated inward and toward the bottom line. It was not until George W. Bush came to power in January 2001 that an American administration was ready to see the world differently, but it was not until September 2001 that the administration saw the necessity and opportunity of making the international score the nation's focus.[12]

The tension between those counting costs and those counting power often plays itself out in the hegemon's choice of how to deal with the world. One broad response to the world is the *unilateralist approach*—the hegemon essentially goes it alone, relying on its own resources, seeking to promote its own interests. It may invite and receive cooperation from others, but it makes few concessions to receive this cooperation. Unilateralism often promises to be a high cost approach, but holds out the prospect of producing outcomes most in line with the interests of the hegemon. A *multilateralist approach*, on the other hand, attempts to build a coalition of states in support of a particular policy. That allows the hegemon to use the power resources of other actors (and thus reduce its costs), but in so doing the hegemon usually has to accommodate the interests of others, thus compromising its own interests to some degree. President George W. Bush's war against Iraq in 2003 is an example of a unilateralist approach: The president announced that if the United Nations did not support the attack, the United States would go ahead in any case with whatever allies would join (only the British played a meaningful combat role). After the war, however, when controlling Iraq proved difficult, the United States swung toward a more multilateralist approach, asking for help from various states. Those states in turn demanded, as the price for their participation, that the United States create a greater role for the United Nations and incorporate the perspectives and interests of its members into policy on the ground, which it did to some degree.

Interestingly, in 1945 the United States was the hegemon as well, but it lost that status relatively quickly.[13] Today, it seems likely to retain its hegemonic status longer because of the nature of the power challenges it faces.[14] A hegemon always faces the prospect that another state's economic power, military capabilities, and diplomatic prestige will grow to rival the hegemon's. No state has reached that point today, but China may do so within the next two to three decades. The Soviet Union began to do so after 1945. The hegemon may also find that another state is able to coordinate the resources and policies of a bloc of states, thus making their power partially its own, posing a greater challenge to the hegemon's interests. The Soviet Union was able to do this with the East European states (until 1989) and to a lesser degree with China (until roughly 1960). Today, the only candidate for such bloc coordination is the European Union, but it is still unable to coordinate its members' foreign policies and many member states remain tied to the United States by the NATO alliance. Finally, the hegemon may find that another state is the home of a powerful, transnational *ideology*, thus mobilizing effective support for its policies *within* other nations, even where its partisans do not control the government. In the Cold War, the Soviet Union was often able to mobilize Communist party members and sympathizers in support of its policies. Today, however, the principal mobilizing ideology is militant Islam, of which al Qaeda is the most well-known manifestation. The defeat of the Taliban in Afghanistan left militant Islam with no state patron, but it continues to demonstrate effective though still limited impact from North Africa to Indonesia.

In the first nuclear age, the Soviet Union was able to tap into its own power, the power of a bloc of states, and a mobilizing ideology. It quickly became a global counter to the hegemon. Now, in the second nuclear age, no one state challenging the hegemon has been able (or appears likely) to hold all three modes of power in its hands, making a relatively long-term American hegemony likely. At the same time, however, the diverse nature of the challenge to American power means that no one policy (such as containment was in the Cold War) will be effective. Those interested in the international score will be forced to pursue three different major strategies in dealing with the rising hegemon

(China), the European Union bloc, and militant Islam. That will likely tax the attention, creativity, and the resources of the hegemon—and create growing anxiety among those counting the costs.

In addition, nuclear weapons or nuclear ambitions exist in each of those arenas. China is a nuclear power, as are France and Britain in the European Union (and Germany has the capability to become a nuclear power relatively quickly). Islamic militants have called for the development of an "Islamic bomb" and al Qaeda has actively sought to acquire such a capability. And al Qaeda has declared global war on the United States and has already mounted a spectacular attack on its homeland. Indeed, since the dawn of the nuclear age in 1945, al Qaeda is the only actor who seems intent on staging a nuclear attack against the United States.

In order to discuss the nature of nuclear relations in a hegemonic world, we find it useful to picture the second nuclear age as a wheel as sketched in Figure 7–1. The United States is at the hub, the sole superpower, but instead of having essentially one state to deal with to define nuclear relationships (the general condition during the Cold War), it has to interact with a variety of actors—with the Russians, with American allies, with China, with the emerging nuclear weapons states, with the international community as a whole, and with terrorist organizations. The United States would be involved

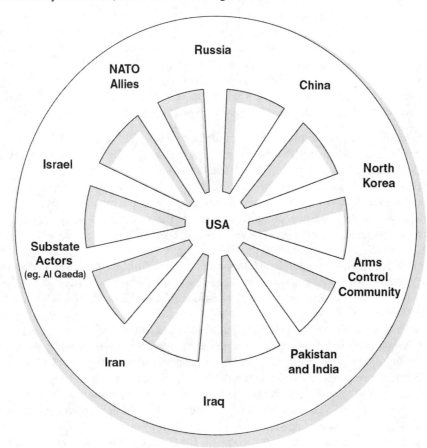

Figure 7–1 Nuclear Relations in the Second Nuclear Age

in every effort to define the new nuclear world given its power and centrality, but given the diversity of issues and actors, the results are likely to be a patchwork of evolving procedures, norms, and agreements, sometimes reinforcing policy in different areas, at other times undermining it. At the same time, the outer rim of the wheel reminds us that the spokes have their own connections that do not flow through the hub, such as the nuclear connection between Pakistan, North Korea, and Iran We will first examine the Russian-American "spoke"—the heart of the nuclear predicament during the first nuclear age, but now just one of the several aspects of the predicament that vie for the hegemon's attention.

THE RUSSIAN-AMERICAN CONNECTION

The most dramatic change of the second nuclear age involved Russia, particularly in its relationship with the United States, where it has gone from adversary to partner, albeit with some suspicion on both sides. There are seven fundamental features of this change.

Sudden proliferation.   The Soviet Union was the first nuclear state to undergo, if you will, a political "fissioning," creating the possibility that the newly independent Belarus, Ukraine, and Kazakstan would become nuclear weapons states by inheriting parts of the Soviet arsenal within their territories. As it happened, a military command structure dominated by the Russian state continued to exercise control over the nuclear arsenal after the Union collapsed, although the leadership of various republics considered how they might gain actual control over the weapons. Subsequently, all weapons were returned to Russia, aided by American pressures and economic incentives.

"Loose nukes."   The economic difficulties of the new Russian state posed critical problems for the control of nuclear materials within Russia. For instance, at the turn of the century, Russia had "30,000 nuclear weapons and 70,000 nuclear-weapons equivalents in highly enriched uranium and plutonium at more than 100 sites across Russia."[15] Security at storage sites for nuclear weapons and fissile materials deteriorated as funds were cut for personnel, maintenance, and repair. Budgetary constraints left spent nuclear materials from nuclear power plants and nuclear submarine propulsion units stored in ramshackle facilities or outdoors in minimally protected areas. Conditions such as these created the possibility of diversion of fissile or radiological materials or the theft of a nuclear weapon itself. In the fall of 2001, for instance, the Russian Defense ministry reported two terrorist attacks on storage sites, both of which were repulsed.[16] As we saw in Chapter 2, relatively small amounts of fissile material (on the order of 20–40 pounds) can make a nuclear device.

In 1991, the U.S. government mounted a multifaceted effort called Cooperative Threat Reduction or the Nunn-Lugar program[17] (named for the two Senators who sponsored it), to buy Russian weapons-grade uranium, to pay for enhanced security for uranium and plutonium stockpiles, to provide benefits for Russian personnel guarding storage sites, to fund the destruction of warheads being decommissioned by arms control agreements, and to find alternative employment for former nuclear scientists. Given the Russian government's chronic budget crisis and the vast amount of materiel to be safeguarded, outside funding and support will be critical for years to deal with this "most urgent unmet national security threat to the United States."[18] The George W. Bush administration, citing its own budgetary problems, has scaled back the funding for these programs.

Faltering arms control.   A general agreement by Reagan and Gorbachev to negotiate a Strategic Arms Limitation Treaty (START) finally bore fruit in July 1991 when the two states agreed to reduce their strategic arsenals to 1,600 strategic delivery systems with 6,000 warheads (START I). When ratification was completed in December, 1994, it began a seven-year period of stepped reductions and close monitoring by both sides of the dismantling and destruction of the delivery systems and warheads. In the meantime, both states had negotiated START II which set a strategic warhead ceiling of 3,500 and prohibited MIRVs on ICBMs. The American Senate ratified the START II treaty in January 1996, but the Russian Parliament stalled. The growing opposition to President Yeltsin pushed the treaty into the swirl of domestic politics, and Russian critics had a litany of complaints: the United States continued to pursue a missile defense system; NATO was expanding eastward; the START treaty was unbalanced, as the United States would have a powerful, accurate MIRVed SLBM force while the Russian navy would not. Financial exigencies, in any case, would force Russia to reduce the size of its arsenal; START II would ensure parallel American reductions as well. The Russian parliament finally ratified START II in 2000.

American interest in traditional arms control waned with the arrival of the presidency of George W. Bush. Bush said that further reductions did not need formal agreements—which would involve "endless hours of arms control discussions." Rather, the two sides could just issue reciprocal pledges to reduce and trust the other to follow through. This was a far cry from the spirit of Reagan's "trust, but verify." The Russians demurred; treaties bind countries while one American president's pledge can be revoked by his successor. After several meetings with the new Russian President, Vladimir Putin, Bush accepted a formal agreement which was signed in Moscow in 2002. His comments, however, caught the new, casual attitude toward arms control: "I looked the man in the eye and shook his hand. But if you need to write it down on a piece of paper, I'll be glad to do that. We don't need to use arms control negotiations to reduce our weaponry in a significant way."[19] The new agreement set warhead ceilings in a range from 1,500 to 2,200, to be reached over ten years.

And that is likely to be the end of the process of strategic arms reduction with the Russians as far as the Bush administration and perhaps successor administrations are concerned, for these ceilings are the lowest level that the Pentagon and its congressional allies are likely to accept. As we saw in Chapter 6, these were only the ceilings for *deployed* warheads. The United States insisted that the agreement allowed them to keep the decommissioned warheads in its reserve stocks. The Russians protested, arguing that the decommissioned warheads were to be destroyed. Russia's economic weakness will likely mean that the U.S. interpretation of the agreement will stand—with bad feeling. Public opinion polls in Russia reported that 17 percent of Russians believed that President Bush sought "to improve relations between the two countries and bring them closer together, while 66 percent think what he's seeking is to strengthen his country's position at the expense of others."[20]

More alienating for the Russians was the Bush administration's determination, in spite of Russian objections, to scrap the ABM treaty which prohibited the testing and deployment of the slowly evolving missile defense system the president wanted to deploy. The hawks within the Bush administration "wanted to drop the A.B.M. treaty altogether as a demonstration that America accepts no artificial limits on its national interest."[21] The president said that September 11 attacks "make it clearer than ever that a Cold War ABM treaty that prevents us from defending our people is outdated, and I believe dangerous." In December 2001, he informed Putin that the United States would exercise its right to withdraw from the agreement in six months time. It did so. The Russian reaction was to suggest that some provisions in the START agreements might not apply. START and the Moscow treaty expire in 2009 and 2012 respectively. Washington at least does not seem to be particularly concerned.

The Iranian connection.   Russia agreed to help Iran rebuild a partially constructed nuclear reactor that was damaged during the Iran-Iraq war of 1980–1988. The United States rejects Iran's claim that its nuclear power industry will be dedicated to meet a growing demand for electricity, believing instead that the Iranian goal is the development of nuclear weapons. The Russians have rejected American requests to halt the construction and not ship nuclear fuel rods, arguing that as Iran is a signatory of the NPT, mandated inspections (particularly with a more aggressive International Atomic Energy Agency) should be effective in detecting Iranian cheating on its NPT obligations. Moreover, Russia pledged to safeguard the plutonium created by the reactor. Russian interests in Iran are geopolitical and economic. It is a near neighbor, with ties to the new Islamic republics on Russia's southern border. The construction project provides needed cash, as do military sales to Iran—another irritant to Washington.[22] Furthermore, in the controversy over Iranian plans to enrich uranium, Russia has tried to devise a compromise, such as having an Iranian facility within Russia to do the enrichment. Russia will likely continue to fend off American protests.

American unilateralism regarding proliferation   The Russian government has continued to express concern about the coercive approach the United States has taken toward states that the latter has labeled "rogue nations." Although it endorsed the first Gulf War against Saddam Hussein, Russia (like many other members of the Security Council) grew increasingly restive with the continued trade embargo on Iraq as it appeared to Russia that Iraq had been divested of its nuclear and other weapons of mass destruction. An end to the embargo would also help Russian economic interests. When the Bush administration made the case in the spring of 2003 that Saddam still had prohibited weapons of mass destruction and constituted a threat to international peace and security, Russia (and France, China, and a majority of the other members of the Security Council) rejected the American demand that the United Nations use force to overthrow Saddam, and subsequently criticized the United States for waging an unnecessary second war against Iraq. Similarly, the Russians have urged Washington to be more accommodating to North Korean demands in order to deal with its threatened proliferation.

The Chechnya quagmire.   Soon after the breakup of the Soviet Union, Islamic peoples in the southern Russian province of Chechnya re-energized their search for greater local autonomy; the more radical insisted on independence. A bloody and brutal insurrection tore through the region when the Russian government granted few concessions and periodically used massive and indiscriminate force. The ongoing war has seen several peace plans, expressions of American and international concern for Russian heavy-handedness, and Russian insistence that the world look on the insurrectionists as terrorists, to be crushed just as American and other forces were attempting to destroy the al Qaeda and Taliban terrorists holding out in Afghanistan.

The nuclear dimension of the Chechen war emerges when commentators speculate that the most likely scenario for the theft of nuclear materials would be by Chechen rebels who then might use what they had stolen or sell the materials on the black market to other actors. To this point, the Chechens have relied on more traditional methods such as suicide truck bombs and the seizure of a Moscow concert hall and a school building to bring the war to Russia. Perhaps, however, as a warning of what might come, a Chechen rebel group did inform Russian authorities that a radiological bomb had been placed in a Moscow park. Though it was defused before it exploded—as the Chechens had apparently planned—the bomb served notice that insurrectionary groups might deploy these kinds of weapons.

Prestige and security issues. The possession of nuclear weapons has long been part of a state's claim to being a major power, thereby ensuring that its views will be heard and its interests heeded. For Russia, all the other supports for its claim have washed away. As one American official monitoring the Russian arsenal said, "The Russians acknowledge in the open press and face to face that their ticket to the big time, their ability to sit at the big people's table, rides on the fact that they still have this nuclear capability. And that is, very frankly, their only claim to superpower status."[23] An attempt to preserve and build such prestige is likely to be active for some time. A large proportion of Russia's population lives with the historical memory "that their Motherland was, virtually overnight, deprived of its name, its flag, nearly half of its territory, its defining ideology, its governing structure and its protective alliance."[24] Nuclear weapons provide the last link with its past stature.

At the same time, nuclear weapons continue to address certain security concerns. In 1999, Poland, the Czech Republic, and Hungary joined NATO—at their request, as they had security concerns about their future relations with Russia—and other states in Eastern Europe have expressed similar desires. The Russian government denounced the expansion as a provocation—if the Cold War was over, why would such a military alliance continue to exist and move itself closer to Russia's frontiers? NATO's response has been to seek ways to bring Russia into a working relationship with NATO (the Partnership for Peace program) and to circumscribe NATO nuclear activities in the East European member states. The Russian response has been begrudging acceptance of the new NATO. All the same, NATO makes a Russian nuclear deterrent necessary. Given the weakened state of conventional Russian forces that must provide security for the homeland against U.S., European, or Chinese threats, it is likely that Russia will maintain as large a nuclear arsenal as it can afford, rather than size an arsenal to meet a different objective such as minimal nuclear deterrence as practiced by the Chinese.

MULTILATERAL ARMS CONTROL COMES UNDER CHALLENGE

Like the Russian-American nuclear relationship, multilateral arms control has shown similar erratic progress. India and Pakistan openly proliferated in 1998, North Korea probably did so by 2003, and Iraq had created an energetic though disorganized program to produce nuclear weapons by the late 1990s (and may well have done so if it were not for the Gulf War of 1990–1991). And the United States began to turn its back on broader arms control measures. It did negotiate and sign the Comprehensive Test Ban treaty (the CTB) along with scores of other states in September 1996. When ratified, the treaty would obligate its signatories "not to carry out any nuclear weapon test explosion or any other nuclear explosion." It set up an organization and procedure for monitoring state compliance and dealing with issues as they emerged. The treaty, like the Partial Test Ban treaty, has an escape clause permitting each state the right of withdrawal if it found its supreme interests jeopardized by adherence to the treaty.[25] A number of states indicated the conditions that would trigger their withdrawal. Worried about Congressional opposition, the Clinton administration said that it would withdraw if the U.S. stockpile of warheads could not be judged safe and reliable without testing.[26]

Clinton's assurance was not enough for conservatives in the Senate, where the treaty had to be ratified in order to become binding on the United States. Republican leaders prevented a vote from being taken until a coalition of nays could be created, then rushed the treaty to the floor of the Senate for a vote in October, 1999, with no time for committee hearings or meaningful floor debate. The treaty received 48 votes in support, 51 against. Treaty ratification in the Senate fails if more than a third of the votes are against the treaty, but here was *a majority against* the treaty. The new sentiment within the political elite was that of Senator Jesse Helms: the United States, he declared, could not and should not rely on others or on treaties to safeguard the United States.[27]

American rejection effectively scuttles the treaty, as the treaty's entry into force depends upon ratification by 44 specific nations—those having nuclear reactors. The Clinton administration tried to salvage what it could by announcing that it would not conduct any tests. The Chinese, British, French, and Russians issued similar statements. The Bush administration has continued this self-imposed moratorium. If it or a successor administration chose to test nuclear weapons, the only constraint would be the Partial Test Ban Treaty's barring testing in the atmosphere or under water.

The Non-Proliferation Treaty, on the other hand, fared better in the 1990s, but it too was buffeted by disquiet. The treaty stipulated that a general conference be held in 1995 to consider making the treaty permanent. Meeting in April and May, many states, most notably India, criticized the existing nuclear powers for making little progress toward the Treaty's declared goal of general nuclear disarmament. The Arab states sought to pressure Israel into signing the NPT in order to force its denuclearization. These two groups of states threatened to block making the treaty permanent. A clear majority (including the existing nuclear powers) wanted permanency, but they did not want to force a vote that would clearly divide the conference and thus appear to rupture the general consensus that proliferation was undesirable. The compromise was that the 175 delegations indicated that they "understood" that the treaty was permanent, that all nations would be urged to sign the NPT, and that at future five-year review conferences, a key issue would be nuclear disarmament by the existing nuclear weapons states.

The Clinton and Bush administrations have had to deal with states that accepted the NPT but have covertly attempted to produce nuclear weapons. The documented cases of treaty violations are Iraq (a signatory in 1969) and North Korea (a signatory in 1985), with strong suspicions being cast on Iran (a signatory in 1970). The United States has become increasingly insistent that signatories adhere to their pledge not to go nuclear and that the International Atomic Energy Agency act more vigorously in the inspection process to detect diversion of fissile materials to weapons-making. For years, the Agency adhered to the treaty guidelines and inspected only the sites that the signatory had designated as falling under the purview of the NPT, but after the experience with Iraq (where inspections prior to the Gulf War consistently found Iraq in compliance with its obligations to the NPT), the Agency developed a more aggressive approach in its inspections and in the mid-1990s invited the treaty's signatories to accept an additional protocol that gave the IAEA the power to watch for and investigate undeclared sites and activities. By mid-2005, nearly 100 states had signed the Additional Protocol, including Iran (who, as we shall see below, was pressured by Europe and the United States to do so).

The irony of the NPT is that while it has enhanced its ability to detect proliferation activities, that very ability will tempt would-be proliferators to renounce the treaty, for by the traditional standards of international law, states that do not agree to a treaty are not bound by its provisions. North Korea's withdrawal from the NPT in 2003 freed it from legal constraint, just as India and Pakistan's never signing the treaty did. Iran has manipulated the threat of withdrawal as well.

The North Korean withdrawal did not free it from political challenge, however, as the United States insisted on imposing a new nuclear rule: *No state that the United States deemed hostile would be permitted to have nuclear weapons.* Washington has added a codicil in light of Iran's pursuit of uranium enrichment—a program the Iranians claimed was solely for powering their planned energy-producing nuclear reactors. The codicil declared that *no state that the United States deemed hostile would be permitted to have a uranium enrichment or plutonium reprocessing capability.* We discuss below how the United States set out to impose those new rules.

Another Clinton administration initiative received a warmer reception from the Bush administration. In 1993 Clinton proposed a Fissile Materials Cutoff Treaty that would ban the further production of fissile materials for nuclear explosives. The United Nations Committee on Disarmament has repeatedly taken up the proposal but has been unable to reach agreement, particularly on the issue of verification, which would have to be extensive in that states would still be permitted to produce fissile materials for power generation and for nuclear-powered submarines. As negotiations stalled, the United States, Russia, France, and Britain declared that they had voluntarily stopped production (China may have done so but has not made a public statement to that effect), and then in 2004 the Bush administration proposed negotiating a treaty having no specific verification procedures. While one could see this as a serious attempt to create a new international norm against the production of weapons-grade material—and hence to prevent any further proliferation—it also fits within the Bush administration's attempt to keep rogue states from proliferating without offering meaningful concessions to bring that about.

Given America's concentration on rogue states, its general disinterest in broader arms control measures, and its perception of the cumbersomeness of negotiations—and a hegemon's distaste for having to bargain—formal, negotiated arms control measures have probably reached a plateau. Barring a nuclear crisis, it is unlikely that there will be any deepening of the *negotiated* arms control regime. Indeed, if anything, the regime is likely to erode from the following pressures:

1. Institutional interests and strategic doctrines of the Russian and American military services will keep deployed strategic warheads at roughly 2000, marking a permanent failure to work toward total disarmament pledged by the NPT. This openly undermines the treaty.

2. The recent uptick in open proliferation (India, Pakistan, and North Korea) has eroded the negative connotations of nuclear weapons and enhanced the idea that states derive power, prestige, and bargaining advantages from them.

3. There have been anti-proliferation successes, notably Libya's agreement in 2004 to terminate its nuclear weapons program under U.S. observation. This is a step away from proliferation, but even in this case, the *threat* of proliferation seemed to be a route to get other states to change their behaviors (such as ending the U.S. and United Nations' embargo on Libya) in exchange for the end of the proliferation effort. Thus a putative proliferation effort may be an attractive bargaining chip.

4. Globalization and technological advances have combined to make it possible for would-be proliferators to purchase overtly and covertly the materials needed to produce weapons-grade fissile materials. These components can be manufactured by relatively small, private compa-

nies, but A. Q. Khan, the "father" of Pakistan's bomb, also demonstrated that an unofficial but governmentally tolerated program could supply components and technical advice. (We discuss this in greater detail in Chapter 8.)

5. The American effort during the 1980s to aid Afghans in liberating Afghanistan from Soviet troops and the Marxist government they supported, and the current American (and NATO) war on Taliban and al Qaeda forces still operating in Afghanistan have made Pakistani cooperation vital for the United States. Cooperation came at a nuclear price: The United States periodically had to overlook known Pakistani efforts to create nuclear weapons (in spite of American laws restricting aid to would-be proliferators). It had to tolerate the refusal of the Pakistani government to punish A. Q. Khan meaningfully. The lesson for others is that American geo-political interests will trump its interest in preventing proliferation, making American demands for non-proliferation by others seem hypocritical and suggesting that states who can align themselves with American geo-political interests will have 'permission' to develop nuclear weapons.

Set against these pressures to unravel the arms control regime are several harbingers of hope. First, India and Pakistan have edged toward the creation of nuclear rules of the road and possibly a tacit understanding about the size of their nuclear arsenals, a topic we take up when we examine that spoke of the wheel. Second, there has been an increased effort to identify and intercept technology transfers of components for nuclear weapons programs and missile delivery systems. In 2003, President Bush announced the Proliferation Security Initiative, an agreement by several states to interdict the suspected shipment of missiles and WMD agents or components through their territory or on their ships and to seek permission from others to do so on a case-by-case basis. In the same year, the head of the International Atomic Energy Agency, Mohammed ElBaradei, proposed a new international treaty that would place all plutonium separation and HEU production activities under multilateral rather than state control and have similar control of spent fuel rods and radioactive waste. In 2004, in an unusual move, the United Nations Security Council directed in Resolution 1540 that states pass laws prohibiting non-state actors (like al Qaeda) from having access to weapons of mass destruction or their precursor materials, and that states develop controls for such weapons and precursors. Here was perhaps the first instance of an attempt by fifteen states (the members of the Security Council) to create new rules of the road by directive rather than the cumbersome process of gaining assent through the negotiation of a treaty.[30]

Of course, the willingness of powerful individual states to sanction others for their nuclear activities remains one way to safeguard the arms control regime, but such a threat has had a checkered history. Periods of American sanctioning of Pakistani nuclear efforts were undercut by domestic pressures (as in continuation of agricultural exports to Pakistan at the behest of the American agricultural lobby) and by the fact that Pakistani aid was crucial in Afghanistan. Furthermore, sanctions or the threat of them can be the very thing that spurs proliferation. In December 1995, for example, U.S. spy satellites noticed activity in an area suspected of being a possible test site for Indian nuclear weapons. The U.S. government quietly pressed India not to test, and India did not. That success, however, had the following consequences. When the nationalist Bharatiya Janata Party came to power in March 1998, it decided to test the weapons in part to show that the new government, "unlike previous regimes, will not give in to international pressure."[31] Moreover, experience with American intelligence capabilities allowed the new government to disguise its preparations so that international pressure prior to the test would be avoided.

COERCIVE ANTI-PROLIFERATION AND COERCIVE DENUCLEARIZATION

The ultimate sanctions to enforce an arms control regime are *coercive anti-proliferation* and *coercive denuclearization*. Coercive anti-proliferation occurs when a state uses threats or punitive actions, including military attack, to prevent another state from acquiring nuclear weapons or the capacity to make them. Coercive denuclearization occurs when a state attempts to remove *existing* nuclear weapons and its associated production capacity by similar means.

In 2003, the United States tried to enlist the United Nations in a campaign of threat and then military invasion to destroy Iraq's nuclear weapons capability (and to remove presumed stores of chemical and biological weapons). At least that was initially the principal argument that the Bush administration advanced for its attack on Iraq, although American officials admitted that it might be years before Iraq's nuclear program actually produced a nuclear device.[32] The administration did advance other justifications (ridding Iraq of a bloody tyrant and of an authoritarian, anti-democratic regime, and implanting democracy in their stead)—justifications that assumed more prominence when no such weapons or actual programs to construct them were found.

Ironically, in this particular case, the attempt at coercive anti-proliferation probably *undermined* the arms regime in three fundamental ways: First, the attack on Iraq was unnecessary because there were no Iraqi nuclear weapons nor the capability to produce them, and that was, despite the intelligence cited by President Bush, the view of many analysts within the American intelligence network[33] and the consensus of the IAEA leadership. An arms control regime that seems to provide *a pretext* for an unwarranted attack will likely be perceived as a danger by other states. Second, the attack was in defiance of the clearly expressed opposition of many governments, some of whom opposed the idea of coercive anti-proliferation in principle, and some who rejected the newly enunciated American rule about the impermissibility of nuclear weapons in the hands *of certain states*. Third, the enormous cost of the American attack and occupation and its uncertain outcome may lead states contemplating proliferation to conclude that the United States will not dare use this level of force again.

Iraq in 2003 was the first time the United States chose to use force to uphold its new rule that hostile states would not be permitted to go nuclear. This is not to say that the United States had not contemplated such action before. We saw in chapter 5 that it considered attacking Chinese nuclear facilities in 1964. In 1994 it apparently came close to attacking North Korea's facilities to prevent the production of a plutonium bomb.[34] Today, coercive anti-proliferation (or coercive denuclearization) remains an option for its dealings with Iran and North Korea. We need to look more closely at those spokes of the wheel.

NORTH KOREA AS A ROGUE NUCLEAR STATE

The American designation of "rogue states" initially referred to states that seemed determined to contravene the norms of the international system, at least those norms that the United States felt important to uphold. The George W. Bush administration modified the term, characterizing them as states that "support terrorism, disregard international agreements they have signed, and are not democratic" and "reject basic human values and hate the United States and everything for which it stands."[35] Bush added another dimension in his 2002 State of the Union address when he declared that there was an "axis of evil" among certain rogue states, implying a connection and coordination between Iraq, Iran, and North Korea that posed a grave danger to the United States, particularly because of their nuclear ambitions and overt hostility toward the United States.

North Korea (more properly known as the Democratic People's Republic of Korea or DPRK) was a product of World War II. A Japanese possession at the time, it was divided into two military occupation zones (like Germany, Austria, and Vietnam). As the Cold War crystalized, the Soviet-occupied north became the Communist DPRK while the U.S.-occupied south became the Republic of Korea. In 1950, American military intervention repelled a Northern attempt to re-unify the peninsula by force. A U.S. re-unification effort failed when China intervened against U.S. forces. The war remained stalemated for two years, with the battle line roughly at the boundary between the northern and southern occupation zones. We saw in Chapter 5 how the Eisenhower administration threatened a nuclear escalation unless the Communists agreed to an armistice. They did agree in 1953, but the two Koreas remained heavily militarized and the North's rhetoric and periodic challenges to the South and to U.S. forces stationed there suggested that war might erupt at any moment. At the same time, the North feared that the South and the United States would resume the war.[36]

By the late 1980s, South Korea had developed into an economic powerhouse while the North's collapsing economy fueled questions about the survivability of Communist control—and what its leadership might do to prevent that collapse. During the early 1990s, the G.H.W. Bush administration became concerned that the North had begun to use its nuclear power program as the route to the development of nuclear weapons.[37] As the evidence became clearer that the North had begun to reprocess plutonium, the administration began to pressure the North to meet its commitments to the NPT (which it had signed) but the North seemed belligerently unresponsive. The Clinton administration inherited the standoff when it came into office in January 1993. It initially adopted a series of threats, implying that some form of sanctions would be imposed on the North unless it came back into compliance with the NPT, but it did offer to consider a change in its relationship with the North if the latter complied.

The North responded defiantly, threatening to devastate South Korea, particularly its capital Seoul, which lies just south of the demilitarized zone separating the two states. But mixed in with the defiant words were suggestions that the North might consider a compromise, hinting that it might end its nuclear program in exchange for an end to the American trade embargo, diplomatic recognition, and compensation for giving up the North's nuclear reactor program. Those offers were hard to hear in Washington. Clinton officials who did hear them had to be concerned that the North was simply trying to blackmail the United States into paying for something the North Korean government had already committed itself to by signing the NPT—a non-nuclear weapons state. Others feared that the North had not abandoned its hope of reuniting the peninsula on its own terms, including possibly the use of force, and would look for a pretext to launch an offensive.

By the summer of 1994, the prevailing view within the Clinton administration was that war was imminent on the peninsula.[38] American intelligence judged that the North had reprocessed enough plutonium to produce two bombs; whether they had been manufactured was unknown. Any American effort to coerce North Korea (for instance, by demanding that the United Nations Security Council impose sanctions on Korea for being in violation of the NPT) might trigger the threatened Northern attack. Alternatively, the United States might be pushed into an attack on the North's nuclear facilities to keep nuclear weapons from appearing in the North's inventory, but even pinpoint attacks on the reprocessing facility might trigger a massive invasion of the South, which would collide with U.S. forces stationed near the demilitarized zone.

At this point, two developments came together which pushed the United States in a different direction. Former president Jimmy Carter inserted himself in the crisis, flying to North Korea to see if there was a peaceful solution. Carter on his own declared that sanctions against the North would not be sought; Kim Il Sung, the North Korean leader, indicated that a deal could be struck if the North was compensated. Second, within the Clinton administration, a group of officials who had been advocating a different approach to the North—one that emphasized making mutual concessions rather than seeking to coerce the North into compliance—had gradually gotten more support, helped by the realization that a very costly war on the peninsula was in the offing. They argued that a package deal had to be proposed to the North, one where both sides would implement mutual concessions more or less simultaneously, rather than demand that the North put itself back into full compliance with the NPT before the United States would negotiate any further. For this group, the immediate goal was to end the North's *further* production of weapons-grade plutonium. In compensation, the U.S. would offer to construct alternative nuclear reactors that made plutonium reprocessing more difficult. Additional confidence-building measures would occur as the reactors were built. The *final* part of the package would be the North's ridding itself of the plutonium (or bombs) that it had *already* produced in exchange for completion of the reactors and the signing of a non-aggression treaty by the United States.

The death of the North Korean leader Kim Il Sung did not derail progress in the negotiations as his son and successor, Kim Jong Il, continued the elder Kim's approach. Within months, there was an Agreed Framework accepted by both sides, with a series of carefully laid out steps. The North agreed to *eventual* denuclearization, while the United States agreed to treat the North as a state with which it could do business, part of which was to meet the North's demands for respect and security. That is, in the interest of mutual security, the United States would overlook the past, overlook the repressive nature of the regime, and overlook the possibility that the agreement would prolong the life of a communist regime. To the Clinton administration, that seemed a reasonable price to pay to avoid war on the peninsula or to face a North Korea armed with many nuclear weapons in the not-too-distant future—as well as armed with a growing arsenal of missiles whose ranges were lengthening slowly but surely.

Indeed, after the signing of the 1994 Accord, the Clinton administration began to work on the missile issue. In 1998 the North tested a long-range missile whose subsequent refinements would likely produce a variant capable of reaching the United States. In addition, the U.S. government had growing concerns about the export of North Korean missile technology to Iran and Pakistan. The United States requested that the North give up its program; the North responded by asking what the United States would do in return. An agreement began to take shape—so much so that President Clinton planned to fly to North Korea—but by then the Democrats were leaving office and, when they received no encouragement from the incoming Bush team, they put the talks on hold.

The Bush administration, hostile to the very idea of negotiating with the North, let alone paying the North to meet its treaty obligations, reluctantly accepted the 1994 Accord but was not eager to do more along these lines. Indeed, the new president, as he had with Vladimir Putin, drew upon his personal reaction to Kim Jong Il in formulating his perspective on negotiating with the North. In August 2002 Bush spoke with Bob Woodward, a reporter for the *Washington Post*.

> The president sat forward in his chair. I thought he might jump up he became so emotional as he spoke about the North Korean leader.
> "I loathe Kim Jong Il!" Bush shouted, waving his finger in the air. "I've got a visceral reaction to this guy, because he is starving his people. And I have seen intelligence of these prison camps—they're huge—that he uses to break up families, and to torture people."

. . .

He wondered how the civilized world could stand by and coddle the North Korean president as he starves his people. "It is visceral. Maybe it's my religion, maybe it's my—but I feel passionate about this." He said he also realized that the North Koreans had massive military might poised to overrun the U.S. ally South Korea.

"I'm not foolish," the President continued. "They tell me, we don't need to move too fast, because the financial burdens on people will be so immense if we try to—if this guy were to topple. Who would take care of—I just don't buy that. Either you believe in freedom, and want to—and worry about the human condition, or you don't."[39]

Bush made it clear where he stood when he publicly consigned the North to the "axis of evil" and the Nuclear Posture Review identified the North as a potential target. By the fall of 2002, the North Korean government was responding in kind, declaring that the U.S. stance "was a clear declaration of war against the DPRK." Because the United States was "behaving so arrogantly and impertinently," "the DPRK was entitled to possess not only nuclear weapons but any type of weapon more useful than that so as to defend its sovereignty and right to exist from the ever-growing nuclear threat by the U.S."[40]

Amidst the swirl of vituperation, American intelligence developed evidence that the North was engaged in the surreptitious enrichment of uranium while still adhering to the 1994 agreement that shut down the plutonium process. As best the intelligence services could determine, the uranium program had begun around 1998. When confronted with the intelligence findings in October 2002, the North Korean government admitted it was enriching uranium (although months later it denied that it was doing so).

What was at work here? Had the North played the United States for the sucker, gaining concessions while cheating on its ostensible agreement not to go further into the nuclear weapons field? The Bush administration's public stance was that North Korea was in flagrant violation of its agreements. U.S. implementation of the 1994 accord was suspended. It demanded that North Korea put itself in full compliance with its NPT obligations and permit the IAEA to conduct intrusive verification inspections. Then and only then would the United States consider North Korea's demands, including the resumption of the fulfillment of the 1994 accord. The standoff has continued. North Korea watched the U.S. invasion of Iraq—for having a program to build weapons of mass destruction—and declared that "the bloody lesson of the war in Iraq for the world is that only when a country has physical deterrent forces and massive military deterrent forces that are capable of overwhelmingly defeating any attack by state-of-the-art weapons, can it prevent war and defend its independence and national security."[41]

We cannot at this point tell you what was in the mind of the North's leadership. Perhaps they were determined to proliferate. To that end they might have decided in 1994 to prevent an American bombing of their nuclear facilities by reaching an agreement but to use the resulting detente to develop a covert uranium enrichment program to produce a nuclear arsenal.

Or perhaps they are devious negotiators. The 1994 agreement focused on the existing reactor that produced plutonium as a byproduct of its operation; it did not ban the North from acquiring other types of fissile materials (though doing so might violate the spirit of the agreement). Perhaps the North drew the conclusion that if the Americans were willing to pay to stop the plutonium reprocessing, they would be willing to pay again to stop uranium enrichment.

Or was the enrichment of uranium a hedge against the possibility that the United States might renege on the 1994 agreement? Was there reason for an inherently suspicious regime to think that the

United States might not live up to its agreement? The 1994 agreement stipulated that the United States organize a consortium (known as KEDO, consisting of the U.S., Japan, and South Korea) to provide two light-water reactors by 2003. KEDO experienced innumerable delays. Some were caused by the North's sensitivity to how South Korea would participate in the consortium and some by the North's continuing policy of pin-prick challenges to the South such as sending a submarine into South Korean territorial waters. Some delays were caused by wrangling between the consortium members over funding and responsibilities. By the late 1990s it was clear that the target date of 2003 for the completion of the reactors would be missed; construction of the reactor buildings had not even begun. The North Korean government might have asked itself, Was the American government stalling for time, hoping that internal events in the North would bring down the communist regime, just as in Eastern Europe and the Soviet Union? Moreover, President Clinton had pledged that the United States would supply large amounts of fuel oil to tide the North over while the existing reactors were not used and until the KEDO reactors came on line. Republicans in Congress balked at appropriating money for the fuel oil, making the United States chronically late in meeting this aspect of the agreement. Was this another sign of American bad faith?

The North took another confrontational step in 2003 when it withdrew from the NPT, thus ending any international legal prohibition on its development of nuclear weapons. It began reprocessing the plutonium, enough so that it claimed in October 2003 to have a half-dozen nuclear weapons. After insisting on bilateral talks with the United States, the North relented (probably under Chinese pressure), agreeing to meet American demands that the issue needed the participation of China, Japan, Russia, and South Korea. The American position, however, had reverted to what it had been before 1994—the North had to denuclearize first, then the United States would discuss a change in the relationship between the two states. North Korea declared further talks would be pointless.

China continued to press both sides to reach some form of accommodation. Its historic concern for security on its periphery has been compounded by the fear that the politico-economic collapse of North Korea would send waves of refugees into northeast China. China's distaste for democracy meant that it could support Kim if he kept control in the North. In return, China could insist on concessions from the North. As a major trade partner of the United States and the source of much of the funding for the U.S. government's growing budget deficits, China has leverage on the United States as well. In the fall of 2005, the Chinese persuaded the United States and North Korea to agree to a general declaration of principles in which the North agreed to give up its nuclear weapons and nuclear capacities, rejoin the NPT, and permit IAEA inspections to resume. The United States would "normalize relations" with the North, implying that the United States would end efforts to block the North's access to trade, loans, and economic aid; establish diplomatic relations; and provide security guarantees. Implicit as well in normalization is a pledge that the United States would not seek regime change in the North.

This was a step back toward the 1994 agreement, but three critical ingredients still had to be worked out: (1) *The phasing of the steps*. The United States had given up its insistence that the North had to get rid of its nuclear program in a verifiable manner before the United States would consider discussing normalization of relations. The 1994 agreement envisioned relatively simultaneous actions that would provide immediate but partial benefits to both sides. What phasing would Washington and Pyongyang accept? (2) *Nuclear power plants*. The North Koreans announced that at the end of the day, they would have to have light-water reactors to generate electricity. The United States has insisted that because of past North Korean cheating, it should have no reactors. (And given the American stance vis-a-vis Iran, discussed below, it has an incentive to insist on this demand). (3) *Verification.* The Americans are likely to insist on very intrusive inspections to verify the North's fulfillment of any agreement. While North Korea has in the past accepted verification by the IAEA (with some critics asserting that the North did so because it was unaware of the sophisticated technology available to detect and identify minute traces of radioactivity), the hyper-sensitive regime may balk this time. What kind of compromise would be possible here?

In the meantime, the North must continue to appear to proliferate, albeit slowly, for that is both its source of bargaining power with the United States and its means of deterring an American attack, yet it also puts the nation at risk from an American attack. The North must, as it has in the past, stress self-reliance, nationalism, and a do-or-die attitude in order to maintain internal control, but that may be read by the United States as the North's unwillingness or inability to ever make real concessions, forcing the United States to contemplate an attack. The Bush administration is also locked into a posture of confrontation. It seems to want to remove both nuclear weapons and the Kim regime from the North. The North is not likely to concede both.

There are only three basic outcomes open to the United States: to negotiate mutual concessions to bring about denuclearization, to take unilateral action such as the bombing of North Korean nuclear sites, or to acquiesce in the status quo— permitting a rogue nation to keep its nuclear weapons.[42] You will be able to observe the outcome of this confrontation unfold over the next several years and judge the consequences for the second nuclear age. Successful proliferation by the North may encourage other states to emulate it, perhaps in a more circumspect fashion—and will certainly force Japan and South Korea to think anew about a nuclear weapons program. Or the United States might find the right combination of threats and inducements to produce denuclearization without having to wage war—a war that looks much more costly than the invasion of Iraq was. Or perhaps the internal processes within the North will continue to erode the regime's ability to control its society, promoting internal chaos and change with unforeseeable consequences for relations on the peninsula.

IRAQ AND SADDAM HUSSEIN

Iraqi interest in nuclear weapons began in the 1970s before Saddam Hussein came to power. By the late 1980s, Saddam's Iraq had an extensive but covert nuclear weapons program under way, largely in response to the war with Iran. Its purchases of dual-use equipment aroused suspicions, but the first Bush administration chose to cultivate good relations with Saddam as a counterweight to Iran, America's nemesis in the region since 1979. The Iraqi invasion of Kuwait in August 1990 changed the picture.[43] While oil interests were involved, in President G. H. W. Bush's mind the critical issue was the flagrant violation of the norm against aggression. Iraq's refusal to heed the UN demand for withdrawal produced an American-led offensive in early 1991 that quickly drove the Iraqi forces from Kuwait and threatened to destroy them.

The United States held out an offer of terminating the war short of that outcome if Saddam accepted a number of conditions, the most important for our analysis was that Iraq had to divest itself of all weapons of mass destruction and the means to produce them, and do so under the supervision of the United Nations. This was a form of punishment for the invasion and the refusal to withdraw from Kuwait as demanded by the United Nations. The extent of the Iraqi *nuclear* effort came as a surprise, but the International Atomic Energy Agency—with the American government supplying intelligence behind the scenes—uncovered the extensive program (albeit one fraught with internal prob-lems).[44] By the mid-1990s the IAEA had dismantled the program. That is not to say that nuclear ambitions were expunged from the thinking of Iraq's leadership. It is to say that Iraq did not dare re-constitute the program, even after it had effectively blocked further IAEA inspections in 1998. And even if it had dared, it probably could not have done so easily. An Iraqi scientist interviewed after the 2003 war indicated that the inspections were devastating: "We would have to start from less than zero… . The truth is, we disintegrated."[45] Iraq had no nuclear program when the United States in-vaded in March 2003.[46]

However, the *image* of nuclear weapons in the hands of rogue states became part of rallying cry for the second Bush administration to build support for an invasion of Iraq. In the late summer of 2002, for instance, Vice President Dick Cheney in a series of speeches argued that Saddam Hussein would attempt to rearm Iraq with nuclear weapons, and as he was a "sworn enemy of our country," the weapons in his hands would constitute a "mortal threat" to the United States. The administration attempted to build its case that Iraq did indeed have a nuclear weapons program by reformulating in-telligence information to make a case that would energize the public, the Congress, and the United Nations. When Secretary of State Powell appeared before the UN Security Council in February 2003 to make the case for an invasion, among his justifications were his conviction of Saddam Hussein's determination "to get his hands on a nuclear bomb" and evidence of Iraq's ordering of high quality aluminum tubes that Powell concluded were to be used to make centrifuges to enrich uranium—thus confirming Saddam was determined to restart the forbidden nuclear program. The tubes had been or-dered (and intercepted). What the tubes were for was a matter of dispute. The International Atomic Energy Agency had concluded that the tubes were for artillery rockets, a standard item in the Iraqi in-ventory. The post-war search of Iraq found no evidence to support Powell's interpretation. No matter the tenuousness of the evidence, however, the Bush administration argued that the risk that Saddam Hussein posed to the United States and to Iraq's neighbors was enough to warrant coercive anti-proliferation measures.

Michael Shrage has argued that the real issue was not whether Iraq possessed weapons of mass de-struction. Rather, the problem was that Iraq had crafted a strategy of *strategic ambiguity*, both deny-ing the existence of such weapons and acting in ways to suggest that it had them (as in forcing an end to the inspections in 1998 with the numerous presidential palace complexes still unvisited). In doing so, Saddam Hussein preserved *the threat* to use such weapons against his foes, hoping thereby to de-ter the United States and to bolster Iraq's power in the region, yet at the same time the ambiguity made it more difficult for the United States to launch an attack. In Schrage's view, the Bush adminis-tration's invasion of Iraq brought about "the end of America's tolerance for state-sponsored ambigu-ities explicitly designed to threaten American lives." Unilaterally ending the ambiguity by force, he acknowledged, "may not make the world a safer place. But policies that permit rogue states to wield greater influence by creating greater uncertainty about their weapons of mass destruction are guaran-teed to make the world an even more dangerous place."[48]

The U.S. military victory opened up Iraq for a renewed and thorough American WMD inspection (which found nothing). It also opened up Iraq for a U.S.-led reconstruction effort to produce a demo-cratic state, at peace with its neighbors, with no weapons of mass destruction, and friendly toward the United States. Whether this Bush administration goal can be achieved remains to be seen. As we write these words, other outcomes seem as likely: Iraq may undergo a violent civil war that fragments the country into three weak states of Kurds, Sunni Arabs, and Shi'ia Arabs—at odds with each other, bitterly anti-American, and potential havens for terrorists. Or it will be a unitary state maintained by force—undemocratic, perhaps still passably friendly toward the United States, but living in a dangerous region in which nuclear weapons might still appear as attractive means to safeguard the Iraqi state's interests.

IRAN AND NUCLEAR NATIONALISM

Iran's interest in nuclear weapons began under the Shah, partially cloaked behind a program to build nuclear power plants to generate electricity.[49] American officials tolerated if not encouraged Iranian interest as the Nixon administration viewed the Shah as a check on Soviet influence in the region. American plans collapsed in 1979 when a politico-religious movement led by the Ayatollah Khomeini overthrew the Shah. The seizure of the U.S. embassy in December 1979 put the new Islamic republic on a collision course with the United States. The war with Iraq followed in 1980 with its massive casualties, the Iraqi use of chemical weapons, and an Iraqi bombing of the partially finished, German-built nuclear reactors. Khomeini's view that the nuclear weapons were fundamentally anti-Islamic hampered Iranian progress toward a weapon despite the war. After the war, Iran renewed its nuclear power program, but with some circumspection as Washington suspected that Iran was engaging in a surreptitious nuclear weapons program. Both the G. H. W. Bush and the Clinton administrations badgered the Russians about rebuilding the reactors, but the Russians persisted. Iran pointed to its signature on the NPT as guaranteeing that it had no interest in weapons.[50]

In the summer of 2002 the picture became more ominous. An Iranian opposition group announced that it had discovered a secret uranium enrichment plant under construction near the city of Natanz. Under the NPT, Iran would be obligated to declare the site to the IAEA when it was ready to begin production, but not before. Faced with the revelation, the Iranian government acknowledge the presence of this site and revealed others; it invited an IAEA inspection, which exposed a large scale centrifuge program using uranium hexafluoride. Scheduled for completion in 2005, the enrichment process could produce enough weapons-grade uranium for several bombs a year—or it could simply enrich uranium to reactor grade as a part of Iran's nuclear power generation program. Iranian officials asserted that Iran could not be dependent on others for nuclear fuel.

The U.S. posture toward Iran has evolved toward ever-more stringent demands. Initially, the United States insisted that Iran accept the Additional Protocol allowing the IAEA to mount intrusive inspections anywhere it suspected nuclear activity. This would both pressure Iran to remain away from weapons activities and likely provide an early tipoff that Iran was moving in that direction. The discovery of the centrifuge project led President George W. Bush to declare that the international community would not accept an Iran armed with nuclear weapons. There quickly followed the American insistence that Iran could not have a uranium-enrichment capability.

The Iranian government has insisted that it must develop nuclear energy to serve the needs of its rapidly growing population, pointing out that depletion of its oil and gas reserves is inevitable. It has claimed its right as a sovereign nation to do so, its right under the NPT to do so, and, using the language of nationalism(a language that has deep resonance in Iran given its history of manipulation by foreign states and corporations), its right as a free and independent people to do so. And it has vigorously denied any intention of producing nuclear weapons.

As we pointed out in Chapter 3, one route to nuclear weapons is for a government to make a series of decisions that eventually gives the state a nuclear reactor and fuel-cycle capabilities, leaving it to later governments to make the decision to create nuclear weapons. Iran's case is more complex, however, than the French and Israeli examples, for Iran is not a democracy like the other two states. Its popularly elected government does not have a free hand as its policies must be acceptable to the Guardian Council, a group of high-ranking, unelected Islamic clerics. Moreover, the Council also determines who is eligible to stand for election, thus shaping the government's composition no matter who wins the election. The Council reflects a bitterly hostile view of the United States for religious reasons (the United States is the Great Satan, as is Russia) and for political reasons (the United States has called for regime change in Iran—meaning the dis-empowerment of the Council). At the same time, popular support for the Council is highly variable. As we write this, both the Council and the government still seem to support Khomeini's assertion that nuclear weapons are undesirable. However, as Iranian President Mahmoud Ahmadinejad warned in 2005, "If some [a clear reference to the United States] try to impose their will on the Iranian people through resort to a language of force and threat with Iran, we will reconsider our entire approach to the nuclear issue."[51] He and members of the Council have tried to build Iranian nationalism as a counter to American threats.

The British, French, and Germans have been in the forefront of a movement to achieve a compromise; they have pressed Iran to accept safeguards that will make weapons development difficult. Europe and the United States, however, have emphasized two different means of persuading the Iranians. The Europeans have offered economic rewards (such as economic aid and increased trade). The Bush Administration repeatedly reiterated that rogue states should not be rewarded for doing what the NPT obligates them to do (although it recently softened its stance, suggesting it might in the future support some economic rewards such as membership in the World Trade Organization). Moreover, the attack on Iraq served as a warning about the possible use of military force to ensure compliance with American insistence that rogue states remain nuclear-free. In the background is Israel's clear unease about Iranian activities and its demonstrated willingness to act as it did against the Iraqi reactor in 1981.[52]

Over the past half-decade, a pattern emerged in the confrontation. The European Union states and the United States would generally reach a compromise position between themselves and then confront Iran with a demand. In 2003, for example, the issue was whether Iran would agree to sign the IAEA Additional Protocol giving the IAEA the power to investigate any suspected facility at any time. The U.S. threatened that unless Iran complied, the United States would take the issue before the 35-member Governing Board of the International Atomic Energy Agency and insist that, as Iran was not in compliance with its NPT obligations, the IAEA must lay the issue before the UN Security Council. The Security Council has the power to sanction states found to be out of compliance. Iran has fought to keep the issue out of the Council's hands, for sanctions would isolate the nation and possibly drive its poorly functioning economy into an irreversible tailspin, threatening the survival of the regime.

There was no guarantee, however, that the IAEA Governing Board would be willing to refer the matter to the Security Council. The IAEA's head, Mohammed ElBaradei has consistently sought negotiated solutions. The Board might, however, judge the situation serious enough to warrant referral—or do so to pass the buck. And there was no guarantee that the Security Council would endorse coercive anti-proliferation policies either. It had refused to do so regarding Iraq, and Russia or China (both with strong interests in maintaining good relations with Teheran) might veto any sanction unless Iran was in egregious violation of its treaty commitments. Or, if hauled before the Security Council, Iran could always withdraw from the Non-Proliferation Treaty, ending both the IAEA's right to make any inspections and the treaty's constraints on Iran. Yet the United States would, nonetheless, have to threaten referral to the Council for it needed the leverage provided by the international community if it hoped to secure Iranian compliance without military action.

The 2003 crisis was resolved by a stopgap compromise: Iran signed the Protocol but reaffirmed its right to have a full nuclear power program, including the capability to enrich uranium. "Iran," declared its foreign minister, Kamal Kharrazi, "has a high technical capability and has to be recognized by the international community as a member of the nuclear club. This is an irreversible path."[53] In 2005 and 2006, the crisis centered on whether Iran would begin the enrichment of uranium, something the Iranians had agreed in the fall of 2004 to suspend temporarily. The United States and the European coalition demanded Iran not go ahead with enrichment, for that would given them the fissile materials for nuclear weapons if they chose to enrich to weapons grade. The Europeans and Russians proposed a variety of schemes for an external party (Russia has volunteered) to supply reactor-grade uranium to Iran and remove it from Iran once it was depleted, or to have an Iranian-owned facility be built in Russia to produce the enriched uranium, but with Russian monitoring of what was shipped to Iran. Iran has insisted that it will control all aspects of the fuel cycle. The IAEA dealt with the standoff in January 2006 by deciding to refer the issue to the Security Council, but hold off for several weeks to allow further negotiations. As we write these words, the Council has yet to act and Iran has declared it will not be coerced.

Iran's options are to accept some form of monitoring and control of its enrichment efforts or to go it alone, risking sanctions or military action by states unable to accept the prospect of a nuclear-armed Iran. (At the present time, United States and Israel have declared that they cannot accept Iranian control of the fuel cycle.) Iran does retain some potent threats. It can cause trouble in its neighbor Iraq and in Israel (by way of the Palestinian groups it supports such as Islamic Jihad), or it can disrupt oil supplies by curtailing its own production or by impeding shipping in the Persian Gulf. Those responses might prove more costly to the United States and Europe in the short run than allowing Iran to go ahead with low level uranium enrichment monitored by the IAEA. And Iran can threaten withdrawal from the NPT (but still remain nuclear weapons free). And it can threaten to declare as national policy that it will become a nuclear weapons state.

It is hard to tell where the Iranian ayatollahs and politicians line up on the question of nuclear weapons for Iran. Most likely they are internally divided, which makes a nuclear power program that does not foreclose on a nuclear weapons program an understandable compromise. External pressure to end both programs, or to make the power-production component dependent upon foreign sources of supply for enriched uranium, will inevitably be rejected by those seeking nuclear weapons and by many Iranians who see such pressure as unwarranted challenges to their independence and sovereignty, challenges to be resisted no matter one's feelings about the desirability of going nuclear. To the degree that Iranians in the street see the pressure as a Western or American attempt to return Iran to a dependent status, or—as the clerics are likely to allege—another salvo in the war against Islam by a godless enemy, they may press their government at least to keep the nuclear option open.

THE ISRAELI WILD CARD

"Under no circumstances," warned the Israeli Defense Minister, Shaul Mofaz, in November 2003, "would Israel be able to tolerate nuclear weapons in Iranian possession."[54] In March 2005, the London *Sunday Times* reported that Israeli military planners had drawn up plans to attack the widely dispersed and hardened Iranian nuclear facilities, and that American officials were briefed on the plans.[55] Iranian President Ahmadinejad then stoked the fire by calling for the destruction of Israel—a long-standing goal, apparently, of many Iranian clerics with whom the Iranian president is allied. It is not possible to tell you if the Israeli government is in earnest about using force if the United States and the European Union states are unable to get Iran to give up its nuclear program. An attack would pose a difficult assignment for Israeli military planners and any attack would likely arouse much of the Islamic world. But Israel has taken threats to its security in the past as needing a forceful response. It is likely that once Iran decides to enrich to weapon-grade uranium, Iran may have a deliverable nuclear device within five years, possibly less. And it has worked to develop missiles with ranges reaching Israel.

When President George W. Bush was asked about a possible Israeli strike against Iranian facilities, the president made this reply:

> Well, of course, first of all, Iran has made it clear it doesn't like Israel, to put it bluntly. There's more diplomacy, in my judgment to be done. But clearly, if I was the leader of Israel and I listened to some of the statements by the Iranian ayatollahs about the security of my country, I'd be concerned about Iran having a nuclear weapon. And in that Israel is our ally, in that we've made a very strong commitment to support Israel, we will support Israel if their security is threatened.[56]

The president's words might be read as an attempt to roll the Israeli theat into the U.S. position: If Iran doesn't accede to American demands to give up uranium enrichment, the United States will not and cannot restrain its Israeli ally, and we all know how Israel responds to perceived threats to its existence.

Historically, U.S. presidents have tolerated if not welcomed a nuclear Israel. Its possession of nuclear weapons does pose a constant dilemma for U.S. non-proliferation goals, for Iranians can say (as they do) that they have *a right* to have nuclear weapons to counter Israeli threats to their existence. The United States and Israel have explored with Israel's Arab neighbors the possibility of creating a nuclear-free zone in the Middle East, but the talks flounder on Israel's insistence that all its neighbors end the state of belligerency with Israel and recognize its right to exist first and on Arab insistence that Israel first meet the legitimate demands of the Palestinian people. Recently U.S. officials have suggested that Israel join the NPT, but only as a non-nuclear weapons state, meaning that they would have to first divest themselves of their stockpile of 100–200 nuclear weapons. That seeming call for Israeli denuclearization is blunted by the fact that India and Pakistan were invited to join the NPT on the same terms. In as much as both are likely to reject denuclearization, the U.S. position essentially becomes, if Pakistan and India won't give up their weapons, why should anyone expect Israel to do so?

INDIA AND PAKISTAN

The decision by the Indian government in May 1998 to test five nuclear weapons marked not only the end of India's opaque status, but muted a powerful voice for global nuclear disarmament. Pakistan's rapid response in testing its nuclear weapons created the potential for a severe regional crisis.[57] While there were several war scares (discussed below), the two states have agreed to negotiate a variety of measures that the superpowers had discussed or adopted during the first nuclear age, ranging from notification of missile tests to creating procedures and communication links that would help deal with accidental or unauthorized use of nuclear weapons.[58] Both declared unilateral moratoria on further testing of their nuclear weapons and both settled quickly into minimum deterrence postures as their strategies. India went further to proclaim a no-first-use policy. Pakistan did not do so, as it viewed its nuclear weapons as a needed counterweight to Indian conventional military superiority. As they had in the past, however, each continued to define the other as a threat to its national security.

As we might expect, both gave some thought to how nuclear weapons might be made part of foreign policy—or how the other might be tempted to do so.[59] The Indian Defense Minister, George Fernandes, for instance, argued that Pakistan now felt that its nuclear weapons would force India to accede to Pakistan's demands to turn Kashmir over to Pakistan. Eastern Kashmir is an Indian province today because its Hindu prince opted to join India at the time of partition of the British colony of India into two separate states (1947), much to the dismay of the largely Muslim population and over strong protests by Pakistan. Pakistani generals had in fact thought that nuclear weapons would provide them with an opportunity to become more aggressive in promoting the liberation of Kashmir.

The ongoing conflict over Kashmir, the growth of an insurrectionary movement there covertly backed by Pakistan and increasingly influenced by jihadist Islamic sentiments, and the fact that India and Pakistan have waged war against each other three times since independence create a unique and complex nuclear relationship. In 1999, Pakistani regular forces and insurrectionists attempted to seize control of a section of the disputed Kashmir border, triggering an Indian counter-offensive and raising the specter of a nuclear confrontation. While that line re-stabilized, insurgent groups, probably operating under the direction of the intelligence branch of the Pakistani armed forces, staged a number of attacks within Indian Kasmir, including an attack on the provincial government building.

The situation escalated dramatically in mid-December, 2001, when five jihadis attacked the Indian parliament building in an attempt to blow it up while parliament was sitting.[60] They killed nine guards in the failed attempt before being killed. India accused Pakistan of harboring and supporting the group responsible. By the end of the month, Indian forces were mobilized along the border and people spoke of an impending war. The United States and Britain (as they had in the earlier confrontations) mobilized a diplomatic effort to stay the Indian hand and to press the Pakistani government of General Pervez Musharraf to clamp down on the militants. The crisis resolved itself temporarily in January 2002 along these lines but without changing Pakistan's posture that Kashmir was part of Pakistan and India's assertion that it would hold Pakistan responsible for terrorist actions against India. Another terrorist strike occurred in May 2002, this time in Kashmir, and the Indian army began preparations for military action. Intense American pressure apparently tipped the scales against an Indian move. During this rolling crisis of 2002, there had been expectations on both sides that nuclear weapons might be used, and Indian and Pakistani officials talked about losing cities with millions of inhabitants.

The United States remains heavily engaged in the region. It needs Pakistan to prevent al Qaeda and Taliban forces from retreating into western Pakistan. It needs Pakistan to keep control over its nuclear establishment to prevent it from becoming a source of aid to would-be proliferators or terrorists. It needs to watch the crowded streets and the scattered villages of Pakistan to monitor a restive militant Islamic movement that is perturbed that the government is working with the United States to crush the Taliban and al Qaeda forces, and that is dedicated to ending the secular political-military elite's control of Pakistan. If such a movement were to come to power, it would likely trigger an immediate crisis with the United States as nuclear weapons would be in the hands of militants with a declared hostility to the United States.

In India the United States sees a new counterweight to the growing power of China, one that demands more American attention and support (and runs the risk of alienating Pakistan, America's traditional ally on the subcontinent). In the summer of 2005, the United States agreed in principle to supply India with nuclear power technology in spite of the fact that it was not a signatory of the NPT. The Bush administration apparently concluded that a partnership with an India determined to remain a nuclear weapons state was worth the damage to non-proliferation norms. Perhaps this new relationship will force the United States to ensure that nuclear rules of the road are crafted and adhered to in this region—if it can find the time and resources given its multiple nuclear concerns. And it needs to be concerned with how both states will react to its policies toward Iran.

RULES OF THE ROAD UNDER PRESSURE

Another spoke in the wheel of American nuclear relations concerns the rules of the road—those agreements or unwritten understandings about how states in general and nuclear-armed states in particular are to behave toward each other. The key rule of the first nuclear age prohibiting aggression has remained (and was clearly reinforced in the 1991 Gulf War against Iraq). The concern about indirect aggression that propelled the United States into Vietnam has, however, abated. Although states continue to involve themselves in others' internal conflicts, particularly in Africa, their interests are intensely local. On the other hand, there has emerged, painfully and slowly, a relatively new rule that declares that states cannot commit or permit genocide to occur in their societies and that the international community has an obligation to intervene to prevent it.[61]

One might well question whether the American invasion of Iraq in 2003 was a challenge to the basic "no aggression" rule. The Bush administration's insistence that this was a "preemptive war" was, we suggest, a recognition of the dangerous territory the administration was entering. The "no aggression" rule does *not* permit *preventive* war—attacking today in the *belief* that, at some point in the future, the target of the attack would strike one's country. Yet to many that is all that the Bush administration could really offer as a reason for its attack. The basic "no aggression" rule is likely to erode further if the United States uses force to impose the new rule declaring that states hostile to the United States will not be permitted to have nuclear weapons or the capabilities to produce them. A world in which aggression is permitted the hegemon but not others may be unjust, but it is tenable as long as hegemony prevails and the hegemon is willing to pay the price. Hegemony, however, will disappear and rules, once broken, have far less power to shape behavior, which may prove quite detrimental to the former hegemon.

The more specific *nuclear rules of the road*, laboriously fashioned by the United States and Soviet Union, have been absorbed into the general practices of states at peace with each other. Where the Cold War nuclear rules of the road need important updating are in the new nuclear rivalries (such as India and Pakistan), in the asymmetrical nuclear relationships (such as the United States and North Korea), and in the potential for new actors such as terrorist groups to acquire nuclear weapons. We might imagine that there would be renewed interest in the oft-proposed rule of no first use of nuclear weapons. While such pledges have been made yesterday and today, there have always been significant hold-outs. NATO planned to respond with nuclear weapons to a Soviet conventional assault into Germany, and Pakistan today has refused to make such a pledge as it believes that nuclear weapons would be necessary to defeat India's greater conventional capabilities. India, on the other hand, has reiterated the no-first-use pledge and called for its general adoption. From the start, however, skeptics (or cynics) claimed that a would-be aggressor state would be among the first to give such a pledge in order to lull its potential victim into believing it planned no hostile actions, and it would be the state most likely to use nuclear weapons first to ensure its victory.

It is likely, however, that while states may not make the pledge, the leadership in every nuclear weapons state will be loathe to be the first to use nuclear weapons except in dire circumstances—a testament to how strong the nuclear taboo is. That repugnance may have a relatively short life, however. We are rapidly approaching a confluence of technology, a distaste for casualties, and a felt need to "get at the root of the matter quickly" that will press the holders of nuclear weapons, preeminently but not exclusively the United States, to consider their use against selective targets. Nuclear use by a terrorist group or rogue state against the United States or any other target will accelerate the confluence, but even without such an event, we expect the temptation to grow over the next several decades. Sophisticated intelligence collection (particularly by satellites and drones and communication intercepts) coupled with precision-guided munitions provide the ability to hit designated targets with near pin-point accuracy in real time. Low yield nuclear weapons, especially when coupled with earth-penetrating delivery systems, hold the promise of devastating power applied to the target alone and confinement of most of the high levels of radioactivity below the earth's surface.[62] Moreover, while the ability to mount such an attack may be quite costly overall, it is not likely to produce high casualty figures for the attacking force or extensive collateral damage at the target site.

The attractiveness of low-yield, high-accuracy nuclear weapons increases as the targets become increasingly individualized, as they have in an era that focuses on regime change and the killing of specific terrorist operatives—as the attempts to kill Saddam Hussein as a prelude to the invasion of Iraq and the repeated strikes against Osama bin Laden and other al Qaeda leaders demonstrate. A leader seeking refuge in a sparsely populated, hard-to-reach area or in a deep underground bunker or a cave complex may appear as an ideal target for such weapons.

A second form of target that appears attractive for low-yield, highly accurate nuclear attack is a concentration of critical weapons systems, enemy personnel, or the facilities to build nuclear weapons. For instance, the ability of such weapons to shatter a command and control facility can defeat the enemy by metaphorically lopping off its head, reducing its resistance to further attack and its ability to mount its own attacks. Alternatively, if the enemy has hardened shelters for chemical, biological, or nuclear munitions, low-yield nuclear weapons might seem to be the answer for quick, sure-kill strikes that produce minimal collateral damage and long-term fallout. And we would imagine that any targeting of a state's nuclear facilities (say, Iran's) will at least engender a consideration of such nuclear weapons.

Any use of nuclear weapons would break the nuclear taboo that has grown with the weapons since 1945. Their use might be preceded by an attempt to make a case for the necessity of such weapons in moral and pragmatic terms, hoping to convince the using nation's public and secondarily other publics and governments that a change in the rules of the road is warranted—that nuclear weapons of this size and discrimination are really just like the conventional weapons already used in the thousands. The moral argument will be made that breaking the nuclear taboo in this limited extent is far less reprehensible than the actions committed by or likely to be committed by the individual being targeted or by the organization they direct. Alternatively, the use might come first and justification delivered after the fact, with decision-makers (and they are certainly to be at the highest level) perhaps calculating that a success makes moral and reasonable what otherwise is will be a heavily contested issue. Success, of course, is never guaranteed, and this may be one occasion when high-level policy-makers—even the most adverse to asking questions— will truly probe the plan's details and assumptions.

The temptation to consider any nuclear weapon in the first nuclear age always had to confront the possibility that its use would bring a confrontation with another nuclear power (not to speak of the enormous propaganda advantage handed the other side). And in that confrontation, with the nuclear threshold having been crossed, there was the great potential that the other thresholds would fail and the participants would be plunged into a catastrophic nuclear exchange. Recall that in 1961, Paul Nitze urged President Kennedy to write off the intermediate stages of Poodle Blanket to defend Berlin as he believed that any initial use of nuclear weapons would quickly escalate to a massive exchange; therefore the United States should attack the Soviet Union first to minimize the damage to itself. *In the second nuclear age*, on the other hand, that threshold of a *general* nuclear exchange has likely been pushed far up the escalation ladder, so to speak, and the threshold to "nuclear lite" (such as the use of comparatively weak bunker-busting warheads) has probably been weakened. Nuclear use, decision makers might reason, can be contained, and what is containable is, in the nuclear world, often seen as morally and pragmatically acceptable.

Nonetheless, a first use will be of such momentous import that we would expect the user to declare the existence of new rule that it will claim guided its behavior. Such a rule will try to justify the use and define the limits of acceptable use. Given the history of rules written by fiat, the first user will try to ensure that it can repeat its actions but impose constraints on the use of tactical nuclear weapons by others. There has already been a suggestion of such a rule: The United States has indicated that it might use nuclear devices if its forces are attacked with chemical and/or biological weapons. When the Presidents Bush made such threats during the two wars with Iraq, it is unlikely that they were promising to obliterate Iraq (that is, attack its cities) in retaliation for CB attacks. Rather, the targets (if their threats were real) would likely be suspected CB storage facilities and massed delivery systems, or the leadership of the state and the military. The attack on the World Trade Center in 2001 probably added the avoidance of mass-damage terrorism to a justification for tactical nuclear attacks against specific sites judged to be harboring the directors of such attacks—in this case, terrorist leaders. That is, if American leaders felt that an attack similar to that against the World Trade Center could best be prevented by a low-yield nuclear attack against the suspected site harboring someone like Osama bin Laden, the nuclear taboo would be under great strain.

Given the threat of another 9/11-type attack, such a rewriting of the rule could come at any time. In May 2003, the U.S. Congress, at the behest of President Bush, repealed the ban on the development of nuclear weapons with payloads of under five kilotons. In December, 2003, the government urged nuclear weapons labs to undertake the necessary research.

CHINA AND THE NUCLEAR FUTURE

Several years from now, when students pick up the 10th edition of this book, they are likely to find an extensive discussion of nuclear relations between China and the rest of the world. It is reasonable to expect that China's economy will grow to rival that of the United States. It is less certain whether its political system will evolve sufficiently to accommodate such growth.[63] The Chinese Communist Party will have every incentive to keep oligarchic political control in its own hands. Historically, authoritarian systems like China's have maintained control by providing a continuing flow of economic payoffs to the citizenry, or through high levels of terror directed against the citizenry to shatter any possible coalition that might be directed against the party's control, or by pointing to a mortal threat to the nation's survival. The Chinese learned from the Soviet experience that a command economy could not sustain itself, nor could it sustain citizen loyalty to the party or, ultimately, could it sustain the state itself. They learned from Mao Zedong's Great Leap Forward and the Cultural Revolution that terror unhinged the economy and jeopardized party control as the party itself broke into warring factions. In the semi-free-market system emerging in China, however, concentrations of wealth will begin to create potential rivals and ways of mobilizing individuals (such as employees and consumers) that lie outside the party's control. Those concentrations are likely to have a strong interest in influencing the party's lawmaking, and, at some point, a strong interest in supplanting the party's control of the state.

The party's choices (other than the difficult one of converting the political system to a democracy in which the party's candidates must compete with non-party candidates in free elections) are limited essentially to finding an internal scapegoat or to exploiting nationalism and the threat from abroad. There is a ready-made issue (one, incidentally, that would confront any Chinese leaders): the future of Taiwan.[64] This island state was once a part of China, but the Chinese civil war ended in 1949 with the defeated Nationalist party in control of Taiwan, and Communist China insisting that Taiwan must be restored to China. As the Nationalists wanted a unified China as well (only under their control), there was no disagreement from either camp that Taiwan was part of China. However, the intervening years produced two fundamental changes: First, the United States became committed to the defense of Taiwan (and it is here that some of the consideration of the use of nuclear weapons occurred in the 1950s). That commitment generally remains. Second, the Taiwanese themselves came to prosper and adopt a political orientation that stressed their autonomy from China, an orientation that has led many Taiwanese to consider independence from China. The Beijing government has warned that if the Taiwanese were to take steps toward independence, China would have to intervene—and that would mean a confrontation with the United States.

Nuclear weapons would likely play a role in such a confrontation. In July 2005, a high-ranking Chinese general, Zhu Chenghu, "warned that his country could destroy hundreds of American cities with nuclear weapons if the two nations clashed over the question of independence of Taiwan." Spokespersons for the Chinese government said the general was speaking for himself, but the view that "we could deter you by threatening to use nuclear weapons" may be pervasive within the military and party.[65]

Balancing this belligerence is China's active attempt to find a solution to the problem of North Korea's nuclear weapons program. As we have seen, China has pressed both the United States and North Korea to accommodate each other's core interests to produce what probably is China's optimal solution: First, to have a non-nuclear North—and with that, continued nuclear abstinence by South Korea and Japan and a continuation of U.S. policy not to have nuclear weapons stationed in Korea. And second, to leave the Kim regime in control of the North. Such a solution would reinforce China's desired image as a positive and powerful influence in international politics. At the same time, it may give China leverage on the Taiwan problem, not because of U.S. gratitude for resolving the Korean crisis (the Bush administration wants an outcome of no nuclear weapons and no Kim), but because all states would recognize that solutions to Asian problems—and therefore stability in Asia—rest with China, and therefore its interests must be, to one degree or another, accommodated.

THE LOOMING CHALLENGES TO THE NUCLEAR FUTURE

Our discussion of China's role in nuclear relations has edged toward the future, when China might be a principal actor in world politics, creating a new environment in which states will need to (re)fashion their nuclear relations. We conclude our discussion with a brief survey of several other areas of concern, areas that are likely to have a powerful impact on relations between nuclear-armed actors in the future.

The first is that the United States may have both focused too narrowly on one area of concern, and has overextended itself in its endeavors. As the hegemon, the United States must deal simultaneously with a host of nuclear issues, each of which demands time and resources if it wishes to shape the result. Since 2001, the fixation on al Qaeda and then Iraq has meant that only two spokes of the wheel have received sustained attention, and the results have been disproportionate to the costs. This attention has been in the service of rule enforcement—that no state hostile to the United States may possess nuclear weapons or, in its more extensive guise, may possess nuclear power plants or the facilities to produce bomb-grade uranium or plutonium. We can debate the wisdom of such a rule (as we do in Chapters 12, 13, and 14 of this book), but we need to recognize that most sovereign states will reject dictation by others. They will want a voice in formulating rules.

It may have been America's misfortune to have made the military enforcement of its new rule on a state without a nuclear program (and hence of no immediate threat to the United States), although Washington correctly perceived that Iraq's militarily weakness would make rule enforcement not particularly costly in its invasion phase, and perhaps that made Iraq a more attractive target than North Korea or Iran. It may also be America's misfortune that it is attempting to create a new polity and economy for Iraq—another common temptation of a hegemon—as a way of permanently preventing proliferation there. That effort has proved to be a costly enterprise, perhaps one that has absorbed attention and resources far beyond their worth if enforcement of the nuclear rule were *the* policy goal.

Setting aside for the moment the question of the desirability of coercive anti-proliferation or denuclearization—that is, the utility and morality of destroying a state's nuclear capability by an attack on the state or its facilities or by compelling the state to undertake the destruction itself to avoid such an attack—it is likely that in the short run, the United States cannot undertake such actions against North Korea or Iran even if it were agreed that here truly are places where the rule should be imposed. It simply is stretched too thin to handle the task and deal with the aftermath. Once Iraq is stabilized, however, it may be able to contemplate coercive actions. As that does not seem likely in the near future, precious months will slip by.

The United States therefore has the choices of (1) abandoning the rule, (2) relying on negotiations that offer meaningful concessions in return for the other's acceptance for the rule, or (3) dragging out the confrontation with rogue states until Iraq resolves itself, hoping to stall those states' steps toward nuclearization long enough until it is able to impose the rule. The first two options are likely to be quite distasteful for an administration such as George W. Bush's that defines its opponents as evil and fiendish enemies. Therefore, a rapid and successful conclusion in Iraq is essential. As we write this, it is not clear that that will be possible. And even "success" might be something that carries a threat, for a united, plausibly democratic Iraq might be both hostile to the United States and interested in acquiring a nuclear arsenal, especially if Iran has some nuclear capability.

Clear failure in Iraq would have broad repercussions. States hostile to the United States would likely come to doubt that the United States would use force again. Without the threat of force, the

American bargaining position would be weakened and some form of proliferation or proliferation capability is likely to be left in the hands of hostile states. To counter this impression, American leaders may feel compelled to take a harder stance, to push a confrontation more than they might have otherwise done, creating a fearsome crisis and possible nuclear use. Or, equally undesirable, a mindless cost-counting might lead to an isolationist America, minimally involved in shaping the nuclear future.

Our second concern for the future centers on *the growth of a mobilizing ideology*, in this case militant or jihadist Islam. Traditional patterns of world politics are often disrupted by the emergence of an ideology that calls for revolutionary change across state borders and by the reaction of governments that see themselves threatened by the militants and their ideology. Iranian Islamic militancy after the 1979 revolution produced such conflict, particularly with the United States and its neighbors (most directly Iraq) but the militancy was contained in that it was a Shi'ia movement (a minority within the Islamic world) and isolated by language and culture (Iranians are mostly Farsi-speaking rather than Arabic-speaking). Current jihadist Islam as represented by al Qaeda is more Sunni-Arab centered, and has a far broader geo-political vision in that it envisions a pan-Islamic state stretching from Gibraltar to India, perhaps further. Like its Iranian predecessors, militant Islam usually identifies the United States and the West as its enemies, along with the local governments that suffer from "Westoxification"—the Iranian militants' term, popularized during Ayatollah Khomeini's rule, for secular, Western-influenced elites. It calls for the expulsion of the West from Islamic lands.

There is a reasonably good chance that a jihadist movement will come to power in an Arab state. (The success of Hamas in the Palestinian elections in January 2006 may be the harbinger of the future). Would a jihadist state seek invariably seek nuclear weapons? Our evidence is scant. The Taliban government of Afghanistan (not themselves jihadists in that their focus seemed confined to Afghanistan), apparently accepted al Qaeda's interest in acquiring nuclear weapons. Islamic militants coming to power in Pakistan would, of course, inherit a nuclear arsenal; coming to power in Egypt would give them a society with the capability to go nuclear relatively quickly. But in general there is no reason to expect a jihadist movement in control of a state to be any more or less interested in acquiring nuclear weapons than a traditional state, or any more or less interested in using such weapons.

A jihadist state that does attract the support of believers beyond its borders may, however, have an easier time gaining access to nuclear know-how and materials through a network of sympathizers. Individuals connected with the Pakistani nuclear weapons program argued that Pakistan had an obligation to help other Islamic nations acquire nuclear weapons and that Pakistan's weapons were "the property of the whole Ummah [Muslim community]."[66] There is some evidence that some Pakistanis consulted with the Taliban in Afghanistan and with al Qaeda about weapons of mass destruction prior to September 2001.[67] (A small number of ideologically committed Americans connected to the Manhattan Project agreed to provide similar information to the Soviet Union about the bomb.)

If jihadists do come to power, they are likely to so in one state rather than sweeping into power across the region. While likely to be quite hostile to the West, their primary focus will center on neighboring states, and that relationship is likely to be hostile, a hostility fueled by historic conflicts that now have an intense ideological divide. In the main, then, we would expect to find local cold wars between jihadist states and their neighbors, with the possibility of a local war, perhaps initiated by latter (as Iraq did in 1980 against jihadist Iran). The acquisition of nuclear weapons *by either side* might seem attractive for security reasons or to prosecute such a war effectively.

A young jihadist state that does attempt to go nuclear today is likely to face an early confrontation with the United States. This will be a new experience for both parties. The current American confrontation with Iran may not tell us much about how that confrontation will play out, as Iran today is a mature jihadist state rather than one drawing on and being driven by the fervor of a revolutionary movement. Iran may be more likely to compromise with an opponent as it now has vested interests to protect. Indeed, even the Ayatollah Khomeini had to accept a cease-fire with Iraq rather than hold out for his oft-stated goal of destroying Saddam Hussein's regime. It is useful to recall, as well, that the young jihadist Iran was able to mobilize hundreds of thousands of its youth for human wave attacks against Iraqi positions, where they died in large numbers but were able to repel the Iraqi invaders, obviating the need for more powerful weapons.

Our third concern for the future is the *internal collapse of a nuclear weapons state*. Having gotten through the collapse of the Soviet Union is no guarantee that other nuclear-armed authoritarian states will be able to manage such a transition, minimizing the possibility of the use of nuclear weapons or their dispersion into a variety of hands. The most likely candidates for collapse are North Korea, Pakistan, and in the more distant future, China, particularly if the Chinese Communist Party fails to find a way to permit greater political participation by a vast array of individuals, especially in the regions on the periphery of the Chinese heartland. The thin democracy in Russia remains suspect as well, especially as its current president, Vladimir Putin, seems intent on bringing more unchecked power into his own hands.

The Soviet case suggests that top-down systems may have an effective life span of some 70 years (or roughly three to four generations of leadership and citizenry) before they undergo a profound legitimacy crisis. North Korea and China will enter that point soon, but as the Chinese have successfully switched to a far less top-down economy, they may have put the testing point off for at least a generation. These two states may be able to manage their political crisis of confidence without nuclear accident as the Soviet Union did (and with support from the international community, it should be noted).

North Korea, however, is part of a divided nation, one where reunification is a popular goal on both sides of the DMZ. A South Korea, watching its northern half suddenly spiral into economic and political turmoil, may decide that it must intervene regardless of American wishes, and be confident that it will not be challenged by the North's allies, as the North essentially has none. The South's actions might trigger a nuclear response by elements of the North Korea political and military leadership, a nuclear response that would likely engulf U.S. forces in the South.

Pakistan has alternated between a parliamentary democracy and a military dictatorship (and various conflations of the two, as in the current Pervez Musharraf government) since independence in 1947. Militant Islam has a strong following in Pakistan, and al Qaeda operates along the Afghan-Pakistan border. The government has tried to walk a thin line between aiding the United States in its war against al Qaeda and not causing the militants to rise in open rebellion against the government. In addition, Kashmir remains the festering sore for Pakistan, and it has been an attraction for Islamic militants. An internal power struggle in Pakistan raises the possibility of nuclear use against domestic rivals, but to the extent that India fears jihadists coming to power in Pakistan, India might be strongly tempted to unleash a preventive attack against Pakistani nuclear facilities and weapons. Alternatively, we might imagine that the first *terrorist* nuclear or radiological attack might be staged by Kashmiri jihadists in alliance with al Qaeda against India.

Our fourth concern for the future is *the inevitable advance of missile technology*. As we noted in Chapter 6, missiles are likely to be the delivery system of choice for nuclear weapons states in the long run, and missile ranges will increase, giving smaller nuclear weapons states the ability to strike at the homelands of the major nuclear powers. Historically, "weak" states have had to cope with the presence of threatening major powers on their periphery, as the major power could deploy its naval, air, and ground power adjacent to the weak state and threaten its territory with no fear of meaningful retaliation against the major power's homeland. Long-range nuclear missiles change that equation, and in so doing create a new context for world politics.[68] North Korea, for instance, has been expanding the range of its missiles. Armed with such weapons, the North may calculate that the United States would be unwilling to challenge a second invasion of South Korea, fearing that if it did so, it would risk the destruction of its cities from long-range nuclear missiles. What might a major power do to prevent such a circumstance? Does the development of such long-range missiles (tests of which will be easily detected) drive the major power toward some form of preventive war, possibly including the use of nuclear weapons to destroy missile production and storage facilities? Would we expect the United States to attempt to impose a new rule: no state hostile to the United States will be permitted to deploy missiles beyond intermediate ranges (roughly 1,500 miles).

The current policy response has been two-fold: to attempt to hinder the development or sales of such delivery systems by export controls, diplomatic pressures, and threats, and to seek to buy off such developments (as in the last-minute effort of the Clinton administration to reach a missile agreement with North Korea). Missile technology, like nuclear technology, is unfortunately ubiquitous. Attempts to negotiate controls on ranges permitted to a nation's missile force run into the same problem as the NPT: the United States, Russia, China, France, and Britain are not about to divest themselves of missiles with intercontinental ranges as they are defined as essential for keeping the nuclear peace. If those weapons are important for those nations, they will be important for other countries as well.

CONCLUSION

The simple yet terrifying world of the first nuclear age held out the prospect of the incineration of large numbers of people and their cultures. In the second nuclear age, the problems are more complex but, while disturbing, do not foreshadow the end of the world. The United States has sought to keep the Russian arsenal under control, challenge hostile states with nuclear pretensions, and destroy terrorist networks with nuclear aspirations. It has become ambivalent about the worth of arms control measures and has leaned more heavily toward unilateral efforts to ensure its security, from the invasion of Iraq to the renunciation of the ABM Treaty in preparation for the deployment of a rudimentary anti-ballistic missile system. It has increasingly exploited its hegemonic position.

For all its power, however, it has not been able to dictate outcomes. Iraq still remains in turmoil, and the United States would likely face a grave threat if that state collapses, as well it might. The United States does not have the power to will a functioning, effective democracy into being. Moreover, by its attempt to impose a new rule on certain states—that they shall not be permitted to have nuclear weapons or even nuclear power plants and nuclear fuel production capability—the United States is in a confrontational relationship with Iran and North Korea. The Bush administration's range of options is identical to those of its predecessor a decade ago: (1) to negotiate mutual concessions with the rogue state to bring about denuclearization, (2) to take unilateral action such as the bombing of North Korean nuclear sites (and run the risk of a massive North Korean attack on the

South), or (3) to acquiesce in the status quo—that is, to permit a rogue nation to keep its nuclear weapons.[69] For all the Bush administration's unilateralist moralism, it is, as the President averred, "not foolish."

The end of the Cold War and the first nuclear age did not end the nuclear predicament. The world today is a much safer place for all its inhabitants, but nuclear weapons continue to exist. We can look back on our nuclear past with some degree of satisfaction, as humans were able to produce a future for themselves and their progeny. But they were unable, just as we will be unable, to solve the nuclear predicament. Nuclear weapons will always exist, either in fact or in thought. Thus the question of 1945 is still with us: Can we continue to keep nuclear weapons from being used?

In the following chapters, we begin our look at what can be done. Our strategy will be to examine carefully the pressing issues of terrorism and proliferation, and then to explore our resources for making decisions about nuclear weapons, particularly the guidance that ethical considerations might offer and how our culture as a whole helps us see (or misperceive) the nuclear predicament. Chapters 12, 13, and 14 revisit the perspectives and issues that we have covered, suggesting three options to shape the future.

ENDNOTES

[1]This account is drawn from Tim Trevan, *Saddam's Secrets: The Hunt for Iraq's Hidden Weapons* (London, UK: HarperCollins, 1999), pp. 96–109, and a telephone interview with Robert Gallucci, August 25, 2003.

[2]Trevan, *Saddam's Secrets*, p. 154.

[3]For studies of Gorbachev and the end of the Soviet states, see Mark Galeotti, *Gorbachev and His Revolution* (New York: St. Martin's, 1997); Archie Brown (ed.), *The Demise of Marxism-Leninism in Russia* (New York: Palgrave Macmillan, 2004); George W. Breslauer, *Gorbachev and Yeltsin as Leaders* (Cambridge, UK: Cambridge University Press, 2002); Anders Aslund, *How Russia Became a Market Economy* (Washington, DC: Brookings Instititution, 1995); Steven L. Solnick, *Stealing the State: Control and Collapse in Soviet Institutions* (Cambridge, MA: Harvard University Press, 1998). For Gorbachev's account, see his *Memoirs* (New York: Doubleday, 1996) and *Conversations with Gorbachev* (New York: Columbia University Press, 2002).

[4]For descriptions of the end of Communist control in Eastern Europe, see David Pryce-Jones, *The War that Never Was: The Fall of the Soviet Empire, 1985–1991* (London: Weidenfeld & Nicholson, 1995), Michael Dobbs, *Down with Big Brother: The Fall of the Soviet Empire* (New York: Alfred Knopf, 1997); and Raymond Pearson, *The Rise and the Fall of the Soviet Empire* (New York: Palgrave, 2002).

[5]For this argument, see Peter Schweitzer, *Victory: The Reagan Administration's Secret Strategy That Hastened the Collapse of the Soviet Union* (New York: Atlantic Monthly Press, 1994). See also Jay Winik, *On the Brink* (New York: Simon & Schuster, 1996) and Jack Matlock, Jr., *Reagan and Gorbachev: How the Cold War Ended* (New York: Random House, 2004). We would suggest that the Reagan administration's deficit spending to finance the military buildup weakened the American economy and left the American government without the financial resources to consolidate the post-Cold War peace.

[6]Quoted by Christopher Andrew, *For the President's Eyes Only: Secret Intelligence and the American Presidency from Washington to Bush* (New York: HarperCollins, 1995), p. 476.

[7]See Paul V. Lettow, *Ronald Reagan and His Quest to Abolish Nuclear Weapons* (New York: Random House, 2005).

[8]For amplification and application of the concept of hegemony, see John Agnew, *Hegemony: The New Shape of Global Power* (Philadelphia, PA: Temple University Press, 2005), Gerry Simpson, *Great Powers*

and Outlaw States (New York, NY: Cambridge University Press, 2004), Demetrios James Caraley (ed.), *American Hegemony: Preventive War, Iraq, and Imposing Democracy* (New York, NY: Academy of Political Science, 2004).

[9]Quoted by David Remnick, "Post-Imperial Blues," *The New Yorker* (October 3, 2003), p. 89.

[10]For a discussion of the responses to the hegemon, see Robert A. Pape, "Soft Balancing Against the United States," *International Security*, Vol. 30 (#1, Summer, 2005), pp. 7–45; and T. V. Paul, "Soft Balancing in the Age of U.S. Primacy," *International Security*, Vol. 30 (#1, Summer, 2005), pp. 46–71.

[11]Paul Kennedy, *The Rise and Fall of the Great Powers: Economic Change and Military Conflict from 1500 to 2000* (New York: Random House, 1987).

[12]For a range of opinions about the G. W. Bush presidency, see Fred Greenstein (ed.), *The George W. Bush Presidency: An Early Assessment* (Baltimore, MD: Johns Hopkins University Press, 2003); Melvin Gurtov, *Superpower on Crusade: The Bush Doctrine in US Foreign Policy* (Boulder, Colorado: Lynne Rienner, 2006); Fred Barnes, *Rebel-in-Chief: Inside the Bold and Controversial Presidency of George W. Bush* (New York: Crown Forum, 2006).

[13]See Peter Beckman, *World Politics in the Twentieth Century* (Englewood Cliffs, NJ: Prentice-Hall, 1984), pp. 207–209, 235–241.

[14]Joseph Nye has suggested that we need to think in terms of two types of power: hard power such as weapons and economic clout and soft power such as culture, philosophies, and prestige. See *Bound to Lead: The Changing Nature of American Power* (New York: Basic Books, 1990).

[15]Robert J. Norris and Hans Kristensen, "Russian Nuclear Forces," *Bulletin of the Atomic Scientists*, Vol. 61 (March–April, 2005), pp. 70–72.

[16]Graham Allison, "Could Worse Be Yet to Come?" *The Economist*, Vol. 361 (November 3, 2001), pp. 19–21; for a much expanded version of Allison's concerns, see his *Nuclear Terrorism* (New York: Times Books/Henry Holt, 2004).

[17]For a history and updates, see Senator Richard Lugar's website, www.lugar.senate.gov/nunnlugar.

[18]David Broder, "A Small Price for National Security," Durham *Herald-Sun*, November 14, 2001, p. A13.

[19]Barry Schweid, "U.S. to Scrap More Nukes," Durham *Herald-Sun*, November 14, 2001, p. A11.

[20]Masha Lipman, quoted in *The Washington Post National Weekly Edition*, (June 3–9, 2002), p. 27.

[21]Bill Keller, "The World According to Powell," *The New York Times Magazine*, November 25, 2001, pp. 74, 90.

[22]Seymour M. Hersh, "The Iran Game," *The New Yorker*, December 3, 2001, pp. 42–50.

[23]Vice Admiral Dennis A. Jones, quoted by James Brooke, "Former Cold Warrior Has a New Mission: Nuclear Cuts," *The New York Times*, January 8, 1997, p. A12.

[24]Deputy Secretary of State Strobe Talbott, "Dealing with Russia in a Time of Troubles," *The Economist* Vol. 349 (November 21–27, 1998), p. 55.

[25]For the text of the treaty, see *SIPRI Yearbook 1997* (Oxford, England: Oxford University Press, 1997), pp. 414–31; the escape clause appears on p. 430.

[26]Jonathan Weisman, "Who's Minding the Store," *The Bulletin of the Atomic Scientists*, Vol. 53 (July/August 1997), p. 37.

[27]For an analysis, see Terry L. Deibel, "The Death of a Treaty," *Foreign Affairs*, Vol. 8x (q, September/October, 2002), pp. 142–161.

[28]For a review, see John Simpson, "The Nuclear Non-Proliferation Regime after the NPT Review and Extension Conference," Stockholm International Peace Research Institute, *SIPRI Yearbook 1996: Armaments, Disarmament, and International Security* (Oxford, England; Oxford University Press, 1996), pp. 561–609.

[29]For a review, see John Carlson, "Can a Fissile Material Cutoff Treaty be Effectively Verified?" (January/February 2005); http://www.armscontrol.org/act/2005_01–02/Carlson.asp.

[30]Chaim Braun and Christopher F. Chyba, "Proliferation Rings," *International Security*, Vol 29 (#2, Fall 2004), p. 39.

[31]BJ Party president, Kushabhau Thakre, quoted in *New York Times*, May 12, 1998.

[32]Condoleezza Rice, for instance, told PBS's Gwen Ifill on July 30, 2003 that a National Intelligence Estimate statement concluded that "if left unchecked Saddam Hussein would possibly have a nuclear weapon by the end of the decade."

[33]See Paul Pillar, "Intelligence, Policy, and the War in Iraq," *Foreign Affairs*, Vol. 85 (March–April 2006). Pillar served as the CIA officer coordinating the Agency's intelligence on Iraq in the run-up to the war.

[34]Leon Sigal, *Disarming Strangers: Nuclear Diplomacy with North Korea* (Princeton, NJ: Princeton University Press, 1998), pp. 75–77, 90–127.

[35]These appear in the 2002 National Security Strategy statement; see Nicholas Leman, "Without a Doubt," *The New Yorker*, October 14 & 21, 2002, p. 175. He reports that then-National Security Advisor Condoleezza Rice mentioned the first three when he asked her to define a rogue state; he speculates that the last reflects President Bush's perspective.

[36]Recent reports on the DPRK include Bradley K. Martin, *Under the Loving Care of the Fatherly Leader: North Korea and the Kim Dynasty* (New York: Thomas Dunne Books, 2004); Bruce Cummings, *North Korea: Another Country* (New York: The New Press, 2003); Kong Dan Oh and Ralph C. Hassig, *North Korea Trough the Looking Glass* (Washington, DC: Brookings Institution, 2000).

[37]For studies of the North Korean nuclear program, see Jasper Becker, *Rogue Regime: Kim Jong Il and the Growing Threat of North Korea* (Oxford, UK: Oxford University Press, 2005); and Gary Samore (ed.), *North Korea's Weapons Programme* (Basingstoke, UK: Palgrave Macmillan, 2004).

[38]The following draws on Sigal, *Disarming Strangers*. See also the account by the participants: Joel S. Wit, Daniel B. Poneman, and Robert L. Gallucci, *Going Critical: The First North Korean Nuclear Crisis* (Washington, DC: Brookings Institution, 2004).

[39]Bob Woodward, *Bush at War* (New York: Simon & Schuster, 2002), p. 340.

[40]"North Korea's Nuclear Weapons Program," *Vantage Point*, Vol. 25 (November 2002), pp. 4, 5.

[41]North Korean State Radio, May 12, 2003; Foreign Broadcast Information Service translation.

[42]Robert Gallucci interview, August 25, 2003.

[43]For the Gulf War, see Lawrence Freedman and Efraim Karsh, *The Gulf Conflict, 1990–1991: Diplomacy and War in the New World Order* (Princeton, NJ: Princeton University Press) and Michael R. Gordon and Bernard E. Trainor, *The Generals' War: The Inside Story of the Conflict in the Gulf* (Boston, MA: Little, Brown, 1995).

[44]As the Iraqis had used chemical weapons against the Iranians in the 1980–1988 war, the United Nations inspectors had a clear target. A biological weapons program was suspected but it was not effectively uncovered until 1995 when one of Saddam's sons-in-law defected and revealed the program.

[45]Sabah Abdul Noor, a key member of the Iraqi program; quoted by Barton Gellman, "An Arsenal on Paper," *Washington Post National Weekly Edition* (January 19–25, 2004), p. 8.

[46]See Charles Duelfer's report, *Comprehensive Report of the Special Advisor to the DCI, September 30, 2004*: http://www.cia/reports/iraq-wmd_2004/Chapt4.html#sect1.

[47]See, for instance, his speech to the Veterans of Foreign Wars, August 26; www.whitehouse.gov/news/releases/2002/08/20020826.

[48]Michael Shrage, "No Weapons? No Matter. We Called Saddam's Bluff," *Washington Post*, May 11, 2003, p. B2.

[49]For Iran's history, see Nikki Keddie, *Modern Iran: Roots and Results of Revolution* (New Haven, CT: Yale University Press, 2003); Christopher de Bellaigne, *In the Rose Garden of the Martyrs: A Memoir of Iran* (New York: HarperCollins, 2005).

[50]For discussions of Iranian efforts, see Anthony Cordesman, *Iran's Developing Nuclear Capabilities* (Washington, D.C.: CSIS Press, 2005), Roger Howard, *Iran in Crisis? Nuclear Ambitions and the Ameri-*

can Response (London: Zed Books, 2004). International Institute for Strategic Studies, *Iran's Strategic Weapons Programmes* (London: Routledge, 2005).

[51]Speech to the United Nations, September 18, 2005. Islamic Republic of Iran Broadcasting Online News Network, www.iribnews.ir/Full_en.asp?news_id=198053&n=12.

[52]For the Osirak attack, see Rodger W. Claire, *Raid on the Sun* (New York: Broadway Books, 2004).

[53]Quoted in the *Durham (NC) Herald Sun* (June 13, 2004), p. A4.

[54]Quoted in Sammy Salama and Karen Ruster, "A Preemptive Attack on Iran's Nuclear Facilities: Possible Consequences," Center for Non-Proliferation Studies, September 2004, www.cns.miis.edu/pubs/week/040012.

[55]London *Sunday Times*, March 13, 2005; www.timesonline.co.uk.

[56]Press conference of 17 February 2005; www.whitehouse.gov/news/releases/2005/02/20050217-2.html.

[57]See Robert Wirsing, *Kashmir in the Shadow of War* (Armonk, NY: M. E. Sharpe, 2003); Lowell Dittmer (ed.), *South Asia's Nuclear Security Dilemma: India, Pakistan, and China* (Armonk, N.Y.: M. E. Sharpe, 2004); Strobe Talbott, *Engaging India: Diplomacy, Democracy, and the Bomb* (Washington, D. C.: Brookings Institution, 2005); and Arpit Rajain, *Nuclear Deterrence in Southern Asia: China, India, and Pakistan* (Thousand Oaks, CA: SAGE, 2005).

[58]Memorandum of Understanding, February 21, 1999; reprinted in A. Subramanyam Raju (ed.), *Nuclear India: Problems and Perspectives* (New Delhi: South Asian Publishers, 2000), pp. 188–189. Both states had agreed in 1989—before their become nuclear weapons states—not to target each other's nuclear facilities even if at war.

[59]Paul Mann, "Tensions Remain High in Volatile South Asia," *Aviation Week & Space Technology* (February 28, 2000), pp. 62–63.

[60]See Steve Coll, "The Stand-Off," *The New Yorker* (February 13 & 20, 2006), pp. 126–139 and Alexander Evans, "India, Pakistan, and the Prospect of War," *Current History* (April 2002), pp. 160–165.

[61]For discussions of genocide and international responses, see Peter Ronayne, *Never Again? The United States and the Prevention and Punishment of Genocide since the Holocaust* (Lanham, MD: Rowman & Littlefield, 2001); Samantha Power, *"A Problem From Hell": America and the Age of Genocide* (New York: Basic Books, 2002); Michael N. Barnett, *Eyewitness to a Genocide: The United Nations and Rwanda* (Ithaca, NY: Cornell University Press, 2002); and Michael N. Barnett and Martha Finnemore, *Rules for the World: International Organizations in Global Politics* (Ithaca, NY: Cornell University Press, 2004).

[62]See Michael Levi, "Nuclear Bunker Buster Bombs," *Scientific American*, Vol. 291 (August 2004), pp. 66–73 for a skeptical view of the possibilities.

[63]For an introduction to contemporary China and its international status, see June Teulfel Dreyer, *China's Political System: Modernization and Tradition*, 5th ed. (New York: Pearson/Longman, 2006), David Shambaugh (ed.), *Power Shift: China and Asia's New Dynamic* (Berkeley, CA: University of California Press, 2006), Jeremy Paltiel, *The Empire's New Clothes: Cultural Particularism and Universal Value in China's Quest for Global Status* (New York: Palgrave Macmillan, 2006); Paul T. Bolt and Albert Willmer (eds.), *China's Nuclear Future* (Boulder, CO: Lynne Rienner, 2005); and Ted Fishman, *China, Inc.:How the Rise of the Next Superpower Challenges America and the World* (New York: Scribner, 2005).

[64]See Richard C. Bush, *Untying the Knot: Making Peace in the Taiwan Straits* (Washington, D.C.: Brookings Institution, 2005); Nancy Bernkopf Tucker (ed.) *Dangerous Strait: The U.S.-Taiwan-China Crisis* (New York, N.Y.: Columbia University Press, 2005); and Edward Friedman (ed.), *China's Rise, Taiwan's Dilemmas, and International Peace* (New York: Routledge, 2006).

[65]Trudy Rubin, "An Uneasy Codependence," *Durham Herald Sun*, October 3, 2005, p. A9. The second quotation is a statement by Wang Jisi, Dean of the School of International Studies, Beijing University.

[66]David Albright and Holly Higgins, "A Bomb for the Ummah," *Bulletin of the Atomic Scientists*, Vol. 59 (March/April, 2003), pp. 49–55.

[67]Albright and Higgins, "A Bomb for the Ummah."

[68]For one speculation, see Paul Bracken, "America's Maginot Line," *The Atlantic Monthly* Vol. 282 (November 1998), pp. 85–93. Seymour Hersh has argued that Israel had a similar strategy: to threaten the Soviet Union with nuclear attack of it did not restrain its Arab allies; *The Sampson Option: Israel's Nuclear Policy and American Foreign Policy* (New York: Random House, 1991).

[69]Robert Gallucci interview, August 25, 2003.

8

Nuclear Proliferation

In January 2004, Siegfried Hecker, a metallurgist and expert on the construction of nuclear weapons, was invited by the North Korean government to visit its secret site for research on nuclear weapons, Yongbyon Scientific Research Center, along with other Western nuclear scientists. The purpose of the invitation, surprisingly, was for the North Koreans to prove to other nations, especially the United States, that the North *had* nuclear weapons. The North Koreans first showed Hecker and the others that some nuclear fuel rods that had been under UN inspection several months earlier had been removed from the inspection site, suggesting that the North was reprocessing plutonium for nuclear weapons. Hecker objected that this did not prove that the nuclear fuel had been reprocessed and the weapons constructed.

In response, the officials showed Hecker two clear jars, one containing a greenish powder and the other a piece of metal. The officials claimed the powder was a compound of plutonium and the metal was cast plutonium, demonstrating that they had the fuel for a nuclear weapon. Hecker, still skeptical, asked to hold the jars. He knew that plutonium was twice as dense as iron and warm due to its radioactivity. The jar with the metal was both heavy and warm. The officials, using a Geiger counter, showed him that the material was radioactive. Hecker still insisted that this was not proof that a nuclear device existed. In later testimony to the U.S. Congress, Hecker reiterated that he could not conclusively say that the metal he was shown was plutonium or, more importantly, that it had actually been crafted into a bomb.[1]

North Korea seemed desperate to prove to the United States and the outside world that it had nuclear weapons—that it had in fact *proliferated*. Why would it want to do this when proliferation went against a long-standing international norm? One likely reason is that nuclear weapons are a deterrent only when other nations know they exist. Specifically, the North wanted to deter the United States from attacking it, having seen the United States attack Iraq. But another possible reason was that North Korea was seeking more concessions from the United States and other nations with which it was then negotiating about its nuclear weapons program. Proliferation would put more bargaining chips in the North's hands. If these were the North's motivations, Hecker's response may have increased the anxiety in Pyongyang. If the North believes that it must finally convince the United States that its nuclear arsenal does exist, the next step would likely be to test a weapon. That would create a major crisis with the United States.

North Korea shows the dangerous face of nuclear proliferation. A nuclear-armed North presents a number of dangerous possibilities. First, the North is a highly militarized society with little contact with the outside world. It lives in tension with its neighbor South Korea and has massive numbers of troops on their border. It also exists in a state of desperate poverty and extreme paranoia. This combination creates the serious possibility that North Korea might go to war using its nuclear weapons. The North could deliberately choose to use its nuclear weapons, or, perhaps more likely, due to its state of fear and lack of adequate controls, it could eventually use them in mindless desperation or accidentally. Second, the North's possession of nuclear weapons could lead its neighbors, such as South Korea and Japan, to acquire nuclear weapons of their own. This additional proliferation could greatly increase tensions in the area, for example, between rivals China and Japan, with the potential to further increase the risk of war, including nuclear war. Third, given its economic desperation, the North might sell its nuclear weapons to others, as it has sold missile technology to Iran, Pakistan, and Egypt in the past. A nuclear weapon might fetch a high price on the international black market, leading to more proliferation among irresponsible or unstable nations. The North might even sell a nuclear weapon to terrorists.

At the same time, North Korea's efforts to acquire nuclear weapons are likely based on the same logic or reasoning that has led others to acquire them, namely, the logic of deterrence. A nation acquires nuclear weapons, in part at least, to keep itself from being attacked with nuclear weapons (or with overwhelming conventional force) by others: the Russians by the United States, the British and French by the Russians, the Chinese by the Russians, the Indians by the Chinese, the Pakistanis by the Indians, and the Israelis by their Arab opponents. North Korea regards the United States as a serious military threat. In his 2002 State of the Union address, President Bush declared North Korea to be a part of the "axis of evil," along with Iraq and Iran, and then proceeded in March 2003 to overthrow the government of Iraq. It is not surprising that North Korea believes it might be next. What better way to deter attack than to threaten nuclear retaliation? Would the United States have attacked Iraq, if the Iraqis had had nuclear weapons? Just to ask the question suggests that proliferation can help deter such an attack.

Thus, North Korea illustrates both the dangers of nuclear proliferation and the strong security motivations nations have to become nuclear powers. Nuclear proliferation is the spread of nuclear weapons to nations beyond those already possessing them.[2] The traditional nuclear powers, the United States, Russia, Britain, France, and China, were at one time nuclear proliferators. Israel, India, Pakistan, and now possibly North Korea, are more recent nuclear proliferators. Iran seems to be seeking to become a proliferator. The main concern with nuclear proliferation has been that it makes nuclear war more likely and that any war waged with nuclear weapons will be far more devastating for the combatant nations and, as well, nations that are not directly involved. September 11 has demonstrated an additional problem. Some terrorists are interested in doing as much damage as possible to the United States and other developed nations, and there is nothing like nuclear weapons for doing damage. Nuclear proliferation increases the risk that nuclear weapons will fall into the hands of terrorists who might be all too willing to use them. In this chapter, we explore the dangers of nuclear proliferation. In Chapter 9, we consider the related danger of nuclear terrorism.

A concern about nuclear proliferation is sometimes linked with concerns about proliferation of other weapons which, along with nuclear weapons, have been called Weapons of Mass Destruction (WMD). WMD are generally understood to include nuclear weapons, chemical weapons, like poison gas, and biological weapons, like anthrax. Recent U.S. policy, especially following 9/11, has shown great concern about the proliferation of all three. There are historical reasons these weapons are grouped together under the WMD label, mainly that their use would involve the death of a large number of civilians; indeed, civilians are likely to be the primary target. But, in fact, nuclear weapons are far more deadly than either chemical or biological weapons.[3] Nuclear weapons can destroy entire cities. In addition, there are effective defenses against chemical and biological weapons, but none against nuclear weapons. For these reasons, it is appropriate to give greater attention to the proliferation of nuclear weapons than to the proliferation of other WMD, and this is the course followed in this chapter.[4]

Though nuclear proliferation is generally thought to be a great danger, precisely why is it dangerous? How dangerous is it? What is the best way to control it? These are the main questions we consider in this chapter. Before addressing these questions, however, we first consider the politics of nuclear proliferation—how nuclear proliferation occurs and why. This will help us to understand the nature of nuclear proliferation and what might be done to stop it.

PROLIFERATION'S PROGRESS

The history of weapons is one of rapid emulation. If a nation could afford what was deemed a war-winning weapon, it would enter the inventory. But one of the most important facts about proliferation in the first nuclear age is that, despite expectations to the contrary, it progressed slowly. In 1963, President John Kennedy said, "[P]ersonally I am haunted by the feeling that by 1970, unless we are successful, there may be ten nuclear powers instead of four, and by 1975, fifteen or twenty."[5] But such expectations were not realized. Rather than accelerating, the pace of nuclear proliferation during the first nuclear age actually slowed. Consider, for example, new nations testing a nuclear weapon. Counting decades since 1945, the first decade saw three nations test a nuclear weapon (the United States, the Soviet Union, and Great Britain), while the second saw two (France and China), and the third decade, only one (India), with Israel likely achieving a nuclear weapons capability without testing.[6]

In the fourth and fifth decades, 1975–1995, no new nations tested nuclear weapons, but South Africa did assemble a small arsenal of nuclear devices.[7] Many nations that had the technological capability did not become proliferators. In the sixth decade (1995–2005), however, with the advent of the second nuclear age, there has been one, and possibly two cases of proliferation, namely, Pakistan and North Korea. This suggests that the pace of proliferation may be picking up. Opportunities for proliferation may be increasing, such as the possible black-market availability of Russian weapons or fissile material. But more important, motivations to proliferate may be on the rise. For example, North Korean nuclear weapons may encourage Japan and South Korea to become proliferators.

At the same time there have been cases suggesting that the overall move toward proliferation has been constrained.[8] For example, in 1993, South Africa announced that it had dismantled the six or seven nuclear weapons it had built in the 1980s and would sign the Nuclear Non-Proliferation Treaty.[9] In 1991, Brazil and Argentina signed a pair of agreements by which each assured the other (and the rest of the world) that it was not attempting to develop nuclear weapons.[10] At that time, both nations had recently adopted democratic, civilian governments after a period of military rule, during which each feared that the other was trying to outrace it to get a bomb.[11] Another case where proliferation was avoided involves the new nations created by the breakup of the Soviet Union, which dispersed the Soviet arsenal. Ukraine, Belarus, and Kazakhstan were "born nuclear,"[12] but in the years following, through a process of negotiation and inducement, the new nations choose to return the weapons to Russia.

Then there is a different kind of anti-proliferation success story in the case of Iraq. Iraq had "pursued a range of technologies, built an impressive collection of buildings at many sites, and purchased hundreds of thousands of pieces of special equipment and hundreds of tons of specialty materials from abroad."[13] Its defeat in the 1991 Persian Gulf War led to a very intrusive weapons inspection regime, accepted by Iraq as part of the terms of the cease-fire. It is estimated that had the program not been interrupted by the Iraqi defeat, a bomb would have been produced by 1996.

Another, more recent success story is Libya. Libya used to be among those the United States referred to as rogue states. The United States bombed the capital city, Tripoli, in April 1986 in response to Libyan sponsored terrorist acts against U.S. troops in Europe, and Libya responded in 1988 with the terrorist destruction of Pan Am flight 103 over Lockerbie, Scotland. Libya was also developing nuclear weapons and other weapons of mass destruction. But on December 19, 2003, Libya announced that it would give up its program for developing WMD and sign the Nuclear Non-Proliferation Treaty. Libya stated that it would undertake this "in a transparent way that could be proved, including accepting immediate international inspection." The leader of Libya, Colonel Qadaffi asserted: "The security of Libya does not come from the nuclear bomb; the nuclear bomb represents a danger to the country which has them."[14] He said in addition: "Libya has secured itself more by discarding such programs. ... The whole world pledges and honors the security of Libya because Libya has forged the road on the path to peace."[15]

Despite these successes, there are a number of factors in the second nuclear age, some mentioned earlier, that increase the likelihood of nuclear proliferation.[16] One is the accelerating growth of global economic integration, which makes it easier for a nation to acquire the industrial technology to make nuclear weapons. Another is that the end of the Cold War has turned the Soviet nuclear threat into a Russian nuclear proliferation threat, namely, the threat that Soviet nuclear weapons or material will find their way to other nations or terrorists.[17] This is the so-called "loose nukes" problem. Due largely to economic difficulties following the breakup of the Soviet Union, Russia has not been able to afford to maintain tight security on its nuclear weapons and fissile material, raising the risk of their being stolen, and it has not been able to afford adequate pay for its military personnel, raising the risk that they will seek to sell nuclear weapons or materials on the black market.

A more startling development in the second nuclear age has been the creation of what Chaim Braun and Christopher Chyba have called "proliferation rings"—groups of individuals and governments who have traded nuclear secrets, materials, and technologies, and delivery systems in return for cash or needed items.[18] The most prominent has been the A. Q. Khan network in Pakistan and the North Korean government's network. Abdul Qadeer Khan, for instance, had overseen the development of Pakistan's nuclear weapons. He had worked for a Dutch company making gas centrifuges, and is alleged to have stolen crucial blueprints before returning to Pakistan to begin work on the Pakistani bomb. In the early 1990s, perhaps earlier, he ran a quasi-private supply network, dispensing blueprints and components to enrich uranium as well as designs of nuclear weapons. His activities came to public notice in February 2004 with the seizure of a cargo ship bound for Libya with such materials. Included in the shipment, described by one investigator as a "sweetener" in the deal he had made with the Libyan government, was a detailed plan for constructing a working ten-kiloton nuclear weapon, allegedly originally from China. (The seizure of this shipment is part of what led Libya to give up its nuclear weapons program.) It soon became clear that the Khan network had supplied nuclear materials and know-how to at least two other nations, Iran and North Korea. Other customers may have included Syria, Egypt, Saudi Arabia, Sudan, Malaysia, Indonesia, and Algeria. Khan, a Pakistani national hero for his role in developing Pakistan's nuclear weapons, confessed to his activity on Pakistani TV and was quickly pardoned by Pakistan's president, Pervez Musharraf. Khan remains in Pakistan, unavailable for questioning by Western intelligence agents about the full extent of his nuclear dealings and the opportunities for proliferation he has bestowed around the world.[19]

The emergence of proliferation rings, the existence of loose nukes in the former Soviet Union, and the general growth of industrial and nuclear know-how and capabilities have set the stage for a new round of proliferation, of which North Korea and Iran may be the harbingers of an unfolding future. We can gain a perspective on the future by summarizing proliferation's progress since 1945. Figure 8-1 does so, and suggests three general predictions about the future: continued slow and steady proliferation, a rapid proliferation explosion, and, lastly, accumulating de-proliferation.

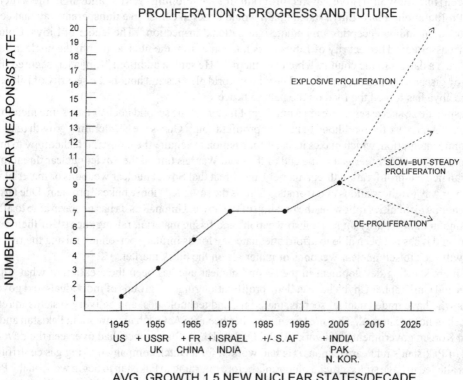

Figure 8–1   Chart of proliferation past and future

OPPORTUNITY AND MOTIVATION

Each of these predictions in Figure 8–1 rests on different assessments of why nations choose to proliferate or to remain non-nuclear, or in a few cases, to give up nuclear weapons. In the main, writes Mitchell Reiss, "nuclear proliferation is a function of two variables: technological capability and political motivation. Both must be present for a country to acquire nuclear weapons. The capability without the motivation is innocuous. The motivation without the capability is futile."[20]

The first variable, technological capability, should be understood more broadly, as the *opportunity* to acquire the weapons. Opportunity is largely a function of a nation's technological capability to build the weapons. States with modern, industrial economies generally have most of the capability needed to produce nuclear weapons, provided that they can acquire or produce fissile material. Globalization, furthermore, allows states with less indigenous industrial capability (such as Iraq or Iran) access to businesses and governments who can supply the missing components for a weapons program. In the second nuclear age, globalization creates increasing opportunities for a nation (or terrorist group) to acquire nuclear weapons or fissile material on the international black market or by theft. Terrorists may well be able to create very crude (but deadly effective) nuclear weapons so long as they have access to fissile material; it is the creating of the fissile material that is clearly beyond their technological capability.

While the lack of technology will still constrain many states, the critical factor for proliferation is *motivation*. With motivation and the diversion of economic resources that political motivation can generate, proliferation is likely (albeit on a prolonged timetable for many). As we have seen throughout this book, national security concerns have driven *some* leaders of *some* states to acquire nuclear weapons. They perceive nuclear weapons as offering the ultimate deterrent. Nations fear attack or blackmail from other nations, and they believe that having a nuclear deterrent can avoid this. To this extent, the desire to acquire nuclear weapons is defensive. But nations may also be motivated to seek nuclear weapons for aggressive purposes. Nations may desire nuclear weapons to defeat an opponent in a war of aggression or to use the threat of such an aggressive war as a form of nuclear blackmail to achieve some aggressive end. In other words, nations may seek nuclear weapons not only for deterrence, but also for *compellence*.

A second motivational force has been the search for prestige; nuclear weapons denote who has great power and who does not. Having prestige can translate into political advantages in diplomacy and negotiation. Moreover, the political process within a nation may also encourage proliferation; leaders responsive to the electorate or to powerful elites may court political support by going nuclear. India's decision to conduct nuclear tests in 1998 reflects these two aspects of motivation as well as the security factor. India gave a justification for its decision in terms of national security and defense: it needed a demonstrable nuclear capacity, beyond the nuclear ambiguity created by its 1974 test, in order to counter the nuclear capacity of China. A senior advisor to the Indian Prime Minister defended the decision to test by claiming that in South Asia there was "a huge gap, a vacuum" in the geographical domain of nuclear deterrence, which India felt the need to fill.[21] India felt that while the United States would protect Japan from China's nuclear threat, no one would protect India. India had to act to protect itself.

But defense and national security may not have been the only motivation. The Indian Prime Minister at the time, Atal Bihari Vajpayee, proclaimed that with the nuclear tests, India had taken "its rightful place in the international community."[22] India thinks of itself as a great nation, but did not see itself as receiving the recognition it was due because, unlike other great nations, it did not have a nuclear arse-

Figure 8–2   The Indian nuclear tests in 1998 had strong popular support.
Copyright © AP Images. Used with permission.

nal. The initial overwhelming and enthusiastic support of everyday Indians for the testing suggests that feelings of national pride and self-respect played a major role in the decision. And Vajpayee's political party—recently brought to power—would benefit from this flowering of Indian nationalism.

In sum, proliferation will always be a temptation for some political leaders. Given the spread of technology and knowledge about nuclear weapons, the constraints once imposed by the technological demands have eroded significantly. That alone increases the likelihood of proliferation. The end of the Cold War has, ironically, played a role in increasing the temptation. The steep decline of Soviet/Russian power has lead to stronger incentives, and weaker disincentives, for non-nuclear nations to acquire nuclear weapons. As Robert Jervis has noted, "former Soviet clients may at once be more desperate (lacking a superpower patron) and more autonomous (lacking a superpower to restrain them)."[23] North Korea is an example. With the end of the Cold War came an end to the relative certainties of the Cold War. The Cold War imposed an alliance system, which tended to make regional conflicts subservient to the East-West conflict. Now some nations may feel, in comparison, abandoned and left to define anew their interests and relations with others. For example, India's decision to retest nuclear weapons in 1998 may have been partly motivated by its feelings of isolation resulting from the loss of its alliance with the Soviet Union. These changes may increase the motivation some nations have to acquire nuclear weapons.[24]

Having pointed these factors out, we might well surmise that many nations are likely to go nuclear over time, as states or their leaders will constantly be concerned about national security, their international clout, and their domestic support. As the opportunity to go nuclear is available to many states, perhaps the "explosion" prediction in Figure 8-1 is our most likely future. What might set off a sudden rush to nuclearize? We have suggested that a successful nuclearization by North Korea will put great pressure on South Korea and Japan to follow suit. Such regional proliferation might be self-limiting, as all the major rivals in the region would then be nuclear powers. On the other hand, Japan's entry into the nuclear club may encourage other middle-range powers to contemplate following suite in order to maintain their international standing. Germany would be a logical candidate. Proliferation in the heart of Europe may, however, trigger another round of regional proliferation there, drawing in perhaps Poland, Ukraine, and Italy. Or, perhaps more likely, the proliferation of India, Pakistan, and North Korea might encourage other leaders to believe that nuclear weapons can elevate their relatively low level of power to a status where their interests and concerns receive much greater attention than before from the great powers. For instance, while there have been other factors that have encouraged the Clinton and Bush administrations to seek better relations with India, some would see India's emergence as a nuclear power as the key that moved the United States into a new posture.

If there is no proliferation explosion, the "slow but steady" prediction would seem most likely. Our table projects that there will be one or two more nuclear powers by 2015, reaching a total of three by 2025. At present, given current policies and practices within and between states, we do not see the de-proliferation prediction as likely. Thus, proliferation is likely to be our future. Is there a significant danger in that future?

THE DANGERS OF NUCLEAR PROLIFERATION

Conventional wisdom holds that nuclear proliferation makes the world a more dangerous place, that it undermines rather than enhances international security. The reason is that nuclear proliferation is thought to increase the risk of war, as well as the level of destructiveness of war. Indeed, this increased danger is assumed whenever nuclear proliferation is labeled a "problem," as it normally is. The conventional assumption that nuclear proliferation makes the world more dangerous may be correct, but the matter deserves examination. Clearly this line of argument seems inconsistent with another bit of received wisdom, namely, that nuclear deterrence is an effective means of achieving national security. A common belief is that nuclear deterrence worked during the first nuclear age, keeping the United States and the Soviet Union from war.[25] These two assumptions of conventional wisdom appear inconsistent: one claims that nuclear deterrence does work (for us, the nuclear powers) because it enhances our security, but that it does not work (for them, the potential proliferators) because it would increase their insecurity. It is odd, notes Kenneth Waltz, that "a happy nuclear past leads many to expect an unhappy nuclear future."[26] Why should nuclear deterrence work for some but not for others?

In response to this apparent inconsistency, we need to resolve it either by showing that it is merely apparent or by rejecting as erroneous one of the two assumptions that compose it. We consider the latter alternative first. Consider the assumption that nuclear proliferation makes the world more dangerous. Some argue that nuclear proliferation may, in fact, make the world safer, as it made the cold-war relationship between the United States and the Soviet Union safer. From this perspective, the view that nuclear proliferation is dangerous "flies in the face of the inherent logic of nuclear deterrence, as well as the history of the Cold War."[27] Kenneth Waltz argues that the long Cold War peace between the superpowers is attributable largely to nuclear deterrence, since nuclear deterrence distinguished the Cold-War era from earlier historical periods when great-power wars were more frequent. If nuclear deterrence worked for the superpowers, it should work for others.[28]

Waltz provides a theoretical argument showing that nuclear deterrence increases security for whatever nations practice it. Not only are nuclear weapons tremendously destructive, but effective defense against them is impossible (whether they are delivered by a ballistic missile or a rented truck). Any nation with a modest number of nuclear weapons can threaten to inflict "unacceptable damage" upon an opponent. As a result, "the presence of nuclear weapons makes states exceedingly cautious." Being certain that an opponent could destroy it, a nation would be much less likely to start a war or to act in ways that might lead to war. Such caution would characterize any nation facing a nuclear-armed foe. Thus, when two opponents have nuclear weapons, each would be especially cautious, and war would be less likely. Waltz concludes: "Nuclear weapons, responsibly used, make wars hard to start. Nations that have nuclear weapons have strong incentives to use them responsibly. These statements hold for small as for big nuclear powers."[29] The theoretical conclusion thus bolsters the historical point, explaining why in fact the Cold War was the long peace. In addition, it provides reason to believe that the same effects would hold for potential proliferators.

Most of those who believe that proliferation is dangerous accept the claim that nuclear deterrence produced, or helped to produce, the long superpower peace of the first nuclear age. They seek to avoid the inconsistency by showing that what appears to be an inconsistency dissolves on closer inspection. Their strategy for doing this is to cite a number of differences between the Cold War superpowers and potential proliferators to show how nuclear deterrence would work in one case but not in the other. According to Joseph Nye, the claim that nuclear deterrence works well

> assumes governments with stable command and control systems, the absence of serious civil wars, the absence of strong destabilizing motivations such as irredentist passions, and discipline over the temptation for preemptive strikes during the early stages when new nuclear weapons capabilities are soft and vulnerable. Such assumptions are unrealistic in many parts of the world.[30]

Because these features are lacking in the case of many potential proliferators, these nations, were they to acquire nuclear weapons, are much more likely than were the Cold-War superpowers to get themselves into a nuclear war, if not deliberately then accidentally.[31] The risk of inadvertent or unauthorized use of nuclear weapons is greater in the case of many potential proliferators. Thus, the national security nuclear weapons promoted for the superpowers could not be expected to apply for many potential proliferators.

Consider the proliferators India and Pakistan, each of which conducted a series of nuclear tests in 1998.[32] The relations of these two nations differ in important ways from the Cold-War relations of the superpowers. First, India and Pakistan share a long and disputed border, while the superpowers did not. Second, the two Asian nations have had three wars between them in the recent past, whereas the superpowers had no recent history of direct conflict.[33] Third, the superpowers had developed elaborate national technical means of verification to determine what military activities each other was up to, while India and Pakistan have not. Fourth, the superpowers developed a secure retaliatory capability, which India and Pakistan lack. These differences make nuclear war between India and Pakistan more likely than it was between the United States and the Soviet Union. It has been reported that "every time the Pentagon has conducted a war game between a nuclear-armed India and Pakistan, the result is a nuclear exchange, something that does not happen between … Russia and the United States."[34]

Waltz responds to such arguments by claiming that the prospect of nuclear destruction is so powerful an influence on a nation's behavior that the prospect would induce extra caution even in the face of these sorts of differences between the superpowers and potential proliferators. The differences are not great enough to show that nuclear deterrence would not work for potential proliferators. The fact that India and Pakistan have avoided war since 1998, despite periods of great tension between them, may lend some support to Waltz's position. It could well be that in the absence of their nuclear weapons, India and Pakistan would have gone to war in this period.

Waltz's counter-arguments speak to leaders' making conscious decisions to wage nuclear war, but there is also the issue of accidental or inadvertent nuclear war. In this regard, there are important technological differences between the superpowers and today's proliferators in terms of the safety and security of nuclear weapons and the systems for their command and control. The superpowers developed over time a robust system of command and control to prevent the use of the weapons accidentally or without authorization and to make the weapons less vulnerable to destruction in a surprise first strike.[35] Many potential proliferators, especially developing nations, would not have such systems. A defender of the Waltzian position might respond, however, that the current nuclear nations have it within their power to correct this problem by providing technological assistance to proliferators in constructing nuclear systems. For example, the United States could provide proliferators with arming technology that avoids unauthorized use (the so-called permissive action link or PAL, discussed in Chapter 4).[36]

The critics who see current proliferators as quite different than the United States and Soviet Union also point to the differences in political cultures, where there may be an "absence of those patterns of behavior and modes of thought that produced prudence in the Soviet-American relationship." Do potential proliferators lack the capacity for prudence characteristic of the superpowers? A positive answer, John Weltman argues, "would assume that the capacity for political rationality is a narrow, culturally based attribute."[37] This criticism is emphasized by Waltz, who argues that the kind of rationality needed to make nuclear deterrence work is simply the human tendency to act cautiously in the face of extreme danger. "Many Westerners who write fearfully about a future in which Third World countries have nuclear weapons seem to view their people in the once familiar imperial manner as 'lesser breeds without the law.'"[38]

But consider that the extent to which a nation is inclined to act prudently or rationally is a function not only of what individual leaders choose to do, but also of the organizations through which they act. To say that nonwestern nations are less inclined to act rationally than western nations is not to imply that their leaders or culture are inferior. Instead, it may simply to imply that their organizations of political and military control are different. Scott Sagan, who discusses the characteristics of military organizations and their implications for nuclear danger, develops this point.[39] Sagan argues that often "the biases, routines, and parochial interests of powerful military organizations, not the 'objective' interests of the state, can determine state behavior."[40] There are two main reasons that organizations do not act rationally. First, the rationality of their behavior is bounded by the routines and standard operating procedures they adopt. Second, the process by which the conflicting goals of the different bureaucracies determine their behavior is highly political, resulting in behavior that is, from an outside perspective, often "systematically stupid."[41] Thus, given the strong influence of the military in the governments of most potential proliferators, proliferation can be expected to create new dangers.

But we suggest that this argument, when used to support the claim that nuclear weapons would be dangerous in the hands of potential proliferators, has critical limitations. First, it does not show how potential proliferators are different from the Cold-War superpowers in ways that matter. Organizational and political factors can influence the actions of the superpowers as well as the actions of potential proliferators. As we saw in Chapter 3, there were occasions during the Cold War when the

United States came close to using nuclear weapons.[42] Moreover, the superpowers did not behave during the first nuclear age as Waltz's theory suggests they should have. In his view, nuclear deterrence works because the parties to the relationship have the capacity to destroy each other, and this policy is easily maintained by relatively small nuclear forces that avoid "war-fighting" weapons and doctrines that threaten the nuclear weapons of the other side. But, as we saw in Chapter 4, the superpowers did not follow this script. Instead, they assumed that "deterrence required much larger forces than the minimum deterrence requirement," and they "opted for precisely the war-fighting nuclear doctrines that are regarded as unnecessary, inappropriate and destabilizing by most deterrence theorists."[43]

This suggests that the superpowers' nuclear behavior was not at the level of prudence and rationality that the conventional assumption suggests it was. Perhaps the organizational characteristics Sagan attributes to new proliferators determined superpower nuclear policy as well. From this perspective, the Cold War was a time of nuclear danger rather than relative nuclear safety. The long peace of the Cold War was more a matter of luck than of the effectiveness of nuclear deterrence. The implication is that the possession of nuclear weapons is dangerous, whether the possessors are the Cold-War superpowers (and other Cold-War proliferators) or current potential proliferators. Nuclear proliferation is dangerous because nuclear deterrence is a dangerous policy, whoever practices it. The proper argument, from this perspective, is not that proliferation is dangerous because most potential proliferators are different in their behavior from the established nuclear powers, as most critics of proliferation maintain. The proper argument is that the possession of nuclear weapons is dangerous whoever the possessor and whether the proliferation occurred in the first or the second nuclear ages.

The second critical limitation of Sagan's argument is that it is too broad in its characterizations. It is not attuned to the details of individual cases. Though the possession of nuclear weapons may tend to be dangerous, it will be more dangerous in some cases than in others. For example, it can make a great difference whether the proliferator is the first of a pair of military opponents to acquire nuclear weapons or the second, because a one-sided nuclear relationship may be much more dangerous than a two-sided relationship of mutual assured destruction.

The fact that one must look at the details of the particular case is recognized by all of the participants in the debate. Those sanguine about proliferation, such as Waltz, acknowledge that proliferation would be dangerous were it to occur rapidly, while those critical of proliferation admit that proliferation might in some cases even have beneficial effects outweighing the dangers.[44] Our assessment is that, in general, the proliferation of nuclear weapons tends to increase danger and lessen security, even if there are in some cases factors that mitigate or even outweigh that tendency. Most dangerous would be a future proliferation explosion, as represented in Figure 8-1, in which a number of new nuclear states, unpracticed in the use of nuclear weapons and nuclear diplomacy, would suddenly emerge on the scene. As regional proliferation would be most likely under an explosion scenario, the traditional balances of power and relationships in the region may be undermined. Threats involving the new nuclear states may suddenly pull in outside powers as would-be mediators, a role for which they are unlikely to be prepared, whose entrance into the issue may compound passions and problems. A slow-but-steady proliferation, on the other hand, reduces these problems by giving states time to adjust to the new condition. Nonetheless, we judge that any nuclear proliferation likely to occur would be dangerous because it would increase the likelihood of nuclear use. We should therefore seek to limit or prevent nuclear proliferation altogether. How can we best achieve that end?

ANTI-PROLIFERATION POLICY

Various kinds of anti-proliferation policies may be adopted, as we discussed in the last chapter. The range of policies is suggested by a U.S. official: "We are determined to use every resource at our disposal—using diplomacy regularly, economic pressure when it makes a difference, active law enforcement when appropriate, and military force when we must."[45] For our analysis in this section, we identify four general kinds of anti-proliferation policy:

1. obtaining the consent of the potential proliferator not to acquire the weapons.
2. denying the potential proliferator the necessary means to acquire the weapons.
3. coercively preventing the potential proliferator from acquiring the weapons.
4. coercively depriving a proliferator of the nuclear weapons it has already acquired.

We shall refer to these as policies of (1) *cooperative anti-proliferation*, (2) *denial anti-proliferation*, (3) *coercive anti-proliferation*, and (4) *coercive denuclearization*. Policies of denial anti-proliferation, coercive anti-proliferation, and coercive denuclearization are all noncooperative in the sense that they seek to stop proliferation against the will of the potential or actual proliferator. We examine this trio of anti-proliferation policies first.

Denial anti-proliferation policy seeks to thwart proliferation by restricting access to necessary material or intellectual ingredients of the bomb-making process such as fissile materials, sophisticated centrifuges, or working plans for a weapon. An example of this approach is the Nuclear Suppliers Group, a group of industrialized nations that has agreed to limit the access of non-nuclear nations to the nuclear-related technology its members command.[46] This works imperfectly at best, inasmuch as the guidelines are ambiguous and nuclear-export interest groups in the various nations have tried to water down or evade the various prohibitions. In addition to such mutual arrangements, nuclear nations have adopted their own individual forms of denial anti-proliferation policy.

Another type of denial policy is the Bush administration's creation in 2003 of the Proliferation Security Initiative, an agreement among interested states to monitor and attempt to interdict the shipment of missiles and nuclear components through their territory and to allow their ships to be boarded at sea or diverted to a friendly port for inspection. The participating states have had some success, as is suggested by the discovery of the shipment to Libya, discussed earlier in the chapter. States that are not members of the initiative can refuse to halt transit and reject the boarding of their flagged ships.

But policies of denial are difficult to implement and to make effective. One reason is they conflict with other national interests, as well as with economic interests within states, as mentioned above. Another reason is that Nuclear Non-Proliferation Treaty (discussed below) allows nonnuclear states to possess technology and materials needed to generate nuclear power, but which can also be used to build weapons. In addition, "Technology is no longer a barrier to weapons proliferation, but merely a hurdle" because "technological progress and the dissemination of knowledge make building nuclear weapons a more manageable task now."[47] Advances in technology and its global dissemination mean that proliferation can no longer be stopped solely by an attempt to restrict technology access. Moreover, as one commentator argues: such an attempt "amounts to treating the symptoms while ignoring the disease. ... Over the long run, the 'cure' for the problem of nuclear proliferation lies ultimately with the reduction of national nuclear propensities [to proliferate]."[48] Policy needs to consider not just opportunity, as denial does, but also motivation.

Coercive anti-proliferation policy is the threat or use of force to insure that a state does not become a proliferator. If it involves a threat of force, it works on motivation. One form of coercive anti-proliferation is the imposition of economic sanctions. Economic sanctions seek to coerce potential proliferators into giving up their plan to acquire nuclear weapons, changing their motivation to proliferate by imposing economic hardship on them.[49] The U.S. Congress, for example, passed the Nuclear Non-Proliferation Act in 1978. It denies foreign aid to any nation that attempts to construct a nuclear explosive. The coercive power of this Act has been undercut in notable cases, however. The Reagan administration's need for Pakistan as a staging area in the war against the Soviet forces in Afghanistan undercut the United States' attempt to keep Pakistan from developing nuclear weapons, as did the exemption carved out by U.S. agricultural interests which permitted continued food aid in spite of proliferation efforts. Similar backsliding can be seen in the recent U.S. reaction to nuclear acquisition by India.

Another form of coercive anti-proliferation policy is the threat of force to deter proliferation.[50] The purpose of such threats is to get a potential proliferator to abandon its nuclear ambitions by persuading it that the costs the threatener seems willing to impose if the program continues are greater than the costs of giving up the program. As you read these words, you may be watching the United States or Israel engaging in such threat-making to persuade the Iranian government to end whatever plans it may have for a nuclear arsenal. Of course, the very threats may inflame nationalist passions, making it much more difficult for the target government to abandon a nuclear program, and for many, such threats prove that nuclear weapons are exactly what it needs to prevent such coercion. As with most deterrent effort, the nation making the threats generally hopes that they succeed, for it does not relish the costs or possible consequences of having to carry them out.

At the extreme, a state may use force to insure that another does not acquire nuclear weapons. The 1981 Israeli attack against a nuclear reactor in Osirak, Iraq is one example of this form of coercive anti-proliferation; Osirak was part of an early effort by Iraq to acquire nuclear weapons. We discuss later a more recent example of coercive anti-proliferation, the war launched in 2003 by the United States against Iraq.

But in some cases, a state may try to use force to reverse a case of proliferation, to deprive a proliferator of its nuclear weapons. This is *coercive denuclearization*. Such a policy may work on either motivation or opportunity. It seeks to deny the opportunity to proliferate by reversing an accomplished proliferation, destroying the proliferator's nuclear weapons and its capacity to build more. On the other hand, the use of force to affect motivation occurs when a nation seeks to overthrow a government that has become a proliferator. This would be a policy of "regime change" and its goal would be to install a different regime that would have a different motivation regarding the possession of nuclear weapons. Regime change is, of course, what the United States achieved in Iraq in 2003, but this was an effort in coercive anti-proliferation rather than coercive denuclearization because Iraq had not acquired nuclear weapons at that point. While the United States misjudged Iraq's capabilities (there was no program to produce nuclear weapons), it knew (and said so at the time) that Iraq did not have nuclear weapons. The administration claimed that the danger lay down the road, when the presumptive ongoing program would deliver such weapons into Saddam Hussein's hands. If the United States or another state attempts through a policy of coercive denuclearization to use force to rid an opponent of its existing nuclear weapons, it will likely be a last ditch anti-proliferation effort, applied when and because all other forms of anti-proliferation policy have failed. Those who in recent years have recommended using force to eliminate the nuclear weapons presumably already possessed by North Korea are endorsing a policy of coercive denuclearization.

Such a policy runs great risks, of course, as was recognized during the first nuclear age when American or Soviet policy-makers contemplated the possibility of launching a disarming first strike. Against a nuclear-armed foe with a modestly robust deterrent force, such a policy seemed to court unimaginable devastation from the retaliatory second strike. Moreover, the initial strike would have had to use nuclear weapons in order to have a reasonable prospect of destroying sufficient enemy weapons or delivery systems before they were launched, with all the global consequences that might follow. Today, however, the more militarily-potent states may calculate that they can stage a *conventional* attack against a budding nuclear arsenal with a fair prospect of destroying most if not all the opponent's nuclear weapons. If this thinking were to become palatable, states would be tempted to act relatively quickly to disarm their opponents, before they assembled a large enough arsenal, some of which would likely survive the attack (or be undetected) and thus able to be used in some retaliatory manner.

The threat or use of military force as an important part of an anti-proliferation effort, whether it has the form of coercive anti-proliferation or coercive denuclearization, is known as *counterproliferation*. Its advocates recommend moving from a "passive" to an "active" anti-proliferation policy.[51] The idea of counterproliferation was introduced into U.S. policy in the Clinton administration in its *Counterproliferation Initiative* (CPI) of December 1993. The second Bush administration has shifted U.S. policy further toward counterproliferation, partly in response to the terrorist attacks of 9/11.[52] The 2002 *National Security Strategy of the United States* reflected the Bush administration's posture:

> *Proactive counterproliferation efforts.* We must deter and defend against the threat before it is unleashed. We must ensure that key capabilities—detection, active and passive defenses, and counterforce capabilities—are integrated into our defense transformation and our homeland security systems. Counterproliferation must also be integrated into the doctrine, training, and equipping of our forces and those of our allies to ensure that we can prevail in any conflict with WMD-armed adversaries.[53]

As we noted in Chapter 6, counterproliferation demands a willingness to wage *preventive* war. Because preventive war lies generally outside American military and political traditions, the Bush administration has chosen to call this "preemption." The difference is this: Imagine that it's the Wild West; you are in a confrontation with another gunfighter. A true preemptive strategy dictates that you wait until you see your opponent begin to draw his gun from its holster. A preventive strategy, on the other hand, has you reaching and firing first, with no indication that your opponent was about to fire, on the assumption that some day your opponent would try to kill you. (This is the bolt-from-the-blue scenario of the Cold War.) The problem with preventive strategies in the Cold War was two-fold. First, your opponent, suspecting that you might have such a thought in mind, may adopt same strategy and launch preventive war first. The prudent gunfighter shoots first and asks questions later. Second, the catastrophic loss of life resulting from a preventive war would have been unnecessary, as the history of the Cold War showed that neither state wished to engage in war with the other.

In the second nuclear age, however, relatively weak rogue states have no capability to do significant damage to the American homeland and have no nuclear-armed allies who are willing to extend the nuclear umbrella to protect them. Against these states, preventive war as a counterproliferation tactic seems to have received the Bush administration's blessing:

> The United States has long maintained the option of preemptive actions to counter a sufficient threat to our national security. The greater the threat, the greater is the risk of inaction—and the more com-

pelling the case for taking anticipatory action to defend ourselves, even if uncertainty remains as to the time and place of the enemy's attack. To forestall or prevent such hostile acts by our adversaries, the United States will, if necessary, act preemptively.[54]

Furthermore, as we saw in Chapter 6, coercive denuclearization, though it can be implemented against lesser powers with conventional weapons, makes the *first use* of nuclear weapons against potential and actual proliferators an attractive option. The reason is that nuclear weapons may still be able to do some things that conventional weapons cannot. For example, so-called bunker-busters or earth-penetrating weapons (EPWs) armed with nuclear warheads, which can be used to destroy facilities buried deep under ground, are being developed by the United States. Such warheads could destroy underground bunkers that might shelter the weapons and weapons-building equipment that coercive denuclearization seeks to destroy.

But a coercive anti-proliferation (and denuclearization) policy, especially if pursued through the use of military force, suffers from serious difficulties. One problem is that using force against nuclear facilities "may precipitate ecological disasters and nuclear war," with the massive destruction that this would entail.[55] Another problem is that such force may prove ineffective, even counterproductive.[56] The Israeli bombing of the Iraqi nuclear facility at Osirak seems to have strengthened Iraqi determination to acquire a bomb, and the extensive Iraqi nuclear facilities discovered to have survived the 1991 Persian Gulf War suggest some of the limits of an intensive bombing campaign, especially when intelligence is sparse about the extent and location of the nuclear program in question. In addition, nations that witness a use of military force for anti-proliferation purposes may draw the conclusion that they need nuclear weapons to forestall such an attack on them, increasing their motivation to proliferate.

COOPERATIVE ANTI-PROLIFERATION

Because both coercive and denial policies have serious limitations, a cooperative approach may offer a better alternative. Cooperative anti-proliferation is achieved by striking a bargain through offering a potential proliferator an inducement for foreswearing the nuclear option. The switch from noncooperative to cooperative forms of anti-proliferation policy is a switch from seeking a military or a technical solution to the proliferation problem to seeking a political solution.[57] It involves nations working together, accommodating each other, rather than one nation seeking to impose its will on another. As such, it seems to promise a more effective anti-proliferation policy. The main form that cooperative anti-proliferation policy has taken is the Nuclear Non-Proliferation Treaty, but before discussing the specifics of this treaty, we consider two other forms of cooperative anti-proliferation policy, namely, nuclear security guarantees and the programs of "cooperative threat reduction."

Nuclear security guarantees, widely used in the first nuclear age, are a form of incentive offered to potential proliferators to induce them not to acquire nuclear weapons. They are promises by nuclear nations to protect nonnuclear nations from nuclear threats. By offering nuclear security guarantees, nuclear nations extend a "nuclear umbrella" over non-nuclear nations. Nuclear security guarantees can be effective because they respond to a main motive nonnuclear nations have in acquiring nuclear weapons, namely, concerns about their own security. A nation receiving nuclear security guarantees can be protected by nuclear deterrence without its having nuclear weapons. Security guarantees would overcome what is called the *self-help character* of the international system. The international system leaves it to each nation to look after itself, to help itself, to provide for its own security and protection. Security guarantees modify this system because, under them, some nations accept responsibility for the protection of others.

During the first nuclear age, the nuclear security guarantees provided by the United States to West Germany (through the NATO alliance) and to Japan helped to keep these nations from becoming nuclear proliferators. One author notes that all the proliferators after the five declared nuclear nations had "special security problems unmet by the Cold War alliance system."[58] As discussed earlier, one of the motivations India had for its 1998 series of nuclear tests was its fear of being outside of an alliance system that could afford it a measure of nuclear protection. Without such protection, it felt it had to go it alone and develop its own nuclear capacity.

But there are problems with nuclear security guarantees as an anti-proliferation policy. One problem is that some nations needing security guarantees to induce them not to proliferate are those that the nuclear nations are reluctant or loathe to protect, like so-called rogue nations.[59] Another problem is that nuclear security guarantees are expensive to maintain and create risks that those providing them will be dragged into a war, even a nuclear war, of which they would not have otherwise been a part. Those very risks undermine the credibility of a nuclear security guarantee; would the United States, for instance, really come to the aid of a state under threat if the cost might be dramatically high? It was apparently partly this concern that during the Cold War led France to become a nuclear proliferator despite the security guarantees it was offered by the United States.

Ironically, successful nuclear security guarantees may *promote* proliferation. For the United States to provide widespread security guarantees, for example, it would have to support an expanded military establishment in order to make its threats to protect other nations credible. It military posture, as Hedley Bull suggests, would have to be high rather than low, making it appear more provocative to other nations.[60] This could encourage proliferation by showing potential proliferators the importance of nuclear weapons. It would provide them an example of how valuable and effective the nuclear nations take nuclear threats to be. As one commentator notes: "The more one emphasizes the success of deterrence in a world of insecurity, the more alluring the deterrence system is bound to appear."[61]

The converse of this argument may also hold, of course. If the United States does not offer nuclear security guarantees and adopts a low military posture, this could help to discourage proliferation by showing other nations that nuclear weapons are not that important. But a lack of security guarantees could encourage proliferation by leaving nations to achieve nuclear security on their own. The more the United States downplays the importance of nuclear weapons in its own policy, "the more it also degrades the extended U.S. nuclear guarantee, which might over the long run contribute to decisions in Berlin and Tokyo to acquire a nuclear weapons capability."[62] The dilemma is that whichever policy the United States adopts regarding the provision of nuclear security guarantees, the policy will encourage nuclear proliferation as well as discouraging it.

Cooperative threat reduction is another form of cooperative anti-proliferation policy. As discussed earlier, there has been great concern during the second nuclear age about the vast amounts of sometimes poorly protected fissile materials in the former Soviet Union. The quickest route to proliferation may be for a potential proliferator or a terrorist group to acquire some of these materials by theft or by purchase on the black market. As a result, the United States undertook in 1991 an initiative to work cooperatively with the new Russian state to better safeguard its vast nuclear stockpile. Informally known as the Nunn-Lugar initiative after the two senators, Sam Nunn and Richard Lugar, who promoted the idea in Congress, the program helped in the early 1990s to insure that the Soviet weapons in the non-Russian states resulting from the breakup of the Soviet Union were returned to Russia. Since then, it has had some success in helping to dismantle some Russian nuclear warheads and launchers, to provide greater security at Russian nuclear storage sites, and to find employment for some of the nuclear scientists from the old Soviet Union, who, without such help, might have been tempted to go to work for potential proliferators. U.S. political support for the initiative has been sometimes rocky, due in part to concern that U.S. money should not be used to support activity of the Russian military, but overall the consensus has been that this is a worthwhile effort that can, for relatively small amounts of money, do much to make the world safer from nuclear weapons. Indeed, there has been much criticism that the United States is not supporting the program as vigorously as it should.[63]

THE NUCLEAR NON-PROLIFERATION TREATY

The main form that cooperative anti-proliferation policy has taken, however, is the Nuclear Non-Proliferation Treaty (NPT), which we introduced in the last chapter. The NPT, like security guarantees, works to weaken the motivation nations have to acquire nuclear weapons, a motivation often due to their concern to protect themselves from the actual or potential nuclear threats from their regional opponents. Security guarantees address this problem by extending nuclear deterrence from nuclear nations to non-nuclear nations. The NPT does this by insuring non-nuclear nations that their opponents will not acquire nuclear weapons.

The United States, Great Britain, and the Soviet Union sponsored the negotiations that produced the 1967 NPT, initially signed by 62 nations and coming into force in 1970. Some states such as France, China, India, Pakistan, Argentina, Brazil, and South Africa refused to sign at the time, though some of these signed later. The current number of signatories is 189. The treaty identified the world's nuclear nations as the United States, the Soviet Union, Great Britain, France, and China. As part of the treaty, nuclear nations promised to provide the non-nuclear signatories with technology and fuels for nuclear power generation, and the non-nuclear nations agreed to allow international inspections of the power plants to insure that they were not being used for weapons development.

The treaty served several different interests. First, the nuclear nations sought to protect their nuclear monopoly and to promote the interests of their nuclear power export industries without exposing themselves to the dangers of further nuclear proliferation. Second, the non-nuclear nations sought to become part of a system that would both insure that their regional opponents would not acquire nuclear weapons and would guarantee them access to peaceful nuclear technology. Third, the non-nuclear nations sought to rein in the nuclear arms race being pursued by the nuclear nations, especially the United States and the Soviet Union. These goals are evident in the treaty's ten articles. Articles I and II forbid the transfer of nuclear weapons devices and technologies from nuclear nations to non-nuclear nations, and Article IV explicitly exempts nuclear power technologies from this ban. Article III obligates non-nuclear nations to submit all of their nuclear facilities to inspection and monitoring by the International Atomic Energy Agency (IAEA). Article VI commits the nuclear nations to work toward nuclear disarmament, and Article VII permits the establishment of regional nuclear-free zones. Article VIII establishes procedures for amending the treaty and mandates treaty review conferences every five years. Article IX offers treaty membership to any nation that accepts IAEA safeguards, and Article X provides that any signatory may withdraw at any time after giving three months' notice. (Recall that North Korea has done this.) Article X also provides for a comprehensive review conference after 25 years to determine whether the treaty should be continued indefinitely. This conference, which occurred in 1995, will be discussed below.

What have proved to be the strengths and weaknesses of this treaty? Consider the role it played during the first nuclear age. Given the relatively slow rate of proliferation in that period, the treaty seems to have had some success in controlling proliferation. This undoubtedly reflects the fact that many nations recognized that it was in their interests to avoid nuclear weapons as long as an effective mechanism existed to deny them to their regional opponents. The treaty's principal weakness during this period was its failure to prevent the nuclear arms race between the nuclear superpowers. This is sometimes referred to as "vertical proliferation," which is the accumulation of additional nuclear weapons by states that already have them. In contrast, the standard form of proliferation we have been discussing in this chapter is referred to as "horizontal proliferation." Article VI of the NPT commits the nuclear nations to engage in a process leading to nuclear disarmament, but, as we saw in Chapter 4, there was a huge increase in the size of the superpowers' nuclear arsenals in the years after the treaty went into effect.

In the second nuclear age, the weaknesses of the treaty have become more pronounced. First, its inability to control vertical proliferation remains. Despite some progress late in the first nuclear age and early in the second in reducing the size of the nuclear arsenals of the United States and the Soviet Union (then Russia) under a series of arms agreements, the arsenals remain very large, and there is no serious consideration of complete nuclear disarmament. Former U.S. Secretary of State Madeleine Albright and former British official Robin Cook assert that an effect of the continuing failure of the nuclear nations to move closer to disarmament would be to "encourage states that do not have nuclear weapons to rebel against nonproliferation norms out of dissatisfaction with what they perceive as a double standard: some states get nuclear weapons, while others do not."[64] The long-term viability of the NPT may depend on the overcoming of this weakness, for non-nuclear nations may not feel themselves bound by an agreement on which the nuclear nations have reneged.

The NPT's second weakness has been that states that are not signatories are not bound by its terms. India and Pakistan were and are legally free to proliferate. As regional rivals, neither could afford to be caught without nuclear weapons if the other developed them—and India had unmet security needs facing a nuclear-armed China. Israel likewise remains outside the constraints of the treaty. It has developed nuclear weapons but has neither tested them nor publicly acknowledged their existence. It engaged in "opaque proliferation," a condition made possible by the fact that it is not necessary to test a fission device to have confidence that it would work. In a sense, India was an opaque proliferator as well; while it did test a nuclear device in 1974, it claimed that it would not build any more weapons, but some, especially the Chinese and the Pakistanis, assumed this claim to be disingenuous. The same might be said of Pakistan; for much of the 1990s India considered Pakistan as already having nuclear devices, although Pakistan neither made such a claim nor tested a nuclear device until 1998.

Opaque proliferation, also known as "part-way proliferation," is "a tactic for having it both ways; for making use of some of the deterrent power of nuclear armaments without driving neighboring countries into the nuclear business or incurring whatever sanctions the international community can impose for a breach of the nuclear rules."[65] An opaque proliferator may get the deterrent value of having the weapons simply because other nations suspect it does, while it avoids the political costs of being a proliferator by not being public about it. While Israel is not a signatory to the NPT, other nations that are might seek to become opaque proliferators in order to keep their violations of the treaty from being public.

The third weakness of the NPT has been in its failure to adequately deal with nuclear power generation as a seed-bed for proliferation. The limitations of the NPT in controlling this route to horizontal proliferation show up most starkly in the recent cases of North Korea and Iran, but in truth, power generation and research reactors were the pathways to nuclear weapons for proliferators like India,

Pakistan, and Israel. As we pointed out at the start of this chapter, North Korea presents the dangers of nuclear proliferation in their most extreme: A North Korea with nuclear weapons might cause a cascade of proliferation among other nations in its region, including Japan, thereby setting up a nuclear arms race between Japan and China, and the North might sell nuclear weapons to other potential proliferators or to terrorists. But the North Korean case represents a weakness inherent in the NPT. As mentioned earlier, the NPT represents a bargain between the nuclear haves and the nuclear have-nots, asserting "the inalienable right of all parties to the treaty to develop research, production, and use of nuclear energy for peaceful purposes without discrimination." North Korea has used that right to provide itself with nuclear weapons (or to be "a screwdriver away" from having the weapon) despite the NPT's provision for inspections. Iran appears to be doing the same.

Thus any nation that controls what is called *the nuclear fuel cycle*, that is, has the capacity to create enriched uranium for its nuclear power plants, will have the capability, through more intensive enrichment, to produce weapons-grade uranium. The capacity to create fissile material inheres in either the capacity to enrich uranium or the capacity to reprocess the plutonium in the used fuel rods from a reactor to extract Pu-239. The Bush administration has argued that North Korea (as well as Iran) cannot be permitted to have such capacities, even though they are permitted by the NPT, because the North has violated the NPT's provisions about inspections of its nuclear facilities and has, by its own confession (or profession), constructed nuclear weapons.[66] But, from the point of view of a nation that relies on nuclear power, controlling the nuclear fuel cycle is an important security matter, even if it has no interest in developing nuclear weapons, because if it depends on other nations for the enriched fuel for its reactions, those other nations have the power to cut it off.

New agreements to control the fuel cycle have been explored in recent years as a means of cooperatively reducing the opportunities to proliferate. In 2004, the Bush administration proposed amending the NPT to close the loophole that allows nuclear activities that can be used to develop a bomb under the cover of nuclear power generation, but the proposal has not drawn wide support in the international community.[67] Mohamed ElBaradei, the head of the International Atomic Energy Agency, has proposed that all uranium enrichment and plutonium reprocessing be under international control and that the uranium be enriched only to reactor grade. Such proposals remain in the discussion stages but the dilemma of dealing with Iran is likely to force some of them to the forefront.

The nuclear fuel cycle is central to American and European concerns about Iran's potential to develop nuclear weapons. Iran has a program to enrich uranium, and has claimed that it wants to do so only for the sake of its nuclear power industry. But Iran has engaged in deception about its nuclear activities in the past, and this has led the United States and others to suspect that it, like North Korea, has a secret nuclear weapons program. Iran, however, claims its right under the NPT to engage in uranium enrichment activities for the sake of its nuclear power generation. Three European nations (the EU-3: Germany, Britain, and France) have been negotiating with Iran to give up its uranium enrichment activities, not by denying that Iran has the right under the NPT to engage in such activities, but by offering it trade and diplomatic incentives if it would, for instance, end its domestic enrichment program and accept reactor-grade uranium from foreign suppliers.[68] As of early 2006, Iran has refused their offers. The United States, skeptical that Iran would ever voluntarily agree to halt its nuclear activities, has sometimes talked of a applying coercive anti-proliferation strategy to Iran, possibly seeking a military solution like the Israeli bombing in 1981 of the Iraqi reactor at Osirik. But the Iranian nuclear program is so well dispersed, including sites in heavily urban areas, that a military solution seems both unacceptable and unachievable.[69]

Many of the nuclear have-nots have voiced their disquiet with the NPT by pointing out, for example, that the nuclear haves have themselves failed to meet their NPT treaty obligations of seeking nuclear disarmament, as called for under Article VI. This failure was a key issue at the 1995 conference in New York to renew the treaty, attended by 175 of the 178 signatories of the treaty.[70] The disgruntled nonnuclear nations did not seek to scrap the treaty, but rather to renew it in a qualified form. First, they wanted the treaty to be extended not indefinitely—as desired by the nuclear haves—but only for another 25-year period, after which a second renewal would be required. In this way they hoped to prod the nuclear nations to meet their disarmament commitments. Second, they proposed that a series of additional conditions be incorporated into the treaty, conditions such as requirements that the nuclear nations support the Comprehensive Test Ban treaty, that the NPT become truly universal (that it bring in the undeclared nuclear nations), and that stockpiles of weapons-grade fissile material be eliminated.

The nuclear nations opposed these qualifications. But agreement was reached, and each side got part of what it wanted. The nuclear nations got an indefinite extension of the treaty. The nonnuclear nations got a commitment to some of the qualifications they had sought in a series of twenty "principles and objectives." The principles and objectives, however, are not part of the formal treaty but are in a separate document, and, as such, they are not legally binding, only "politically binding." The nonnuclear nations also got a strengthened review process in the form of substantive review conferences to be held every five years. But the discontent of the nonnuclear nations has continued, as the review conferences in 2000 and 2005 have not shown the nuclear nations any closer to disarmament. Clearly, though, the nuclear nations achieved their objective of treaty renewal in 1995, but their tolerance of the discriminatory situation and their lack of willingness to take seriously their disarmament obligations under the treaty, if this continues in the future, may cause serious problems with the effectiveness of the treaty and its ability to curtail proliferation.

The treaty will also come under strain if the proliferation increases in Figure 8-1 hold true, even if we avoid the proliferation explosion. At the present time, there are only a few states that are not signatories of the NPT. No potential proliferators are outside the NPT at this time. (North Korea has withdrawn from the treaty and claims to be an actual proliferator, but efforts are underway to have it rejoin the treaty.) Given that we predict 4–5 states are likely to proliferate in the next 20 years (the slow-but-steady model), those proliferators will have to be states who renounce the treaty or who become nuclear weapons states clandestinely. Such actions are likely to be a shock to the treaty sufficient to imperil it; other than North Korea, no signatory has renounced the treaty and become a nuclear weapons state. Iran is shaping up as a crucial test. If the NPT collapses, all the formal constraints on proliferation will fall to the wayside and the general sense that proliferation is contrary to the mores of the international system is likely to evaporate. This would set the stage for explosive proliferation and move the world closer to the third nuclear age.

IRAQ 2003: COERCIVE ANTI-PROLIFERATION AT WORK

The NPT is a multilateral, cooperative anti-proliferation effort, involving an agreement among most of the nations of the globe. But in recent years, especially after 9/11, the United States has come to rely increasingly on unilateral, coercive anti-proliferation policies. The most significant of these has been the war against Iraq.

In March 2003, the United States invaded Iraq for the primary stated purpose of stripping it of its weapons of mass destruction, including its capacity to develop nuclear weapons. Because the United States responded to a *presumed capacity* rather than the actual existence of nuclear weapons, we do not yet have an example of full-fledged *coercive denuclearization* against a state armed with nuclear weapons. Nonetheless, the Iraq case is instructive, perhaps not so much for what it tells us about how a policy of coercive denuclearization might work, but for how the Iraq war might make coercive denuclearization highly *unlikely* in the future; if that is the case, then the United States will have lost the ability to make an effective *threat* of coercive denuclearization. The effectiveness of such a threat may be very important, for, if effective, it may keep others from contemplating proliferation. Absent the effective threat, the constraints on proliferation may be attenuated.

As of the beginning of 2006, when we write these words, the war in Iraq continues, with 135,000 U.S. troops (and several thousand from Great Britain and smaller contingents from other nations) fighting a resistant insurgency and al Qaeda-led terrorism. In this section, we discuss the Iraq war in more detail than we have earlier, and we examine the lessons that should be drawn from it about the prospects of coercive anti-proliferation or denuclearization policy through military force. Because the United States went into the Iraq War against the will of much of the international community, we shall refer to the efforts of the United States to eliminate the Iraqi nuclear weapons program as a policy of unilateral coercive anti-proliferation.

As we pointed out in Chapter 7, the approach taken by the United Nations when Iraq invaded Kuwait in 1990 opened the door to a new standard: States that violated fundamental rules (in Iraq's case, waging a war of aggression) forfeited the right to possess nuclear weapons and other weapons of mass destruction. The UN created a new response as well: the forcible destruction of the nuclear weapons capability of a nation, written into the cease-fire agreement terminating the war. Iraq had to admit inspectors from the International Atomic Energy Agency (IAEA) and from a new organization UNSCOM (to look for chemical and biological weapons) with leave to investigate any site in the search for WMD production facilities. Initial Iraqi attempts to remove materials and machines while stalling the inspectors at the gates surrounding the facilities, or by keeping them at bay with the threat of violence, drove the Security Council to adopt Resolution 707, which denied Iraq the right to have any nuclear weapons-related items or capabilities.

The inspection regime continued until 1998, effectively destroying Iraqi stores of chemical and biological weapons and the Iraqi programs and facilities to create nuclear weapons. Although the Iraqi government increasingly hampered inspections and forced their suspension in 1998, insisting that the inspectors had in fact accomplished their mission and that Iraq was free of WMD, the head of the IAEA, Mohamed ElBaradei, declared in 1999 that there was no evidence that Iraq had "nuclear weapons or any meaningful amounts of weapon-useable nuclear material, or that Iraq has retained any practical capability (facilities or hardware) for the production of such material."[71] However, David Kay, the chief IAEA inspector, argued that, while Iraq may at that point have been stripped of its capacity to make nuclear weapons, as long as Saddam Hussein remained in power, Iraq would have nuclear ambitions.[72]

The inspection regime had been held in place by sanctions imposed on Iraq, principally prohibitions on the sale of Iraqi oil (later, modified to permit sales under stringent conditions), and by the threat of renewed attack on Iraq. The end of inspections did not end the sanctions or the threat, as the UN judged that Iraq, having forced the withdrawal of the inspectors, was not in compliance with its obligations. The Clinton administration chose not to challenge this new status quo and within the incoming Bush administration there was no consensus on what to do with Iraq.[73] The al Qaeda attack on September 11, 2001 changed the picture. National security now became central, but al Qaeda and its host state, Afghanistan, became the target of the moment. The intense concern about Iraq shared by some of Bush's key advisors went to the back burner.

By early 2002, the rout of the Taliban government in Afghanistan and the apparent destruction and dispersal of al Qaeda shifted the administration's attention again toward Iraq, with the President authorizing the planning of a military invasion. Washington began to talk about the need for "regime change" as a way of dealing with rogue states who threatened international peace and security, and Iraq was exhibit number one. Recall that the United Nations Security Council in 1992 had declared that "the proliferation of all weapons of mass destruction constitutes a threat to international peace and security." Now the administration asserted that it would act to prevent such proliferation.[74] After the war, then National Security Advisor Condoleezza Rice explained that President Bush had ousted Saddam Hussein because of the "possibility" that the dictator "might use" weapons of mass destruction or hand off the devices to terrorists "to mount a future attack beyond the scale" of September 11. "That terrible prospect could not be put aside. You don't leave that threat in the middle of the Middle East."[75]

This new orientation toward Iraq replaced the earlier policy of *containment*. During the first nuclear age, as we have seen, the United States adopted a policy of containment toward the Soviet Union, the rogue state of its day. Containment was designed to prevent an expansion of Soviet influence or control in the belief (or perhaps more accurately, the hope) that deprived of success, the regime would mellow, losing its interest in threatening the security of the United States or its neighbors. In the more extreme version, successful containment would, advocates predicted, crack Communist Party control and lead to its replacement by a more liberal, pacific regime. Containment was a strategy of patience—and also a strategy of necessity, as attempting to force a regime change on the Soviet Union would have produced another world war, and, beginning in the 1950s, a nuclear one at that. But in 2003, the United States faced the vastly weaker Iraqi state, perceived itself already at war with international terrorism, and was dominated by impatient advisors and a president with little experience in any aspect of foreign relations.

Impatience with the multilateral nature of containment was reflected in the Bush administration's reluctance to work through the United Nations. Secretary of State Colin Powell urged that the administration attempt to mobilize the United Nations as the vehicle to confront Iraq, in spite of clear signs that key members of the Security Council with veto power (Russia, China, and France) did not see Iraq as the threat that the President did. To have any hope of receiving the blessing of the United Nations to confront Iraq with military force would necessitate persuading the Security Council that (a) Iraq had chemical and biological weapons of mass destruction and a program to acquire nuclear weapons (a point about which the evidence was at best very ambiguous) and (b) the use of military force to bring about regime change in that state was the only meaningful alternative open to the international community. Powell struggled against the hawks in the administration who did not want to be delayed or encumbered by the United Nations. The hawks wanted speedy military action against Iraq by the United States and whatever other nations were willing to sign on to an American plan (what came to be called "the coalition of the willing").

Powell, worried about what would happen in an Iraq occupied by the United States and concerned with preserving a united front against Iraq and not alienating America's allies, pushed for an approach through the United Nations. Like many policy disputes, the clash appears to have ended with a compromise: Powell was given the opportunity to rally the UN while the hawks got a military buildup in the region, poised to force the end of Saddam Hussein's regime. The United Nations members sought ways to meet American demands, focusing on the question of whether Iraq did in fact possess prohibited weapons of mass destruction. With reluctant American approval, the Security Council ordered a reinvigorated inspection regime and the Iraqi government acquiesced. The Bush administration then grew impatient with the so-far fruitless inspections and had a sizable military force on the southern borders of Iraq that had to be used or suffer the erosion of its effectiveness. Powell returned to the Security Council to argue that the United Nations must bring about the removal of the Iraqi government because the evidence (at least from the administration's perspective) showed continuing programs of weapons of mass destruction, a link to al Qaeda, and the existence of a brutal dictatorship that constituted a threat to international peace and security. Key members of the Security Council (principally China, France, and Russia) refused to endorse an invasion. The United States, in league with Britain, attacked on March 19, 2003, beginning with air strikes and following quickly with a ground invasion. In 21 days, American forces took Baghdad.

The swift and successful toppling of Saddam's regime allowed for an unfettered search for WMD. None were found. No weapons, no programs to produce them. (The pre-war claim of links between Iraq and the al Qaeda terrorists were not verified either.) Given that these central justifications offered for the war had no merit, the Bush administration shifted its emphasis to promoting the virtues of removing a brutal tyrant and of bringing democracy to Iraq, which the president claimed would unleash a movement to democratize the entire region. But restoring order to Iraq has proved difficult. A home-grown insurgency against the U.S. presence and against the democratic regime that the United States had hoped to implant in Iraq has gathered strength, abetted by Islamic militants who entered Iraq to contest the U.S. presence in the country. Firmly mired in Iraq, the Bush administration argued that that nation was now the battlefront against global terrorism, one that the United States had no choice but to fight and to win.

Given the shifting explanations for why the United States needed to invade Iraq and the costs of pacifying the country, can we expect that the United Nations collectively will act to prevent rogue states—or any states with a history of hostile relations with major powers or their neighbor—from acquiring nuclear weapons? Such a willingness likely depends on two problematic elements. First, are national intelligence systems capable of detecting the existence of WMD programs and their products? This is important because it is likely that there will be more willingness to confront a state in the early stages of proliferation rather than waiting until nuclear weapons enter its arsenal. (Recall that the United Nations did back the return of the inspectors to Saddam's Iraq.) The poor performance of U.S. intelligence, presumably having the most resources and the greatest incentive to get it right, must raise reservations about this capability. Second, a willingness to confront a proliferator depends upon how compellingly one can demonstrate that the proliferator intends to endanger international peace and security. Discerning a state's intentions is a difficult job in many circumstances. This may have been easier in Iraq due to its invasion of Kuwait in August 1990 and its flagrant lies in 1991 about not having programs to produce WMD. But reading hostile intentions in the behavior of the other two states in the axis of evil, Iran and North Korea, may be more difficult.

The Bush administration did identify a rough measure of whether a nation was a threat to international peace and security. It was whether it had shown great and unrelenting hostility toward the United States. If it had, and if, in addition, it had or was attempting to develop WMD, the administration claimed that the United States could not wait to see whether its judgment about intention was correct, for then the United States might have waited too long. American allies and other nations resisted the notion that the United States was to be the sole judge of the intentions of other states. Coercive anti-proliferation measures are likely to lack broad support as long as the United States insisted on being the sole judge in such matters.

Is it likely that the United States will continue to enforce this new rule, even if it has to do so unilaterally? Nothing succeeds like success. If the American public and political leaders judge the outcome of the invasion of Iraq a success in terms of accomplishing its mission at an acceptable cost, then there will be an incentive to continue rule enforcement. But, while the outcome in Iraq is currently unclear, the question of whether the United States will enforce the rule is already upon us, as the United States has identified North Korea and Iran as two states in the same category as Iraq. It is unlikely that the Bush administration will do more than harass and fitfully negotiate with those two states until the outcome in Iraq is clearer. Continuing pressure and threats are a signal that the administration has not abandoned the rule. The re-election of the Bush Administration in 2004 suggests more of the same policy approach. A Democratic administration, the one that might have been elected in 2004 or might be elected in 2008, might be (or have been) more averse to enforcing this rule and more likely to emphasize a cooperative anti-proliferation approach, such as providing rewards for abandoning nuclear weapons in the manner that the Clinton administration tried in 1994 with North Korea.

As long as the United States remains mired in Iraq, its ability to enforce the rule in North Korea, Iran, or elsewhere is severely limited. Moreover, given that the cost of the Iraq war in terms of lives, both military and civilian, and resources is already high, and will be much higher if the war ends up leaving the region politically unstable, this and future administrations will have a much more difficult time selling a policy of coercive anti-proliferation or denuclearization that relies on war and regime change. If so, we would have to rely on other, more multilateral kinds of anti-proliferation policy.

We judge it to be relatively likely that the invasion of Iraq in 2003 marks the first and last attempt at unilateral coercive anti-proliferation on this magnitude. The United Nations as a whole seems dead set against such a project. We judge it unlikely that the American public or political leaders will be willing to do it again. This leaves the possibility of coercive anti-proliferation efforts through limited military strikes, such as against nuclear facilities (like the Israeli strike at Osirak). But even these will be blanketed in controversy. Such strikes may, for example, involve a release of significant amounts of radioactive contamination, both locally and globally. In addition, such a strike would still be a form of aggression, an unprovoked attack, a preventive military intervention, and so would be seen by many, both at home and abroad, as another egregious break with principle. Further, such a strike could be catastrophic, if, for instance, North Korea were to respond by destroying Seoul, the capital of South Korea, as it probably is able to do.[76]

Ironically, Iraq itself may provide another important test of the U.S. position on nuclear weapons. What happens if the U.S. project of democratization succeeds in Iraq and a democratically elected Iraqi government decides that, in the face of an Iranian potential to create nuclear weapons and the Israeli possession of such weapons, Iraq too must have them? There is no reason to expect that a democracy, particularly a fledgling democracy, will overlook its historical hostilities with its neighbors simply because it is a democracy. Nor is there reason to expect that it will be any more inclined to turn its back on the indigenous scientific and technological prowess that brought it close to nuclear weapons in the first place, simply because it is a democracy. As we have seen, British, French, Israeli, and Indian democracies found reason to proliferate, even in peacetime.

SUMMARY

Nuclear proliferation is a central concern of the second nuclear age. Though nuclear proliferation proceeded more slowly than expected during the first nuclear age, with fewer nations acquiring nuclear weapons than had been feared, the pace has picked up in the second nuclear age. The second nuclear age seems to provide both increased opportunity and increased motivation for non-nuclear nations to acquire nuclear weapons. Increased opportunity is due largely to the dissolution of the Soviet Union and the resultant potential availability of fissile material, as well as advances in technology and its increasing availability through international trade. Increased motivation comes, again, largely from the fall of the Soviet Union, which has created an international climate where some old constraints on potential proliferators have fallen away and nonnuclear nations may have increased fears about their security.

There are three approaches to anti-proliferation policy: coercion, denial, and cooperation. Other nations can seek to *coerce* a nonnuclear nation (for example, through military force) either not to acquire nuclear weapons or to surrender weapons it already possesses; they can seek to *deny* the nonnuclear nation the wherewithal to build weapons; or they can seek to work *cooperatively* with the nonnuclear nation to get it to agree not to acquire weapons. Coercive anti-proliferation and denuclearization are the kinds of policies often favored in recent years by the United States, but the effectiveness of such policies is questionable and they can have strong negative consequences. Denial anti-proliferation policies are widely practiced, but their ability to constrain proliferation is limited. Cooperative anti-proliferation policies may have the greatest promise, especially in the long run, but it takes two to cooperate. Their chief form is the Nuclear Non-Proliferation Treaty. The treaty was quite successful in the first nuclear age, but less so in the second. Two of its weaknesses are that the nuclear nations have not lived up to their commitments under the treaty to pursue nuclear disarmament, undermining support for the treaty among non-nuclear nations, and the treaty does not prohibit non-nuclear nations from engaging in nuclear activities ostensibly related to nuclear power generation, such as uranium enrichment, that can be used as a cover for the development of weapons. This last problem has been seen recently in the cases of North Korea and Iran.

Because of the increased likelihood of nuclear proliferation in the second nuclear age, it is more likely that nuclear weapons will be used in the future. But further nuclear proliferation is not inevitable. Cooperative anti-proliferation policies, combined with policies of denial and coercion, can help to weaken the impetus toward greater proliferation. In the final chapters of the book, we discuss from a broader perspective how we should treat the nuclear danger we face. But now we must consider the other chief danger of the second nuclear age, one related to the proliferation danger, namely, the danger of nuclear terrorism.

ENDNOTES

[1]Glenn Kessler, "North Korea's Nuclear Bluff?" *The Washington Post National Weekly Edition*, January 26, 2004, p. 18.

[2]More precisely, this is so-called horizontal proliferation, in contrast with vertical proliferation, a distinction discussed later in the chapter. Portions of this chapter are adopted from Steven Lee, "Nuclear Proliferation and Nuclear Entitlement," *Ethics and International Affairs* 9 (1995), pp. 101–131, with the permission of the journal.

[3] Biological weapons, like nuclear weapons, have the potential for lethality on a large scale, but this potential has not and may never be developed.

[4] For a discussion of this issue, see Joseph Cirincione, "The End of 'WMD'," Carnegie Endowment for International Peace, http://carnegieendowment.org/publications/index.cfm?fa=print&id=17166, accessed 7/7/2005, and Allison Marfarlane, "All Weapons of Mass Destruction Are Not Equal," MIT Center for International Studies.

[5] Quoted in Mitchell Reiss, *Without the Bomb* (New York: Columbia University Press, 1988), p. 16.

[6] The case of Israel suggests that nuclear testing may not be the best way to gauge proliferation. The nuclear properties of matter are now well known and computers are powerful, so it is no longer necessary to actually test a device in order to have confidence that it will work. See Theodore Taylor, "Nuclear Tests and Nuclear Weapons," in Benjamin Frankel (ed.), *Opaque Nuclear Proliferation* (London: Frank Cass, 1991), pp. 175–90. Indeed, as we saw in chapter 3, even in the infancy of atomic physics and computers, scientists were so certain that the gun assembly design would work that they did not feel the need to test it before dropping it on Hiroshima.

[7] Also in this period, Pakistan may have developed a rudimentary capability.

[8] For a discussion of why some nonproliferating states have not gone nuclear, see Mitchell Reiss, *Bridled Ambition: Why Countries Constrain Their Nuclear Capabilities* (Washington: Woodrow Wilson Center Press, 1995).

[9] David Albright, "South Africa Comes Clean," *The Bulletin of the Atomic Scientists 49*, no. 4 (May 1993), pp. 3–5. South Africa is a special case, however, because the Apartheid government was motivated to dismantle its weapons to keep them out of the hands of Black majority government that was soon to take power.

[10] Jean Krasno, "Brazil, Argentina Make It Official," *The Bulletin of the Atomic Scientists 48*, no. 3 (April, 1992), pp. 10–11. But some question has arisen about whether this agreement will hold. In early 2004, a dispute arose when Brazil refused to allow inspectors from the International Atomic Energy Agency to inspect a facility under construction near Rio de Janeiro for enriching uranium. See Peter Slevin, "Brazil Shielding Uranium Facility," *Washington Post*, April 4, 2004.

[11] This suggests that the process of democratization may be effective in reducing the likelihood of proliferation, although this may be countered by the observation that three of the five principal nuclear powers are democracies (as are India and Israel).

[12] Scott Sagan, "The Perils of Proliferation," *International Security 18*, no. 4 (Spring, 1994), pp. 68–69.

[13] David Albright and Robert Kelley, "Has Iraq Come Clean at Last?" *The Bulletin of the Atomic Scientists 51*, no. 6 (November/December, 1995), p. 60.

[14] Quoted in "U.S. Seeks Better Enforcement of Nuclear Non-Proliferation Treaty" U.S. Department of State International Information Programs, listserv 1.8e, August 27, 2004.

[15] Quoted in "Qadhafi Urges End to All WMD", CNN.com, April 27, 2004.

[16] Some of the novel features of proliferation in the 1990s are discussed by John Simpson, "Nuclear Non-Proliferation in the Post Cold War Era," *International Affairs 70*, no. 1 (1994), pp. 17–39.

[17] There have been stories about plutonium being smuggled out of the states of the former Soviet Union and put on the black market. For some early accounts of this see William Broad, "A Smuggling Boom Brings Calls for Tighter Nuclear Safeguards," *New York Times*, August 21, 1994, and Gary Milhollin, "Plutonium Plunder," *Boston Globe*, September 4, 1994.

[18] Chaim Braun and Christopher Chyba, "Proliferation Rings," *International Security*, Vol. 29 (Fall, 2004), pp. 5–49.

[19] See William Broad, David Sanger, and Raymond Bonner, "A Tale of Nuclear Proliferation: How Pakistani Built His Network," *New York Times*, February 12, 2004, and William Broad and David Sanger,

"As Nuclear Secrets Emerge in Khan Inquiry, More are Suspected," *New York Times*, December 26, 2004.

[20]Mitchell Reiss, *Without the Bomb*, p. 247.

[21]Jaswant Singh, quoted in Barbara Crossette, "Why India Thinks Atomic Equation Has Changed," *New York Times*, June 15, 1998, p. A6.

[22]Vajpayee, quoted in Steven Weisman, "Nuclear Fear and Narcissism Shake South Asia," *New York Times*, May 31, 1998, sec. 4, p. 16.

[23]Robert Jervis, "The Future of World Politics: Will It Resemble the Past?" *International Security 16*, no. 3, p. 63.

[24]See, for example, Benjamin Frankel, "The Brooding Shadow: Systemic Incentives and Nuclear Weapons Proliferation," in Zachary Davis and Benjamin Frankel (eds.), *The Proliferation Puzzle* (London: Frank Cass, 1993), p. 37.

[25]We have, however, raised questions about this in Chapter 5 and will do so again in Chapter 11.

[26]Kenneth Waltz, *The Spread of Nuclear Weapons: More May Be Better*, Adelphi Paper No. 171 (London: International Institute for Strategic Studies, 1981), pp. 3–4.

[27]John Mearsheimer, "The Case for a Ukrainian Nuclear Deterrent," *International Security, 18*, no. 4 (Spring, 1994), p. 57.

[28]Waltz, *The Spread of Nuclear Weapons*.

[29]Waltz, *The Spread of Nuclear Weapons*, pp. 5, 17, 30.

[30]Joseph Nye, "Maintaining a Nonproliferation Regime," in George Quester (ed.), Nuclear Proliferation: *Breaking the Chain* (Madison, WI: University of Wisconsin Press, 1981), p. 32.

[31]Lewis Dunn, "What Difference Will It Make?" in Herbert Levine and David Carlton (eds.), *The Nuclear Arms Race Debated* (New York: McGraw-Hill, 1986), pp. 330–331. On the general risks of accidental nuclear war, see Scott Sagan, *The Limits of Safety: Organizations, Accidents, and Nuclear Weapons* (Princeton, NJ: Princeton University Press, 1993) and Bruce Blair, *The Logic of Accidental Nuclear War* (Washington, DC: Brookings Institution, 1993).

[32]While India conducted a nuclear weapons test in 1974, prior to 1998 it was thought to have no nuclear arsenal.

[33]But the United States did use military force against the Soviet Union in the period after the World War I in an unsuccessful attempt to defeat the communist revolution and aided rebels fighting Soviet forces in Afghanistan as recently as the 1980s. On the other hand, they were allies in World War II.

[34]Steven Erlanger, "India's Arms Race Isn't Safe Like the Cold War," *New York Times*, July 12, 1998, sec. 4, p. 18, citing Joseph Cirincione, director of the Non-Proliferation Project at the Carnegie Endowment for International Peace.

[35]Although the superpowers did not develop the robust command and control system until a number of years into the Cold War, and the risk of nuclear war between them was much greater in those early years than it came later to be. There was also the factor that we elsewhere refer to as "nuclear learning." The United States and the Soviet Union learned over time how to behave with nuclear weapons in ways that lessened the risk of war between them.

[36]John Weltman, "Nuclear Devolution and World Order," *World Politics 32* (January, 1980), p. 189.

[37]Weltman, "Nuclear Devolution," p. 189.

[38]Waltz, *Spread of Nuclear Weapons*, p. 11.

[39]Sagan, "Perils of Proliferation."

[40]Sagan, "Perils of Proliferation," p. 68. You might remember here the anecdote from Chapter 4 about General LeMay's assertion that he would be the one to make a decision to launch a first strike against the Soviet Union.

[41]Sagan, "Perils of Proliferation," pp. 71–72.

[42]On this point, see also Sagan, "Perils of Proliferation," pp. 96–97.

[43]Sagan, "Perils of Proliferation," p. 86. Steven Miller, "The Case Against a Ukrainian Nuclear Deterrent," *Foreign Affairs 72* (Summer, 1993), p. 71.

[44]For example: Waltz, *Spread of Nuclear Weapons*, p. 26; Lewis Dunn, "What Difference Will It Make?" p. 335.

[45]John Bolton, U.S. Undersecretary of State for Arms Control and International Security, writing in the *Financial Times* in September 2004, quoted in Paul Reynolds, "Nuclear Weapons: Can they Be Stopped," *BBC News Online*, September 22, 2004.

[46]Simpson, "Nuclear Non-Proliferation," pp. 25–26.

[47]Frankel, "Brooding Shadow," p. 39.

[48]Stephen Meyer, *The Dynamics of Nuclear Proliferation* (Chicago: University of Chicago Press, 1984), p. 165.

[49]Economic sanctions may be a fairly mild form of coercion, but they can have devastating effects on the population of the nation being sanctioned, if that nation's government hoards available resources to itself and diverts them away from the population. This occurred in the case of the economic sanctions imposed on Iraq during the 1990s.

[50]Sergie Kortunov, "Nonproliferation and Counterproliferation: the Role of BMD," *Comparative Strategy 13*, p. 138.

[51]See Kortunov, "Nonproliferation and Counterproliferation," p. 138.

[52]"Counterproliferation Policy and Doctrine," http://www.counterproliferation.org- /policy/index.html, accessed 11/29/04.

[53]National Security Strategy of the United States, www.whitehouse.gov/nsc/nss.pdf, p. 18.

[54]National Security Strategy of the United States, p. 19. As we mentioned, the Bush Administration has chosen to refer to its policy of preventive was as one of preemptive war.

[55]Simpson, "Nuclear Non-proliferation," p. 38.

[56]For a discussion of the weaknesses of the Bush administration's counterproliferation policies, see George Perkovich, "Bush's Nuclear Follies," *Foreign Affairs 82*, no. 2 (March/April 2003), pp. 2-9.

[57]Simpson, "Nuclear Non-Proliferation," p. 19.

[58]Avner Cohen, "The Lessons of Osirak and the American Counterproliferation Debate," in Mitchell Reiss, *International Perspectives on Counterproliferation*, working paper #99 (Washington, DC: Woodrow Wilson Center, 1995).

[59]Richard Betts, "Paranoids, Pygmies, Pariahs and Nonproliferation," *Foreign Policy 26* (spring 1977), p. 165.

[60]Hedley Bull, "The Role of the Nuclear Powers in the Management of Nuclear Proliferation," in Levine and Carlton, *Arms Race Debated*, p. 368.

[61]Barrie Paskins, "Proliferation and the Nature of Deterrence," in Nigel Blake and Kay Pole (eds.), *Dangers of Deterrence* (London: Routledge & Kegan Paul, 1983), p. 128.

[62]Brad Roberts, "From Nonproliferation to Antiproliferation," *International Security 18*, no. 1 (Summer, 1993), p. 172.

[63]See Jason Ellis and Todd Perry, "Nunn-Lugar's Unfinished Agenda," *Arms Control Today 27*, no. 7 (October 1997), pp. 14–22, and Richard Lugar, "Eliminating the Obstacles to Nunn-Lugar," *Arms Control Today* (March 2004).

[64]Albright and Cook, "Commentary: We Need a Global Attack on Nuclear Proliferation," *Los Angles Times*, June 7, 2004.

[65]For a discussion of opaque proliferation, see Avner Cohen and Benjamin Frankel, "Opaque Nuclear Proliferation," in Frankel, *Opaque Nuclear Proliferation*. "Part-way proliferation" is discussed by Michael Mandelbaum, *The Nuclear Future* (Ithaca, NY: Cornell University Press, 1983), p. 93.

[66]For a discussion of the problem of the nuclear fuel cycle, see Jon Wohfsthal, "The Nuclear Third Rail: Can Fuel Cycle Capabilities be Limited?" *Arms Control Today* (December 2004). For the case of North Korea, see Barbara Demick, "Split Develops Over North Korea's Right to Civilian Nuclear Power," *Los Angles Times*, August 24, 2005.

[67]Wohfstal, "The Nuclear Third Rail."

[68]See Dilip Hiro, "Iran's Nuclear Ambitions," *The Nation*, http://www.thenation.com/doc/20050912/Hiro, accessed 9/1/05.

[69]See David Sanger, "The U.S. vs. a Nuclear Iran," *New York Times*, December 12, 2004.

[70]See William Epstein, "Indefinite Extension--with Increased Accountability," *The Bulletin of the Atomic Scientists 51*, no. 4 (July/August, 1995), pp. 27–30.

[71]Marvin Miller, "The Iraqi Nuclear Program: Past, Present, and Future?" in Steven L. Spiegel, Jennifer D. Kibbe, and Elizabeth G. Mathews (eds.), *The Dynamics of Middle East Nuclear Proliferation*, (Lewiston, NY: Edwin Mellen, 2001), p. 86.

[72]"Frontline" interview (April 1999); www.pbs.org/wgbh/pages/frontline/shows/unscom/ interview/kay.

[73]See Richard Wolffe, "A Man with a Mission," *Newsweek*, October 27, 2003, p. 33.

[74]To the degree that you believe that the United States acted from other motives (such as access to oil or the unfinished Bush family concerns with Saddam Hussein), you might see the American interest in a rule regarding security and nuclear weapons as a pretext to pursue those other motives. But once states begin describing their actions in terms of rule, that very fact begins the process of rule construction.

[75]Stewart M. Powell, "Rice Launches Iraq PR Campaign," Durham, NC, *Herald-Sun*, October 9, 2003, p. A6.

[76]One incentive for the American government to press Iran for a clear demonstration that it is not developing nuclear weapons is to head off an Israeli attack against Iranian facilities since such an attack may unleash a new round of intense instability in the region, forcing the United States to make difficult choices to re-stabilize the situation.

9

Nuclear Terrorism

Within weeks after the terrorist attacks of 9/11, an alert circulated among the top security agencies in the U.S. government that terrorists had obtained a ten-kiloton nuclear weapon from the Russian arsenal and were planning to detonate it in New York City. The information had come from a source code-named "Dragonfire," who claimed that the device was already in the city. The alert was plausible because experts had long suspected that one or more weapons of this size were missing from the Russian arsenal. Security officials desperately sought to determine the truth of the information on which the alert was based and to thwart a potential detonation. In order to prevent panic, few people were notified, not even the mayor of New York. A team equipped with detectors carried in briefcases scoured the city but turned up no signature of a nuclear device. After some very anxious days, it was determined that the information was false.[1]

A ten-kiloton nuclear weapon is nearly as powerful as the weapon detonated on Hiroshima in 1945. We saw in Chapter 1 the consequences of that blast. A ten-kiloton nuclear explosion in a major U.S. urban area would immediately kill hundreds of thousands of people or more. Within a half-mile radius of the explosion, everything would be flattened, and beyond that buildings would be severely damaged. Wind-borne radiation would spread from the site killing many more and contaminating an area of more than a thousand square miles. Evacuees would number in the hundreds of thousands. Recovery time would be in years.[2] It is reasonable to assume that such destruction would permanently alter the fabric of our national political, social, and economic lives. In 2005, we saw the effect on the United States of the destruction wrought by two major hurricanes. The overall harm to the nation from a terrorist nuclear explosion in an urban area, in lives, in economic damage, and in our sense of security, would be far beyond this and far worst than the attacks of 9/11.

But the real horror in this story of the post-9/11 nuclear alert lies in the fact that the information supplied by Dragonfire might have been correct. It was plausible. A terrorist nuclear detonation on U.S. soil could occur at any time. After the Cold War and prior to 9/11 we had become complacent about the existence of nuclear weapons, despite the tremendous damage they could cause, because they had not been used since 1945. International terrorism makes the possibility of their use suddenly more real. The possibility of nuclear terrorism has resurrected the deep fear of nuclear weapons that many thought we had left behind with the first nuclear age.

In this chapter, we will first discuss the nature of terrorism, then examine the prospects for nuclear terrorism, and finally consider how the threat of nuclear terrorism can be reduced.

TERRORISM

We have claimed that the terrorist attacks of September 11 were a defining event of the second nuclear age. This may seem an odd claim because nuclear weapons were not involved in those attacks. But the attacks reveal in stark form a new danger, the prospect of nuclear terrorism. Those attacks might have been undertaken with nuclear weapons, for clearly the September 11 attackers had an interest in killing a large number of civilians. The best way to do that is with nuclear weapons.[3] Even in the 1990s, prior to 9/11, a group of prominent thinkers on nuclear weapons observed that, despite the common perception that the end of the Cold War had lessened the nuclear danger, "the risk of a nuclear detonation on American soil has increased."[4] September 11 demonstrates how and why that risk has increased significantly. Nuclear terrorism can no longer be regarded as a remote possibility.

To understand the threat of nuclear terrorism we face today, it is helpful to begin by considering the chief international terrorist organization that threatens the world today, and which was responsible for the 9/11 attacks, al Qaeda ("al Qaeda" means "the base" in Arabic).[5] Al Qaeda arose out of the struggle waged by Afghans and other Muslims, a *jihad* or holy war, against the Soviet Union's invasion of Afghanistan in 1979. By 1989, the Soviets had withdrawn in defeat. That defeat was due in part to a young Saudi Arabian, Osama bin Laden, who was able to help fund the jihad partly through his own family's wealth and partly through a world-wide support network among Muslims that he developed. (Much of the support also came from the United States, which was eager to have the Soviet Union suffer a defeat in Afghanistan.) bin Laden and his organization, which came to be called al Qaeda, began to turn its attention to the United States following the stationing of U.S. forces in Saudi Arabia beginning in 1991. The troops were permanently stationed in Saudi Arabia after the first Gulf War in order to deter Iraq from again invading its neighbors to the south, Kuwait and Saudi Arabia. The United States was greatly concerned about such a possibility given the dependence of the West on Saudi and Kuwaiti oil. bin Laden and other Muslims saw it as sacrilegious for non-Muslim troops to be stationed in a nation that contained the religious sites most holy to Muslims. bin Laden's hostility toward the Saudi royal family, who colluded with the Americans, led him and al Qaeda to seek sanctuary in the Sudan, where he planned to direct his campaign against the new enemy.

In 1992, al Qaeda promulgated a *fatwa*, a religious edict, calling for a jihad against the Western occupation of Islamic lands, singling out the United States for special attention. Through the first two-thirds of the 1990s, there were a series of attacks against United States and other Western interests by Islamic extremists, and al Qaeda seems to have been involved in many of these. In 1996, bin Laden and al Qaeda were expelled from the Sudan and found new refuge in Afghanistan, with the acquiescence or support of its neighbor Pakistan. The organization, with the support of the Taliban government, had greater freedom of operation there, and they established a series of camps to train jihadists (or holy warriors), mostly from abroad, to struggle against what al Qaeda claimed to be the Western enemies of Islam. In February 1998, bin Laden and al Qaeda issued another fatwa, which called on Muslims to murder Americans anywhere on earth because the United States had declared war on Islam. Interviewed on American TV shortly afterwards, bin Laden asserted: "We do not have to differentiate between military or civilian. As far as we are concerned, they are all targets."[6] A few months later, al Qaeda carried out the first major act of terrorism for which it had complete responsibility, the near-simultaneous bombings of the American embassies in Narobi, Kenya and Dar es Salaam, Tanzania, killing 224, most of them Africans, and injuring over 5,000. This was followed two years later by an attack on the American destroyer *USS Cole* in Aden, Yemen, on October 12, 2000. A small boat pulled along side the destroyer and exploded, killing 17 U.S. sailors.

But al Qaeda was setting its sights on an attack in the United States, and on September 11, terrorists commandeered four U.S. airliners and sought to fly them into symbolic targets. On that sunny Tuesday morning, two of the airliners were flown into the World Trade Center towers in lower Manhattan, one was flown into the Pentagon, and the fourth, whose apparent target was the U.S. Capitol, crashed in rural Pennsylvania, brought down by a struggle between the hijackers and some of the passengers. Almost 3,000 people were killed. Few think that this will be the last effort by al Qaeda to cause mass casualties in the United States.

Al Qaeda, however, is not the only international group that may be interested in practicing nuclear terrorism. To get a fuller view of the phenomenon, we need to understand what terrorism is in general. According to one publication of the U.S. government:

> There is no single, universally accepted, definition of terrorism. Terrorism is defined in the *Code of Federal Regulations* as "...the unlawful use of force and violence against persons or property to intimidate or coerce a government, the civilian population, or any segment thereof, in furtherance of political or social objectives." (28 C.F.R., Section 0.85)[7]

This definition is a good starting point. A terrorist uses unlawful force or violence to intimidate or coerce in pursuit of political or social objectives.

But additions to this definition are required. First, terrorists seek to create terror within a civilian population. Terrorist violence is violence directed at civilians because, through such violence, terror is created in the civilian population. The main purpose of the terrorists in creating the terror is to achieve their political or social objectives by getting the government to respond to its terrorized population by giving in to the terrorists' demands. The main purpose of a government, after all, is the physical security of its population, and when that security is undermined, the government must seek to reestablish it. Second, while the term "terrorist" is usually applied to individuals or groups, such as al Qaeda, that are working independently of established governments (so-called non-state actors), it is a mistake to limit the term in this way. Governments can also practice terrorism in their use of violence. In addition to the terrorism of non-state actors, there is government terrorism, committed either against its own civilians (state terrorism) or against civilians in other nations (war terrorism).[8]

In the case of state terrorism, a government rules by practicing terrorism against its own people, the objective generally being to preserve or extend its domestic power. In the case of war terrorism, governments practice terrorism against the populations of other states to achieve military objectives in war. For example, the bombings of Hiroshima and Nagasaki (as well as the conventional bombings of other cities in World War II) are acts of terrorism. In these attacks, the United States and its allies used violence against civilians to achieve the objective of getting their governments to surrender. This idea that terrorism is used by governments as well as the non-state actors we call terrorists is important, and we discuss it further in Chapter 11. Caleb Carr points out that governments are reluctant to admit that they can be terrorists as well. "They don't want to lose the weapons of terror—and they don't want to admit to having used it in the past."[9] It should also be noted that terrorism occurs not only when violence is actually used against civilians, but also when it is publicly threatened against them. For example, if a group hijacks a plane full of civilians and threatens them to achieve its demands, it is engaging in terrorism, even if none of the civilians are killed.

Including the ideas that terrorism is violence directed at civilians, that it can be practiced by governments as well as by non-state actors, and that it includes threats as well as the actual use of violence leads to the following revised definition.

> Terrorism is the use (or threat) of force or violence against civilians in order to achieve political objectives through creating terror in the civilian population; the political objectives may be getting a government to meet certain demands (terrorism by non-state actors and war terrorism) or getting the civilians themselves to accept the authority of the government perpetrating the violence (state terrorism).

It is important to note that the terrorist use or threat of violence is *unjustified*; otherwise, normal police activities might count as terrorism, because the police use force (or the threat thereof) to deter or stop crime. In fact, it is because police use of force is generally justified that it does not generally create terror in the population.

Consider some implications of this definition. First, it implies that those who attack military targets are not terrorists. Thus, for example, the al Qaeda operatives who bombed the *USS Cole* would not be terrorists, though they are often referred to as such.[10] Neither would the insurgents in Iraq be terrorists, so long as they restrict their attacks to U.S. and Iraqi security and military forces (as in their use of IEDs, improvised explosive devices). Second, people who terrorize but have no social or political objective for their actions are not terrorists. For example, serial killers, such as the pair of snipers who killed a number of people in the Washington, D.C. area in the fall of 2002, may terrorize a civilian population, but they are not strictly speaking terrorists, unless their intention is to use the terror to obtain some political or social goal, beyond whatever perverted satisfaction they may take in the killings themselves. If the killers' purpose were, for example, to force a police crackdown that would lead the population to revolt against the government, then they would be terrorists.

Note that the political objectives that are necessary for an act of violence to be an act of terrorism need not be the only motive or reason with which terrorists act. For example, in the last several years terrorists have been increasingly acting out of a strong religious motive.[11] The main example of this trend is, of course, al Qaeda, which is a fundamentalist Islamic group. For such groups, religious motives have become mixed with the motives resulting from the political objectives they pursue. When al Qaeda attacked the World Trade Center towers, its objective, as we said, appears to have been, at least in part, to get the United States to remove its troops from Saudi Arabia. But the suicide hijackers may also have acted out of a sense that they were instruments of divine retribution against the infidel, whom they blamed for thousands of Muslims deaths. Another kind of motive terrorists may have is an expressive one. They may want through their actions to express their outrage at the targets of their attack. Connected with this, terrorist acts often have a symbolic target; they are directed against symbols of a detested government, as when the 9/11 terrorists chose the World Trade Center and the Pentagon as targets symbolic of U.S. power. But these motives can coexist. If a violent attack against civilians has a religious, expressive, or symbolic motive, it may have a social or political motive as well.[12] As with human actions in general, motives are generally mixed.

Perhaps the most important implication of this definition is that it treats terrorism as a matter of tactics rather than as a matter of objectives. In other words, the definition is tactical rather than political, because, though it stipulates that terrorists have political objectives, they are terrorists whatever those objectives are.[13] The definition is tactical because it refers only to the methods adopted by the terrorists, not to their political objectives. Terrorism is about means and not about ends. Terrorism should be a politically neutral term, in the sense that it should apply to anyone who uses violence against civilians for political or social objectives, whatever those objectives, and, in particular, regardless of whether the objectives are moral or immoral. In contrast, a political definition would contain an ideological component, in the sense that it would classify perpetrators of violence as terrorists based on the nature of the objectives they seek. According to a political definition, for example, violence against civilians committed for a good cause might not count as terrorism. A tactical definition precludes this possibility. People often claim that one person's terrorist is another person's freedom fighter. This claim is true only under a definition that includes political objectives as part of it. Under a tactical definition a terrorist is a terrorist is a terrorist.

The term "terrorism" is often used exclusively to label one's opponents or those who "break the law" (that is, those who act against established governments). This approach is based on a political rather than a tactical definition. Anyone can be a terrorist: not just those on the other side, but those on your side as well; not just non-state actors, but governments as well. It is important to avoid what is called the rhetoric of terrorism, the use of the term to label only one's enemies.[14] Because "terrorism" has powerfully negative connotations, one can score rhetorical points by using it to label only the other side.

Although it is important to appreciate that the term "terrorism" can apply both to states and to nonstate actors (like al Qaeda), the focus of our discussion in this chapter will be on its application to nonstate actors. We discuss nuclear terrorism by states in Chapter 11.

A BRIEF FOR TERRORISM?

Is there a case to be made for terrorism? How do terrorists and their supporters seek to justify their actions, and should the justifications be accepted? Non-state actors, particularly al Qaeda, have offered two main arguments for terrorism.[15] First, supporters claim that the terrorism is a justified response to the effort by the United States to impose its culture on the rest of the world, to the detriment of other cultures. The United States "imposes a single method, thought, and way of life, as the people of the entire world are clerks in its government offices and employed by its commercial companies and institutions." Moreover, that way of life is one of "abomination and licentiousness" perpetrated upon others by means of "cheap media and vile curricula." Second, supporters claim that the United States has been responsible for the deaths of millions of Muslims, in Iraq, Palestine, and elsewhere. As a result, Muslims "have the right to kill four million Americans—two million of them children," according to one al Qaeda spokesman. Clearly, the sense of grievance to which al Qaeda is responding runs deep.

There are two ways for critics of terrorism to respond to these arguments, to deny that they provide an adequate justification for terrorism. First, they may challenge the claims that the United States is responsible for the contamination of Muslim cultures and the deaths of four million Muslims. One way to challenge these claims is to say that Muslims themselves are largely responsible for these consequences. As regards culture, the point would be that Western culture can spread only with the consent of those who partake in it. As regards the claim about four million Muslim deaths, the figures can be disputed, but there is the fact that the United States did wage war against Islamic Iraq and did support the oil embargo imposed on Iraq due to its noncompliance with the terms of the Gulf War surrender. Children did die, but those deaths were arguably the result of Saddam Hussein using what revenues were available for other purposes. The second way critics can respond is to argue that, even if the United States is responsible for the cultural contamination and the deaths attributed to it, this does not justify terrorism, which is the killing of many innocent people, people in no way personally responsible for the deeds to which the terrorism is a response. Nothing can justify the killing of innocent persons, not even reprisal for the alleged killing of innocent persons. (In Chapter 11, we consider in greater detail the possible justifications for terrorism by both states and non-state actors.)

Historically, of course, no matter the cause, terrorism has often been the weapon of the weak or of the few. It is a tactic of necessity, particularly when passions are strong, the environment is repressive, and the cause looks hopeless from the perspective of conventional politics. It can, or so it seems on the surface, mobilize others through "the propaganda of the deed," calling forth new supporters and partisans through the very act of terror. The repressive reaction to terror on the part of governments is often overblown, pushing more individuals into at least a tolerance of terrorists in their midst if not actual support for them. Terrorism can appeal to individuals, because it is often seen as the work of committed, single individuals. It can justify itself as a means of expression, perhaps the only means, open to the individual, acting apparently alone, defiant and unimaginably powerful. Terrorism can justify itself as the only action available to the weak and oppressed.

In reality, the vision of the heroic individual is only partially correct. Behind most terrorists is an organization, an organization that recruits, trains, and assigns individuals to missions; provides them with the logistics and support; and raises the funds, materials, and information needed to wage a war of terror. Without an organization, terror becomes a personal crusade, much like the Unabomber undertook in sending explosive packages and letters to individuals, and leaving little impact. Nuclear terrorism in particular demands an effective, relatively extensive organization, staffed with individuals having specialized skills. For instance, a stolen nuclear weapon is useless unless one knows how to arm the weapon and by-pass the security devices designed to thwart an unauthorized use. Because the number of such devices in the hands of terrorists would be limited, there will be a premium on ensuring a delivery to the target, which likely necessitates a careful casing of the route and one or several trial runs, all demanding an organization, one that has honed its skills and avoided detection. Effectiveness in terms of waging nuclear terror probably depends as well on some stability in the organization, a condition hard to maintain when it is under constant assault as al Qaeda has been. That is not to say that al Qaeda is incapable of staging a nuclear attack; it is only that the odds of its being able to do so are diminished as long as an effective assault continues.

Radiological terrorism (the dirty bomb approach), on the other hand, is likely to need much less organizational effort, discipline, and skills, either to acquire the raw ingredients or to deliver the explosive device to a target. The tradeoff is in its greatly reduced power to kill and to leave a physical scar that would remind the victims of the group's power and purpose.

The organizational structure of terror makes it a modern political phenomena, with the self-regarding aspects of organizations that crode whatever slim justification terrorism might otherwise have. In particular, organizations seek to maintain themselves, not necessarily for the programmatic goals that they espouse, but because organizations do not plan for or accept their demise. They offer benefits to the members within them such as friendship, a sense of purpose, and rewards (from salaries to prestige to accolades for a job well done). For the ambitious, they offer a career path that spurs action and fidelity to the organization's norms, particularly loyalty (which is also a requisite for survival of terrorist organizations). The routines of the organization—in this case, creating terror—become ends in themselves. Reasons for doing something become lost in the mechanical practice of terror, and the organization loses its ability or interest in asking, is this appropriate, will it accomplish our goals, does it cross the line in our moral universe? For example, al Qaeda in Iraq—the Abu Musa al-Zaqari organization—has staged attacks against fellow Muslims as a part of its attempt to drive the United States out of Iraq, earning the condemnation of others, including Islamic jihadists for crossing the line. Terrorism is particularly troubled by this problem of line-crossing because it makes civilians—including children—its targets. (All organizations that mete out violence face the same problem to one degree or another; Chapter 11 will discuss these issues further.)

THE NUCLEAR COMPONENT OF TERRORISM

The real fear is that terrorists will use nuclear weapons. There is also concern about the prospects of terrorists using other so-called weapons of mass destruction, specifically chemical and biological weapons. But, to repeat the point made earlier, it is misleading to put nuclear, chemical, and biological weapons in the same category. Nuclear weapons are capable of far more destruction than either chemical or biological weapons. Of course, nuclear explosions are not the only way terrorists might make use of nuclear materials.[16] For example, terrorists might seek to destroy a nuclear power reactor by crashing an airplane into the protective dome surrounding the reactor or to cause a melt-down in the nuclear waste stored on-site at most nuclear power plants. These actions would not cause a nuclear explosion, but could spread radioactive material over a wide area, causing some deaths and making an area downwind from the power plant uninhabitable, such as occurred at the Chernobyl nuclear power plant in the Soviet Union in 1986. Or they may use a "dirty bomb" or "radiation dispersal device."[17] But, though it may be easier for terrorists to explode a dirty bomb, or perhaps to destroy a nuclear reactor, than to explode a nuclear weapon, these alternatives do not pose anything like the risk of destruction nuclear explosions pose. These alternative forms of terrorism involving nuclear materials are, in terms of their levels of destruction, in the same category as the terrorist use of either chemical or biological weapons; they are weapons of mass disruption. Therefore, we will spend the remainder of the chapter focusing on nuclear terrorism involving the explosion (or threatened explosion) of a nuclear weapon.

Because any use of nuclear weapons is likely to kill a large number of civilians, these weapons have been referred to as terror weapons. Their very use is an act of terrorism, and any use of them makes their user a terrorist.[18] A person may commit terrorism with conventional weapons, but it is hard to avoid committing terrorism with nuclear weapons.[19] Thus, nuclear weapons are the ideal weapon for terrorists—they can do the work of terrorism very effectively. But there may be other reasons that terrorists would choose to use nuclear weapons besides their effectiveness at killing people and creating terror. For example, terrorists may seek to demonstrate that they have the ability to acquire and use the most devastating of weapons against the strongest power in the world, because such a demonstration would increase their bargaining leverage with the United States and its allies, and with Muslim states, and would serve as a potent recruitment device.

How likely is nuclear terrorism? Experts differ in their answer to this all-important question. Many think that it is very likely or virtually inevitable. Eugene Habiger, a retired general who was in charge of U.S. strategic nuclear weapons and ran the nuclear anti-terror program for the Energy Department, asserts that "it's not a matter of if; it's a matter of when."[20] Graham Allison, a well-repected academic who has written on the issue of nuclear terrorism, states: "It is my considered judgment, on the current path, a nuclear terrorist attack on America in the decade ahead [written in 2004] is more likely than not."[21] Journalist Bill Keller notes that "the best reason for thinking it won't happen is that it hasn't happened yet, and that is terrible logic."[22]

Author Jessica Stern offers five reasons why nuclear terrorism is now more likely.[23] First, nuclear weapons would be seen as especially valuable by terrorists because their use would demonstrate scientific prowess or carry a sense of divine retribution. Second, terrorists are now more likely than in the past to be interested in committing acts of extreme violence, partly due to the increasingly religious nature of the terrorists' motives. Third, the breakup of the Soviet Union has made nuclear weapons or fissile nuclear material more available for theft or purchase on the black market. Fourth, there is an increasing pace of nuclear proliferation to states that may support terrorism. Fifth, technological advances, such as the internet used as an organizing tool, make nuclear terrorism easier.

To these considerations can be added evidence that al Qaeda has in fact been seeking to obtain nuclear weapons. The *9/11 Commission Report* notes that "al Qaeda has tried to acquire or make nuclear weapons for the past ten years."[24] One specific bit of evidence they cite is that Osama bin Laden's associates

> received word that a Sudanese military officer ... was offering to sell weapons-grade uranium. After a number of contacts were made through intermediaries, the officer set the price at $1.5 million, which did not deter Bin Ladin. Al Qaeda representatives asked to inspect the uranium and were shown a cylinder about three feet long... Al Qaeda apparently purchased the cylinder, then discovered it to be bogus.

The report points out that the apparent failure of this effort to obtain nuclear materials provides little comfort, given what it shows about al Qaeda's efforts to obtain such materials, most of which would presumably not be known to us. In addition, bin Laden has publicly declared that al Qaeda's acquiring a nuclear weapon is a religious duty, and he received in 2003 religious approval from a Saudi Muslim cleric to use a nuclear weapon against the United States.[25] On the other hand, the fact that the organization paid for bogus material indicates that it did not have the skills needed to evaluate what was being offered.

But more is required to explode a nuclear bomb than obtaining fissile nuclear material, or a bomb itself, by theft or on the black market. Graham Allison asserts that al Qaeda has "demonstrated an organizational capacity to plan, coordinate, and implement operations well above the threshold of competence necessary to acquire and use a nuclear weapon."[26] But other experts would question this judgment, arguing that obtaining and exploding a nuclear weapon is more difficult than is usually appreciated. Al Qaeda may be unable to succeed in its efforts despite its demonstrated organizational ability. Enriching uranium is extremely difficult, requiring technical apparatus and expertise probably beyond a group of nonstate actors.[27] As a result, terrorists would have two choices, either obtain enriched uranium or plutonium and construct a bomb from it or obtain a ready-made bomb. Each poses serious problems. While it might be easier to obtain fissile nuclear material than a ready-made bomb, constructing the bomb would be fraught with difficulties. There would probably not be enough fissile material to use in a test of the device, and a test would likely be detected in any case, alerting the world to an impending danger. Terrorists would likely adopt the gun-type device as their weapon design (see Chapter 2), but while U.S. scientists felt that there was no need to test the device before its use against Hiroshima, that confidence had been based on extensive design work and testing of the gun itself. If, on the other hand, terrorists obtained a ready-made bomb, say one from the old Soviet arsenal, they would have to figure out how to bypass the built-in security features designed to keep anyone from exploding the bomb without authorization. No matter the means of acquiring a nuclear weapon, transporting the bomb to the intended location would be an additional hurdle. The fissile nuclear material and/or the bomb itself would have to be moved across multiple borders without detection.

These considerations remind us of the twin factors of opportunity and motivation, discussed in Chapter 8 on proliferation. An act of nuclear terrorism would require that the terrorists had both sufficient motivation and sufficient opportunity to obtain and use a nuclear weapon. It is helpful to consider each of these at somewhat greater length.

Under the category of opportunity we should include both the ability of the terrorists to obtain a ready-made bomb or the fissile material (and the expertise) to construct one and the ability to defeat the safety mechanisms (in case of a ready-made bomb) or to construct the bomb (if only the materials are obtained). It seems clear that the ability of terrorists to do these things is greater now than it has been in past decades, and so that their opportunity to commit acts of nuclear terrorism is better than it used to be and these opportunities are likely to increase in the future. Much of the greater opportunity is due to the same factors creating greater opportunity for nuclear proliferation, for, as we noted in Chapter 8, there is a close connection between nuclear proliferation and nuclear terrorism. The sources of nuclear weapons or of fissile nuclear material more readily available to potential proliferators are also more readily available to potential nuclear terrorists. The potential thieves or buyers of Russian nuclear weapons or fissile nuclear material could be potential nuclear terrorists as well as potential nuclear proliferators.[28] The increase in opportunity for nuclear terrorism, tied to the end of the Soviet Union, is a special problem of the second nuclear age. It is ironic that the efforts of the Mujahidin or Muslim holy warriors to defeat the Soviet Union in Afghanistan, supported strongly by the United States, has led, through its contributing to the demise of the Soviet Union, to the descendents of the Islamic jihadists in al Qaeda having greater opportunity to engage in nuclear terrorism.

The crucial question, of course, is whether this increase in opportunity is enough to make it likely that terrorists could obtain or construct a nuclear weapon, and use it, if they chose to do so. Does increased opportunity mean sufficient opportunity? As the earlier discussion indicates, experts are divided on the answer to this question.

If al Qaeda had the opportunity to explode a nuclear weapon in an act of nuclear terrorism, would they do so? The evidence from the *9/11 Commission Report* clearly indicates that al Qaeda is seeking the option to commit nuclear terrorism, but this does not show that they would actually commit such an act if that had the option to do so. The question of motivation may seem simple to answer, but it is not. As one commentator notes, "We are in the paradoxical position of having a clearer understanding of the interior of the atom than we do of the interior of the mind of the terrorist."[29]

There are some reasons to think that the terrorists of al Qaeda may not be sufficiently motivated to use nuclear weapons, despite their demonstrated efforts to obtain fissile nuclear material. First, there is the *nuclear taboo*, a strongly held rule or norm against their use that emerged in the period since

1945.[30] It is an added reason for nations, and perhaps non-state terrorist groups as well, not to use nuclear weapons. The willingness of al Qaeda to commit acts of massive slaughter, as shown by its actions on 9/11, strongly suggests that the nuclear taboo alone would not deter them. Another reason to think that al Qaeda may lack motivation to use nuclear weapons is a possible concern for the reaction by the United States. Creating massive civilian casualties in the Unites States may be seen by al Qaeda as being too provocative and too costly to the organization, given the massive U.S. response it would lead to. It may reason that the prolonged and low intensity war against the United States in Iraq and Afghanistan is preferable. According to this argument, it may be possible for al Qaeda to be deterred from nuclear terrorism by the threat of retaliation, a point we take up again shortly.

These two reasons why terrorists may lack the motivation to use nuclear weapons are bound up with the concept of rationality. To say that acts are rational is to say that, given an actor's beliefs, the acts promote the actor's objectives at the cost the actor is willing to pay. Acts that are irrational for most people may be rational for terrorists because the objectives (and beliefs) of the terrorists may differ from those of most people. So, to understand whether nuclear terrorism may be rational for terrorists, we must understand what the objectives (and the relevant beliefs) of the terrorists are. Brian Jenkins claims that the main objective of terrorists is to make their grievances known, not just to kill people. He notes, "Simply killing a lot of people has seldom been a terrorist objective.... Terrorists want a lot of people *watching*, not a lot of people *dead*."[31] It is true that the objective of creating terror requires that people be left alive to be terrorized, but this requirement is consistent with a very large number of deaths. Moreover, Jenkins made these comments a number of years ago, prior to rise of al Qaeda. As 9/11 shows, the objectives of al Qaeda seem to include killing large numbers of people,[32] and, in its call to kill Americans wherever they may be found, it seems to lump people with government as the enemy. Killing large numbers of the enemy may, in al Qaeda's eyes, be necessary because of the maximalist goals that they pursue: driving the west from Muslim lands and—in more extreme visions—returning Islamic control to the vast swaths of land in Europe and Asia once held by Islamic rulers. From this perspective, it would be rational for al Qaeda to have nuclear weapons and, given likely resistance by the west to withdrawing its influence—or, with much greater difficulty, its culture—from Islamic lands, their motivation to use nuclear weapons would be strong.

The second question is whether terrorists in general, and al Qaeda in particular, make decisions in an irrational fashion. That is, do they perceive with some accuracy how others may react, or do they make absurd assumptions that the method they have chosen to reach their goal is sure to do so. For instance, suppose that al Qaeda believed that flying four planes successfully into their targets, including the Capitol or the White House, would surely compel the United States to leave the Middle East and abandon Israel. Of course, the American response was to wage unrelenting war against al Qaeda—just the opposite of what the goal was. Wouldn't any rational decision-making process have come to the same conclusion? Or are terrorists particularly defective as rational thinkers? Jerrold Post has argued, that, even though terrorists in the main do not suffer from profound distortions in their thought processes, which would make their actions irrational, they are nonetheless likely to suffer from "a pattern of psycho-social vulnerabilities that renders [them] particularly susceptible to the powerful influences of group and organizational dynamics."[33] Post's point is that there are certain personality characteristics that lead people to join terrorist groups and that these characteristics, along with the isolated nature of the group itself, predispose the group to make decisions, such as the decision to use nuclear weapons, that might not be what most of its members would individually regard as appropriate or rational. "There is a tendency for individual judgment to be suspended so that conforming behavior results."[34]

This is not to deny that a terrorist group might be led by a deranged individual. For example, Chizuo Matsumoto founded an apocalyptic Japanese cult, Aum Shinrikiyo in 1987, renaming himself Shoko Asahara and proclaiming that the world was coming to an end. Cult members would be saved, of course, but they had to follow Asahara's authoritarian rules; those who did not were murdered. The world outside the Aum communes were filled with the enemy: the United States, those who were entranced by the lures of materialism, and the Japanese government that was investigating the deaths of cult members. Moreover, the mass of citizenry, oblivious to what they should be doing to prepare for the approaching end, were accumulating more and more bad karma which would prevent them from surviving the final days. Better that those individuals should die now, Asahara told his closest followers, for their deaths would preserve the possibilities of a future for them. Ashara had ordered Aum members—many of whom were well educated with scientific backgrounds—to prepare chemical, biological, and nuclear weapons. There are reports that Aum was unsuccessful in its attempt to purchase a nuclear device in Russia, but it did manufacture the deadly nerve gas sarin. An initial use of the gas in 1994 had no effect. In March 1995, a gas attack killed 12 and sickened 5000 the Tokyo subway system. (An inefficient dispersal system for the gas kept the casualties low.)

Was the gas attack an irrational behavior? "It is still not entirely clear," conclude Daniel Benjamin and Steven Simon,

> what Asahara thought the attack would accomplish. Did he mean it to confirm his repeated claims that chemical weapons were being used by others? Did he expect his followers to interpret it as proof of his apocalyptic warnings? Did he think it would set off the global Armageddon he had been predicting, or cripple Japan's government and thereby open the door to Aum Shinrikyo's government-in-waiting? None of these explanations is implausible, given what is known about Asahara's mental state and worldview in 1995.[35]

The first two questions suggest that the gas attack was a rational but perverted attempt to maintain his stature as a leader, someone to be listened to and heeded. The third is based on a delusional understanding of the world, and hence not rational. Nonetheless, Asahara gave the order to use the weapon and the five who carried out the attack complied. It appears that if a nuclear weapon were available, it would have been used.

Finally, in considering rationality in decision making, we note that a number of observers have noted that under the American assault after 9/11, al Qaeda has become a franchiser. It has encouraged local jihadists to create their own networks and devise their own campaigns of terror. Like a franchiser, it supports them with funding, training, and possibly a supply of recruits, as well as with the "brand name," as it vested al-Zarqawi 's group with the label, al Qaeda in Iraq. Al Qaeda's top leadership would still provide guidance for its franchisees, but there would be a good deal of local autonomy (a condition reinforced by the U.S. attempt to disrupt the al Qaeda leadership). We suspect, however, that many al Qaeda cells or sympathizers would pay heed to the already expressed wishes or observations from the top leadership, such as "Muslims need a nuclear weapon" or "the use of nuclear weapons is permitted against oppressors," and that this would spur them into devising their own programs to acquire and use such weapons. Thus, in a franchised terror movement with a long-standing interest in nuclear weapons, the decision to obtain *and use* a nuclear weapon may drift down into a local commander's hands rather than remain with the top leadership. At that level, local interests and issues, in particular a desire to prove oneself in the eyes of the top leadership, may form the basis for the decision.

Factors in the second nuclear age thus lead us to conclude that some terrorists are probably more motivated to use nuclear weapons, and that they probably have a greater opportunity to acquire usable nuclear weapons, either ready-made or through constructing them. The key question is whether their motivation, and especially their opportunity, has increased enough to make it likely that nuclear terrorism will occur. The answer to this question is a matter of debate, but we would side with those experts who claim that the risk of nuclear terrorism is significant. Whether or not the risk is great, however, the stakes are so high that we should make serious efforts to avoid nuclear terrorism. But what form should our efforts to avoid nuclear terrorism take?

REDUCING THE OPPORTUNITY FOR NUCLEAR TERRORISM

It is essential to understand that the risk of nuclear terrorism cannot be eliminated. So long as nuclear weapons exist, there is a finite risk that they will be used. In the second nuclear age, nuclear terrorism has simply become one of the most likely forms that the use of nuclear weapons would take. What we can do, all that we can do, is to reduce the risk of the use of nuclear weapons, and of nuclear terrorism in particular. It is also essential to understand that almost all people—and this includes terrorists—want some form of control of nuclear weapons that would prevent their use against things they value. Except for the few Asaharas of the world who might welcome massive losses of human life and habitat as a prelude to a new world, almost all leaders and followers would want to be spared being the victims of a nuclear attack. All want arms control that protects themselves, or their community, or the meaningful treasures of their lives. The challenge is to find a common ground on which the mutual prevention of tragic loss can be based.

What kinds of policies should be adopted to reduce the risk of nuclear terrorism? Whatever policies we adopt should have two components. First, they should reduce the risk of terrorism in general because, in most cases, a lesser likelihood of terrorism should mean a lesser likelihood of nuclear terrorism.[36] Second, the policies should reduce the risk of specifically *nuclear* terrorism, making it less likely that, if terrorism occurs, it will involve nuclear weapons. Reducing either kind of risk will depend upon reducing opportunity and motivation. Two basic strategies from the first nuclear age suggest themselves: deterrence and prevention. These strategies could be applied to reduce the risk of terrorism in general or nuclear terrorism in particular. In our discussion of deterrence, we will consider their application to nuclear terrorism. Deterrence would work on the terrorists' motivation to commit acts of nuclear terrorism, seeking to avoid nuclear terrorism by making terrorists fear the negative consequences to them or their interests of their using nuclear weapons. Prevention would work primarily on the opportunity terrorists have to engage in nuclear terrorism, making it more difficulty for them in any effort they might undertake to succeed in a policy of nuclear terrorism.

It is often claimed that deterrence cannot be an effective strategy against nuclear terrorism. There are two reasons for this. First, terrorists, being nonstate actors, have no territory that can be threatened with a retaliatory attack. Second, contemporary terrorists are often suicidal; they give up their own lives in the commission of their terrorists acts. For example, the 9/11 terrorists all died in their attacks. If a terrorist is willing to die, it seems that no threats could stop him or her from committing acts of terrorism. If so, nuclear terrorism poses a radically new threat. Throughout the first nuclear age and into the second, deterrence was relied on to avoid the use of nuclear weapons. Many believe that it was deterrence that kept the world from nuclear war. So, if deterrence cannot work with the new nuclear threat posed by terrorists, we may be in serious trouble. Nuclear terrorism may reveal the limits of nuclear deterrence.

But there may be some role for deterrence in avoiding nuclear terrorism. We suggested earlier in the chapter that al Qaeda may regard causing mass casualties in the United States as too provocative an action to take, given their experience of the U.S. reaction to 9/11. If so, al Qaeda is to some extent deterred from nuclear terrorism. This possibility is strengthened by noting that while there may be many agents of al Qaeda willing, like the 9/11 attackers, to commit suicide, the organization itself may not be willing to do so. If the leaders of the organization thought it might be in jeopardy by a massive U.S. reaction to an act of nuclear terrorism, this might stay their hand from committing nuclear terrorism.[37] Michael Levi has argued that al Qaeda can be deterred from nuclear terrorism if the United States made it clear that a massive retribution would follow not only a successful act of nuclear terrorism, but a failed act as well.[38] Because any particular attempt at nuclear terrorism has a significant risk of failure, this added threat could work as a deterrent.

Consider further the idea of deterrence to avoid nuclear terrorism. Can we draw conclusions from the apparent effectiveness of deterrence during the Cold War? Perhaps not, given the important differences between the two cases. Cold War deterrence took place in an environment in which the two contenders were not directly engaged in warfare against the other. But there is now a war between the United States (and the West more generally) and international terrorists. So what we are talking about today is intra-war deterrence. Moreover, in this war, both sides have relatively maximalist goals; the United States seeks to eradicate the terrorists, and the terrorists would like to do serious harm to the United States. Cold War deterrence was symmetrical (Mutual Assured Destruction), while deterrence of terrorism is asymmetrical, with the United States possessing nuclear weapons and the terrorists seeking to acquire them. But the most important difference is, as suggested above, that the terrorists, having no territory and social assets to defend, seem to have nothing against which to threaten retaliation.

Could deterrence be effective? What is there of value to the terrorists that the United States could target in its threatened retaliation against a terrorist use or attempted use of nuclear weapons, and would such threats be credible? Consider the sorts of things, in general, that could be the targets of threatened retaliation in an attempt to deter an adversary. Those things include: (1) the leaders as individuals; (2) the organizations the leaders control; (3) the wealth of societies, their populations and their built capital, their industry, resources, and housing; and (4) the cultural icons that give meaning to values and beliefs.

First, those leading terrorist groups such as al Qaeda are likely to have some concern for their personal survival. They are likely to have come to see themselves as indispensable, as exceptional figures in history that need to survive to carry out their mission. This is not to say that they are afraid to die, but simply that they see themselves as too important. They are likely to ask themselves, "Would my death due to a savage American retaliation be too great a cost for this movement to free the Islamic world?" But there is a problem with the credibility of such threats, given, for example, how effectively bin Laden has been able to avoid being killed or captured by the United States since 9/11.

Second, al Qaeda may fear its own destruction, the destruction of the organization. This is the point mentioned earlier when we suggested that al Qaeda might avoid being too provocative in its attacks against the United States in order to avoid an all-out American assault on its organization. But there are two problems with the effectiveness of such a threat. One is again the credibility of the threat. If the United States has not been able to completely destroy al Qaeda in the period since 9/11, can it credibly threaten to do so in retaliation for their use of a nuclear weapon? Another problem is that al Qaeda may not greatly fear its own destruction because it does not seem to be a top-down, control-seeking organization. Its strength seems to lie in its willingness to allow autonomy for its sub-groups (such as al Qaeda in Iraq), and it is likely to believe, as young movements tend to do, that its mission will survive independently of the organization because of the way in which it represents the tide of history. In addition, the calculations of success by Islamic jihadists, as with other fundamentalist groups, seem to rest on intensely non-materialist considerations. In answering to God and God's demands, one enters a different frame of reference than materialists like Marxists or U.S. presidents use. If Islamic terrorists lean toward the apocalyptic perspective, like the Aum leadership, then deterrence may fail when the terrorists believe they are doing God's work in bringing forth some form of apocalyptic bloodbath. So, on balance, the threat to destroy the terrorist organization is not likely to be very effective, at least by itself.

Third, the threat to the populations and built capital of societies seems to be an area in which there are no effective threats available because the terrorists, being nonstate actors, lack control of a territory and so would not fear such retaliation. The societies that might be targeted in a threatened retaliation are not ones for which the terrorists have any special responsibility, and those societies may be, in their eyes, part of the problem, as they may be seen as too heavily saturated with the unacceptable western influences. On the other hand, it would be cultural myopia on the part of the West to think that Islamic terrorist leaders would be devoid of any concern about the fate of Muslim societies. There is the concept of the Umma, the Islamic community that cuts across borders. It is what apparently influenced the proliferation activities of A. Q. Khan. And given that Osama bin Laden seems to want to restore Islamic peoples to their rightful power—one that history accorded them for centuries in the past—he and others may be loathe to risk large portions of that community. One test of the depth of this regard would be observing the way in which al Qaeda treats fellow Muslims. Perhaps the adoption into the al Qaeda fold of Abu Musab al-Zarqawi, leader of al Qaeda in Iraq and responsible for the deaths of many Iraqi civilians, is a sign that the concern for fellow Muslims is being overwhelmed by a desire to wage war against the Americans. In addition, credibility is an issue in the case of this threat as well. Would the United States really carry out a threat to attack societies in the Middle East, given their lack of direct responsibility and the large numbers of civilians who would die?

Fourth, the United States could threaten to attack the symbols of Islam, such as the Islamic holy sites in Mecca. For political reasons, the United States could not publicly threaten such attacks, but the terrorists, already prone to think of the United States as implacably hostile and materialistic, may believe that there is an implicit threat to retaliate against such symbols should they use nuclear weapons. This would give such threats some credibility, but would they be effective? Would the terrorists care enough about their possible destruction? They may, so there may be some deterrence here.

Our overall conclusion is that there is probably some deterrent effect to be had by threatening at least some of these forms of retaliation for a terrorist use of nuclear weapons. If one can assume both an element of rationality in the leadership of al Qaeda (and in the leadership of its franchisees) and its ability to avoid the temptations of group-think, as discussed earlier, deterrent threats may help to stay their hand from a nuclear attack. As a result, the basic policy question is now two-fold: how does the United States reinforce deterrence thinking among terrorists; and conversely, how does it avoid actions that weaken it.

But there is one concern raised by a discussion of the impact of deterrence on the threat of nuclear terrorism. A primary motivation for nations to obtain nuclear weapons, as discussed in the last chapter, is to provide security in a context in which their adversaries are threatening to destroy them with nuclear weapons of their own. Nuclear deterrence is a means to security. So, it seems, part of the logic of deterrence would be to provide extra motivation for terrorists, under relentless attack from the West, to acquire nuclear weapons with which to practice deterrence on their own. Why should we not expect terrorists to consider acquiring nuclear weapons as a route to their own security, not for use, but to deter the American effort to annihilate them? Perhaps that may be the evolving thought for terrorists—nuclear weapons are to deter. There is irony in the resulting dilemma for American policy: the more that the United States seeks to destroy al Qaeda, the more likely it is that they will seek to acquire nuclear weapons.

Though deterrence may be expected to have some effect at avoiding nuclear terrorism, its effect may not be very great. It cannot, for example, be expected to be as effective as deterrence was during the first nuclear age. Deterrence must be supplemented with prevention. Prevention has become the key idea in dealing with the problem of nuclear terrorism. Author Graham Allison refers to nuclear terrorism as the "ultimate preventable catastrophe."[39] Speaking of nuclear terrorism, William Perry, former U.S. Defense Secretary, notes that "we're racing toward unprecedented catastrophe" and that "this is preventable, but we're not doing the things that could prevent it."[40] What are the things that could prevent it?

Prevention, unlike deterrence, works primarily on the decreasing the opportunity terrorists have to acquire and use nuclear weapons. There are a number of measures that might be taken to prevent nuclear terrorism by reducing the opportunity of terrorists to acquire and use a nuclear weapon. Some of these are directed at terrorism in general, and some are directed specifically at nuclear terrorism.

(1) Passive defense: This refers to activities designed to make potential terrorist targets harder to attack. Much of the United States' anti-terrorism effort since 9/11 (and even before that) has been devoted to such activities, such as erecting concrete barriers to stop car bombs and requiring tighter security checks to enter buildings or board airplanes. Also included among passive defense against terrorists are strict border and immigration controls. But such measures, while important in stopping terrorists with conventional weapons, may not be sufficient to stop nuclear terrorism, for two reasons. First, in the case of nuclear weapons, one failure to stop an attack could still produce catastrophic damage. Second, local barriers do little to avoid damage from nuclear terrorism, since the weapons are so destructive that large parts of cities can be destroyed from anywhere within the city. Passive defense in the case of nuclear terrorism requires keeping nuclear weapons out of the United States. One of the most likely ways in which a nuclear weapon might be introduced into the nation is in a large steel shipping container, the means by which most imported goods enter the country. Two thousand such containers enter the United States every hour, and fewer than 2 percent are inspected.[41] A crude nuclear weapon could be put in a shipping container overseas and exploded in a major American port. This is an area where inspection efforts must be greatly improved.

There is an interesting irony here. In our discussion of nuclear terrorism, we have been speaking mostly of efforts of the United States to avoid a terrorist nuclear attack on itself. But, as the United States becomes more proficient in its passive defenses, such as preventing terrorists from bringing nuclear weapons into the country, the terrorists may be more likely to attack other nations. This problem may be accentuated by a new "use it or lose it" rule: terrorists may rightly conclude that the longer a nuclear device remains in their keeping, the more likely its existence will become known. That fear, coupled with an appearance of U.S. effectiveness in stopping nuclear weapons at the border, will pin the target on U.S. allies. This displacement effect means that passive defensive measures undertaken to protect the United States should increasingly become the routines of states closely associated with the United States. A further irony here is that, to some extent, the United States is safer from nuclear terrorism to the extent that other nations are more vulnerable to it because terrorists would be inclined to go for the easier target.

But, however effective passive defensive measures may be, they are insufficient. There are simply too many potential terrorist targets and too many ways for terrorists to sneak themselves and their implements of destruction into the United States and other target nations. Anti-terrorist efforts need to be active as well as passive. The fight needs to be brought to the terrorists. This can be done in different ways.

(2) Covert disruption: This refers to efforts, mainly by law enforcement and intelligence agencies, to interfere with terrorists' activities and to disrupt their organization in ways that are not generally publicly obvious. Such efforts include the many aspects of intelligence work, such as the monitoring communications among terrorists, the use of informants to infiltrate terrorist groups, and covert activities such as assassinations of terrorists and sowing dissension within a terrorist group.[42] In addition, many kinds of legal measures can help to disrupt terrorist groups and activities, such as more thorough investigations of terrorist suspects, seeking stronger banking and financial controls to keep money out of the hands of terrorists, and prohibiting the dissemination of information that may be useful to terrorists.[43]

The U.S. government has vigorously pursued methods of covert disruption since 9/11. Some of the legal measures were included in the U.S. Patriot Act, passed by Congress in the immediate aftermath of 9/11. But the Act, and other legal measures since adopted, raises concerns about the erosion of civil liberties. How is the balance to be struck? How much, if at all, should civil liberties be curtailed in the fight against terrorism? This is a hotly debated issue. Some argue that the government has gone too far, indeed that, because we are fighting terrorists to preserve our freedoms, abandoning them in that fight would be handing victory to the enemy.[44] This concern was seen in late 2005, when the reauthorization of some aspects of the Patriot Act was held up by the Senate in an effort to get the Bush administration to weaken some of the provisions deemed especially threatening to civil rights, such as those allowing government access to the library records of private individuals. But defenders of the full range of the government's anti-terrorism efforts, including President Bush, argue that the government's most important job is making its citizens secure, so that measures to achieve this should go forth, even though they threaten civil liberties. There is a third group in this debate, one that is also concerned about the violations of civil liberties, but that argues that the government's anti-terrorism measures that violate civil liberties are largely ineffective in any case, so there is no real need to choose between effective anti-terrorism and civil liberties. They argue that measures like the Patriot Act are largely a matter of political posturing. Anti-terrorism efforts that violate civil liberties should be avoided not only because they violate those liberties, but also because they are of little effect.

(3) Overt military disruption: This refers to military efforts to destroy terrorist groups and their ability to take action. These efforts generally take place outside the United States, in the places overseas where terrorists have sanctuary. The Afghanistan war, launched by the United States in the immediate aftermath of 9/11 is a prime example. Al Qaeda, responsible for the 9/11 attacks, had its main base of operation in Afghanistan, supported by the Taliban, the regime then in control of most of Af-

ghanistan. As a result of that war, the Taliban were overthrown and al Qaeda largely driven to the remote frontier area bordering Pakistan or over the border. Some al Qaeda and Taliban elements continue to fight an insurgency against the new Afghan regime and have demonstrated a worrisome staying power.[45] As discussed in earlier chapters, the Afghanistan war was the first instance of a new military policy adopted by the Bush administration after 9/11 to use military force to attack terrorists and regimes that aided terrorists before the terrorists could attack the United States. The 2003 Iraq War, discussed in Chapter 8, was another instance of this policy. But many questioned the alleged connection between the Iraq war and the war on terrorism, pointing out that there is no compelling credible evidence that Saddam Hussein was aiding al Qaeda, as the Taliban were, and that the war, especially as it has dragged on, may well have increased the risk of terrorism by serving as a training ground and recruiting device for al Qaeda. In addition we, like others, have argued that the Iraq War is not a preemptive war, but a preventive war, since there was no imminent attack by the terrorists it was meant to thwart. (This distinction is discussed in Chapter 4.) In any case, the signal failure of the United States to produce stability after the overthrow of Saddam Hussein's regime or to defeat the resulting insurgency quickly may well have spelled the end, for the time being, of the "preemptive" war policy.

(4) Anti-proliferation efforts: The last form of anti-terrorism is directed specifically at stopping nuclear terrorism. As mentioned in Chapter 8, there is a close connection between the problems of nuclear proliferation and nuclear terrorism. The more nations that have nuclear weapons, the more likely it is that terrorists could steal one or the fissile material needed to construct one. This is especially the case because new nuclear nations may not have the kinds of safeguards against such theft or the kinds of tight controls over the weapons and the fissile material that established nuclear nations have. In addition, nuclear proliferators could deliberately pass on a nuclear weapon to terrorists. Thomas Schelling notes: "The best way to keep [nuclear] weapons and weapons-material out of the hands of nongovernmental entities is to keep them out of the hands of national governments."[46] As a result, all efforts to avoid nuclear proliferation, discussed in Chapter 8, are directly or indirectly efforts to avoid nuclear terrorism.

COPING WITH MOTIVATION

These four approaches we have reviewed are forms of prevention that work on the opportunity terrorists have for nuclear terrorism. But there are also forms of prevention that work, like deterrence does, on motivation. We will look briefly at two of these.

First, we might try to dissuade terrorists from engaging in terrorism in general, and nuclear terrorism in particular, by accommodating some of the terrorists' demands, or, as some would describe it, by "giving in" to their demands. In other words, we could negotiate with the terrorists. Most people would react strongly against such an idea. They would argue that terrorists could not be trusted to keep their word, even if they would negotiate with us. In addition, they would argue that it is simply morally reprehensible to give in to terrorists' demands; further, it is self-defeating because they would see our willingness to meet their demands as a sign of weakness and they would be emboldened and would respond simply by increasing their demands. History would seem to suggest, however, that many if not most insurrections and civil wars are resolved by negotiation.

So, there may be some reason to consider negotiation as part of an anti-terrorist strategy, especially if terrorists get nuclear weapons. Al Qaeda has claimed in the past that it would establish a truce with nations that stop attacking Muslims and stop intervening in their affairs.[47] If there proved to be a deal available on such terms, it might be in the interest of the United States to consider it, if others efforts to stop terrorism could not be assured of success. Allen Zerkin, a specialist in conflict management, suggests that "we should seek to determine if bin Laden would withdraw his *fatwa* against Americans in exchange for certain policy changes, if al Qaeda would settle for less than its maximum demands and if its far-flung followers would honor a truce." Zerkin believes that al Qaeda might be willing and able to satisfy these conditions and that, given the stakes, it would be worth our while to seek to find out if they would.[48] If, however, a limited settlement was not available, the full demands of al Qaeda would be a heavy price for the United States to pay, likely requiring the United States to disengage from much of the world, abandon Israel, and withdraw its influence from all Muslim nations. At the moment, the threat of a few small-scale nuclear attacks, even doing their worst, does not seem to be enough to compel the United States to contemplate such an outcome.

Second, we might seek to deprive potential terrorists of the motive to become actual terrorists and/or potential supporters of terrorism to become actual supporters. How might this be done? Short of meeting the terrorists' demands, can nations at risk from terrorism change the world in some way that would significantly reduce the number of new terrorists that might arise and the support that terrorists receive? Addressing this question requires understanding something about the causes of the terrorist struggle being undertaken by groups like al Qaeda, and this is a very controversial subject. Two ideas about the principal causes of such terrorism, and the resultant policy recommendations, have been much discussed. The first is that the chief cause of such terrorism is the lack of political freedom in the nations from which it arises, so that what the United States and others should do is promote democracy in these nations. The second is that the chief cause is poverty in the nations from which the terrorists come, so that the United States and others should mount a massive campaign to reduce poverty in the world. We consider briefly each of these ideas.

The idea that the chief cause of terrorism is lack of political freedom is based on the following sort of argument. Most of the Muslim nations, and the Arab nations in particular, are ruled by authoritarian and feudal governments, many of which are propped by oil revenues. The leaders in these nations often seek to deflect internal criticism away from themselves by allowing the population and the press to vent their anger at the West and at Israel as the main source of their troubles. Thus, these nations have become breeding grounds for terrorist movements, both in creating grievances and in directing those grievances toward foreign targets. If democracy were to come to these nations, so the argument goes, the populations would feel more in control of their politics, and would no longer need to vent their anger at the outside targets, and support for terrorism would decline. Hence, the United States and others should seek to bring democracy to these nations. This has been the general approach articulated by the Bush administration as to the importance of Iraq for the future. Creation of a functioning democracy there, a democracy blessed with oil revenues, would begin the process of democratizing to the region. There are two problems with this view. First, it is not clear that it is correct. For example, in many of these nations, the population is much more radical than its leaders, and democracy might bring to power radical regimes that would aid and promote terrorist groups. Second, even if the view is correct, it is not clear that the United States can do much effectively to bring democracy to these nations. It is certainly not a short-term project. Democracy promotion has had limited success to date, and the jury is still out on whether the United States can effectively bring democracy to Iraq. Even if successful there, it seems unlikely that other states would transform themselves quickly into democracies, which would leave the problem of terrorism today and tomorrow untouched.

The second idea is that poverty is the chief cause of terrorism, so that a main component of an anti-terrorism effort is to reduce world poverty. Sometimes this idea is expressed in terms of the image of "draining the swamp" out of which terrorism develops. Is the terrorism of groups like al Qaeda caused by poverty? Some argue that this is not the case, that the 9/11 terrorists and members of other terrorist groups are by and large educated and middle class.[49] In response to this, it could be argued that because the leaders are middle class does not mean that the grievances they represent are not rooted partly in poverty. But on the other side of the issue, while Africa contains some of the most extreme poverty in the world, poverty which many claim is the fault of the West, it appears not to be a breeding ground for international terrorists.[50]

But arguments that poverty or lack of political freedom is not a direct cause of terrorism may miss the point. The arguments may show that these are not sufficient to produce terrorism, but it still could be that these, in conjunction with others, make important, possibly critical, contributions to the emergence of terrorism and the motivations of those who practice it. For example, in the case of poverty, middle-class, educated people in the developing world may come to abhor the poverty of many of their fellow citizens, and, blaming the economic domination by the West for this poverty, turn to terrorism against the West and their own rulers who seem to be in league with the West. If so, reducing poverty in the developing world could reduce likelihood of terrorism. The same might be true of the lack of political freedom.

But the developed world should make greater efforts to reduce poverty and increase political freedom in the developing world anyway, even if it has no connection with terrorism. Perhaps some of the poverty and lack of political freedom in the developing world is the result of the developed world treating the developing world unjustly. For example, some argue that a main reason that authoritarian and feudal governments have survived so long in many Muslim nations is that United States has supported those governments against the wishes of their citizens. In addition, it may be in the long-term self-interest of Western nations, apart from concern about terrorism, to alleviate poverty and promote political freedom in the developing world. Indeed, some of the demands of the terrorist groups may be for actions that the West should be taking anyway. If so, then the United States and the West should be meeting these demands not out of concern about terrorism, but out of concern for what is just and what is in its long-term self-interest.[51]

Efforts to alleviate global poverty may help the struggle against terrorism not by changing the minds of the terrorists themselves, but by convincing many would-be supporters of the terrorists not to provide their support. The idea is that the terrorists' critique of the West may sound plausible to many would-be supporters because they blame the West for the poverty they either experience themselves or see around them. Were the West seen by them to be leading a vigorous effort to combat that poverty, the terrorists' case would lose that plausibility for many. An appropriate analogy is that one can fight cancer not by attacking the cancer cells directly, but by cutting off the blood flow to those cells. Indeed, fighting poverty may be simply one way among many that the West can encourage moderation in Islam generally. All such efforts should be pursued. One popular theory holds that part of the tacit support that many Muslims give to the terrorists is due to the humiliation many Muslims feel at the dominance and success of the West and their own consequent sense of backwardness. This is related to the point made earlier about the lack of political freedom in the Muslim world. There seems to be something to this theory, and this suggests that the United States and other nations in the

West should do what they can to alleviate that sense of humiliation, though it is not clear exactly how they would best go about this.

There is another important point to be made regarding the effort to curtail terrorism in general and nuclear terrorism in particular. Many of these efforts can be effectively pursued only through international cooperation. Terrorists can easily move across borders. As a result, efforts to disrupt terrorist activities can only work well if many nations are involved together in the fight. Any successful anti-terrorist program must be an international, multilateral effort. If a nation takes unilateral actions that are opposed by much of the rest of the world, whether in its fight against terrorism or in its other business, this is likely to cripple its anti-terrorism efforts overall. This has been a problem with the Bush administration's war on terrorism.

We offer one final observation. In our discussion about combating terrorism, we have been largely assuming that the current source of Islamic terrorism does not run very deep in Islamic societies. We have been speaking as if a combination of actions against the terrorists themselves and efforts to dissuade or mollify potential supporters of the terrorists can succeed in defeating the terrorist effort. But one could instead take the view that the virulent anti-Western and anti-American sentiment that drives the terrorists runs deep in Islamic society. This view could be supported by reference to the so-called "clash of civilizations" position taken by the author Samuel Huntington.[52] According to this position, the ideological clash of the Cold War has given way to a clash among civilizations, defined largely in terms of religious faith, such as the West and Islam. These civilizations, in his view, are destined to clash, and the current terrorist campaign by the Islamic fundamentalists is just one form of that clash. The problem is that the clash is not simply between the West and the fundamentalists, but between the West and Islam itself. Thus, we might expect that the cultural well-spring from which Islamic terrorism draws its energy is much deeper than we had imagined. The clash itself will be difficult to avoid, and terrorism may for the indefinite future be one of its manifestations.

SUMMARY

Terrorism is the tactic of using violence against civilians to create terror in a population to promote the political demands of the terrorists. Terrorism can be practiced by non-state actors, such as the members of al Qaeda, or by nations, and it can be practiced by nations either against their own populations (state terrorism) or other populations (war terrorism). This chapter has discussed the terrorism, and potential nuclear terrorism, of groups of non-state actors, such as al Qaeda.

The use of nuclear terror by such groups is a matter of motivation and opportunity. The motivation for terrorists to go nuclear is probably quite high. Nuclear weapons are the terror weapon par excellence, so one would expect terrorists to be drawn to them. In addition, 9/11 suggests that that terrorists have an interest in killing large numbers of people, and there is no more effective and dramatic way to do this than with nuclear weapons. Some, however, would argue that it would not be rational for al Qaeda to use nuclear weapons, and that this organization can be expected to act rationally, given its interests in survival as an organization.

On the side of opportunity, the second nuclear age presents terrorists with increased opportunity to acquire or construct a nuclear weapon. While enriching uranium is a technical feat beyond the ability of a non-state group, there are plenty of poorly guarded nuclear weapons and loose fissile material in the world, especially in the former Soviet Union, that terrorists might be able to get their hands on. In addition, the terrorists could avail themselves of the enriched uranium and plutonium in nuclear power reactors.

What policies could be adopted to reduce the risk of nuclear terrorism? Clearly, anti-proliferation efforts are important; terrorism and nuclear proliferation must be fought together. Though deterrence was the main mechanism to avoid nuclear use in the relations among nuclear nations, such as the United States and the Soviet Union in the first nuclear age, deterrence may not seem to be as effective a way to avoid nuclear terrorism. This is because Islamic terrorists often commit suicide in their attacks and have no national territory to retaliate against. But we would argue that deterrence still has some role to play in dissuading nuclear terrorism. There are various other approaches to preventing terrorism in general, and nuclear terrorism in particular, such as forms of passive defense, disrupting terrorist groups through legal and intelligence means, and disrupting their efforts with military force overseas. In addition, some argue that we should seek to negotiate with the terrorists, or that we should launch massive campaigns to reduce global poverty and bring greater political freedom to the developing world. But one thing is clear: the anti-terrorist effort is not something any one nation, no matter how powerful, can undertake on its own. By the nature of the problem, an international effort is necessary.

Our conclusion is that the risks of nuclear terrorism have increased in the second nuclear age, making it more likely that nuclear weapons will be used in the future. Nuclear terrorism, however, is not inevitable. We can take measures that will reduce the danger. But none of these measures, no matter how vigorously pursued, guarantee that there will be no act of nuclear terrorism. In the second nuclear age, as in the first, the risk of the use of nuclear weapons cannot be eliminated. Thus the nuclear predicament survives the end of the Cold War.

This chapter concludes our discussion of the nature of the nuclear threat in the second nuclear age. We now turn, in the next two chapters, to questions about nuclear weapons and human values, looking in Chapter 10 at nuclear weapons and cultural values, and in Chapter 11 at nuclear weapons and moral values. The final three chapters of the text consider three different approaches to our nuclear future. They raise the question of what we should do now and in the future to reduce to the greatest extent we can the risk of nuclear use.

ENDNOTES

[1] Massimo Calabresi and Romesh Ratnesar, "Can We Stop the Next Attack?" *Time*, March 11, 2002. This episode is also discussed in Graham Allison, *Nuclear Terrorism: the Ultimate Preventable Catastrophe* (New York: Times Books, Henry Holt, 2004), pp. 1–2.

[2] J. Peter Scoblic, "How Conservatism Leaves Us Vulnerable to Nuclear Terrorism," *The New Republic* on line, http://www.tnr.com/docprint.mhtl?i=20050808&s=scoblic080805, accessed 8/1/05.

[3] Though terrorists may have other reasons as well for using nuclear weapons, as we discuss below.

[4] Graham T. Allison, et al., *Avoiding Nuclear Anarchy* (Cambridge, MA: The MIT Press, 1996), p. 3 (italics removed).

[5] This account of al Qaeda is taken from *The 9/11 Commission Report* (New York: Norton), pp. 47–70. (The report is also available online.)

[6] *The 9/11 Commission Report*, p. 47.

[7] http://www.fbi.gov/publications/terror/terror99.pdf; accessed September 30, 2003.

[8]The distinction among small group terrorism, state terrorism, and war terrorism is made by Michael Walzer, "Five Questions about Terrorism," *Dissent 49*, no. 1 (winter 2002), also published in Michael Walzer, *Arguing about War* (New Haven, CT: Yale University Press, 2004), pp. 130–142.

[9]Caleb Carr, "Wrong Definition for a War," *Washington Post*, July 28, 2004, p. A19.

[10]Shannon French, "Murderers Not Warriors," in James Sterba (ed.), *Terrorism and International Justice* (New York: Oxford University Press, 2003), p. 43.

[11]Jessica Stern, *The Ultimate Terrorist* (Cambridge, MA: Harvard University Press, 1999), p. 8.

[12]In addition, it may be hard to separate motives. For example a religious motive may be closely connected with the political or social motive.

[13]The distinction between tactical and political definitions of terrorism is drawn by C.A.J. Coady, "Terrorism, Just War, and Right Response," in Georg Meggle (ed.), *Ethics of Terrorism and Counter-Terrorism* (Frankfurt: Verlag, 2005).

[14]See Thomas Kapitan, "The Terrorism of 'Terrorism'," in Sterba, *Terrorism*, pp. 47–66.

[15]The arguments in this paragraph are taken from a series of articles published online in 2002 by a spokesman for al Qaeda. Excerpts from these articles were published by the Middle East Media Research Institute, http://www.memri.org/bin/opener.cgi?Page=archives&ID=SP38802, accessed 9/23/05. Quotations in this paragraph are from this document.

[16]For a discussion of some of these other ways, see Bill Keller, "Nuclear Nightmares," *New York Times Sunday Magazine*, May 26, 2002, and Allison, Nuclear Terrorism.

[17]See Stern, Ultimate Terrorist, pp. 54–57, and Brian Jenkins, "Is Nuclear Terrorism Plausible?" in Paul Leventhal and Yonah Alexander (eds.), *Nuclear Terrorism: Defining the Threat* (Washington: Pergamon-Brassey's, 1986), p. 26.

[18]Thomas Schelling, *Choice and Consequence* (Cambridge, MA: Harvard University Press, 1984), p. 315.

[19]A small nuclear explosion in an isolated area might not kill any civilians, but such an explosion and the threat it implied of the further use nuclear weapons in populated areas would create a great deal of terror. As we noted earlier, the threat to kill civilians is itself a form of terrorism.

[20]Quoted in Keller, "Nuclear Nightmares."

[21]Allison, *Nuclear Terrorism*, p. 15.

[22]Keller, "Nuclear Nightmares."

[23]Stern, *Ultimate Terrorist*, pp. 8–10. Stern offers these reasons also to show that terrorism with chemical and biological weapons is now more likely.

[24]The quotations in this paragraph are taken from the *Report*, pp. 380 and 60.

[25]Dafna Linzer, "Nuclear Capabilities May Elude Terrorists, Experts Say," *Washington Post*, December 29, 2004. p. A1.

[26]Allison, *Nuclear Terrorism*, p. 25.

[27]This difficulty and others are discussed in Linzer, "Nuclear Capabilities."

[28]Stern, *Ultimate Terrorist*, pp. 87–106.

[29]Jerrold Post, "Prospects for Nuclear Terrorism: Psychological Motivation and Constraints," in Paul Leventhal and Yonah Alexander (eds.), *Preventing Nuclear Terrorism* (Lexington, MA: Lexington Books, 1987), p. 91.

[30]Nina Tannenwald, "The Nuclear Taboo," *International Organization 53*, no. 3 (Summer 1999), pp. 433-468. The idea of the nuclear taboo will be discussed further in Chapter 11.

[31]Jenkins, "Is Nuclear Terrorism Plausible," pp. 28, 29, 30.

[32]If the 9/11 terrorists had wanted to minimize the number of people who died, that is, if their point were simply to destroy the World Trade Center towers as symbols rather than to kill people, they could have

scheduled their attack for evening hours or on a weekend. They wanted to do a great deal of destruction and kill a large number of people, and nuclear weapons would be a good way to do this.

[33]Post, "Prospects for Nuclear Terrorism," p. 93.

[34]Post, "Prospects for Nuclear Terrorism," p. 101.

[35]Daniel Benjamin and Steven Simon, *The Age of Sacred Terror*, (New York: Random House, 2002), p. 438.

[36]This would not be the case if vigorous efforts to suppress terrorism drive the terrorists to respond with more extreme methods than they would otherwise have used, such as setting off nuclear weapons

[37]Complicating matters here is the belief of many experts that al Qaeda is now not so much an organization but an idea, with local terrorists acting autonomously, though in its name. So there may be no executive control from the organization on the actions of the local groups.

[38]Michael Levi, "Old Guard," *The New Republic Online*, posted 4/13/05, http://www.tnr.com/docprint.mhtml?i=w050411&s=levi041305.

[39]In the title of his book, *Nuclear Terrorism: The Ultimate Preventable Catastrophe*.

[40]Quoted in Nicholas Kristof, "An American Hiroshima," *New York Times*, August 11, 2004.

[41]Keller, "Nuclear Nightmares."

[42]Some of these tactics, especially assassination, raise important moral and legal questions, but we do not have the space to explore these here.

[43]Some of these are discussed in Stern, *Ultimate Terrorist*, pp. 148–154.

[44]This point of view is nicely represented by the Eisenhower administration in the early days of the Cold War. In the 1953 Nation Security Paper NSC-162/2, the administration argued that it was the objective of U.S. security policy to meet the Soviet threat while at the same time avoiding "seriously weakening the United States economy or undermining our fundamental values and institutions." U.S. Department of State, *Foreign Relations of the United States: 1952: 1954,* vol. 2, part 1 (Washington D.C.: U.S. Government Printing Office, 1984), p. 578.

[45]Osama bin Laden escaped to Pakistan, where he remains at large as of early 2006.

[46]Schelling, *Choice and Consequence*, p. 325.

[47]Allen J. Zerkin, "Is Al Qaeda Asking to Negotiate?" *Los Angles Times*, September 19, 2005.

[48]Zerkin, "Is Al Qaeda Asking to Negotiate?"

[49]See Sebastian Mallaby, "Does Poverty Fuel Terror?" *Washington Post National Weekly Edition*, May 27, 2002.

[50]Walzer, "Five Questions." But Africa has its share of domestic terrorists, such as the Rwandans who massacred 800,000 of their fellow citizens in the 1994 genocide in Rwanda.

[51]See Michael Walzer, "Terrorism: A Critique of Excuses," in Walzer, *Arguing about War*, p. 62. But Walzer seems to take a different position in "Five Questions."

[52]Samuel Huntington, *The Clash of Civilizations and the Remaking of World Order* (New York: Simon and Schuster, 1998).

10

Living in the Nuclear Age
The Social and Cultural Impact of Nuclear Weapons

What is your greatest fear? What is it deep down, within you, that frightens you the most, that physically, emotionally, and mentally paralyzes you? Some believe that if you can locate the source of that fear you should embrace it, let it permeate your very being. That is the only way to be freed from its grip. But that may come at a heavy price, as Christopher Nolan's hugely popular 2005 film, "Batman Begins," powerfully implies. Starting from the apparently correct assumption that the public was ready for a Batman character that is a plausible real-world figure, director Nolan scraped away the cartoon façade that accrued to the Batman legend over the previous four films and a T.V. series, stripping down the story to an elemental battle between a man and his own night terrors. Nolan's Batman, like Steven Spielberg's re-make of "The War of the Worlds," in many ways are metaphors of our day, responding and reflecting in popular culture our post 9/11 anxieties. Nolan's conception of Batman as an almost obsessed crusader for justice whose single-minded fixation makes him only slightly saner than his enemies, clearly has contemporary resonance. The film's central theme is the debilitating effect of fear and the ways it can be exploited. Again, parallels to our time are enticing. Batman and his enemies each seek to capitalize upon the things that terrify us, and Batman must rise above his own childhood fears before he can claim his place as the savior of Gotham City.

The story begins in this version with the adult Bruce Wayne in the middle of that journey, in the far reaches of Asia, where he first encounters a clandestine brotherhood, called the League of Shadows, reminiscent of al Qaeda, with its singleminded, moralistic hatred of the decadence of the West. Led by a warrior sensei, Ra's al Ghul, and his aide Henri Ducard (played by Liam Nesson), the League invites Bruce into its fold, but he declines in a violent confrontation. Thereafter he returns to Gotham City, where he assumes the dual identity as the city's wealthiest patron and its avenging angel, but an angel with a dark side. Nolan's Batman is tormented by demons both physical and psychological. In an uncertain world, one the director models with an eye to our own where the weapon of choice of the

276

League is a vaporized gas that induces self-destructive fear and paranoia, this is a hero caught between justice and vengeance, heroism and violence, a desire for peace and the will to unbridled power.

Before Batman defeats the League, the victimized people of Gotham City are being enveloped by a state of mass panic. This is mirrored by scenes in Spielberg's version of "War of the Worlds", also released in 2005—an unraveling of society, with disoriented people, afraid for their lives, hiding in their basements or fleeing the cities. The enemy here are extraterrestrials but they are clearly metaphors as well. In H.G. Well's 1898 novel, written at the end of British colonialism, this was a war between two worlds, between competing colonialisms, the Martians fleeing a dying planet, a war for survival itself. Spielberg has other preoccupations in mind, other parallels. He commented after the movie's release, that it was "about Americans fleeing for their lives, being attacked for no reason,"[1] having no idea who is attacking them and what they want. And there are explicit allusions: to 9/11 posters of missing people, clothing and paper dropping from the sky as remnants of vaporized people or crumbling buildings.

There is ambivalence in this film as well. Although the invaders from space are cruel and genocidal, the humans are quickly transformed into selfish and violent victims living in a state of anarchy, willing to kill each other for another moment of life. Like the novel, the film probes the similarities between victim and attacker, but also what was at stake and what effects the attackers ultimately had. Through them, as both Wells and Spielberg realized, humanity was robbed of its confidence in the future.

Let us examine another popular cultural artifact to probe how fear has become the flavor of choice in our day. Philip Roth in his important new political novel, *The Plot Against America*, (2004) imagines an alternative American history, in which America has gone fascist, and ordinary life is subverted by ideologically driven national politics and mass hatreds. Hitler's allies control the White House, anti-Semitic mobs roam the streets brutalizing and killing, reminiscent of the Brownshirts in Nazi Germany, and the lower-middle-class Jews of Weequahic in Newark, New Jersey, cower behind locked doors waiting for the inevitable.

In Roth's version of history, the Republicans nominate Charles A. Lindbergh for president in 1940 and he defeats F.D.R. in a landslide on an isolationist plank. Lindbergh, in real life as in the novel, was an admirer of Adolf Hitler, a recipient of the Nazi Service Cross of the German Eagle and was hostile to Jews and what he believed was their excessive influence. We know that fascism took over most of Europe in those years and Roth posits an ingenious "what if" and skillfully closes the gap between far-fetched hypothetical and possible reality. He shows how quickly the rights and democratic values of American life are lost under the authoritarian guidance of President Lindbergh and his "Just Folks" program which sets out to break up Jewish families by scattering Jewish children into the Christian heartland. Although Roth never makes reference to the present, if you are not careful the reader may find himself thinking of the potential civil liberty abuses contained in the Patriot Act, the unfortunate abuses of the Geneva Conventions of War in Iraq and Guantanamo and other worrisome aspects of our present situation in the Middle East.

The novel, on many levels, is dark, fable-like, disturbing, preposterous and, as Paul Berman writes in his *New York Times* book review "creepily plausible." Roth seems to be playing with the emotions of the reader. You think fascism is only for other countries? And then you turn the pages and find yourself astonished and afraid, like the young narrator of the novel, Philip, who begins the novel with the lament that "fear presides over these memories, a perpetual fear" (p. 1).[2] Fear of what, you may ask? Of Nazis? They are gone. Of Lindbergh? He never got anywhere in politics. Fear of what? Anyone living in our times may not have an explicit answer to that question but lives in the matrix of that fear, nonetheless.

We began this chapter by asking you to consider your greatest fear and to reflect on whether fear has somehow become the cultural metaphor of our era. If it has, what form has it taken and how has this been expressed in our sixty-year experience living with nuclear weapons?

To this point in the book we have discussed at great length the history, politics, policies, and doctrines of the nuclear ages—the *what happened* and *why* perspectives. We would now like to ask you, the reader, to reflect on what you have read, to consider its meanings and implications and how they personally affect you. Are you thinking that this is a trivial issue in the post-cold war second nuclear age, or are you numbed by the awesome power of destruction presented by nuclear weapons, or are you very upset and frustrated that nations and groups still possess or want to possess them, or do you embrace the weapons as the savior of your way of life? We want to invite you to enter the discourse of this chapter in a different frame of mind. To think, or better perhaps, to "sense" differently. We have to realize that we remain human in the face of nuclear weapons and how helpful and unhelpful our human-ness is in confronting the future.

How can we break out of the syndrome of numbing and resignation that is at least partially caused by living in a world with nuclear weapons? How can we recognize that we are all to some degree affected by these weapons, whether we know it or not, whether we want to admit it or not? We believe that intellectual and emotional engagement are required to help provide the will and intentionality necessary to break through the barriers impeding action. That is why this chapter takes the form that it does. It attempts to capture and evoke the essence of what it means to live in the nuclear age. At times the prose may be emotional, metaphorical, angry, and startling, very different from the style of the other chapters. This was done because we are struggling somehow to touch the wellsprings of the issue; to stimulate our own and our readers' consciousness to reveal the true impact and significance of the nuclear danger. We did so as well because this emotive approach expresses what we feel as informed observers of the nuclear predicament and as ordinary citizens who want to learn not only how to live with the predicament but also how to begin to solve it.

We have seen how Hiroshima is a watershed event that has permanently altered our scientific, technological, political, and military landscapes. It has not, however, been widely perceived to have had a comparable impact on our perceptions of self, reality, history, future, and faith. This is not surprising, for often the more important a human event, the more its significance eludes us. Precisely because of its dimensions, the meaning of Hiroshima is difficult to penetrate. The awesome nature of the technology of destruction itself and the resulting psychic "numbing" has inhibited our ability to comprehend the transformations that have occurred. Human beings master new technical skills quickly but are slow to interpret the effect that new technologies have on their nature, their changing values, and their ways of thinking and behaving.

This is particularly true in the second nuclear age, at least until the September 11 attacks. Since the fall of the Berlin Wall in 1989, we have almost managed to forget that we are still living with the specter of nuclear weapons and that for many decades we lived with a fear characterized by apocalyptic anxiety. For most of the last five decades, the nightmare of the massive use of nuclear weapons and possibly even a fiery end seemed real and there were discernable cultural and psychological impacts that we will trace below. Then these fears dissipated somewhat with the end of the Cold War rivalry of the two superpowers. September 11, as we have argued in earlier chapters, has reawakened these fears, making the reactions to the first nuclear age particularly salient again. The problem remains, however, that the nuclear threat is the one we find most difficult to comprehend. Graham Allison noted in his recent book *Nuclear Terrorism* that although 40 percent of Americans reported in 2003 that they worry about a nuclear attack by terrorists, the average American, and even policy makers, have not given the threat sufficient thought and analysis. Nuclear weapons have been with us for so long that although we fear them we don't really think about them and their impact on society and politics. Consequently, we have less of a sense that something must be done to control and even eliminate them, if possible.

It is difficult to recapture the sense of nuclear anxiety that ran through the years of nuclear brinksmanship. It might seem, in the light of the collapse of the Iron Curtain and the subsequent dismantling of the Soviet Union in December 1991, as if a new era of optimism has overtaken the nuclear fears of the Cold War. Indeed, there are genuinely hopeful possibilities in the second nuclear age. However, as we have demonstrated, there are reasons to be cautious. We should not equate dramatic changes in the political configuration of the superpowers with the needed changes in the deep cultural and psychological structures of our world. Although the tension of the Cold War between Russia and the United States has eased, we should not forget that each possesses thousands of nuclear warheads, many under less control than in the past. The danger of nuclear proliferation seems greater; the weapons may soon be in the hands of reckless leaders or terrorist groups. September 11 has given legs to these fears. Since Nagasaki, nuclear weapons have never been used in a war, but they have nearly been on a number of occasions, as we pointed out in earlier chapters. We can hardly put permanent faith in the mixture of restraint and good fortune that has prevailed. The events of recent years, particularly the threats of international terrorism, should give us pause. We have to resist the tendency to believe that nothing needs fundamental changing. A closer examination of the situation has revealed that we still face dangers and that, in fact, we still are anxious about the dangers. The threat of nuclear destruction has receded in our imaginations, replaced by a less focused, less specific anxiety. We have traded one threat for a panoply of others. We now find ourselves afflicted by what existential philosophers call angst: the non-specific worry, the pervasive fear of the ill-at-ease. We, and many other nations, continue to be on edge. And there are good reasons: cities around the world are crumbling, dangerous gaps are opening up between rich and poor; population and consumption are growing without heed to the gradual and inevitable decline of non-renewable resources. And September 11 demonstrated that the United States is hated by many people around the world who want to do us irreparable harm. They may hate us because of who we are and the values we represent or because they perceive the United States as a global bully or because they have distorted a great religious tradition into an ideology of nihilism and death. We are not responsible for what happened to us on that fateful Tuesday, but happen it did. On some level, everything has changed. There have always been death seekers and evil people. The new danger, however, is posed by the extraordinary access the death seekers have to weapons of mass destruction. As the novelist Melvin Jules Bukiet recently put it: "There's a sense that Los Alamos can be found in the family attic these days, everyone has it; everyone's doing it. This is the war of the rest of our lives."[3] There may be a merging, therefore, of nuclear fear with fear of other serious threats such as chemical and biological warfare, a flu pandemic, environmental destruction and global warming. As journalist Peggy Noonan wrote: "We are lucky because for some reason ...the terrorists didn't use a small nuclear weapon floated into New York on a barge in the East River. We are lucky that this didn't turn nuclear, chemical or biological. For ...the next time, and there will of course be a next time, the attack likely won't be 'conventional'."[4]

In any case, the threat of nuclear weapons can be an important warning that draws our attention to the tribalistic and technobureaucratic patterns of dehumanization at work in our emerging postmodern world. By closing ourselves off from the human costs of the devastating weapon, by not thinking about them, we are more able to do the same in relation to other experiences of collective suffering—for example, the 1990s genocides in Bosnia and Rwanda, or the genocide in the Darfur region of Sudan (2003 to present). The habit of denial, of numbing, becomes a way of coping with large human disasters, even if we are not primarily responsible for them. However altered in its expression, the fear of the future initiated by Hiroshima and reinforced by 9/11 remains.

We therefore believe, with journalist Roger Rosenblatt, that even when the implications of the event are not obvious, "Hiroshima survives in the mind, which broods, denies, forgets and eventually must deal with what it saw.... What the people saw after Hiroshima was a fearful vision of the future."[5] It is in this spirit that the young French Algerian Albert Camus wrote a prescient essay in 1946: "We can sum it up in a single phrase: mechanized civilization has just achieved the last degree of savagery.... Already it is hard enough to breathe in this tortured world. But now we are being offered a new form of anguish, which may well be final...."[6] Camus, like Einstein, understood something of history and something of the nature of the transformation created by Hiroshima. It is that vision and transformation we will be discussing below, in terms of the effect nuclear weapons have had on how Americans define their sense of self-worth and ability to control their own lives; their behavior in the social and political arenas; their willingness conceptually and politically to confront the nuclear dangers; and their relationship to such "ultimate" questions as death, immortality, and eschatological hopes for the future. As the journalist Robert Manoff commented: "Nuclear weapons have not and never will be an inert presence in American life. Merely by existing they have already set off chain reactions throughout American society and within every one of its institutions."[7]

At first glance, in the light of the physical and social destruction that would occur if nuclear weapons are ever used again, it seems trivial to concern ourselves with the effects of living under the shadow of the bomb. On second thought, however, a better understanding of how people cope with an unprecedented threat may bring us closer to the heart of the predicament, because it is people who design and build nuclear weapons, who plan strategies and doctrines for their use, and who will either live or die with them.[8]

NUCLEAR DENIAL

The point we would like to stress is the overriding significance, in varying degrees, for each generation after Hiroshima of this threat of historical extinction. Some have responded by being attracted to the weapons; still others, maybe the majority, suffer from an inability to properly confront and deal with their ubiquitous threat—a phenomenon that Robert Jay Lifton calls "psychic numbing." Daniel Lang observed in the *New Yorker* as early as 1946 that many Americans were coping with the atomic threat "by simply refusing to think about it."[9] People try to avoid facing the nuclear danger through several mechanisms. Some simply blot the idea from their consciousness in an extreme form of defensive avoidance. A significant percentage of patients informed that they have cancer, for example, refuse to accept this information as true. The simplest type of defensive avoidance is not exposing oneself to the threatening information—refusing to visit a doctor when one recognizes danger signs—choosing not to read or think about nuclear weapons. The presence of this behavioral tendency is supported by a 1963 public opinion poll, which indicated that people who are most anxious about a nuclear holocaust are often the most badly informed about the weapons.[10]

Others practice displacement activities—they engage in endeavors that are far removed from the life-threatening situation. They immerse themselves in family, work, physical activity, and so on, thereby facilitating the repression of the very real danger that exists. Most people, in fact, simply go about their business as usual as if these weapons did not threaten life itself. However many nuclear weapons exist, however big, powerful, and accurate they are, life goes on. We see a version of this behavior in post-9/11 New York City and Washington. It is now several years after the attack and although people in those cities believe they will be targeted again, they go about their daily lives, rushing to meetings or lunch, shopping, having their nails done, filling sports arenas, as if they did not have a target on their backs. People are still walking briskly through life with their diversions and their plans. There is a disjunction between what they believe will happen and how they act. A high-level intellectualization of this tendency may be deterrence theory itself and those who advocate its implementation in policy. Credible and potent deterrence as an end to the threat of nuclear war may, in fact, be partially a method to rationalize not thinking about nuclear weapons—a way to avoid or obscure their danger. Others take the position that precisely because nuclear weapons are so horrible, they never will be used, or they resign themselves to the belief that nothing can be done to significantly lessen the danger. Still others fall back on a reliance on history: No nuclear weapons have been used in war since 1945. Here history ironically conspires to inhibit the possibility of meaningfully confronting these weapons and recognizing them as fundamentally different from conventional ones. Because the weapons are so horrible and unreal and because, except for the survivors of Hiroshima and Nagasaki, no one has actually experienced the effects of a nuclear explosion and few have even witnessed one, nuclear weapons are particularly difficult to deal with.

THE DOMESTICATION OF NUCLEAR LANGUAGE

Consequently, we domesticate these weapons and we normalize them in the language that we use. Rather than speak about their deadly power, we render them trivial and benign. We have learned to live with the unthinkable and not to think about it. An expression, "to nuke," has become part of the English language. In the spring of 2005 the phrase "the nuclear option" was widely used in Washington and the media to refer not to the use of nuclear weapons but to the threat made by Senate Republicans to eliminate the filibuster option in Senate deliberative procedures during confirmation hearings for federal judges. A popular computer game is entitled, "Duke Nukem." This tendency was explicit in the naming of the two atomic bombs dropped on Japan—the first, "Little Boy," suggesting an innocent little child, the second, "Fat Man," after Winston Churchill. Secretary of War Henry Stimson referred to the weapon in his diary as "the thing," "the dire," "the awful," or "the secret." At Los Alamos, the code name for the bomb was the "Gadget." The Pentagon's atomic-war plans in the early years after Hiroshima bore such code names as Pincher, Broiler, Grabber, and Sizzle. By sanitizing the language of nuclear weapons, we have etherized ourselves to their lethal implications.

Many have pointed to the anesthetizing quality of the language of nuclear weapons, often referred to as "nukespeak."[11] We need to recall here the power of language, that language affects thinking and meaning, and that meaning provides an interpretive frame for reality. Just as there are no uninterpreted facts, there is no unmanipulated language. And we are trapped by the very language that we use. Such words as superiority, inferiority, margin of safety, victory, defeat, and defense make sense when we speak about conventional weapons, but they may have little relevance in the nuclear world. The word "defense" is itself powerfully ironic. At almost the very moment in 1947 when the name of the War Department was changed to the Department of Defense, America lost the capacity to truly defend itself. Today, when there are still thousands of nuclear weapons in the world, it is questionable whether they defend in the traditional sense, in the sense of warding off danger.[12] Yet we use such beguiling metaphors as "nuclear shields," and many people still advocate for missile "defense" systems. Because our perception of reality is largely shaped by the language we use to describe it, using the language of conventional weapons creates the false impression that nuclear weapons are simply bigger and therefore better than conventional ones.

In the nukespeak of the first nuclear age, we find terms like nuclear yield, peacekeeper, surgical strike, city busting, escalation dominance, hardware, delivery systems, reentry vehicles, buses, window of vulnerability, and window of opportunity.[13] Suffering is rendered invisible by sterile words like "megadeaths"; nuclear war is called a "nuclear exchange." Bombs are called "thermonuclear devices." The neutron bomb is called an "enhanced radiation instrument." People are referred to as a nation's "values." Targeting them is referred to as "countervalue targeting." Deployment of weapons to kill people is called "defense." The euphemisms are either emptied of fear or are implicitly reassuring, referring to familiar activities and evoking images that suggest protection and stability, such as umbrella, window, and hardware. In them we find nothing about millions of people incinerated or vaporized, nothing about millions of corpses. Rather, the weapons come to seem ordinary and manageable. Thus the language used to describe them reinforces and contributes to our ability to repress the anxiety produced by the weapons.

People are psychologically resilient enough to come to terms with almost anything. But such adaptation is achieved at a price. The inner knowledge on the part of the post-Hiroshima generations that human beings are capable of initiating a nuclear holocaust creates an undercurrent of anxiety and an uncertainty about human continuity. "Our tragedy," William Faulkner said in his 1950 Nobel Prize address, "is a general and universal fear so long sustained by now that we can even bear it. There are no longer problems of the spirit. There is only the question: When will I be blown up?"[14] To lose the future means to lose the past as well and may be associated with the growing sense of profound historical dislocation—with the decline or disintegration of formerly vital symbols of stability and continuity associated with family, religion, community, and nation. As journalist and critic Dwight MacDonald commented: "Now that we confront the actual, scientific possibility of The End being written to human history and at a not so distant date, the concept of the future, so powerful an element in traditional… thought, loses for us its validity."[15] Consequently, there has been a retreat among the "nuclear haunted" generations, particularly the case in the first nuclear age but certainly true again post-9/11, to the narrowest sliver of the present, to the "illusory" protection of self-interest. On the surface, most people simply go about business as usual as if the threat of technological annihilation did not exist. However, if one probes deeper, one finds evidence that beneath the apathy and repression there resides a pervasive anxiety.[16]

Ever since Hiroshima, the bomb has been a presence and a factor in social, cultural, and intellectual life, even when people have attempted to accommodate to it or to avoid it. In fact, in the years immediately after Hiroshima, the public seemed not to want to deal with the threat of the bomb directly and preferred instead to immerse itself in a culture that supplied numerous diversions and consumer pleasures. To the extent that popular culture dealt with the threat, it did so indirectly through the genre of science fiction films with titles like *The H-Man, The Blob, It,* and *Them*; the revival of *King Kong*; *the Invasion of the Body Snatchers*; dozens of English dubbed movies produced in Japan about radioactive monsters from the deep; and Nevil Shute's 1957 best seller, *On the Beach*, subsequently made into a film. Sublimated nuclear warnings and fears were also present in other less popular films like *Killers from Space, The Beast from 20,000 Fathoms*, and *The Beginning of the End*.

Now the threats are not only coming close, they are hitting us directly. Meteors the size of a small country come down and obliterate the eastern seaboard, volcanoes engulf Los Angeles and creatures from Mars destroy the White House in *Independence Day*. The biggest-grosser of all time, *Titanic*, was really about the destruction of a "world," the sinking of an unsinkable ship and with it the drowning of illusions of safety, invulnerability and permanence. In more recent years there were films like the new version of *Godzilla, Broken Arrow, Peacemaker, Crimson Tide*, and *Armageddon* where nuclear weapons were used to save the world from a meteor about to collide with the earth and the movie version of Tom Clancey's novel *The Sum of All Fears*, where neo-Nazis get their hands on an Israeli nuclear weapon and viewers get to see Baltimore destroyed.

There was also a tendency to trivialize the bomb. Within days of the Hiroshima bombing, bars were selling "Atomic Cocktails," department stores were running "Atomic Sales," tasteless jokes were making the rounds concerning the Japanese suffering from "Atomic Ache," songs were being recorded with titles like "Atom Polka," and MGM was promoting an actress as "The Anatomic Bomb." In 1946 the General Mills Corporation offered an "Atomic 'Bomb' Ring" for 15 cents and a Kix cereal box top. Some 750,000 children ordered rings that year.[17]

Yet there were some more direct and serious confrontations. The 1950s was also the time of bomb shelters and "duck-and-cover" instructions to schoolchildren. Tom Lehrer was singing in 1958 "We Will All Go Together When We Go," at the time of the Berlin crisis, which was discussed in Chapter 5, and Robert Lowell was about to write "Fall 1961," a powerful poem about extinction in nuclear war. The major reaction of the era, however, was to look at the threat with a sidelong glance. People were too close to the initial shock of this horrendous technology of war to deal with it in any other way. As one cultural observer noted in those early years, attempts to make light of the bomb or to avoid serious consideration of its impact were caused by "paralyzing fear."[18]

In the 1960s and 1970s, however, individuals began reacting to the bomb in more explicit ways. The behavior of this particular post-Hiroshima generation was distinctive in ways that suggest roots in nuclear-induced anxieties. These decades, when many of those born in the late 1940s and 1950s reached maturity, were rebellious ones. People questioned authority and challenged sacred institutions and policies—be they related to government, foreign policy, universities, or civil rights. This kind of activity has a plausible connection to the nuclear fear and may in fact be in large part a logical reaction to it. It may be interpreted as a protest against the absurdity of annihilation by a generation devoid of assurance of living on eternally as a species and angry at the "establishment" for passing on this rather hopeless legacy.[19] The 1962 Port Huron Statement, the founding document of the New Left group Students for a Democratic Society (SDS), for example, reflected this sentiment. "Our work is guided by the sense that we may be the last generation in the experiment with living."[20]

Similarly, many members of this generation chose to turn their backs on their class interests and rejected materialism, the conventional family, organized religion, the accepted social, and cultural mores of society and preferred instead a more "natural" life in rural and urban communes, in the joys of vegetarianism and holistic healing, organic farming, and so on. More contemporary versions of this utopian tendency are found among "survivalist" groups who are preparing for the "event" so that they can somehow survive it and among those who advocate space colonization as a method to en-sure biological survival. Those who "opt" out may be seeking survival in a return to nature, in mysti-cal traditions, in a commitment to communalism, in a revival of nineteenth century rugged individualism, or in space travel; but they all agree on the fundamental rejection of and desire to es-cape from the harsh realities of what appears to be a self-destructive world,[21] even extending into the second nuclear age. The mass suicide of dozens of "Heaven's Gate" followers in 1997 in California may have been an extreme example of this tendency.

Others were so deeply disturbed by the world they were about to inherit that they responded with cynicism and mockery. Some observers as early as 1945–1946 anticipated an era in the near future of hedonistic self-indulgence caused by nuclear-induced anxiety.[22] A striking pattern of behavior that emerged in the 1960s and 1970s, for example, was a dramatic rejection of the social and sexual mores of society. During those decades there was a great preoccupation with intensified forms of experi-ence via drugs, sex, rock music, meditation, dance, religion, and even politics. During times of crisis and anxiety, people tend to gravitate towards physical and immediate pleasures.[23] Consequently, some form of hedonism may also be a plausible reaction to the threat of nuclear holocaust. When ex-istence itself is threatened, people seek to do more with or to their bodies, to stretch the possibilities of human pleasure. The nuclear generation that came of age in the 1960s and 1970s had about it a sense of urgency, both to produce political and social change and to cram all the personal pleasure and experience possible into what might be a short lifetime.[24] A very large number of people regarded the future as so deeply terrible that it hardly warranted planning for and they preferred to concern themselves with more immediate, gratifying, and manageable pleasures. As one young person re-flected: "It's terrifying to think that the world may not be here in a half-hour, but I'm still going to live for now." Or, as another remarked: "Sometimes when I think that there may be no future at all, I feel just like letting myself go. Why wait?"[25]

There are obviously other plausible explanations for this behavior. For example, student protests are a recurrent feature of social history. The unpopular Vietnam war and military draft were further inducements to political activism. Changes in sexual mores may have been as much due to advances in birth control technology as anything else. Attitudes toward work and career are affected by eco-nomic considerations and demographic realities. The levels of anxiety and apathy were intensified by the very size of the Baby Boom generation that faced stiff competition in an America of apparent shrinking economic opportunities. Apathy and alienation may have been caused as much by the reve-lations concerning World War II death camps, the assassinations of the Kennedys and Martin Luther King, and Watergate as by the nuclear threat.[26]

Nevertheless, we maintain that one important factor contributing to the behavior of that genera-tion was their nuclear-induced anxiety. As Erich Fromm has argued, one can appropriately speak of the nuclear generation as being composed of new types of persons who turn away from life and trans-form all life into objects, including themselves. "Sexuality becomes a technical skill"; love is equated with genital stimulation; radio personalities promote the virtues of "good sex"; "joy, the ex-pression of intense aliveness, is replaced by 'fun' or 'excitement'; and whatever love and tenderness people have is directed toward machines and gadgets. The world becomes a sum of lifeless artifacts," from artificial food to artificial hearts. Life has become technique.[27]

The complex psychological link between atomic destruction and Eros raises some interesting possibilities. The first postwar atomic test in 1946 in the Bikini atoll in the North Pacific led a French fashion designer to name his new revealing bathing suit the "bikini." Dr. Helen Caldicott has underscored the phallic symbolism of the bomb and missiles in terms of "missile envy." Elongated missiles, erupting and ejecting their warheads, are phallic symbols. Even some of the names associated with these weapons are laden with psychosexual allusions; missile erector, thrust, deep penetration, soft lay down.[28] There may be a perverse identification with the bomb on the societal level, an anticipation of oblivion experienced as ecstasy, as a cosmic orgasm, related to the objectification of immediate and intense sensory pleasures on the individual level. Even our omnicidal weapons have become objects of psychosexual adoration. We see this nuclear high portrayed sarcastically in the 1964 Stanley Kubrick film *Dr. Strangelove: Or, How I Learned to Stop Worrying and Love the Bomb*, in which a pilot straddles the bomb on its way to its target while uttering a wild Texas yodel.

According to Fromm, why is there objectification of sexuality in American culture? It may be because of the profound threat posed by nuclear weapons, the threat of meaninglessness, of an absurd mass death caused by a horribly nondiscriminating weapon. Long-term, substantial, and authentic commitments of an emotional and social nature are problematical risks under the best of circumstances; in an unstable, unpredictable world that may end, they carry such risks or show so few promises of dividends that many people find commitments and social conventions increasingly difficult to accept. They prefer to direct their libidinous energies to objects that can be manipulated, controlled, interchanged and collected. In a world characterized by impermanence, people seem to revert to the false security and pleasure provided by "stuff," to the "haven" of the cluttered room.

They also may revert to self-inflicted pain. The phenomenon of extreme body decoration—the tattooing, piercing, scarring and branding that borders on self-mutilation and that became increasingly popular in the 1990s, is itself an expression of uncertainty. Body piercing fashion has been marked by a kind of escalation, a sort of ring race. Highly visible contravention of the social rules reveal a new and more subtle lesson about cultural unease. In a strange way, these trends can be seen as attempts to get the body back, a way of coping with anxiety, an attempt at getting cultural insecurity under control. The decline of straightforward anxiety into this extreme anxiety is the movement of a culture that has lost faith in its promise of security. To decorate the physical body, especially in painful ways, is to reclaim its natural reality. The statement is simple: I exist; I am in pain; therefore I am material; I am alive. Here body mutilation, a self-conscious toying with primitiveness, is a political act. It marks a rejection of modernity, a rejection of the increasing meaninglessness of life. It is a symptom of the multi-layered forms that anxiety about the future now often takes.[29]

This tendency to objectify pleasure and pain is depicted with great force in Dan DeLillo's panoramic 1997 novel, *Underworld*. In this 827-page work, DeLillo's wake for the Cold War, the discontinuity of American cultural life is primarily caused by nuclear weapons. Everything changed in 1945 when the power of the atom was unleashed and fear was institutionalized five years later when the Soviet Union began to achieve rough parity. Cosmic might was now being wielded by mortal hands and by the state. The prologue of the novel is called "The Triumph of Death." In the end, the bombs did not go off and death didn't triumph. It just ruled the social and psychological landscape for 50 years. Nick Shay, the protagonist of the novel, works for a company called Waste Containment, a powerful and suggestive metaphor for life in the post-nuclear age. We live with and must process, like Nick, the sludge, the excreta, the junk of the nuclear age. There is human waste that can be disposed of. But then there is nuclear waste that never goes away, that threatens our health, our existence. In the epilogue, Shay visits the Museum of Mishapens in Semipolatinsk, the test site of 500 nuclear explosions. He sees fetuses preserved in Heinz pickle jars. "There is the two-headed specimen. There is the normal head that is located... perched on the right shoulder."[30] All our better feelings took a beating during these decades, according to DeLillo. An ambient mortal fear constrained us. Love, even parental love, got harder to do.

THE PSYCHOLOGICAL IMPACT OF NUCLEAR WEAPONS

There certainly are other causes contributing to this behavior, including the anomie pervasive in a sprawling, urbanized, technological society without the familiar supports provided by family, community, religion, and shared values. Yet central is the anxiety deriving from the sense that all forms of human connection are perhaps pointless because they are subject to a sudden, total end. The psychological consequences of this atmosphere of futurelessness are just beginning to reveal themselves. What are the implications for childhood development, personality formation, individual values, expectations, and self-projection? What are the effects on the family structure? What is the impact on cultural values and social mores?[31]

Studies have indicated "the ubiquitous presence of the bomb at some level of people's minds."[32] Michael Carey, a psychoanalytic researcher, conducted a research project in the early and mid-1970s to determine what impact the nuclear air-raid drills of the 1950s and other aspects of nuclear weapons had on people of his generation. He found that many of his subjects described a general feeling of death anxiety that manifested itself in frequent dreaming about nuclear catastrophe. Others described extended periods of avoidance or the feeling that nothing is permanent, that nothing can be depended on, that life is absurd,[33] as Bob Dylan mused in his 1963 song, "Talkin' World War III Blues."[34] Similarly, the 1980 *Rock Music Song Book* listed over 40 songs that have as their theme imminent nuclear disaster with titles like "So Long Mom," "We Will All Go Together When We Go," "Political Science," "The End," "Eve of Destruction," "Judgement Day," "A Hard Rain's Gonna Fall," "Waiting for the End of the World," and "I'm Scared."[35] Nuclear fear has been a prominent theme in the songs of rock groups like Van Halen, Iron Maiden, and the Sex Pistols. After years of neglect, movies and television began in the 1980s to be drawn to the themes of how a nuclear conflict might begin (*War Games*), and its impact on specific communities ranging from Sheffield, England (*Threads*), to Kansas City (*The Day After*), to northern California (*Testament*).[36]

A 1982 Gallup Poll reported that some 47 percent of the respondents believed that nuclear war is likely within five years, and about half of those felt that they would not survive such a war.[37] Recent public opinion polls indicate that a majority of Americans expect the United States to be attacked again by terrorists, this time using weapons of mass destruction. We live in a world with thousands of nuclear weapons and dangerous germs and chemicals that can be harnessed and used to kill entire populations. It takes only a few hundred or thousand bright, resourceful, determined people to harness and deploy these weapons. September 11 left a deep psychic wound on the American consciousness. Below the sense of fatalism and acceptance—it's going to happen anyway so why worry about it—that seems to characterize the response of so many Americans is a deep-seated apprehension and numbing fear. In fact, growing up in a social environment that seems to tolerate and ignore the nuclear threat tends to foster those patterns of personality development that can lead to a sense of cynical resignation and apathy. The opposite of love is not hate, as writer Elie Wiesel has often reflected, it is indifference.

For children and adolescents, optimism about a livable future largely depends on the sense of security provided by the adult world. Eric Erikson has emphasized the importance for the child of gaining a sense of basic trust early in life. Without it, one's self confidence and creativity can be damaged. Without this sense of security, the perception of the self as competent, as an active agent who can change reality, may be underdeveloped.[38]

Again, DeLillo in *Underworld*, has a schoolteacher in the 1950s (a nun) issue her class dog tags. "Then Sister told them to place their dog tags out above their shirts and blouses so she could see them. …The tags were designed to help rescue workers identify children who were lost, missing, injured, maimed, mutilated, unconscious or dead in the hours following the onset of atomic war. … She said, 'Woe betide the child who is… wearing someone else's tag.'"[39] Nuclear war never happened during the Cold War, but a generation of children "ducked and covered" hoping to be shielded from the end of the world. Notwithstanding the absurdity of the exercise, they could not be shielded from the sense that life was not secure and that it was pervaded by an unknowable terror.

A study performed by a special task force of the American Psychiatric Association by Drs. John Mack and William Beardslee between 1978 and 1981 and similar studies conducted by the *Houston Post*, the *Boston Globe*, and other scholars demonstrated a consistent apprehension among children and adolescents, an alarm about what nuclear war might do to all of us.[40] What comes through is their sense of powerlessness, of the insecurity of life, but also an anger and frustration directed at the adult world that created this situation. Collectively, these young people indicate that the nuclear threat is too terrible to contemplate; when they do think about it they feel angry and helpless. They learn to cope either by living for the present, by persuading themselves that nuclear war will never happen, or that, if it does, they will be on the winning side, by putting hope in bomb shelters or missile defense initiatives and, probably, most of the time, by repressing the fear. Some representative comments are indicative of their feelings. An 11-year-old girl commented: "I don't know, I feel there's a nuclear war going on inside me. It's terrible."[41] One 17-year-old young woman said: "As for a career, it seems like it is a waste to go to college and to build up a career and then get blown up someday."[42] Another said: "Mommy, I don't think I'll ever have a baby."[43] A teenage woman reflected in 2001 on the ways she is feeling differently about her future after September 11. She thinks about it "every day."[44] Finally a nine-year old remarked: "I sometimes think that I'd rather be dead because then I could go up to heaven and I wouldn't have to worry about all this stuff about nuclear war."[45]

The implications of such studies have become the subject of some disagreement. Robert Coles, a Harvard University child psychiatrist, believes that the children who were most affected by the nuclear threat tended to be from middle- and upper-class families whose parents are themselves involved in the nuclear freeze or disarmament movements. Working-class children, by and large, were not emotionally touched by this fear. Class, for Coles, seems to be a primary determinant in how children sort themselves out on the issue.[46] For many American children, poverty and inequality seem to be more pressing concerns.

Obviously, the nuclear threat does not exist in a vacuum. It coexists with a wide range of other factors that affect psychological and emotional development. Yet, because of its extraordinary nature, it seems likely, and there is growing evidence to support the claim, that at least among large segments of the population, it has contributed to, if not substantially accounted for, much of what is psychologically troubling to many people on the societal level—feelings of dislocation, unidentified dangers, insecurity, aimlessness, and loneliness. The threat of nuclear war may be a possible contributor to the increase in family disruption, drug abuse, heightened loneliness, and despair, and behaviors such as body mutilation. Parental authority may be weakened because children sense that parents cannot fulfill their primary responsibility, that of providing security. Because the permanence of any relationship is thrown into question, the institution of the family itself may be threatened. There may be a greater reluctance to marry and to bring children into the world. There is also some evidence that the nuclear shadow has altered normal economic planning. Several studies have shown that the fear of nuclear war has diminished people's willingness to save for future use. The image of futurelessness may also be contributing to the high divorce rates and the decision of many people to avoid long-term commitments by living together. As writer and biologist Lewis Thomas reflected: "What I cannot imagine, what I cannot put up with...is what it must be like to be young. How do the young stand it? How can they keep their sanity? If I were very young, sixteen or seventeen years old, I think I would begin perhaps very slowly and imperceptively to go crazy."[47]

These responses to nuclear threats seem to be particularly potent in the United States. When we examine public reactions around the globe, particularly in Europe, we may see something quite different. Europeans often argue that Americans have an unrealistic expectation of security, the product of living for centuries "protected" by two oceans. Europeans claim that they know what it is like to live with ambiguity and to live adjacent to evil powers—hence their greater tolerance for threats that may be posed by the ayatollahs of Iran, al Qaeda, or North Korea. Americans talk of threats while Europeans talk of challenges.[48] A poll of European and American opinion taken in the summer of 2002 clearly revealed this transatlantic gap in perceptions of threat. Asked to identify which threats to vital interests were extremely important, the results indicated many more Americans than Europeans worried about the threat posed by international terrorism (91 percent versus 65 percent), Islamic fundamentalism (61 percent versus 49 percent), tensions between India and Pakistan (54 percent versus 32 percent), the development of China as a world power (59 percent versus 19 percent) and political turmoil in Russia (27 percent versus 15 percent).[49] September 11 clearly impacted the peoples of the two continents differently. Americans know they were attacked and expect to be the target again whereas Europeans have never really believed they are next. They have empathy for American suffering but that empathy may be circumscribed by a different world view and perspective. Two of the issues that most clearly divide Europeans and Americans today are a philosophical disagreement over where mankind stands on the continuum between the laws of power and violence and the laws of reason and rights and America's role as the policeman of the continuum.

THE BOMB AND THE CULTURAL IMAGINATION

Literature provides further evidence for the presence of a debilitating alienation and angst felt by many in contemporary society. It is through literature and poetry and what might be called "high-cultural" reflections that people strive to express, often in new comparisons and metaphors, things beyond the sphere of easy perception and observation. This is especially true when language tries to lead to where our senses and our intellect find it hard to follow. Humans can speak only in metaphor of the infinite and the unfathomable. If people wish to describe the indescribable, they can often only do so by "poetry." Even science, when it reaches its deepest fundamentals, is forced to use the symbols and metaphors of "poetry." It is the intellectuals, writers, and poets among us who have the fine-tuned sensibilities to perceive and articulate what many of the rest of us are only beginning to feel and understand.

In E. L. Doctorow's novel, *The Book of Daniel* these themes of alienation, despair, and meaninglessness are brilliantly explored. The novel is a thinly fictionalized version of the Ethel and Julius

Rosenberg spy case of the late 1940s and early 1950s. The defendants and their two coconspirators were alleged to have been participants in a plot aimed at obtaining national defense information for the Soviet Union. But the crux of the matter was the accusation that the Rosenbergs had stolen the secrets of the atomic bomb and passed them on to the Soviet Union. From the moment of their arrests until their executions on June 19, 1953, in the electric chair at Sing Sing Prison, they proclaimed their innocence. They were the only Americans in U.S. history ever executed for espionage by judgment of a civil court. This was also the first double execution of a husband and wife in American history. The peculiarities and poignancy of the case have inspired not only numerous histories, but also poems, plays, novels, television documentaries, and, a major motion picture based on Doctorow's powerful novel. It still speaks to us of great contemporary concerns: the abuse of secrecy by governmental agencies; the inability of national leaders to properly confront the realities of nuclear weaponry; and the hysteria of the Cold War years.

Doctorow incorporates the Rosenberg story into a larger family drama: that of a son searching to determine the truth about his parents and through this quest finally coming to terms with their values and legacy; and that of a daughter who is psychologically crushed by their fate, a victim of the hysteria created by the nuclear fear. Rage and meaninglessness are at the heart of *Daniel*, a book about children whose parents were convicted and executed for conspiracy to commit atomic espionage. The rage exists both on the personal level, since the two children obviously feel greatly aggrieved, and on a broader political plane. While the book avoids explicit evidence as to the guilt or innocence of the executed couple, it expresses enormous outrage over their fate. The double execution of the Rosenbergs that *The Book of Daniel* powerfully depicts cannot be understood outside of the context of Cold War hysteria, blacklisting, McCarthyism, Red-baiting, and anti-Semitism that characterized this period of American history. The political and psychological travail of the children may serve as an analogue for an entire generation of post-Hiroshima youths searching for meaning within absurdity. It may also provide a warning concerning the dangers of racial profiling and scapegoating as applied to Muslims and people of Middle Eastern origins in the United States today.

Meaninglessness and absurdity of different sorts have become almost stereotyped characterizations of twentieth-century life, central themes in modern art, politics, and theater. In what other age would Franz Kafka's haunting characters, unaware of place and identity, metamorphosized into grotesque, alienated insects, have been so celebrated? The possibility of nuclear holocaust makes us doubt that anything we create will last. We find examples of what Lifton calls the "new ephemeralism" in the literary works of Norman Mailer, the poetry of Alan Ginsberg, the novels of Gunter Grass, Kurt Vonnegut, Ken Kesey, Thomas Pynchon, Joseph Heller, and William Burroughs—even the unlikely connection of a pseudo-kabbalistic mysticism and nuclear dread in a novel by Chaim Potok entitled *The Book of Lights*.[50] The theme of waste, particularly nuclear waste, provides the landscape for Delillo's *Underworld*, a novel of betrayal and innocence abused. Poets have applied themselves to the theme of living in the nuclear age perhaps more imaginatively and consistently than film makers and fiction writers. They can attempt to get at the meaning of nuclear weapons in a more creative, imagistic fashion. Many well-known poets such as Robert Penn Warren, Marc Kaminsky, Campbell McGrath, Philip Levine, and Denise Levertov have focused on the issue. McGrath in "Nagasaki, Uncle Walt, the Eschatology of America's Century," examined how the atomic bombings had affected his entire generation. He noted that young people had "invested so much in World War III it seems a shame to miss it."[51] In the visual arts, as Lifton has pointed out, "we find increasing acceleration in shifts in styles and movements ... from pop art... to kinetic art, to minimalist, to conceptual art, to photorealism."[52] Furthermore, there are artists who directly grapple with the themes of destruction and impermanence. Some conceptual artists, like Peter Hutchinson, who placed works under water, designed art out of perishable materials that were meant to gradually disintegrate as if to underscore the ephemeral nature of contemporary civilization. In a world that could witness the destruction of a city in seconds or, in the view of some, could countenance the deterioration of traditional democratic freedoms in the United States during the Rosenberg case, and other episodes since, there are no permanent values, no permanent institutions.

DEATH AND DYING

Even the security or sense of purpose provided by the anticipation of a meaningful death has been seriously undermined. The prospect of nuclear war poses a basic challenge to what has been one of humanity's most universal problems—the attempt to come to terms with death and dying. Death is anticipated as a severance of connection—or severance from the inner sense of organic relationship to nature and particularly to the people most necessary to feelings of continuity and relatedness. Death therefore threatens to bring about that which is most intolerable: total severance, total nothingness.[53]

Existentialist philosopher Martin Heidegger and others have pointed out that people understand themselves largely in terms of the deaths they anticipate. If, for example, an individual is a devout theist who believes in reward and punishment and life after death, that person will understand and presumably live his or her life differently than an individual who is a committed secularist. Their philosophies of life are different because their views of death are different.[54]

Individual death is not the only death that affects the way people live. Because humans are social beings who define themselves naturally as parts of families, societies, kinship groups, religions, nations, and humanity as a whole, how they view themselves will depend largely on whether they anticipate the continuing existence of these social entities. In the prenuclear age, the individual obviously dies, but the social unit, the nation, the family, the species, was understood as outliving death.[55]

But in the nuclear age, we must anticipate nuclear death as a collective experience, what Norman Cousins called "irrational death"—death of a new kind, a nondiscriminating death without warning, death *en masse*. While all deaths are individual, in the mass deaths of the twentieth century, be they at Auschwitz or at Hiroshima and Nagasaki, and obviously on a much smaller scale on 9/11, the individual is lost in a faceless, mindless, random destruction. Writer Norman Mailer described the transformation as follows:

> For the first time in civilized history, perhaps for the first time in all history, we have been forced to live with the suppressed knowledge that the smallest facets of our personality or the most minor projections of our ideas...might be doomed to die as a cipher in some vast statistical operation in which our teeth would be counted, and our hair would be saved, but our death itself unknown, unhonored and unrewarded, a death which could not follow with dignity as a possible consequence to serious actions we have chosen, but rather a death in a gas chamber or a radioactive city; and so...in the midst of civilization...our psyche was subjected itself to the intolerable anxiety that death being causeless, life was causeless as well, and time deprived of cause and effect had come to a stop.[56]

If the type of death we anticipate is important because it affects how we view ourselves in the world, then the pervasive fear of nuclear annihilation does not necessarily tell us anything about death per se, but rather it reveals something about the perception humans have of their place and worth in the world.[57]

Nuclear weapons challenge a basic belief in the importance of the individual. They challenge possibly the most central tenet of the Judeo-Christian world view: Each individual is unique and important and created in the image of God. If you save one life it is like saving the entire world, the Talmud teaches. "God so loved the world that He gave His only begotten son," John says. Now, we are haunted with the image of human beings as objects, as matter, to be burned, radiated, turned into ashes or vapor. In the nuclear age, vaporization has replaced organic decay as the metaphor of death. When the bomb fell on Hiroshima, people not only witnessed a weapon of unprecedented destructive power; they saw one more proof of their insignificance. What meaning can one's individual life have when all human life might vanish at any time? We live in a world of "virile weapons and impotent men," the French historian Raymond Aron wrote in 1983, a world that has engendered feelings of powerlessness and profound meaninglessness; a world where humans find themselves severed from virtually all their notions of connection and worth, including their struggle to maintain symbolic paths to immortality. And this is not a trivial matter. The need for symbolic immortality, as psychiatrist Robert Jay Lifton has argued, seems to be basic to humans. It "can be expressed biologically... by living on through one's community, nation, race, species; theologically, in the notion of life after death or in the spiritual conquest of death; creatively, through one's work, books, poems, paintings and influences large and small, that exist beyond one's death; or through identification with eternal, cyclical nature."[58] In each case, the individual contributes to something of value that survives him. Death is not the end.

Nuclear weapons, however, challenge these notions of symbolic immortality and connectedness because they threaten not only biological death but also ontological death, what Jonathan Schell refers to as the "second death "—a rendering into nothingness of that which constitutes the world and human relatedness to it, including memory, history, the sense of individuality, and belief in the inevitability of progress. Nuclear weapons, unlike all other weapons, even the incredibly destructive chemical and biological weapons, have the power to turn everything into nothing. In a nuclear war-ravaged world, as Schell has powerfully argued, we cannot imagine the survival of nations, culture, works, or innocence, and even the idea of an afterlife may not be sufficiently convincing to quell the anxieties of total severance.[59]

Joyce Maynard, in *Looking Back: A Chronicle of Growing Up in the Sixties*, wrote that "what especially alarmed me about the bomb... was the possibility of total obliteration. All traces of me would be destroyed. There would be no grave and if there were, no one left to visit it."[60] Woody Allen, whose humor is so obsessed with death, put it another way: "Eternal nothingness is O.K. as long as you are dressed for it." The devastation of nuclear war, of course, belies the notion that one can be ready and "dressed" for immortality. Yet, despite doubts, many are still inclined to want to believe in an afterlife. Again, Allen: "I don't believe in an afterlife, although I am bringing a change of underwear just in case."[61] A nuclear holocaust would make this hedging of one's theological bets quite ineffective. Even the immortality symbolized by nature, as Schell has argued, would be threatened by the destruction of a nuclear war. Writer Lewis Thomas expressed the pathos experienced by the fear of omnicide as follows: "I cannot listen to Mahler's Ninth Symphony with anything like the old melancholy mixed with high pleasure I used to take from the music. Now...I cannot listen to the last movement...without the door-smashing intrusion of a huge new thought: death everywhere, the dying of everything, the end of humanity... ."[62]

NUCLEARISM

Pathos, however, has not been the only response to this anticipation of the "death of death." Some have perversely identified with these weapons of mass destruction. Lifton refers to this phenomenon as "nuclearism," "the passionate embrace of nuclear weapons as a solution to [human] anxieties, especially anxieties concerning the weapons themselves... ."[63] The fact that nuclear death threatens the profound meaning of life itself may in part account for the attraction some feel for these weapons and their use, for this serves as a way of denying the very anxiety they experience. Most people fear death, and some deal with this fear by actually toying with death as a way of gaining power or control over their mortality. On a trivial level, video games enable players to vaporize planets and stars. A rock group calls itself the B-52s. The Grateful Dead until the death of its leader Jerry Garcia on August 9, 1995, the fiftieth anniversary of the Nagasaki bomb, remained a persistent cultural artifact of the 1960s.

This counterphobic mechanism may indeed also be operating in many of the scientists, engineers, nuclear planners, and theorists who make up the nuclear "priesthood." They and all who are attracted to these weapons, in one of the ultimate human ironies, may seek in the technology of nuclear destruction a source of power, of life.[64] At the root of this tendency is the struggle to achieve power by controlling death. As anthropologist Ernest Becker argued in *The Denial of Death*, there is a tendency of wanting to kill in order to affirm one's own life. By killing an enemy we have symbolically killed death, we have attempted to forestall our own deaths.[65] It may also have something to do with the fetishising and worship of technology that seems peculiar to recent times. Technology, the systematic study (logos) and exercise of skill (teknai), has been with us as long as we have used tools. We have not always believed, however, that we could destroy the world using the tools we have invented, or that we could usher in new forms of consciousness through the virtual realities of cyberspace we developed. Now our tools seem tools no longer. We do not use technology; it uses us, it stands over us, sometimes threatening, sometimes seductively beckoning.

There is nothing about nuclear necrophilia, however, that suggests deliberate evil. Those who are attracted to nuclear weapons and even nuclear war may be influenced by the powerful urge to avoid evil, to avoid anxiety, as Becker pointed out in *Escape From Evil*: "Men cause evil by wanting heroically to triumph over it, because man is a frightened animal...who will not admit his own insignificance, that he cannot perpetuate himself and his group forever... ."[66] So if we accept Lifton's concept of "nuclearism," and the notion that it has little to do with evil, then we may also have to accept that it is humanity's genius or character which propels it to the possible ultimate misfortune. As Erich Fromm argues in *On Disobedience* and *The Heart of Man*, the fundamental choice for humans, inasmuch as they seek fulfillment, is to choose either acts of creation or acts of destruction, either to love or to kill. "Only part of us is sane," Rebecca West writes, "only part of us loves pleasure and the longer day of happiness, wants to live to our nineties and die in peace....The other half of us is nearly mad. It...loves pain and its darker night despair, and wants to die in a catastrophe that will set life back to its beginnings and leave nothing of our house save its blackened foundations."[67]

This life-denying tendency has also found expression among certain fundamentalist Christian groups who, in their literal reading of biblical imagery, equate nuclear holocaust with Armageddon and seem to welcome the event as a confirmation of their view of human sinfulness and as a necessary "cleansing."[68] They infuse new meaning in such biblical passages as "The heavens shall pass away with a great noise, and the elements shall melt with fervent heat, the earth also and the works that are therein shall be burned up."[69] They construct a loose tie between religious end-of-the-world imagery and nuclear threat. In that way they do precisely what other religious thinking cannot do: provide an immortality system that includes nuclear disaster as a vehicle for the end of human history and the beginning of a new spiritual era.

This type of anticipatory religious thinking may also help account for the phenomenally successful "Left Behind" series of novels by Tim LaHaye and Jerry B. Jenkins that have sold tens of millions of copies since 1995. The twelfth and last book in the series, *The Glorious Appearing* was published in 2004. They are loosely based on the fundamentalist doctrines of "premillennialism" or "dispensationalism"—in essence, the idea that Christ will return to earth in the not-so-distant future and sweep soul-saved Christians into rapture, leaving nonbelievers to face the horrors of the apocalypse before the everlasting reign of God is established.

In an age of ultimate weapons capable of annihilating the human race, apocalyptic fantasies are understandable, but they are exceedingly dangerous. Apocalyptic belief is a way of overcoming what Mircea Eliade calls the "terror of history" and is the result of a desperate search for order.[70] It must be comfortable and assuring to believe that one's future and that of the world will be taken care of by God in a flash near the end of time as part of a divine plan. A 1980 Jehovah's Witnesses circular said, for example, "that...the approach of Armageddon should not be a cause for fear, but for real hope! Why? Because Armageddon is God's way to cleanse the earth of all wickedness, paving the way for a bright, prosperous new order!"[71]

There is a connection, as well, between nuclear threat and the worldwide spread of fundamentalism. Fundamentalism in general, including its political forms, stems from the loss, or fear of loss, of fundamentals. Nuclear weapons fueled that fear. A version of the same thinking motivates al Qaeda and Osama bin Laden. As *New York Times* columnist Thomas Friedman wrote: "Their deed was their note: we want to destroy America, starting with its military and financial centers. Which part of that sentence don't people understand? … These terrorists aren't out for a new kind of coexistence with us. They are out for our non-existence".[72] In a videotaped statement after the attacks, Osama bin Laden claimed that God had struck America through the terrorists.[73] What is going on isn't a battle between Islam and the West but a human conflict between what Freud describes as a battle between the life-affirming forces of eros, versus the forces towards Thanatos, towards death. Islam is the context but at their core the terrorists are deeply nihilistic, death-loving people. The problem with all apocalypticism, however, is that no one has to plan for the future because God has already determined the final battleground and knows who the enemies will be in that cosmic conflict. It doesn't matter what the peacemakers do, it doesn't matter how many arms treaties come about between Russia and the United States. In al Qaeda's eyes, it doesn't even matter what the United States ultimately does in the Middle East. The die is already cast and we simply have to play our appropriate roles. This is theological determinism with a vengeance. It must be distinguished from older images of the "end of days." "Terrifying as these may be,they are part of a world view or cosmology—man is acted upon by a higher power...who destroys only for spiritual purposes (such as achieving 'the kingdom of God'). That is a far cry from man's destruction of himself with his own tools, and to no purpose."[74]

This impulse to make the weapons themselves objects of pseudo-religious adoration and anticipation may be the ultimate idolatry. The prophets of monotheism did not denounce pagan religions as idolatrous because of the worship of several gods, but rather because people spent their energies and intellects on building objects and then worshipped these objects as idols, as gods. The ultimate idolatry, and hence the ultimate alienation, may be nuclearism because it is the weapons themselves, objects of human creativity that still stand over and threaten the future of the species itself, which inflame mutual distrust and which have become our nemesis, more than any ideological differences between nations.

NUCLEAR NORMALITY: LIVING WITH NUCLEAR PEACE

What may have emerged in the post-Cold War period until 9/11 is a species of nuclear normality, an unrealistic interlude, a sense of relief rather than "numbing," the idea that we are now living in a world that has seen or will soon be able to see reduction of the likelihood of nuclear war to an "acceptable" level, even though the threat has not been removed totally. September 11 brought us back to reality. What may emerge, however, is a "new realism," the notion that our best hope for the future lies in living with the weapons in this new era of nuclear anxiety. That will be seen as appropriate "realism." Imagining that we could be involved in actively shaping history will run up against our sense of powerlessness and normality. "That's the best that we can hope for," may emerge as the new refrain. Finding the will and imagination to think about a world without nuclear weapons; to develop effective disarmament solutions; to control proliferation; to effectively prosecute the war on terror; to find creative ways to implement a rational world order, may remain difficult to generate because there is no longer a recognized "evil empire" threatening our collective well-being, although there is a threat of international terrorism.

Our response to this terrorism may also be problematic. In the imagery of an "evil empire" in the Cold War and its contemporary analogue in the "evil" of terrorism, the threat seems more political than technological and nuclear weapons-centered. People often reach for the easy answer. It wasn't the weapons themselves that threatened us—in fact, they helped keep us safe so we could make it to the great transformation of 1990–1991. Rather, it was the existence of evil people armed with nuclear weapons. And that relief or illusion lasted until September 11 when we "rediscovered" that bad people still exist and they want nuclear weapons. But, there is the danger that we may assume there is a relatively quick and relatively cheap fix to this problem. If we can eliminate the bin Ladens and the Saddam Husseins of the world and pacify their power bases and their countries then the threat dissipates. Many are adopting something like the National Rifle Association's take on guns and crime—criminals kill, guns don't. Separate the criminals from the guns, the evil people from nuclear weapons, and we can live in a nuclear armed peace. After all, we don't expect the British to attempt to end civilization or that the United States would do so.

And then there is the additional irony that we may be distracting ourselves from directly facing our predicament, as we did in the 1950s, by engaging in displacement behavior of various kinds as we obsess on the tragedy of 9/11. Some Americans are thinking about and agonizing over what responsibility the nation must carry for that tragedy—a completely unjustified atrocity that was not deserved—as though being victimized requires accepting some guilt. We are not guilty. We are investigating the failures of policy and security of 9/11 and while we investigate and analyze we may be contributing to the next tragedy. We have created a new version of the "Red Scares" of the 1920s as domestic threats are turned into actions and policies that threaten civil liberties of people with Middle Eastern origins or appearances. Our focus seems to be on the war against terror and on domestic security and although important they are not the only sources of the danger we face. The more we focus on 9/11, the more we engage in displacement behavior motivated by fear or manipulated by leaders, the less energy, will, and intelligence will be available to focus on realistic risk assessments and prevention techniques to foil the next attack, or on ideas on how to limit proliferation or how to reduce further the thousands of nuclear weapons still extant.

Why aren't we addressing the real dangers? In part it is because people are just not good at facing future threats. We face the dangers of today while thinking of the dangers of yesterday. And our concern is that as the immediate dangers recede somewhat it becomes even more difficult to think oneself through to the unthinkable. We may become complacent again, distracted by "homeland security" campaigns, multi-colored terror alerts, confusing public warnings about the risk of attack alongside soothing official exhortations to enjoy life and live life normally, or emboldened by successful wars against weak opponents like Iraq, and susceptible to the false illusion that security may be near. Some believe that politicians have willfully exploited the terror threat for political gain. This alleged political manipulation of fear may result in increasing levels of anxiety for some and indifference and numbing for others. In either case, it blunts our ability to accurately gauge what we may truly be facing.

This feeling of nuclear normality perpetuates the illusion that we can, in fact, expect to live with nuclear weapons. Language again conspires to obscure the uniqueness of nuclear weapons. We speak today of "weapons of mass destruction"—the triumvirate of nuclear, chemical and biological weapons. This terminology creates a generalized notion of danger but does not encourage specific reflections on the unique characteristics of these technologies. Nuclear weapons really should stand alone. Chemical and biological weapons do not threaten the end of history, the "second death" that Schell talks about. The term, weapons of mass destruction, represents a way of taming weapons by renaming them. The language obscures and muffles the reality. This new sense of nuclear normality, combined with the seduction of "realism" may convince us that the greater degree of security we are enjoying in the short term is, in fact, real security. We may, therefore, be more unwilling to take the kinds of political and military risks that would lead us to a nuclear-free world. If we are lulled into complacency by nuclear normality we may miss a critical opportunity to fundamentally address the predicament; we may miss what the Greeks referred to as a Kairos moment, one so crucial because it has a profound effect on all that follows.

SUMMARY

In this posture of "living with the bomb," then, we encounter various combinations of normality, resignation, numbing, cynicism, and even anticipation—along with large numbers of people, most of them well intentioned, going about tasks that may contribute to a potential nuclear catastrophe. Whatever can be said for or against our time, it is burdened with a knowledge that otherwise rational people have carried out the extermination of entire populations if it suited their purpose; that professionals with pride in their professions lent their expertise to mass murder; that students and professors continued to learn and teach; and that many good citizens, far from raising a wild cry of outrage, accepted these policies as an eminently sensible means of waging a war or establishing socialism in one country, or eliminating a superfluous population.[75] Polls show that Americans have generally supported nuclear weapons developments and even first use of the weapons. According to Gallup surveys, a majority supported using the atomic bomb in Korea in 1951 after China entered the conflict; in Vietnam in 1954 when the French were surrounded; and against China in 1955 during the first

Quemoy-Matsu crisis. During the 1980s with antinuclear sentiment rising, polls showed over-whelming support for a no first-use pledge—but a later survey found a near majority backing use of the bomb against Iraq in 1991,[76] and again in 2003 if it used weapons of mass destruction against our troops.

Nuclear arsenals, meanwhile, remain largely in place. Although the United States and Russia have agreed to destroy thousands of warheads, each will still retain thousands of the newest and most accurate variety even after the next round of arms cuts. Russia remains unstable, proliferation is a growing problem and there are terrorist groups who want nuclear weapons and may use them if they get them, while in America there are constant calls for spending more on future weapons technology and missile defense.

Just as the Hiroshima and Nagasaki decisions were prefigured in the fire bombings of Hamburg, Dresden, and Tokyo, in the policy of unconditional surrender and in laboratories in Chicago and New Mexico, we are preparing today for the crises of tomorrow. Yet, there are choices to be made. The Deuteronomist implored: "I have set before you life and death, blessing and cursing: therefore choose life, that both you and your seed may live."[77]

There may, in fact, be an ironic advantage to living in the second nuclear age. If we can reorient "our ways of thinking," the Hiroshima experience and our responses to 9/11 can help us avoid war. The paradox is a fundamental one: The existence of weapons that threaten the globe and its history with destruction, may also, however indirectly, be a stimulus to forestalling the catastrophe, if their meaning can be grasped. The ubiquitous specter of the bomb, as we have seen, intrudes to some degree in our work, our play, our capacities to love and nurture, in our public and private lives, in our very ability to deal effectively with nuclear weapons. The problem is compounded by the difficulty most people have in appreciating how malignant the bomb actually is. We ask you, the reader, to consider how this tendency may be operating in your own life. Yet, confront we must. As the ancient rabbis advised, "It is not incumbent upon us to finish the task; neither are we free to exempt ourselves from it."[78] Chapter 11 will suggest some ways we can start this work, beginning with an appreciation of the moral dimensions of nuclear weapons and their use and the unique moral problems they pose.

ENDNOTES

[1]*New York Times*, (July 11, 2005).

[2]Philip Roth, *The Plot Against America* (Boston: Houghton Mifflin Company, 2004), p. 1.

[3]Quoted in, Netty Gross, "The Writer After 9/11", *The Jerusalem Report*, July 14,2003, vol. xiv, no. 6, p. 41.

[4]Peggy Noonan, *A Heart, A Cross, and a Flag,* (New York:Wall Street Journal Books, 2003), p. 2.

[5]Roger Rosenblatt, *Witness: The World Since Hiroshima* (Boston: Little, Brown and Co., 1985), pp. 4–5.

[6]Albert Camus, "Combat," 8 August 1945, (Gallimard, 1950), pp. 109–110.

[7]Robert Karl Manoff, "The Media: Nuclear Security vs. Democracy," *Bulletin of the Atomic Scientists*, (January, 1984), p. 29.

[8]See Sibylle Escalona, "Growing Up With the Threat of Nuclear War: Some Indirect Effects on Personality Development," *American Journal of Orthopsychiatry*, vol 52, no. 4, (October 1982), p. 600.

[9]Quoted in Paul Boyer, *By the Bomb's Early Light* (New York: Pantheon Books, 1985), p. 282.

[10]Jerome D. Frank, *Sanity and Survival in the Nuclear Age* (New York: Random House, 1967), pp. 30–33.

[11]Stephen Hilgartner, Richard C. Bell, Rory O'Connor, *Nukespeak* (New York: Penguin Books, 1983); Lifton, *Indefensible Weapons*, pp. 106–107; and Paul Chilton, "Nukespeak," *Undercurrents, 48* (1982), p. 12.

[12]See Richard Barnet, "Fantasy, Reality, and the Arms Race," *American Journal of Orthopsychiatry*, vol. 52, no. 4 (October, 1982).

[13]Hilgartner, Bell, O'Connor, *Nukespeak*.

[14]Ibid., p. 251.

[15]Ibid., p. 236.

[16]See Robert Jay Lifton, Indefensible Weapons (New York: Basic Books, 1982) and *In A Dark Time* (Cambridge Mass: Harvard University Press, 1984).

[17]See Boyer, *By the Bomb's Early Light*, pp. 10–12.

[18]Ibid., p. 12.

[19]Michael Mandelbaum, *The Nuclear Revolution* (New York: Cambridge University Press, 1981), pp. 207–229.

[20]Quoted in Lifton, *Boundaries* (New York: Random House, 1967), p. 96.

[21]See Christopher Lasch, *The Minimal Self: Psychic Survival in Troubled Times* (New York: W.W. Norton, 1984).

[22]See Boyer, *By the Bomb's Early Light*, pp. 281–282.

[23]See Mandelbaum and Lifton works previously cited.

[24]See Mandelbaum and Lifton works previously cited.

[25]Quoted in Milton Schwebel, "Effects of the Nuclear War Threat on Children and Teenagers: Implications for Professionals," *American Journal of Orthopsychiatry*, vol. 52, no. 4 (October 1982), p. 611.

[26]See Mandelbaum, *The Nuclear Revolution*.

[27]Erich Fromm, *The Anatomy of Human Destruction* (New York: Holt, Rinehart and Winston, 1974), pp. 350–351.

[28]Dr. Helen Caldicott, *Missile Envy* (New York: Bantam Books, 1984).

[29]Mark Kingwell, *Dreams of Millennium: Report from a Culture on the Brink* (Boston: Faber and Faber, 1996), pp. 182–186.

[30]Don DeLillo, *Underworld* (New York: Scribner, 1997), p. 466.

[31]See Richard Barnet, "Fantasy, Reality, and the Arms Race," *American Journal of Orthopsychiatry*, vol. 52, no. 4 (October 1982), p. 582.

[32]Lifton, *Indefensible Weapons*, p. 47.

[33]Ibid., pp. 48-49.

[34]Bob Dylan, "Talkin' World War III Blues," quoted in Lifton, *In a Dark Time*, p. 87.

[35]Ibid.

[36]See Boyer, p. 361.

[37]Quoted in Barnet, "Fantasy, Reality and the Arms Race," p. 583.

[38]See Sibylle Escalona, "Growing Up With the Threat of Nuclear War" and Lifton works cited previously.

[39]DeLillo, *Underworld*, p. 717.

[40]John Mack, "The Perception of U.S. Soviet Intentions and Other Psychological Dimensions of the Nuclear Arms Race," *American Journal of Orthopsychiatry*, vol. 52, no. 4 (October, 1982), pp. 590–599; *Houston Post* (December 13–15, 1981); *Boston Globe* (October 29, 1981); *The New York Times*(May 27, 1982); P.L. Blackwell and J.C. Gessner, "Fear and Trembling: An Inquiry into Adolescent Perceptions of Living in the Nuclear Age," *Youth and Society*, vol. 15 (1983), pp. 237–255; B.M. Kramer, S.M. Kelich, and M.A. Milburn, "Attitudes Toward Nuclear Weapons and Nuclear War: 1945–1982," *Journal of Social Issues*, vol. 39 (1983), pp. 7–24; A. Rapoport, "Preparation for Nuclear War: The Final Madness," *American Journal of Orthopsychiatry*, vol. 54 (1984), pp. 524–529; Susan Hargraves, "The Nuclear Anxieties of

Youth," *Peace Research,* vol. 18 (1986), pp. 46–64; and J. Thompson, *Psychological Aspects of Nuclear War* (Chichester: John Wiley, 1985).

[41]Reprinted in Lifton, *In a Dark Time*, p. 89.

[42]Quoted in Caldicott, *Missile Envy*, p. 335.

[43]Ibid., p. 336.

[44]Quoted in Noonan, *A Heart, A Cross, and a Flag*, p. 38.

[45]Quoted in Lifton, *In a Dark Time*, p. 89.

[46]Robert Coles, "Children and the Bomb," *The New York Times Magazine* (December 8, 1985), pp. 44, 46, 48, 50, 54, 61–62.

[47]Joel Slemrod, "Savings and Fear of Nuclear War," *Journal of Conflict Resolution*, vol. 30 (September, 1986), pp. 403–419; Bruce Russett and Miles Lackey, "In the Shadow of the Cloud," *Political Science Quarterly*, vol. 102 (Summer, 1987), pp. 259–272; Lewis Thomas, *Late Night Thoughts on Listening to Mahler's Ninth Symphony* (New York: Viking Penguin, 1983), p. 168.

[48]See, Robert Kagan, *Of Paradise and Power: America and Europe in the New World Order*, (New York: Alfred A. Knopf, 2003).

[49]Ibid., pp. 34–36.

[50]Lifton, *Indefensible Weapons*, p. 77.

[51]Robert Jay Lifton and Greg Mitchell, *Hiroshima in America* (New York: G.P. Putnam's Sons, 1995), pp. 380–381.

[52]Lifton, *Indefensible Weapons*, pp. 71–72.

[53]See Robert Jay Lifton, *Boundaries* (New York: Random House, 1967) and *The Broken Connection* (New York: Simon and Schuster, 1979).

[54]David Weinberger, "A Phenomenology of Nuclear Weapons," *Philosophy and Social Criticism*, no. 3/4, vol. 10 (1984), pp. 98–99.

[55]Ibid., p. 101.

[56]Norman Mailer, *Advertisements for Myself* (New York: G.P. Putnam's Sons, 1959), p. 338.

[57]Weinberger, pp. 102–105.

[58]Robert Jay Lifton, *Home From the War* (New York: Simon and Schuster, 1973), p. 25.

[59]Jonathan Schell, *The Fate of the Earth* (New York: Avon Books, 1982).

[60]Joyce Maynard, *Looking Back: A Chronicle of Growing Up in the Sixties* (New York: Doubleday & Co., 1973), p. 13.

[61]Woody Allen, *Getting Even* (New York: Warner, 1972), p. 31.

[62]Thomas, *Late Night Thoughts*, p. 167.

[63]Lifton, *Boundaries*, pp. 26–27.

[64]See Robert Jay Lifton and Richard Falk, *Indefensible Weapons* (New York: Basic Books, 1982).

[65]Ernest Becker, *The Denial of Death* (New York: The Free Press, 1973).

[66]Quoted in Louis René Beres, "Vain Hopes and a Fools Fancy: Understanding U.S. Nuclear Strategy," *Philosophy and Social Criticism*, no. 3/4, vol. 10 (1984), p. 46.

[67]Rebecca West, *Black Lamb and Grey Falcon* (New York: Viking Press, 1982), p. 1102.

[68]See Lifton, *The Broken Connection*, pp. 339–343.

[69]11 Peter 3:10.

[70]Mircea Eliade, *Cosmos and History* (New York: Harper, 1959).

[71]Quoted in Lifton, *In a Dark Time*, p. 66.

[72]Thomas L. Friedman, "Yes, But What?" *New York Times*, October 5, 2001, p. A23.

[73]Quoted in Bruce Lincoln, *Holy Terrors: Thinking about Religion after September 11*, (Chicago: The University of Chicago Press, 2003), pp. 102–103.

[74]Lifton, *The Broken Connection*, p. 335.

[75]See Richard Rubenstein, *The Age of Triage* (Boston: Beacon Press, 1983) and *The Cunning of History* (New York: Harper & Row, 1975); Irving Horowitz, *Genocide: State Power and Mass Murder* (New Brunswick, NJ: Transaction Books, 1976); Robert Jay Lifton, *Death in Life* (New York: Random House, 1967); and Ronald Aronson, *The Dialectics of Disaster* (London: Verso, 1983). The connection between culture and mass death is examined in some of the following: Jules Henry, *Culture Against Man* (New York: Vintage Books, 1965); Ernest Becker, *Escape from Evil* (New York: The Free Press, 1975); George Steiner, *Language and Silence* (New York: *Atheneum*, 1967); and Isidor Wallimann and Michael Dobkowski, ed., *Genocide and the Modern Age* (New York: Greenwood Press, 1987).

[76]Lifton and Mitchell, *Hiroshima in America*, p. 305.

[77]Deuteronomy 30:19.

[78]*Pirkei Avos* 2:16.

11

Nuclear Weapons and
Moral Values

During the transition between the first and second nuclear ages, in December 1994, the General Assembly of the United Nations requested that the International Court of Justice, also known as the World Court, issue a ruling on the question of whether "the threat or use of nuclear weapons in any circumstance [is] permitted under international law." On July 8, 1996, the court delivered its ruling, maintaining "that the threat or use of nuclear weapons would generally be contrary to the rules of international law applicable in armed conflict, and in particular the principles and rules of humanitarian law." This was an historic opinion. For the first time an authoritative body had ruled that the possession of nuclear weapons merely for the sake of deterrence was generally contrary to the requirements of international law.

As a result of its view that the use or threatened use of nuclear weapons is generally illegal, the Court found that the nuclear nations have "an obligation to pursue in good faith and bring to a conclusion negotiations leading to nuclear disarmament in all its aspects under strict and effective international control."[1] The obligation that nuclear states have to pursue nuclear disarmament need not be based on any treaty commitment they have individually made. It is inherent in their membership in the international community, in virtue of which they are bound by international law.

Law and morality have always been closely linked. Law often follows morality and is often designed to give force to the important moral values of a community. The same is the case for international law. There are moral norms that are regarded as applying to the relations among nations, expressing the moral values of the human community. These norms are at the basis of much of international law. Thus, the World Court ruling has important implications for understanding how morality applies to the possession and use of nuclear weapons. The Court asserted that its ruling is based on "the principles and rules of humanitarian law," in particular, on one of "the cardinal principles contained in the texts constituting the fabric of humanitarian law [which] is aimed at the protection of the civilian population and civilian objects and establishes the distinction between combatants and non-combatants."[2]

But the Court's judgment that the use and threatened use of nuclear weapons are contrary to international law was not unqualified. The Court asserted:

> In view of the current state of international law, and of the elements of fact at its disposal, the Court cannot conclude definitively whether the threat or use of nuclear weapons would be lawful or unlawful in an extreme circumstance of self-defense, in which the very survival of a State would be at stake.[3]

Note that the Court did not say that the use or threatened use of nuclear weapons would be legally justified under such extreme circumstances, but rather that it cannot determine that such uses would be unjustified. Nevertheless, this is an important qualification, and it reflects a similar area of doubt in the moral assessment of nuclear weapons. This area of doubt is one of the most troubling and difficult features in the discussion of nuclear weapons. As Richard Falk puts it, the Court's conclusion "most accurately reflects the complex and contradictory mixture of normative elements including the tension between the logic of prohibiting all weaponry of mass destruction and the logic of self-defense."[4] The moral as well as the legal assessment of nuclear weapons often leads to conflicting results.

The morality of nuclear weapons has from time to time become an important part of the public debate over military policy. One such time was over two decades ago, during the first nuclear age. In May 1983, the National Conference of Catholic Bishops issued a controversial pastoral letter on nuclear weapons, *The Challenge of Peace: God's Promise and Our Response*. The bishops debated the issues through two earlier drafts and heard expert testimony from a wide variety of witnesses, including high-level representatives of the administration of then-president Ronald Reagan. The bishops' letter focused on the morality of nuclear weapons policy, and, because of the attention it received, it introduced moral issues into the public debate about nuclear weapons to an extent unprecedented since 1945. The bishops asserted: "In the nuclear arsenals of the United States or the Soviet Union alone, there exists a capacity to do something no other age could imagine: we can threaten the entire planet." This is close to a passage from the World Court opinion in which the Court asserts that nuclear weapons "have the potential to destroy all civilization and the entire ecosystem of the planet."[5] As a result of this potential, the bishops continue: "Nuclear weapons... raise new moral questions. No previously conceived moral position escapes the fundamental confrontation posed by contemporary nuclear strategy."[6]

In Chapter 10, our attention shifted from the physical, military, and political realities of the nuclear predicament discussed in the earlier chapters to the human values implicated in the existence of nuclear weapons and the resulting debate about nuclear weapons policy. In Chapter 10 we considered the implications of nuclear weapons for cultural values generally. In this chapter, we consider more specifically the moral dimension of the nuclear predicament: What do nuclear weapons imply for the moral values that have been developed to apply to war? How should nuclear weapons be viewed in terms of those values?[7] Because nuclear weapons are unique among weapons in their destructive effects, they give rise to special moral problems. As the bishops claim, nuclear weapons have raised new moral problems for our understanding of war. This must be counted as one of the changes that, as Einstein suggested, has yet to be fully reflected in our ways of thinking. The purpose of this chapter is to understand the nature of this change.

Our world was altered forever on August 6, 1945, when the atomic bomb exploded on Hiroshima. This change was, in part, a moral change. Speaking of Hiroshima, Fred Cook asserted: "the ruthless employment of that power to obliterate 80,000 men, women and children in one blinding flash meant that all considerations of morality, all moral restraint, had now become archaic concepts." The bombing meant "that naked force had been enthroned over the world as never before."[8] Have nuclear weapons made morality obsolete, as Cook suggests? Do moral restraints no longer apply to war when nuclear weapons are involved? We consider in the first section below what morality has to say about war, both conventional war and nuclear war. (Since the advent of nuclear weapons, nonnuclear war has come to be called *conventional war*.) In the second section we examine the key moral question raised by nuclear weapons in the first nuclear age, namely, what morality has to say about nuclear deterrence. In the third section we discuss in greater detail the moral problems posed by nuclear weapons in the second nuclear age. The bishops wrote their pastoral letter at a time of high Cold War tension between the United States and the Soviet Union, in the depths of the first nuclear age, and the International Court of Justice made its ruling at the cusp of the transition between the two nuclear ages. Do the moral principles on which the bishops and the Court based their conclusions still have the same implications in the very different international environment in which we now find ourselves?

MORALITY, WAR, AND NUCLEAR WAR

We have seen in earlier chapters the tremendous increase in destructive power introduced into war by nuclear weapons, from the actual destruction caused to Hiroshima and Nagasaki to the much greater destructive potential of the nuclear arsenals developed since 1945. In Chapter 1, we got a glimpse of what the world might be like if this potential were to be actualized in a nuclear war. But, to help us understand what morality has to say about nuclear war, we must first consider what morality has to say about conventional war.

There are three possible moral responses to conventional war. First is the position of the *moral pacifist*, which is that war is morally unacceptable in any form, due to the violence and death it entails. Second is the position of the *moral realist*, which is that morality does not apply to the relations among nations, so that morality is irrelevant or inapplicable to war.[9] No moral objections can be raised to war. Third is a position that is, in a sense, part way between pacifism and realism. This is the position that some wars (and some ways of fighting a war) are just or morally acceptable and some are not. This position is known as *just war theory*, and it is the approach to the morality of war traditional in Western thought. Just war theory differs from pacifism and realism in that it makes moral distinctions between different kinds of war and different ways of fighting a war. Pacifism regards all war and ways of fighting a war as morally unacceptable, while realism regards no war and no ways of fighting a war as morally unacceptable (because it makes no moral judgments about war). Thus neither realism nor pacifism distinguishes morally acceptable from morally unacceptable wars or ways of fighting in war. But just war theory does. While our discussion of the morality of war focuses on the just-war-theory approach, we encourage you to consider as you read the rest of the chapter what the realist or pacifist would say about the matters discussed.

Before we can examine the morality of war through the eyes of just war theory, however, we should briefly discuss morality in general. Morality is composed of rules for guiding human actions, especially those actions involving our relations with other people. Morality prescribes how individuals and groups (such as nations) ought to behave in relation to other individuals or groups. To act morally is to act in a way that takes into account the interests of others. Contrasting with morality is the idea of *self-interest*. When individuals or groups act out of self-interest, they consider as primary their own interests rather than the interests of others. "National security" is a term often used to refer to national self-interest. Another term referring to self-interest is *prudence*. To act prudently is to act in one's own interest rather than the interest of others.

Often there is no conflict between acting prudently and acting morally. When there is no conflict, there is nothing morally wrong with acting prudently. But morality and prudence sometimes provide conflicting guidance for our actions. For example, while there have been strong moral objections expressed to the bombing of Hiroshima, for reasons we discuss later, the bombing is also said to have been in the self-interest of the United States because it saved the lives of American troops and ended the war more quickly. When morality and prudence conflict, we must choose one or the other. Thus, moral behavior can sometimes require sacrifice of self-interest. This becomes crucial when considering the actions of nations at war, where a great deal is at stake in terms of national self-interest, perhaps even a nation's survival. Just war theory traditionally has not required great sacrifice of national self-interest, but nuclear weapons seem to change this.

Another feature of morality is its universality. This is especially important when considering the morality of war. War often involves a clash between different societies, and different societies may disagree about what is morally right or wrong. Because of this diversity of moral views, it may seem that morality is not universal, but rather that, like other cultural values, it varies with and is relative to the social group. This would make talk about the morality of war pointless. (This is the position of the moral realist.) But the fact of the social diversity of moral beliefs does not show that morality is not universal. When people from different societies argue about what is morally right, they appeal to what they take to be universal moral principles in an attempt to persuade others to adopt their own moral view. If morality were relative to the social group rather than universal, then arguments between members of different social groups about moral views would be as pointless as arguments about which flavor of ice cream is best. Preferences for flavors of ice cream, unlike moral claims, are clearly a matter of individual taste.

In any case, there is, as a matter of fact, nearly universal agreement among the nations about when a war is just or unjust and what conduct in war is right or wrong. Just war theory has its traditional source as a doctrine of Christian moral thinking, but in its development it has become increasingly secularized, so as to represent Western culture more generally. Through the spread of international law of war, which in large measure is based on just war theory, it has come to be a universal expression of our understanding of the morality of war. Nearly all nations have expressed support for the international laws of war, the law that was appealed to by the World Court in its ruling about the legality of nuclear weapons. To say that nations have expressed support for these laws is, of course, not to say that they have consistently abided by them.

Just war theory seeks to assess the morality of war by appealing to universal moral rules or standards. Just war theory provides arguments, which means that it gives reasons for its claims by appealing, directly or indirectly, to those standards. One important set of standards for moral arguments about war are *human rights*. Among our human rights is the right against aggression. At the individual level, a person has a right not to be attacked by others. But what if a person is attacked and has his or her rights violated in this way? A person who is attacked has a right of *self-defense*. Thus it is sometimes morally justified for an individual to use force against others. Our basic human right against aggression implies that no one is morally allowed to use force against others, except in self-defense against aggression. We might say that a person's right not to be attacked is forfeited when that person first attacks another.

Consider some other aspects of the morality of individual self-defense. First, it is not morally acceptable to use force self-defensively, if there is any other reliable way to stop the attack, such as by talking the attacker out of attacking or by leaving the scene of the attack. This is because force should not be used unless it is necessary to stop the attack. Second, it is not morally acceptable to use more force than is needed to stop the attack. For example, if the person can stop the attack by disabling the attacker, it would be morally wrong to kill the attacker instead. Again, this is because any extra force would not be necessary in stopping the attack.

Third, it is not morally acceptable to use a degree of force in self-defense that would do much more harm to the attacker than the attacker intends to inflict. For example, a person cannot kill an attacker who intends only to inflict a bloody nose. Defensive force should not be so great as to inflict an amount of harm that significantly exceeds the harm the defensive force is seeking to avoid. The reason is that an aggressor forfeits a right against force being used against him or her only to the extent of the intended aggression. An aggressor does not forfeit his or her right to life by intending to give the victim a bloody nose. Fourth, it is not morally acceptable to use defensive force against those who are not engaged in the aggression, even if using such force would help to stop the attack. For example, a defender cannot injure the attacker's child, even if doing so would stop the attack. This is because only the aggressor forfeits his or her right against force. Nonaggressors retain that right.

If we apply these ideas to the use of force among nations, we get the rough outlines of just war theory. Consider three central moral questions that just war theory must address:

Q1. When may military force be used?

Q2. How much military force may be used?

Q3. Against whom may military force be used?

If we follow the above points about individual self-defense, we get these answers:

A1. Military force may be used to defend a nation from aggression only when there is no alternative method of stopping the aggression. This follows from the first point above.

A2. The amount of military force that may be used is limited by both how much force is needed to stop the aggression and how much harm the aggressor intends. This follows from the second and third points.

A3. Military force may be used against only those who are involved in the attack. This follows from the fourth point.

These are roughly the answers that just war theory provides.

As (A1) implies, there is an important moral difference between aggressive and defensive wars. Only defensive wars are morally justified. This means that what is usually referred to as a single war (for example, the U.S. Civil War or World War II) is, from a moral perspective, two wars, a war fought by an aggressor, which is not morally justified, and a war fought by a defender, which may be morally justified. The two wars of World War II were the war fought by the Allies, which, as a defensive war, was morally justified, and the war fought by the Axis powers (Germany, Italy, and Japan), which, as an aggressive war, was not.

Just war theory provides a set of rules used to determine whether military actions are morally justified. As discussed above, many of these rules can be derived from the basic human right against aggression, understood as applying to nations as well as to individuals. The rules of just war theory may be divided into two kinds, namely, rules about *when* a war may be fought and rules about *how* a war may be fought. First are the rules concerning when it is morally acceptable for a nation to go to war. These rules, which address (Q1), are known by their Latin name as rules of *jus ad bellum*, that is, morality *of* war. The rules of *jus ad bellum* stipulate that it is morally acceptable to go to war, only if the war has a just cause, as it does when it is a case of self-defense, and is fought with the intention of serving that cause. In addition, going to war must be a last resort, all peaceful avenues for ending the aggression having been exhausted. Both these points are included in (A1) above. Moreover, it must be reasonable to expect that the war will do more good than harm, there must be a real chance of success, and it must be declared by those with the legal authority to do so.

Second are rules about how a war may be fought, how much force may be used and against whom the force may be directed. These address (Q2) and (Q3), and are known as the rules of *jus in bello*, morality *in* war.[10] Because these rules concern how a war should be fought, not whether it should be fought, they are the rules relevant to the questions about use of nuclear weapons. The rules regarding how much force may be used are based on the *principle of proportionality*, and those regarding against whom the force may be directed are based the *principle of discrimination*. In just war theory the rules of *jus in bello* apply equally to the aggressor and the defender.

The principle of proportionality is related to (A2). This principle is not directly derived from the human right against aggression, but rather is related to the moral requirement that defensive force should be kept to a minimum. The amount of force employed in fighting a war should be the least amount necessary to achieve the just objective of the war (stopping aggression). In addition, the use of force in self-defensive war produces harm as well as the good of stopping the aggression, and the amount of force employed should not so great as to produce an amount of harm that would greatly exceed the amount of good. In other words, the amount of harm produced by self-defensive force should be at most roughly proportional to the amount of good it would produce. A minor aggression would not justify massive attack in response. Although the term "proportionality" may suggest mathematical precision, the application of this principle clearly cannot be based on precise calculations. The principle of proportionality applies not only to individual military actions within the war (where it is part of *jus in bello*) but also to the war as a whole (where it is a part of *jus ad bellum*). The basic idea is that the deadly and destructive force employed in war should not be gratuitous, more than is necessary, nor should it be excessive in relation to the end to be achieved. An example of a policy that threatened force contrary to the principle of proportionality is the 1950s U.S. policy of massive retaliation, discussed in Chapter 4.

According to the principle of discrimination, force should be employed in a way that discriminates between combatants and noncombatants. Generally speaking, combatants are military personal, and noncombatants are civilians. Force is not to be directed against noncombatants, because they are not engaged in the fight. (The rule is also referred to as the principle of noncombatant immunity.) A noncombatant should not be attacked, because he or she is *innocent* of involvement in the aggression that justifies the military response. This notion of innocence is central to the principle of discrimination. The principle is based on the idea of an individual right against aggression, as discussed earlier. A person should not be attacked unless he or she is attacking others. Hence, noncombatants should not be attacked. This principle follows the idea in (A3) that defensive force may be used only against the attacker or, more broadly, against those who are participating in or directly contributing to the aggression. This would include the enemy's military personnel and leadership hierarchy, and also, perhaps, those who are supplying the means of making war, such as munitions workers. But obviously most people in the society would be innocent of direct involvement in the aggression, and it would not be morally acceptable to attack them. A nation at war should not only minimize the number of people it kills (following the principle of proportionality), but it should not kill certain kinds of people (noncombatants) at all. The principle of discrimination explains why many regard the bombings of Hiroshima and Nagasaki as not morally acceptable, even though they may have saved lives overall, because most of those killed in those cities were noncombatants.

Two further points should be made about the principle of discrimination. First, some critics have challenged the applicability of this principle on the grounds that in modern war the entire population of a nation may be mobilized in support of the war effort, so that there are no innocent persons. But this is simply not the case.[11] For example, young children and most old people are surely innocent, in the sense that they do nothing to support the war effort. There may be a legitimate question about precisely where to draw the line between combatants and noncombatants; we discussed this issue in Chapter 4 when we considered the role that different groups play in the conduct of modern war. But however hard it is to draw a precise line, there is a line to be drawn. The second point is an important qualification of the principle of discrimination. If the killings of noncombatants in war were never morally acceptable, virtually all major military attacks would be ruled out, because few attacks can avoid the risk or even the certainty that noncombatants will be killed as a side-effect of the attack. But the principle of discrimination rules out only *intentional* or *reckless* killings of noncombatants. If a battle were planned so that attacks are directed only against combatants, and efforts are made to minimize any risks to noncombatants, the attack would be morally acceptable in terms of the principle of discrimination. This shows the importance for just war theory of judging military actions in terms of the intentions behind them.

At this point, we may briefly consider again the position known as moral realism. As mentioned earlier, moral realism is the position that morality does not apply to war.[12] Realists argue in criticism of just war theory that because nations at war often ignore moral limits, moral limits do not apply to what they do, and there is no need for even conscientious leaders to worry about the morality of their war-time actions. But this is a poor argument. Consider an analogy with the law. If certain people consistently break the law, the law still applies to them. Otherwise, we could not even say that they had broken the law. Thus, people or nations cannot make moral rules inapplicable to their actions by ignoring them, or it would be impossible to act immorally. As a matter of fact, we frequently pass moral judgment on acts done in war, for example, we label actions in war as aggression or massacre precisely in order to morally condemn them, and if moral realism were true, it would make no sense to do so.[13]

Whatever the strength of arguments for it, the popularity of moral realism is not hard to understand. First, many people view morality as an external imposition on the activity of war, that is, an attempt by someone on the outside (the moralist) to interfere with the legitimate business of military leaders. This is a mistake. The rules of just war theory are recognized, accepted, and generally practiced by military leaders. They are not an external imposition. A second explanation for the popularity of realism is the belief that if nations respect moral limits in war, they put themselves at a great disadvantage, perhaps risking their very survival. But this is not generally the case. Just war theory allows nations to defend themselves and allows them to attack the opponent's military forces in ways that do not put noncombatants unduly at risk. In most circumstances, there would be little military advantage in violating the rules of just war theory. The same holds for the morality of individual self-defense. Respecting the moral limits would not normally place those under attack at a significant disadvantage in defending themselves.

Now consider what the rules of just war theory, in particular, the rules of *jus in bello*, have to say about the use of nuclear weapons in war. Would the use of nuclear weapons in war ever be consistent with the limits set by *jus in bello*? Would the use of nuclear weapons in war accord with the principles of discrimination and proportionality?

Consider first the principle of discrimination. In Chapters 1 and 4, the concept of total war was introduced. Total war is war in which an opponent's whole society, not just its military forces, becomes a target of attack. Total war violates the principle of discrimination, for a society is composed in large measure of noncombatants. Advances in technology over the past century, especially the development of aerial bombing, have made total war possible. Aerial bombing allows a nation to attack the homeland and economy of the opponent without having to defeat its military forces on the battlefield. In addition, aerial bombing has historically been inaccurate, increasing the likelihood that noncombatants would be killed.

World War II was total war even prior to Hiroshima. Great sections of German and Japanese cities such as Dresden, Hamburg, and Tokyo were deliberately destroyed with firebombs. The principle of discrimination was disregarded, as John Ford argued in 1944: "For in practice, though one may adhere verbally to the distinction between innocent and guilty, the obliteration of great sections of cities, including whole districts of workers' residences, means the abandonment of this distinction as an effective moral norm."[14] Ford argues that such bombing ignores the principle in substance. The government's claim that the intention behind the bombing was the destruction of the economy supporting the military effort rather than the killing of noncombatants shows respect for the principle only in a formal sense. The principle of discrimination requires that efforts be made to minimize the number of noncombatants killed, and bombing large cities cannot count as meeting this requirement. To minimize the number of noncombatants killed, the bombing of large cities must be avoided.

According to the principle of discrimination, it is not morally acceptable for a nation to use bombs in a way that kills large numbers of noncombatants. Bombs must be used only against military targets. Because nonnuclear bombs can be used in a discriminate way, by aiming them at places away from large civilian populations, their use in war is sometimes morally acceptable. But nuclear bombs are different. Using them even against military targets does not, in general, avoid killing civilians. Nuclear explosions produce windborne radioactive debris (fallout), which can kill people at great distances from the site of the blast. In addition, nuclear bombs kill people across time, through increasing risks of cancers and genetic mutations. People in Japan are still dying from the effects of the atomic blasts at Hiroshima and Nagasaki. As the World Court said, the use of nuclear weapons "cannot be contained in either time or space." This fact makes it likely that many noncombatants will be killed, no matter where a nuclear weapon is aimed. Thus, virtually any use of nuclear weapons would be an abandonment of the principle of discrimination.

How does the use of nuclear weapons fare in terms of the principle of proportionality? Nuclear weapons are so destructive that their use in any numbers would cause catastrophic harm. Such terrible destruction would likely be disproportionate to whatever goals the war was fought to achieve, including the halting of aggression. In the case of nuclear war between nuclear powers, the destruction would be reciprocal; the use of nuclear weapons by one side would lead to retaliation in kind. It is hard to imagine what military gain could compensate for such destruction.

Two objections may be made to these arguments. Against the argument concerning discrimination, the objection would be that some nuclear weapons could be used in a way that posed little risk to civilians. A low-yield (or tactical) nuclear weapon exploded in the air (so as to create little fallout) over isolated military targets might do little harm to noncombatants. Against the argument concerning proportionality, the objection would be that the use of a low number of such weapons in a discriminate way might not result in a disproportionate level of destruction.

To be persuasive, these objections must show that the kind of nuclear war they envision is probable, not merely possible. To guide our action, the principles must be applied to what is reasonable to expect as an outcome of a use of nuclear weapons, not to a merely possible outcome. In considering the likelihood of such outcomes, we must recognize differences between the first and second nuclear ages. In the first nuclear age, the main concern was a nuclear war between the two superpowers, the United States and the Soviet Union. The problem at that time was the risk of escalation from a limited nuclear war to a large-scale nuclear war, one involving the use of hundreds or thousands of nuclear weapons. Even those who believed at the time that a nuclear war between the superpowers might be kept limited did not believe that we could ever be very sure in some particular case that it would be. Given the number of nuclear weapons that existed, the animosity between the two sides, and the technical difficulties in keeping a nuclear war limited, there was always a serious possibility that any use of nuclear weapons between them would escalate into a large-scale nuclear war. Thus, during the first nuclear age, any use of nuclear weapons between the superpowers carried a substantial risk of an outcome that was more than just war theory could allow, in terms of both discrimination and proportionality.

One other possible outcome of nuclear war in the first nuclear age should be mentioned. A large-scale nuclear war would have had serious effects on the global environment. For example, such a war could have depleted the upper-atmospheric layer of ozone, which protects the earth from the sun's ultraviolet radiation, to such an extent that lethal levels of this energy might get through. Or, such a war might have raised so much smoke and dust into the atmosphere that the sun would be blotted out for months, leading to a devastating "nuclear winter."[15] This conceivably could have lead to the extinction of the human species—what Jonathan Schell called "the second death."[16] The possibility of human extinction, or "omnicide," as it was sometimes called, put a decision to use nuclear weapons potentially in a catastrophic violation of the principle of proportionality. Human extinction would represent not only the greatest level of harm to those who it killed; it would destroy the possibility of future generations. Nuclear war would then have destroyed everything of human value. This possibility shows, again, the unprecedented moral import of nuclear weapons.

But what about the use of nuclear weapons in the second nuclear age? Though the United States and Russia still have large arsenals of nuclear weapons, they are not now enemies, and the risk of nuclear war between them is much lower. The main sources of the possible use of nuclear weapons in the second nuclear age arise from nuclear proliferation and nuclear terrorism, creating the possibility that new nuclear nations, such as India and Pakistan, or terrorists, would use nuclear weapons.[17] In either case, nuclear use would be limited because there would be relatively few nuclear weapons available for use. If nuclear use could be limited, even if only by the exhausting of the nuclear weapons available for use, then perhaps it would not violate the principles of discrimination and proportionality. This suggests that there might, in the second nuclear age, be some nuclear wars that are morally acceptable.

But the use of nuclear weapons by new nuclear nations is not likely to be morally acceptable. First, such use would very likely not be limited enough to be in accord with the principles of discrimination and proportionality. New nuclear nations are unlikely to have the advanced technology to make small nuclear weapons and deliver them accurately. The weapons these nuclear proliferators have are likely to be morally and crude, and these states will have no means to deliver them accurately. Any use of such weapons will almost certainly involve so much civilian destruction as to violate the principles of discrimination and proportionality. Moreover, the use of nuclear weapons by terrorists would not be morally acceptable, given that terrorists would target their weapons on civilians and thereby violate the principle of discrimination. What was true of the United States and the Soviet Union at the beginning of the first nuclear age is now true of new proliferators and terrorists, namely, that the small number of nuclear weapons they held means that they would want to use the weapons to the greatest effect, which means on populations centers.

Second, even if the use of nuclear weapons by new nuclear nations could be limited enough to be morally acceptable in itself, such a use of nuclear weapons could lead to a relaxation of the restraints on their use by other nations, leading to future nuclear wars that themselves would be morally unacceptable. Any use of nuclear weapons would violate the *nuclear taboo*, the global tradition or norm that has developed since 1945 against the use of nuclear weapons. Were the nuclear taboo to be violated, there might be much less restraint on the use of nuclear weapons in the future. Thus, even if an instance of nuclear use in the second nuclear age, considered in isolation, could be limited enough to be morally acceptable (which in itself there is strong reason to doubt), it would be morally unacceptable when considered in context of its long-term consequences because it would seriously increase the risk of future nuclear wars. On the other hand, the breaking of the nuclear taboo could, as we have suggested elsewhere, have the opposite effect, hardening attitudes against nuclear use and making future nuclear wars less likely. In any case, there remains a good chance that any use of nuclear weapons could make future use more likely, and this provides another reason to regard nuclear use in the second nuclear age as morally unacceptable.

The conclusion is that any use of nuclear weapons is morally unacceptable. Nuclear weapons are morally different. Nuclear war cannot be waged within moral limits. Just war theory can provide no guidance for those waging nuclear war, except to demand that it not be waged at all. In the face of nuclear weapons, just war theory has, in effect, lost its intermediate position between realism and pacifism. As far as nuclear weapons are concerned, just war theory joins hands with pacifism, ruling out war altogether. Some argue that just war theory implies "nuclear pacifism."

But the above discussion so far does not exhaust the question of the morality of nuclear weapons, because nuclear weapons have a use other than their use in war. Fortunately, since 1945, nuclear weapons have been used not to *wage* war, but to *deter* war. By threatening nuclear war, the policy of nuclear deterrence seeks to insure that there will not be a nuclear war. Deterrence is the main military reason for having nuclear weapons. The moral acceptability of nuclear weapons turns, then, on whether nuclear deterrence is morally acceptable.

THE MORALITY OF NUCLEAR DETERRENCE

Nuclear deterrence seems, morally speaking, to be a totally different matter than nuclear war, for nuclear war would cause catastrophic destruction while nuclear deterrence, if it works, causes none at all. Nuclear deterrence is, moreover, designed, at least in part, to avoid nuclear war. For these reasons, nuclear deterrence would seem to be a morally acceptable policy. Yet, the World Court in its ruling found both nuclear threat and nuclear use to be unacceptable.

Nuclear deterrence is a policy of threat to attack with nuclear weapons any opponent who engages in aggression.[18] The nuclear threat, to be effective, must involve a real intention to use the weapons in response to aggression, and not be a bluff. Sometimes, of course, threats are bluffs, but if a nation's threat to use nuclear weapons were a bluff, the risk would be too great that the opponent would discover this and no longer be deterred. Credibility is crucial for an effective deterrence policy, and a policy of bluff would not be credible. So, in the light of our conclusion that the use of nuclear weapons in war is morally unacceptable, the question becomes, is it morally acceptable to intend to do what would be morally unacceptable to do (that is, retaliate with nuclear weapons)?

For many contemporary thinkers in the just war tradition, the answer to this question is clearly no. For example, one commentator argues:

> If an action is wrong no matter what the circumstances, it is wrong to intend to do it in any, no matter how carefully limited and specified, circumstances. If exploding nuclear weapons is morally wrong in any circumstances, it is morally wrong to intend exploding them in any, no matter how carefully circumscribed the conditions.[19]

If using nuclear weapons is not morally acceptable, the intention to use them is not either. The importance given to intention in just war theory is the basis of this line of argument. As we saw earlier, the intention to attack noncombatants is what violates the principle of discrimination. The theory holds that such an intention by itself, even in the absence of the act, is morally unacceptable. Given that it is not morally acceptable to use nuclear weapons in war, it follows that nuclear deterrence is not morally acceptable either.[20]

Something stronger may be said here, especially in the case of nuclear use during the first nuclear age. Given the tremendous destructive power of nuclear weapons and the large size of the nuclear arsenals, nuclear deterrence during the Cold War was a form of terrorism.[21] The nuclear threat by the superpowers in the first nuclear age was a threat of *assured destruction*, that is, a threat to destroy the opponent's civilian population and economic infrastructure. As discussed in Chapter 4, nuclear deterrence during the cold war took the form of mutual assured destruction (MAD), where both superpowers made a threat of assured destruction. The threat to kill civilians is a form of terrorism. In Chapter 9, terrorism was defined as harming or threatening harm to civilians for the sake of political ends, and this is what practitioners of nuclear deterrence as assured destruction do. Such nuclear threats are akin to the threats made by individuals who hijack a plane threatening to kill the passengers. The hijackers are terrorists simply in virtue of making this threat, even if the threat is never carried out. Likewise, nations that make a nuclear threat of assured destruction are engaging in terrorism, even if the threat is never carried out.[22]

The U.S. Catholic bishops, in their pastoral letter, have a different view of the moral acceptability of nuclear deterrence. The bishops appear to hold both that the use of nuclear weapons is not morally acceptable and that nuclear deterrence is morally acceptable. They endorse the basic just war principle that "no *use* of nuclear weapons which would violate the principles of discrimination or proportionality may be *intended* in a strategy of deterrence."[23] They do not, however, draw the conclusion that nuclear deterrence is not morally acceptable, arguing instead for "a strictly conditioned moral acceptance of nuclear deterrence."[24] The condition is that nuclear deterrence must not be seen as a permanent solution but rather as an interim step on the way to disarmament. Their position is in some ways similar to, though apparently more lenient than, that of the World Court in its ruling on nuclear weapons. Both the bishops and the Court find the threat to use nuclear weapons to be severely problematic from a moral or legal perspective, but both qualified this negative judgment, the Court by the admitting that the threat might be legally justified in cases where a nation's survival was at stake, and the bishops acknowledging that the threat was conditionally morally acceptable. Moreover, the condition that the bishops put on the moral acceptability of deterrence is also endorsed by the Court, namely, that nuclear states have an obligation vigorously to pursue nuclear disarmament.

Critics of the bishops' letter have called attention to the apparent inconsistency between the strictures of their just war position and their conditional acceptance of nuclear deterrence. Why were the bishops led to accept deterrence despite its seeming to be at odds with just war theory? They were clearly impressed with what deterrence seems to be able to achieve. Following Pope John Paul II, they argued: "The moral duty today is to prevent nuclear war from ever occurring and to protect and preserve those key values of justice, freedom and independence which are necessary for personal dignity and national integrity."[25] Nuclear deterrence, they believed, is the only policy that could achieve this until alternative arrangements for keeping the peace are found. Apparently this made nuclear deterrence morally acceptable to the bishops despite their recognition that, contrary to the requirements of just war theory, nuclear deterrence involves an intention to do what is not morally acceptable, namely, kill large numbers of civilians.

The bishops appear to place more emphasis on the serious consequences that they believe would follow from abandoning nuclear deterrence than on the deterrent intentions in relation to the principle of discrimination. Several writers on the morality of nuclear deterrence have explicitly adopted this moral view.[26] For these writers (and perhaps the bishops), abandoning nuclear deterrence would have grave consequences in terms of national survival, and these consequences are sufficient to override the just war principles. Abandoning nuclear deterrence would open a nation to a nuclear attack or aggression through nuclear blackmail. Concern with this superseded the moral concern about the intention to do what is not morally acceptable, emphasized by just war theory.

The bishops' conclusion and the World Court ruling represent the paradoxical nature of nuclear deterrence. The *jus in bello* rules of just war theory, as well as the closely connected legal traditions of international humanitarian law, seems clearly to condemn nuclear deterrence. But nuclear deterrence, at least as it was practiced during the first nuclear age, seems uniquely able to avoid nuclear war, as well as nonnuclear aggression. When a nation is facing an opponent with nuclear weapons, as the World Court's ruling suggests, nuclear deterrence may be a policy necessary for its very survival. In other words, the just war rules of *jus ad bellum*, which permit a nation to take military action in self-defense, allow a nation under nuclear threat to make a nuclear threat in response. This is what we may call the *paradox of nuclear deterrence*: nuclear deterrence seems at once both morally acceptable in terms of *jus ad bellum* and morally unacceptable in terms of *jus in bello*. The paradox is that nuclear weapons put the two parts of just war theory, *jus ad bellum* and *jus in bello*, on a collision course. The way in which the bishops and the Court qualified their moral and legal condemnation of nuclear deterrence is a recognition of this paradox. Such a paradox may have arisen for the first time in the history of military technology with the advent of nuclear weapons.

One way to escape the paradox is to question one of the assumptions on which it is based. There are two assumptions: that nuclear deterrence is not morally acceptable (according to *jus in bello*) and that it is necessary for a nation's survival (thus permitting it under *jus ad bellum*). The latter assumption depends on the further assumption that nuclear deterrence *works*, that it succeeds in avoiding nuclear war and other forms of aggression. But this assumption may be open to challenge.

How well did nuclear deterrence work between the superpowers during the first nuclear age? This is a difficult question indeed. We might argue that deterrence worked well by pointing out that there was neither nuclear war nor aggression between the United States and the Soviet Union. But factors other than nuclear deterrence may explain this. If someone points out to a person wearing elephant repellent in New York City that such measures are unnecessary because there are no elephants in the city, the response could be, "See how well it's working!" Just as we cannot conclude from the absence of elephants that the repellent works, we cannot conclude from the absence of war or aggression that nuclear deterrence worked. The question whether nuclear deterrence deters war is somewhat like the controversial question whether capital punishment deters murder, except that in the case of capital punishment, there is a much greater amount of historical evidence on which to base an answer.

The question is one of risks and probabilities. No policy could have guaranteed that there would be no war or aggression. The question is whether nuclear deterrence made war and aggression less likely than it otherwise would have been. There are ways in which nuclear deterrence may have lessened the risk of war, such as by decreasing the likelihood of deliberate aggression, but there are also ways in which it may have increased the risk of war. It created the risk of accidental nuclear war and encouraged suspicion and mistrust, which may have increased the risk of war from miscalculation. The answer to the question whether nuclear deterrence works requires a balancing of such considerations.

NUCLEAR MORALITY IN THE SECOND NUCLEAR AGE

During the first nuclear age, there was general agreement that the use of nuclear weapons was not morally acceptable, especially in the light of the risk that any use could escalate to a large-scale nuclear war. As a result, the main controversial moral issue, as we have discussed, was whether nuclear deterrence was moral acceptable. This issue remains during the second nuclear age. Mutual nuclear deterrence continues to be practiced, if not between the United States and Russia, then between other pairs of nations, such as the United States and China, or India and Pakistan. But, because there is now little risk that the use of a single nuclear weapon would escalate to a large-scale nuclear war, the United States is now considering policies that envision the use of nuclear weapons in circumstances short of retaliation for a nuclear attack. These are still deterrence policies because they seek to use an expanded threat of nuclear use to deter certain forms of hostile behavior on the part of opponents. But these policies raise new moral issues because they increase the risk that nuclear weapons will be used, with all of the moral implications this has. A second, related set of moral issues that has come into prominence in the second nuclear age concerns efforts to halt the spread of nuclear weapons. This set of issues is related to the first set because the expanded threat of nuclear use is one way to control proliferation. Given the importance of controlling nuclear proliferation, it is crucial for nations to make efforts to put a stop to it, but there are moral limits on what nations may do in this regard. These are the two sets of moral issues regarding nuclear weapons we will examine in this section.

On January 8, 2002, the U.S. government released portions of a new version of the *Nuclear Policy Review*, the first since 1994 (discussed in Chapter 6). This document, discussing in broad outlines the role that nuclear weapons should play for the United States in the twenty-first century, was formed in large measure by two events. The first is, of course, the collapse of the Soviet Union and the end of the

Cold War in 1991, the event that inaugurated the second nuclear age. The foreword to the document states:

> First and foremost, the *Nuclear Posture Review* puts the Cold War practices related to planning for strategic forces behind us. ...The U.S. will no longer plan, size, or sustain its forces as though Russia presented merely a smaller version of the threat posed by the Soviet Union. ...The *Nuclear Posture Review* shifts planning for America's strategic forces from the threat-based approach of the Cold War to a capabilities-based approach.

This last sentence apparently means that the United States will seek to guarantee that adversaries will have the capabilities to attack taken away from them, not simply that they be deterred from attacking by our threat of retaliation. The second formative event is the terrorist attacks of 9/11.

> Second, we have concluded that a strategic posture that relies solely on offensive nuclear forces is inappropriate for deterring the potential adversaries we face in the 21st century. Terrorists or rogue states armed with weapons of mass destruction will likely test America's security commitments to its allies and friends. In response, we will need a range of capabilities to assure friend and foe alike of U.S. resolve.[27]

As a result, the *Nuclear Policy Review* asserts, nuclear weapons need to play a different role than they did during the first nuclear age. Nuclear deterrence is still of great importance, but deterrence may take different forms. In addition, nuclear weapons need to be part of an offensive capability for those cases where deterrence proves ineffective. Michael Gordon poses the question faced by the authors of the *Review*: "Should the purpose of nuclear weapons in the post-Cold-War world be essentially to deter a nuclear attack on the United States? Or should nuclear weapons be developed for fighting wars, including conflicts with nonnuclear adversaries?"[28] This is Ivo Daalder's account of the answer to this question given by the *Review* authors:

> Throughout the nuclear age, the fundamental goal has been to prevent the use of nuclear weapons. Now the policy has been turned upside down. It is to keep nuclear weapons as a tool of war-fighting rather than a tool of deterrence. If military planners are now to consider the nuclear option any time they confront a surprising military development, the distinction between nuclear and nonnuclear weapons fades away.[29]

Another feature of the new policy is a recasting of the relationship between nuclear and conventional weapons. In one respect, nuclear weapons are to be given greater emphasis because they will be used to do some of the jobs that conventional weapons have traditionally been used for. For example, the new approach includes using nuclear threats to deter not only nuclear attack, but also attack with chemical or biological weapons. The new approach will continue a policy of the United States since the early 1990s, "a position of calculated ambiguity as to whether it would actually use nuclear weapons in response to a chemical or biological attack, even if the aggressor did not possess nuclear weapons."[30] In the area of nuclear use, the *Nuclear Posture Review* "stresses the need to develop earth-penetrating nuclear weapons to destroy heavily fortified underground bunkers, including those that may be used to store chemical and biological weapons."[31] These would be the first new nuclear weapons developed since the 1980s.

In another respect, nuclear weapons will be given less emphasis. The size of the U.S. nuclear arsenal will be reduced. In November 2001, the United States and Russia agreed to cut their nuclear arsenals to a range of between 1,700 and 2,200 warheads by 2012. This is a significant cut for the United States, which at the turn of the century held 6,000 nuclear weapons. Of course, part of the reason for such reductions is that there is no longer a Soviet Union to deter. But another reason is that conventional weapons will be used in places where a nuclear weapon might have been used in the past. Developments in conventional weapons and in the accuracy of delivery systems will allow conventional weapons in some cases to produce a level of destruction that only nuclear weapons could have produced in the past. As an indication of this, there are plans to convert some Trident submarines so that they can fire conventional cruise missiles, and change the warheads in some ground-based intercontinental ballistic missiles from nuclear to conventional.[32]

It may seem paradoxical to suggest, as the *Nuclear Policy Review* does, that nuclear weapons in the second nuclear age will be given both a greater and a lesser emphasis. But this is simply the result, narrowing or dissolving the *firebreak* between nuclear and conventional weapons. The firebreak is a wide and easily recognized gap between the type of situations in which nuclear weapons would be used and in which conventional weapons would be used. During the first nuclear age, it was thought important to keep this firebreak wide and clear to reduce the risk that a conventional conflict would escalate into a nuclear conflict. But in the second nuclear age, the *Nuclear Policy Review* calls for a blurring of the line between the types of situations in which each kind of weapon might be used. Nuclear weapons will sometimes function as conventional weapons used to, and conventional weapons will sometimes function as nuclear weapons used to.

Consider one kind of case envisioned by the new nuclear policy. The United States may engage in preventive war with nuclear weapons against rogue states that are seen as developing a threatening WMD arsenal. (The 2003 war by the United States against Iraq is an example of a preventive war, though one carried out with conventional weapons only.[33]) Nuclear weapons would be used in such a war, for example, to destroy underground bunkers in which WMD may be stored, bunkers that conventional bombs might not be able to destroy (hence the need for the earth-penetrating nuclear warheads, mentioned above). It is important to remember that this policy not only expands the range of potential use of nuclear weapons, but also expands nuclear deterrence. One goal of the policy is to deter rogue states from developing WMD by the threat to attack them with nuclear weapons if they do. The idea is that by making it more likely that nuclear weapons would be used where in the past only conventional weapons would have been used, a more effective deterrent of the behavior of rogue states would be achieved.

Interestingly, this leads nuclear policy in a direction of some strategic ideas proposed during the first nuclear age, ideas such as flexible response, countervailing strategy, or nuclear war-fighting (discussed in chapter 4). The point of these cold-war policies, like the point of the current policies, was to threaten the use of nuclear weapons in a broader range of circumstances to create a better, more credible deterrent. For example, the thinking was that this policy was needed to deter a conventional attack by the Soviet Union against Western Europe.

The moral problem raised by the new nuclear policy (as well as by similar policy ideas in the first nuclear age) is that it increases the risk that nuclear weapons will be used. In a sense, this is deliberate. The thinking is that increasing the number of situations in which the weapons would be used makes those situations less likely to occur. This is why the policy is said to be a better deterrent. Some proponents of the new nuclear policy might argue, as mentioned earlier, that a policy of increasing the risk of the use of nuclear weapons is morally acceptable now, whereas it would not have been during the first nuclear age, because any use of nuclear weapons now would not carry the risks of escalation to large-scale nuclear war that it did during the cold war. The new policy could better deter rogue states from developing WMD, and this would make us all safer.

Thus, the policy is a kind of gamble. The upside of the gamble is that increasing the risk that nuclear weapons will be used will lead to a better deterrent of dangerous rogue-state behavior. The downside of the gamble is that the deterrent threat will fail and nuclear weapons will be used. The downside of the gamble is intensified by the belief that rogue states may not be deterrable, so that the expectation of the policy makers is that deterrence will fail and the weapons will have to be used. The moral objection to the policy is that this is not a gamble that should be taken, not simply because the gamble may be likely to fail, but also because the result of failure, the use of nuclear weapons, is morally unacceptable in itself. It is morally problematic to engage in a gamble with those kinds of stakes. The reasons for this were discussed earlier. One is that any use of nuclear weapons violates the principle of discrimination in just war theory. Another reason is that any use of nuclear weapons could undermine or destroy the nuclear taboo, which has helped keep us from nuclear war for 60 years. Any use of nuclear weapons may make the use of nuclear weapons much more likely in the future. The new nuclear policy may be akin to betting the farm, and betting the farm is morally problematic because, even if you think that the odds are in your favor, it could lead to a catastrophic outcome.

Now we consider the set of issues concerning the morality of efforts, on the part of the United States and other powers, to control the proliferation of nuclear weapons, as well as other weapons of mass destruction. (WMD include nuclear, chemical, and biological weapons.) The second nuclear age is characterized by great concern about the potential of rogue states or terrorists to attack the United States, as occurred on 9/11, especially when those attacks may involve WMD, and the moral issues in question arise largely in response to these concerns. Rogue states or terrorists may acquire and use WMD against the United States or its allies. The risk of this increases with the proliferation of WMD, so it is important to control such proliferation, and important moral issues arise from anti-proliferation efforts. Such efforts include, at an extreme, the waging by the United States of preventive war, possibility with nuclear weapons.

First, then, what, if anything, does just war theory have to say about efforts to stop WMD proliferation? An important preliminary question is whether it is morally acceptable to proliferate. Is it morally wrong for a nation without nuclear weapons or other WMD to acquire them? Note that all nuclear states were at one time proliferators. Speaking generally, it could be argued that, if it is morally wrong to become a nuclear proliferator, it is, by parity of reasoning, morally wrong for a nuclear state to retain the nuclear weapons it has acquired by having become a proliferator in the past. The moral obligation for nuclear *nonacquisition* on the part of potential proliferators seems to go hand in hand with a moral obligation for nuclear *deacquisition* on the part of nuclear nations. In addition, this is, as we saw in Chapter 8, what the Nuclear Nonproliferation Treaty requires of the nuclear powers.

But here the paradox of nuclear deterrence comes into play. During the first nuclear age, the superpowers saw nuclear deterrence as necessary for their survival. As we argued earlier, their *jus in bello* moral obligation to abandon nuclear weapons was set against the *jus ad bellum* moral acceptability of nuclear deterrence for the sake of self-defense. The same argument may apply to potential nuclear proliferators. Their national survival may be threatened by nuclear weapons already in the hands of opponents. Thus, the nuclear weapons program of Nazi Germany threatened the United States, U.S. nuclear weapons threatened the Soviet Union, Soviet bombs threatened China, Chinese bombs threatened India, and Indian bombs threatened Pakistan. The paradox applies to potential nuclear proliferators as well, and their obligation not to acquire nuclear weapons must be set against the moral acceptability of their doing so due to the risk to their survival, if they do not.

But the moral question we would like to consider for the remainder of this section is: What are the moral limits on anti-proliferation policies? Anti-proliferation policies are efforts by a nation to stop another from acquiring nuclear weapons. What is a nation morally permitted to do in seeking to stop such proliferation? One central moral concept in this regard is *fairness*. Unfair actions are generally morally wrong, and it seems unfair to allow some nations to have nuclear weapons, but not to allow others. Is it fair of the United States, which has nuclear weapons, to stop other nations from acquiring them? It seems that the nuclear "haves" are being unfair in their efforts to stop further proliferation. On this view, any anti-proliferation policies by nuclear nations like the United States appear to be morally problematic.

Following this logic, Indian policymakers have often argued that the nonproliferation regime (that is, the set of international laws and rules set up mostly by the nuclear nations to stop nuclear proliferation) is unfair. India has used this argument to justify its not signing the Nuclear Non-Proliferation Treaty and its 1974 and 1998 nuclear tests. In fact, this argument based on unfairness explains an apparent inconsistency in India's pronouncements regarding nuclear weapons. India has long claimed (1) that the nuclear nations should abandon their nuclear weapons and (2) that India has the right to develop such weapons. This only seems like a contradiction. Each of these claims is a different way to avoid an unfair situation: Either no nation should have nuclear weapons or every nation should have the right to acquire them.

But this unfairness argument needs to be more carefully thought out. Recall from Chapter 8 that there are three kinds of anti-proliferation policy: a nation can either *coerce* another not to acquire nuclear weapons (for example, through force or threat of force), *deny* the other some knowledge or material necessary for building a bomb, or seek to acquire the other nation's *cooperation* in not proliferating. The unfairness argument seems clearly to apply if the nation with nuclear weapons is using coercion to stop proliferation, for then it would be seeking to halt proliferation against the will of the potential proliferator. The unfairness argument may or may not apply to anti-proliferation policies based on denial, depending on what form the denial takes. But the argument does not apply in the case of a cooperative anti-proliferation policy, for then the potential proliferator is invited voluntarily to refrain from acquiring nuclear weapons. From a moral perspective, the unfairness argument seems to rule out coercion, and perhaps denial, as acceptable forms of anti-proliferation policy for nations with nuclear weapons. It seems, then, that the only form of anti-proliferation policy that is clearly morally acceptable for the United States is a cooperative one.

This is another argument against the new nuclear policy discussed earlier in this section. The new nuclear policy has extended the threat to use nuclear weapons to seek to deter nuclear and other WMD proliferation. This is a policy of coercive anti-proliferation or denuclearization, and as such, is now seen to be morally problematic for a reason in addition to that described earlier, which was that such an extension of deterrence is a gamble that is not morally acceptable. Now we see that it is morally problematic also because it is a coercive policy in a situation where coercion is unfair. But here we considering coercive anti-proliferation in general, which may involve threat and use of conventional as well as nuclear weapons.

Consider a coercive anti-proliferation policy involving the use of military force, conventional or nuclear, against recent or potential proliferators. When the reason for such a war is to eliminate weapons of mass destruction, especially nuclear weapons, then it is a form of anti-proliferation policy. Is it morally acceptable to engage in war to stop proliferation? In response to 9/11, the Bush administration announced a policy of "preemptive" war and put this policy into practice in 2003 in Iraq. The policy is to attack nations that either harbor terrorists or are developing WMD that might be used against the United States or its interests. The attack is to occur not in retaliation for the use of such weapons, but before the weapons are used, which is why the policy is referred to as one of "preemptive" war.

Is such a policy morally acceptable? The kind of war recommended by the policy would not be defensive, as just war theory requires, because it would not be in response to an attack. In fact, as we have said, the term "preemptive war" is a misnomer. There is an important distinction in just war theory between *preemptive war* and *preventive war* (this difference was also discussed in Chapters 4 and 8). A preemptive war is a war initiated by a nation under threat of imminent attack. It is a defensive war, even though it involves striking the first blow, because the nation attacked is itself in the process of attacking. So, it may be morally justified. But a preventive war is another matter. A preventive war is a war undertaken against an opponent who, it is feared, might attack some time in the future.[34] A preventive war is morally unacceptable because it violates the rights of the nation attacked. A nation has a right to be free from attack unless it first attacks another (or is about to attack, as in the case of preemptive war). But the anti-proliferation policy of the Bush administration proposes to attack a nation because that nation may in the future use WMD against the United States. As such, it represents, from the perspective of just war theory, a form of anti-proliferation policy that is not morally acceptable.[35]

But this matter bears further discussion. Some would argue that one of the ways in which nuclear weapons have changed things morally is that they have made obsolete the traditional prohibition of preventive war. If a hostile nation has nuclear weapons, its opponents cannot wait for it to strike first, given the immense damage nuclear weapons can accomplish. In justifying the war against Iraq, President Bush's National Security Advisor Condoleezza Rice said that we would not want "the smoking gun" of the Iraqi plan to attack the United States to be "a mushroom cloud."[36] Nations no longer have the moral luxury to hold off on military action until an attack occurs and they can respond in self-defense. To stop a potential attack by WMD, preventive war must be permitted. If this is the case, then the earlier claim that coercive anti-proliferation policy is not morally acceptable may be false. It is difficult to decide whether this argument is sufficient to lead us to abandon the traditional opposition of just war theory to preventive war. For this argument to be strong enough, it seems that a nation contemplating a preventive attack would have to be fairly sure of three things: (1) that if it waits for the opponent to attack first with its WMD, the damage would be catastrophic; (2) that if the preventive attack is not undertaken, the feared future WMD attack by the opponent would be very likely to occur; and (3) that there are no acceptable means, apart from the preventive attack, to avoid the WMD attack. For example, (3) would require that the nation could be fairly sure that the opponent's attack could not be deterred.[37] Critics of the argument would argue that is unlikely that a nation contemplating a preventive war could be fairly sure of all these three things.

But is the current form of cooperative anti-proliferation policy, based, in the case of nuclear weapons, mainly on the Nuclear Non-Proliferation Treaty (NPT), morally acceptable? The NPT was discussed in Chapter 8, but here we consider it from a moral perspective. Because the nonnuclear signatories of the NPT have agreed in signing the treaty not to acquire nuclear weapons, it seems like it would not be unfair to seek to hold them to that agreement.[38] But just as the nonnuclear signatories should be held to their obligations under that treaty, so should the nuclear signatories. The nuclear nations, under Article VI of the treaty, agreed "to pursue negotiations in good faith on effective measures relating to cessation of the nuclear arms race at an early date and to nuclear disarmament." So, far, the nuclear nations have not lived up to this commitment. The nuclear nations give every indication of expecting to hang on to their nuclear weapons indefinitely. So the fairness argument comes in again here. It may not be fair to require nonnuclear signatories of the treaty to avoid proliferation, though they have agreed to do so, because the nuclear nations have not fulfilled their part of the bargain. Perhaps the only way for the nuclear nations fairly to enforce nonproliferation on the nonnuclear signatories of the NPT would be for the nuclear nations to adhere to their commitments under Article VI of the treaty and vigorously pursue nuclear disarmament.

SUMMARY

Morality is a set of values concerning how humans should act, especially in their relationships with others. It can be presented in terms of rules of conduct that individuals or nations should observe in their interactions with others. Just war theory is the traditional approach to the morality of military matters. Just war theory contrasts, on the one hand, with pacifism, which views war as morally unacceptable, and, on the other, with moral realism, which holds that morality does not apply to war. Just war theory finds some wars and some conduct in war morally acceptable and some not. The rules of just war theory are divided into two groups: *jus ad bellum*, rules about when a nation is morally permitted to go to war, and *jus in bello*, rules about how a nation is morally permitted to fight in war. The basic idea of *jus ad bellum* is that only defensive war is permitted; wars of aggression are not allowed. The basic ideas of *jus in bello* are, first, that civilians are not to be attacked in war (the principle of discrimination) and, second, that the amount of benefit resulting from a military action should be greater than the amount of harm the action causes (the principle of proportionality).

Nuclear weapons are unique among military technologies in their destructive capabilities. As a result, when the rules of just war theory, specifically *jus in bello*, are applied to the idea of using nuclear weapons in war, the conclusion is that their use is not morally acceptable. Nuclear weapons would cause too much destruction overall (violating proportionality), and too much harm to civilians (violating discrimination). Even the use of one nuclear weapon could lead through escalation to the use of many. This conclusion applies in both the first and second nuclear ages, though the problem of escalation is less in the second age.

But nuclear deterrence, in both nuclear ages, raises a special moral problem. Deterrence, if it is successful, causes no actual harm, but, of course, success is not guaranteed. The threat may get carried out. According to the rules of *jus in bello*, nuclear deterrence is not morally acceptable because the policy involves the threat, and so the intention, to use nuclear weapons, which would itself be morally wrong. No one can guarantee that the threat would not get carried out, the intention acted on. But, at the same time, according to the rules of *jus ad bellum*, a nation is morally permitted to defend itself, and if a nation's opponent has nuclear weapons, the nation may feel the need to acquire nuclear weapons and practice nuclear deterrence for its own defense. Thus, nuclear deterrence is both prohibited and (in some cases) permitted. This is the paradox of nuclear deterrence. The moral problem of nuclear weapons is that they, in this way, force the two branches of just war theory into sharp opposition to each other. This sort of problem has led Michael Walzer to observe: "Nuclear weapons explode the theory of just war. They are the first of mankind's technological innovations that are simply not encompassable within the familiar moral world."[39]

The moral paradox remains in the second nuclear age, even though concern about the dangers of nuclear deterrence has been pushed into the background with the end of the superpower confrontation. The paradox is inherent in the existence of nuclear weapons, and they cannot be disinvented. Nuclear deterrence continues to be practiced, if not between the United States and the Soviet Union, then between other pairs of nations. But, in addition, the second nuclear age brings new moral problems to the fore. The main concern about nuclear weapons now is their proliferation (along with that of other weapons of mass destruction) to rogue states or terrorists, who might not be deterred, and so might use them. This raises questions about the morality of anti-proliferation efforts. One of these is an application of the fairness argument. It may not be fair for current nuclear powers to demand that other nations not acquire nuclear weapons when they themselves refuse to give up theirs and, in particular, do so in the face of their commitments under the Non-Proliferation Treaty to disarm.

In addition, there is a question about the morality of the U.S. policy of "preemptive" war meant to stop proliferation or to stop successful proliferators from using their newly acquired weapons. Such wars, which are in general preventive rather than preemptive, are not acceptable under the rules of *jus ad bellum* because they are not a defense against an attack. But this raises the question whether the great destructive power of nuclear weapons might require that just war theory be revised to permit such wars. Also, the new nuclear policy adopted by the United States in the second nuclear age needs examination. The 2002 *Nuclear Policy Review* called for a widening of the circumstances in which nuclear weapons might be used, including, for example, their use against WMD facilities of rogue states. There are serious moral problems with this policy because it makes the use of nuclear weapons more likely and risks undermining the nuclear taboo that has helped keep the world free from nuclear use since 1945.

POSTSCRIPT: ON THE RELATION BETWEEN MORALITY AND NATIONAL SECURITY

In the final section of this book, the next three chapters, we compare three possible nuclear futures and policies needed to get us to each of them. So, it is appropriate to summarize at this point how morality can be a guide to nuclear policy choices. The distinction between morality and prudence is crucial in understanding this. By "prudence" we mean national self-interest, or, as it is more often called in the military context, national security. Prudence is as much a guide to action as morality is, and policy makers certainly appeal much more to prudence, in the guise of national security, than to morality in making their policy choices. In fact, given what they say about how they make their decisions and how they justify them, leaders take national security as their principal or exclusive guide, giving morality little attention. (In this respect, policy makers often seem to be moral realists.) Indeed, most of the argument in the next three chapters will be couched in terms of national security rather than morality.

We mentioned earlier that, though morality and prudence sometimes conflict, they are often in accord. Indeed, in the case of national self-interest, as in the case of individual self-interest, the more we look at the long term rather than the short term, the more morality and self-interest seem to converge. For example, in an individual case, while cheating may be in a person's short-term self-interest, it is much less likely to be in his or her long-term self-interest. In the long-term, morality and self-interest seem to converge, or at least to come closer than they appear from the short-term perspective. In the case of national security, the long-term convergence between morality and self-interest is especially strong as far as nuclear weapons policy is concerned. The reason is the tremendous destructive power of nuclear weapons. From the moral side, it is, as we have seen, of great importance that nuclear weapons not be used, because they would likely kill many civilians and because of the high level of overall harm they are likely to cause, given the number of nuclear weapons that exist in the world and the risk of escalation.[40] From the side of national security, the risk of escalation means that any use of nuclear weapons is likely, at least over the long term, to lead to nuclear attack against the nation using them. In addition, given the present state of international interdependence, reflected in the idea of "globalization," destroying one part of the world with nuclear weapons is likely to do significant harm (at least of an economic sort) to one's own nation. Thus both morality and prudence strongly recommend choosing a nuclear weapons policy that minimizes the likelihood that nuclear weapons will be used.

Of course, policy considerations, especially from the side of national security, are much more complicated than this simple account implies. For example, there would be strong disagreements among policymakers about the relative importance of the goals a nuclear weapons policy is meant to achieve and differences over how risky certain policies are. But the account does suggest that if policy makers think of national security in the long term, they will be making decisions that are at least close to those they would make were they choosing on the basis of morality. But there may be one important respect in which morality and national security are partly at odds. Because of the moral paradox generated by nuclear weapons, as discussed earlier in the chapter, morality would place a strong value on getting rid of all nuclear weapons, at least if and when this could be done in a way that would not pose a great risk to national self-interest. This may place morality more on the side of the kind of policy discussed in Chapter 14, which seeks the elimination of nuclear weapons.

ENDNOTES

[1]The quotations in these two paragraphs were taken from Mike Moore, "World Court says mostly no to nuclear weapons" and Peter Weiss, "And now, abolition," both in *The Bulletin of the Atomic Scientists* (September/October 1996), pp. 39, 41, 43.

[2]Quoted in Moore, "World Court," p. 41.

[3]Moore, "World Court," p. 41.

[4]Richard Falk, "Nuclear Weapons, International Law, and the World Court: A Historic Encounter," *The American Journal of International Law* 91 (1997), p. 70.

[5]Quoted in Moore, "World Court," p. 41.

[6]The passages in this paragraph from the Catholic Bishops are in U.S. Catholic Bishops, *The Challenge of Peace* (Washington, D.C.: U.S. Catholic Conference, 1983), p. 39.

[7]A number of important books discussing morality and nuclear weapons in the first nuclear age appeared in the 1980s. Among these are: Douglas Lackey, *Moral Principles and Nuclear Weapons* (Totowa, NJ: Rowman & Allenheld, 1984); Douglas MacLean (ed.), *The Security Gamble* (Totowa, NJ: Rowman & Allenheld, 1984); Russell Hardin et al. (eds), *Nuclear Deterrence—Ethics and Strategy* (Chicago: University of Chicago Press, 1985); Michael Fox and Leo Groarke (eds.), *Nuclear War—Philosophical Perspectives* (New York: Peter Lang, 1985); Avner Cohen and Steven Lee (eds.), *Nuclear Weapons and the Future of Humanity* (Totowa, NJ: Rowman and Allanheld, 1986); *Nuclear War—the Moral Dimension* (New Brunswick, NJ: Transaction Books, 1986); Joseph Nye, *Nuclear Ethics* (New York: Free Press, 1986); John Finnis, Joseph Boyle, and Germain Grisez, *Nuclear Deterrence, Morality and Realism* (Oxford: Oxford

University Press, 1987). See also, Steven Lee, *Morality, Prudence, and Nuclear Weapons* (Cambridge: Cambridge University Press, 1993).

[8]Fred J. Cook, "The Enthronement of Naked Force," in Paul Baker (ed.), *The Atomic Bomb: the Great Decision* (New York: Holt, Rinehart, and Winston, 1968), p. 75.

[9]Moral realism is different from the realism discussed in chapter 8 on proliferation. The realism discussed in chapter 8 is a form of political rather than moral realism. Political realism holds that leaders do not act on moral principles in international affairs, while moral realism holds that moral principles do not apply to international affairs.

[10]For a discussion of *jus ad bellum* and *jus in bello*, see U.S. Catholic Bishops, *Challenge of Peace*, pp. 26–34, and William O'Brien, *The Conduct of Just and Limited War* (New York: Praeger, 1981), pp. 13–70.

[11]For an excellent argument to this effect, see John C. Ford, "The Morality of Obliteration Bombing," in Richard Wasserstrom, ed., *War and Morality* (Belmont, CA: Wadsworth, 1970), pp. 15–41.

[12]For a valuable discussion of realism, see Richard Wasserstrom, "On the Morality of War: A Preliminary Inquiry," in Wasserstrom, *War and Morality*, pp. 78–85.

[13]This argument is made forcefully by Michael Walzer in his book *Just and Unjust Wars* (New York: Basic Books, 1977).

[14]Ford, "Morality of Obliteration Bombing," p. 39.

[15]See Paul Ehrlich *et al.*, *The Cold and the Dark* (New York: Norton, 1984).

[16]Jonathan Schell, *The Fate of the Earth* (New York: Avon Books, 1982), section II.

[17]There is another possibility for nuclear use in the second nuclear age, namely, the use of a nuclear weapon by a traditional nuclear nation against a nonnuclear nation. This has become more of a possibility in the second nuclear age because the user might not, as would have been the case in the cold war, risk nuclear retaliation by one of the superpowers in defense of the nonnuclear nation. But such a use would not be morally acceptable for some of the same reasons that use of nuclear weapons by a new nuclear nation would not be, as we discuss below.

[18]Is the nuclear threat a threat to retaliate with nuclear weapons against any form of military aggression or against a nuclear attack only? Different nuclear strategists have a different response to this question. Some of this is discussed below.

[19]R. A. Markus, "Conscience and Deterrence," in Walter Stein (ed.), *Nuclear Weapons: A Catholic Response* (New York: Sheed and Ward, 1961), pp. 71–72.

[20]In opposition to this argument, some thinkers in the just-war tradition have argued that nuclear deterrence is morally acceptable. But they usually do so on the basis of the claim, contrary to our earlier argument, that some uses of nuclear weapons in war are morally acceptable as well. See, for example, Paul Ramsey, *The Just War* (New York: Scribner and Sons, 1968).

[21]Thomas Schelling, *Choice and Consequence* (Cambridge, MA: Harvard University Press), p. 315.

[22]For a discussion of these issues, see Lee, *Morality, Prudence, and Nuclear Weapons*, chapter 2.

[23]Bishops, *Challenge of Peace*, pp. 46–62.

[24]Bishops, *Challenge of Peace*, p. 58.

[25]Bishops, *Challenge of Peace*, p. 55. For an excellent critical discussion of the bishops' letter, see Susan Okin, "Taking the Bishops Seriously," *World Politics* 36, no. 4 (Summer 1984), pp. 527–554.

[26]See, for example, Walzer, *Just and Unjust Wars*, chapter 17, and Gregory Kavka, "Some Paradoxes of Nuclear Deterrence," *Journal of Philosophy* 75 (1978), pp. 285–302.

[27]Nuclear Posture Review [Excerpts],

[28]Michael Gordon, "Nuclear Arms: For Deterrence or Fighting?" *New York Times*, March 11, 2002.

[29]Ivo Daalder, quoted in Gordon, "Nuclear Arms."

[30]"America as a Nuclear Rogue," editorial, *New York Times*, March 12, 2002.

[31]Michael Gordon, "U.S. Nuclear Plan Sees New Targets and New Weapons," *New York Times*, March 10, 2002.

[32]Eric Schmitt, "New Command Would Meld Missile Defense and Offense," *New York Times*, June 25, 2002, and "Threats and Responses: Strategies; U.S. Considers Conventional Warheads on Nuclear Missiles," *New York Times*, February 24, 2003.

[33]Of course, as things turned out, Iraq had no WMD. The Bush administration referred to the Iraq war as a preemptive war rather than a preventive war, but the war was clearly preventive rather than preemptive. The Iraq war was discussed in Chapter 8.

[34]An example of a preventive war is the war Japan began by attacking Pearl Harbor.

[35]The Afghanistan War and the Iraq War are morally distinct in this respect. The Afghanistan War was arguably neither preemptive nor preventive, but defensive in the classic sense, because the United States had been struck first on 9/11 by forces using that nation as a base. The Iraq War was preventive and so morally wrong.

[36]This general discussion of preventive war should be kept separate from the specific case of the United States war against Iraq. Even if some preventive wars are justified there are legitimate questions about whether the Iraq War would be such a case.

[37]In the early 1950s, the United States considered a preventive war against the Soviet Union as the Soviet Union was beginning to develop its nuclear arsenal. Presumably, part of the reason such a war was not undertaken was that the U.S. leaders believed that the Soviet Union could be deterred from launching a future nuclear attack against the United States.

[38]Of course, if the nuclear states have applied coercion to get some nonnuclear states to sign the NPT, this argument may not apply to those nonnuclear states.

[39]Walzer, *Just and Unjust Wars*, p. 282.

[40]Recall that the escalation may be immediate, as it likely would have been in the first nuclear age, or over a longer period of time, as it likely would be in the second age, resulting from the breaking of the nuclear taboo.

12

Coercive Denuclearization

In the fall of 2003, Bob Woodward of *The Washington Post* interviewed President George W. Bush. The United States had, at the President's direction, already waged war successfully against Iraq and was now concentrating on the occupation. The President reflected on his decisions:

> September the 11th obviously changed my thinking a lot about my responsibility as president. Because September the 11th made the security of the American people the priority ... a sacred duty for the president. It is the most necessary duty for the president, because if the president doesn't take on that duty, who else is going to?

It changed his attitude toward "Saddam Hussein's capacity to create harm," he said, adding that "all his terrible features became more threatening. Keeping Saddam in a box looked less and less feasible to me." Saddam was a "madman," the president said. "He had used weapons of mass destruction in the past. He has created incredible instability in the neighborhood." Saddam had invaded Iran in the 1980s and Kuwait in the 1990s.

Bush added, "The options in Iraq were relatively limited when you are playing the containment game."[1]

The President's ruminations reflect one possible American response to the nuclear predicament in the second nuclear age. The United States had to deal directly, forcefully, and—if need be—unilaterally with the Saddams of the world who have nuclear weapons. Was this the only policy available to the United States? Was it the best response? Does it continue to be the best response? In this and the following two chapters, we join the debate about how best to cope with the nuclear predicament from this point forward. We explore three different policy options and urge you to consider the strengths and weaknesses of each.

Our perspective is American-centric in that we speak principally about what the United States might do. While we do this because most of our readers are Americans, there is a more pragmatic point. In a hegemonic world, while the United States cannot necessarily make the world the way it wants, without American leadership the odds of producing any outcome other than sheer drift are reduced. It is equally true that the hegemon cannot effectively shape the world without the participation of others. They, too, have a responsibility to evaluate the options open to the United States and make clear their hopes and concerns.

Given the nature of the predicament, a perfect solution is beyond our reach. Moreover, there is no way to know in advance what is the best—even though imperfect—option. On the other hand, doing nothing—that is, making no attempt to devise a conscious strategy to deal with the predicament—is, we believe, the worst choice we might make, for it is most likely to produce the third nuclear age, the age of nuclear use. Once we cross that threshold, prospects for the relatively unconstrained use of nuclear weapons increase dramatically.

Each option offers a different, sometimes quite different, response to the nuclear predicament. Nonetheless, each option tries to cope with what this book has argued are the fundamental features of the nuclear predicament. Each recognizes *the permanent nature of the nuclear predicament*: Nuclear weapons will always exist in their weapons form, or in the available raw materials that may at the time be devoted to the peaceful production of nuclear energy, or in the ineradicable knowledge that nuclear weapons can be built and that the technologies to do so are available. Each option recognizes *the anarchical nature of the international system*: Because no state or world government guarantees any state's security, states will acquire weapons to defend themselves, thus making the possession of nuclear weapons a continually attractive option for some states. Each option recognizes that in an anarchical world, *states will periodically come into intense conflict with each other.* Their leaders will often believe that a state's power and prestige will determine its success in that conflict. Therefore, the possession of and brandishing of nuclear weapons may usefully augment power and prestige. Finally, each option recognizes *the uncertainty of the second nuclear age*: The existing nuclear rules of the road, laboriously crafted in the first nuclear age, seem not to speak to new circumstances, and traditional arms control has floundered. The new element in world politics, global terrorism, has not yet been successfully dealt with. Uncertainty may make nuclear weapons seem all the more necessary.

Each of the policy prescriptions also reflects another argument of this book: Nuclear weapons always exist *in particular contexts*. Those contexts will shape future decisions to produce and use such weapons. Thus any long-term strategy to create a desired nuclear future must also consider how we might need *to shape the context* in which states make decisions about nuclear weapons.

SHAPING THE CONTEXT FOR DECISIONS ABOUT NUCLEAR WEAPONS

The context that we believe gives the peoples of the world the best chance to deal with nuclear weapons has these characteristics. First, there has to be *increased security* for the states and peoples of the world, as security fears play an important role in the acquisition and possible use of nuclear weapons. Perversely, going nuclear created insecurity for others. Proliferation is therefore both a sign of and a cause of insecurity. Preventing proliferation may be a part of the answer, but alone it cannot resolve the concern about security.

Second, there must be *mechanisms that encourage the discovery of just, equitable, and reasonable solutions* to the issues that divide states and peoples. Issues spawn conflict between states. States may contemplate the use of force to resolve the conflict, thus increasing the likelihood that nuclear weapons will seem desirable for bargaining or to compel the settlement of an issue—or to prevent others from imposing an unfavorable settlement. Some issues may, of course, be beyond the capacity for any such mechanisms to handle, but without them disputes may metastasize, making force seem the only way to respond. Such mechanisms usually must be negotiated rather than imposed, and negotiated in advance. The United Nations has historically been a major step in that direction.

Third, we should support the development of societies and polities to *meet the just and reasonable aspirations of their citizens*. We suspect that open, tolerant societies, democratic in political organization, offer the best opportunity to meet those aspirations, and in so doing, reduce the likelihood of conflict between states and peoples. Democratic polities—particularly broadly representative democratic polities—are less likely to use force against each other. As Spencer Weart argues, their political culture emphasizes a search for accommodation when parties disagree rather than attempting to establish a hierarchy of power and command.[2]

Additionally, open societies have greater capacities for empathy, the ability to recognize that while others may see the world differently, they, at heart, are much like us. While a begrudging *tolerance* allows us to put up with others, *empathy* allows us to listen respectfully to the perspectives of others, thus making accommodation possible. Indeed, empathy allows for making concessions to others without insisting on a strict quid pro quo—just as we treat friends in our daily lives and respond to the plight of unknown others ravaged by hurricanes and tsunamis. Empathy makes it much more difficult to consider the use of any weapon of mass destruction against the other.

In laying out these considerations, you may have already sensed that there are important tensions. To fulfill one hope may make the accomplishment of another more difficult. For example, U.S. efforts to promote democracy in states whose leaders are autocrats will threaten the security of those regimes. They may respond with hostility and fear, seeking to thwart U.S. efforts by increasing their military power (perhaps by going nuclear) or by supporting non-state actors such as terrorists. Similarly, in certain circumstances, some of these sought-for attributes may be dangerous. Empathy may lead us to believe that our opponent really does not intend us grievous harm, when in fact that is exactly what is intended and every concession or show of good faith on our part encourages a more energetic attack on our position. No policy can satisfy all goals and avoid all dangers. You will need to consider what you might be willing to sacrifice or de-emphasize in order to achieve a particular outcome you find more desirable. While we might disagree on the desirability of such a trade-off, we do need to recognize its existence and weigh the alternatives carefully.

GENERAL ASSUMPTIONS FOR DEVISING A NUCLEAR FUTURE

Each of the specific policies that we present in this and the next two chapters shares several basic assumptions. We identify them here, for you need to be aware that in making these assumptions, we do limit the range of possibilities for thinking about the future. First and foremost, we assume that any policy should *actively attempt to reduce the likelihood of the use of nuclear weapons*. While it might be argued that in certain cases, some use of nuclear weapons might be salutary—after all, two atomic bombs seemed to bring the Pacific War to a close and may have made post-war governments more cautious in their foreign policies—we judge a benign outcome from nuclear use to be far less probable than a tragic outcome.

Second, we assume that any policy should *thwart dangerous nuclear proliferation* as much as possible. Expanding the number of nuclear weapons states or actors increases the risks of use and makes more complex—and hence potentially more uncontrollable—the dynamics between nuclear armed states that come into conflict. Recall that the Cold War simplified the calculus: A threat against a superpower or its allies meant a superpower confrontation, and that helped stay the hand of decision makers. While it might be argued that proliferation might serve some stabilizing purposes, only one destabilizing act is likely to produce a sea-change in world politics, most likely for the worst.

Third, we assume that there is a pressing need to *respond to a state or less-than-state actor (such as a terrorist group) that creates serious threats to the existence of other states or to their core interests*. States or other actors that seek radical change in the international system are likely to contemplate the acquisition of and the use of nuclear weapons, creating the peril we seek to avoid. Their intended victims will of necessity think along those lines as well. While it might be argued that it is impossible to prevent serious conflict in an anarchical world, we would argue that the hallmark of the twentieth century was a gradual recognition by many states—including the major powers—that wars of territorial expansion are too devastating to combatants and non-combatants alike. Therefore, states and groups that sought the violent overthrow of the status quo were actors who had to be confronted. That should remain our guidepost as well.

COERCIVE DENUCLEARIZATION'S PREMISES

The policy option this chapter considers is essentially a continuation of the Bush administration's approach. We will call this the *coercive denuclearization* option, rolling coercive anti-proliferation and coercive denuclearization into a package for the purposes of this discussion. After laying out its features, we provide an assessment.

Coercive denuclearization begins with the premise that when the United States itself is threatened or under attack, the security of *all* states is threatened, for if states or terrorist organizations pursue a hostile policy toward the hegemon, they surely will contemplate attacking weaker states. And if they are successful in their challenge to the United States, they *will* attack weaker states that do not comply with their demands.

Hostile states or terrorist groups recognize that they cannot defeat the United States in a traditional military contest. Therefore, they will seek creative means of attack, designed to bypass the defenses of a nation (as in al Qaeda's use of hijacked aircraft to attack buildings in the United States) or to challenge U.S. military power in low-cost operations (as in al Qaeda's use of a two-man rubber raft in the suicide attack on the destroyer *USS Cole* or Iraqi insurrectionists' use of Improvised Explosive Devices against American vehicles). Such attacks define success in terms of destroying American targets of a symbolic nature and in undermining U.S. prestige and determination by producing military and civilian casualties. *Political* success would come if the United States withdrew from the engagement or terminated its policy rather than to continue to suffer such losses. The withdrawal of U.S. forces from Mogadishu, Somalia, in 1993 and the abandonment of its attempt to impose a solution on the Somali civil war are emblematic of the outcome sought by such states and actors—and is often cited by bin Laden as how America can be compelled to withdraw from Islamic territory.

In some cases, states or terrorist groups will target U.S. allies. Success there can erode U.S. prestige and power as it raises questions about the desirability of an alliance with the United States. Success can cause the ally to end its support for U.S. policy, as the train bombings in Madrid in 2004 apparently influenced an election outcome, which brought an end to Spanish participation in the American-led occupation of Iraq. Even threats can have a similar result. North Korea has threatened to bathe Seoul, South Korea, in a sea of fire if war breaks out, and has warned that it might initiate war in response to what it deems to be unbearably provocative American acts. South Korea has subsequently leaned on the United States to be more accommodating in the negotiations regarding the North's nuclear weapons program.

A policy of coercive denuclearization adds one final, critical premise: *Nuclear weapons or radiological devices will always attract the interests of hostile states and terrorist groups*. While such weapons are very unlikely to be able to compel the surrender of the United States, they can clearly meet the objective of causing mass devastation in order to shape public opinion which in turn might force the United States to change its policies. Even the threatened possession of such weapons can enhance the prestige of the holder, draw in new recruits, and add great weight to the counsels within other governments who advocate accommodating the interests of the hostile state or terrorist group.

A POLICY OF COERCIVE DENUCLEARIZATION

At its heart, then, a policy of coercive denuclearization begins with a basic demand: *Any state hostile to the United States must provide clear evidence that it does not have nuclear or radiological weapons or the capability to acquire such weapons and that it eschews any plan to acquire them in the future*. At a minimum, hostile states cannot have plutonium reprocessing capabilities nor uranium enrichment capabilities, even for peaceful electrical power generation. Ideally, they should not have nuclear power generators, but as a concession, the United States might tolerate nuclear power generators if there is tight international control over fuel sources and spent fuel rods. Hostile states must be Non-Proliferation Treaty (NPT) signatories and accept the Additional Protocol giving the International Atomic Energy Agency wide investigative powers to detect any movement toward nuclear weapons. They must be in compliance with all NPT obligations. Their international trade must be transparent enough to ensure that nuclear weapons and associated technologies are not entering from outside sources.

In return, the United States would tolerate the existence of a hostile regime as long as it clearly denies itself the capability of inflicting nuclear harm on the United States or its allies. Furthermore, the United States may offer hostile states that meet this requirement—as Libya has—some tangible rewards in terms of lowered levels of U.S. hostility. In the long run, however, because authoritarians hostile to the United States are likely to succumb to the nuclear temptation at some point, for its own security the United States must look to *eventual* regime change in such states and ultimately to the development of democracy within them.

As we have seen, some hostile states already have programs in place to produce nuclear weapons or have in fact produced nuclear weapons. Coercive denuclearization demands that the United States act to remove those weapons or weapons-producing capabilities. In confronting hostile states having nuclear weapons or nuclear weapons programs, the United States must consider the full range of measures available to it to bring about denuclearization, *including the waging of preventive war*. In most cases, it will begin with diplomatic and economic pressure. While the United States will invite other states to participate in the actions it deems prudent and necessary, it must ultimately make the decision as to the particular means it will employ and it will proceed with a coalition of one if necessary. Moreover, it will take the lead in designating the specific focus of concern, for while there may be more than one state creating a nuclear threat (such as Iran and North Korea from the 1990s onward), the United States will invariably bear the brunt of any denuclearization effort and needs therefore to gauge its resources carefully.

In pursuit of denuclearization, the United States can offer some tangible rewards. These might include access to economic benefits and membership in international organizations. In some cases, it may offer a tacit pledge to forego the pursuit of regime change as long as the current incumbent or coterie controlling the government is in power and keeps the state non-nuclear.

In the pursuit of denuclearization against recalcitrant states, the United States would make clear that if it attacks, it will target the leadership of the state along with the weapons, their delivery systems, and the means of production of those weapons. To accomplish these missions, the United States reserves the right to use nuclear weapons, including first use, if it judges the circumstances warrant. Indeed, if it suspects that a nuclear strike is in preparation or contemplated by the opponent, it will strike first, with nuclear weapons if necessary.

Regarding terrorists, coercive denuclearization necessitates that the United States attack and destroy any terrorist organization that seeks to acquire or does acquire nuclear capabilities (or radiological devices), as such possession must be deemed equivalent to preparing an attack on the United States. The United States cannot wait until it or an ally suffers a nuclear terrorist attack. Nor can it assume that deterrence will work with terrorist organizations. Moreover, any terrorist organization that makes the United States and its citizens targets of any kind of attack must be destroyed. Prudence requires the United States to assume that such organizations will inevitably attempt to acquire nuclear and radiological weapons. Furthermore, any nation sheltering such organizations will be subject to attack if it refuses to expel terrorists from their territory.

Finally, a policy of coercive denuclearization would continue to provide support for the norms of the first nuclear age. The United States will continue to *discourage nuclear proliferation* by any state and to *insist upon the safeguarding* of existing nuclear weapons and fissile materials. It will continue to aid Russia in securing its nuclear arsenal and fissile materials and the other successor states in which radiological materials are poorly secured. It will permit access to enriched uranium for power production but insist on tight controls over such material. The United States will rely on the general patterns created in the first nuclear age (such as SALT/START and the rules of the road) to tide the world over until the problem of hostile states and non-state actors with nuclear weapons is resolved. While we can begin to lim the likely nuclear crises of the future—particularly how the United States accommodates itself to the growing power of China, especially if China is controlled by authoritarians—the policy of coercive denuclearization recognizes that *the critical issue of the moment* is nuclear or radiological weapons in the hands *of the declared enemies of the United States*.

In addition, a policy of coercive denuclearization necessitates that the United States continue to develop and deploy an anti-ballistic missile shield to offer some protection to itself and its allies. Such a shield, along with robust homeland defense measures, will significantly degrade the ability of hostile states to harm the United States.

In its broader foreign policy, the United States will generally support the expansion of democracy, for ultimately, the security of the United States can best be achieved by having a world of such states. Maintaining active support for democratization provides the United States with a bargaining chip in dealing with hostile states: it will not push such policies if a hostile state clearly refrains from any attempt to go nuclear. Moreover, the United States will support the existing leadership of non-democratic but friendly states armed with nuclear weapons (such as General Musharraf's Pakistan), if the alternative is likely to be the acquisition of power by an anti-democratic regime hostile to the United States, even if that acquisition of power is by democratic means. Furthermore, in the war against terrorist organizations or in efforts to deal with hostile, nuclear-armed states, the United States will not penalize those states whose assistance is crucial by demanding that they accept democracy or even strict adherence to non-proliferation.

THE BUSH POLICY OF COERCIVE DENUCLEARIZATION

The presentation of this policy echoes the George W. Bush administration's approach to Iraq, al Qaeda, Iran, and North Korea—albeit without the heavy idealism and moralism that the President and many of advisors have entwined around the realist premise that "September the 11th made the security of the American people the priority ... a sacred duty for the president," as the president told Bob Woodward. As we saw in earlier chapters, the Bush policy has been a mix of force and diplomacy, of unilateral and multilateral efforts to deal with the emerging nuclear environment. It accepted preventive war to counter the assumed proliferation by Saddam Hussein's Iraq. It continues to wage war against al Qaeda. In both cases, it emphasized decapitation strategies to kill the top leadership, regime change through democratization, and the direct use of U.S. military power. The next steps in coercive denuclearization against Iran and North Korea lie before us as we write these words.

Has coercive denuclearization proved a success? The record is incomplete but worrisome. Iraq is denuclearized—but then there were no nuclear weapons (nor other weapons of mass destruction) to begin with. North Korea, however, has advanced ever-closer to being more than just a declared nuclear weapons state and Iran has not ended its plans to enrich uranium, thus preserving its dual track ability to become a nuclear weapons state in the future. Libya, on the other hand, did agree to denuclearize (although the agreement to do so may have been more the result of British diplomacy and the long-standing U.N. sanctions than to any recent demonstration of U.S. military power).

For better or worse, the United States chose to use military force to achieve the denuclearization of Iraq. It had the alternative of using the combination of continued economic sanctions and inspections (backed by a threatened use of force) to enforce denuclearization, but it mistakenly concluded that neither were working. Ironically, this route to effective denuclearization had been made possible by Saddam's invasion of Kuwait in 1990 and George H. W. Bush's decision to build a coalition to liberate Kuwait. Those advantages are not available in confronting Iran or North Korea.

So far, while the denuclearization of Iraq has been completed—or, more accurately, verified—the Bush administration is still searching for an end-game. America remains in Iraq, its forces under attack, with no clear sign (as we write these words) that Iraq will become a stable state, at peace internally and with its neighbors. Indeed, it seems equally likely that Iraq may remain contested terrain between the Kurds, Shi'ia Arabs, and Sunni Arabs, with internal insurrection and an active al Qaeda war being waged against the United States and the Iraqi government, all the while drawing in jihadists from other societies. Under such circumstances, it will be difficult for the United States to withdraw its forces, which may mean many more years of costly involvement in Iraq.

The clear implication is that *if* Iraq continues to be a costly and seemingly never-ending mess, rogue state leaders are likely to conclude that the United States will not have the stomach to undertake another preventive war to bring about the coercive denuclearization. Equally open to question would be whether air strikes alone will serve as an alternative means of achieving coercive denuclearization, for the targets (North Korea and Iran) have dispersed their weapons or facilities and both can retaliate against their neighbors for U.S. actions. Such retaliation by the target states would likely embroil the United States in prolonged conflict—in other words, in more costly messes if not worse. But without *the threat* of coercive denuclearization (coupled with the Bush administration's demonstrated distaste for making concessions to rogue regimes), the U.S. government may be stuck with an ineffective policy—or worse, with a highly dangerous one, for it may drive the U.S. government to attack precisely to give credibility to its demand that certain states not have nuclear weapons.

How did it happen that the United States came to this uncomfortable point? Is there something egregiously flawed with a policy of coercive denuclearization itself? It is always difficult to suggest definitive conclusions while events continue to enfold, but it appears to us that there were two critical, interrelated missteps by the Bush administration in Iraq. The first was *the lack of meaningful planning for the post-war occupation period*. The Bush Department of Defense had little doubt that the Iraqi ground and air forces could be quickly and decisively routed by the deployment of overwhelming power at the times and places chosen by the United States. They were correct in their assessment. Iraq was overrun in less than a month. But it quickly became apparent that the Department of Defense had done little to prepare for the post-war occupation.[3] It had dispatched a force too few in number to secure the country. It had not planned to impose martial law immediately in order to prevent the systematic destruction of Iraq's infrastructure by looters. It decided to break up the only mechanisms of control within Iraq (the army and the Ba'ath party) without having in place a replacement structure except for a small group of hand-picked Iraqi leaders who generally had no following in Iraq. It relied on U.S. combat infantry personnel to provide local security—without extensive training in how to interact with Iraqis and without adequate numbers of Arabic-speaking interpreters. And it continued to be exceedingly reluctant to change its approach when problems quickly emerged.

The second misstep paralleled these. President Bush proved to be a relatively unengaged policy maker. That is, while he did insist that he make the important decisions, he was not the kind of President to question proposed plans or ideas from respected subordinates or to ask about the possible consequences of the choices before they were implemented. In spite of warnings from Secretary of State Colin Powell, the President never insisted that his advisors present and critique the plans for the post-war period. To be fair, the last item on the agenda in White House planning sessions inevitably was the occupation phase, and as a rule there is never enough time for the last agenda item[4]—unless the president insists that it be given time. Bush did not, and others did not want to do so, not only because they—particularly Vice-President Cheney and Secretary of Defense Rumsfeld—felt that the occupation needed little planning, but more importantly, they saw any discussion of occupation planning as another avenue through which those opposed to the war would try to derail the march toward war.

These two missteps are not necessarily inherent in a coercive denuclearization policy. Presidents can be far more effective leaders; bureaucracies can plan much more effectively (as, in fact, the State Department had done prior to the invasion of Iraq; the Defense Department essentially disregarded State's effort). The two missteps were compounded, however, when President Bush decided that coercive denuclearization of Iraq would be coupled with *democratization* as the follow-on policy. That goal, exceptionally difficult to achieve in a nation whose political life had few of the traditions or ethos of a democratic polity, now had to work within the chaos of an ineptly handled occupation and a growing insurgency. However laudable a goal that democratization might be—and here the president articulated an idealism long part of the U.S. foreign policy tradition—the critical question for us is this: Does democratization of Iraq pose such a daunting, perhaps impossible, task that by coupling it to coercive denuclearization, the Bush administration has made it *exceedingly difficult if not impossible to persuade the Congress or the American public to pursue a policy of coercive denuclearization again*?

Consider what the policy might have been. The United States undertakes coercive denuclearization at the point of a bayonet because keeping nuclear weapons (or, more broadly, WMD) out of Iraqi or out of other hostile states' hands is desirable in its own right. The nature of Iraq's political system is a subordinate issue. An Iraq run by anyone, authoritarian or democrat, who, after the war, submits to continued, unhindered, and wide-ranging inspections and on-demand destruction of prohibited materiel is what the goal of coercive denuclearization calls for, and it is the *only* goal. That is achievable—*and was achieved after 1991 in Iraq*. It might be agreeable to have a democracy in Iraq or elsewhere rather than an authoritarian regime, and if democratization can occur at modest cost, it might be a useful adjunct or bonus. But to insist, as the Bush administration has, on democratization and on U.S. forces remaining within the country until the new political system can survive on its own, may be elevating democratization above the security interests of the United States.

The Bush administration was correct, however, in its selection of targets for its first effort at coercive denuclearization. Iraq was the weakest of the three rogue state with nuclear ambitions. That was an important choice, because a policy of coercive denuclearization must show success each and every time it is deployed. In fact, the optimal payoff for this policy is if it brings about denuclearization *without going to war*. The irony is that the Bush administration *had achieved that success*, first in the fact that Saddam had no WMD programs, and second, in the fact that Saddam had agreed in early 2003 to allow intrusive inspections to resume in order to avoid being attacked by the United States.

There are a number of likely explanations for why the Bush administration could not see the success of its own policy. 9/11 may have panicked the president; there simply could not be another successful attack during his watch. The president and his advisors had concluded that his father, George H. W. Bush, had failed to deal with Saddam when the United States had him on the ropes in the spring of 1991; it was a mistake that had to be corrected.[5] The president has a strong tendency to see issues in terms of personalities; Saddam was a loathsome individual heading a very violent regime. Such personalities seemed to matter more than ever now; Osama bin Laden had personally built a powerful organization of dedicated individuals who found a way to by-pass the nation's defenses. With the administration's mind-set, the inability of the United Nations' inspectors to find WMD before the American attack seemed *to confirm* that Iraq had very well-hidden WMD—and therefore the threat was all the greater as such a skillful, duplicitous regime would surely use them in the future.

Of the major powers, only Great Britain chose to see Iraq as such a threatening state. Prime Minister Blair was concerned that Iraq might use its WMD and, perhaps more importantly, he judged it vital to stand with Britain's most important ally on a policy the Bush administration seemed committed to no matter what others did. The post-invasion turmoil in Iraq has soured the British public and elite toward a policy of coercive denuclearization. That turmoil has confirmed for many other governments the wisdom in their initial refusal to support the policy.

MAKING COERCIVE DENUCLEARIZATION ATTRACTIVE AGAIN

Any future effort by a U.S. administration to rally either domestic or international support for coercive denuclearization will, at a minimum, have to demonstrate (1) that a nuclear weapons program or the weapons themselves do in fact exist, (2) that an attack (and occupation, if necessary) will solve the problem at a reasonable cost, and (3) that without U.S. action, the opponent is likely to use nuclear weapons against the United States or its allies or other states. The Iraq experience makes this a formidable task. It may be, of course, that Iraq will turn out to be judged a success and it may be that the United States will have learned how to implement coercive denuclearization far more effectively. But success is likely to take some time, and time is in very short supply as North Korea claims to have nuclear weapons (and has given every indication short of an actual test that it does have them) and Iran is alleged to have intense nuclear ambitions. Thus, in the short run, the United States—if it wishes to keep coercive denuclearization as a live policy option—needs to keep the North Korean and Iranian nuclear programs contained long enough to produce a palpable success in Iraq, which in turn might give U.S. demands that there be no nuclear weapons in those other states sufficient clout to get such an outcome without war. If success in Iraq eludes the United States, the Bush administration will have likely removed coercive denuclearization from America's policy repertoire just when it may be most needed. Indeed, in having committed the United States to enforce the rule of no nuclear weapons for rogue states in *this particular instance*, the Bush administration may have made the world far more dangerous for the United States. Rogue states may make highly provocative decisions regarding nuclear weapons or in the promotion of their foreign policy interests, setting the stage for a frightful crisis.

In its defense, the Bush administration might argue that it had to take advantage of its hegemonic position—just as the Truman administration did in 1945—to attempt to write new rules. While those new rules might trample on the rights or desires of some nations, they would, if successful, make the international system safer. No one could seriously argue, it would claim, that a nuclear-armed Iraq, Iran, and North Korea would provide greater stability in their regions. Future generations would hold the administration culpable for letting slip the opportunity to prevent such dangerous proliferation. The lack of preparation for the occupation, it might ruefully admit, undercut the initial effectiveness of its imposition of the rule in Iraq and reduced the salutary effects on other rogue states. But it was the right rule, at the right place, at the right time. And it continues to be the right policy. Moreover, America's demonstrated willingness to use force may still lead Iran and North Korea to accommodate the rule. And Iraq may still confound the critics by emerging as a democratic state, at peace with itself and its neighbors, without nuclear weapons. Just as the Cold War took 50 years to win—and the prospects for doing so looked questionable during the first two decades—shaping an effective nuclear peace in the second nuclear age will take time and perseverance. Coercive denuclearization must remain, its proponents would argue, a central component in U.S. foreign policy.

Thus, for better or worse, nuclear weapons in the hands of Iraq, North Korea, and Iran *is* the issue of the moment, and if we do not focus, we lose our ability to shape a future that reduces the *known and palpable* threats to the United States and to others. Coercive denuclearization fits squarely into traditional world politics. One state insists that other states behave in certain ways (in this case, to divest themselves of nuclear weapons and the means to make them) or they will be attacked. What we need to do now is to ensure that there is room for negotiation, which gives the alleged possessor of nuclear weapons the opportunity to seek some agreement. In practice, that would mean accepting a North Korean offer to accept real denuclearization and a rigorous inspection regime in exchange for U.S.

concessions regarding aid, recognition, and security for the regime. If negotiations fail, then force will become necessary, but it must be clear that negotiations have failed because the rogue state resisted every effort to find a settlement, or that it was simply playing for time, waiting for the moment when its nuclear arsenal was large enough to give it a means of retaliation against U.S. interests if the United States were to attack.

SHOULD WE CONTINUE A POLICY OF COERCIVE DENUCLEARIZATION?

Like any policy, coercive denuclearization has its flaws. It may have a particular flaw given our current circumstance. We suspect that just aerial bombardment of presumed nuclear weapons storage and production facilities in North Korea or Iran would not guarantee complete denuclearization—but it would guarantee that a state of war would exist between the United States and North Korea or Iran—a condition that poses real risks to American interests. Thus invasion on the Iraq model may be the only real option—and real threat—available to the United States.[6] *It is, however, open to question whether the United States could now or in the immediate future undertake such an invasion*. That is the first and most fundamental flaw in a continued coercive denuclearization policy.

This is not to say that *the threat* of coercive denuclearization would necessarily be an ineffective one. It may produce a desirable response—as it did in Iraq when Saddam Hussein permitted the inspectors to return with unfettered access in 2003. But of course he had no WMD and no nuclear infrastructure, and he had already suffered defeat at the hands of the United States. Whether it would produce a similar response by a state with nuclear weapons or a nuclear infrastructure is surely open to doubt today.

A second flaw with coercive denuclearization is that it may *absorb too much of the attention of policy makers and too many of the resources available to the United States*. As a consequence, other nuclear threats, such as the safeguarding of Russian warheads and fissile materials, aiding new nuclear states in managing their nuclear relationship, and waging the war against terrorists, are likely to receive inadequate attention and resources. As we write this, al Qaeda's top leadership is active, al Qaeda still mounts operations, and Afghanistan remains contested territory in spite of a reconstituted (and democratic) Afghan government and in spite of a NATO force attempting to defeat the regrouped Taliban and al Qaeda forces. There is little reason to believe that al Qaeda has given up on its goal of acquiring a nuclear or radiological device—or in planning some form of attack against a nuclear power plant or holding-pond for spent fuel rods. If one judges, as we do, that the most likely scenario for nuclear use against the United States in the short run will come from a terrorist strike, one might be quite concerned that a policy of coercive denuclearization against rogue states has diverted too much away from the more likely threat.

In particular, one should note that any terrorist nuclear strike, even one far from U.S. shores, or *even a failed attempt*, is likely to be a success. Terrorists will have demonstrated *the ability to acquire* nuclear or radiological weapons, and will have given every reason for us to believe that they will *do so again*. A successful attack elsewhere, be it a port in Spain, or a Shi'ia city in Iraq, or an airport in the Philippines, will send shockwaves through the United States and its allies.

Bluntly said, coercive denuclearization may foolishly distract us from the war against terrorists. Thus, the more we concentrate on rogue states rather than terrorists, the more risk we take upon ourselves; to date only terrorists seem to be willing to stage a nuclear attack against the United States. The trade-off is that rogue state nuclear weapons are likely to be far more powerful and their methods of delivering such weapons to targets more varied and better funded. Thus, by pursuing coercive denuclearization against rogue states, we might be able to reduce the overall damage that an enemy might cause, but at the expense of making a terrorist-created nuclear event more likely.

A third flaw in a policy of coercive denuclearization concerns the *robustness of deterrence*. Part of the Bush administration's argument for the necessity of coercive denuclearization rests on the claim that rogue leaders like Saddam Hussein cannot be deterred. Madmen will use nuclear weapons, they claimed, as they do not care about the possible retaliation against themselves or their society, or they are not able to make reasoned judgments about the high likelihood of retaliation. Either we force those leaders to get rid of their weapons and the ability to produce them or we or our allies must expect to be struck. So goes the argument. Is it a reasonable argument? Did the Bush administration actually believe it? The lesson of the World War II is that even a reputed madman such as Adolf Hitler was deterred from using poison gas, even when Germany was about to be overrun. The lesson of the first nuclear age is that it is highly unlikely that the leader of a nuclear-armed state will be either a madman or have the latitude to act madly. Moreover, despots as well as democrats can be deterred, as American relations with Stalin's USSR and Mao's China demonstrated. Even the Reagan administration's strategic reformulation concluded that there was one thing that would stay the Soviet hand: its leaders' fears that they and the Communist Party might lose control over their society. The fact that Saddam Hussein did not restart his WMD programs is an indication that despots in weaker states can be deterred as well.

More telling, the Bush administration itself cast doubt on its claim that tyrants could not be deterred when it asserted that the demonstrated American willingness to attack Iraq would deter *other* tyrants from acquiring or using nuclear weapons.[7] Indeed, the fact that the Administration pointed to Muramar Qadaffi's offer to destroy Libya's nuclear weapons program rather than suffer the fate of Iraq (be it a slow death through economic isolation or a rapid demise through preventive war) is a telling indication of how strong deterrence can be.

Of course, there *is* a probability—even if low—that a deranged individual who is immune to the rationales of deterrence might come to power and be able to slip the restraints imposed by his or her own political elites and bureaucracy. That leader may initiate a nuclear attack. The real issues are these, however. First, is it reasonable to use a high-risk, high-cost policy response like coercive denuclearization to deal with all cases in which there is a small risk that a real madman has control over the nuclear decision. Second, coercive denuclearization policy itself runs the great risk of forcing a *rational* decision maker to contemplate using his or her nuclear arsenal when faced with an impending attack by the United States. As U.S. threats against North Korea mount, for instance, a rational North Korean leader, deeply dissatisfied with the American refusals to offer meaningful rewards for ending the North's nuclear program, might order the first test of a nuclear device, wanting it to serve as a warning, and if that seemed unlikely to stay the American hand, to use a nuclear device against South Korean positions just south of the DMZ. Dangerous actions to be sure, but understandable responses by a *rational* leader seeking to force the United States to abandon its plans for an attack on the North.

A fourth flaw of coercive denuclearization flows from the preceding discussion: *very costly retaliation may occur*. Attempting to denuclearize a state armed with nuclear weapons obviously increases the likelihood that nuclear weapons will be used, as the target is thrown into the Cold War-era dilemma of "use them or lose them." The United States, fearing this, may decide to use nuclear weapons first to ensure destruction of that capability. Even if the United States acted *before* nuclear weapons were available to the targeted state, other retaliatory responses are likely. Iraq, after more than a decade of sanctions and a very punishing war, was a hobbled society. The two other targets of coercive denuclearization are not. They have meaningful retaliatory capacities: North Korea might invade the South (and Seoul would likely be heavily attacked by conventional weaponry), threatening to overrun U.S. forces; and Iran might openly intervene in Iraq and would likely close the Persian Gulf to all oil shipping. These states might have a great incentive to do so preemptively, fearing that the United States was about to open hostilities to bring about denuclearization—*and to bring about regime change*, as that has been the precedent set by the Bush administration.

CONCLUSION

This chapter makes the case for a policy of coercive denuclearization as the centerpiece in an effort to shape the nuclear future. Such a policy defines the chief threats to the future as (1) nuclear weapons in the hands of states controlled by authoritarians who are intensely hostile to the United States and (2) in the hands of terrorist organizations that find shelter or succor in weak states. The more time that rogue states or terrorists have to build a nuclear arsenal, the greater the threat becomes, as those leaders will be tempted to use their new weapons, either to blackmail others or to wage war against them. U.S. interests, U.S. allies, and the United States itself will inevitably become targets. While deterrence may work most of the time, if it fails, it will be with rogue leaders. And deterrence is very likely to be completely ineffective with terrorist leaders.

Negotiations with rogue leaders are fraught with danger. Negotiations are unacceptable with terrorists, if for no other reason than the fact that terrorists have little or no incentive to honor agreements. Negotiations that end up leaving either nuclear weapons or the capability of manufacturing them in the hands of such authoritarians are unacceptable. While concessions might be made in return for complete and verifiable denuclearization by rogue regimes, negotiated denuclearization will only occur if there is a credible threat to attack the rogue state and do so unilaterally. The United States must threaten and—when needed—wage war to compel the denuclearization of such states. Iraq may have been the wrong place at the wrong time, and the Bush administration's failures to plan effectively for the occupation/democratization phase may have dramatically increased the costs of coercive denuclearization, but good policy is still good policy even if ineptly applied. And even an ineptly implemented policy in time may prove successful, restoring credibility to the threat to wage preventive war.

At the end of the day, it may well be that in order to protect the future, the United States must actively work for the democratization of other societies, particularly those hostile to the United States. Democracies are not an absolute barrier to waging nuclear war, nor are they a real barrier to the development of nuclear weapons. But they are likely to be more peaceful states than those run by authoritarians. In a world of democracies, nuclear weapons (and even nuclear proliferation) lose some of their threatening face.

Coercive denuclearization, like all policies, has its drawbacks. War-waging is never cost-free, and against a state with nuclear weapons, it may prove very costly indeed. Even to threaten war against such a state runs the risk of high levels of damage to U.S. interests and American allies (and, more generally, to the world's peoples). This policy, of the three we examine, may be the most likely to bring about some form of nuclear use, either by the United States or by the target, or by states fearful of being the target. But that is the risk one must take if one wants to confront directly and immediately certain states that threaten international peace and security—before they have large arsenals of nuclear weapons that allow or encourage those states to pursue their ambitions aggressively. As President Bush said to a reporter, "The worst thing that could happen would be to allow a nation like Iraq, run by Saddam Hussein, to develop weapons of mass destruction, and then team up with terrorist organizations so they can blackmail the world. I'm not going to let that happen."[8]

Even if this is a convincing case for coercive denuclearization, however, we need to ask if there were policy alternatives available in 2003 that might have produced an acceptable outcome for the United States. More importantly, are there options that might do so today? In the next chapter we consider a policy that looks much like the one pursued by the United States during the Cold War, a policy of attempting to manage the international environment in the hope that time would dissolve the frightful dilemmas of the nuclear age.

ENDNOTES

[1]Bob Woodward, *Plan of Attack* (New York: Simon & Schuster, 2004), p. 27.

[2]Spencer R. Weart, *Never at War: Why Democracies Will Not Fight One Another* (New Haven, CT: Yale University Press, 1998).

[3]For a discussion, see George Packer, *The Assassins' Gate: America in Iraq* (New York: Farrar, Straus, and Giroux, 2005); Larry Diamond, *Squandered Victory: The American Occupation and the Bungled Effort to Bring Democracy to Iraq* (New York: Times Books, 2005); and L. Paul Bremer III with Malcolm McConnell, *My Year in Iraq: The Struggle to Build a Future of Hope* (New York: Simon & Shuster, 2006).

[4]See Woodward, *Plan of Attack* for the fleeting attention given to Phase IV planning (the post-invasion period).

[5]See J. Goldberg, "Breaking Ranks," *The New Yorker* (October 31, 2005), pp. 55–56.

[6]Israel might be willing to stage an aerial operation against Iran, but the likely Iranian counterstrike would include actions in Iraq and the Persian Gulf—forcing a high degree of American involvement, but at the initiative of the Iranians. American war-fighting currently emphasizes being on both the strategic and tactical offensive.

[7]Benjamin R. Barber, *Fear's Empire: War, Terrorism, and Democracy* (New York: W. W. Norton, 2003).

[8]Interview with Trevor McDonald, April 2002, quoted in Bob Woodward, *Plan of Attack* (New York: Simon and Schuster, 2004), p. 118.

13

The Management Option

Mohamed ElBaradei, Director General of the International Atomic Energy Agency (IAEA), may have noted the irony when he and the agency received the Nobel Peace Prize in October, 2005. In announcing the prize, the Norwegian committee that makes the selection noted that the committee "has concentrated on the struggle to diminish the significance of nuclear arms in international politics, with a view to their abolition. That the world has achieved little in this regard makes active opposition to nuclear arms all the more important today."[1] The message seemed to be that while the IAEA was the bright spot in the darkness, the agency had to redouble its efforts. The Non-Proliferation Treaty does commit its signatories to eventual abolition, a goal that seems as elusive as when the ink was barely dry on the treaty some 30 years ago. The IAEA, however, is principally in the business of maintaining the nuclear status quo—to prevent the spread of nuclear weapons—rather than pushing for abolition.

Moreover, ElBaradei and the IAEA have their share of critics. The Director in particular has been the target of periodic U.S. criticism that he and the agency have been lethargic in exposing treaty violations by the North Koreans or the Iranians or the Iraqis and lethargic in compelling them to comply with their obligations. In the past, the Nobel committee has used the peace prize to bolster support for individuals and organizations who encounter such criticism from powerful international actors and to put more bargaining chips in their hands. ElBaradei did seem energized. The prize, he told a reporter, increased "my resolve to speak without fear, to speak—to use the power. As you know, I have been having a difficult time when you have to look a government in the face and tell them, 'You are not telling us the truth,' or 'You need to comply with your commitment.'"[2]

ElBaradei and the IAEA stand at the heart of the dilemma regarding nuclear weapons. Given the constant proliferation pressures, how best can we ensure that states comply with their agreements not to proliferate? Should the international community emphasize persuasion—which necessitates considering the interests of the state involved—or confrontation—which emphasizes the importance of the community's interests? A year earlier, ElBaradei had reflected on the issues the international community faced regarding nuclear weapons. At their heart, he argued, was the lack of security. "New generations," he said, "struggle at regional and global levels to cope with renewed fears and in-

337

securities, in unfamiliar forms and dimensions: The resurrection of old conflicts, the rise of terrorism, and the ever-present and ever-evolving threat of weapons of mass destruction." Without "the necessary political dialogue among concerned States to address underlying issues of insecurity, and to build confidence and trust," he argued, the acquisition of nuclear weapons will remain attractive. Unfortunately, "the international community has not been successful to date in creating a viable alternative to the doctrine of nuclear deterrence as the basis for international security. Nuclear weapons will not go away until a proven collective security framework exists to fill the vacuum."[3] Ensuring compliance with the NPT was important, but it did not get at the larger issue of security for all. How might that be done?

This chapter offers for your consideration a second policy option for the United States. It begins with the same basic set of assumptions and preferences introduced in Chapter 12: The nuclear predicament is essentially permanent, the international system does not now offer the kind of security that many governments offer their citizens, and states will continue to come into conflict with each other, making nuclear weapons attractive and, unfortunately, making nuclear use possible. Furthermore, this option assumes that American goals should be to promote security for all, a peaceful and equitable resolution of conflicts between states and peoples, and tolerant, democratic societies. Those attributes are, we judge, most likely to create the conditions for a lasting peace in which nuclear weapons play little or no role.

This chapter argues for adoption of the *management option*. It draws its inspiration from the basic U.S. Cold War approach to nuclear weapons and to nuclear weapons states, modified to reflect the circumstances of the second nuclear age. It stands in significant contrast to coercive denuclearization.

THE PREMISES AND PROPOSALS OF THE MANAGEMENT OPTION

The management option assumes that *nuclear weapons should remain in the arsenals* of the existing nuclear weapons states as they give some assurance against an uncertain future. Practically speaking, it is difficult to imagine that any political leader in an existing nuclear weapons state would be willing to take the political risk to call for the divesting of those weapons—nor should she or he. Rather, leaders need to spend their political capital in other ways, as discussed below.

This management option assumes that *a strategy of minimum deterrence* will effectively safeguard the existence of the state and help protect its core interests. Jonathan Dean, a diplomat with extensive experience in arms control, has suggested that an inventory of 200 warheads for each of the five major nuclear weapons states would be enough for minimum deterrence.[4] Recall that this accords with Robert McNamara's insight in the early 1960s and reflects the current practice of the Chinese, French, and British, as we saw in Chapter 6. While 200 warheads might be a reasonable target, the question of how much is enough can only be answered by the states themselves, and that will take negotiations. Indeed, it is likely to take negotiations to convince the nuclear weapons states of the very desirability of permanent, mutual minimum deterrence postures—but that reflects management's emphasis on giving stakeholders a say in setting the rules for the international system. A minimum deterrence posture still depends, however, upon the threat to use nuclear weapons in retaliation for a nuclear attack on the state or on its allies. A state needs enough weapons to guarantee catastrophic levels of destruction no matter what the opponent does.

The management option also demands that the United States and Russia begin a *significant reduction in their tactical nuclear stockpiles* through negotiations. Large numbers of tactical weapons are not necessary for deterrence, and their possession only tempts their holders to consider how they might be used. Furthermore, the management option insists that all decommissioned strategic and tactical warheads *should be destroyed* rather than placed in reserve or in storage, with suitable verification procedures in place to monitor both the destruction and the size of the remaining warhead inventory.

Finally, all nuclear weapons states must make *a pledge of no first use* of nuclear weapons except when its homeland or the homeland of a declared ally is under direct attack. This pledge should come through a negotiating process in which both nuclear and non-nuclear states lay out their security fears (which make nuclear weapons necessary for some and desired by others). Hopefully, these discussions will point to additional ways in which the security concerns of all states might be addressed.

The United States would take the lead—as it did during the Cold War—in creating a *multilateral, negotiated framework of acceptable behaviors (or rules of the road) for nuclear and non-nuclear weapons states*. To facilitate such an agreement, the United States would agree in advance that it would renounce a policy of unilateral coercive denuclearization when the framework had been agreed. (That is, its current policy would be a bargaining chip.) Indeed, it would treat rogue states as states to be negotiated with (using a mixture of threats and promises) with the intention of gaining their active acceptance of the negotiated rules of the international system. It could draw on its Cold War experience with confidence-building measures such as hotlines, on-site inspections, and notification of troop exercises to provide mechanisms by which the rules could be safeguarded.

The negotiated rules would *reaffirm the NPT injunction against any further proliferation and validate energetic investigation of suspected violations*. The United States should further propose (1) that the NPT obligations extend to the entire international community, including the non-signatories and (2) that renouncing the NPT is not permitted. This represents a significant change in treaty practice, as traditionally treaties only bind those who agree to the treaty. As a concession to gain support for this modification, the United States would agree to be guided by the international community (as represented by the UN Security Council) in terms of the response that it and the other members of the United Nations would make in case of a violation that the accused state refused to rectify. The existence of such a pledge in 2003 would have meant that the United States would have waited perhaps six more months until the inspections had been completed in Iraq and, then, given that there were no nuclear or other WMD in Iraq or programs to produce them, the U.S. government would have been guided by the consensus of the international community whether Saddam Hussein's regime constituted a meaningful threat to international peace and security. The invasion of Iraq would have been far less likely—and that comports with a management approach. (All will understand, of course, that the United States—like any other state—will ultimately decide for itself the course of action it will undertake if it believes its supreme national interests are at stake, treaty or no treaty, rule or no rule.)

There will still be states hostile to the United States and its interests, and hostile to their own neighbors. That hostility will have to be managed, rather than eradicated, and in this endeavor, the United States can also draw on its Cold War experience. It would take active measures to contain the influence of hostile states. Active containment coupled with the deterrence provided by a strong conventional military establishment is likely to maintain an acceptable level of peace and security. Management would draw comfort from the fact that the containment of both China and the Soviet Union eventually led to the erosion of hostility toward the United States and to significant changes in the nature of those states' political and economic systems. Ultimately, if history is any guide, those transformed states are likely to see *the value for themselves* in upholding the rules of the road, just as the Russians and Chinese acquiesced in the United Nations attack on Iraqi forces in 1991 to reverse Saddam's aggression against Kuwait.

Compliance with whatever rules are agreed to is, of course, more likely when states have had a say in defining the rules and when they perceive that others share in the sacrifices that come with accepting rules. In that regard, *U.S. nuclear weapons* (and conventional weapons) *must be on the negotiating table*. That is, the security fears of others will need to be addressed in order to meet a U.S. objective of constraining the behavior of others. Indeed, the United States must be conscious of the security dilemma it poses to others. If it attempts to make its military strength overwhelming, others will see that as a threat to their security, to which they will respond by increasing their military strength and threat potential, thus eroding the margin of security that Americans desire. Management approaches cannot end the security dilemma; they can, however, effectively dampen its effects by promoting less threatening international behaviors by all states.

Finally, the United States generally *must eschew regime change* as an active component of its foreign policy, as this is surely a key contributor to the insecurity of some states. It can, as a bargaining chip, offer to refrain from actions that promote regime instability to secure acceptable international behavior. It may be a particularly attractive chip because the United States did demonstrate in Iraq and Afghanistan that it could quickly bring down a regime. Americans would continue to *hope*, of course, just as they did during the Cold War, that internal pressures and processes within non-democratic states would eventually bring about an evolution to greater democracy. They would not, however, engage in a general crusade to export democracy.

IMMEDIATE MANAGEMENT TASKS AND TESTS

The management option takes a long-term, macroscopic perspective. It denies that there are quick fixes. It requires a steady, constant attention to the world—to all of the world. A policy of coercive denuclearization, in contrast, looks for relatively quick payoffs and focuses intensely on a particular problem, usually centered on one state. Nonetheless, there are five key issues upon which a management approach itself *must initially and quickly focus*. To make rapid progress, the United States will need to take the initiative in raising the issue and proposing a specific response.

First, the United States should lead a formal effort *to reaffirm the central rule of the first nuclear age* that the use of force to change the international status quo is unacceptable. It should get a reaffirmation from the international community that cross-border aggression will be met with collective force (as was done in 1990-1991 in response to Iraq's invasion of Kuwait). Second, the United States should begin building a consensus that external support for violence in another state is an act of aggression and will be opposed by the international community. That will mean a confrontation with jihadist Islamic movements and their supporters.

The leverage that the United States can bring to the issue would be a pledge not to use war to bring about regime change as it did in Iraq in 2003, for that violates the spirit of the general rule—unless that state sponsors insurrectionary movements in another state or terrorist groups. Second, it would insist on a settlement of the Palestinian issue in which a Palestinian state emerges in the West Bank, a state whose borders closely match those of the 1967 boundaries and with no Jewish settlements within Palestinian territory. In return, the international community, including Israel's neighbors, would recognize Israel's right to exist in peace and would agree that external support for violence within Israel would be treated as aggression against the state of Israel and would be resisted by the international community. Making Israel and Palestine an integral part of the nuclear future is essential if one wants to be able to confront Islamic extremism (as British Prime Minister Tony Blair recognized). It also opens the way for Israelis and the region to deal openly with the issue of Israeli nuclear weapons.

Second, the United States must quickly *formulate a series of proposals for real rewards for hostile states to end their nuclear weapons programs*. Fortunately, the United States has a large number of resources at its disposal. Recall that in its negotiations with North Korea, the United States was able—at least initially—to strike a deal through offering immediate material rewards (light-water nuclear reactors, fuel oil deliveries) and through promises of more to come (an end to the North's economic and diplomatic isolation and security guarantees against a U.S. attack). There is no surety that such rewards will be attractive enough to prevent proliferation or that a hostile state will be interested in negotiation or in living up to any agreement it signs. But making clear that there can be substantial payoffs for remaining demonstrably non-nuclear is the first step in effective management.

If the Bush administration were correct in its assessment that nuclear weapons in the hands of a dictator like Saddam Hussein constituted a mortal threat to the United States, then the U.S. government's spending of more than $200 billion to achieve coercive denuclearization gives us a sense of what the United States should be willing to pay for security without war, without the loss of lives by either side, and with a greater confidence that its efforts would produce the outcomes it desired. It is likely, in fact, that paying for denuclearization and the creation of necessary safeguards to preserve it would turn out *to be far less expensive*.

Third, the United States needs *to reinforce the IAEA and the provisions of the NPT*. The United States should first try to bring all states into the NPT, but with acknowledgment and acceptance of India, Pakistan, and Israel's status as nuclear weapons states. This will be difficult for Israel, who has found it useful to remain an opaque proliferator, and for Israel's neighbors such as Egypt who could tolerate Israel's ambiguous status, but now might face internal pressure to become nuclear powers in response. To meet these security fears, the United States would urge all signatories of the NPT to agree (1) that any NPT member in full compliance with IAEA requirements would not be attacked by another NPT-member state unless the member violates commonly accepted norms governing international relations; and, furthermore, (2) that all NPT signatories pledge to come to the aid of an NPT-member state under unwarranted attack. The United States, in making this proposal, should pledge up front to refrain from attacking NPT states in compliance and to come to the defense of any NPT signatory. Such a U.S. pledge should provide the needed security guarantees to tide worried nations over until the international community as a whole takes the pledge. As a part of a formal security guarantee to Israel, the United States should insist upon a step-by-step plan for eventual Israeli denuclearization.

Fourth, the United States should lead the way in *the creation of a new international organization*, working independently of but in coordination with the IAEA, that would (1) monitor all trade in technologies and materiels that have nuclear-weapons applications, (2) interdict such trade when in violation of international treaties, (3) help secure all nuclear and fissile materials in the custody of the successor states of the Soviet Union or any other state requesting such assistance, (4) render harmless all decommissioned nuclear materials, and (5) provide emergency funding and technical aid when needed to help safeguard a state's nuclear establishment in unusual circumstances.

Fifth, the United States, acting with the United Nations, would seek a U.N. resolution or treaty that *criminalizes the possession of nuclear (or radiological) weapons by any non-state actor* and mandates that all states provide aid to a United Nations member seeking to arrest such actors once it is established that such actors have nuclear or radiological weapons or are actively engaged in an effort to acquire them. Furthermore, the resolution or treaty would *declare that any state that provides such weapons or the wherewithal to create them has committed an act of aggression against the international community* and will be dealt with as an aggressor state. Moreover, the agreement should also specify that any government that *involuntarily* permits nuclear materials to fall into the hands of terrorists is culpable for whatever havoc the terrorists cause, and the international community will sanction that government until it makes full restitution.

THE PROBLEM OF TERRORISM

Terrorism poses a particular problem for the management orientation. Terrorists reject the ends sought by a management option: the preservation of the status quo while allowing slow, hopefully cumulative, change to occur. Terrorists usually reject the means employed by the management approach: the negotiation of solutions acceptable to both sides. Terrorists usually reject the other state, elite, or culture as having no legitimacy at all (a stance mirrored by governments in their view of terrorists), thus making negotiations with terrorists morally unacceptable and pragmatically dubious. The terrorists' method of violence and blackmail—while surely not foreign to international relations—fails as a negotiating tactic, for they generally cannot offer any positive rewards for meeting their demands other than the suspension of terrorist acts. That, of course, may be compelling, but compulsion is not negotiation.

Terrorists with nuclear ambitions represent a particular kind of challenge, for the destructive reach of such weapons multiplies the number of lives threatened and expands the range of a society's assets that are imperiled. A management approach must give this threat a high priority. The policy of the United States under a management approach would be that *any non-state actor seeking such a capability (let alone possessing it) would be the principal target of U.S. counter-terrorism* in which the United States would seek the destruction of the terrorist group. In contrast to the Bush administration policy, a management approach would have put far more military (and economic) resources into the operations against al Qaeda and the Taliban in Afghanistan. It would do so immediately.

As all members of the international community have a mutual interest in the adequate safeguarding of nuclear materials to prevent their diversion into terrorists' hands, they should *provide aid* (as in the Nunn-Lugar program) to states having difficulty in protecting their fissile materials. Indeed, a strong anti-terrorism policy would mandate accomplishing this task in the shortest period of time.

Currently, these general guidelines would mandate that the United States—ideally with the aid of the international community or particular states—would wage war against al Qaeda (which has proclaimed its nuclear intentions and has tried to procure bomb-making materials). It would also mandate some form of cooperation with the Russian government in its attempts to destroy those elements of the Chechen insurrectionary movement that have displayed a radiological threat against the Russian government, while at the same time pressing the Russian state to offer greater autonomy to non-terrorist Chechens. This kind of cooperation is fraught with difficulties. Russian counter-terrorism has at times been indiscriminate, fueling outrage against Moscow. Moreover, states under attack by terrorists may claim on the flimsiest of evidence (or even planted evidence) that their opponents have nuclear ambitions, and thus ensure external support.

The fundamental problem as we write these words, however, is the chaos in Iraq. The management approach can offer no easy solution for Iraq. Historically, when a management approach has waged war against insurgents and attempted to promote the development of a democratic polity (as it did in Vietnam during the Cold War), it has had mixed success. In those circumstances, management is often whipsawed between the fear, on the one hand, that its withdrawal without military success would undermine whatever rules it was attempting to safeguard, and, on the other, the fear that escalation (even if it were politically possible) would expand the war in ways detrimental to the interests of the United States. Its usual policy response was to continue its present course of action—with mixed success.

Switching to a management orientation may, however, free up thinking about what is most important in Iraq. In this case, it would be to reduce the likelihood that terrorists (or anyone else in Iraq) would acquire and use nuclear weapons, and to prevent Iraq from becoming a sanctuary for terrorists. A second-order goal would be to prevent Iraq from becoming a threat to its neighbors, which in turn might spur proliferation. That is, the United States would manage with a hard-nosed political purpose—to shape the nuclear environment of the world we live in. A democratic, unified Iraq might suit that end, as might a fragmented state, ruled undemocratically. A democratic, unified Iraq is not proof against nuclear temptations. Indeed, Iraqi political parties might view the acquisition of nuclear weapons as a way in which they could appeal to Iraqi nationalism—a nationalism battered by Iraq's defeat and occupation by the United States—just as India's BJ Party rode to victory with nationalism and chose to proliferate openly. On the other hand, a divided Iraq, free of U.S. occupation, might better police its regions (particularly the Sunni center) and thus eliminate terrorists, but the cost would likely be enhanced fears in the region (such as the Turks' concern about their own restive Kurds) and the unresolved issues that always occur with partition (such as those that continue to divide India and Pakistan).

Beyond the issue of Iraq lies the more general question of how to deal with terrorists, particularly those who may plan to acquire a nuclear or radiological capability. Is the reliance on military power the only or even best way to deal with the nuclear threat terrorists might mount? It might be that a "shoot-on-sight" policy that mounts an unrelenting, high-violence campaign against terrorists with nuclear ambitions *might have some deterrent effect*. That is, clear variations in the level of violence directed against different terrorist groups might imply that if a terrorist group stays away from nuclear or radiological weapons, U.S. policy might be more restrained. Restraint might be shown in, say, an unwillingness to cause collateral damage in attempts to kill the terrorist leadership; the Clinton administration, for instance, withheld some cruise missile strikes against bin Laden because large numbers of family members or other non-combatants were reported in his company. That might be a price worth paying if it ended terrorists' nuclear efforts.

We have come to the heart of the question of whether terrorists can be deterred, which we discussed in Chapter 9. If we have reason to believe that even a detested and feared enemy could be deterred (as Americans and Soviets came to believe about the other during their Cold War), then the management option might consciously seek to deter terrorists. To do so, there would have to be appropriate answers to four questions:

1. Are there things that even terrorist leaders would be loathe to lose? For Islamic jihadists, those precious things may run the gamut of their own lives to the lives of their families (or tribes or

clans), to the nation or peoples that they call home, to objects or sites of great significance, such as the sacred sites of Islam. Of course, we are likely to find it utterly repugnant to consider threatening such targets, but recall that the threat of nuclear devastation in the Cold War led us to promise the destruction of millions of Russian lives and the culture embedded in their urban areas.

2. Can we threaten those valued things in persuasive, credible ways but in doing so avoid intensely negative repercussions? Threatening to kill terrorist leaders is likely to be a credible threat— few would doubt that the United States would attempt it, although there may be some doubt about its ability to do so. On the other hand, a threat to destroy Islamic holy sites is credible in that they can be easily targeted, but as such sites are in countries aligned with the United States (Saudi Arabia and Iraq) and their destruction would be a body-blow to the hundreds of millions of Muslims who around the world who are uninvolved with terrorism, it would be incredible that the United States would want to raise the Islamic world against it in an unquenchable firestorm. Just making the threat would likely swell the ranks of the jihadists and thus create far more terror efforts than we have experienced to this point, even if the jihadist leadership got the message that by continuing terror they risked the things they valued. Threatening family, tribe, and nation of origin might have greater credibility, but as terrorists may put themselves at odds with their own people—or see their own people as expendable in the cause—such threats may carry not much weight. And those threats are likely to alienate the targets who may rightly claim that they oppose the terrorists as much as the United States does.

3. Does the leadership have sufficient control over its weapons and followers to hold off a nuclear attack if it so decided? Deterrence is meaningless if subordinates or affiliated groups can make their own decisions about whether a nuclear device would be used. The evolving nature of al Qaeda—an evolution forced in no small part by U.S. attacks—suggests that there is less central control than would be necessary for deterrence.

4. To the degree that attacks against terrorist leaders and followers succeed, can the die-hards who are left be deterred as "easily" as the leadership might have been earlier? The time of the greatest risk in the use of nuclear weapons by terrorists may come precisely at the end of military campaigns against them.

Overall, effectively deterring terrorist use of a nuclear weapon appears far more difficult than the deterrence created during the Cold War. Recall as well that the deterrence that prevailed during the Cold War may *not* be the reason why there was no nuclear use; the fact that neither side wanted to wage a war against the other may have been a far more important cause of the nuclear peace. Now, however, actors with nuclear ambitions *have* chosen to wage war against the United States. Does that mean that it must be bitter war to the end? Does it mean a constant race to either prevent the acquisition or delivery of a nuclear device against a target, while the terrorists ceaselessly try to do so, believing that it might tip the scales so dramatically in their favor that the United States and others must make stunning concessions? After all, the terrorists do not need to compel a surrender of the United States. A limited number of nuclear weapons might force the United States to withdraw from the Middle East, abandoning its Islamic allies and Israel. Or at least al Qaeda may so believe.

If deterrence is uncertain, is *any* negotiation with terrorists possible?[5] It is possible, and it has been used. For instance, Israel has refrained from killing all leaders of Hamas, the Palestinian organization that sends suicide bombers against Israeli civilians, in return for suspensions of the bombing campaign. Israel has accepted cease-fires with groups it labels as terrorists. (And has retaliated against Hamas leaders when the cease-fires have been broken.) Is it possible to construct a similar deal—say, a U.S. agreement not to target the top leadership of al Qaeda in return for the organization's agreement not to go nuclear? While such an agreement is possible, verifying it would be next to impossible and therefore would not be accepted by the United States even if proposed by al Qaeda. Thus the negotiation/deterrence track seems closed to the United States as a way of preventing nuclear use. All that is left is the race to destroy the terrorists (or to prevent the use of a nuclear device) before their nuclear ambitions are realized. Nuclear weapons in the hands of terrorists creates a novel situation in which the management option may be ineffective. Management's most meaningful claim may be that it can head off situations where terrorists come to possess nuclear weapons.

THE POWER OF A MANAGEMENT APPROACH

A management policy assumes that the best way to handle a problem (be it the nuclear predicament or anything else) is to contain and restrain undesired behaviors. A management orientation must emphasize multilateralism, as management depends upon some degree of cooperation by others. Ultimately, it needs some cooperation from opponents as well. Management attempts to provide other states with a reason for restraint even while remaining in opposition.

Management is likely to be less costly than coercive denuclearization and other unilateralist approaches, but it still has costs. It takes constant attention, the provision of meaningful rewards for compliance, and a willingness to live with moral ambiguity (such as a need to negotiate with evil empires and dictators and in so doing possibly prolong their existence). It demands the maintenance of a nuclear arsenal and the strategies and tactics to wage nuclear war if it is forced on the nation. Management, with luck and skill, postpones a deadly confrontation, counting on a mellowing of the antagonisms that separate states to produce stability in international politics. That mellowing in turn may create the conditions for the emergence of democratic polities and more moderate foreign policies when elites cannot point to foreign threats as the rationale to maintain authoritarian control and aggressive actions abroad. Management often cannot provide immediate solutions to pressing problems; it does provide a means to prevent the worst today in the hope that the solution can be crafted tomorrow.

Coercive denuclearization, on the other hand, generally presents itself as a solution to the problem rather than the means to ride out the problem. Powerful states are often tempted to believe that if they want a particular outcome, they can have it. The Bush administration's attempt to bring about a fundamental restructuring of Iraq (and possibly of all non-democracies in the Middle East) reflects this belief in action. Other states may urge the hegemon on, for its actions may serve their interests while allowing them to benefit without doing much to achieve it. This free-rider phenomenon is a rational response, and there is little the hegemon can do about it. On the other hand, some states, even erstwhile allies, may judge the hegemon's actions as being too provocative, potentially ineffective, and contrary to their interests. But given the hegemon's power, they are not likely to oppose the hegemon actively. Hegemons thus often end up shouldering most of the costs, resenting their friends and allies who often fail to act to promote what the hegemon believes to be the common good. The hegemon's power can make it victorious on the battlefield but that power may prove to be insufficient to win the peace, as that takes the cooperation of the vanquished and those on the sidelines. In other words, at some point, even hegemons often have to come back to management policies, where negotiation rather than fiat is the order of the day.

A management approach, however, does not just hope that "things will work out." Managers must invest time and energy; they must make the case to others that there is a common problem and others have meaningful parts to play. A management approach to nuclear weapons can point both to reason and to experience (the Cold War) to support its argument that management can reduce the risk of nuclear use and of proliferation. Management relies on the destructiveness of nuclear weapons to create a "crystal-ball effect."[6] Because it is known that the use of nuclear weapons would be very destructive, potentially catastrophic results would be clearly *foreseen* by any leader in a position to start such a war *as if they were gazing into a crystal ball.*

This is a relatively new phenomenon. Prior to 1914, leaders often assumed that wars would be relatively quick and therefore modest in cost, certainly not something that would risk their nations' very survival. This belief was alive during the early weeks of World War I. Even after those four years of slaughter and the death of three empires, some leaders had visions of swift victories in the opening months of World War II. But that war proved to be longer and more destructive than contemplated, leaving the post–1945 generation of leaders with a clearer vision of what the next war might bring. The advent of nuclear weapons in the closing days of the war made things clearer yet. As we saw, this clarity made deterrence possible and the negotiation of the rules of the road imperative during the Cold War.

But we have said that the crystal ball may not give terrorist leaders that image. Perhaps it will not give rogue state leaders a clear image either. Perhaps Indian and Pakistani leaders have a different image in their crystal balls. How does the management approach propose to deal with these immediate problems?

MANAGEMENT'S RESPONSES TO CONTEMPORARY NUCLEAR ISSUES

Management means that the United States must strike a deal with both Iran and North Korea as it did with the Soviet Union during the Cold War. Ideally, it would like to remove nuclear weapons from their hands. In return, it must offer something of similar worth to the other side. Offering not to attack or to seek regime change is not likely to be enough (in part because both states may have concluded that after Iraq, the U.S. government may not be willing to use coercive denuclearization again). Positive concessions are likely to be necessary. Recall that in the Cold War, the United States offered the Soviet Union prestige—the recognition of its status as a superpower—and thereby treated the Soviet Union as an equal, particularly in negotiations regarding arms control and the rules of the road. This was an open recognition that Soviet interests could not be disregarded, just as the United States insisted that American interests could not be disregarded by the Soviet Union.

In the case of Iran, while seeking to contain Iranian influence within the region, the United States must be willing to accord Iran the status of a meaningful player, no matter who controls the state; it needs to be consulted about affairs in the region, from Afghanistan to Iraq. The United States should offer at least to end its economic and diplomatic embargo in return for Iran's pledge to remain a non-nuclear weapons state and Iran's acceptance of transparent, meaningful monitoring to demonstrate its compliance with all its NPT and IAEA obligations. As Iran has in the past tried to hide its nuclear efforts, even if they were for peaceful purposes only, the United States should insist on Iran's suspension of any enrichment or reprocessing activities whatsoever for a period of time (say, five to seven years). Instead, Iran would agree to purchase such fuels internationally and have spent fuel rods returned to their source. Iran would be guaranteed access to such fuels at market prices and without hindrance.

Bringing North Korea into a managed relationship will be more difficult because it has nuclear weapons or the materials needed to construct such weapons. It is those weapons that makes North Korea of grave concern to the world at large. (Iran, on the other hand, has oil as a bargaining chip and a residual of respect as the first revolutionary Islamic state of the modern era.) Getting North Korea to agree to end its nuclear weapons program and then divest itself will take more patience and rewards. To demand that North Korea completely, irrevocably, and transparently divest itself of its weapons as a precondition to negotiations (as the Clinton administration initially insisted and the Bush administration has generally insisted) is to ensure no negotiations.

The North has repeatedly expressed an interest in a deal with the United States. We suggested in Chapter 7 that the failure of the 1994 agreement cannot be laid solely on the North's doorstep. The United States, as a democracy, is a difficult state to negotiate with because of competing bureaucratic interests and a vigorous political opposition, both of which have means to derail negotiations or hinder fulfillment of a negotiated agreement. Nonetheless, the 1994 approach still seems to be valid (if for no other reason than the alternatives of the use of force or just ignoring the North's proliferations seem to be far more risky). The outlines of an agreement are there: A series of reciprocal steps leading ultimately to the end of the North Korean nuclear weapons and the program to produce them. The United States would end its economic and political isolation of the North, provide security guarantees, and end efforts to bring about regime change. It would provide the North with transition energy supplies, and complete the construction of the power-generating reactors. Those reactors would be fueled by foreign-supplied fissile materials for a stipulated period, after which the parties would consider the restoration of North Korea's indigenous fuel-creation program, but under IAEA safeguards.

In addition to dealing with these two critical problems, the management orientation forces the U.S. government to pay attention to other issues that have important nuclear implications. The most important of these concern Taiwan and the India-Pakistan relationship. Regarding Taiwan, the essential question for the United States is, How important it is to avoid a confrontation with the People's Republic of China? Certainly in the short run, the United States needs China in order to deal with North Korea. This is particularly true if it insists that the North end its nuclear weapons status with few meaningful rewards from the United States. In the long run, if China becomes a superpower as many expect, it is to America's advantage to avoid having a series of hostile confrontations that compound the tensions that will surely emerge when the international system returns to a condition of superpower bipolarity. The island of Taiwan, long a part of China but independent since 1949 because the United States took up the defense of the island, lies at the heart of the problem. U.S. policy has had two tracks: Warning the Taiwanese that they will forfeit U.S. protection if they press too hard toward independence (even if that is what a democratically elected Taiwanese government wants), and warning Beijing that the United States would not stand by if it used force against the island. It also means ensuring—as it did in the 1970s—that Taiwan makes no move toward acquiring nuclear weapons, as that may be the trigger for a Chinese invasion. But to keep Taiwan nuclear-free means that the United States must continue to defend Taiwan from such an invasion.

America's 50-plus years of commitment to Taiwan means that it is a relationship, like that with Israel, that the United States cannot easily walk away from. American policy has been to maintain the status quo—an acknowledgment that there is but One China but two separate systems. China's astounding economic growth coupled with its traditional nationalist pretensions to be *the* power in Asia constantly press against this status quo. And given that China helps fund a large part of the American government's budget deficit, alienating China now poses economic risks. The future of Hong Kong, a former British colony now being integrated into China in a step-by-step process, may provide the framework for Taiwan's acceptance to returning to One China. Or it may make Taiwanese insist on independence no matter the cost.

A management option for the United States thus must struggle with these difficult non-nuclear issues (just as it had to struggle with the question of Berlin during the Cold War), for nuclear weapons are never far in the background when states see vital interests at stake. Because management is oriented around the status quo and creative ways to preserve it, it may not easily conceive how to move beyond the status quo in order to produce a safer nuclear future. It faces a similar dilemma with India and Pakistan.

Both states are important for American interests. Pakistan is part of the battleground against al Qaeda and the Taliban in Afghanistan, and its own jihadist elements, were they to come to power, would have a sizable nuclear arsenal. India is an emerging counterweight to China and is a potential economic powerhouse in its own right. Ironically, the open proliferation by both in 1998 may have been a productive step as it removed ambiguity and forced both to deal with each other as nuclear states. Pakistan and India comprise the first pair of nuclear states in serious conflict that lie wholly outside the traditional nuclear-state framework established during the Cold War. They have adopted minimum deterrence strategies from the start—another first. They have a serious disagreement over the status of Kashmir, and there are Pakistani Kashmiris who seem intent on waging a terrorist campaign against India. This is a relatively novel situation. The Cold War for all its real fears, animosities, specific conflicts, and near uses of nuclear weapons never had a significant dispute revolve around territory claimed by a nuclear power as part of its nation.[7] What is reminiscent of the historical Cold War is the asymmetrical prestige relationship, with the Indian government seeing Pakistan as a backward state, and Pakistan insisting on being seen as an equal. Both states seem to be interested in a management approach, at least at the nuclear level (as we saw in Chapter 7). But tensions will continue to revolve around the Indian-occupied part of Kashmir.

Does adopting the management option mean that the United States must play an active role in the management of nuclear South Asia? In one respect, it may have no choice as both states have an incentive to draw others into their conflict, to get outsiders to pressure the opponent. They may also look to outside actors to head off a nuclear confrontation and to furnish both with ways to back down from a confrontation if it were to take place. With the Bush Administration's decision in 2005 to create a new nuclear relationship with India, the United States becomes more firmly connected to the issues of South Asia, even if the United States has had little intrinsic interest in the problem of Kashmir. Unless the United States invests some attention to the Kashmir issue, however, it will leave the working out of the rules of the road between India and Pakistan to the tensions and fears of the moment. The Cuban Missile crisis nearly produced war (and likely nuclear use) between the United States and the Soviet Union. Too many such experiences in the second nuclear age are not likely to end in a similarly pacific manner. The problem is that, like Taiwan, there is at this point no solution that both sides will accept as permanent in South Asia. Thus, the management approach must try to prevent open conflict, hoping that time and changes in government and public sentiment will provide new avenues to a resolution.

In addition to dealing with regional conflicts and the so-called rogue states, the management orientation argues that there is a constant need to renew the non-proliferation regime. That renewal would include:

1. Adopting minimal deterrence postures, which move closer to the NPT treaty commitment to get rid of nuclear weapons entirely.

2. Ratification of the Comprehensive Test Ban Treaty by the United States and persuading all states to do so.

3. Negotiating and ratifying a treaty cutting off the production of all fissile materials suitable for nuclear weapons, with a consideration that the production of all reactor-grade uranium should be put under international supervision and control by the IAEA. States would further agree that as long as any nation was in compliance with its international obligations (as judged by the U.N. Security Council), it would have unfettered access to reactor grade uranium at the market price.

4. Expansion of controls on missile technology transfers and negotiations to limit missile ranges and numbers.

DRAWBACKS OF THE MANAGEMENT OPTION

Every option has its drawbacks; each makes significant compromises and runs some risks in its attempt to produce a desirable future. We identify six here.

First, *the posture of minimum deterrence is inherently risky* where all states have few nuclear weapons. A would-be attacker might be more tempted to launch a disarming first strike, accepting some loss in the limited retaliation, and then with ten or so remaining warheads, blackmail its opponent into making significant concessions rather than stand to lose its cities one after the other. To prevent this in a minimum deterrence world, states would likely establish firm nuclear alliances so that the warheads of their ally could be called upon to deliver the crippling retaliation. But that very alliance would be highly threatening to a state without an ally or having an ally whose reliability was in question. Assured destruction capabilities on the order of 2000 warheads greatly lessen the likelihood of miscalculation (and discourage potential nuclear alliances for the purposes of attack).

Why not rely on a much higher number of warheads in the nuclear arsenal as the United States and Soviet Union did in the Cold War? The proponents of the management option would point out that there has been a radical change since the Cold War: Though Russia has inherited the large Soviet nuclear arsenal, no one sees Russia as a counter-weight to the United States. It is not likely to challenge the United States. No other state approaches the warhead level of the United States, even after the Moscow treaty reduces it to roughly 2000. The Chinese in the near future will need to decide whether such American strategic dominance is tolerable. To the degree that China sees itself as *the* competitor with the United States, its current strategic inequality will be worrisome politically and militarily. To avoid a Chinese buildup—one that threatens the annihilation of the United States—the United States will have to reduce its inventory. To avoid a potentially dangerous spillover arms race between China and India, and then between India and Pakistan, the United States needs to reduce its arsenal. And, given the perennial question of Russia's stability, it is probably prudent to seek a reduction of its arsenal as well. That will necessitate reciprocity. Management would be willing to avoid the risks of a new arms race at the possible price of increased risk during a crisis.

The second major drawback of the management approach is that *it will provide significant rewards to authoritarian leaders*. By threatening to go nuclear, they can (and will) force concessions from the United States and others that (a) may make their regimes proof against external pressures to change, (b) may provide the regime with enough rewards to buy off internal discontent, while (c) maintaining their conventional military establishments and the threats those establishments pose to their neighbors. The United States would be in the unsavory position of having to oppose or remain uninvolved with indigenous democratization movements to avoid jeopardizing a regime's pledge not to go nuclear. North Korea is clearly the exemplar here. Iran may choose to pursue this strategy as well. Because management almost guarantees some degree of success to authoritarians who threaten to go nuclear, others may adopt such a stratagem. Thus the management approach may in fact encourage the explosive proliferation we discussed in Chapter 8.

Equally serious, any regime that begins the proliferation, even for negotiation purposes, may find new incentives to continue the proliferation efforts. Leaders may discover that the first step sparks a nationalism that benefits them—and that could turn on them if they were to renounce a nuclear program, seemingly under U.S. pressure. The Indian and Pakistani publics, for instance, generally celebrated the 1998 weapons tests by their governments and their governments turned a deaf ear to American requests for restraint. Similarly, Iranian leaders may have wrapped their nuclear program so tightly in the flag that they cannot easily give up the program; the elected Iranian leadership's dependence upon the public's votes probably compounds the problem. Beyond the nationalist pressures, there will be the bureaucratic pressures coming from the organizations charged with creating the weapons and from their military backers to keep the weapons or the program to produce them. Thus, management may induce unwanted proliferation pressures and reap the harvest of states that cannot call off the proliferation no matter the rewards the United States offers.

Third, the management approach *makes the unwarranted assumption that all proliferation is inherently dangerous*. As we saw in Chapter 8, there is some reason to doubt this claim; states with nuclear weapons have generally behaved responsibly with them, precisely because of the enormous threat they pose and the retaliation that can follow. For the United States, however, there is a great difference if Germany or Brazil proliferates rather than Iran. Why would one squander one's political capital to try to prevent the former with as much vigor as one attempts to prevent the latter? Rather, the United States should seek to use its influence to ensure that other states—particularly Russia in the case of German proliferation—do not feel imperilled. Attempting to head off all proliferation may also blind us to the stabilizing benefits that might accrue. For instance, if North Korea insists on remaining a nuclear state, it may be important to allow (if not encourage) the South and Japan to proliferate, in order to set up a regional balance, one where U.S. nuclear power is not directly involved. A management option built around the NPT stigmatizes all proliferation. It might be far better to ask, how does the proliferator propose to behave, and can we expect continued compliance with the rules? If so, proliferation loses some of its threatening aspects.

Fourth, the management approach is built upon *a dubious premise that states collectively will do the right thing or will do it in time*, from sanctioning would-be proliferators to waging war to roll back aggression (as the international community did against Iraq in 1991). Sometimes they will, particularly when the challenge to the international order is egregious (as Iraq's seizure of Kuwait was). But when the issue is more complex and various nations' interests are engaged in different ways, collective action is far more difficult. Consider the U.S. war on Iraq in 2003. Many states disagreed with the U.S. call to drive Saddam and the Ba'ath party from Iraq, not so much because they disputed the claim that Saddam had a WMD program or capability, but because they could not see how their particular interests would be best served by an attack on Iraq. For many, Saddam was too weak to pose a threat and the lure of commercial agreements with Iraq, particularly regarding oil, too strong.

Similarly, there is a diverse set of opinions among the six states challenging North Korea's proliferation effort, an effort that none doubt, though they may doubt exactly how far the North has gone in creating a nuclear arsenal. Getting the North—and other states like it—to back away from nuclear weapons will ultimately depend upon two things: (1) a united group of influential states confronting the North, waving (2) the threat of collective force to achieve denuclearization if negotiations fail. Because management relies on a multilateral approach, it must first gain acceptance for whatever approach it takes. For a variety of reasons, many states will oppose the use of force. Of course the United States can act on its own, but to be committed to the management option means that at every step along the way, the United States often has to accept constraints and delays to maintain the support of other states. Those constraints and delays are likely to make any use of force much less effective (or too late), forcing the United States to deal with a state that has successfully proliferated (or in the case of North Korea, begun to amass an arsenal). In those cases, the risk of a nuclear use increases and the cost of buying an end to proliferation balloons.

Fifth, *management unwisely assumes that others will bargain in good faith when they choose to bargain.* The Korean and Iranian cases are instructive in the negative. Though the North might claim it was technically in compliance with the 1994 agreement, its attempt to enrich uranium clearly lay outside any reasonable expectation for the behavior of a state that had agreed to end its production of fissile materials by way of reprocessing plutonium. Iran for many years insisted that it was in compliance with all NPT reporting requirements, but the secret existence of the uranium enrichment facility suggested that Iran was violating at least the spirit of the NPT (the relatively benign interpretation) or was in fragrant violation of its obligations. How could one reasonably hope to manage through negotiations with states like these?

The emphasis on negotiation often assumes that states or groups hold essentially the same goals (such as promoting "life, liberty, and the pursuit of happiness") but disagree over how to achieve those goals. Such disagreement might be profound and bitter, but negotiation is acceptable because having similar overarching goals holds out the prospect that there may be some formula that will allow both sides to get something of what they want. When one confronts a leader who has a radically different view of the world than others—as Hitler did—negotiations will be based on blackmail ("make concessions or be grievously harmed!") and provide nothing more than a respite in which the aggressor grows stronger from the concessions and the defenders of the status quo, weaker. At some point , the aggressor uses force to achieve its next demand because the defenders of the status quo have failed repeatedly to defend that status quo. When the defenders do take up arms, it often is a surprise to the aggressor—and the ensuing war becomes a bitter fight to the finish. Doing that in a nuclear-armed world is a recipe for calamity.

Sixth, *management proposes to do too much.* In attempting to cover all the bases (from Taiwan to loose nukes in Russia to terrorist ambitions to acquire nuclear weapons to rogue states), it may do too little, too late in the one area that mattered to prevent the arrival of the third nuclear age. In the Cold War period, management had a central focus (the Soviet Union) and a palpable, single nuclear threat to deal with. It still managed to become bogged down in costly side shows (Korea, Vietnam), spend billions needlessly on nuclear weapons systems, and come close to nuclear Armageddon in Cuba.

Yet it worked out reasonably well. Now, having so many things on its plate, the management option may be a recipe for disaster.

CONCLUSION

A nuclear world is our permanent condition. The management option attempts to postpone the moment when leaders give serious attention to the option of using a nuclear weapon—or better yet, to remove nuclear weapons from their options list in the first place. It does so in the belief that with time, we can find a solution to the predicament. The Cold War suggests that this can be done. The most powerful authoritarian regime transformed itself into a less internationally threatening state and a democracy to boot. Management holds out the promise that it can buy us the time for a similar process to work for most of the international community. It recognizes threats—a full panoply of threats—but it cautions about over-reaction. It understands that all states seek security, and that there must be a mutual consideration of security issues. As a policy, it is well suited for a hegemon, who starts with the power and the resources to encourage and purchase adherence to negotiated norms, and, when needed, to enforce the rules. Its long-term strategy is modest but perceptive: to create conditions where few states see the necessity of nuclear arsenals, few need to make nuclear threats, and no one sees an advantage in using nuclear weapons. Under those conditions, it can tolerate the future erosion of its hegemony—an erosion that it cannot stop but whose potentially negative consequences it can minimize by having institutionalized patterns of international relations that provide it with security when its heyday has passed.

At the same time, the management option makes nuclear weapons an important part of its arsenal, though at much reduced numbers. It makes managing a worldwide set of nuclear relationships its top priority. It is concerned about rogue states and terrorists. It sees them as problems to be resolved more than solutions to be imposed, because it is conscious of the bottom line and it recognizes that imposed solutions are often the very things that increase an interest in proliferation and nuclear threat-making. And at heart, it realizes that its solutions will often be imperfect and fragile.

In a nuclear-armed world, imperfect and fragile solutions should be cause for great concern. In Chapter 14, we examine another response to the nuclear predicament, one that claims to perfect and strengthen our nuclear future.

ENDNOTES

[1]Statement of October 7, 2005; www.nobelprize.org/peace/laureates/2005/press.

[2]Interview with Marika Griehsel, October 7, 2005; www.nobelprize.org/peace/laureates/2005/elbaradei-telephone

[3]Mohamed ElBaradei, "Nuclear Weapons and the Search for Security," Statement to the 54th Pugwash Conference, Seoul, Korea, October 6, 2004 (html://www.iaea.org/NewsCenter/Statements/2004/ebsp2004n010.html).

[4]Jonathan Dean, "The Road Beyond START: How Far Should We Go?" (Washington, D.C.: The Atlantic Council of the United States, 1997).

[5]We cannot always expect that terrorist groups will announce their attentions in advance or serve notice about their capabilities by leaving a device in a city park. This policy demands an intelligence capability to ferret out the ambitions or capabilities of terrorists or the activities of a state or organization (such as the A. Q. Khan network) that may provide those capabilities to non-state actors. Because of the transnational char-

acter of many terrorist or insurrectionary groups, that intelligence would have to be coordinated among a number of foreign intelligence agencies. The intelligence would always be imperfect (as intelligence always is), leading to some false assessments of nuclear activity, either judging incorrectly that a group has nuclear ambitions or judging incorrectly that it has none. There would have to be scrupulous regard by policy-makers for the independence of intelligence evaluation, as well as the evaluators' acceptance of the fact that conflicting estimates will be resolved by the policy-makers. Evaluators and policy-makers must also recognize that a foreign state confronting a terrorist challenge may be prone to see (or even invent) a nuclear or radiological threat in its opponent's actions or plans in order to gain allies in its war against its terrorist opponents. How a terrorist group accused of having nuclear ambitions or capabilities could demonstrate its innocence of the charge remains a vexed question.

[6]See The Harvard Nuclear Study Group, *Living with Nuclear Weapons* (New York: Bantam, 1983), pp. 43–44.

[7]Portions of the Ussuri River separating the Soviet Union/Russia and China have been in dispute for decades and were the site of a short-lived, local, but quite violent clash between the two states in 1969. But the amount of territory involved is small and subsequent negotiations paved the way for an amicable settlement. See Tai Sung An, The Sino-Soviet Territorial Dispute (Philadelphia, PA: Westminster Press, 1973); and David Marks, "The Ussuri River Incident as a Factor in Chinese Foreign Policy," *Air University Review*, July-August, 1971 (http://www.airpower.maxwell.af.mil/airchronicles/aureview/1971/julaug/marks.html).

14

Abandoning Nuclear Weapons

Ten years ago, in December 1996, five years after the Cold War ended, 58 high-ranking retired military leaders from 17 nations, including many from Russia and the United States, issued a statement supporting the abandonment of nuclear weapons.

> We military professionals who have devoted our lives to the national security of our countries and our peoples, are convinced that the continuing existence of nuclear weapons in the armories of nuclear powers, and the ever-present threat of acquisition of these weapons by others, constitute a peril to global peace and security and to the safety and survival of the people we are dedicated to protect... [Nuclear weapons] represent a clear and present danger to the very existence of humanity. ... That threat has now receded, but not forever—unless nuclear weapons are eliminated.

Their statement continued: "long-term international nuclear policy must be based on the declared principle of continuous, complete, and irrevocable elimination of nuclear weapons." This is their conclusion:

> We have been presented with a challenge of the highest possible historic importance: the creation of a nuclear-weapons-free world. The end of the Cold War makes it possible. The dangers of proliferation, terrorism, and a new nuclear arms race render it necessary. We must not fail to seize the opportunity. There is no alternative.[1]

What is most significant about this strong endorsement of the abandonment of nuclear weapons is not the novelty of the policy being recommended. Complete nuclear disarmament had been recommended by many before, going back to Albert Einstein in the period immediately following the first nuclear explosion. What was unprecedented about this recommendation is the people who made it. Never before had such a large and prominent group of former military leaders, most of whom had been in charge of nuclear weapons themselves, called for complete nuclear disarmament. Their endorsement of the abandonment of nuclear weapons carried a special weight. With this statement, the abolitionist position moved from the theoretical preserve of academics and visionaries, where it had largely resided before, to the practical world of hard-headed military practitioners.

In the years right after the end of the Cold War, it seemed that the minds of many had been opened to the virtues and the possibility of complete nuclear disarmament. For example, in 1997, Michael Mazarr observed that during the Cold War

> the concept of disarmament provided one of the clear litmus tests of an analyst's ideological stance—and to some, his or her sanity as well. Those who broached the idea ... thereby defined themselves as members of what was viewed as an unserious and irrelevant fringe of the Washington policy community.

But after the Cold War, calls for disarmament were being taken more seriously. "As with so many national security issues in the United States, the end of the Cold War has fractured old consensuses and called into question well-established ideologies and belief systems."[2] As nuclear weapons have changed our way of thinking about military matters, it appeared to some that the second nuclear age had changed our way of thinking about nuclear weapons.

Such optimism, however, was premature. In the more than 15 years since the end of the Cold War, the world has barely moved toward the goal set by these former military leaders. The latest agreement on nuclear arms reductions between the United States and Russia, the Moscow Treaty on Strategic Offensive Reductions of 2002, was disappointing to many who advocated eventual nuclear disarmament. That treaty required that each power reduce its nuclear warheads on operational missiles and bombers to 2,200 by 2012, but no reduction timetable was established, no requirement that the two nations remain at that lower level was included, and the nations were allowed to keep additional warheads in storage rather than dismantle them. In addition, the Bush administration has expressed its opposition to the Comprehensive Test Ban treaty and has withdrawn from the antiballistic missile treaty. Due to proliferation and terrorism, the nuclear danger now seems greater than it was at the end of the Cold War.

This chapter proposes that the United States respond to the military leaders' suggestion by setting a goal of complete nuclear disarmament—the abolition or abandonment of nuclear weapons by all nations—and crafting its foreign policy to achieve that objective. This goal, the chapter argues, is a better response to the situation we face in the second nuclear age than both the management option and a policy of coercive denuclearization, proposed in Chapters 12 and 13. The management option holds that although nuclear weapons should be deemphasized, they should be kept around nonetheless. For this policy, a minimal form of nuclear deterrence, isolation of rogue states, and expanding the negotiated rules of the road are the best way to reduce the risk of nuclear use and nuclear war; it is preferable to coercive denuclearization, which sees the retention of a large nuclear arsenal and the threat and use of military force against particular states as the best way to insure that nuclear weapons are not used.

This debate about nuclear policy, the question whether coercive denuclearization, the management option, or abandonment is the most effective way to achieve international security and avoid nuclear use, makes clear once again that our situation is a predicament. Part of the nuclear predicament is that nuclear weapons create great danger for our civilization and for billions of the earth's inhabitants. This is why nuclear disarmament may seem to be the obvious response. If nuclear weapons create the problem, then the response must be to rid ourselves of them. We must get beyond nuclear deterrence, which mandates the existence of such weapons. But the other part of the predicament is that we have nuclear weapons to avoid, through nuclear deterrence, the very certain dangers the use of nuclear weapons pose. The main purpose of nuclear deterrence, after all, is to avoid nuclear war. So getting rid of the weapons may make our situation more dangerous. There is danger on all sides.

Albert Einstein warned at the dawn of the nuclear age that nuclear weapons had changed everything except our way of thinking. As a result, he feared that catastrophe lay ahead. We have successfully negotiated the superpower rivalry of the Cold War, but we may have gone from the frying pan into the fire. The catastrophe Einstein feared is still a possibility, and nuclear use may be more likely than it was during the Cold War. This reminder of Einstein's warning brings us back to the point at which this book began. Einstein was one of the first to recognize the nuclear predicament because he was among the first to be caught up in it when his letter to President Roosevelt initiated the effort to build the bomb. As a pacifist, Einstein was certainly strongly opposed to the creation of such a terrible weapon. Yet he was led to sign the letter by the deep fear, which he shared with many of the refugees from fascism who would work on the Manhattan Project, that Nazi Germany might get the bomb first. Einstein may have recognized the need for nuclear deterrence, reasoning in this way: Such a weapon must never be used, and to ensure that it will not be used, the Allies must acquire the bomb in order to deter its possible use by Germany. After World War II, Einstein proposed his own solution to the nuclear predicament, which we consider later. But more fundamentally, Einstein, as among the first to encounter the nuclear predicament, has given us the perpetual challenge to search for the best possible nuclear policy.

TWO OPTIONS FOR THE ABANDONMENT OF NUCLEAR WEAPONS

If nuclear weapons did not exist, they could not be used. This suggests at first glance that the proper response to the nuclear predicament lies, as the former military leaders cited at the beginning of the chapter believe, in the abandonment of nuclear weapons: complete and universal nuclear disarmament. As we saw in Chapter 4, one of the questions that leaders had to answer at the dawn of the nuclear age was whether nuclear weapons should be built and stockpiled in times of peace. The answer was that nuclear weapons should be part of the military arsenal in times of peace, and out of this decision developed the doctrine of nuclear deterrence. But now, in the second nuclear age, we face this question again. The answer, however, is not as simple as the first sentence of this paragraph suggests.

What exactly is nuclear disarmament? As Michael Mazaar notes: "The question of nuclear-weapon capability is one of degree, not an either/or proposition; no major industrial power will ever have 'zero' nuclear-weapon capability."[3] A nation may have no fully assembled nuclear weapons, but have components that could be assembled into a functioning warhead in a short time, in which case that nation could be said metaphorically to be "a screw-driver away" from a functioning weapon. Would such a nation be disarmed of nuclear weapons? There is no clear answer. It is a matter of how we want to define "nuclear disarmament." The end state of nuclear disarmament means, at a minimum, that there are no functioning nuclear weapons, but does it also mean not being a screw-driver away from a functioning weapon, and, if so, how far away must it be? There is a continuum from a nation's having a functioning nuclear weapon to its being very far away from having such a weapon. As Jonathan Schell has noted, this can be thought of in terms of the amount of time it would take a nation to construct a functioning nuclear weapon, should it choose to do so.[4]

The kind of policy one recommends to reach the abandonment of nuclear weapons will depend on what definition is adopted, where the line is drawn between being disarmed and not being disarmed of nuclear weapons. We begin our analysis with two different definitions, leading to two different policy choices, which we label Nuclear Disarmament I and Nuclear Disarmament II.

> Nuclear Disarmament I: The nations of the world have disarmed themselves of their nuclear weapons when they have no functioning weapons, even though they may have extensive nuclear capability and be only a screw driver away from having a weapon.

> Nuclear Disarmament II: The nations of the world have disarmed themselves of their nuclear weapons only when they are very far away in time from having a functioning nuclear weapon (should they choose to make one)—that is, only when they have little existing nuclear capability.

When a nation is disarmed of its nuclear weapons in the first sense, it has merely eliminated its nuclear weapons, but when it is disarmed in the second sense, both its nuclear weapons and most of its nuclear capacity have been eliminated. But is there a meaningful practical difference in these two conditions, one that would affect the policy choices of the United States? There is. If all the nations of the world were to divest themselves of their nuclear weapons but retain the ability to rebuild on short notice, each would have a "virtual nuclear arsenal." That is, each would have an arsenal *in effect*, though not in fact.[5] Each could therefore make meaningful nuclear threats against its opponents, and it could still practice a form of nuclear deterrence, threatening to destroy its opponents in retaliation for an attack.[6] In Jonathan Schell's apt phrase, a nation with a virtual nuclear arsenal could practice "weaponless [nuclear] deterrence."[7] Thus the abandonment of nuclear weapons in the first sense does not by itself move us beyond nuclear deterrence.

Would this be better than the management option, which would (at least as presented in Chapter 13) rely on minimum deterrence—that is, on the possession of some 200 warheads by each of the nuclear powers? Would management make nuclear use less likely? The most likely use of nuclear weapons would come during a crisis between states, especially if both have nuclear weapons. In the last chapter, we pointed to the *crystal ball effect*: Leaders can clearly see the massive devastation they are likely to receive if they attack a nuclear-armed opponent. Minimum deterrence postures would provide relatively clear views of such devastation. A policy of Nuclear Disarmament I might not. But the crystal ball effect has the greatest impact when in situations like the Cold War standoff between the superpowers. Perhaps the effect has been weakened in the second nuclear age, at least for some states. With increased proliferation and the creation of new pairs of nuclear-armed states in conflict, we might have a repetition of the Indian-Pakistani crises of the late 1990s and early 2000s, where the opponents seemed to be relying less on the crystal ball rather than on relatively blind assumptions about other disadvantages nuclear use might have. This would be especially true where newly proliferating states have few nuclear weapons, and thus might either fear a disarming first strike or be tempted to launch one. In addition, given a growing number of nuclear nations, a one-way war (a war between a nuclear and a non-nuclear state) becomes more likely.[8] Here the crystal ball may not operate at all.

But this argument against the effectiveness of minimum deterrence does not by itself show that Nuclear Disarmament I would be more effective. Weaponless deterrence also depends on the crystal-ball effect. Under weaponless deterrence, what is supposed to keep nations from rebuilding and then using their nuclear weapons is the same perception that is supposed to keep them from using their nuclear weapons under minimum deterrence, namely, their ability to foresee in the crystal ball the utter catastrophe that could result. But the crystal ball seems cloudier under weaponless deterrence than under minimum deterrence. Under weaponless deterrence, leaders might believe that if they secretly rebuilt their nuclear weapons they could use them to destroy the ability of their opponent to rebuilt and retaliate. Thus, the crystal ball does not yield as clear a perception of catastrophe as it does under minimum deterrence. In other words, crisis stability is weaker under weaponless deterrence than under minimum deterrence.

This point is sometimes expressed by saying that nations would have a temptation under Nuclear Disarmament I or weaponless deterrence to "break out," that is, to seek an advantage by secretly rebuilding their nuclear weapons and suddenly threatening their opponents with them in order to achieve some advantage. Even if there is an established regime of mutual inspections among nations, as there almost certainly would be for any disarmament regime, a nation might believe that it could rebuild its weapons in secret without being caught by the inspectors. The crisis instability would be accentuated because some nations, fearing that their opponents may be secretly rebuilding nuclear weapons, would begin to rebuild their own as a hedge against this threat. It is clear that such a situation would be pregnant with the possibility of nuclear use.

If weaponless deterrence poses this risk, are there compensating features that could nonetheless make it more attractive than the minimum deterrence of the management option? One strong argument advanced for minimum deterrence over the high warhead levels of coercive denuclearization would be that under minimum deterrence "the risk of accidental or unauthorized use would decline dramatically." But it would "not disappear altogether,"[9] as there are still warheads in the inventory. Nuclear Disarmament I, on the other hand, would apparently eliminate this risk, because there would be no weapons to be accidentally used. So, in comparing minimum deterrence and Nuclear Disarmament I in terms of the risk of nuclear use, we must decide whether crisis instability (greater under Nuclear Disarmament I) or the risk of accidental nuclear war (greater under the minimum deterrence of the Management Option) is a more weighty consideration. This would be a difficult judgment to make.

NUCLEAR DISARMAMENT II AND THE PROBLEM OF INTERNATIONAL COOPERATION

Neither Nuclear Disarmament I nor minimum deterrence under the management option seems to offer a compelling response to the threat of nuclear use and the catastrophes that nuclear use might bring. Does a policy of Nuclear Disarmament II, where states might have a capability to produce nuclear weapons but would require a significant period of time to do so, offer a stronger response? To answer this question, we need to take a slight detour and bring to the fore a topic that underlies any attempt to move away from threat-based approaches to keeping the nuclear peace.[10] Consider this observation by Salvador de Madariaga:

> The trouble with disarmament was (and still is) that the problem of war is tackled upside down and at the wrong end. … Nations don't distrust each other because they are armed; they are armed because they distrust each other. And therefore to want disarmament before a minimum of common agreement on fundamentals is as absurd as to want people to go undressed in winter. Let the weather be warm, and they will undress readily enough without committees to tell them so.[11]

If states distrust each other—and that has been a common characteristic of the anarchical international system—they will arm, and in so doing perpetuate the distrust. To disarm unilaterally, without a sense that there are rules of the road that will protect the disarmed and some mechanism to enforce the rules, would seem to be madness. This might not be a serious problem for Nuclear Disarmament I, for it makes the disarmament universal and provides the assurance that, though there will be no weapons on hand, they can be quickly rebuilt if needed. It is like the homeowner who does not carry a gun but keeps one in a locked cabinet and the ammunition in another. Disarmament II, on the other hand, would have the homeowner drive several hours to purchase a weapon every time it might be needed. That might not sound reasonable to a homeowner in a neighborhood that seems prone to violent break-ins.

What would make it possible for states to accept the terms of Disarmament II? Only when the level of cooperation and trust between states is high would states feel confident enough in the benign intentions of others to abandon most of their nuclear capacity. The clothes would be shed only when the weather had sufficiently warmed. Nuclear Disarmament II would ensure continued warm weather, for the threat of nuclear blackmail or incineration would have melted. But something has to happen to get the temperature to rise.

If we were able to achieve Nuclear Disarmament II, states would be safer than under Nuclear Disarmament I not only because the level of international cooperation and trust would be greater, but also because "break out" would be more difficult (and these points are not unrelated). Because nations had destroyed not only their nuclear weapons, but also their nuclear production facilities, break out would take much longer, which means that the risk of getting caught rebuilding would be much greater. This greater risk of getting caught would both dissuade nations from attempting breakout and keep them from fearing that their opponents would be able to do so successfully.

But, could nations achieve the level of cooperation and trust necessary to bring about Nuclear Disarmament II? Plans for the dismantling of nuclear weapons and nuclear capabilities can be relatively easily drawn up, as the success of the START program between the United States and Russia testifies. The technological answer is rather clear. What is missing is a political answer.

THE POLITICS OF NUCLEAR DISARMAMENT

Is it possible to devise a politics that could make states feel comfortable in abandoning their nuclear capacity? There seem to be two requirements: Avoiding the likelihood of conventional war and guaranteeing that nations do not interfere with the legitimate interests of one another. Conventional war must be avoided because, so long as it remains a significant possibility, states will be greatly tempted to rebuild their nuclear weapons, the losing side in order to turn defeat into victory and the winning side in order to deny the losing side this advantage. But in attempting to avoid conventional war we come to the paradox that we have lived with for more than a half-century: One may need to be prepared to wage nuclear war to deter a conventional war. Nuclear states are afraid to engage in any kind of military conflict with each other out of fear that the conflict could escalate into nuclear war. This is the logic behind the Cold War policy of extended deterrence and the threat of first-use of nuclear weapons in Europe, discussed in Chapter 4. The very effort to lessen the likelihood of nuclear war—and what better way to do that than to remove nuclear weapons from the hands of states—may make conventional war more likely. But conventional war can lead to nuclear war.

The second requirement in building trust between nations sufficient to permit Nuclear Disarmament II is to guarantee that nations will not interfere with the legitimate interests of other nations. In order to insure noninterference from others, nations have traditionally acquired military forces, conventional and nuclear, and practiced deterrence. So armaments ward off interference, but armaments also create the possibility of such interference, because they can be used for aggression as well as defense. This incompatibility is at the heart of the nuclear predicament. The nuclear predicament is a situation in which efforts to achieve national security through nuclear threats and deterrence end up threatening national survival through the risk of nuclear catastrophe. These efforts seem self-defeating, since they pose the serious risk of destroying the nation whose interests they are designed to serve. It seems that a nation cannot both ensure the avoidance of nuclear catastrophe and guarantee that its legitimate interests will not be interfered with.

But these incompatibilities among the goals exist only in an international climate in which there is insufficient trust and cooperation among nations. These incompatibilities assume a background of international hostility and mistrust. They exist only in cold weather, not warm. If there were sufficient trust and cooperation, nations would not feel so strong a need to deploy military forces and practice deterrence to protect their interests. When conflicts of interest arose, the expectation would be that they would be settled peacefully. Consider one small example of how cooperation among nations can avoid conflicts of interest leading to war. In pursuit of economic prosperity, many nations might seek to mine the resources of the deep oceans. If nations simply try to compete with each other in staking out areas of the ocean containing valuable minerals, this might lead to war. But if all nations agree in advance on some scheme of dividing up ocean plots or profits from ocean mining, then the conflict would be handled cooperatively and war would be unlikely to result. The Law of the Sea Treaty has established the basis for the cooperative resolution of this kind of conflict.

What is needed is a scheme of international cooperation (including effective means by which conflicts can be resolved without the use of military force) that is sufficiently deep to remove the fear of aggression. Moreover, the scheme of cooperation would have to involve all nations, not simply the nuclear powers, because military conflict anywhere on the globe could lead to nuclear war, due to nuclear powers' being dragged into the fray, and nonnuclear nations could become nuclear proliferators. When we speak of the peace that nuclear deterrence is said to have brought to the world since 1945, we often forget the continuous series of bloody military conflicts that occurred between or within other nations (or between a nuclear and a nonnuclear nation). We must put a stop to all such bloodshed not only because of the great human suffering it represents, but also because the most effective response to our nuclear situation requires this. Nuclear weapons have created a situation in which security for one requires security for all, not just among nuclear powers, but also among all nations.

This line of thinking shows precisely why nuclear abandonment is viewed as utopian. Given the assumption that we are for the foreseeable future fated to live in a world of often antagonistic, sovereign nations, how could a level of cooperation and trust sufficient to remove the likelihood of conventional war and states' interference in each others' interests be achieved?

PATHWAYS TO COOPERATION

There are two general methods of cooperative, nonviolent conflict resolution among nations. First, the nations in conflict may themselves negotiate a resolution, through a formal or an informal negotiating process. We will call this *direct cooperation*. Second, the nations may have previously created or accepted an institutional arrangement, the purpose of which is peacefully to resolve conflicts between them. We will call this *indirect cooperation* because the nations may not agree with the particular resolution, but are bound to accept it because they have agreed to live under a common institutional framework that has dictated that resolution. For example, if two neighbors are in conflict over their property line, a cooperative resolution might come directly through negotiations between them or indirectly through the legal system of that community, of which the neighbors are a part.

Though force or threat of force need not come into play with direct cooperation, it can come into play with indirect cooperation. Courts, backed up by the police, can use threats or force to ensure that the neighbors comply with the legal system's determination of the property line. Similarly, in indirect cooperation between nations, the nations would have previously agreed to accept the authority of the institution for conflict resolution, and part of that agreement may be to allow the institution to use force or threat of force against them if they do not accept the institution's peaceful resolution of particular conflicts in which they are involved.

How might it come about that nations could, either directly or indirectly, cooperatively resolve their conflicts? This is a question of what would constitute a *cooperative world order*.[12] One possibility is that nations might have such good relations that all conflicts between them are, as a matter of course, resolved through direct cooperation. Consider the United States and Britain. They do not require an independent institutional framework to resolve their conflicts because it is simply unimaginable that their conflicts could ever lead to war. The political, economic, and cultural ties between the United States and Britain are so close that no leader of either nation would ever, at this point in time, seriously consider using force against the other. When conflicts arise between them, pushing things to the point of force is never a real option. A resolution is formally negotiated or arrived at through informal give and take.

In the case of nations whose relations are not that close, direct cooperative resolution of conflicts cannot always be counted on to succeed. When relations are not close, it is not unthinkable that the nations could seek to resolve their conflict with force. Only indirect cooperation can guarantee no war. What are called for are independent institutions for resolving such conflicts, supranational institutions with some authority over nations and some ability to enforce their decisions. The backbone of this would be a stronger form of international law than currently exists. Nations would remain largely sovereign, but some of their sovereignty would be ceded to an international authority.

But perhaps such a limited surrender of national sovereignty to an international authority would not be sufficient to achieve the goals of avoiding conventional war and the interference of states in each others' affairs. If so, nuclear abandonment under Nuclear Disarmament II would not be possible consistent with our assumption that states will remain sovereign for the foreseeable future. Such a thought may have motivated the solution to the nuclear predicament proposed by Albert Einstein.

EINSTEIN'S PROPOSAL REFORMULATED

Einstein worked hard after the war with his fellow scientists and the public at large in seeking to bring about recognition of the need for a world government, a strong global authority that would hold sovereignty over the world's nations. This was the situation as he saw it:

So long as there are sovereign nations possessing great power, war is inevitable. That is not to say when it will come, but only that it is sure to come. That was true before the atomic bomb was made. What has been changed is the destructiveness of war.

This, then, was Einstein's solution: "Mankind can only gain protection against the danger of unimaginable destruction and wanton annihilation if *a supranational organization has alone the authority to produce and possess these weapons.*"[13] It was not a utopian dream, as it paralleled the U.S. government's initial proposal for the control of nuclear energy presented by Bernard Baruch in the late 1940s, which we described in Chapter 3.

The nations of the world could voluntarily create a world government with full police power, that is, the power to enforce resolutions of conflicts. In support of its police power, Einstein suggested, the world government would need the authority to possess nuclear weapons, an authority it would deny its member nations. Thus, under this scheme, nuclear weapons would be abandoned by nations, but not by the world government. The world government would presumably use nuclear threats to keep nations from using force against other nations or interfering in each others' affairs.

There are two obvious problems with such a vision of a world authority. First, it is probably politically infeasible in the foreseeable future. Nations would not likely agree to a world government with full police power because it would extinguish their valued independence and sovereignty. Nor is it at all likely that one nation could establish a world state by world conquest. Not even the United States, the militarily strongest nation in absolute, and perhaps in relative, terms that has ever existed, has the power (let alone the will) to achieve this. Moreover, the fear that nations would have of a world government, especially one with nuclear weapons, is not unjustified. Such great and unchallengeable power could be abused. The world government might turn into a tyranny. So, it is hard to imagine that the nations of the world would ever voluntarily submit to the authority of a true world government (or that one could be forced upon them). The infeasibility of such a solution is precisely why we adopted the assumption that the best nuclear policy has to be consistent with the existence of sovereign states.

In addition, Einstein's solution does not even count as the abandonment of nuclear weapons, because they would still be possessed by the world government. Even if we assumed that a world government were feasible, its possession of nuclear weapons would mean that the risk of nuclear use would remain, and might be expected, as some state leaders at some point in time are likely to refuse to comply with a world government's decisions.

But consider the possibility of a weaker form of world authority, one that could provide an effective means of conflict resolution among nations, but would not involve extensive police power, and, especially, would not possess nuclear weapons. If such an authority came into being, it might represent a form of cooperation among nations that would lead to a level of international trust sufficient to bring about Nuclear Disarmament II and constitute it as the best nuclear policy to adopt. Under this form of world authority, nations would not be forced to surrender their nuclear weapons because of nuclear threats from the authority, but would over time give up their weapons and their nuclear capability through negotiation because the need for the weapons would no longer be as strongly felt.

But is there reason to think that achieving this more limited form of world authority is any more feasible than achieving a world government with extensive police power? Perhaps it is feasible, if we conceive of its coming about in a different way. Instead of the nations deliberately surrendering a significant part of their sovereignty at one large global negotiating session, they might slowly and only half consciously surrender their sovereignty by acquiescing in the development of rules of progressively stronger international law. Even now, without the central enforcement mechanism necessary for a world government, international law often serves as an effective mechanism of control over the behavior of nations and for resolving disputes among them. This is due, in part, to the fact that other nations can "punish" violators of international law by applying various kinds of sanctions, especially economic sanctions, and this, in conjunction with growing economic interdependence, makes compliance with international law generally in the national self-interest.

This could lead to the gradual and limited empowering of a central authority to enforce a resolution of conflicts, as suggested by Stephen Toulmin.

> [G]reater interdependence makes it increasingly disadvantageous for states to act as "outlaws," even in advance of formal machinery for the enforcement of international law...[A]s Vico and the Epicureans both foresaw, the pragmatic demands of the actual situation may nonetheless lead to the progressive crystallization of supranational institutions and constraints, without any need for the sovereign nations involved to agree explicitly on any formal treaty or contract.[14]

Toulmin suggests an analogy. When humans discovered how to use fire, its destructive potential in the hands of one's enemies must have seemed as frightening as nuclear energy in the hands of our enemies seems to us. But fire was brought under community control through a legal invention: the concept of "arson." The use of fire was safely naturalized into human life through the development of new institutions and public attitudes, by which the misuse of fire was stigmatized as anti-human and punished as a crime.[15]

A strengthened but limited world authority of the sort envisioned might, over time, allow Nuclear Disarmament II to come into being. It could be the warm weather that would lead the nations to remove their defensive coats of their own volition. But, if it succeeded, the main contributing factor to the reduction in the risk of nuclear use would not be the abandonment of nuclear weapons themselves, but rather the creation of the cooperative world order. In fact, it would be the cooperative world order that would make it politically possible for nations to then consider abandoning the weapons. It is the extensive network of international political institutions, and the level of trust that they could in time engender, that would lead to the greatest reduction of the risk of nuclear catastrophe. The nuclear weapons themselves would be abandoned mainly as a side effect or as a symptom of the larger success.

In this process of disarmament, considerations of the morality of nuclear weapons should have an impact as well. People have always recognized the morally problematic nature of nuclear weapons. This attitude is expressed by retired U.S. General George Butler, one of the leaders in the group of military officers issuing the statement favoring abandonment cited at the beginning of the chapter. In speaking of the abandonment proposal, he observed that the United States has a responsibility in "dealing with the conflicted *moral* legacy of the Cold War," that we must "work painfully back through the tangled *moral* web of this frightful 50-year gauntlet."[16] But so far, especially in the first nuclear age, it has been hard for this recognition of the immoral nature of nuclear weapons to have an impact on policy. The reason is the moral paradox of nuclear deterrence discussed in Chapter 11. Possession of the weapons for deterrence was seen as the necessary for national survival, itself an important moral consideration, so concerns about the immorality of practicing nuclear deterrence had to take a back seat. But, were a sufficiently cooperative world order to come into existence, the weapons would no longer be seen as necessary for security. Then, there would no longer be the conflict between the moral horror the weapons engender in us and the moral concern that we had to have them for our self-defense. The moral paradox would have been largely removed, and we would look upon the weapons only with horror. Possession would no longer be seen as legitimate. Once the defensive need for the weapons dissipated, they would be seen as lacking legitimacy, and this perception would hasten their abandonment.

MAKING ABANDONMENT HAPPEN: A POLICY FOR THE FUTURE

Getting to nuclear abandonment under Nuclear Disarmament II would be a long-term project. How would American foreign policy begin the process? This option would envision the following:

1. For the immediate future, the United States would adopt the management option presented in Chapter 3. That option proposed to continue a formal negotiating process for the mutual reduction of nuclear armaments to a relatively small number, something approaching what all could agree would likely ensure minimum deterrence. But the explicit purpose of the negotiations would be to set the stage for the eventual abandonment of nuclear weapons. Having abandonment of nuclear weapons as the ultimate goal would give the management option a needed focus—a way of helping to prioritize its efforts and providing a benchmark against which to judge its specific proposals.

2. It would be important, however, not to take the abandonment of nuclear weapons as the chief goal in the short run. Rather, as this chapter has stressed, a much higher level of international cooperation is the chief goal, with abandonment as an consequence of achieving this. To get rid of nuclear weapons or even bring about a significant reduction in their numbers below minimum deterrence levels without a parallel and ever-increasing level of international cooperation might make our situation worse. The management option, while it does encourage cooperation, does so with a stick in hand. The trust required for the abandonment of nuclear weapons would require that threats and punishment were less salient. One way to help bring this about would be for stronger states to offer concessions in negotiations in excess of the concessions offered by the other side. The United States currently has the capacity to make such unequal concessions.

3. Whereas the management option stresses negotiation and offering concessions in return for concessions—and in so doing increase the possibilities for international cooperation and trust—the abandonment option necessitates a particular general concession by the United States: All American actions would have to reinforce the nuclear taboo. Nuclear weapons are not to be used. Therefore, such things as the development of bunker-busting nuclear weapons (possibly tolerated under the management option) would be explicitly and completely rejected by the United States, as would planning to use nuclear weapons as part of coercive denuclearization efforts. There would be no brandishing of nuclear weapons, and the United States would sanction states that engaged in such activity. De-emphasizing the importance of nuclear weapons in world politics would need the hegemon's endorsement and support.

WHAT ABOUT OUR CURRENT PROBLEMS?

As we have said, the overall goal of nuclear policy should be to reduce as far as possible the risk of the use of nuclear weapons, which requires effectively avoiding nuclear proliferation, dealing successfully with state and nonstate actors (such as terrorists) that pose security threats, and avoiding the risk of nuclear blackmail. In the long term, abandonment may be the best policy to achieve these goals. But things are dangerous in the short term, so we must ask how a policy of (eventual) abandonment helps to achieve these goals in the short term. The answer to this question has already largely been addressed in Chapter 13 because the management option is the way-station toward abandonment. The positives and negatives of the management option are the roughly the same in the short term as the positives and negatives of a policy of abandonment because the way to eventual abandonment moves through the management option.

Consider one aspect of this issue, the effectiveness of a policy of moving toward abandonment in the short-term goal of dealing successfully with state and nonstate actors posing security threats. This has, or course, been the chief concern of United States policy since 9/11. This is a question of what you do, in a generally cooperative world, with the non-cooperators, those who, for whatever reason, find it in their national or group interest to pose security threats to (other) states. Some of the non-cooperators are so-called rogue states, states who challenge militarily their neighbors or more distant major powers. Nonstate terrorists, such as members of al Qaeda, are, of course, non-cooperators par excellence. Terrorists pose a special threat when they receive support from a rogue state or they are able to use the territory of a failed state (a state with an ineffective government that cannot control what goes on in its territory). To avoid the security threats posed by rogue states or terrorists, military force may be necessary.

This is, of course, also the view of advocates of coercive denuclearization, but they tend to prefer that the military force be imposed unilaterally by the United States (perhaps with support from a "coalition of the willing"). While military force may be necessary, it is not necessary that it be imposed unilaterally. It can be imposed under the authority of a recognized, legitimate international organization, such as the United Nations. Such multilateral use of force would have advantages over unilateral use. It is likely to be more effective because it would be sanctioned by the international community and seen as an expression of the community's norms. Opposition from within the state attacked may also be weaker, and the international cooperation involved in the decision and the use of the force is likely to move the process of increasing international cooperation along. In addition, international authorization would reduce the risk that the force is being used for an illegitimate ulterior purpose, as might be the case with the unilateral use of force.

The use of military force against rogue states might be preventive, that is, designed to protect against future rather than imminent threats, rather than defensive or preemptive. Preventive attacks, precisely because they are not defensive, are morally questionable and are viewed with suspicion by the rest of the world, for anyone can use it as a pretext to wage war. If preventive attacks are necessary, the only way to do them effectively and legitimately is to do them through international authorization which is a form of judgment about the plausibility of the allegation of threat. This approach, if adhered to by the United States and Britain in 2003, would have prevented their invasion of Iraq—and would have bolstered the development of cooperation and trust since the international community would have demonstrated that its organization had the power to prevent an attack. At the same time, the renewed inspection regime would have reinforced the point that Iraq had to remain in compliance with its international obligations. If, on the other hand, the Security Council had been persuaded that Iraq posed a serious threat to its neighbors and the United States and therefore had authorized the invasion, it is likely that there would have been far more troops on the ground and a more

successful occupation and reconstruction of Iraq than has occurred. The odds for effective democratization of Iraq might have been significantly enhanced as well.

This form of cooperative international behavior might effectively deal with international terrorism as practiced by al Qaeda. The United Nations quickly passed a resolution "condemning the
Taliban for allowing Afghanistan to be used as a base for the export of terrorism by the Al-Qaida network and other terrorist groups and for providing safe haven to Usama Bin Ladin, Al-Qaida and others associated with them, and in this context supporting the efforts of the Afghan people to replace the
Taliban regime."[17] The United Nations sponsored an international security force to safeguard the
new government and restore order throughout the state. (This task that has proven to be difficult, but
more from the U.S. distraction in Iraq than any hindrances imposed by the international community.)
This strongly suggests that any war against terrorism is much more likely to be effective if it is pursued, especially in regard to any necessary military force, with international authorization and cooperation.

But all this talk of international cooperation around military matters seems to be, in the early years
of the twenty-first century, against the grain. The talk about disarmament agreements seems, as a dis-
missive critic might say, so Cold War. The tide seems to be moving away from that kind of policy. The
United States under the Bush administration has shown little interest in negotiating any agreements
regarding nuclear arms and has formerly withdrawn from a major existing nuclear treaty, the
Anti-Ballistic Missile Treaty, in addition to having made the unilateral decision to go to war in Iraq.
American policy has been moving in the direction of coercive denuclearization rather than the
management option, let alone a policy of eventual nuclear abandonment. But nuclear policy, like any
policy, should be judged on its potential effectiveness in meeting the problems for which it is designed, not in terms of whether it is historically in ascendancy. The policy of nuclear abandonment
may not be the best policy, but if this is the case, it is not because it is currently out of favor by the nation's leadership. And, in any case, history has a funny way of turning things around.

THE FOURTH NUCLEAR AGE

We are now in the second nuclear age. At the start of this book, we spoke of a third nuclear age, one
initiated by the next use of nuclear weapons. We see in that use the potential for a new world in which
nuclear weapons return to center stage in the relations between nations, where proliferation pressures
dramatically escalate, and nuclear-driven crises become the order of the day. But there is the possibility of another nuclear future, beyond the second and possible third nuclear age. It would be a time
when the threat from nuclear weapons had declined to close to zero. (It is characteristic of the nuclear
predicament that it can never be at zero.) This may be referred to as the *fourth nuclear age*. If we can
reach the fourth nuclear age, it may be as the successor to the third nuclear age, or it may, if we are
lucky and wise in our policy choices, directly follow the current second nuclear age. If the fourth nuclear age comes, it will come gradually over time, something only our great grandchildren may see,
unlike the third nuclear age, which, should it come, will come any moment with a bang.

Many people, of course, would argue that the fourth nuclear age is a practical impossibility, that
the policy of nuclear abandonment either would not work or cannot be achieved. They may be right,
which would leave us to choose between coercive denuclearization and the management option. But
one virtue of the policy of nuclear abandonment is that committing to it as a goal does not entail any

significant immediate risks because progress toward it would have to be slow. The point in time when nuclear weapons and nuclear capacity would finally be eradicated, a time that critics see as a special time of danger, would come only when the world was ready for it—when the level of international cooperation and trust would sustain us through that point of potential danger. It may, as the critics maintain, be impossible to achieve the necessary level of cooperation and trust, but trying for it does not impose much if any extra risk, and we can achieve it only if we try.

CONCLUSION

We have asked you to consider three basic options available to the United States in dealing with the nuclear predicament. Each has its strengths and weaknesses. None offers a guarantee that it will keep the world free from nuclear use, nor perfectly safeguard the interests of the various states and peoples of the world. But we must chose to do something, else we will find that others, perhaps less well intentioned, and the workings of circumstance will dictate the contours of the second nuclear age. That might seem comforting—let someone else do the worrying. But one of the responsibilities of being a citizen of the greatest nuclear power is to do the worrying—and the acting—to create a world worth handing on to our children and the world's children.

ENDNOTES

[1]International Generals and Admirals, "Statement on Nuclear Weapons," reprinted in *The Washington Quarterly 20*, no. 3 (Winter 1997), pp. 125–130. Quotations are from pp. 125, 126, 127.

[2]Michael Mazarr, "Introduction," special issue on nuclear arms control, *Washington Quarterly 20*, no. 3 (Summer 1997), p. 82.

[3]Michael Mazaar, "Virtual Nuclear Arsenals," *Survival 37*, no. 3 (Autumn 1995), p. 23.

[4]Jonathan Schell, *The Abolition* (New York: Alfred Knopf, 1984).

[5]Mazaar, "Virtual Nuclear Arsenals."

[6]In a fuller discussion of the idea of a virtual nuclear arsenal, we should consider the role of a delivery vehicle for the weapon. If a nation was a screwdriver away from a nuclear weapon but could not delivery it against an opponent, it would not have a virtual nuclear arsenal because it could not use the weapon against anyone or credibly threaten anyone with it.

[7]Schell, *The Abolition.*

[8]The only nuclear war to have occurred was such a war, the one between the United States and Japan.

[9]Michael Mazaar, "Virtual Nuclear Arsenals," p. 13.

[10]For an elaboration of this argument, see Steven Lee, *Morality, Prudence, and Nuclear Weapons* (Cambridge: Cambridge University Press, 1993), especially, Chapter 7.

[11]Salvador de Madariaga, quoted in Michael Quinlan, "The Future of Nuclear Weapons in World Affairs," *The Washington Quarterly 20*, no. 3 (Winter 1997), p. 141.

[12]There is a large literature on world order studies. One classic example is Richard Falk, *A Study of Future Worlds* (New York: Free Press, 1975).

[13]Einstein, *Ideas*, p. 150, emphasis supplied.

[14]Stephen Toulmin, "The Limits of Allegiance in a Nuclear Age," in A. Cohen and S. Lee (eds.), *Nuclear Weapons and the Future of Humanity* (Totowa, NJ: Rowman and Allanheld, 1986), p. 365.

[15]Toulmin, "Limits," p. 365.

[16]George Lee Butler, "The General's Bombshell: Phasing Out the U.S. Nuclear Arsenal," *The Washington Quarterly 20*, no. 3 (Summer 1997), pp. 133, 134 (emphasis added).

[17]Security Council Resolution 1378 (2001) of November 14, 2001; (http://www.unama-afg.org/docs/_UN-Docs/_sc/_resolutions/sc1378.pdf).

Epilogue

What If?

The Third Nuclear Age would begin with the next detonation of a nuclear weapon, one used deliberately against an opponent. In that brief moment, the world faces great risks. Leaders and peoples may dramatically change how they view the world and the role of nuclear weapons in it. We might hope that they would collectively recoil in horror and recommit themselves to the Cold War's great truth: If nuclear weapons are to exist, they are not to be used. We fear, however, that even if it were just one explosion, the odds are strong that more would follow, for there are likely to be new answers to very familiar questions: What do we do to prevent our nation from being the target of the next detonation? How will others attempt to exploit their possession of nuclear weapons to advance their political purposes? How might we? How can we head off explosive proliferation? For those seeking to restore the nuclear taboo, however, there is but one, quite novel, question: how do we shut the door on further explosions? In other words, are we prepared, like a fire department, to put out the fire?

We might imagine that our preparations would have to be wide ranging. Consider, for instance, the question of who staged the attack. The role of breaker-of-the-nuclear-taboo might be played by a number of actors: from a terrorist group with extraordinarily ambitious political goals, to a regional power attempting to forestall what it judges to be an impending conventional assault that will overwhelm it, to the leadership of a major nuclear-weapons state determined to eradicate a terrorist group's leadership or to compel the reunification with lost territory (such as Taiwan). If a terrorist group—already operating outside the conventions of traditional international politics—were the first user, its use of a nuclear device might further stigmatize nuclear weapons as being particularly immoral and unacceptable and lead to redoubled cooperative efforts to prevent any further use by anyone else. The result of this scenario would be a strengthening of the nuclear taboo. At the same time, however, the result might be a significant weakening of the nuclear taboo. There may be a number of observers who conclude that a crude nuclear device can work reliably and that a reliable delivery system (say, a shipping container) is available to anyone, bypassing the need for aircraft or missiles. They may be tempted to emulate.

If a regional power were the first user, the rest of the international community—particularly the major nuclear powers—might rally strongly to prevent the next use. Or members of the international community might instead take hesitant, partial steps, believing that, however regrettable, nuclear use happened within "an understandable context of normally conflictual regional politics," one in which prudent states would be wary of becoming too deeply involved. And if a major nuclear-weapons state were to use the weapon, there are likely to be responses ranging from explicit approval, to embarrassed silence, to vocal condemnation, to active defense, possibly including the use of nuclear weapons, of the target of the nuclear attack. In sum, the reaction to the next use of nuclear weapons could be quite varied, with no assurance that, whatever the response, further use of nuclear weapons would cease.

Given the wide range of possible scenarios for the fire next time, we might despair of being truly ready to cope with that fire. The hegemon (the United States), however, because of its great power, carries greater responsibility to be the linchpin for any effort to stop further nuclear use. If it is skilled (and lucky) the hegemon will be able to provide a respite—a moment after the fire is temporarily doused, but with hot embers still there to reignite the house—when it can help to shape the contours of the third nuclear age. So what the hegemon is prepared to do when the next use of nuclear weapons happens may be *the* most critical factor for the future.

We invite you to consider what kind of preparations the United States should make for the next use of nuclear weapons. What would give us (and the rest of the world) the greatest chance of stopping further nuclear use and reconstituting nuclear relations so that it would not happen again? We will conclude our survey of the nuclear predicament with the following observation: The policy choice we Americans make today about dealing with nuclear weapons in the second nuclear age will determine how the United States will, in fact, respond to the fire next time. Here is our assessment of how three different fire departments, if you will, are likely to respond.

A policy of coercive denuclearization and first-use. Coercive denuclearization is essentially a *fire-prevention* strategy—to keep nuclear weapons out of "the wrong hands." While advocates of this policy would not like to see nuclear use anywhere, they are most concerned by first-use by rogue states or terrorists. First-use by those actors would confirm the aptness of the U.S. policy (at least in the minds of its advocates) and would likely call forth an even greater effort to halt or prevent further use by them. Such an effort could include the strongest of threats and the use of force, possibly including selective nuclear use of its own (akin to starting a back fire to contain a forest fire). Whether such dramatic action would be sufficient to prevent any further use by terrorists or rogue states cannot be known in advance. In contrast, if there were first-use by *other* actors, the United States, under a policy of coercive denuclearization, would surely condemn the use, but likely tolerate it, if it were limited and it seemed that the user had no other choice to protect its interests—assuming that neither the United States nor an ally were the target of the attack.

A management orientation and first-use. The approach taken by advocates of the Management Option would be to douse any fire quickly and lay arson charges against the perpetrator. That is, the United States, under this policy, would likely insist that there be no further nuclear use and that all hostilities immediately cease. The United States is likely to threaten to aid the victim of the attack "in suitable ways" in order to prevent the initiator from taking advantage of its nuclear strike and to give the victim the ability to accept a cease-fire. Furthermore, the United States would likely choose to overlook the causes of the conflict and the nature of the regimes involved. Its initial premise would be that *ending further nuclear use takes priority over everything else* and, second, that under its leadership, the international community must *devise terms of settlement of the original conflict and impose them on both parties*, terms that might give greater weight to the claims or proposals *of the victim* of a nuclear attack.

A management policy works best, of course, if the rules are laid out before hand, because they help to guide state behavior (in this case, to make nuclear use unattractive). But, while the policy would require that the United States announce its support of such rules in advance and attempt to enlist others' support, to do so may be politically divisive domestically (as it commits the United States to take very difficult actions) and dangerous (as it would take away the flexibility that would be desirable to have in such a crisis). The rules might also effectively remove the legitimacy of the nuclear option for states like Israel and Pakistan, who, were they to use the weapons, would be punished in the settlement phase even if they used nuclear weapons to repel a massive conventional invasion. It may be important also to announce that any nuclear use by any less-than-state actor anywhere would be treated as an act of war against the United States. Finally, under a management policy, the United States is likely to resist using nuclear weapons itself unless it must do so to enforce the rules.

Abandonment and first-use. We have suggested that a policy of the abandonment of nuclear weapons is likely to be implemented initially through an interim adoption of the management approach, so, in the near future, the response to first use under a policy of abandonment would echo the response of the management approach. But the emphasis may be different. Now management's perceptions of the issue would be conditioned by abandonment's central goal: nuclear weapons must be abandoned. If that is where the international community is to end up, then there can be little political or moral justification for their use now. First use, should it occur, is likely to be perceived as a horrifying practical demonstration of why nuclear weapons must ultimately be abandoned, making clear that they are profoundly immoral implements of destruction. Their users would be treated as international outcasts.

But should the first use occur not in the short term, but decades from now, after the goal of abandonment had been largely achieved, the consequences might be much worse. If nations had achieved Nuclear Disarmament II, under which no nation would possess nuclear weapons or have the production capacity to build them quickly, the use of nuclear weapons would be a dramatic indication of the failure of the policy. The user would have "broken out" of its weaponless condition, presumably undetected by others until the moment of detonation. Some states would surely scramble to restore nuclear weapons to their arsenals, while others might redouble their efforts to restore the status quo of a nuclear weapons-free world. To guard against this outcome, abandonment would have to be based on an extensive regime of detection and verification, so that a break-out attempt would likely be detected in time to be effectively dealt with before a nuclear weapon was rebuilt. There would have to be smoke detectors in every room and periodic inspections by the fire marshal. The proponents of abandonment would, of course, argue that first use would be *much less likely* under abandonment than under the other two policy options.

As we have seen, there is no foolproof answer to the nuclear predicament. Indeed, nuclear weapons, nuclear states, and terrorism pose challenges that can never be solved in any final sense, and every choice we make has its dangers. The choice that you help to make (or that you allow others to make in your name) will shape our collective nuclear future. Our hope is that the discussion we have presented over the course of this book will have put you, the reader, in the position intelligently to consider our way forward in the perilous world that has been our lot since 1945. What nuclear policy choices do you recommend, and what arguments would you make for them?

Glossary

ABM Antiballistic Missile; a missile designed to destroy warheads on incoming missiles.

ABM Treaty Treaty between the United States and the Soviet Union signed in 1972 restricting the testing and deployment of ABMs; the United States announced its intention to withdraw from the treaty in 2001.

Alpha Particle The Helium-4 nucleus consisting of two protons and two neutrons.

Appeasement A policy of offering real concessions to an opponent in return for its pledge to behave in a particular way in the future.

Arms Control A policy of seeking agreements to stabilize an arms race in both its qualitative and quantitative dimensions; may involve reductions in force levels or restraints on the development, testing, and deployment of weapons.

Arms Race An upward-spiraling competition between two or more nations, each trying to equal or exceed the number and quality of weapons held by an opponent.

Arms-Race Stability A military situation in which an arms race is unlikely to arise, because neither side believes that building new weapons would provide it with a significant military advantage or help it overcome a significant military disadvantage.

Assured Destruction A form of deterrence, made possible by nuclear weapons, where a nation is able to destroy the society of its opponent even after receiving a surprise first strike. This strategic doctrine was first promulgated by Secretary of Defense Robert McNamara in the 1960s.

Atomic Number (Z) The number of protons in the nucleus of an atom.

Atomic Weight (A) The sum of the number of protons and neutrons in an atom's nucleus; very close to the actual weight of the atom.

B-2 Bomber Current generation U.S. bomber; although subsonic, its very low radar profile make it almost impossible to detect and destroy

B-52 Bomber First-generation intercontinental bomber; in the U.S. inventory for over 50 years, it carries a very large payload, including cruise missiles, and is quite reliable.

Beta Rays A form of radiation consisting of electrons.

Blitzkrieg "Lightning war;" the use of motorized and armored units along with airpower to break through enemy defenses quickly, isolate enemy units, and defeat them piecemeal.

BMD Ballistic Missile Defense; a component of National Missile Defense (which also is planned to include cruise missile and theater high altitude defenses) consisting of a variety of systems (for example, anti-ballistic missiles) capable of destroying enemy missiles or warheads after their launch.

Bolt from the Blue An unexpected attack launched by one nation against another.

CBRNE Chemical, biological, radiological, nuclear, and enhanced explosive weapons.

CBW Chemical and Biological Weapons.

CENTCOM United States military command responsible for military operations in the Middle East and Central Asia.

Coercive Anti-Proliferation A policy of using threats of military force or force itself to deprive a potential nuclear proliferator of the capacity to build nuclear weapons.

Coercive Denuclearization A policy of using threats of military force or force itself to deprive a nuclear proliferator of the nuclear weapons it already possesses, along with the capacity to build them.

Cold War The intense rivalry between the United States and Soviet Union following World War II in which war was a possibility but was not deliberately sought by either nation. The Cold War, which we have called the first nuclear age, lasted until the 1991 dissolution of the Soviet Union.

Collateral Damage The unintentional (but often foreseen) destruction of civilian population or infrastructure resulting from attacks against adjacent military targets.

Combatant A person serving in the military forces of a nation at war or otherwise closely involved in the nation's war-making activity (such as a munitions worker).

Combined A military command or operations is combined when it involves forces of the United States and an ally, for example, the United Kingdom.

Command, Control, Communication and Intelligence (C^3I) The systems required to obtain timely intelligence, maintain reliable communications during crisis, and direct and control a nation's armed forces in a war.

Compellence Using threats to get another nation to make positive concessions; compellence is contrasted with deterrence, which uses threats to get another nation *not* to do something, such as engage in aggression.

Confidence Building Measures Measures undertaken by a nation to reassure its opponent that it does not intend a sudden attack, including arrangements such as a "hotline" providing direct communication between leaders, onsite inspection of critical areas, and national technical means of inspection (q.v.).

Containment Any policy attempting to restrict the expansion or influence of another nation; usually associated with U.S. foreign policy toward the Soviet Union during the Cold War, beginning in the late 1940s.

Conventional Forces Those components of a nation's military forces not involving nuclear weapons or other weapons of mass destruction.

Cooperative Anti-Proliferation A policy of stopping nuclear proliferation by getting the agreement of the potential proliferators not to proliferate. The principal example of this is the Nuclear Non-Proliferation Treaty.

Cooperative Threat Reduction A policy adopted in 1991 by which the United States aids Russia in securing its nuclear weapons and fissile material from possible theft, also known as Nunn-Lugar after the two Senators who sponsored it.

Coulomb Force The force of attraction or repulsion between electrical charges.

Counterforce Weapons Weapons best suited, because of their speed and accuracy, for the destruction of an enemy's military forces.

Counterproliferation A policy of using military force or the threat of such to keep a potential proliferator from acquiring nuclear weapons or to deprive a proliferator of the nuclear weapons it has already acquired.

Countervalue Weapons   Weapons best suited for the use against what an enemy values, a euphemism for its industry, recovery capability, and population. In contrast with counterforce weapons, countervalue weapons are often relatively slow and inaccurate.

Crisis Stability   A military situation in which war is unlikely to arise in a crisis because neither side perceives that the other would achieve an advantage from striking first, and so has little fear that the other side would do so.

Critical Mass   The mass of fissionable material required to produce a self-sustaining fission reaction.

Cruise Missile   An air-breathing, computer guided pilotless aircraft that can carry either nuclear or conventional weapons.

Crystal Ball Effect   The cautious-making influence on a nation's military policy of the ability of its leadership to foresee, as if in a crystal ball, its total ruination in the event of a nuclear war.

CTBT   Comprehensive Test Ban Treaty, a 1996 treaty prohibiting all nuclear weapons testing. The treaty is not yet in force because not all 44 nuclear-weapons-capable states have signed and ratified the treaty, which is required.

Decapitation   The elimination by surprise attack of an adversary's top leadership in order to make it incapable of defending itself.

Decoupling   The loss by a nation of its willingness to use nuclear weapons in the defense of its allies.

Denial Anti-proliferation   A policy which seeks to avoid nuclear proliferation by denying to would- be proliferators the knowledge, technology, or fissile material they need to construct a nuclear weapon.

Détente   Generally speaking, a policy by a nation to seek better, more cooperative relations with an opponent. This was, specifically, the Nixon administration's policy toward the Soviet Union.

Deterrence   Persuading another nation by threat of military retaliation not to engage in aggression, especially the launching of a nuclear attack.

Dirty Bomb   A conventional explosive device containing radioactive material, the use of which radioactively contaminates the immediate vicinity of the explosion.

Disarmament   The reduction or elimination of a nation's war-making capacity, brought about voluntarily, as by mutual agreement, or through force.

Disarming First Strike   A surprise nuclear attack that attempts to destroy a large enough portion of an enemy's nuclear arsenal to forestall nuclear retaliation.

Electronic Volt (eV)   A unit of energy appropriate for measuring the energies of electrons in atoms and molecules.

EMP   Electromagnetic Pulse; a surge of electromagnetic energy, destructive of sensitive electronic equipment, created by a nuclear explosion.

EUCOM   U.S. military command responsible for military operations and forces in Europe and Africa.

Extended Deterrence   Use of the threat of nuclear retaliation to deter a conventional or nuclear attack on one's allies as well as a conventional attack on one's homeland.

Failed State   A nation in which the government has broken down and can no longer either perform the functions of caring for and protecting its people or effectively control violence or the use of armed force in all or part of its territory.

Fallout   Radioactive particles carried by the wind away from the site of a nuclear explosion, posing a threat to living organisms downwind.

Firebreak   A gap in the process of escalation in a war between the use of conventional weapons and the use of nuclear weapons. The wider this gap, the smaller the risk that a conventional war would escalate to a nuclear war.

First Strike   The initiation of war by a nuclear strike against an opponent.

First Use   A declared policy of being willing to use nuclear weapons in response to a conventional attack on one's self or one's allies.

Flexible Response   A doctrine proposed by Secretary of Defense Robert McNamara in the early 1960s under which the United States would have a variety of options with which to respond to provocation or aggression by the Soviet Union, other than the single one of launching a massive nuclear strike.

Forward-Based Systems   A nation's nuclear delivery systems (such as aircraft) located outside the nation's borders near an opponent nation.

Gamma Ray   A form of electromagnetic radiation with a frequency much higher than that of the visible spectrum.

Geosynchronous Satellites   Satellites with orbits high enough that they orbit the earth once a day, thereby remaining over a fixed spot of the earth's surface.

Ground Zero   That land or water area at which a nuclear weapon detonates. This term is also used to refer to the site of the September 11th terrorist attacks.

Gun-Type Nuclear Explosive   The simplest and most reliable nuclear fission weapon, so reliable that it was used untested on Hiroshima; but it is not as efficient or as powerful as implosion-type fission weapons.

Half-Life   The amount of time it takes for half of a sample of a radioactive isotope to decay to a stable, nonradioactive form. The more unstable the isotope, the shorter the half-life.

Hibakusha   The Japanese term used to refer to the surviving victims of the atomic explosions over Hiroshima and Nagasaki.

Horizontal Proliferation   The traditional meaning of the term *proliferation*, namely, the acquisition of nuclear weapons by states not already possessing them.

ICBM   Intercontinental Ballistic Missile.

INF Treaty   Intermediate Nuclear Forces Treaty, a 1987 treaty between the United States and the Soviet Union abolishing all intermediate and short-range missiles (300–3,500 miles) deployed by the two nations in Europe.

International Atomic Energy Agency (IAEA)   The United Nations agency charged with monitoring compliance with international treaties and agreements on the production and use of nuclear materials.

Isotope   A term used to distinguish between different forms of an element whose masses differ from one another because their nuclei contain different numbers of neutrons.

JCS   Joint Chief of Staffs, consisting of the commanding officers of each of the U.S. military services plus a chairman, who serve as the principal military advisors to the U.S. government.

Joint   In the United States, "joint" refers to a military command or operations involving more than one of the military services, that is, Army, Air Force, Navy, or Marines.

Jus ad Bellum   Justice *of* war; that part of just-war theory concerning the conditions under which it is morally acceptable for a nation to go to war.

Jus in Bello   Justice *in* war; that part of just war theory concerning the morally acceptable ways of fighting a war.

Just-War Theory   The traditional set of standards for judging the mortality of military activity, recognized by military authorities themselves and embodied in international law.

Kiloton (Kt)   A unit of energy for measuring the prompt yield of nuclear explosions, equal to the energy released by one thousand tons of TNT.

Linkage   Making decisions about arms control or nuclear policy based on a consideration of the nonnuclear actions of one's opponent, such as, during the Cold War, Soviet intervention in the Third World or its human rights practices.

MAD   Mutual Assured Destruction (q.v.).

Manhattan Project   The code name for the U.S. project to build atomic weapons during World War II.

MARV   Maneuverable reentry vehicles; ballistic missile warheads that have the capability to maneuver during reentry, increasing the difficulty of ballistic missile defense.

Massive Retaliation   A doctrine from the mid-1950s under which the United States threatened to retaliate instantly by means and at places of its own choosing in response to a variety of aggressive actions by communist states.

Megaton (MT)   A unit of energy for measuring the prompt yield of a nuclear explosion; equal to the energy released by the explosion of one million tons of TNT.

Minimum Deterrence   A nuclear weapons policy that involves the deployment of relatively small numbers of deliverable nuclear warheads, invulnerable to a first strike, and lacking an extensive counterforce capability.

Minuteman   U.S. land-based solid-fueled intercontinental ballistic missile based in underground silos; can be equipped with multiple warheads.

MIRV   Multiple Independently Targeted Reentry Vehicle; separate nuclear warheads mounted on one missile, each capable of being directed to a different target.

Multiplication Factor (k)   A parameter describing the growth or decay in the number of free neutrons in fissionable material. If k is greater that one, the fission reaction will grow exponentially.

Mutual Assured Destruction   A nuclear standoff, such as existed between the United States and the Soviet Union during the Cold war, in which each of two adversaries has an assured destruction capacity in relation to the other; that is, each has the ability to destroy the other even after receiving a surprise attack; often referred to by its initials MAD.

National Command Authority   The president of the United States and the Secretary of Defense or their successors, who have the authority to order the use of nuclear weapons.

National Security Council (NSC)   Established in 1947 as the formal advisory body to the president on major national security issues.

National Technical Means   A collective name for monitoring capabilities such as satellites used to verify arms control.

NATO   North Atlantic Treaty Organization; a mutual security alliance between the United States and the major powers of Western Europe. Since the end of the Cold War, NATO has expanded to the east.

Noncombatant   A person who is not a combatant (q.v.) and so is morally immune from attack in war, as indicated in just war theory.

NORTHCOM   United States military command responsible for defending the air, land, and sea approaches to the United States.

NPT   Nuclear Non-Proliferation Treaty, a 1968 treaty obligating the five nuclear signatories (the United States, the Soviet Union, Britain, France, and China) not to facilitate the acquisition of nuclear-weapons by other states and the other signatories not to acquire nuclear weapons.

NRO   National Reconnaissance Office: United States Department of Defense agency responsible for space-borne imagery and signals intelligence.

NSA   National Security Agency; the United States agency responsible for foreign signals intelligence and information security for the U.S. government.

Nuclear Fission   A process in which a large unstable nucleus, such as Uranium-235, breaks up into two smaller nuclei, releasing energy. Nuclear fission generates the energy of an atomic bomb and is the fuse for a hydrogen or thermonuclear bomb.

Nuclear Fuel Cycle   The process by which uranium is enriched in the isotope (235) needed for its use as a fuel in a nuclear power generator or a nuclear bomb.

Nuclear Fusion   A process in which two nuclei of hydrogen are brought close enough together so that the strong nuclear force can act to fuse them into a single new nucleus, releasing energy. Nuclear fusion generates the energy of a hydrogen or thermonuclear bomb.

Nuclear Pacifism   The doctrine that the use of nuclear weapons or the threat of their use is morally unacceptable.

Nuclear Security Guarantees   Assurances by a nuclear nation that it will protect a nonnuclear nation should it come under attack by another nuclear nation. The purpose is to keep the protected nation from becoming a nuclear proliferator.

Nuclear Taboo   A general belief or norm of international society that nuclear weapons are not to be used, that their use is completely unacceptable. This norm has apparently grown in strength during the long period since 1945 in which nuclear weapons have not been used. Of great concern is what would happen should this taboo be broken.

Nuclear Terrorism   The use or threatened use of nuclear weapons against civilian targets to achieve political ends. The term is often used specifically to label such a use or threat by a terrorist group, such as al Qaeda, acting independently of a state.

Nuclear Winter   A theory that the spreading blanket of darkness from dust, smoke, and other debris generated by a large number of nuclear explosions could cause world temperatures to plummet for an extended period of time.

Omnicide   The destruction of all human life; the extinction of the human species.

Opaque Proliferation   A situation in which a state acquires nuclear weapons but does not test them and refuses to acknowledge their existence.

PAL   Permissive Action Link; devices on nuclear weapons of the United States and other nations that require the use of a unique code to arm the weapons, a code that must be supplied by the leaders ordering their use; if an incorrect code is entered, the weapon is permanently disabled.

Paradox of Nuclear Deterrence   The view that nuclear deterrence is paradoxical because it is simultaneously morally acceptable, due to the permissibility of self-defense, and morally prohibited, due to the threat it poses to noncombatants.

Patriot missile   A type of anti-missile missile, which proved ineffective in its use in the first Gulf War.

Peaceful Coexistence   A Soviet term for a state of peaceful relations between adversaries, but with continued ideological and economic competition.

Penetration Aids   Devices, such as dummy warheads and radar-intercepting chaff, deployed by ballistic missile warheads in flight to confuse or defeat ballistic missile defenses.

Point Defense   A defensive system designed to protect a very small target area against missile attack.

Polaris missile   First-generation submarine-launched ballistic missile, not as long-ranged or reliable as current SLBMs.

Politburo   The top decision-making group of the former Soviet Union.

Preemptive War (Attack)   A war or attack launched by a nation against an opponent who the nation believes is about to attack it.

Preventive War (Attack)   A war or attack initiated by a nation without provocation against an opponent out of fear that the opponent will otherwise attack or acquire the capability to attack the nation in the future.

Principle of Discrimination   That part of just war theory requiring that military force not be directed against noncombatants, also called that principle of noncombatant immunity.

Principle of Proportionality   That part of just war theory requiring that the amount of force used, either in particular military engagements or in a war overall, not exceed what is proportionate to the military objective.

Proliferation   The acquisition of nuclear weapons technology and capability by nonnuclear nations.

PSI   Proliferation Security Initiative; a 2003 United States proposal for the creation of international agreements allowing the United States and its allies to search planes and ships carrying suspect cargo and seize illegal weapons or missile technologies.

Radioisotope   An isotope of an element that is radioactive.

Realism   The doctrine that morality is irrelevant or inapplicable in international relations, especially war.

Rogue State   A nation that refuses to play by the international rules, as set forth in treaties and international law.

SAC Strategic Air Command; the U.S. Air Force command with responsibility for strategic bombers and ballistic missiles.

SALT Strategic Arms Limitation Talks/Treaty; arms control negotiations that produced two treaties (SALT I and II). The first was signed in 1972 and fixed the number of Soviet and American ICBM and SLBM launchers. The second, signed in 1979, was never ratified, though it was generally adhered to, by the United States; it limited missiles, bombers, and MIRV deployments.

SDI Strategic Defense Initiative (known popularly as "Star Wars"); a ballistic missile defense system proposed by President Ronald Reagan in 1983.

Second Strike A nuclear retaliatory attack launched by a nation after it is struck by a nuclear first attack.

SIGINT Signal intelligence, that is, intelligence gained from intercepting, decrypting and analyzing radio signals.

SIOP Single Integrated Operational Plan; the U.S. government's plan for the use of nuclear weapons in case of war, in place from the 1960s until the 1990s.

SLBM Submarine-Launched Ballistic Missile; such missiles are launched when the submarine is submerged.

SOCOM Special Operations Command; a United States command exercising authority of all special operations forces, civil affairs, psychological operations, and counter terrorism and reconnaissance forces in the United States.

SORT Strategic Offensive Reduction Treaty; a 2002 treaty between the United States and Russia requiring each to reduce its operationally deployed strategic nuclear warheads to 1,700–2,200 by December 31, 2012.

Sovereignty The power and authority of a nation over its own internal affairs, generally recognized by international law.

START Strategic Arms Reduction Talks/Treaty; two treaties (signed in 1991 and 1993) stipulating a phased reduction of United States and Soviet/Russian strategic delivery systems and nuclear warheads over roughly a 15-year period, and banning MIRVs on ICBMs. Both the United States and the Russian have ratified the treaties, but in 2003, in response to the US withdrawal from the ABM treaty, Russia declared it will no longer be bound by START II.

STRACOM Strategic Command; the U.S. military command responsible for strategic nuclear forces and space operations, including nuclear and conventional global strike capabilities, integrated missile defense, and information operations.

Strategic Nuclear Weapons Nuclear weapons designed to be launched over the battlefield against the homeland of an adversary.

Strong Nuclear Force A force that exists between neutrons and protons when they are close together.

Survivability The degree to which a strategic weapons system can survive an enemy attack and still be available for retaliation. The opposite of survivability is vulnerability.

Tactical Nuclear Weapons Relatively small nuclear weapons intended for battlefield use.

Thermonuclear Weapons Weapons whose force is derived at least in part from nuclear fusion, releasing great energy; there is no upper limit to the power of a thermonuclear weapon, only the limit of the delivery system.

Titan An early liquid-fueled U.S. ICBM, the first to be truly intercontinental in range.

TMD Theater Missile Defense; weapons designed to destroy incoming warheads that had been launched by an enemy's battlefield or theater delivery systems.

Total War A war with the aim of complete destruction of the enemy nation, in which all possible means are employed without restraint; in total war noncombatants may become objects of direct attack on a large scale.

Triad The U.S. reliance of ICBMs, SLBMs, and bombers as its strategic delivery systems.

Trident   Current generation U.S. submarine-launched ballistic missile, truly intercontinental in range.

Trinity   Code name for the first nuclear device denoted on July 6, 1945, at Alamogordo, New Mexico.

UAV   Unmanned Aerial Vehicle: a remotely piloted aircraft, small in size but capable of carrying both strike weapons and surveillance equipment and loitering aloft almost indefinitely; its size and small radar profile make it very difficult to attack and destroy.

Verification   The process of determining if a nation is in compliance with its treaty obligations; often performed by satellites and other national technical means.

Vertical Proliferation   An increase in the number of nuclear weapons held by states that already possess nuclear weapons.

WMD   Weapon(s) of Mass Destruction; a category of weapons, in distinction from conventional weapons, that traditionally has included nuclear, chemical, and biological weapons.

Worst-Case Analysis   A military planning tool that assumes that the enemy will take the most damaging course of action possible.

Index